Visual C++™ 4

UNLEASHED

Viktor Toth

SAMS
PUBLISHING

201 West 103rd Street
Indianapolis, IN 46290

Ildikónak

Copyright © 1996 by Sams Publishing

FIRST EDITION

International Standard Book Number: 0-672-30874-6

Library of Congress Catalog Card Number: 95-72334

99 98 97 96   4 3 2

Interpretation of the printing code: the rightmost double-digit number is the year of the book's printing; the rightmost single-digit, the number of the book's printing. For example, a printing code of 96-1 shows that the first printing of the book occurred in 1996.

Composed in AGaramond and MCPdigital by Macmillan Computer Publishing

Printed in the United States of America

Publisher and President	*Richard K. Swadley*
Acquisitions Manager	*Greg Wiegand*
Development Manager	*Dean Miller*
Managing Editor	*Cindy Morrow*
Marketing Manager	*Gregg Bushyeager*

Acquisitions Editor
Grace Buechlein

Development Editor
Anthony Amico

Software Development Specialist
Cari Skaggs

Production Editor
Carolyn Linn

Technical Reviewer
Daniel Boyle

Editorial Coordinator
Bill Whitmer

Technical Edit Coordinator
Lynette Quinn

Formatter
Frank Sinclair

Editorial Assistants
Sharon Cox
Andi Richter
Rhonda Tinch-Mize

Cover Designer
Jason Grisham

Book Designer
Alyssa Yesh

Production Team Supervisor
Brad Chinn

Production
Carol Bowers
Chris Cleveland
Bronte Davis
Mike Dietsch
Jason Hand
Sonja Hart
Ayanna Lacey
Kevin Laseau
Steph Mineart
Casey Price
Bobbi Satterfield
Andrew Stone
Todd Wente
Colleen Williams

Overview

Part IV OLE in MFC Applications 501

Part V Advanced Programming Topics 599

Part IV OLE in MFC Applications 501

Preface

Writing about programming used to be very different from what it is today. In 1986, shortly before I left my native Hungary, I completed a book about the Commodore 16 home computer for a Hungarian publisher. In fewer than 400 pages, I provided a complete reference for that machine, down to the last tiny bit in the computer's ROM, the last transistor in its circuit diagram.

Assuming that it were possible to develop such a comprehensive reference for today's Windows 95-equipped desktop computers, that work would fill not only volumes, not only several bookshelves, but probably several large bookcases. The subject of "system calls" used to be a topic for a brief appendix in a typical programming book from the early 80s. Although these books are not yet old enough to have their pages turn yellow with age, the words in them seem to come from prehistoric times; today's programmer has to know more APIs than the number of system calls listed in many of these works!

Visual C++ is the fundamental programming tool for Windows. Writing about this programming environment requires covering most Windows programming topics in reasonable detail. One of the basic decisions an author has to make before embarking on such a task is to define the target audience.

This book is not for the novice programmer. Knowledge of the C and C++ programming languages, as well as a basic understanding of Windows programming fundamentals, is assumed.

This book is not a replacement for the excellent tutorial manuals that you find on your Visual C++ CD-ROM. What this book provides is a detailed introduction into many specific programming topics. Such introductions are often hard to find; function references and MFC class descriptions are a poor substitute for simple examples and helpful tips.

When I first started working with Visual C++ 1, I was thoroughly impressed by the power of the development environment. It took only a few short days with the Scribble tutorial application to get up to speed with MFC programming; afterwards, within less than a week, I was able to put together a Windows-based action game complete with multimedia sound effects.

With this experience behind me, it was not easy to understand why so many programmers, including people with years of C and C++ programming experience, had difficulty with Visual C++. Eventually, I think I understood the root of the problem. Many of these programmers have not had any prior exposure to Windows programming. The MFC Library does a wonderful job hiding many of the complex details of the Windows API; however, this also means that without prior exposure, you never have a chance to learn some fundamental concepts.

Let me show you an example. If you ever wrote a non-MFC Windows application, you must be familiar with the concept of the *message loop*. Essentially, all Windows applications have a WinMain function that looks something like this:

```
int WinMain(...)
{
    // Initialize main window
    ...
    while (!GetMessage(&msg, NULL, 0, 0))
        DispatchMessage(&msg)
    return msg.wParam;
}
```

The while loop in this function is the application's main message loop. All messages posted to the application are processed here and dispatched to the appropriate message handler functions.

As a programmer with Windows experience, you must also be familiar with the msg structure and what Windows messages generally look like. So if I tell you that the MFC Library provides its own version of WinMain, and that after initialization, it calls your CWinApp-derived object's Run member function that implements the message loop, you should have no problem understanding how MFC applications process Windows messages.

However, if you never wrote a non-MFC Windows application before, you might as well think that I wrote the above paragraphs in my native Hungarian. Message loop? Message structure? Message handlers? Dispatching? What do all these concepts mean?

This was my reasoning when I decided to devote a sizable portion of my book to Win32 programming topics. These topics form the very foundation upon which Visual C++ is built; without a thorough understanding of Win32 fundamentals, Visual C++ programming becomes a nightmare.

Not that this part is meant exclusively for those with little prior Windows programming exposure. Hopefully, even seasoned Windows programmers among you will find some of these chapters useful when you wish to understand more about such Win32 topics as structured exceptions, virtual memory, or programming with the Registry.

These topics do not require the Microsoft Foundation Classes; therefore, I liberally used simple, pedestrian examples that can be easily edited, compiled, and run from the command line. This simplicity is characteristic of all the examples I used in this book. My goal was not to demonstrate how good a programmer I am by adding all kinds of bells and whistles to these programs, but to illustrate specific programming concepts.

Take, for example, MAPI. If you have not done any MAPI programming before and wish to add some messaging features to your application, what would you prefer as your first exposure to MAPI? A comprehensive MFC-based example with a hundred kilobytes of source code? Here is what I offer instead:

```c
#include <windows.h>
#include <stdio.h>
#include <mapi.h>

LPMAPILOGON lpfnMAPILogon;
LPMAPISENDMAIL lpfnMAPISendMail;
LPMAPILOGOFF lpfnMAPILogoff;

MapiRecipDesc recipient =
{
    0, MAPI_TO,
    "Bill Clinton", "SMTP:president@whitehouse.gov",
    0, NULL
};

MapiMessage message =
{
    0, "Greetings",
    "Hello, Mr. President!\n",
    NULL, NULL, NULL, 0, NULL, 1, &recipient, 0, NULL
};

void main(void)
{
    LHANDLE lhSession;
    HANDLE hMAPILib;

    hMAPILib = LoadLibrary("MAPI32.DLL");
    lpfnMAPILogon =
        (LPMAPILOGON)GetProcAddress(hMAPILib, "MAPILogon");
    lpfnMAPISendMail =
        (LPMAPISENDMAIL)GetProcAddress(hMAPILib, "MAPISendMail");
    lpfnMAPILogoff =
        (LPMAPILOGOFF)GetProcAddress(hMAPILib, "MAPILogoff");

    (*lpfnMAPILogon)(0, NULL, NULL, MAPI_ALLOW_OTHERS, 0,
                     &lhSession);
    (*lpfnMAPISendMail)(lhSession, 0, &message, 0, 0);
    (*lpfnMAPILogoff)(lhSession, 0, 0, 0);
    printf("Message to the White House sent.\n");

    FreeLibrary(hMAPILib);
}
```

This program, in all its 42 lines, is a fully functional command line-based MAPI application. It demonstrates how to load the MAPI library, use MAPI data structures, and call MAPI functions. Nor does compiling this program require a 1000-line make file (I always considered such huge make files somewhat obscene in *examples*); you can compile it from the command line by simply typing cl cmdmsg.c.

I actually use simple examples like this one regularly when I try to understand a new programming topic. Even when I find a suitable sample application somewhere, I often mutilate it by removing all nonessential fluff. After all, when I wish to learn about MAPI, I am not really interested in menus, resource files, or how to construct fancy dialogs.

This simplicity is perhaps most evident with my favorite Windows program, the Windows equivalent of the infamous Hello, World! program with which Kernighan and Ritchie introduce their bible on C programming. It has often been said that Windows programming is so complex, even the simplest of applications requires hundreds of lines of code. If you ever hear this again from diehard DOS or UNIX programmers, just show them the following program:

```
#include <windows.h>

int WINAPI WinMain(HINSTANCE d1, HINSTANCE d2, LPSTR d3, int d4)
{
    MessageBox(NULL, "Hello, World!", "", MB_OK);
}
```

Although the lines themselves are longer, this program has the exact same number of lines as the command line original:

```
#include <stdio.h>

void main(void)
{
    printf("Hello, World!\n");
}
```

As this example so well demonstrates, Windows programming *can* be made simple.

You will also notice that very few of the programming examples in this book are *code fragments*. I always found that a program that you can actually compile and run, no matter how simple it is, helps further your understanding of a subject a great deal more than code fragments. Such executable programs are also proof that the author actually tested the concepts presented; indeed, on the attached CD-ROM, you will find a ready-to-run executable for every example in this book. (I hope they will run on your machine; they run on mine.)

Let me say a few words about the topics and organization of this book. Part I is about the Developer Studio, which is the name for the new Visual C++ IDE (Integrated Development Environment). Some of its features are familiar to Visual C++ programmers, while other features, such as the Component Gallery or the WizardBar, are brand new. In this part, I also cover the two most important components of the Developer Studio, the AppWizard and the ClassWizard; additional topics include browsing and debugging applications, and using the Developer Studio in conjunction with other Microsoft development tools.

Part II is about programming in Windows with specific emphasis on 32-bit Windows programming. Many of the basic concepts of Windows programming are covered, and so are advanced 32-bit concepts such as thread management, virtual memory, structured exceptions, and the Registry.

Part III introduces the Microsoft Foundation Classes Library. Documents and views, dialogs, controls (including the use of OCXs), device contexts and GDI objects, serialization, collections, and miscellaneous classes are the topics of the 10 chapters that comprise this part.

Part IV is about OLE. In accordance with my philosophy of providing the fundamentals before presenting cookbook-like MFC recipes, I begin this part with a review of OLE fundamentals. A non-MFC example of a mere 300-some lines that is nevertheless a fully functional OLE automation server highlights some of the basic ideas presented in the first chapter. In the remaining four chapters, the use of MFC is explored in developing OLE containers, OLE component servers, OLE drag and drop applications, and OLE automation servers.

Part V contains an assortment of chapters about a variety of Visual C++ programming topics. ODBC, MAPI, TAPI, DAO, or OpenGL are just some of the acronyms that make up the subject of the chapters here.

At the beginning of this preface I mentioned how different programming books are today from those written a mere decade ago. Another difference is the rapidly changing nature of development environments. When I began my programming career, I used books on the FORTRAN language that were written 10 years earlier and were still perfectly useful; can you imagine trying to write a Windows 95 program using an MS-DOS programmer reference published in 1985?

Not only does this rapidly changing environment make the lives of programmers more difficult, it also takes its toll on authors. We can no longer afford the luxury of working on a book for a year or more; such a book would be rendered obsolete by new software versions even before it was published. I can only hope that despite the short time I had for developing this book, it does not contain too many glaring errors or omissions, and that it becomes a useful addition to your library.

Finally, I would like to thank my wife, Ildiko, for her unwavering support. Without her patience and understanding, the grueling routine of 14-hour work days and 7-day workweeks during the last two months would not have been possible.

About the Author

Viktor Toth is a Hungarian-born author and self-employed software developer. His professional career started in 1979, when he wrote his first Hungarian-language book on Ernő Rubik's Magic Cube. Between that time and 1986, he developed many scientific and business applications for clients in Hungary, Austria, Germany, and the United Kingdom. He wrote applications in Fortran, a variety of assemblers, Simula-67, C, and Pascal, just to name a few languages. In 1986, he authored his second book, a technical reference for programmers of the Commodore 16 home computer.

Viktor Toth became a resident of Canada in 1987. There, he continued his self-employed career. He coauthored several studies as a consultant for the Canadian government and wrote numerous applications in C and C++, assembler, dBase, and other environments. After briefly experimenting with other graphical systems such as the long-forgotten GEM, he eventually wrote his first Windows application in 1990 and has not looked back since.

Viktor Toth is coauthor of Sams Publishing's *Windows 95 Programming Unleashed.*

Viktor lives with his wife in their ever-smaller apartment in Ottawa, surrounded by several hundred pounds of computing equipment (his), knitting yarn (hers), and books. They hope to move soon to a house where they can add some cats to the family inventory.

What Is New in Visual C++ Version 4?

Whether Visual C++ 4 is revolutionary or merely evolutionary is subject to debate; but it certainly represents a major improvement over previous versions. If you liked the earlier versions, you must love Version 4; if you did not use Visual C++ before, it has never been easier to begin.

The improvements over earlier versions are in several areas. The new Integrated Development Environment (IDE) application, the Developer Studio, has a variety of new features. Among these are the improved ClassWizard, AppWizard, and an entirely new tool, the Component Gallery. The Microsoft Foundation Classes Library also has a new version that improves on earlier versions in many ways; it also adds support for the new Data Access Objects (DAO), another new redistributable component that ships with Visual C++. The C/C++ compiler component of Visual C++ also underwent some major revisions; in particular, the compiler supports several new elements of the emerging ANSI C++ standard, such as namespaces, run-time type information, and the Standard Template Library.

What Is New in the Developer Studio?

The new Developer Studio offers a variety of new and improved features for managing projects and subprojects, editing code and resources, managing classes, and for code reuse and code generation.

The Project Workspace

The Project Workspace window offers three views on projects: in ClassView, project classes, member variables, and functions are shown; in FileView, files comprising a project are visible; and in ResourceView, resource file components can be manipulated.

A workspace can now contain several projects. These can be top-level projects or subprojects.

Improved Editor

The new source code editor offers improved compatibility with Brief and other popular editors.

The ClassWizard and the WizardBar

The new ClassWizard offers support for OLE control development. Many ClassWizard features can easily be accessed in the WizardBar, a toolbar that is displayed in source editor windows.

Component Gallery

The Component Gallery is a major new component in Visual C++. Classes that are created through ClassWizard or entire projects created through AppWizard can be added to the Component Gallery and later inserted from here into other applications. The Component Gallery comes with many useful tools, including OLE controls and other components that add various useful features to your project.

Custom AppWizards

The new Visual C++ offers the capability to create custom AppWizards. Custom AppWizards can be based on existing AppWizard code or can be entirely custom made. Appropriately, creation of custom AppWizards is made easy by a custom AppWizard specifically written for this purpose.

Resource Editing

An improved Resource Editor now adds toolbars to the set of resource file components it can handle. Toolbar buttons can now be easily added, removed, or manipulated without having to modify corresponding structures or arrays in your code.

The dialog editing capabilities have also been improved; more accurate placement of dialog controls is now possible with the help of guides and margins. The Resource Editor can now also import Visual Basic forms.

Debugging

The integrated debugger has redesigned windows. It also offers a new feature, *DataTips*; positioning the mouse cursor over a symbol in an editor window during debugging causes a tooltip-style window to appear, displaying the current value of the symbol.

Integration with Other Tools

The Developer Studio offers a high level of integration with other Microsoft development tools such as the Microsoft Developer Library, Microsoft FORTRAN, Microsoft Test, and Microsoft SourceSafe.

Source Control

Visual C++ cooperates with source-code control systems that conform to the Microsoft Common Source Code Control Interface, such as Microsoft's own Visual SourceSafe.

The InfoViewer

The InfoViewer is a new, integrated tool for browsing online documentation. In addition to browsing the documentation that comes with Visual C++, it can also browse other titles, such as the Developer Network Library. It also has improved features, such as keyword browsing—the ability to search for highlighted words when the F1 key is pressed. (This feature was previously available only in source code windows.)

What Is New in the MFC Library?

The new MFC Library, MFC Version 4, offers several new classes and improved support in a number of areas.

Data Access Objects

The new MFC Library contains a series of new classes that encapsulate Data Access Objects (DAO). DAO is the technology used in Visual Basic, Microsoft Access, and other products to access databases through the Microsoft Jet engine.

OLE Controls

Support for the development of OLE controls, previously available in the form of a separate development tool (the Control Development Kit, or CDK), has now been fully integrated. The MFC supports OLE controls through a series of new classes. It also provides control container functionality through new member functions added to the CWnd class.

Synchronization Classes

The new MFC Library provides wrapper classes for a variety of synchronization objects, including events, mutexes, semaphores, and critical sections.

Windows 95 Common Controls

MFC support, previously available in add-on classes that were released in beta form as part of the Visual C++ subscription product, is now officially part of the MFC Library. In addition to classes that wrap control functionality, a series of new view and other classes have also been defined that support views based on list, tree, and rich-text edit controls.

What Is New in the C/C++ Compiler?

The C/C++ compiler component of Visual C++ has been improved to provide better support for new features in the ANSI draft standard.

Namespaces

The compiler now supports namespaces. In addition to the single global namespace provided by the language, applications can define additional namespaces that provide unique scopes for globally defined objects. A namespace can be defined using the namespace keyword:

```
namespace A
{
int n;
}
```

Namespaces can be used explicitly or implicitly. Explicit use involves a syntax that is similar to the syntax used when referring to class members: for example, A::n. Implicit use requires the using keyword:

```
using namespace A;
printf("%d", n);
```

Run-Time Type Information

The new compiler supports ANSI-style Run-Time Type Information, or RTTI. RTTI is enabled through the /GR compiler command line option. RTTI introduces several new language elements. The typeid operator can be used to identify the type of an object. This operator returns an object of type type_info. For example:

```
class A { ... };
class B : public A { ... };
...
A *pa = new A;
B *pb = new B;
const type_info& ta = typeid(*pa);
const type_info& tb = typeid(*pb);
```

A series of new casting operators provides a replacement for old-style C casts while removing ambiguities. These operators include dynamic_cast, static_cast, const_cast, and reinterpret_cast.

The Standard Template Library

Visual C++ now provides support for the Hewlett-Packard public domain implementation of the Standard Template Library. Note that the STL is not installed by the Visual C++ setup program. Simultaneous use of STL and the MFC in the same application requires the use of namespaces due to conflicting declarations in the two libraries. ANSI recommends the use of the namespace std as the standard library namespace.

Run-Time Library Source

The source of the debug version of the C/C++ run-time library is now available. Using this source, it is now possible to step into run-time library functions during debugging.

Performance Improvements

The new compiler offers several performance improvements. The *minimal rebuild* option selects only those files for rebuild that are actually affected by changes in header files (as opposed to rebuilding all dependent source files). The incremental linker has been improved to handle more cases incrementally. The compiler's new incremental compilation feature detects portions of a source file that actually changed and limits compilation to these elements, greatly reducing compilation time.

Notational Conventions Used in This Book

Throughout *Visual C++ 4 Unleashed,* a simple notational style is used. All listings are typeset in a monospace font for ease of reading. In the text, the same monospace font is used for all function names, variable names, filenames, keywords, and other symbols that occur in programs. A monospace italic font is used for placeholders, such as function or method parameters, indicating that a symbol must be substituted in their place by the user. In some listings, a vertical line is used to mark code that must be added manually, to distinguish from code that was automatically generated or code that was added earlier. In the book, many new terms are introduced; the first occurrence of such terms is highlighted by the use of an italic font.

The Visual C++ Development System

PART

I

Visual C++ and the Developer Studio

IN THIS CHAPTER

The Visual C++ Developer Studio application is the centerpiece of the Visual C++ development system. It offers a variety of features, provides access to most Visual C++ development system components, and also provides a front end for other Microsoft development products, such as Microsoft Test, Microsoft SourceSafe, or the Developer Library CD-ROM.

This new Developer Studio (Figure 1.1) sports a much-improved source editor, an excellent resource editor, an integrated help system, project build options, and access to other integrated components such as the AppWizard, the ClassWizard, the integrated debugger, and the profiler.

FIGURE 1.1.

*The Developer
Studio.*

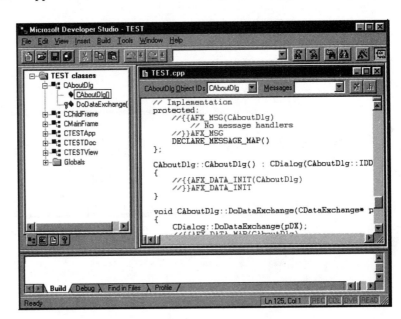

Although the Developer Studio represents the interface of choice for accessing the features of Visual C++, the C/C++ compiler and other components of the development system can also be used from the command line. In some cases, such as when compiling simple test programs, it is actually easier to do than to use the graphical interface.

In this chapter, we begin our tour of Visual C++ by reviewing the Developer Studio and its basic features. In the second half of the chapter, we examine the use of Visual C++ command-line tools.

Developer Studio: An Overview

The Developer Studio offers a series of interfaces for projects, source files, resource file components; and a series of tools for building, running, and testing applications. It also offers integrated access to the Visual C++ help system and other media titles, such as the Microsoft Developer Library.

The Project Workspace

For those of us familiar with earlier versions of Visual C++, perhaps the most striking new feature in Version 4 is the new project workspace window (Figure 1.2).

FIGURE 1.2.

The Project Workspace in ClassView.

In addition to the old-fashioned presentation of a project as a collection of source files, you are now provided with two new ways of looking at a project. In *ClassView*, the classes that comprise a project, their member functions and variables, and the project's global variables and functions are presented; in *ResourceView*, the project's resource file components can be viewed.

The ClassView window provides a hierarchical representation of classes when they are embedded in other classes. It also uses different symbols to identify private, protected, and public class members.

Apart from being pretty, the ClassView is also useful. Double-clicking on any item opens the appropriate file for editing and positions the text cursor on the item. For example, double-clicking on a class name opens the file containing the class declaration and positions the cursor at the beginning of the declaration. Double-clicking on a member function name opens the appropriate implementation file and positions the cursor at the beginning of the function definition.

The *FileView* window presents a more traditional view of your project. This view lists all your project source files and dependencies. Double-clicking on any file opens the file for editing.

NOTE

Unlike previous versions of Visual C++, Version 4 does not allow file groupings. This feature is replaced in part by the ClassView window, and in part by the new capability of handling projects and subprojects.

Often you add new files to a project implicitly, such as when you create a new class through ClassWizard. However, if you need to explicitly add a new file to your project, use the Files into Project command from the Insert menu.

Projects and Subprojects

The Project Workspace is not restricted to a single project. You can use the Project command from the Insert menu to insert additional projects into a workspace.

You can add new projects to the workspace as top-level projects or as subprojects. The major distinction is that a subproject participates in the build process; when a project with subproject is rebuilt, its subprojects are rebuilt first.

The use of projects and subprojects allows for a variety of scenarios. For example, a project may have subprojects representing dynamic link libraries. Two top-level projects may represent a client and a server application.

> **NOTE**
>
> You cannot add an existing project to your workspace. The Insert Project command can only be used to add new projects created through AppWizard. One way to overcome this limitation is to create a blank project with the same settings as your existing project and copy the appropriate files into your new project directory. Another approach is to create a new project specifying an external make file.

Project Configuration

A project configuration defines how the executable program or library that a project defines is built. When you create a project through AppWizard, a set of default project configurations is also created. For example, if you create a project for the Win32 Intel platform, AppWizard creates two configurations: one for debug and one for release build. Later, project configurations can be added or removed using the Configurations button from the Build menu (Figure 1.3).

The settings for a specific configuration or set of configurations can be modified using the Settings command in the Build menu. We return to the Project Settings dialog later in this chapter when we discuss building a project.

FIGURE 1.3.

The Configurations dialog.

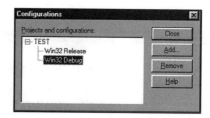

Editing Source Files

The new Visual C++ source editor offers familiar features, such as drag and drop editing and syntax coloring. It is also extensively customizable.

The editor can be made key-compatible with the Brief or Epsilon editors. Key settings can also be customized by the Customize command from the Tools menu and selecting the Keyboard tab in the Customize dialog (Figure 1.4).

FIGURE 1.4.

Keyboard customization.

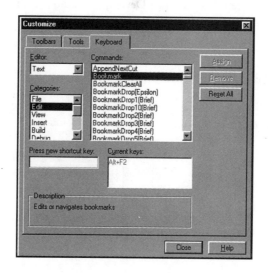

The preset Brief or Epsilon editor configurations can be invoked through the Options command in the Tools menu. In the Options dialog, select the Compatibility tab. In the Recommended options drop-down box, select the desired editor emulation. The four choices include the default Developer Studio configuration, the Visual C++ 2.0 compatibility mode, and the Epsilon and Brief emulations (Figure 1.5).

FIGURE 1.5.

Selecting editor emulations.

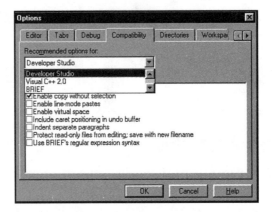

Resources

The integrated resource editor in Developer Studio provides a comprehensive editing facility for all types of resources. This includes the new toolbar editing facility, as well as the capability to insert and edit custom resources.

Resource Editing

Resource editing begins with the ResourceView in the Project Workspace window (Figure 1.6). This window provides a view of all the elements in a project's resource file.

FIGURE 1.6.

ResourceView.

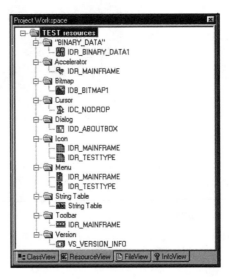

You can insert a new resource by selecting the Resource command from the Insert menu. This command displays a dialog (Figure 1.7) where you can select the type of the new resource. In addition to predefined types, user-defined types also appear in this dialog. You can use this dialog to insert a blank resource; however, when inserting a cursor or a dialog, you can also use a predefined template as the basis for your new resource.

FIGURE 1.7.

Inserting a new resource.

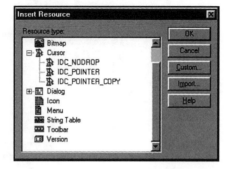

Accelerators (Figure 1.8) are keyboard shortcuts that generate WM_COMMAND messages; the same type of messages as those generated by menu commands and dialog controls. A project can have several accelerator tables; for example, if it uses multiple menus, it may use different accelerator tables for those. To edit a specific accelerator key, double-click the key in this window to invoke its properties.

FIGURE 1.8.

Editing an accelerator table.

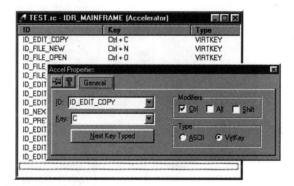

The bitmap editor (Figure 1.9) enables you to create monochrome or color bitmaps. A variety of graphics tools can be used when drawing the bitmap. Use the mouse to select the desired tool and the foreground and background colors, and then draw the bitmap.

While a bitmap is displayed on-screen, a new menu, the Image menu, becomes available in the Developer Studio menu bar. Commands in this menu can be used to manipulate the bitmap; in particular, the Grid Settings command can be used to set up a grid of guide lines. Use this grid when creating a bitmap that consists of many small pictures.

FIGURE 1.9.

Editing a bitmap.

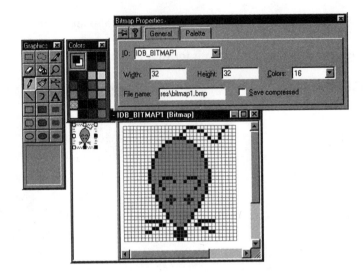

Editing a cursor (Figure 1.10) is very similar to editing a bitmap. However, for cursors, the color palette also contains two special "colors": one that corresponds to the background color, and another that corresponds to the inverse background color.

FIGURE 1.10.

Editing a cursor.

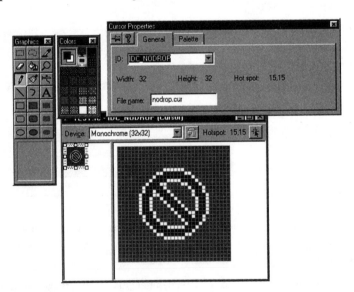

You can also specify a cursor's hotspot. The hotspot is the position in the cursor image that Windows uses to track the cursor and to generate cursor-related events.

The dialog editor (Figure 1.11) is the tool for editing dialog templates. Editing a dialog template consists of selecting controls from the control palette and placing them on the template, and specifying dialog and control properties.

FIGURE 1.11.

Editing a dialog.

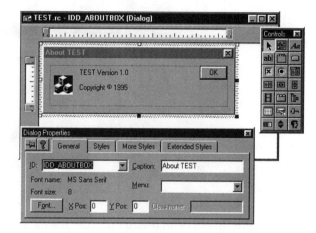

The dialog control palette supports all standard controls as well as most Windows 95 Common Controls. It also provides a tool for placing OLE controls in your dialog.

While a dialog is being edited, a new menu, the Layout menu, is displayed by the Developer Studio. This menu offers several commands that help to adjust the placement of controls in a dialog template. Among these is the Guide Settings command. This command invokes a dialog (Figure 1.12) where you can specify rulers, guides, and grid settings to assist you during dialog template editing.

FIGURE 1.12.

Guide settings for dialog editing.

Editing an icon (Figure 1.13) is very similar to editing a cursor. The only notable difference is the lack of a hotspot in icons. When creating an icon, you may wish to create several versions of the icon. For example, compatibility with Windows 95 requires that your application register a 16×16 icon in addition to the standard 32×32 icon.

FIGURE 1.13.

Icon editing.

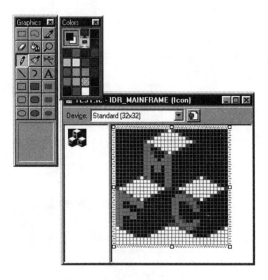

Editing menus is easy and straightforward using the graphical menu editor (Figure 1.14). To insert a new item in either a horizontal menu bar or a vertical popup menu, simply grab the blank item at the end of the menu using the mouse and move it to the desired position, then type the menu text. The menu editor will automatically assign a symbolic identifier to the menu based on the text you typed; however, should you desire another identifier, you are free to change it through the menu item's property sheet. Through this property sheet, you can also adjust the initial settings of a menu item.

FIGURE 1.14.

Menu editing.

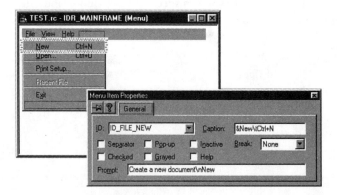

To insert a separator, create a blank menu item and check the Separator box in the item's property sheet. To insert a menu item that has a submenu, create the item and check the popup box in the item's property sheet.

For every menu item, you can also prescribe a prompt string. The prompt string consists of two parts, separated by the newline (\n) character. The first part of the prompt string appears in the status bar of standard MFC applications; the second part is used for tooltips. The string you specify as the prompt string is actually deposited in your application's string table, with an identifier that matches the identifier of the menu item.

A string table (Figure 1.15) is a collection of text strings used in your application. The major advantage of using a string table is that it lets you use the resource file as the depository of all language-dependent elements of your application. If such an application is localized in a foreign language, only the resource file needs to be changed and relinked; it is not necessary to modify and recompile the application's source code.

FIGURE 1.15.

*Editing a
string table.*

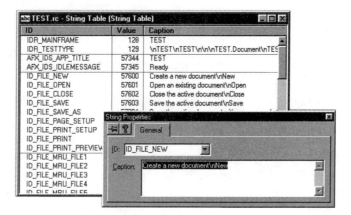

The MFC framework uses the string table extensively for MFC text constants. To edit a string in the string table, simply double-click the item and modify it as needed using the property sheet that is displayed. You can add a new string to the table by double-clicking the blank entry at the end of the list.

A new feature in Visual C++ 4 is the toolbar editor (Figure 1.16). Previously, it was necessary to edit toolbars as bitmaps and manually adjust corresponding structures in your application's source code—a procedure that was cumbersome and error-prone. With the new toolbar editor, you can edit toolbar buttons, assign command identifiers, and prompt strings all within the resource editor.

To add a new toolbar button to the toolbar, grab the blank button at the end of the toolbar using the mouse and drag it to the desired position. To remove a toolbar button, select it with the mouse and drag it out of the toolbar window altogether (pressing the Delete key will only erase the button bitmap instead of removing the button from the toolbar altogether).

FIGURE 1.16.

The toolbar editor.

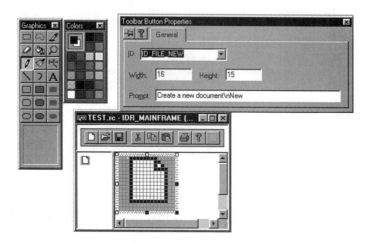

You can assign a symbolic identifier and a prompt string to a toolbar button the same way you assign them to menu items. Note that in order for a toolbar button to be functional, it is not necessary to have a menu item with the same identifier. In other words, your program may have commands that are accessible from a toolbar only.

The version information resource (Figure 1.17) identifies the current version of your executable program or library file. This version information is used by software installation functions; it is also displayed by the Windows 95 Explorer when QuickView is selected.

FIGURE 1.17.

The version information resource.

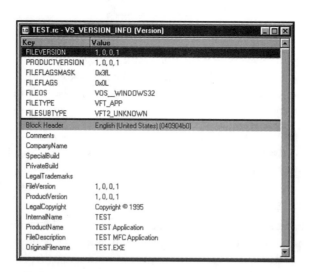

Lastly, the resource editor can also edit custom resources. A custom resource type is identified by a type name enclosed in double quotes. Custom resources are edited through a binary editor (Figure 1.18); more likely, they are resources that are created using an external tool. A good example for a custom resource is a multimedia sound or video file.

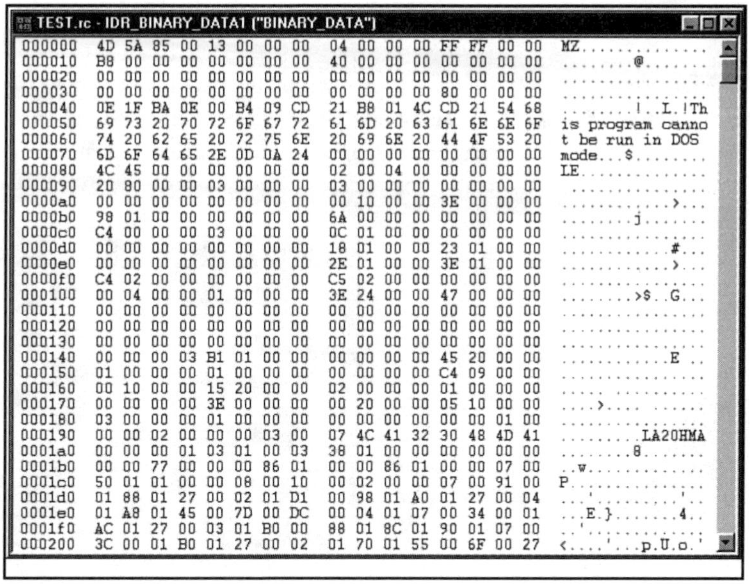

FIGURE 1.18.

Binary editor for custom resources.

```
TEST.rc - IDR_BINARY_DATA1 ("BINARY_DATA")
000000   4D 5A 85 00 13 00 00 00   04 00 00 00 FF FF 00 00   MZ...........
000010   B8 00 00 00 00 00 00 00   40 00 00 00 00 00 00 00   ........@.....
000020   00 00 00 00 00 00 00 00   00 00 00 00 00 00 00 00   ..............
000030   00 00 00 00 00 00 00 00   00 00 00 00 80 00 00 00   ..............
000040   0E 1F BA 0E 00 B4 09 CD   21 B8 01 4C CD 21 54 68   ......!..L.!Th
000050   69 73 20 70 72 6F 67 72   61 6D 20 63 61 6E 6E 6F   is program canno
000060   74 20 62 65 20 72 75 6E   20 69 6E 20 44 4F 53 20   t be run in DOS
000070   6D 6F 64 65 2E 0D 0A 24   00 00 00 00 00 00 00 00   mode...$........
000080   4C 45 00 00 00 00 00 00   02 00 04 00 00 00 00 00   LE............
000090   20 80 00 00 03 00 00 00   03 00 00 00 00 00 00 00    .............
0000a0   00 00 00 00 00 00 00 00   00 10 00 00 3E 00 00 00   ............>...
0000b0   98 01 00 00 00 00 00 00   6A 00 00 00 00 00 00 00   ........j.....
0000c0   C4 00 00 00 03 00 00 00   0C 01 00 00 00 00 00 00   ..............
0000d0   00 00 00 00 00 00 00 00   18 01 00 00 23 01 00 00   ............#...
0000e0   00 00 00 00 00 00 00 00   2E 01 00 00 3E 01 00 00   ............>...
0000f0   C4 02 00 00 00 00 00 00   C5 02 00 00 00 00 00 00   ..............
000100   00 04 00 00 01 00 00 00   3E 24 00 00 47 00 00 00   ......>$..G...
000110   00 00 00 00 00 00 00 00   00 00 00 00 00 00 00 00   ..............
000120   00 00 00 00 00 00 00 00   00 00 00 00 00 00 00 00   ..............
000130   00 00 00 00 00 00 00 00   00 00 00 00 00 00 00 00   ..............
000140   00 00 00 00 03 B1 01 00   00 00 00 00 45 20 00 00   ..........E ..
000150   01 00 00 00 01 00 00 00   00 00 00 00 C4 09 00 00   ..............
000160   00 10 00 00 15 20 00 00   02 00 00 00 01 00 00 00   ..... .......
000170   00 00 00 00 3E 00 00 00   00 20 00 00 05 10 00 00   ....>.... ....
000180   03 00 00 00 01 00 00 00   00 00 00 00 00 00 01 00   ..............
000190   00 00 02 00 00 00 03 00   07 4C 41 32 30 48 4D 41   .........LA20HMA
0001a0   00 00 00 01 03 01 00 03   38 01 00 00 00 00 00 00   ........8.....
0001b0   00 00 77 00 00 00 86 01   00 00 86 01 00 00 07 00   ..w...........
0001c0   50 01 01 00 00 08 00 10   00 02 00 00 07 00 91 00   P.............
0001d0   01 88 01 27 00 02 01 D1   00 98 01 A0 01 27 00 04   ...'.......'..
0001e0   01 A8 01 45 00 7D 00 DC   00 04 01 07 00 34 00 01   ...E.}......4..
0001f0   AC 01 27 00 03 01 B0 00   88 01 8C 01 90 01 07 00   ..'...........
000200   3C 00 01 B0 01 27 00 02   01 70 01 55 00 6F 00 27   <....'...p.U.o.'
```

Resource Localization

The Developer Studio supports multiple language resources in the same resource file. To specify the language for a resource, select the resource identifier in ResourceView, and invoke the Properties command from the Edit menu (Figure 1.19). Note that the resource file can contain several localized versions of the same resource sharing the same identifier. Compilation of localized resources is controlled through preprocessor directives in the resource file. You can utilize localized resources in language-specific build configurations by adding the appropriate preprocessor definitions in the configuration's resource settings in the Project Settings dialog.

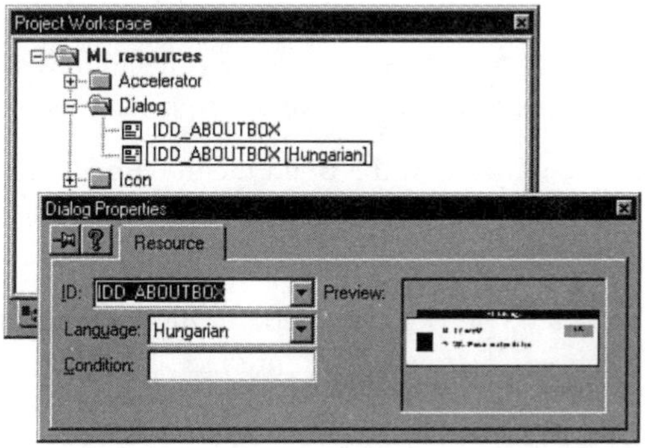

FIGURE 1.19.

Setting the language for a resource.

```
Project Workspace
  ML resources
    Accelerator
    Dialog
      IDD_ABOUTBOX
      IDD_ABOUTBOX [Hungarian]
    Icon

Dialog Properties
  Resource
  ID: IDD_ABOUTBOX          Preview:
  Language: Hungarian
  Condition:
```

Resource Templates

The Developer Studio supports resource templates. Resource templates are predefined resources that are used as templates when new resources are created. For example, when you select the Resource command from the Insert menu, in addition to the default dialog, you can select from a variety of additional dialog templates (Figure 1.20).

FIGURE 1.20.

Using resource templates.

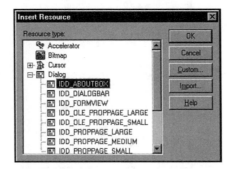

To create custom resource templates, copy the desired resources to a new resource file, and save the file as a resource template file in your msdev\template directory using the Save As command in the File menu. The new templates will appear the next time you invoke the Resource command from the Insert menu.

Building a Project

Building a project means recompiling and relinking the project's components to produce the project's target executable or library file. Every project has a make file associated with it. When a project is being rebuilt, dependencies in the project's make file are evaluated, and components that are affected by changes are recompiled and relinked. To rebuild a project, select the Build command from the Build menu. Incidentally, you can also rebuild a project using the command line nmake.exe utility; to do so, you should enter the project directory and type nmake /f projname.mak, where projname represents your project's name.

The Rebuild All command in the Build menu rebuilds all project components unconditionally; it does so by removing all files that are the results of previous builds and then reevaluating the project's make file.

The Developer Studio provides an interface where a multitude of project build options can be specified or changed. To invoke this interface, select the Settings command from the Build menu (Figure 1.21). On the left side of the Project Settings dialog, you see the list of project configurations; on the right side, a property sheet provides access to many project options.

FIGURE 1.21.

Project Settings: General options.

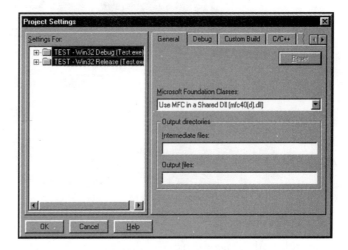

When you initially invoke this dialog, all project configurations are selected in the left side. Correspondingly, any settings that are displayed on the right side are those that are common to all configurations. If you wish to alter settings that are specific to one configuration or another, select the desired configuration first, before making any changes on the right side.

In addition to being able to specify configuration-specific settings, you can specify settings that apply to individual files. To do so, expand the desired configuration by double-clicking its title. The files that comprise that configuration are displayed, and by selecting a specific file, you can alter settings for that specific file. Note that the set of tabs shown on the right side of the dialog changes to reflect your selection; for example, if you select a C++ source file, only the General and the C/C++ tabs will be available.

The first property page on the right side of the Project Settings dialog is the General page. In this page, you specify the MFC Library you wish to link your project with; you can also specify separate directories where intermediate files and output files are deposited.

The next property page shows debugging options. Figure 1.22 shows the Debug property page; or, to be more precise, the first subpage of this property page. Using the Category control, you can select either the General category, shown in Figure 1.22, or the Additional DLLs category. Yes, this is property pages within property pages.

FIGURE 1.22.

Project Settings:
Debug options.

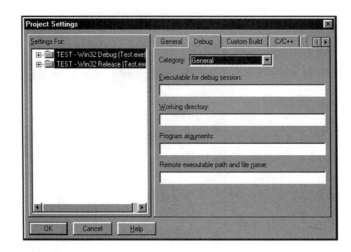

In the General subpage, you can specify the debugging environment in which your program will run. Of particular importance is the executable filename field. Why would you want this to have anything other than the name of the program you are currently debugging? The answer is simple; by specifying an executable in this dialog, you can debug DLLs and other components that are not directly executable from the command line.

For example, if you use Visual C++ to develop a MAPI transport provider, specify the name of the MAPI spooler, `mapisp32.exe`, as the name of the executable, because it is this program that would load your transport provider DLL. If you are developing an OLE control (OCX file), specify an OLE control container application, such as the `tstcon32.exe` application that comes with Visual C++, as the executable.

The third property page in the Project Settings dialog, the Custom Build page, enables you to add customized build steps to a standard make file. For example, if your project contains a grammar specification file that is to be processed by the yacc parser generator, you may wish to add a custom build step for your grammar file, `gram.y`, as shown in Figure 1.23. Note that if your custom build step produces files that further need to be processed, you must also include those files in your project; in the example shown in Figure 1.23, this means that the file `gram.c` had to be added to the project separately.

The fourth property page enables you to set several compiler options. This property page has several subpages, again selectable using the Categories field.

Of particular interest is the Precompiled Headers subpage, which enables you to specify how the compiler creates and uses precompiled header (PCH) files during compilation. The use of precompiled headers is of great importance, as it enhances the compiler's performance very significantly.

FIGURE 1.23.

Using Custom Build options.

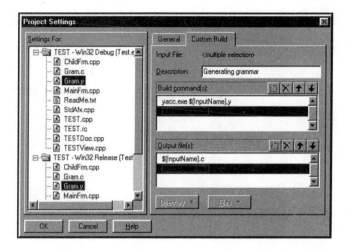

Basically, there are two options; one is self-evident, the other is not. If you select the Automatic use of precompiled headers option, the compiler will look for and identify common headers in your project's files, and generate and use a precompiled header accordingly.

However, automatic precompiled headers are not what AppWizard-generated projects use. Instead, in those projects, the generation and use of precompiled headers is prescribed explicitly. If you wish to copy this behavior, it is important to realize that you should pick one file in your project (for example, stdafx.cpp) that the compiler uses to create the precompiled header (Figure 1.24); all other source files should be set to use the precompiled header (Figure 1.25).

FIGURE 1.24.

Compiler options: creating a precompiled header.

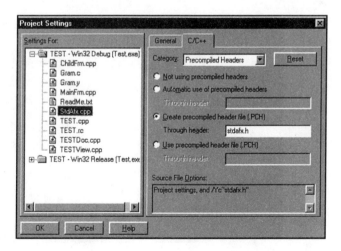

The Project Setting dialog's fifth property page, the Link page, provides access to various link options. This is the third property page with several subpages.

FIGURE 1.25.

Compiler options: using a precompiled header.

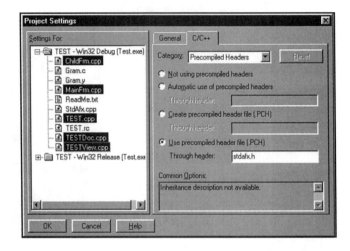

The sixth property page in this dialog, the Resources page, contains fields that control the building of the project's resources.

The seventh property page, OLE Types, controls how OLE type library files (TLB files) are constructed from Object Description Language (ODL) files. This page is relevant for OLE automation servers and OLE control projects.

The eighth and last property page controls the building of a browse information file. If you wish to use the browsing features of Developer Studio, make sure that the Build browse info file box is checked (Figure 1.26).

FIGURE 1.26.

Building the browse information file.

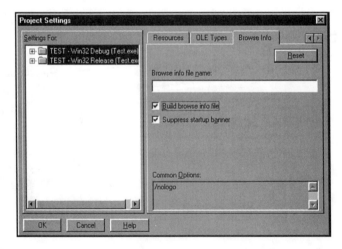

The InfoViewer

A brand new feature of Visual C++ Version 4 is the built-in InfoViewer. The InfoViewer is a Developer Studio component for reading Microsoft MediaView titles (MVB files); most notably, the online documentation that comes with Visual C++ itself.

When Visual C++ 4 is installed on a system on which the Microsoft Developer Library was installed previously, the Visual C++ installation program will add the Developer Library media title to the set of titles that can be browsed using the InfoViewer. Unfortunately, no easy-to-use facility exists for adding other titles.

In my experimentation with Visual C++, I discovered how new titles can be added to the InfoViewer; however, this method, apart from being completely undocumented, requires manually altering Registry contents, so use at your own risk! I used this method successfully to add the MAPI SDK documentation, available for downloading from CompuServe, to the set of media titles that can be browsed using InfoViewer.

Essentially, adding a new title requires adding several subkeys and values under the `HKEY_CURRENT_USER\Software\Microsoft` key in the Registry. The subkeys and values that I needed to add for the MAPI SDK documentation, stored in the file `f:\msdn\mapisdk.mvb`, are as follows:

```
InfoViewer\DocSets\MAPISDK\mapisdk.mvb\MAPISDK=1
InfoViewer\Series\MAPISDK\Title="mapisdk.mvb"
InfoViewer\Titles\MAPISDK.MVB\aux="MAPISDK.AUX"
InfoViewer\Titles\MAPISDK.MVB\Localdir="F:\MSDN"
InfoViewer\Titles\MAPISDK.MVB\Path="F:\MSDN\"
InfoViewer\Titles\MAPISDK.MVB\Series="MAPISDK"
InfoViewer\Titles\MAPISDK.MVB\Title="MAPI Documentation"
```

This method works well for titles that consist of a single MVB file. I have not experimented with titles consisting of multiple MVB files.

Note once again that all the affected Registry keys are under `HKEY_CURRENT_USER`. Even though there is an `InfoViewer` subkey under `HKEY_LOCAL_MACHINE`, you should not alter that key or its subkeys in any way.

WARNING

Editing undocumented Registry entries may yield results incompatible with your version of Visual C++. It is a very good idea to back up the Registry first.

If your effort is successful, the new title shows up in the InfoViewer toolbar (Figure 1.27).

FIGURE 1.27.
The InfoViewer toolbar with a manually added title.

Hopefully, future versions of Visual C++ will make it easier to add or remove InfoViewer titles.

To browse an InfoViewer title, select the InfoView in your Project Workspace window (Figure 1.28). If you have no project open, this is the only view that is visible in that window. To select a specific article, double-click on its title; the InfoViewer will display the article together with a toolbar that contains several navigation buttons.

FIGURE 1.28.

InfoView.

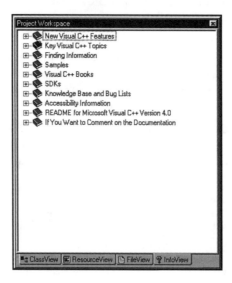

You can set a variety of options for the InfoViewer through the Options command in the Tools menu. InfoViewer search options can be selected through the InfoViewer tab in the Options menu (Figure 1.29); the appearance of text in InfoViewer windows can be specified using the Format tab.

FIGURE 1.29.

InfoViewer options.

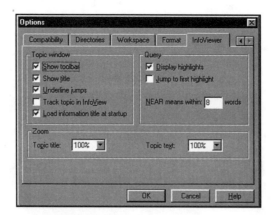

Other Integrated Components

The Developer Studio, in addition to providing the features discussed in this chapter, also provides an integrated interface to some of the major Visual C++ tools.

The AppWizard is a tool for generating skeleton applications. Through the AppWizard, application skeletons for OLE component servers, containers, ODBC and DAO applications, OLE automation servers, OLE controls, and more can be created.

The ClassWizard is perhaps the most often used Visual C++ tool; in addition to being a browser tool for `CCmdTarget`-derived classes, it can also be used to create new classes and add member functions and variables to existing classes.

The source browser provides the capability to review definitions and references of symbols in your application.

The integrated debugger is a highly powerful symbolic debugger for C and C++ applications. It can be used to debug Win32 executables as well as dynamic link libraries.

The Visual C++ Profiler is a performance analysis tool. With the help of the Profiler, you can easily determine which areas of your application represent performance bottlenecks.

Miscellaneous Tools

The Visual C++ development system also includes a set of extra tools that are available from the Tools menu. These tools are stand-alone applications that help you exercise and test programs and components that you develop.

The first of these tools is Spy++, a new application for snooping messages (Figure 1.30). With Spy++, you can display all messages sent or posted to selected windows; you can also specify a subset of messages that you are interested in. Spy can also display the hierarchy of current processes, threads, and windows owned by threads; this way you can select windows for tracing that are normally hidden and could not otherwise be selected on the screen.

FIGURE 1.30.

Microsoft Spy++.

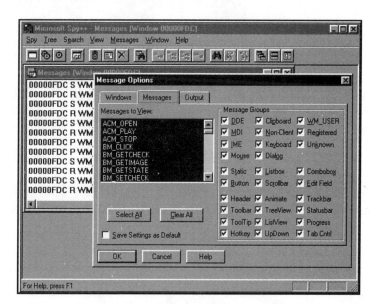

The MFC Tracer application (Figure 1.31) enables you to turn on various MFC trace flags. With these flags on, MFC applications that have been compiled with the debug version of the MFC Library send a variety of debugging messages to debugging output.

FIGURE 1.31.

MFC Tracer.

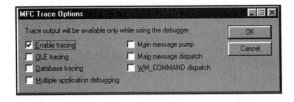

The Register Control option invokes the `regsvr32.exe` program. This program is used to register an OLE control. It does so by loading the control DLL (the OCX file) and calling its `DllRegisterServer` exported function.

The OLE Control Test Container (Figure 1.32) is useful for testing the behavior of OLE controls. You can use this application to insert any registered OLE control, invoke the control's properties and methods, and trace control notifications.

FIGURE 1.32.

OLE Control Test Container.

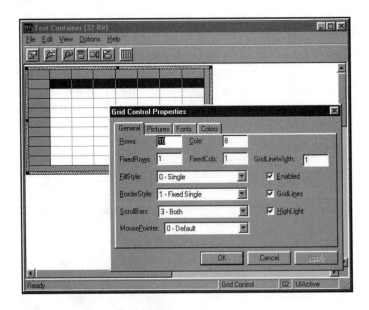

The OLE Object View application (Figure 1.33) is a testing tool that enables you to view all installed OLE types, their properties, interfaces, version numbers, type libraries, and more.

There is a series of additional tools that are not included in the Developer Studio Tools menu. These include DDESpy, a utility to monitor Dynamic Data Exchange activity; the PView process viewer utility; ZoomIn, a utility to capture and enlarge portions of your Windows screen; and WinDiff, a file and directory comparison utility.

FIGURE 1.33.

OLE Object View.

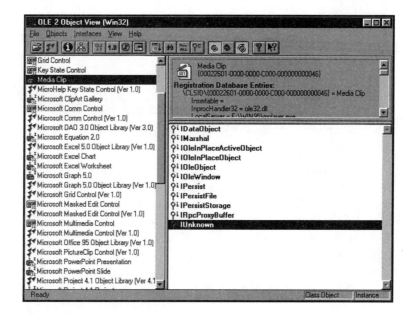

Integration with Other Applications

The Developer Studio, in addition to presenting an excellent interface to many Visual C++ features, also provides integration with other Microsoft development tools. One, I already mentioned; through InfoViewer, the Developer Studio can be used as the reader for the Microsoft Developer Library.

Another product that the Developer Studio provides integration for is Microsoft FORTRAN. If you have Microsoft's FORTRAN PowerStation installed, you can use the Developer Studio to create and build both C++ and FORTRAN projects.

The Developer Studio can also be used in conjunction with Microsoft Test, Microsoft's scripting tool for application testing.

The Developer Studio is also integrated with Microsoft's new source code control system, Visual SourceSafe. If you have Visual SourceSafe installed, a series of additional menu commands appears, providing access to source code control functions.

Command-Line Tools

Is using the wonderful tools of Visual C++ from the command line a heresy? I don't think so. Often it is much simpler to type `cl myprog.c` than to go through the elaborate process of setting up a Visual C++ project, adding your files to it, and recompiling and running your project through the graphical interface.

When would you use the command-line tools? I would like to offer some simple rules of thumb: If your project is complex enough to require a make file, use the graphical interface. If you wish to debug your program interactively, use the graphical interface. If your program has a resource file, use the graphical interface.

However, if you just want to key in a 10-line example from a textbook and quickly test it, you may find it more convenient to do so at the command line. In fact, many simple examples in this book can easily be compiled from the command line (of course, nothing prevents you from loading them as Visual C++ projects).

Many command-line tools depend on the appropriate Visual C++ directories being on the path and on other environment variables being properly set. If you are using Windows NT as your development platform, the Visual C++ installation program offered you the option to register these environment variables so they automatically appear in DOS sessions. If you are using Windows 95, you must run the vcvars32.bat batch file (found in your msdev\bin directory) to register these variables before you can use the command-line tools. Note that it may be necessary to increase the environment size for DOS windows (select the Properties command from the DOS window's control menu and use the Memory tab) before vcvars32.bat can be successfully run.

The vcvars32.bat batch file also accepts an optional parameter that specifies the target system (X86, Motorola 68k, or the PowerPC). Use this parameter to specify a target environment other than Intel X86 on systems with a Visual C++ cross-development edition installed.

The environment variables set by vcvars32.bat include the following: INCLUDE specifies the location of include files for the compiler; LIB specifies the location of library files for the linker; and PATH specifies the location of Visual C++ executables (in addition to any other directories that you may have included there). There are several other environment variables interpreted by the various utilities; for example, the compiler, cl.exe, reads the contents of the CL environment variable for additional command-line options, while the linker reads additional command-line arguments from the LINK environment variable. All Visual C++ programs make use of the TMP environment variable to find the location for temporary files.

The C/C++ Compiler

The Visual C++ compiler is invoked from the command line using the cl command. If invoked with the name of source files on its command line and no other parameters, it compiles those source files, then invokes the linker to create an executable.

If you specify the name of object files or library files on the command line, those will be passed to the linker. For example, consider the following compiler command line:

```
cl hello.c myfunc.obj mylib.lib
```

In response to this command, the Visual C++ compiler will compile `hello.c`, then invoke the linker with `hello.obj` and `myfunc.obj`. It will also pass the name of the library file `mylib.lib` to the linker, which will use this file in addition to any default libraries when searching for library functions.

If you wish to compile a file but not produce an executable, use the `/c` option:

```
cl /c hello.c
```

Note that using the forward slash or the dash is equivalent when specifying command-line options.

Some other useful options include `/MT` (link with the multithreaded version of the run-time library), `/MD` (link with the DLL version of the run-time library), and `/LD` (create a DLL). Of course, the compiler has a myriad other options (type `cl /?` to find out just how many). However, if you need to specify complex options, you're probably better off compiling from the Developer Studio.

The object files produced by the Visual C++ compiler are of the Common Object File Format (COFF).

The Linker

The linker, `link.exe`, is a tool that accepts Common Object File Format (COFF) files, 32-bit Object Module Format (OMF) files, library files, and other input files and produces Win32 executable files or dynamic link libraries. In its simplest form, the linker is invoked with the name of an object file on the command line:

```
link hello.obj
```

The linker accepts many command-line options. Among these is the `/subsystem` option that specifies the type of the resulting executable. For example, specifying `/subsystem:windows` forces the output file to be a Windows executable. However, often it is not necessary to use this option; the linker defaults to `/subsystem:console` if the object files contain a definition for the `main` (or the wide-character version, `wmain`) function, and to `/subsystem:windows` if a `WinMain` (or `wWinMain`) function exists.

If you wish to produce a dynamic link library instead of an executable file, use the `/DLL` option. This option is automatically specified when the linker is invoked by the compiler, and the compiler was run with the `/MD` option.

Many other options control how input files are processed, what default libraries are used, and the type and contents of output files. In additional to executables, the linker can also produce debugging files (such as map files); you can also specify whether the executable is to include debugging information or not.

The Library Manager

The library manager, `lib.exe`, is used to create libraries of COFF object files. It can also be used to create export files and import libraries for DLLs.

In its simplest form, `lib.exe` is invoked with a series of object filenames on its command line. It uses the base name of the first object file as the base name of a library file and creates (or updates) a library consisting of the object files on its command line. The name of the output file can be overridden using the `/OUT` option.

If you wish to later remove the contents of an object file from the library, use the `/REMOVE` option. The `/EXTRACT` option can be used to extract the contents of the object file into a separate file.

To use the library manager to create an export file and an import library, use the `/DEF` option. Note that you rarely need to use this option, as the linker usually automatically creates the export file and the import library. Using the library manager is only required to resolve a situation when a program exports to, and imports from, the same library.

The Program Maintenance Utility

The program maintenance utility, or make tool for short (`nmake.exe`), is used to evaluate dependencies in make files and invoke the appropriate commands to generate targets. For example, a simple make file may look like this:

```
test.exe: test.obj
        link test.obj

test.obj: test.c
        cl /c test.c
```

In all make files, the make tool evaluates targets in the order of their dependencies and updates all targets if they are older than any of their dependencies.

In addition to targets and dependencies, make files can contain many additional features, including macros and inference rules. These features render make files a formidably powerful and versatile tool.

Important options for `nmake.exe` include `/a` (specifying that all targets should be rebuilt unconditionally), `/n` (specifying that the make tool should only display, but not execute, commands), and `/f` (specifying the name of a make file).

Other Command-Line Tools

Other command-line tools that ship with Visual C++ include `rc.exe`, `bscmake.exe`, `dumpbin.exe`, `aviedit.exe`, and `editbin.exe`.

The resource compiler, rc.exe, can be used to compile resource files and prepare them for linking with your project's object files. The resource compiler accepts the name of a resource file (with the .rc extension) and optional switches on the command line. Switches include /d (to define a symbol for the preprocessor), /fo (to specify the name of the output file), and /v (for verbose output). To obtain a complete list of command-line options, run rc.exe with the /? option.

The browse information maintenance utility, bscmake.exe, is used to create browse information (BSC) files from SBR files created during compilation. Browse information files can be viewed from the Developer Studio using its browsing facilities.

The binary file dumper, dumpbin.exe, displays information about COFF object files.

The aviedit.exe program is a simple tool to edit AVI files intended for animation controls. Use this tool to create an animation file from a series of bitmaps.

The binary file editor, editbin.exe, can be used to view and modify certain properties of COFF object files. Among these options is the ability to change a file's base address, the default heap size, and the default stack size.

Summary

The Microsoft Developer Studio is the centerpiece of the Visual C++ development system. It provides a series of different views on your projects through the Project Workspace windows; through this window, a project's class structure, files and dependencies, and resource file components can be examined.

A project workspace may contain one or more top-level projects; each project can have several subprojects, which can further be nested. For each project, Developer Studio maintains a series of configurations; a project configuration consists of settings used to rebuild the project. For example, when you create a new project using the Intel version of Visual C++, by default two project configurations (a debug and a release configuration) are created.

Source files in a project can be edited using the Developer Studio's customizable editor. Resource file components can be edited using the built-in resource editor; these components include accelerator tables, menus, dialogs, toolbars, icons, cursors, bitmaps, string tables, and custom resources.

Project settings can be modified using the Settings command in the Build menu. The Project Settings dialog is a complex dialog with eight property pages and several subpages. Settings for all configurations, specific configurations, a subset of files, or individual files can be specified or altered using this facility. Settings categories include the General, C/C++, Linker, Debug, Resource, OLE Types, Custom Build, and Browse Info categories.

Another useful Developer Studio facility is the InfoViewer; this facility provides access to MediaView titles, such as the Visual C++ online documentation or the Microsoft Developer Library.

The Developer Studio is also integrated with tools such as the AppWizard, ClassWizard, the integrated debugger, profiler, and source browser.

Many Visual C++ components can be used from the command line. For example, a basic Hello, World program can be compiled by typing `cl hello.c`. Other command-line tools include the linker, library manager, and the program maintenance utility (make tool).

Project Creation and the AppWizard

2

One of the great strengths of the Visual C++ development system is its capability to create highly functional application skeletons through the AppWizard tool. The AppWizard can be used to generate skeleton Windows applications with a variety of OLE, database, windowing, help, and other options. The AppWizard can also be used to create Windows DLLs; in addition, specialized AppWizards exist for creating OLE controls and custom AppWizards.

In this section, we review how projects of various types are created using the Developer Studio.

Creating Windows Projects

When you select the New command from the Developer Studio's File menu, you are presented with the choice of creating a new text file, a new project workspace, or a variety of new resource file components (Figure 2.1).

FIGURE 2.1.

The New dialog.

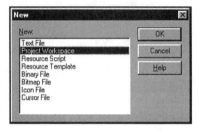

If you select Project Workspace in the New dialog, another dialog, the New Project Workspace dialog, appears (Figure 2.2). In this dialog, you can choose from a variety of workspace options.

FIGURE 2.2.

*The New Project
Workspace dialog.*

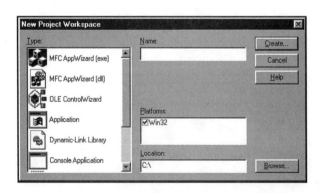

The first two choices listed in this dialog represent AppWizard-generated skeletons for Windows executable programs and for Windows DLLs. Next, we examine these options in detail. Later in this chapter, we take another look at the other project workspace types and how they can be used with new or existing projects.

Types of Windows Applications Created Through AppWizard

If you select MFC AppWizard (exe) as the type of your new project, you are presented with step one of a multistep wizard process (Figure 2.3). In this first step, you can decide the basic characteristic of your new application: whether it will have a single-document-based, multiple-document-based, or dialog-based user interface.

FIGURE 2.3.

MFC AppWizard: Selecting your project's type.

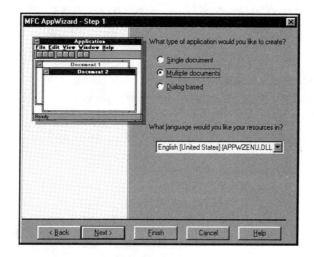

A single-document-based application can present only one file to the user at any given time. A good example for such an application is the Windows NotePad.

A multiple-document-based application, in contrast, can present several documents at once, each in its own child window. Many word processing applications, such as Microsoft's Word for Windows, are multiple-document-based applications.

A dialog-based application presents a single dialog as its user interface. These applications are used when all user interaction can take place through a single dialog template. An example for a dialog-based application is the Windows Character Map.

> **NOTE**
>
> AppWizard-generated dialog-based applications offer substantially fewer MFC features than MFC-based SDI or MDI applications. If you plan to use a document class, view class, or other MFC features, consider creating an SDI application based on the CFormView view class instead of creating a dialog-based application.

During this first AppWizard step, you can also specify the language of your application. Your language selection defines which standard MFC resource set will be included with your project.

You can also use the AppWizard to create a project that supports multiple languages. To do so, create the additional resource files (perhaps by rerunning AppWizard to create dummy projects in the desired language) and add the new resource files to your project. Create additional project configurations, including and excluding resource files as needed.

Document-Based MFC Applications

The creation of single- or multiple-document-based (SDI or MDI) applications through AppWizard are nearly identical procedures, consisting of the same AppWizard steps.

The project files created by AppWizard for SDI and MDI projects are somewhat different; in particular, for an MDI project, AppWizard generates an additional class, CChildFrame, that represents MDI child windows.

After you select one of these document-based options, clicking the Next button takes you to Step 2 of a six-step process. In this step (Figure 2.4), you must specify the level of database support your application will provide. Database support is in the form of MFC's Open Database Connectivity (ODBC) and Data Access Objects (DAO) classes.

FIGURE 2.4.

MFC AppWizard: Selecting database support.

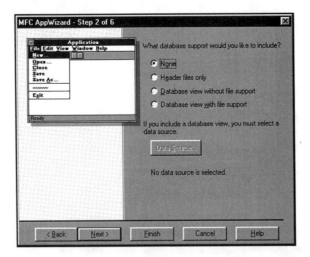

The meaning of the None option is obvious. The Header files only option creates a project with the necessary header files included, but otherwise the project files will be no different from files in a project with no database support.

The remaining two options represent significant additions to your project. First, your project's view class will be a class derived from CRecordView or CDaoRecordView; second, a new class, derived from CRecordSet or CDaoRecordSet, will be added to your project. The new view class is dialog template-based and represents the fields in a record; the recordset class provides an internal representation for those fields and methods to access the underlying tables.

The difference between the Database view with file support and Database view without file support options in AppWizard Step 2 is simple. The former provides menu and toolbar commands to load and save document files; the latter does not. Often, when creating a database application, your application's document class provides merely a transient representation of the database and does not need to be saved; in this case, use the Database view without file support option.

Regardless which of these two options you choose, before you proceed to AppWizard Step 3, you must also specify a data source. The data source is a table or set of tables in a database that can be accessed through the ODBC or DAO mechanism. To select a data source, click on the Data Source button.

AppWizard Step 3 (Figure 2.5) is about support for Object Linking and Embedding features. You can specify whether your application supports OLE compound document functionality as a server, container, mini-server, or container-server. You can also add OLE automation server and OLE control container support; the latter is important if you wish to use OLE controls in your application's dialogs.

FIGURE 2.5.

MFC AppWizard: OLE features.

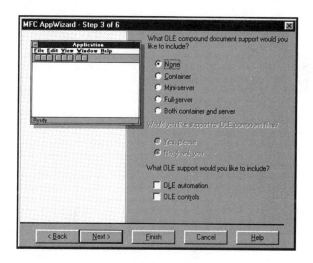

If you select OLE compound document support, you can also specify OLE compound file support.

Depending on which OLE features you select, the AppWizard may generate additional classes for your application. For OLE servers, these additional classes include `CInPlaceFrame` (representing the frame window during in-place editing), and a `COleServerItem`-derived class representing the server object in container applications. For OLE containers, a new `COleClientItem`-derived class is added, representing OLE server items in the container. In both cases, the base class of your application's document class is also modified; it is derived from `COleDocument` in the case of containers, and `COleServerDoc` in the case of servers or container-servers.

Step 4 of AppWizard (Figure 2.6) contains a variety of miscellaneous options. The checkboxes for toolbar support, status bar support, and support for 3-D controls require little explanation.

FIGURE 2.6.

MFC AppWizard: Miscellaneous options in Step 4.

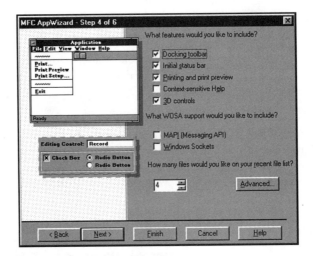

If you clear the Printing and print preview checkbox (it is set by default), your application will not have a Print or Print Preview command in its File menu, nor will it provide support for print preview mode. It is generally a good idea to leave this box checked even if you do not wish to provide the printing commands in the File menu, as long as you intend to use the printing and print preview–related features of MFC.

Setting the Context-sensitive Help checkbox adds a skeletal help project file and help topic files to your application. It also adds the batch file `makehelp.bat` that can be used to regenerate your project's help file.

Adding Messaging API (MAPI) support to your application means two things: first, your application will be linked with the MAPI libraries; second, your application will have a Send menu item in its File menu. Often this is all you need to provide minimal MAPI support for compatibility with Windows 95 application requirements.

Setting the Windows Sockets checkbox adds WinSock libraries and header files to your project. However, you are responsible for adding any specific WinSock functionality.

Of particular interest in AppWizard Step 4 is the Advanced Options dialog, invoked when you click on the Advanced button. Through this dialog, you can specify a variety of additional options that affect your application's appearance and execution in subtle ways.

The Advanced Options dialog is a tabbed dialog. The first tab, Document Template Strings (Figure 2.7), enables you to specify several string values defining your application's default filename extension, filename filter, file type identifier, and more. These strings are combined and stored in your application's string table (in the resource file) under the identifier IDR_MAINFRAME. For example, the string corresponding to the settings shown in Figure 2.7 is this:

```
TEST\n\nTEST\nTEST Files (*.tst)\n.TST\nTEST.Document\nTEST Document
```

FIGURE 2.7.

MFC AppWizard: Advanced document template string settings.

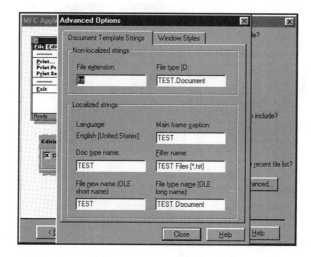

The second tab in this dialog, Window Styles (Figure 2.8), can be used to specify the window styles for the application's frame window. You can also select split window support; when this checkbox is set, your application's views will have a splitter bar.

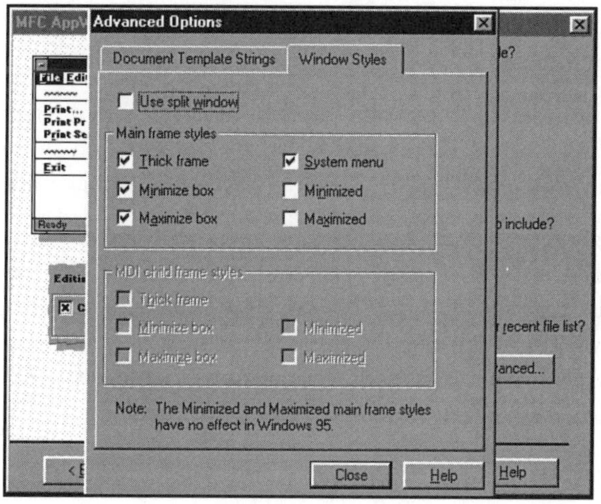

FIGURE 2.8.

MFC AppWizard: Advanced window style settings.

In this part of the Advanced Options dialog, you can also modify settings for child frame windows in MDI applications.

Step 5 of AppWizard (Figure 2.9) enables you to specify two simple options; whether the AppWizard-generated skeleton source should contain comments or not, and whether the MFC Library should be linked to your project as a static library or a DLL.

FIGURE 2.9.

MFC AppWizard Step 5.

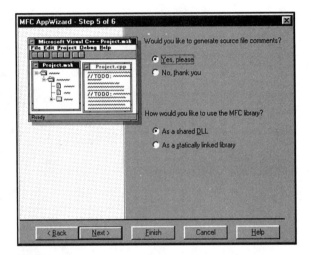

Usually, specifying source file comments is a good idea. In addition to providing meaningful explanations in your code, the AppWizard also generates "TODO" comments, which indicate those points in your code that you need to complete or modify manually.

The final step in the AppWizard process, Step 6 (Figure 2.10), lists the classes that the AppWizard is about to create for your application. You can also modify some aspects of class creation at this stage. For example, you can modify the base class of your application's view class to be based on the CFormView or CScrollView class, instead of the default CView.

To complete the AppWizard process, click the Finish button. This displays the New Project Information dialog (incidentally, giving you one more chance to back out and cancel the AppWizard procedure); this dialog displays information about the skeleton project. This information is also saved in your project directory as your project's readme.txt file.

The classes generated for a basic single-document-based application include a document class, a view class, a frame window class, and a CWinApp-derived class representing the application. The declaration and definition of a CDialog-derived class, representing your application's About dialog, will also be included in the implementation file of your application's CWinApp-derived class. Depending on what additional options you specified (MDI support, database support, OLE features), additional classes may be generated by AppWizard.

FIGURE 2.10.

MFC AppWizard:
Class overview.

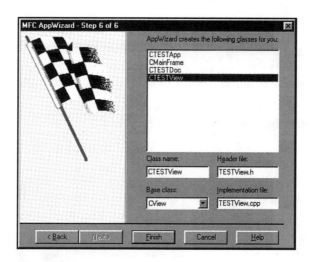

Dialog-Based MFC Applications

The AppWizard process for creating a dialog-based MFC application is much shorter than creating document-based applications. Selecting a dialog-based application in AppWizard Step 1 and clicking on the Next button takes you to Step 2 of a four-step process (Figure 2.11).

FIGURE 2.11.

MFC AppWizard:
Creating a dialog-
based application.

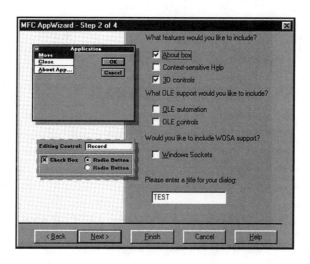

The About box option in this step adds an About command to the dialog's control menu; note that the dialog will not have a menu bar. The Context-sensitive Help option adds AppWizard-generated skeletal help support in the form of a help project file, topic files, and the `makehelp.bat` script for regenerating your application's help file. The 3D controls option needs no explanation.

You can also specify OLE automation and OLE control support. Check the latter if you wish to use OLE controls in the dialog.

The Windows Sockets option adds WinSock header and library files to your project; however, it is up to you to implement any specific WinSock functionality.

You can also specify the title of your application; this text will be displayed in the title bar of the application's dialog box.

Step 3 of the AppWizard process for dialog-based applications is identical to Step 5 for document-based applications (see Figure 2.9). Similarly, Step 4 for dialog-based applications is the same as Step 6 for document-based ones; however, the list of generated classes is different (Figure 1.12). Only two classes are created: one representing the application object, the other representing the application's dialog.

FIGURE 2.12.

MFC AppWizard: Dialog-based application classes.

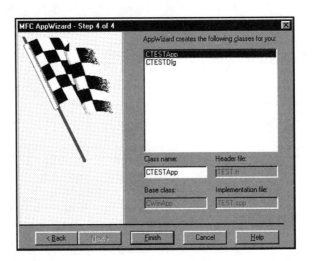

In many cases, you may find that a dialog-based AppWizard-generated skeleton application lacks the features that you wish to see in your program. In such cases, consider using an SDI application based on the CFormView class.

Using AppWizard to Create MFC-Based DLLs

If you use the AppWizard to create an MFC-based DLL skeleton, you are presented with a one-step procedure where you can specify your DLL's characteristics (Figure 2.13).

The first set of options is where you specify how the DLL should be linked with the MFC Library. Linking statically is the most expensive in terms of disk space and memory requirements. The least expensive is creating an MFC extension DLL; however, these DLLs can only be used with MFC applications. A regular DLL linked with the MFC DLL can, in turn, be called from any application.

FIGURE 2.13.

MFC AppWizard: Creating an MFC-based DLL.

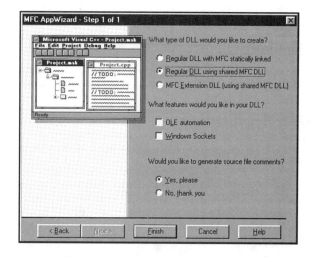

By setting the OLE Automation checkbox, you enable support for using your DLL as an OLE Automation inproc server. (An inproc server is a server that executes in the process space of the client application, as opposed to using a remote procedure call mechanism for communicating with the client.)

Adding WinSock support enables compiling and linking with the WinSock header and library files; however, you must add your own implementation of any WinSock-specific functionality. Finally, you can also specify if you wish to see AppWizard-generated source comments in your DLL.

Other Project Types

The New command in the Developer Studio's File menu, in addition to letting you create skeleton projects with AppWizard, also enables you to create other, blank projects.

Application

Creating an application means creating a project and its make file in support of a Windows-based graphical application. The make file will be blank; you will need to add your project files manually. You can use this option, for example, when you are setting up a Developer Studio project for a set of source files not created with AppWizard. You can also use this option to import files from a project that was created earlier with an incompatible version of Visual C++. However, you should try to open that project's make file (or better yet, a copy of the make file) first; chances are that if it is a make file generated by Visual C++, the Developer Studio will be able to successfully import it and convert it to its new format.

Dynamic Link Library

Creating a dynamic link library means creating the make file and project file for a dynamic link library project. The compiler and linker settings will be configured to generate a DLL file. The project will be blank; you must add or create your source files manually.

Console Application

A console application is a program that runs from the command line in Windows 95 or Windows NT DOS boxes. Creating a console application project means creating a blank project with project files and a make file supporting the generation of a console program. You must add or create your source files manually for this application.

Static Library

A static library is a library file with the `.lib` extension that can be linked with other projects. Selecting the static library option in the New Project Workspace dialog creates a make file and support files for a static library project. The project will be blank; you must add your own source files to create the library.

Make File

You can use the option to create a make file-based project when you wish to specify an external make file or some other executable program that is used to rebuild your project. This option is also useful when adding existing projects as subprojects.

Specialty AppWizards

The New Project Workspace dialog also offers access to special versions of the AppWizard. These include the OLE ControlWizard, the Custom AppWizard, and any custom AppWizards you may have created.

OLE ControlWizard

The OLE ControlWizard guides you through the steps of creating a project that consists of one or more OLE controls. An OLE control project creates an OCX file that is a special DLL file. The first of the two AppWizard steps is used to specify generic properties of your OLE control project; the second step enables you to specify settings specific to individual controls in your project.

Custom AppWizard

The Custom AppWizard enables you to create custom AppWizards (and if terms like "AppWizard-generated AppWizard project skeleton" confuse you, you are not alone). A custom AppWizard can be based on the standard AppWizards for MFC applications or DLLs; it can also be based on an existing project or contain only custom steps you define. If you specify that your custom AppWizard be based on standard steps, a second step of the Custom AppWizard lets you select which AppWizard to use. If your custom AppWizard is to be based on an existing project, you can specify the project's path in the second step. For custom AppWizards consisting entirely of custom steps, Step 2 of the Custom AppWizard is unavailable.

Modifying an Existing Project

A recurring problem with AppWizard-generated projects is how to modify project options "after the fact"—after a project has been created and extensive changes have been made to it. There are two methods that can be used for this purpose: manually updating your project based on dummy AppWizard projects is one, use of the Component Gallery is another.

Modifying a Project Manually

The first method consists of creating two dummy projects, one with the settings you used in your original application, another with the desired AppWizard settings. When the two projects have been created, close the project workspaces, and use the WinDiff utility to compare the two project directories. This comparison reveals any changes or additions that the AppWizard added for the project with the new settings. You can incorporate these changes into your own project manually.

Using the Component Gallery

Many AppWizard options can also be added to a project through the Component Gallery. For example, you can add MAPI support, OLE automation support, or support for OLE controls to an existing project using the appropriate components from the Component Gallery. In some cases, you may be able to use components from your own project to add support for specific features to your application.

Summary

The AppWizard has a central role in the Visual C++ development system for creating skeleton applications.

The AppWizard can be used to create project workspaces for MFC-based Windows applications and Windows DLLs.

Creating a document-based Windows MFC application is a six-step process. In the various AppWizard steps, you can specify database support, support for OLE features; you can determine your application's appearance, add support for context-sensitive help and printing, Windows Sockets and MAPI; and you can modify the list of classes generated by AppWizard.

Creating a dialog-based Windows MFC application is simpler; in addition to controlling your application's appearance, you can add OLE automation and OLE control support and modify the AppWizard-generated list of classes for your project.

In addition to MFC projects, you can also create blank projects for Windows applications, DLLs, console applications, static libraries, and existing make files.

There are also specialty AppWizards. The OLE ControlWizard can be used to create OLE control projects; the Custom AppWizard enables you to create customized versions of the AppWizard based on standard steps, an existing project, or your own custom steps.

If you created a project with the wrong settings, you can modify the project by copying settings from a dummy AppWizard project that was created with the settings you require. Alternatively, many options can also be added to an existing project using components in the Component Gallery.

The ClassWizard and the WizardBar

3

Next to the AppWizard, the ClassWizard represents the second most powerful tool in the Visual C++ development system. ClassWizard represents a unique way of looking at and managing certain types of classes; namely, classes that are command targets, from the MFC class `CCmdTarget`.

ClassWizard Features

The ClassWizard is typically invoked from the Developer Studio's View menu. It can also be invoked from many popup menus; for example, you can invoke the ClassWizard from the popup menu that appears during dialog editing. In such cases, the ClassWizard is invoked in a special mode. It usually appears with the relevant class (that is, the class associated with the dialog template you were editing) preselected. If such a class does not exist, the ClassWizard is invoked in class creation mode where a new class for the selected object (dialog) can be created.

The ClassWizard appears to the user as a large dialog with five tabs. Each of these tabs represents a special ClassWizard function. The Message Map tab presents options for defining and editing message handler functions. The Member Variables tab is where you assign member variables to dialog controls in classes that are associated with a dialog template. The OLE Automation tab offers a choice of OLE automation methods and properties of an OLE server application or DLL. The OLE Events tab is where you add events to an OLE control. Lastly, the Class Info tab presents a review of some of the overall characteristics of your class.

Message Maps

The MFC implements a special mechanism for the processing of Windows messages. These messages, after being received by the application's message loop, travel through the application's `CCmdTarget`-derived class objects in accordance with a set of specific rules. When an object receives a message it can handle, it does so; alternatively, it can also pass on the message for further routing.

Whether an object can handle a message or not depends on whether it has an entry for that particular type of message in its message map. The message map for MFC classes is maintained through the ClassWizard.

Figure 3.1 shows the message map for the property page of an OLE control. (I decided to use a simple OLE control project for the illustrations in this chapter for the simple reason that it is the classes of an OLE control that allow me to demonstrate all features of ClassWizard.)

Take a look at the left side of this dialog. The Object IDs list shows that you can specify message map entries for the class itself, `COCTLPropPage`; however, you can also specify message map entries for specific control identifiers. The `IDC_CBSHAPE` identifier in Figure 3.1 refers to a control (a combo box) in the dialog template that the `COCTLPropPage` class is associated with. If the class is a dialog or property page class, the ClassWizard will list the identifiers of all the controls of the dialog template associated with that class in the Object IDs column.

The list of selectable messages on the right side, in the Messages column, varies depending on which item you pick on the left side. If you select the class name, this list shows all Window Manager (WM_) messages that the class may respond to; if the class has overridable functions, those are also shown here.

If you select a control identifier in the Object IDs column, the list on the right side changes; it shows the list of WM_COMMAND messages that the control can send to its parent.

Adding a handler function for a specific message can be done by clicking on the Add Function button or double-clicking on the message item in the Messages column. Either way, ClassWizard responds with the Add Member Function dialog, shown in Figure 3.2.

FIGURE 3.1.

Editing message maps through ClassWizard.

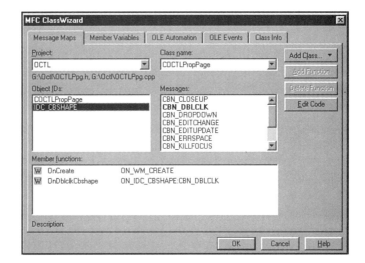

FIGURE 3.2.

Adding a message handler function to a class.

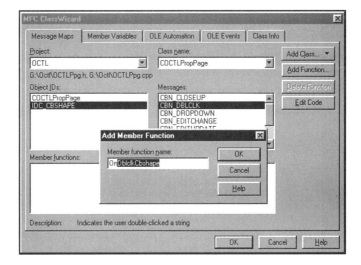

You can edit the suggested member function name or accept it as is; the member function is created when you click the OK button.

The name of the new member function then appears in the Member functions list at the bottom of the ClassWizard dialog. Invisible to you, the ClassWizard also modifies code files; it adds the member function name to the header file for this class and also adds a default member function implementation to the implementation file.

For example, when you add the member function shown in Figure 3.2 to the COCTLPropPage class, its message map declaration in its header file is modified as follows:

```
// Message maps
protected:
    //{{AFX_MSG(COCTLPropPage)
    afx_msg void OnDblclkCbshape();
    //}}AFX_MSG
    DECLARE_MESSAGE_MAP()
```

The ClassWizard identifies the location of the message map in your code by the special comments that enclose it. Message map declarations, for example, are marked by comments that begin with //{{AFX_MSG. Under normal circumstances, you should never modify code that is marked by such comments. It is easy to notice these ClassWizard-specific sections of code in your source files; by default, the Developer Studio editor shows these portions of your application with a special color.

The message map declaration is not the only place that the ClassWizard touched. It also modified the message map definition, in the implementation file of COCTLPropPage:

```
/////////////////////////////////////////////////////////////////
// Message map

BEGIN_MESSAGE_MAP(COCTLPropPage, COlePropertyPage)
    //{{AFX_MSG_MAP(COCTLPropPage)
    ON_CBN_DBLCLK(IDC_CBSHAPE, OnDblclkCbshape)
    //}}AFX_MSG_MAP
END_MESSAGE_MAP()
```

Most importantly, the ClassWizard also added a skeleton implementation of the new function, OnDblclkCbshape. This implementation is simply appended to the file; it is your responsibility to move it elsewhere in order to keep your source file well organized:

```
/////////////////////////////////////////////////////////////////
// COCTLPropPage message handlers

void COCTLPropPage::OnDblclkCbshape()
{
    // TODO: Add your control notification handler code here

}
```

The ClassWizard can also be used to remove handler functions. To remove a message handler, select it from the Member functions list in ClassWizard, and click the Delete Function button.

The ClassWizard will warn you that removing the member function will not cause the automatic deletion of its implementation; indeed, the function will only be removed from the message map declaration and definition. You will have to manually remove, or comment out, your implementation of the function.

Member Variables

In the second tab in the ClassWizard dialog, you can add and modify member variables (Figure 3.3).

FIGURE 3.3.

Editing member variables with ClassWizard.

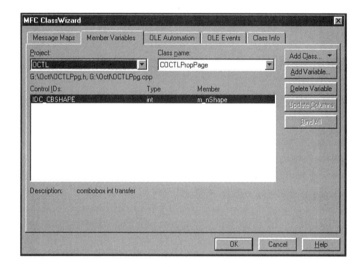

The member variables that you can edit here are those that are associated with controls in the dialog template for your class. (Needless to say, the class must represent a dialog or property page.)

The list in this ClassWizard page lists all control identifiers with which member variables can be associated. Any existing member variables are also shown. To add a new member variable to a control, select its identifier, and click on the Add Variable button (or simply double-click the control name).

In the Add Member Variable dialog (Figure 3.4), you can specify the name and type of the new variable.

Generally, there are two kinds of member variables that can be assigned to a control. Either a member variable representing the control's value, or a member variable representing the control object can be specified. However, for many control types (buttons, for example), only the latter kind of variable is available. You can select whether the variable is to represent the control's value or the control itself in the Category field.

FIGURE 3.4.

Adding a member variable.

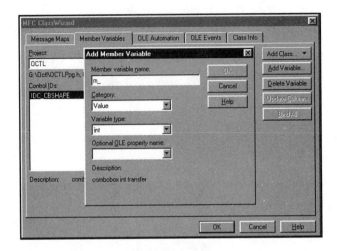

Variables that represent a control's value are typically of a simple type, like CString or int. Variables that represent controls are of a class representing the control's type; for example, CButton or CComboBox.

You can normally add only one member variable for a specific control. However, if a control is of a type that enables member variables representing both the control's value and the object itself, you can add both to the control. Thus, it is possible, for example, to have an edit control with a CEdit member variable through which the control's appearance and behavior are controlled, while at the same time, another member variable of type CString represents the text typed into the same control.

For OLE controls, a new member variable added to the control's property page may represent a control property. This property is identified in the Optional OLE property name field. You can assign a user-defined property name to the member variable, or you can select one predefined property from the list presented in this box.

When you define a new member variable, the ClassWizard updates your application's source code in several places. For example, adding the m_nShape member variable shown in Figure 3.3 is reflected by the following change in the COCTLPropPage header file:

```
// Dialog Data
    //{{AFX_DATA(COCTLPropPage)
    enum { IDD = IDD_PROPPAGE_OCTL };
    int     m_nShape;
    //}}AFX_DATA
```

The ClassWizard also changed the class's implementation file. Initialization for the new variable has been added to the class's constructor:

```
COCTLPropPage::COCTLPropPage() :
    COlePropertyPage(IDD, IDS_OCTL_PPG_CAPTION)
{
```

```
    //{{AFX_DATA_INIT(COCTLPropPage)
    m_nShape = -1;
    //}}AFX_DATA_INIT
}
```

Another function that is modified by ClassWizard is the class's `DoDataExchange` member function. It is in this function where information is exchanged between the control object itself and the variable representing it or its value. In the case of `COCTLPropPage`, this function is modified as follows:

```
//////////////////////////////////////////////////////////////////
// COCTLPropPage::DoDataExchange - Moves data between page and properties

void COCTLPropPage::DoDataExchange(CDataExchange* pDX)
{
    //{{AFX_DATA_MAP(COCTLPropPage)
    DDP_CBIndex(pDX, IDC_CBSHAPE, m_nShape, _T("Shape") );
    DDX_CBIndex(pDX, IDC_CBSHAPE, m_nShape);
    //}}AFX_DATA_MAP
    DDP_PostProcessing(pDX);
}
```

Not only is there a call to the Dialog Data Exchange (DDX) function facilitating the exchange of data between the control object and the member variable, a Property Page (DDP) function is also called; this function exchanges data between the member variable and the OLE control object.

In the case of classes representing records in databases, the ClassWizard may make modifications to other functions as well (for example, the `DoFieldExchange` member function of `CRecordSet`-derived classes).

OLE Automation

The OLE Automation tab of ClassWizard (Figure 3.5) enables you to add or modify OLE automation properties and methods. A property is basically a member variable that is exposed to the outside world through the OLE Automation interface; a method is a member function exposed in a similar fashion. In addition to classes that have OLE automation enabled, classes representing OLE controls also have exposed properties and methods.

Not all classes in your application support OLE automation. Although you can add OLE automation support to a class using the OLE Automation tool in the Component Gallery, you may have to manually update your application's Object Description Language (ODL) file to reflect this change in your application's type library. To find out what needs to be added to the ODL file, consider creating a dummy class with OLE automation support enabled and copying the relevant ODL entries.

You can tell whether a class supports OLE automation by simply looking at the buttons on the right side of the ClassWizard OLE Automation page; if the buttons (except for the Add Class button) are all grayed, the class does not support OLE automation.

FIGURE 3.5.

*Defining OLE
automation
properties and
methods.*

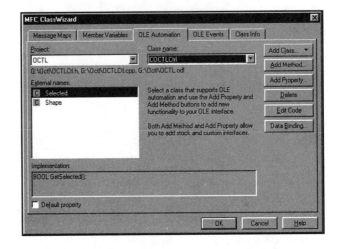

To add an OLE automation method to a class, click the Add Method button. This displays the Add Method dialog, shown in Figure 3.6.

FIGURE 3.6.

*Adding an OLE
automation
method.*

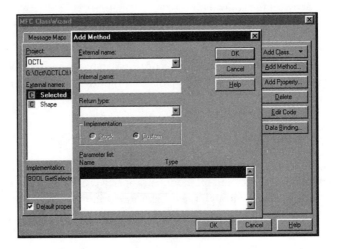

The first thing you specify for a new method is its external name; the name by which it will be known to other applications. If the class represents an OLE control, you can also select the name of a standard method from the drop-down list in the External name field.

By default, the ClassWizard suggests the external name you specified as the method's internal name; that is, the name of the member function that implements the method. You must also specify the member function's return type and its parameter list. To add parameters to the parameter list, simply click in the Parameter list area with the mouse, type the name of the desired parameter, and select its type.

For stock properties (available for OLE controls only) you can also specify Stock Implementation. In this case, the Internal name, Return type, and Parameter list fields in this dialog will not be available.

To add a new property to your OLE automation class or OLE control class, click on the Add Property button in ClassWizard. This button invokes the Add Property dialog (Figure 3.7).

FIGURE 3.7.

Adding an OLE automation property.

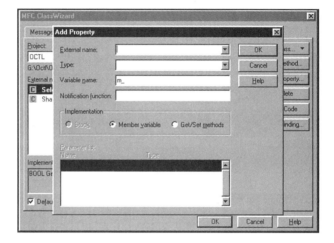

There are two fundamentally different ways of implementing an OLE automation property. An OLE automation property can be represented by a member variable or by Get/Set methods; that is, a pair of functions that set or obtain the property's value.

The first thing to specify for a new property is its external name. Based on the property's external name and its implementation, the ClassWizard will suggest names for the member variable or Get/Set methods that represent the property. For example, if you add a property named X, the ClassWizard will suggest the member variable name m_x or the Get/Set method names GetX and SetX. For properties implemented through member variables, you can also specify a notification function that is called whenever the variable's value is changed. The ClassWizard also suggests a name for the notification function (OnXChanged for property X).

When you are adding a property with a Get/Set method implementation, you may also specify a list of additional parameters that will be added to the declaration of the Get/Set method functions. To specify a parameter, click in the parameter list area using the mouse, type the parameter's name, and select its type.

For OLE controls, you can also add stock properties. If you add a stock property, you may decide to use a stock implementation. In this case the Type, Variable name, Notification function, and Parameter list areas in the Add Property dialog remain unavailable.

In the ClassWizard dialog, once you have a series of OLE automation properties defined for your class, you can designate one as your class's default property.

For OLE controls, you can also specify the level of data binding support you wish to add to the control. Data binding is the capability to bind an OLE control's properties to fields in a database. Use the Data Binding button to designate a property as a bindable property and also to specify the level of data binding the property supports through the Data Binding dialog (Figure 3.8).

FIGURE 3.8.

Data binding support.

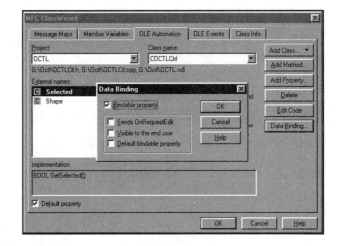

OLE Events

OLE events are events generated by OLE controls. Events represent a mechanism through which the control can communicate with its container.

OLE events for an OLE control class can be added or modified through the OLE Events tab in ClassWizard (Figure 3.9).

FIGURE 3.9.

OLE events.

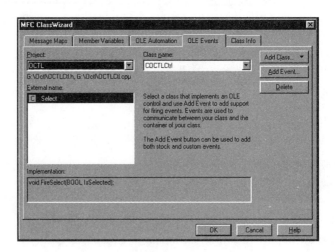

To create a new OLE event, click on the Add Event button. This displays the Add Event dialog (Figure 3.10) where the new event can be specified.

FIGURE 3.10.

Adding an OLE event.

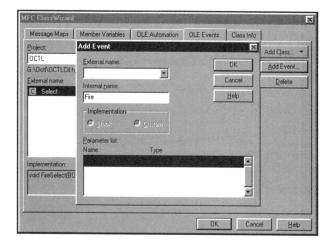

You can either specify a custom event or select one of several stock events. For stock events, you can specify the stock implementation or you can use a custom implementation. Custom implementation is the only available option for custom events.

For every event specified, the ClassWizard generates a function that fires the event. For this function, the ClassWizard suggests a name combining the word `Fire` with the event's external name; for example, for an event named `Select`, the function name suggested by ClassWizard will be `FireSelect`.

When a new event is added, the ClassWizard modifies your class's header file by adding the event to the event map. The event is added in the form of its firing function and its inline implementation. For example, for a custom `Select` event, ClassWizard modifies the event map as follows:

```
// Event maps
   //{{AFX_EVENT(COCTLCtrl)
   void FireSelect(BOOL IsSelected)
     {FireEvent(eventidSelect,EVENT_PARAM(VTS_BOOL), IsSelected);}
   //}}AFX_EVENT
   DECLARE_EVENT_MAP()
```

The event is invoked when you call the firing function from within other functions in your code.

The firing function can also have additional parameters. You can add parameters to the firing function when you add the event itself. In the Add Event dialog, click in the Parameter list area, type the desired parameter's name, and specify the parameter's type.

Class Info

The last page in the ClassWizard dialog is the Class Info page (Figure 3.11). In this page, various properties of classes are displayed, and certain advanced options can be modified.

FIGURE 3.11.

Class Info options.

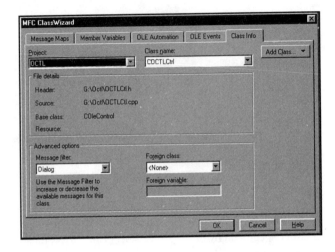

The first of the Advanced options, the Message filter option, enables you to specify which messages should be shown by ClassWizard in the Message Map page. Note that changing the Message filter does not affect your application code in any way; it merely affects what ClassWizard displays.

The Foreign class option is most relevant with database applications. In such applications, the application's view class, derived from CRecordView or CDaoRecordView, is associated with a recordset class, derived from CRecordSet or CDaoRecordSet. In these cases, the foreign class is the name of the recordset class; the foreign variable is the pointer variable in your application's view class that represents a foreign class object. It is necessary for ClassWizard to know the identity of the foreign class because it has to be able to refer to the member variables of the recordset class and update this class's OnFieldExchange member function.

Creating a New Class

By clicking on the Add Class button, you can add a new class to your application. ClassWizard enables you to add a class using an existing implementation, create a class using a type library file, or create a new class from scratch.

Adding a class from an existing implementation really means importing class data to ClassWizard; the class is presumably already part of your project. This function is most useful if you imported a new class to your project by copying its header and implementation files and adding them to your project manually. It can also be used to re-create your application's Class

Information File (CLW file) if it has been damaged. This is the file where ClassWizard keeps all class-related information.

Adding a class from an OLE type library means creating a new class that wraps the interface described in the type library. For example, you can use this feature to add a class that represents an OLE control or OLE automation object (Figure 3.12).

FIGURE 3.12.

Adding a class from an OLE type library.

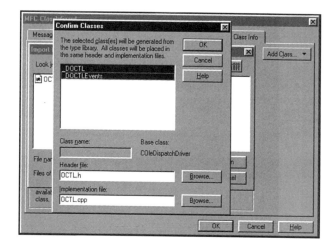

You can also add a new class from scratch. If you select the New option from the Add Class button's popup menu, you are presented with the Create New Class dialog (Figure 3.13).

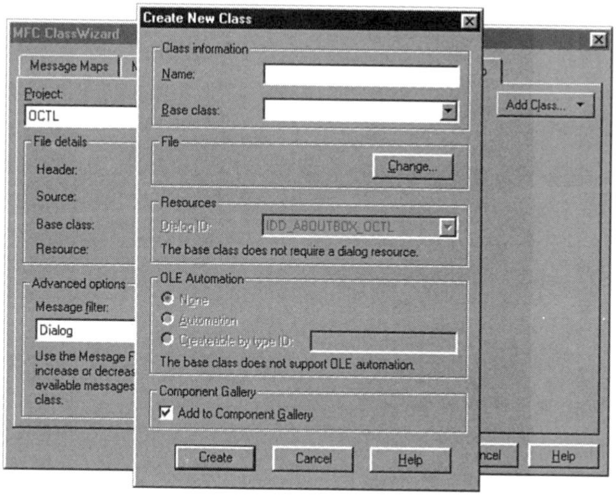

FIGURE 3.13.

Adding a new class.

The first thing to specify for a new class is its name; you should also specify the base class from which the new class is derived. The available selections in the Base class field represent those CCmdTarget-derived classes that are recognized by ClassWizard.

ClassWizard derives a default pair of header and implementation filenames from the class name you specify. For example, if you specified CMyClass as the class name, ClassWizard would suggest MyClass.h and MyClass.cpp as the names for the class's header file and implementation file. However, you can change these names by clicking on the Change button.

If the selected base class represents a dialog template (for example, a dialog, form view, or property page class), the Dialog ID field becomes available. Here, you can select a dialog template identifier from the list of identifiers that are present in your application's resource file.

Similarly, if the base class provides support for OLE automation, the items in the OLE Automation area become available. Note that some classes support OLE automation but do not support creating objects; therefore, the Creatable by type ID field remains grayed.

NOTE

In order for the OLE automation settings to work properly, your application must have been created through AppWizard with OLE automation support enabled. Otherwise, your application will not have an Object Description Language (ODL) file. This will cause many ClassWizard operations to fail and your project may not compile and build properly.

You can also add your newly created class to the Component Gallery. Doing so makes it possible for you to import the class into other projects.

NOTE

If you wish to add a class that is not derived from a class recognized by ClassWizard, you have to create the class's header and implementation files manually and add the files to your project by hand. Such a class will not appear in the list of classes in ClassWizard.

Editing Code

Another common ClassWizard function is the Edit Code function, available in the Message Maps and OLE Automation pages. Clicking on the Edit Code button dismisses the ClassWizard dialog, opens the source file corresponding to the function that was most recently selected in ClassWizard, and positions the cursor over the implementation of the selected function. This is a great convenience feature of ClassWizard.

The WizardBar

A new feature in Visual C++ 4 is that some ClassWizard functions are now available in the form of a toolbar that is part of source code windows (Figure 3.14).

FIGURE 3.14.

The WizardBar.

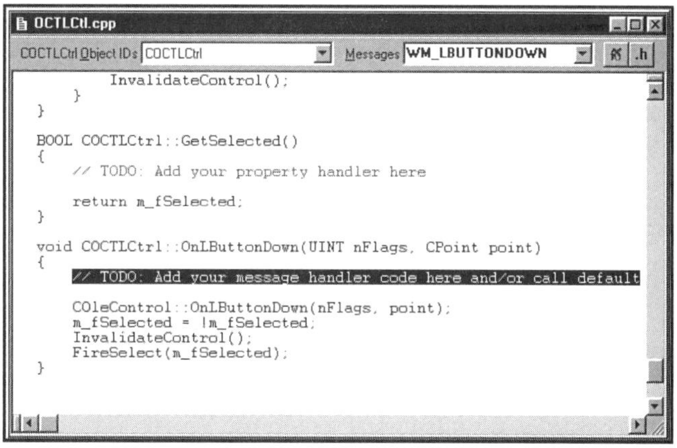

```
█ OCTLCtl.cpp                                              _□×
COCTLCtrl Object IDs COCTLCtrl         ▼  Messages WM_LBUTTONDOWN  ▼  ▨ .h
              InvalidateControl();
       }
}

BOOL COCTLCtrl::GetSelected()
{
    // TODO: Add your property handler here

    return m_fSelected;
}

void COCTLCtrl::OnLButtonDown(UINT nFlags, CPoint point)
{
    // TODO: Add your message handler code here and/or call default

    COleControl::OnLButtonDown(nFlags, point);
    m_fSelected = !m_fSelected;
    InvalidateControl();
    FireSelect(m_fSelected);
}
```

Specifically, the WizardBar provides a convenient shortcut for the ClassWizard functions relating to message handlers. Through the WizardBar, it is very easy to add new event handler functions or to jump to the implementation of a specific event handler.

The combo box on the left side of the WizardBar contains the identifier of the class itself, as well as the identifiers of any controls that can be the source of WM_COMMAND messages. The other combo box contains message identifiers, command identifiers, and the names of overridable functions. These two controls work in a fashion similar to the Message Maps page of ClassWizard. To jump to a specific function in your source code, simply select the appropriate function using these two combo boxes. If the function exists, the cursor will be positioned at the beginning of its implementation; however, if the function does not exist, you will be presented with the option of creating a handler for the specific message or event.

The WizardBar also contains two buttons. The Delete Function deletes the declaration of the specified function. (Note that, just as if you deleted the function from the ClassWizard itself, it remains your responsibility to manually remove the function's implementation.) The Open Header button opens the header file that corresponds to the currently open implementation file.

The Class Information File

By this time, it should be plainly obvious that the ClassWizard, although it is capable of parsing your application's source files, also maintains a fair amount of information that cannot be extracted from source files. All this information is stored in a special file, the class information file; by default, this is a file with the same base name as the name of your project, and the `.clw` extension.

Usually, you do not need to modify your application's class information file in any way. However, there is one exception; and that is the case when you wish to add custom Dialog Data Exchange (DDX) and Dialog Data Validation (DDV) functions and desire ClassWizard support for these.

Information about custom DDX and DDV functions is added to the class information file in a special section marked by the `[ExtraDDX]` header. The specific procedure for adding custom DDX and DDV support to ClassWizard is described in MFC Technical Note 26.

Because of the relative complexity of the procedure, it is usually not beneficial to add custom DDX/DDV support this way unless you intend to reuse your custom DDX/DDV routines in other applications.

Summary

The ClassWizard is a fundamental tool in the Visual C++ development system; through this tool, you can manipulate your application's `CCmdTarget`-derived classes in a variety of ways.

The ClassWizard presents itself in the form of a dialog with five pages. The first of these five pages, the Message Maps page, enables you to define message handler functions for a variety of events, including `WM_COMMAND` messages generated by controls in dialogs. The Message Maps page is also where you specify your implementations for many overridable functions.

At the Member Variables page, you can add member variables that are associated with dialog controls. Two types of member variables can be added for each control; variables associated with the control's value and variables associated with the control object itself. A control can have one variable of each type; however, many kinds of controls do not support variables representing their value. If the member variable represents a control in an OLE control's property page, you can also associate an OLE control property with the variable.

The OLE Automation page presents the selection of OLE automation methods and properties to classes that support OLE automation. For OLE controls, you can also add stock method and properties in addition to user-defined ones. You can also specify the level of data binding that specific properties of an OLE control support.

The OLE Events page is specific to OLE controls and lets you specify what OLE events the control may generate. Adding an OLE event also adds a firing function for the event. You can also stock events to your OLE control.

The Class Info page shows some general information about classes. It can also be used to modify the behavior of ClassWizard as related to this class, by enabling you to change the message filter the ClassWizard applies when displaying the class's message map, and by setting up or changing the foreign class associated with this class.

A new class can be added to the project by clicking the New Class button. New classes can be added from scratch, can be generated from an OLE type library, or can be added from existing header and implementation files. Note that you can only add classes that are derived from base classes that ClassWizard recognizes; other types of classes can be added to your project manually but will not be visible in ClassWizard.

The WizardBar represents a shortcut to some Message Map–related functions in ClassWizard. The WizardBar is visible when source files are being edited and lets you quickly and easily add message handlers or overridable functions to your application, or to position the cursor over an existing message handler or overridable.

Class information is stored in the class information file. While usually this file should not be modified manually, the exception to this rule is when you implement your own set of DDX/ DDV functions and wish to have ClassWizard support for them.

Source Browsing

4

In addition to the ClassWizard, the Source Browser is yet another invaluable development tool in Visual C++. This tool enables you to quickly locate definitions and references of symbols and to explore the relationship between symbols.

Adding Source Browser Information to a Project

The Source Browser tool requires the presence of a browser information file in your project. To add browser information, you must change your project settings; alternatively, you can also invoke the BSCMAKE utility manually.

Changing Project Settings

If you attempt to use source browsing features when no browser information file exists, the Developer Studio warns you of this and offers the option of rebuilding your project with browser information. You can also specify browser information in the Project Settings dialog (Figure 4.1). Select the Settings command from the Build menu to invoke this dialog, and select the Browse Info tab.

FIGURE 4.1.

Adding browse information to a project.

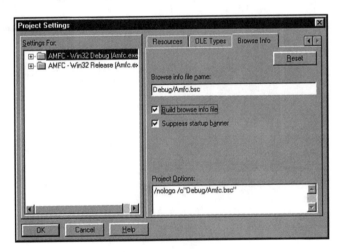

To add browse information to your project, make sure the Build browse info file check box is set. Note that you can apply this setting selectively; for example, you can specify that browse information be added to your project's Debug build, but not to its Release version.

In this dialog, you can also specify additional command-line settings for the bscmake.exe utility.

The BSCMAKE Tool

The BSCMAKE tool, `bscmake.exe`, is the utility that creates browse information (BSC) files. This file is generated from source browser (SBR) files that are created during the link process. BSCMAKE employs a few tricks to improve its efficiency; for example, when it is finished processing an SBR file, it resets that file's length to zero, thus indicating that the file has no new information. This way, BSCMAKE can perform an incremental build of the browse information file during subsequent invocations. You can prevent BSCMAKE from implementing this behavior by specifying the /n command-line switch; when run with this switch, BSCMAKE performs a full build of the browse information file and does not truncate SBR files.

The `bscmake.exe` utility has several command-line options that can be used to improve its performance and limit the size of the BSC file. These options all begin with /E. For example, /Ei can be used to exclude the contents of specified include files from the build; /Er can be used to exclude specific symbols (the name of the include file or symbol to be excluded must be specified on the command line; if you wish to specify multiple filenames, enclose them in parenthesis). Other /E options include /El (exclude local symbols), /Em (exclude symbols in macro bodies), /Es (exclude include files specified with an absolute path either explicitly or through the INCLUDE environment variable).

BSCMAKE by default does not include unreferenced symbols in the browse information file. To include unreferenced symbols, specify the /Iu command-line option. Note that this option has no effect if the compiler generated packed SBR files, which do not contain unreferenced symbols.

To prevent BSCMAKE from repeatedly processing a header file that appears in several source files with preprocessor settings, use the /S option; this option forces BSCMAKE to ignore repeated occurrences of the header files specified on the command line.

BSCMAKE uses the base name of the first SBR file on its command line as the base name for its output file. To specify another output filename, use the /o command-line option.

The following example performs a full rebuild of a source information file. It also prevents BSCMAKE from processing two header files repeatedly:

```
bscmake /n /S (myhd1.h myhd2.h) /o myproj.bsc mysrc1.sbr mysrc2.sbr
```

The Source Browser Window

The features of the Source Browser can be accessed through the Source Browser window. This window is invoked through the Browse command in the Tools menu. This command presents the Browse dialog (Figure 4.2), where you can enter the symbol you wish to look up and specify the type of browse information that you wish to see. If a symbol is presently highlighted in ClassView or in an editor window, the symbol will appear as a default in the Identifier field of this dialog.

FIGURE 4.2.

The Browse dialog.

Note that you can use the asterisk as a wildcard character when specifying the symbol in this dialog.

You can also invoke the Source Browser window from within ClassView in the Project Workspace window. Position the cursor over a symbol (class name, member function name, member variable name, or global symbol) and right-click to invoke the popup menu. Depending on the symbol's type, the popup menu will contain several commands (for example, the Base classes or Called by commands) that take you directly to the Source Browser window. Another shortcut available in these popup menus (and also popup menus in source editor windows) can take you directly to a symbol's declaration, definition, or references; this capability is a shortcut to a key Source Browser functionality.

Definitions and References

Depending on how you invoke it, the Source Browser can provide several views on your application's source code. The first of these views is the Definitions and References window (Figure 4.3).

FIGURE 4.3.

Source Browser: Definitions and References.

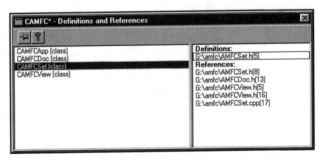

In this window, all definitions and references of the specified symbols are shown. Selecting a definition or reference and double-clicking on it opens the appropriate source (or header) file and positions the cursor directly over the selected definition or reference. Thus, the source browser can be used as an efficient source navigation tool.

File Outline

The File Outline window (Figure 4.4) provides a unique view on a source or header file. This window lists all classes, functions, variables, macros, and types defined in the specified file.

FIGURE 4.4.

Source Browser:
File Outline.

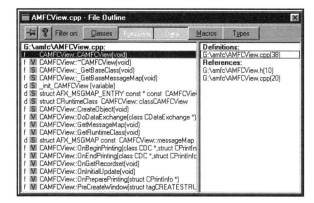

This window also contains a series of buttons that can be used to filter out unwanted symbols. You can specify which types of symbols you wish to see listed by clicking the appropriate button in the window's toolbar.

The type of a symbol is displayed in the form of a lowercase letter in the left pane of the File Outline window. For example, a lowercase *f* means that the symbol is a function. Next to this letter, an uppercase letter on gray background specifies whether the symbol is virtual (for example, a virtual member function) or static.

Base Classes and Members

The Base Classes and Members window (Figure 4.5) is a three-pane window where you can browse the base classes of a specific class; it also shows the selected class's member functions and variables and the definitions and references for those.

In the combo boxes in this window's toolbar, you can specify what combination of virtual, static, nonvirtual, and nonstatic functions you wish to see listed; and also, what combination of static and nonstatic data you wish to see appear.

In the pane displaying class members, the type of a member is marked by the lowercase letter *f* (function) or *d* (data). Another, uppercase letter on a gray background shows whether the member is declared as virtual or static.

FIGURE 4.5.

Source Browser:
Base Classes and
Members.

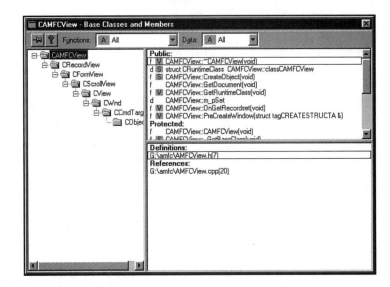

Derived Classes and Members

The Derived Classes and Members window (Figure 4.6) enables you to browse classes derived from a specific class. The appearance and behavior of this window are similar to that of the Base Classes and Members window.

FIGURE 4.6.

Source Browser:
Derived Classes and
Members.

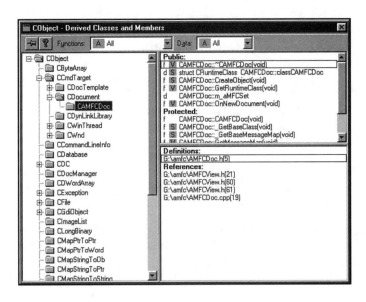

This window is also a very useful tool for familiarizing yourself with the structure of the Microsoft Foundation Classes. For example, as shown in Figure 4.6, you can browse the entire hierarchy CObject-derived classes, exploring their members and their relationships.

Call Graph

The Call Graph window (Figure 4.7) shows a hierarchical view of functions called by the specified function.

FIGURE 4.7.

Source Browser: Call Graph.

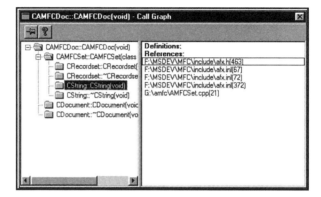

Callers Graph

The Callers Graph window (Figure 4.8) shows the hierarchy of functions that call the specified function.

FIGURE 4.8.

Source Browser: Callers Graph.

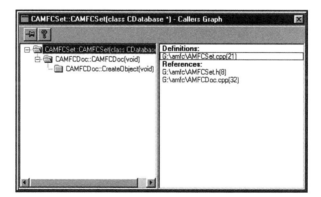

Summary

The Source Browser is an invaluable reference tool component of Visual C++.

Using the Source Browser requires that your project be built with source browser information added. You can select this option in the Project Settings dialog (Browse Info tab). The tool used to build browser information (BSC files) is the `bscmake.exe` utility.

The Source Browser window, invoked through the Browse command in the Tools menu or through various popup menus, presents six different views on your application's source.

The Definitions and References window lists all definitions and references for selected symbols. If you double-click on a definition or reference, the appropriate source or header file is opened with the cursor positioned at the location of the selected definition or reference.

The File Outline window presents a view of all symbols declared or defined in a specified source or header file. Toolbar buttons let you control what type of symbols you wish to see listed.

The Base Classes and Members window is where you browse the base classes of a specific class. The Derived Classes and Member window is where you do the same for classes derived from the specified class.

The Call Graph and Callers Graph windows can be used to list the functions called by a specific function or the functions that call a specific function.

Debugging and Profiling

5

One of the great features of Visual C++ is its excellent integrated symbolic debugger. This debugger has many features, such as Just-in-Time debugging (the ability to debug programs that crash while launched outside the development environment) or remote debugging. It is also fully integrated with other features of the Development Studio, such as the Source Browser or source editors.

When you are faced with the task of having to identify performance bottlenecks in your application, the debugger is often of little help. Fortunately, you can use another tool, the Source Profiler, for this purpose. The Profiler uses the same debugging information as the debugger and analyzes how frequently elements of your code are accessed.

The Integrated Debugger

The Visual C++ integrated debugger is launched when you run an application in debug mode. This is accomplished by selecting the Go, Step Into, or Run to Cursor commands from the Debug submenu in the Developer Studio's Build menu. However, before you can start the debugger, you must ensure that the application you are about to debug has been compiled with debugging information.

Preparing an Application for Debugging

In order for the symbolic debugger to function, you must compile an application with debugging information. If your application is an MFC application that was originally created through AppWizard, chances are that you do not have to do anything; the AppWizard already created a debug configuration for your project and made it the default configuration.

However, if you need to create a debug configuration yourself, you can do so in the Project Settings dialog. You must set the appropriate compiler and linker options that make debugging possible.

To set the compiler options, invoke the Project Settings dialog through the Settings command in the Build menu, and select the C/C++ tab. Select the General category, and select the configuration you wish to use as the debug configuration in the left side of the Project Settings window. To enable debugging, you must alter two settings: in the Debug info field, select Program Database, and in the Optimizations field select Disable (Debug), as shown in Figure 5.1. If you wish to utilize the Developer Studio's Source Browser features, you may also set the Generate browse info check box; for AppWizard-generated debug configurations, this check box is turned off by default to save compiler time.

If you are using the compiler from the command line or from within a custom make file, you may need to set these debugging options manually. To turn off optimization, use the /Od compiler option; to turn on the generation of debugging information, specify the /Zi option.

FIGURE 5.1.

Setting up the compiler for debugging.

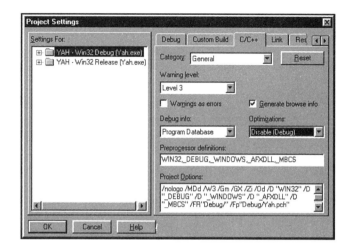

Another setting that is relevant for debugging specifies that your project be linked with the debug version of the C Run-time Library. This is specified by selecting the Code Generation category and picking the desired debug library in the Use run-time library field (Figure 5.2). The equivalent compiler command-line option is /MDd (debug DLL), /MLd (debug single-threaded library), or /MTd (debug multithreaded library).

FIGURE 5.2.

Specifying a debug run-time library.

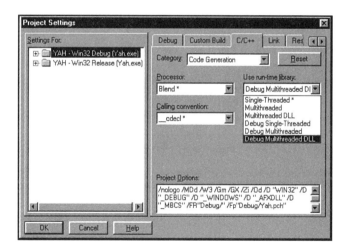

In addition to compiler settings, linker settings must also be modified. This can also be done from the Project Settings dialog. Select the Linker tab and the General category. To turn on the generation of debugging information, set the Generate debug info check box (Figure 5.3).

The command-line equivalent for this option is /debug on the linker command line.

FIGURE 5.3.

Setting up the linker for debugging.

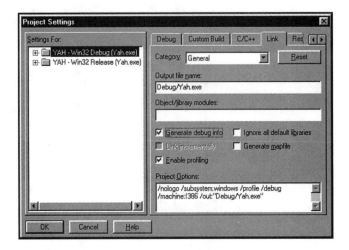

Running an Application with the Debugger

Once you recompile your application with debug settings, you can run it in debug mode by using any of the commands in the Debug submenu in the Build menu.

How an application is run when it is being debugged is also controlled through the Project Settings dialog. A setting of special interest is the Executable for debug session field (Figure 5.4). Use of this field enables you to debug dynamic link library (DLL) projects. Instead of specifying the name of the DLL, you should specify the name of a program that loads and exercises the DLL. For example, to debug an OLE control (which is a special type of a DLL), you can use the Visual C++ utility tstcon32.exe as the debug session executable.

FIGURE 5.4.

Debug options.

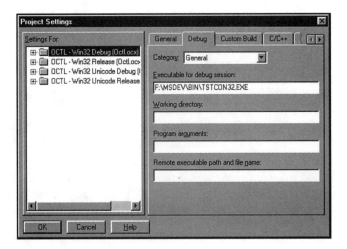

When you begin a debug session, depending on your Developer Studio settings, any one of a variety of debug windows may appear. Other windows (such as the Project Workspace window) that are normally present may also disappear. The Developer Studio menu bar also changes: the Debug menu replaces the Build menu.

The application selected for debugging starts executing until a breakpoint is reached or its execution is interrupted by the Break command from the Debug menu.

Debug Windows

During a debugging session, the Developer Studio presents debugging information in a series of debug windows. These windows, if not displayed, can be invoked through the appropriate command in the Developer Studio's View menu. All of these windows can be displayed as normal windows or as docking windows. If they are used as docking windows, they also appear in the toolbar popup menu—the menu that appears if you right-click in an empty toolbar area.

Source windows are regular source editor windows. However, during a debugging session, special debugging functions are also available through the popup menu that is invoked by right-clicking inside a source window. You can set, clear, or enable/disable breakpoints. You can also execute single-stepping commands. The Disassembly window and the QuickWatch dialog can also be invoked from this menu.

The Variables window (Figure 5.5) presents a look on the variables in the current function. This window has three tabs; the Auto tab shows variables that are used in the current line and the previous line; the Locals tab shows all variables that are local to the current function including function parameters; and the this tab shows the object pointed to by the `this` pointer.

FIGURE 5.5.

The Variables window.

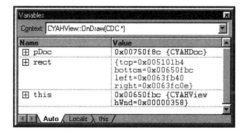

The Variables window can also be used to view variables in the scope of functions that called the current function.

As you single-step through your code, the Variables window shows all changed variables with a different color.

The Variables window can also be utilized to modify the values of data items that are of a simple type (for example, `int`, `double`, or pointer types). To modify a value, double-click on it in the Variables window; if the value can be modified, a text cursor will appear.

The Watch window (Figure 5.6) can be used to monitor the values of expressions. You can enter an expression in the Name field using the keyboard, or you can paste it (or drag it) from a source window.

FIGURE 5.6.

The Watch window.

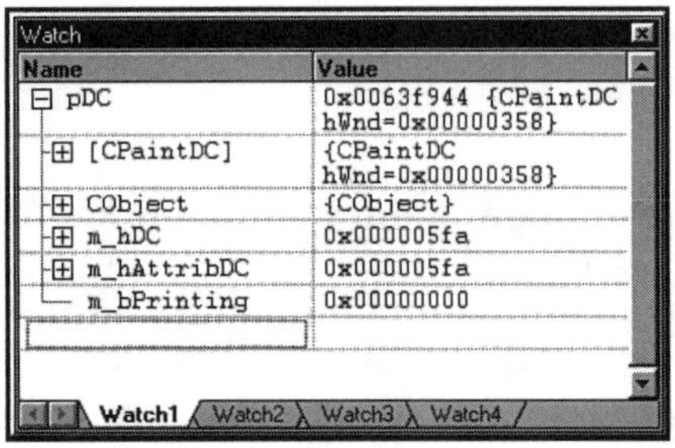

The Watch window has four tabs. You can use these tabs to maintain four different sets of watch expressions (for example, representing the context of four different functions).

The Watch window also uses a different color to mark expressions that change as you single-step through your code. Like the Variables window, the Watch window can also be used to modify the values of data items of a simple type.

The Registers window (Figure 5.7) shows the current values in the registers of the computer's processor, including (optionally) its floating-point registers. This is another window that uses a different color to mark values that change during single-stepping.

FIGURE 5.7.

The Registers window.

The Memory window (Figure 5.8) enables you to view memory contents in the address space of the process that is being debugged.

The Memory window can display memory contents in byte format, word (short hex) format, and double word (long hex) format. If byte format is used, the ASCII characters represented by those bytes are also displayed. You can select the format through the Memory window popup menu; to invoke this menu, right-click anywhere in the Memory window.

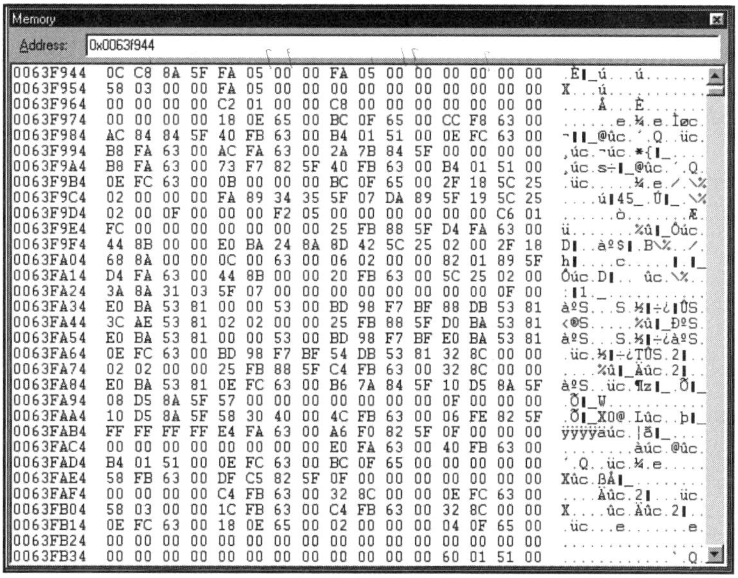

FIGURE 5.8.

The Memory window.

To display memory at a specific location, type an expression in the Address field of the Memory window's toolbar. Note that the Memory window displays memory locations that precede the specified address; if the address is specified as a symbolic expression, this may make it a bit difficult to interpret the Memory window contents. However, the caret (text cursor) is positioned at the correct location, so use this cursor's position as a guide as to where the requested block of memory begins.

The Memory window also uses color to highlight changed values.

The Call Stack window (Figure 5.9) lists the hierarchy of function calls that led to the current function. Double-clicking on a function in this window updates source windows and other debugger windows to reflect the context of that function. Selecting a function in the Call Stack window and pressing the F7 key executes code until the specified function is reached.

The Disassembly window (Figure 5.10) provides a view on the assembly language code that the compiler generates for your application. While this window has the focus, the single-stepping features of the debugger work differently; instead of stepping through source lines, they enable you to step through individual assembly language instructions.

A special feature of the Disassembly window is available through the popup menu that appears when you right-click anywhere within the window. The Set Next Statement command enables you to alter the processor's instruction pointer, setting it to the address of the statement that is under the text cursor. You can use this feature, for example, to skip portions of your code. However, you should use this command with care; do not set the next statement to be one in the body of another function, and make sure that the stack is maintained properly. Otherwise, the results will be unpredictable and the application you are debugging will probably crash.

FIGURE 5.9.

The Call Stack window.

```
Call Stack
⇨ CYAHView::OnDraw(CDC * 0x0063f944 {CPaintDC hWnd=0x00000358}) line 64
  CView::OnPaint() line 187
  CWnd::OnWndMsg(unsigned int 0x0000000f, unsigned int 0x00000000, long
  CWnd::WindowProc(unsigned int 0x0000000f, unsigned int 0x00000000, long
  AfxCallWndProc(CWnd * 0x00650fbc {CYAHView hWnd=0x00000358}, HWND__ *
  AfxWndProc(HWND__ * 0x00000358, unsigned int 0x0000000f, unsigned int
  AfxWndProcBase(HWND__ * 0x00000358, unsigned int 0x0000000f, unsigned
  KERNEL32! bff73663()
  KERNEL32! bff92858()
  00638c2c()
  058f64c9()
```

FIGURE 5.10.

The Disassembly window.

```
Disassembly
    64:         pDC->DPtoLP(&rect);
⇨ 00401207    lea     eax,dword ptr [rect]
  0040120a    push    eax
  0040120b    mov     ecx,dword ptr [pDC]
  0040120e    call    ?DPtoLP@CDC@@QBEXPAUtagRECT@@@Z (004020a8)
    65:         pDC->DrawText(pDoc->m_sData, &rect,
    66:                 DT_CENTER | DT_VCENTER | DT_SINGLELINE);
  00401213    push    00000025
  00401215    lea     eax,dword ptr [rect]
  00401218    push    eax
  00401219    mov     eax,dword ptr [pDoc]
  0040121c    add     eax,00000054
  0040121f    push    eax
  00401220    mov     ecx,dword ptr [pDC]
  00401223    call    ?DrawTextA@CDC@@QAEHABVCString@@PAUtagRECT@@I@
    67:
    68:     }
  00401228    jmp     CYAHView::OnDraw+00000061 (0040122d)
  0040122d    pop     edi
  0040122e    pop     esi
  0040122f    pop     ebx
  00401230    leave
  00401231    ret     0004
```

Breakpoints and Single-Stepping

The two most fundamental features of any debugger are the ability to insert breakpoints into code and the ability to execute code step-by-step.

The simplest way to place a breakpoint in your code is to move the text cursor over the specific location in a source window and press the F9 key. The presence of a breakpoint is marked by a large red dot to the left of the source line (Figure 5.11). Note that you can also set breakpoints in the Disassembly window.

FIGURE 5.11.

Breakpoints in a source window.

```
YAHView.cpp                                                    _ □ ×
CYAHView Object IDs: CYAHView          ▼   Messages              ▼  🔲 .h

        //  the CREATESTRUCT cs

        return CView::PreCreateWindow(cs);
    }

    //////////////////////////////////////////////////////////////////
    // CYAHView drawing

    void CYAHView::OnDraw(CDC* pDC)
    {
        CYAHDoc* pDoc = GetDocument();
        ASSERT_VALID(pDoc);

        // TODO: add draw code for native data here
●       CRect rect;
        GetClientRect(&rect);
        pDC->DPtoLP(&rect);
        pDC->DrawText(pDoc->m_sData, &rect,
                      DT_CENTER | DT_VCENTER | DT_SINGLELINE);

    }

    //////////////////////////////////////////////////////////////////
    // CYAHView printing
```

Much finer control of breakpoint settings can be achieved through the Breakpoints command in the Edit menu. This command displays the Breakpoints dialog, where three different kinds of breakpoints can be set.

Location breakpoints are those that interrupt program execution at a specific location. These are the breakpoints that you set using the F9 key. You can also add a conditional check to a location breakpoint; instead of interrupting your program every time, the breakpoint will interrupt your code only when the specific condition is satisfied.

Data breakpoints interrupt program expression when a specific expression's value changes. For both data and location breakpoints, you can invoke the Advanced Breakpoint dialog (Figure 5.12) by clicking on the triangular button next to the breakpoint identifier. Here, you can specify the context of the breakpoint; the function, source file, and executable file in which it is located.

FIGURE 5.12.

The Advanced Breakpoint dialog.

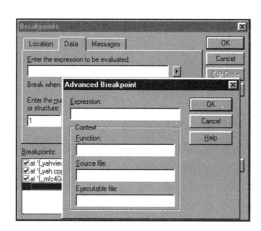

The third type of breakpoint is a message breakpoint (Figure 5.13). Such a breakpoint interrupts your program's execution when a specific message is received by one of your program's window procedures.

FIGURE 5.13.

Setting a message breakpoint.

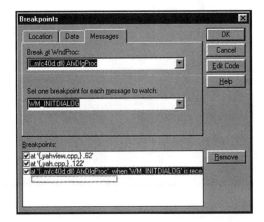

A breakpoint can be active or disabled. When a breakpoint is active, a checkmark appears next to it in the Breakpoints dialog's list of breakpoints. If you click this checkmark, the breakpoint turns inactive.

Program execution can also be interrupted using the Break command in the Debug menu. However, such an interruption is asynchronous by nature and may cause the program to be interrupted deep inside nested system function calls. You can use the Step Out command in the Debug menu to step out of such functions until you reach a recognizable location in your code.

The Step Out command is just one of several single-stepping commands that you can use to execute your program one step at a time. The most basic single-stepping command is the Step Into command; this command executes the next line in your source file or the next instruction in the Disassembly window, stepping into the bodies of functions if the instruction is a function call.

The Step Over command is similar to Step Into except that this command does not step into the body of a function; instead, the function call is completed and execution stops at the next source line or assembly instruction in the calling function.

The Run to Cursor command effectively places a one-shot breakpoint at the cursor's current location in a source window or the Disassembly window; execution continues until the cursor position is reached or until another breakpoint is triggered.

The Step Into Specific Function command can be used to control which function is entered in the case of nested function calls in a single source line.

Many of these commands have keyboard shortcuts; these are shown in Table 5.1. These shortcuts are different from the keyboard shortcuts in Visual C++ 2.0 or earlier versions. (Note that if you selected Version 2.0 compatibility during installation, the keyboard shortcuts will default to those used in these earlier versions, not the ones shown in Table 5.1). You can, of course, also customize these shortcuts by selecting the Customize command from the Developer Studio's Tools menu, and clicking on the Keyboard tab in the Customize dialog.

Table 5.1. Keyboard shortcuts to single-stepping commands.

Command	Function key
Step Into	F11
Step Over	F10
Step Out	Shift+F11
Run to Cursor	Ctrl+F10

While a program is halted, you can specify the instruction at which execution should continue. Use the Set Next Statement command in either a source window or the Disassembly window. Be careful when using this command; never set the next statement to one in a different function.

QuickWatch and DataTips

Often it is necessary to examine the value of a specific symbol that does not appear in the Variables or Watch windows. The Visual C++ debugger provides two features for this purpose: the QuickWatch window and DataTips.

DataTips are similar to the familiar tooltips the show hints for a button or other user-interface object when the cursor rests over them for a brief period of time. If during a debugging session you position the mouse cursor over the name of a symbol that can be evaluated, the symbol's value is displayed in a tooltip-like window (Figure 5.14).

Sometimes, you need to evaluate expressions for which the DataTips feature is insufficient. In these cases, you can invoke the QuickWatch dialog (Figure 5.15) through the QuickWatch command in the Debug menu. If the text cursor was positioned over a symbol name, it automatically appears in the QuickWatch dialog; if an expression was highlighted, that expression appears instead.

The function and appearance of the QuickWatch dialog are similar to those of the Watch window. In particular, you can use this window to alter the values of data items that are of a simple type.

FIGURE 5.14.
DataTips.

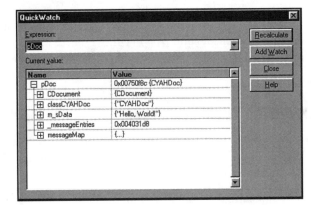

FIGURE 5.15.
The QuickWatch dialog.

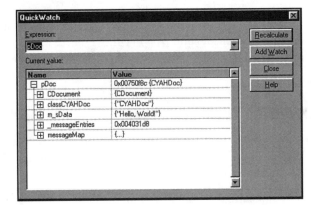

Threads and Exceptions

The Threads dialog (Figure 5.16), invoked through the Threads command in the Debug menu, lists all current threads in your application. This dialog can be used to set the focus to a specific thread when debugging a multithreaded application.

FIGURE 5.16.
The Threads dialog.

The Exceptions dialog (Figure 5.17) specifies how your program responds to exceptions during a debug session. You can select a standard exception or specify a user-defined exception. The Action field specifies how the debugger responds when it is notified of a specific exception.

FIGURE 5.17.

The Exceptions window.

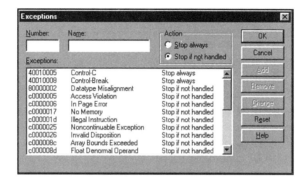

Simple Debugging Techniques

The Visual C++ integrated debugger and the various debugging features in the Microsoft Foundation classes provide for a variety of different debugging techniques.

Using Message Boxes

Sometimes it is not convenient to use the integrated debugger. For example, the presence of the debugger window may interfere with your program's execution, or the bug that you are trying to resolve appears only in the release version of your program. In this case, a well-placed message box may be all you need to catch an elusive bug. For example, when you determined that a two-parameter function named `foo` in your application misbehaves, you can easily verify that the function receives correct parameters by adding a call to `AfxMessageBox` as follows:

```
...
char temp[100];
wsprintf(temp, "Calling foo(x = %d, y = %d)", x, y);
AfxMessageBox(temp);
foo(x, y);
```

Debugging Output

When an MFC application is compiled with debug libraries, many MFC functions generate debugging output. You can also generate debugging output in your own code, using the `TRACE`, or `TRACE0`, `TRACE1`, `TRACE2`, `TRACE3` macros. Debugging output is sent to `afxDump`, a predefined object of type `CDumpContext`, and usually appears in the Developer Studio's Output window; to see debug output, select the Debug tab in this window.

For example, to examine the values passed to the foo function, you could write:

```
...
TRACE2("Calling foo(x = %d, y = %d)", x, y);
AfxMessageBox(temp);
foo(x, y);
```

Note that this type of debugging output appears only if your application has been compiled for debugging. It also requires that your application be launched from the debugger, even if you do not wish to use other debugging features.

Using the TRACE0, TRACE1, TRACE2, TRACE3 macros is recommended when appropriate, as these macros require slightly less memory and resources than TRACE.

The TRACE family of macros is nonfunctional unless an application has been built for debugging.

Assertions

The ASSERT macro can be used to interrupt program execution when a specific condition is false. This macro can be used in debug versions of your application to verify, for example, that a function received proper parameters:

```
void foo(int x)
{
    ASSERT (x >= 0 && x < 100);
    ...
```

The ASSERT_VALID macro is used to verify that a pointer points to a valid CObject-derived object. For example, when you have a function called GetDocument that returns a pointer to an object of CMyDoc, you may verify that this pointer is valid as follows:

```
CMyDoc *pDoc;
pDoc = GetDocument();
ASSERT_VALID(pDoc);
...
```

ASSERT macros, after displaying a message box indicating the line number at which the assertion failed, interrupt program execution. However, in programs that have not been built for debugging, assertion macros do nothing.

Object Dumping

The CObject class has a member function, Dump, that dumps the contents of an object to the debugging output. If you intend to use this feature, implement the Dump member function for classes that you derive from CObject either directly or indirectly.

For example, if your application has a CDocument-derived class, CMyDoc, with two member variables, m_x and m_y, your CMyDoc::Dump implementation may look like this:

```
#ifdef _DEBUG
void CMyDoc::Dump(CDumpContext& dc) const
{
    CDocument::Dump(dc);
    dc << "m_x = " << m_x << '\n';
    dc << "m_y = " << m_y << '\n';
}
#endif //_DEBUG
```

Detecting Memory Leaks and the *CMemoryState* class

The CMemoryState class can be used to detect memory leaks that occur due to inappropriate use of the C++ new or delete operators. To take a snapshot of memory allocation, create a CMemoryState object and call its Checkpoint member function. Later, you can call the DumpAllObjectsSince member function to dump the contents of all objects since the last time Checkpoint was called. For example, to dump any objects allocated by foo that the function fails to deallocate, you could use the following code:

```
...
CMemoryState memState;
memState.Checkpoint();
foo(x, y);
memState.DumpAllObjectsSince();
```

If you do not need to see a complete dump of all allocated objects, you can also use the DumpStatistics member function. DumpStatistics can be called after the difference between two memory states has been evaluated using the Difference member function. This technique requires altogether three CMemoryState objects; the first two are used to take snapshots of the state of memory, while the third is used to evaluate their differences as in the following example:

```
CMemoryState msBefore, msAfter, msDiff;
...
msBefore.Checkpoint();
foo(x,y);
msAfter.Checkpoint();
if (msDiff.Difference(msBefore, msAfter))
    msDiff.DumpStatistics();
```

> **NOTE**
>
> CMemoryState objects cannot be used to detect memory leaks caused by incorrect calls to malloc/free, GlobalAlloc/GlobalFree, or LocalAlloc/LocalFree.

MFC Tracing

The debug version of the MFC Library sends a variety of trace messages to the debugging output. These messages can be enabled or disabled through the MFC Tracer application, tracer.exe. This application can be invoked from the Tools menu.

The MFC Tracer presents a simple dialog interface (Figure 5.18) where you can specify the MFC trace messages that you are interested in.

FIGURE 5.18.

The MFC Trace Options.

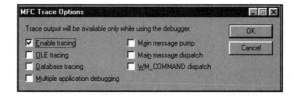

Remote Debugging

Remote debugging enables you to debug code running on another machine. The local and the remote machines are connected through a serial connection or a local area network; the local machine runs the Visual C++ Developer Studio and its integrated debugger, while the application that is being debugged runs on the remote machine with the Visual C++ Debug Monitor (Figure 5.19).

FIGURE 5.19.

Remote debugging.

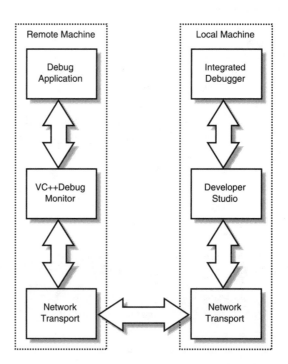

In order to be enabled for remote debugging, the remote machine must run the Visual C++ Debug Monitor application, `msvcmon.exe`. In order for this application to run properly, you must also have the following DLLs installed on the remote computer: `msvcrt40.dll`, `tln0com.dll`, `tln0t.dll`, and `dmn0.dll`. Copy all these files into a directory that is on your path (for example, the Windows system directory).

To use remote debugging, first you must run the debug monitor on the remote computer. The debug monitor appears as a dialog (Figure 5.19) where you can specify its settings. You can use remote debugging over a serial line or using a TCP/IP network connection. Use the Settings button to specify the details of the connection after the desired connection type has been selected.

FIGURE 5.20.

The Visual C++ debug monitor.

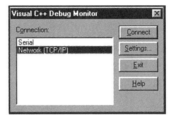

When remote debugging has been fully configured, click on the Connect button. Clicking this button puts the debug monitor in a state where it waits for an incoming connection.

You must also configure the Developer Studio on the local machine for remote debugging. To do so, use the Remote Connection command in the Tools menu. This invokes the Remote Connection dialog (Figure 5.21) where you can specify the type of connection to use for debugging and set connection options using the Settings button.

FIGURE 5.21.

The Remote Connection dialog.

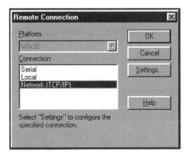

NOTE

When setting up a TCP/IP connection for debugging, you are also asked to specify a password. Make sure that the password you specify is the same on both the local and the remote computer.

The major advantage of remote debugging is that the application runs in a machine unaffected by the presence of the debugger. Remote debugging is ideal, for example, for debugging applications that take over the Windows display and keyboard—like full-screen game applications).

Remote debugging can also be used during cross-platform development. For example, you can use remote debugging to debug a Visual C++ application running on a Macintosh computer. You can also use remote debugging with a remote computer running Windows 3.1 and Win32s.

Just-in-Time Debugging

Just-in-Time debugging represents the ability of the Visual C++ debugger to attach itself to a running program that was just interrupted with an unhandled exception. Just-in-Time debugging is useful to debug applications that have not been launched from within the integrated debugger.

Just-in-Time debugging is turned on using the Options command in the Tools menu. In the Options dialog, select the Debug tab and set the Just-in-Time debugging check box.

Application Profiling

The Visual C++ Profiler is a performance analysis tool that collects reliable statistics on the number of times certain elements of your code are executed, and the amount of elapsed time spent executing them. The Profiler can be used from within the Developer Studio or from the command line.

> **NOTE**
>
> If you installed Visual C++ with default settings, the Profiler may not be installed on your system. In this case, profiling features may not be available. To install the profiler, rerun the Visual C++ installation program.

Setting Up an Application for Profiling

In order to profile an application, you must link it with the appropriate flags. This is accomplished easily, by linking your application with the /profile linker command-line flag. If you are compiling from within the Developer Studio, you can set this flag in the Project Settings dialog; invoke this dialog through the Settings command in the Build menu, select the Link tab, select the General category, and make sure that the Enable profiling check box is set.

The Profiler can be used for *function profiling* and for *line profiling*. Function profiling analyzes the way functions in your program are executed; line profiling performs a similar analysis on a per source line basis. In order for line profiling to work, you must compile your code with debugging information. If you do function profiling, debugging information is ignored.

Profiler Operation

How does the Profiler work? The Profiler actually consists of not one, but three tools that can be executed from the command line. These are the PREP, PROFILE, and PLIST tools. A simplified view of how these tools operate is shown in Figure 5.22.

FIGURE 5.22.

Profiling operation.

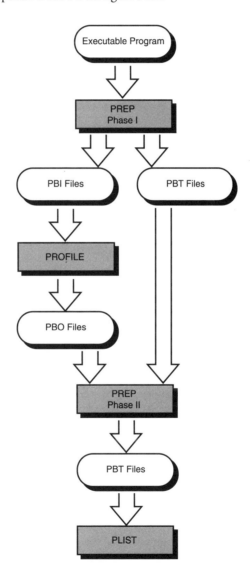

The PREP tool is run twice during profiling. First, it reads the application's executable file and produces a PBI and a PBT file. The PBI file serves as the input to the PROFILE tool; this tool runs and profiles the application, and writes its results to a PBO file. The PBO file and the

PBT file serve as the input when the PREP tool is run for the second time, this time generating a new PBT file; finally, the PLIST tool is used to generate human readable results.

The Profiler is typically run from batch files that invoke PREP, PROFILE, and PLIST as appropriate.

The output of PLIST is a readable (natural language) summary of profiling results.

Running the Profiler

From within the Developer Studio, the Profiler is invoked through the Profile command in the Tools menu. This command invokes the Profile dialog, shown in Figure 5.23.

FIGURE 5.23.

The Profile dialog.

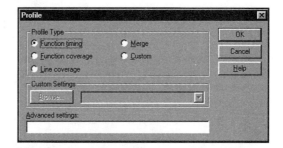

NOTE

If you have remote debugging enabled, you may not be able to invoke the Profile command from the Tools menu. To disable remote debugging, use the Remote Connection command in the Tools menu and select Local as the connection type in the Remote Connection dialog.

Types of Profiling

The Profiler can be used to perform a variety of different types of profiling operations. Some of these can be invoked from the Profile dialog; others require the use of batch files that are typically found in your `msdev\bin` directory.

Function timing evaluates the amount of time your application spends executing specific functions. By default, timing statistics for all functions are generated. You can invoke this type of profiling by selecting Function timing in the Profile dialog.

Function coverage is used to record whether specific functions have been called. You can use this capability, for example, to verify whether certain portions of your code are executed. Function coverage can also be invoked from the Profile dialog.

Function counting evaluates the number of times specific functions are called. To invoke function counting from the Profile dialog, select the Custom profile type and specify the `fcount.bat` batch file (usually located in `msdev\bin`) in the Custom Settings field.

Line counting evaluates the number of times specific lines in your code are executed. To invoke line counting, select Custom in the Profile dialog and specify `lcount.bat` in the Custom Settings field.

Line coverage evaluates whether specific lines in your code have been executed or not. Note that line coverage is much faster than line counting, as after a line has been executed once, the Profiler can remove its breakpoint from that line. Line coverage can be directly invoked from the Profile dialog by selecting the Line coverage option.

In addition to these profiler options, the Profile dialog also provides a Merge option. This option enables you to combine profiler statistics from several sessions (with identical settings).

Advanced Profiler Settings

Profiling your entire application rarely makes sense. By identifying specific sections of your code for profiling analysis, you can also greatly speed up program execution during a profiling session.

There are three ways to fine-tune the profiler. You can modify your `tools.ini` and `profiler.ini` files; you can specify advanced settings in the Profile dialog in Developer Studio; or you can write custom batch files for profiling.

The `tools.ini` and `profiler.ini` files contain profiler related settings in the `[profiler]` section. In this section, you can specify library (LIB) and object (OBJ) files that are to be excluded from profiling. For example, your `tools.ini` file may contain the following lines:

```
[profiler]
exclude:user32.lib
exclude:gdi32.lib
```

When reading `tools.ini` and `profiler.ini`, the Profiler reads settings from both files and merges them. Note that the location of `tools.ini` is defined by the `INIT` environment variable; in contrast, `profiler.ini` can be found in the `msdev\bin` directory.

If you select the Function timing, Function coverage, or Line coverage options in the Profile dialog, you can specify additional parameters that will be passed to the PREP tool in its Phase I invocation. For example, if you wish to invoke the profile to analyze only a specific range of source lines in the file `MyApp.cpp`, you could specify the following in the Advanced settings field:

```
/EXCALL /INC MyApp.cpp(30-67)
```

Finally, you can develop your own custom profiling batch files. Use the batch files that are installed in your `msdev\bin` directory (`fcount.bat`, `fcover.bat`, `ftime.bat`, `lcount.bat`, and `lcover.bat`) as examples for developing profiler batch files.

Analyzing Profiler Data

Normally, the PLIST tool provides profiler output in a human readable form. However, it is also possible to generate output in an exportable tab-delimited format.

This tab-delimited output can be read by other applications. For example, it can be imported into a Microsoft Excel spreadsheet. Provided with your Visual C++ installation is a Microsoft Excel 4 macro file, `profiler.xlm`, that provides some profile analysis tools.

Summary

The integrated debugger in the Developer Studio is launched when you start an application using one of the Debug commands in the Build menu. The debugger offers a variety of views on your application and its memory; these include source windows, the Variables window, the Watch window, the Registers window, the Call Stack window, the Memory window, and the Disassembly window.

To prepare an application for debugging, you must compile and link it with the appropriate flags. This is accomplished automatically for MFC applications that were created with the AppWizard; for these applications, AppWizard creates a Debug configuration and makes it the default configuration.

When an application is being debugged, its execution can be interrupted using a variety of breakpoint settings. Location breakpoints are the most common; however, you can also specify data breakpoints that interrupt program execution when the value of an expression changes, and message breakpoints that interrupt program execution when a specific window procedure receives a specific message.

There are many debugging techniques you can use to debug MFC and other applications. These include the use of the TRACE and ASSERT family of macros, the CObject::Dump function and its override versions, and various MFC tracing options. You can also use objects of type CMemoryState in MFC applications to detect and analyze memory leaks.

A specific debugging technique is remote debugging. Remote debugging enables you to debug an application on a remote computer using a debugger on the local computer. Remote debugging requires that the Visual C++ Debug Monitor be set up on the remote computer. Remote debugging is most useful when debugging applications without interference from the debugger or when debugging applications running on non-Win32 platforms such as Win32s or Macintosh.

Visual C++ also offers the Just-in-Time debugging feature that enables you to invoke the debugger on applications that fail outside the integrated debugger environment.

The Visual C++ Source Profiler is a powerful analysis tool. To enable profiling, your application must be linked with profiling enabled.

The Profiler consists of three tools: PREP, PROFILE, and PLIST. These tools are used to prepare an application for profiling, profile the application, and interpret the results.

The Profiler can be used for line profiling and function profiling. Line profiling can be used to analyze line coverage and hit counts; function profiling can be used to analyze function timing, function coverage, and hit counts.

Function timing, Function coverage, and Line coverage are options available in the Profile dialog in the Developer Studio. In addition, two more batch files, `fcount.bat` and `lcount.bat`, can be used with the Custom option to perform function counting and line counting.

Profiler settings can be refined through the Advanced settings option in the Profile dialog, or through using custom batch files. For example, you can limit profiling analysis to a specific set of functions or source lines.

The PLIST tool normally generates human-readable output. You can override this using the `/T` command-line switch to generated tab-delimited output that can be imported by other applications. A set of Microsoft Excel analysis tools for profiler output is provided in the form of the `profiler.xlm` macro file.

Code Reuse with the Component Gallery

6

One of the great promises of object-oriented programming is improved code reusability. The Visual C++ development system goes a long way toward realizing this promise by providing a repository for reusable code components, the Component Gallery.

One of the nice things about the Component Gallery is that it isn't empty; like Santa's stockings, it is filled with a variety of goodies that are ready to be used with your applications. Examples include reusable components that add clipboard support, splash screen functionality, a password dialog, palette support, and many other features to your programs.

The Component Gallery

The Visual C++ Component Gallery is a repository of a variety of standard and user components. What is a component? A component can be a class complete with its header file, implementation file, and resources; it can also be an OLE control. It can also be a "smart" component supplied by Microsoft or a third-party vendor.

The Component Gallery provides a facility to store and manage these components.

NOTE

Information about the contents of the Component Gallery is stored in a file named `gallery.dat` in your `msdev\template` directory. If this file becomes corrupt for any reason, you can erase it; next time you access the Component Gallery, the default version of this file will be re-created. Obviously, references to any custom components will be lost.

Inserting a Component into a Project

The Component Gallery is invoked through the Component command in the Developer Studio's Insert menu. It appears in the form of the Component Gallery dialog box (Figure 6.1).

Installable components are shown using a series of tabbed panes. The Microsoft and the OLE Controls tabs are added when the Component Gallery is installed; other tabs are added automatically or manually when components from your own projects are added to the Component Gallery.

To add a specific component to your project, select the component, and click on the Insert button. If you wish to receive more information about the component before adding it to your project, click on the Help button (the button marked with a question mark).

Many standard components display configuration dialogs when you select them for insertion. Components may also examine your application's source code to determine whether the selected component is compatible with your application.

Chapter 6

FIGURE 6.1.

*The Component
Gallery.*

Creating Your Own Components

As you work with Visual C++, you develop many components that are potential candidates for reuse. For example, you may create a splash dialog, a CDocItem-derived class of document objects, or a customized About dialog with your company's animated logo, all of which are reusable components.

Adding these components to the Component Gallery is easy; in fact, often you do not have to do anything because these components are added automatically. When you create a new project through AppWizard, all the new classes created by AppWizard are automatically added to the Component Gallery.

When you create a new class through ClassWizard, you can also specify whether the new class is to be added to the Component Gallery. To do so, make sure the Add to Component Gallery check box in the Create New Class dialog is set (it is set by default). When you create the new class, it is automatically added to the Component Gallery.

Unfortunately, I know of no way to add an existing class to the Component Gallery. However, there is a relatively easy workaround; you can make a copy of the class, remove it from your project, and create it again through the ClassWizard, this time with the Add to Component Gallery check box set. When you are done creating this new class, you can copy your old code over the newly created files.

When you are adding a class that is associated with a dialog template (for example, a class derived from CDialog), create the dialog template before you create the class through the ClassWizard. This way, you ensure that the class is properly associated with the dialog template and that the dialog template is part of the component that is added to the Component Gallery.

When a class from your project is added to the Component Gallery, what is actually added is a reference to the files comprising the class. This way, any changes to the class are reflected immediately in the Component Gallery. This also means, unfortunately, that if your project is moved, the contents of the Component Gallery may no longer be valid.

When classes from a project are added to the Component Gallery by AppWizard, a new category of components is created, represented by a new pane in the Component Gallery. You can manipulate these categories, move components between categories, add and remove categories to the Component Gallery, and rename categories and components using the Component Gallery's customization feature. To invoke the Customize Component Gallery dialog (Figure 6.2), click on the Customize button.

FIGURE 6.2.

The Customize Component Gallery dialog.

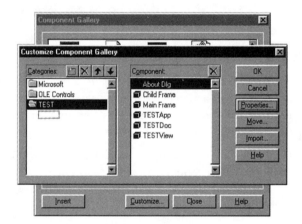

This dialog also lets you view and possibly modify component properties. Selecting a component and clicking on the Properties button invokes that component's property sheet. Most importantly, you can use the General page of the component's property sheet (Figure 6.3) to change the description of a component or to add a description to a custom component.

NOTE

Because every time you run the AppWizard, a new category of components is created in the Component Gallery, it is useful from time to time to invoke the Component Gallery and remove unwanted categories and components.

FIGURE 6.3.

*Adding a
description to a
custom component.*

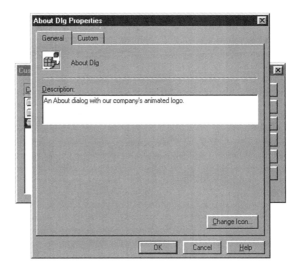

Custom components are limited to simple classes or classes with associated dialog templates. At present, Microsoft has announced no plans to publish the interfaces for creating "smart" components; that is, components that can present a user interface prior to insertion, provide customized property pages, and obtain information about the project. Hopefully, this information will become available with a future release of Visual C++.

Exporting a Component

The ability to add components to the Component Gallery is a great reusability feature; however, the concept of reusability is not limited to a single computer. In order to facilitate sharing components between users, the Component Gallery provides an Export feature for custom components.

To invoke this feature, open the Component Gallery, click on the Customize button, select the desired custom component, and click on the Properties button. In the component's property sheet, select the Custom property page (Figure 6.4). Click on the Export button. The Component Gallery will respond by requesting a filename; by default, exporting components have the .ogx filename extension.

FIGURE 6.4.

Exporting a custom component.

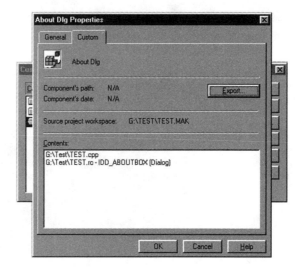

Importing a Component

An exported component can be imported using the Component Gallery's Import feature. To use this feature, invoke the Customize Component Gallery dialog and click on the Import button.

The Import feature can be used to import two types of components; components that were exported earlier (OGX files), and OLE controls (OCX files). When you are importing a component, you are given the choice of either copying the files to the msdev\template directory or not. If you do not copy the file, the component added to the Component Gallery will be a reference to the file at its original location. Needless to say, removing the file will also invalidate the component in the Component Gallery.

Note that when an OLE control is registered, it is automatically added to the Component Gallery.

Standard Components

The Visual C++ development system comes equipped with a variety of standard components. These components can be used to add specific features to your application. In the remainder of this section, I present a few notes about some of these components that I found most useful.

Clipboard Assistant

The Clipboard Assistant component adds basic clipboard functionality to your project. It does so by adding a series of message handlers to the selected class (by default, your application's view class) that implement the cut, copy, and paste commands. Clipboard support can be added for edit controls, rich-text controls, or for an application-specific custom format.

Dialog Bar

The Dialog Bar component can be used to add a dialog bar to a frame window in your project. This component adds a dialog bar object of type `CDialogBar` to the designated frame window. It also creates a dialog template resource for the dialog bar.

Figure 6.5 shows a dialog bar added to a child window using the Dialog Bar component.

FIGURE 6.5.

Child window with a dialog bar.

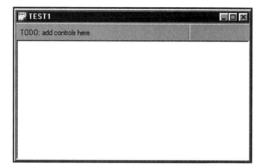

Palette Support

The Palette Support component adds handlers to the selected window class for `WM_QUERYNEWPALETTE` and `WM_PALETTECHANGED` messages. It also adds a `SetPalette` member function to the designated window. Subsequent changes to the palette can be accomplished by simply calling `SetPalette`; the palette will be remembered and properly restored when the window regains focus.

Popup Menu

The Popup Menu component adds popup menu support to the selected class. The popup menu is invoked when the user clicks on the window that the class represents using the right mouse button.

The component adds two member functions, `OnContextMenu` and `PreTranslateMessage`; it also creates a new menu resource with three default commands, Cut, Copy, and Paste (note that the component does not supply the implementation for these commands).

Splash Screen

The Splash Screen component adds a splash screen to your project. The splash screen is displayed when the application starts. This component adds a new class to your application (CSplashWnd) and also a bitmap resource (IDB_SPLASH) that you can customize.

System Info for About Dialog

The System Info for About dialog component modifies your application's About dialog implementation to include system information. It adds an OnInitDialog member function to your application's About dialog class; you must manually add two static controls to your About dialog (Figure 6.6) and modify the code in OnInitDialog to update these controls.

FIGURE 6.6.

About dialog with system information.

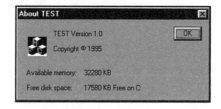

Tip of the Day

The Tip of the Day component adds a Tip of the Day dialog (Figure 6.7) to your project. The dialog is added in the form of a header file (TipDlg.h), implementation file (TipDlg.cpp), and dialog template IDD_TIP. The component also modifies the InitInstance function of your application class to invoke the Tip of the Day dialog when the application is started. The Help menu is also updated to provide a Tip of the Day command.

FIGURE 6.7.

Tip of the Day dialog.

Summary

The Component Gallery is a repository of standard and custom components. A component is a class, an OLE control, or a "smart" component from Microsoft or a third party vendor.

To add a component to your application, select the desired component in the Component Gallery and click the Insert button.

You can create your own components that are to be added to the Component Gallery. All classes of a new AppWizard-generated project are automatically added to the Component Gallery. You can also specify that a new class created through ClassWizard be added to the Component Gallery by checking the appropriate box in the Create New Class dialog. Although no facility exists to add an existing class to the Component Gallery, you can easily create a dummy class that is compatible with your existing class, add it to the Component Gallery, and then copy code from your existing class into it.

The customization feature of the Component Gallery enables you to arrange component categories and components. It also lets you export an existing component so you can give it to other users. To import an exported component or an OLE control use the Component Gallery's import feature.

The Visual C++ development system comes equipped with a series of standard components. These include components for adding clipboard support, support for dialog bars, palettes, popup menus, a splash screen component, a Tip of the Day component, About dialog enhancements, and much more. You can also add classes representing registered OLE controls through the Component Gallery.

PART

IN THIS PART

The Windows Architecture and the Win32 API

Operating System Overview

7

The 32-bit edition of Visual C++ can be used to develop programs for three Win32 platforms: Windows NT (on multiple processors), Windows 95, and Win32s.

Windows NT is Microsoft's high-end portable server operating system. It is a full-featured 32-bit multithreaded operating system with an integrated graphical environment and advanced server capabilities. Its development has been aimed to maximize portability, stability, and security. While its compatibility with well-behaved MS-DOS and Windows 3.1 applications is remarkably good, it falls short of being a 100 percent replacement for your old MS-DOS system; if you wish to run a sophisticated game program, you may have to reboot to the good old DOS command line. (Does DOOM work under Windows NT? Don't ask me; I haven't tried.)

Windows 3.1 is, of course, the omnipresent graphical environment sitting, used or unused, in a directory on just about every PC nowadays. While it delivers some operating system-like features, it is essentially a graphical environment sitting on top of MS-DOS instead of replacing it. Because of limitations in both DOS and the 16-bit Windows 3.1 architecture, the DOS-Windows system combination is inherently unstable, prone to crashes, and exposed to ill-behaved applications. The Win32s subsystem is yet another layer on top of Windows 3.1; it implements a subset of the Win32 system calls that enables many simpler 32-bit applications (or complex ones that were written with Win32s compatibility in mind) to run.

Microsoft's new operating system, Windows 95, offers the best of both worlds. Unlike Windows NT, Windows 95 has been written with backward compatibility as one of the main design criteria. Despite this and the fact that Windows 95 inherited a significant amount of legacy code from Windows 3.1, it has remarkably few shortcomings. Its stability is comparable to Windows NT, its performance exceeds that of both Windows NT and Windows 3.1, and its hardware resource requirements are minimal, comparable to that of Windows 3.1.

Despite the obvious differences between these platforms (the most notable are the restrictions placed on applications intended to run in the Win32s environment), they share most essential features. In particular, most simple applications are expected to be compatible with all three of these platforms with little or no modification. For this reason, I usually discuss operating system or compiler features without regard to the target operating system; if significant platform differences exist, however, I mention those.

Windows and Messages

Windows is often referred to as a *message-passing* operating system. At the very heart of the system is the mechanism that translates just about every *event* (a keypress, a mouse movement, a timer countdown) into a *message*; typical applications are built around a *message loop* that retrieves these messages and dispatches them to the appropriate message handler functions.

Messages, although sent to applications, are not addressed to them; they are, instead, addressed to what are the other fundamental components of the operating system, *windows*. A window is much more than merely a rectangular area of the computer's screen; it also represents an abstract entity through which the user and the application interact with each other.

Applications, Threads, and Windows

What is the relationship between applications and windows? A typical Win32 application consists of one or more *threads*, which are basically parallel paths of execution. Think of threads as multitasking within a single application; for example, one thread in a word processing application may be processing user input, while another is busy sending a document to the printer.

> **NOTE**
>
> Under Win32s, only single-threaded Win32 applications can run.

A window is always "owned by" a thread; a thread may own one or more windows, or none at all. Finally, windows themselves are in a hierarchical relationship; some are top-level windows, others are subordinated to their *parent windows*. Figure 7.1 illustrates this hierarchy.

FIGURE 7.1.

Processes, threads, and windows.

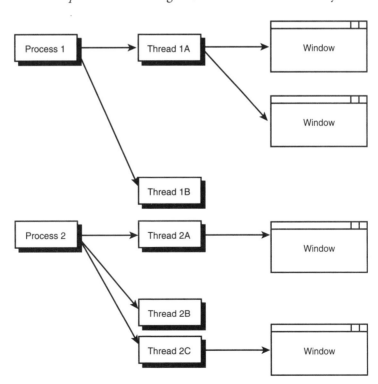

There are many types of windows in Windows—no pun intended!. The most obvious, of course, is the large rectangular area that we typically associate with an application. Also obvious is that a dialog box is a window in its own right; it can be moved around, sometimes sized, maximized, or minimized just like the main window of an application. What is less obvious is that many elements displayed within main windows or dialogs are also windows themselves. Every button, edit box, scrollbar, list box, icon, and even the screen background itself is treated as a window by the operating system.

A very revealing exercise, if you have not done this before, is spending some time with the Spy++ application that comes with Visual C++. Use its Find Window command from the Spy menu and drag the finder tool around the screen to find out how even an apparently simple application window can have many window components. Figure 7.2 shows a typical screen under Windows 95 with each of the multitude of windows within it marked by a thick black border.

FIGURE 7.2.

The multitude of windows during a typical session.

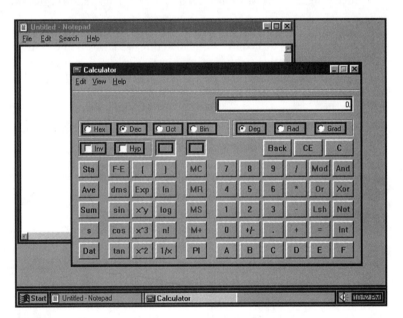

Window Classes

The basic behavior of a window is defined by its *window class*. The window class carries information about the window's initial appearance; the default icon, cursor, and menu resource associated with the window; and perhaps most importantly, the address of a function called the *window procedure*. When an application processes messages, it usually does so by calling the Windows function DispatchMessage for each message received; DispatchMessage, in turn, calls the appropriate window procedure by checking the class of the window the message is for. It is the window procedure that actually processes messages sent to that window.

There are many standard window classes provided by Windows itself. These *system global* classes implement the functionality of common controls, for example. Any application can use these classes for its windows; for example, any application can implement edit controls by using the Edit window class.

Applications can also define their own window classes through the `RegisterClass` function. This enables programmers to implement window behavior that is not part of any of the system-supplied global classes. For example, this is how a typical application implements the functionality of its own main window and registers the main window's icon and menu resource.

Windows also enables subclassing and superclassing an existing class. *Subclassing* substitutes the window procedure for a window class with another. Subclassing is accomplished by changing the window procedure address through the `SetWindowLong` (instance subclassing) or `SetClassLong` (global subclassing) function. The difference? In the first case, only the behavior of a specific window changes; in the second case, the behavior of all windows of the specified class is affected.

> **NOTE**
>
> Global subclassing behaves differently in Win32 and 16-bit Windows (Win32s). In the Win32 case, it affects only windows under the control of the application doing the subclassing; in 16-bit Windows, the effect is global, affecting the windows of every application.

Superclassing creates a new class based on an existing class, retaining its window procedure. To superclass a window class, an application retrieves class information using the `GetClassInfo` function, modifies the `WNDCLASS` structure thus received, and uses the modified structure in a call to `RegisterClass`. Through `GetClassInfo`, the application also obtains the address of the original window procedure, which it should retain; messages that the new window procedure does not process should be passed to this function.

Although the terminology is reminiscent of object-oriented terminology, the concept of a window class should not be confused with C++ concepts (or, in particular, concepts of the MFC library). The concept of window classes predates the use of object-oriented languages in Windows by several years.

Message Types

Messages come in many flavors, representing events at many different levels. Again, the Spy++ tool can help you appreciate the complex message set every single window must process. Use the Spy++ tool to select some simple element, such as a dialog box, to snoop on; then watch the seemingly endless cascade of messages streaming by in the Spy++ window as you move the mouse over a button in the dialog and click it. Table 7.1 shows the list of messages that appear as I dismiss the Word for Windows "About" dialog by clicking on its OK button.

Table 7.1: Messages sent to the Word for Windows "About" dialog when the user clicks the OK button.

Symbolic Identifier	Description
WM_LBUTTONDOWN	The left mouse button was pressed.
WM_PAINT	The OK button is repainted as it is pressed.
WM_LBUTTONUP	The left mouse button was released.
WM_PAINT	The OK button is repainted as it is released.
WM_WINDOWPOSCHANGING	The position of the window is about to change.
WM_WINDOWPOSCHANGED	The position of the window has just changed.
WM_NCACTIVATE	The window's title area has been activated.
WM_ACTIVATE	The window's client area has been activated.
WM_WINDOWPOSCHANGING	The position of the window is about to change.
WM_KILLFOCUS	The window is about to lose focus.
WM_DESTROY	The window is being destroyed.
WM_NCDESTROY	The title area of the window is being destroyed.

As you can see, messages representing every single occurrence, every single action are sent to the window for processing. Fortunately, an application does not have to be aware of the meaning of every single message. Instead of processing all possible messages, an application is free to pick and choose; messages that remain unprocessed are passed to the operating system's default message handler function.

Windows messages consist of several parts. Perhaps it is best to review the MSG structure, shown in Listing 7.1, which is used to represent messages.

Listing 7.1: The MSG structure.

```
typedef struct tagMSG {
    HWND    hwnd;
    UINT    message;
    WPARAM  wParam;
    LPARAM  lParam;
    DWORD   time;
    POINT   pt;
} MSG;
```

The first element of this structure, hwnd, uniquely identifies the window to which this message has been posted. Every window in Windows has such an identifier.

The next element identifies the message itself. This element may have hundreds of different values, indicating one of the many hundreds (literally!) of different messages that Windows applications may receive. Messages can be organized into several groups depending on their function. Message identifiers are usually referred to symbolically (such as, WM_PAINT, WM_TIMER) rather than by numeric value; these symbolic values are defined in the standard Windows header files. (You need only include windows.h; it, in turn, contains #include directives for the rest.)

By far the most populous group of Windows messages is the group of window management messages. The symbolic identifiers for these messages all begin with WM_. This group is so large, it only makes sense to further subdivide it into categories. These categories include DDE (Dynamic Data Exchange) messages, clipboard messages, mouse messages, keyboard messages, nonclient area messages (messages that relate to the title, border, and menu areas of a window, typically those areas that are managed by the operating system, not the application), MDI (Multiple Document Interface) messages, and many other types. These categories are somewhat inexact, and are not always strictly defined; they simply serve as a tool of convenience for programmers trying to form a mental picture of the large set of window management messages. Nor is the set of WM_ messages fixed; it is constantly growing as new operating system capabilities are added.

Other message groups are related to specific window types. There are messages defined for edit controls, buttons, list boxes, combo boxes, scrollbars, list and tree views, and so on. These messages, with few exceptions, are typically processed by the window procedure of the control's window class and are rarely of interest to the application programmer.

Applications can also define their own messages. Unique message identifiers can be obtained through a call to the function RegisterWindowMessage. Using private message types enables parts of an application to communicate with each other; separate applications can also exchange information this way. In fact, in 16-bit Windows, cooperating applications typically exchanged data by sending handles of global memory objects to each other. In Win32, this mechanism does not work because applications no longer share an address space; however, other, more powerful mechanisms (for example, memory mapped files) are available for intertask communication.

Messages and Multitasking

In Windows 3.1, the message loop has another important role in the interaction between the application and the operating system: it enables the application to yield control. As Windows 3.1 is not a preemptive multitasking operating system, it does not wrestle away control of the processor from an uncooperative application. Proper functioning of the system depends on the cooperative behavior of applications; namely, that they calls specific message processing functions frequently. This behavior is still required of applications that are intended to run under Windows 3.1 using Win32s.

Message Queues

This section starts with the simple and moves to the more complex. First, I describe the workings of the 16-bit Windows messaging and task scheduling architecture.

In 16-bit Windows, the operating system maintains a single *message queue*. Messages that are generated by various operating system events—such as a keyboard or mouse interrupt—are deposited into this message queue. When an application makes an attempt to retrieve the next message in the queue through the GetMessage or PeekMessage function, the operating system may perform a *context switch* and activate another application for which messages are waiting in the queue. The message at the top of the queue is then retrieved and returned to the active application via an MSG structure.

If an application fails to make a call to GetMessage, PeekMessage, or Yield (which enables an application to relinquish control without checking the message queue), it effectively hangs the system. Messages keep accumulating in the message queue; as the queue is of a fixed size, eventually it overflows. Windows responds to this by generating a nasty beep every time a new message is received that cannot be placed into the queue; the result is a very ill system that is beeping continuously even at the slightest mouse movement.

In Win32 (that is, both in Windows NT and Windows 95) the message queue mechanism is much more sophisticated. In these preemptive operating systems, the orderly cooperation of competing tasks or threads is no longer guaranteed. Two or more threads can quite possibly attempt to access the message queue at the same time; furthermore, as task switching is no longer dependent on the next available message in the queue, there are no guarantees that a task would retrieve only the messages addressed to it. This is just one of a number of reasons why the single message queue of 16-bit Windows has been separated into individual message queues for each and every thread in the system.

Processes and Threads

The subject of threads came up briefly during the discussion of the relationship of processes and threads versus windows.

In a non-multithreaded operating system, such as most flavors of UNIX, the smallest unit of execution is a *task* or *process*. The task-scheduling mechanism of the operating system switches between these tasks; multitasking is accomplished between two or more processes. If an application needs to perform multiple functions simultaneously, it splits itself into several tasks (for example, by using the UNIX fork system call). This approach has some severe drawbacks: tasks are a limited resource (most operating systems can handle fewer than a few hundred simultaneously executing tasks), spawning a new task consumes a prodigious amount of time and system resources, and the new task loses access to its parent's address space.

In contrast, in a multithreaded system the smallest unit of execution is a thread, not a process. A task or process may consist of one or more threads (usually one designated as the main thread). Setting up a new thread requires little in terms of system resources; threads of the same process have access to the same address space; switching between threads of the same process requires very little system overhead. In fact, I cannot think of any drawbacks a multithreaded operating system has when contrasted with a single-threaded one.

Threads and Messages

Earlier I indicated that ownership of windows is assigned to individual threads. Correspondingly, each thread has a private message queue, in which the operating system deposits messages addressed to windows the thread owns. Does this mean that a thread must own at least one window and contain a message loop?

Fortunately, no; otherwise, the use of threads in typical programming situations would become cumbersome indeed. Threads can exist that own no windows and have no message processing loop whatsoever.

Consider, for example, a sophisticated mathematical application in which a complex calculation needs to be performed on every element of a two-dimensional array (a matrix). The easiest way to do this is to implement a loop in which the calculation is performed repeatedly. Under 16-bit Windows this approach was strictly forbidden; during the execution of the loop, no other applications could control the processor, and the computer effectively froze. In Win32, however, it is perfectly legitimate to set up a separate thread in which such a calculation is performed, while the application's main thread continues processing any messages the application may receive. The only effect on the system is a performance hit—something not entirely unexpected when a complex, processing-intensive calculation is being performed. The thread doing the calculations has no windows, no message queue, no message loop; it does one thing only, and that is the calculation itself.

In MFC, these threads acquire a name of their own; they are called *worker threads*, in contrast to the more sophisticated, message queue processing *user-interface threads*.

Windows Function Calls

While the existence of a message loop is perhaps the most distinguishing characteristic of Windows applications, it is by far not the only mechanism through which an application and Windows interact. Windows, like other operating systems, offers a humongous number of system calls to perform a wide variety of tasks, including process control, window management, file handling, memory management, graphical services, communications, and many other functions.

The "core" set of Windows system calls can be organized into three major categories. Kernel services include system calls for process and thread control, resource management, and file and memory management. User services include system calls for the management of user-interface elements, such as windows, controls, dialogs, or messages. Graphics Device Interface (GDI) services provide device-independent graphical output functionality.

The Windows system also includes many miscellaneous Application Programming Interfaces (APIs). Separate APIs exist for a multitude of tasks; examples include MAPI (Messaging API), TAPI (Telephony API), and ODBC (Open Database Connectivity). The degree to which these APIs have been integrated into the core system varies; for example, OLE (Object Linking and Embedding), although implemented in the form of a series of system Dynamic Link Libraries, or DLLs, is nevertheless considered part of the "core" Windows functionality; other APIs, such as WinSock, are considered "extras" or add-ons.

This distinction between what is core and what isn't is fairly arbitrary. Indeed, from the perspective of an application there is little difference between a core API function that is part of the Kernel module and a function that is implemented in a DLL. Nothing illustrates this better than the conventions used to invoke API functions from the Visual Basic programming language. All API functions are declared identically, as functions in an external DLL. The only difference is the module name: "Kernel" in the case of a Kernel system call, and the name of the DLL in the case of a call to a DLL function.

Kernel Services

Kernel services typically fall into the categories of file management, memory management, process and thread control, and resource management. While far from being an exhaustive list, these categories accurately describe most commonly used Kernel module functions.

The preferred method of file management differs from what is typically used in C/C++ programs. Instead of accessing files through the standard C library functions for stream or low-level I/O, or through the C++ `iostream` class, applications should utilize the Win32 concept of a *file object* and the rich set of functions associated with those. File objects enable accessing files in ways that are not possible using the C/C++ libraries; examples include overlapped I/O and memory mapped files used for intertask communication.

In contrast, the memory management requirements of most applications are completely satisfied through the C `malloc` family of functions or the C++ `new` operator; in a Win32 application, these calls automatically translate into the appropriate Win32 memory management system calls. For applications with more elaborate memory management requirements, sophisticated functions exist for managing virtual memory; for example, these functions can be used to manipulate address spaces that are several hundred megabytes in size by allocating but not *committing* memory.

The most important facet of process and thread management concerns *synchronization*. This problem is new to the Windows environment, as it was not encountered in 16-bit Windows. Under the cooperative multitasking regime of Windows 3.1, applications give up control only at well-defined points during their execution; the execution of competing tasks is *synchronous*. In contrast, in the preemptive multitasking environment, processes and threads cannot deduce knowledge about the execution status of competing threads. In order to ensure that competing threads that are mutually dependent execute in an orderly fashion, and in order to avoid dead-lock situations where two or more threads are suspended indefinitely, waiting for each other, a sophisticated synchronization mechanism is required. In Win32, this is accomplished through a variety of *synchronization objects* that threads can use to inform other threads about their status, protect sensitive areas of code from reentrant execution, or obtain information about other threads or the status of other objects.

Speaking of objects, in Win32, many kernel resources (not to be confused with user-interface resources) are represented as kernel objects. Examples include files, threads, processes, and syn-chronization objects. Objects are typically referred to through *handles*; some functions exist for the generic manipulation of objects, while others manipulate objects of a specific type. Under Windows NT, objects also have security-related properties. For example, a thread cannot manipulate a file object unless it has appropriate permissions that match the file object's secu-rity properties.

The Kernel module also provides functions to manage *user-interface resources.* These resources include icons, cursors, dialog templates, string resources, version resources, accelerator tables, bitmaps, and other user-defined resource types. Kernel system calls are not aware of the pur-pose of a resource; however, they provide functionality to allocate memory for resources, load resources from a disk file (typically, the application's executable file), and purge resources from memory.

Some areas of Kernel module functionality are specific to Windows NT. For example, the NT Kernel module provides a variety of functions through which the security attribute of kernel objects can be examined and manipulated.

Another NT-specific area of functionality is tape backup functionality. Calls are available for erasing and formatting a tape and for reading and writing tape contents.

Accessing the contents of initialization files (INI files) is also accomplished through Kernel module calls such as `WriteProfileString` or `GetPrivateProfileString`. Use of these functions is not recommended, however; instead, new applications should use the Windows Registry for storing initialization information.

The Kernel module also provides the functionality required for 32-bit text-only programs, *console applications.* At first sight, these programs appear as plain old DOS programs; in reality, these are full-featured 32-bit applications that run from the command line and do not make use of the Windows graphical interface. Nevertheless, these applications can still access a rich set of Win32 system calls; for example, a console application can use virtual memory functions or it can be a multithreaded program.

There are many other areas of Kernel module functionality, ranging from the simple (such as operations on large integers) to the complex (such as the use of named pipes).

User Services

The User module, as its name implies, provides system calls that manage elements and aspects of the user interface. These include functions that handle windows, dialogs, menus, text and graphic cursors, controls, the clipboard, and many other areas.

In fact, it is through User module functions that awareness of these high-level components of the user interface becomes possible. The Kernel module provides memory allocation, thread management, and other services required for windows to function; the GDI module provides graphic primitives; but it is the User module that integrates these two areas and provides the concept of a window, for example.

Window management calls include functions to manage a window's size, position, appearance, and window procedure, as well as functions to enable or disable a window and to obtain information about windows. These functions are also used to manage controls, such as buttons, scrollbars, or edit boxes. The User module also contains functions to manage Multiple Document Interface (MDI) child windows.

Menu-related calls in the User module provide functionality to create, display, and manipulate menus, menu bars, and pop-up menus.

Through a family of User module functions, applications can manage the shape and appearance of the text cursor (the mouse cursor) and graphic cursor (the caret).

Management of the Windows Clipboard is also accomplished through User module functions. The Windows *Clipboard* is basically a simple mechanism through which applications can exchange data. An application can place data in the Clipboard in a variety of public or private clipboard formats; other applications can examine the Clipboard and retrieve data in any of the available formats that they can interpret. Most applications provide a set of Edit menu commands (Cut, Copy, Paste) for the explicit manipulation of Clipboard contents.

The User module also provides functions for the management of messages and thread message queues. Applications can use these calls to check the contents of their message queues, retrieve and process messages, and create new messages. New messages can be either *sent* or *posted* to any window. A message that has been posted is simply entered into the message queue of the thread that owns the destination window. In contrast, sending a message directly invokes the window procedure of the destination window; the SendMessage function does not return until the destination window has processed the message. Not only does this mechanism bypass the message queue, it also makes it possible for the sending application to obtain a return value before continuing.

GDI Services

Graphics Device Interface (GDI) functions are typically used to perform primitive device-independent graphical operations on device contexts. A *device context* is essentially an interface to a specific graphical device. It can be used to obtain information about the device and also perform graphical output to the device.

The information that can be obtained through a device context describes the device in detail. The technology of the device (for example, vector or raster), its type, name, resolution, color capability, font capability, and so on, can all be obtained through appropriate device context calls.

Graphical output is performed through a device context by passing the handle of the device context to the appropriate GDI output function. Through the device context, a generic, device-independent graphical call is translated into a set of instructions that realize the output on the specific device. For example, when an application calls the GDI function Ellipse, it is the device context that determines which device driver will actually execute the call; the device driver, in turn, may further refer the call to a hardware accelerator, if the video subsystem has such an accelerator capability.

GDI device contexts can describe a wide variety of devices. Typical device contexts include *display device contexts* (for output that goes directly to the computer's screen), *memory device contexts* (for output into a bitmap stored in memory), or *printer device contexts* (for output that eventually gets translated into printer control codes and sent to the printer).

A very special kind of a device context is the *metafile device context* that enables applications to make a permanent record of GDI output calls. Such a record is device-independent and can be played back on any device later. More than a mere convenience feature, metafiles play a crucial role in the device-independent representation of embedded OLE objects, the very mechanism that makes OLE objects portable and enables container applications to display or print them even in the absence of the server application.

Drawing into a device context usually takes place through logical coordinates. *Logical coordinates* describe objects using device-independent real-world measurements; for example, a rectangle can be described as two inches wide and one inch high. The GDI provides the necessary functionality for the mapping of logical coordinates to physical coordinates.

Significant differences exist in the way coordinate mapping takes place in Win32s, Windows 95, and Windows NT. For starters, both Win32s and Windows 95 are limited to 16-bit coordinates. In Win32s, this is due to the Windows 3.1 limitation that 16-bit integers are used to represent coordinate positions; in Windows 95, the reason is pretty much the same—the restriction exists due to the existence of a lot of legacy code inherited from Windows 3.1. In contrast, Windows NT can handle 32-bit world coordinates, making it an operating system that is much better suited for sophisticated graphical applications—CAD programs, for example.

All three operating systems support simple mappings from the logical to the physical coordinate space. This mapping is determined by the values specifying the coordinate origin and signed extent of the logical and physical space. The coordinate origins basically specify a horizontal and vertical displacement; the extents determine the orientation and scale of objects after the mapping.

In addition, Windows NT offers what are called *world transformation functions*. Through these functions, any linear transformation can be used for mapping the logical to the physical coordinate space; in addition to translations and scaling, output can also be rotated or sheared.

Of the large number of GDI functions, perhaps the ones used most frequently are those that draw various objects; examples include the `Rectangle`, `Ellipse`, `Polygon`, and `TextOut` functions. (These are just a few representative cases; the actual number of these functions is very large.)

Other frequently used drawing functions are the *bit blit* functions that are used to quickly and efficiently copy bitmaps. (Well, maybe not that quickly and efficiently; for applications, such as games, which really require blazing speed, there is a faster, albeit less safe, set of bitmap manipulation functions in the Windows Game SDK.)

Other functions manage device contexts. Device contexts for various devices can be created and destroyed, their state can be saved and reloaded, or information about them can be obtained through these functions.

Another set contains functions that manipulate coordinate transformations. Functions common to all Win32 platforms can be used to set or retrieve the origin and extent of the *window* (the logical coordinate space) and the *viewport* (the coordinate space of the target device). NT-specific functions can be used to manipulate sophisticated world transformation matrixes.

GDI functions can also be used to manipulate palettes. This is mostly useful for applications that strive to achieve color fidelity on devices that offer a limited number of simultaneous colors—256 colors, for example. By manipulating the color palette, these applications (a typical example would be a viewer for graphic files such as GIF or PCX format files) can select a set of colors that best match the colors in the picture about to be displayed, and thus reduce reliance on dithering techniques, providing a better quality image. Palette manipulation can also be used for *palette animation*, a technique that uses palette changes to create the impression of motion on the screen.

Yet another GDI feature is the ability to create and manage *GDI objects*. Brushes, pens, fonts, bitmaps, and palettes can be created and selected into device contexts to determine the appearance of shapes that are drawn subsequently.

Speaking of fonts, the GDI module also provides functionality to handle fonts (including TrueType fonts).

Other functions exist to manage two types of metafiles (the old-style *Windows Metafiles* and the new *Enhanced Metafiles*). Metafiles can be created, saved, reloaded, and replayed into any device context.

The GDI Module also provides the capability to manage regions and *clipping*. Clipping is of utmost importance in the Windows environment because it enables applications to draw to a display surface without regard to the boundaries of the surface (a client window, for example), or the possibility that parts of the surface are obscured by other objects on the screen.

Other APIs

Windows is much more than the capabilities implemented in the three "core" modules. Many other modules, many other APIs, exist—each implementing another specific area of functionality. Here are some of the more commonly used APIs, many of which are discussed in substantially more detail later:

- *Common Control* functions are used to manipulate the new Windows 95 common controls. Needless to say, these functions are only available in Windows 95 or later, or Windows NT 3.51 or later, and Win32s 1.3 or later.

- *Common Dialogs* include system-supplied dialogs for opening a file for reading or writing, selecting a color from a color palette, selecting a font from the set of fonts installed on your system, and specifying a search or search and replace operation. These dialogs can be used as is, or their functionality can be modified through new dialog templates and window procedures.

- *MAPI*, or the Messaging Applications Programming Interface, gives applications access to messaging functions through mail delivery systems like Microsoft Mail. Actually, there are three variants of MAPI that are commonly used: *Simple MAPI* is used by older applications that are *messaging-aware*; that is, applications that do not require the presence of a messaging subsystem but can make use of it if it is there. Microsoft Word falls into this category. Newer messaging-aware and *messaging-enabled* applications (those that rely on the presence of a messaging subsystem) should use *CMC*, the Common Messaging Calls interface. Finally, sophisticated *message-based* workgroup applications may use the full range of MAPI services (*Extended MAPI*).

- *MCI* is the Multimedia Control Interface. Through MCI functions, applications have easy access to the video, audio, and MIDI capabilities of Windows. Most multimedia applications would use MCI functions for media playback; some applications would utilize more sophisticated MCI capabilities for the editing of media files.

- The *OLE API* is a very rich collection of system calls implementing all aspects of OLE functionality. This includes OLE container and server functionality for in-place editing, activating objects, drag and drop, OLE Automation, and OLE custom controls.

- *TAPI* is the Telephony API. Applications can use TAPI for a device-independent method of accessing telephony-based resources (modems, FAX-modems, voice messaging hardware).

There are several areas of network-related functionality; examples include *WinSock,* the Windows Sockets library; *RAS*, the Remote Access Service; and *RPC*, the Remote Procedure Call library.

Error Reporting

Many Windows functions use a common mechanism for error return. When an error occurs, these functions set a thread-specific error value that can be retrieved by calling the GetLastError function. The 32-bit values returned by this function are defined in the header file winerror.h or in library-specific header files.

Functions in your application can also set this error value by calling SetLastError. Application-specific error codes should have bit 29 of the value set; error codes with this bit set are reserved by the operating system for application-specific use.

Using Standard C/C++ Library Functions

Win32 applications can also use the standard set of C/C++ library functions, although some limitations apply.

First and foremost, a Windows application does not normally have access to the traditional stdin, stdout, or stderr streams; the corresponding DOS file handles (0, 1, and 2); or C++ iostream objects (cin and cout). Only text-based console applications can use these standard file handles. (However, Windows applications, too, may have a standard input or standard output open if they are launched with their I/O redirected.)

As I mentioned already, Windows applications should use the Win32 file management functions for file handling. This is not to say that the standard C stream and low-level I/O functions or the C++ iostream library are no longer available; it is simply that these libraries do not have all the capabilities available through the Win32 API. For example, the C/C++ library functions are not aware of a file object's security properties; nor can they be used for asynchronous, *overlapped* input and output operations.

Applications should also refrain from using the MS-DOS-style C library process control functions (the exec family of functions) in favor of CreateProcess.

Most other C/C++ libraries can be used without restrictions. In particular, although the Win32 API offers a richer function set for memory manipulation, most applications do not require any services more sophisticated than those offered by malloc or the C++ new operator. The C/C++ math, buffer, string manipulation, character and byte classification, data conversion, and other routines can also safely be used.

Win32 applications should not attempt to access MS-DOS Interrupt 21 or IBM PC BIOS functions. The APIs that were available for this purpose in 16-bit Windows have been removed. Applications that require low-level access to system hardware are probably best developed using the appropriate DDK (Device Driver Development Kit).

Platform Differences

While the Win32 API is intended to serve as a platform-independent API, some platform differences exist due to limitations in the underlying operating system. Some of these have already been mentioned earlier in this chapter; here, we review and summarize features that are specific to the Windows NT, Windows 95, and Win32s platforms.

Of the three platforms, two (Windows NT and Windows 95) can be used as development platforms with Visual C++. I have decided to include some notes reflecting my experience in actually developing code using these operating systems.

Windows NT

The most complete implementation of the Win32 API can be found in Windows NT. Since Version 3.51, Windows NT offers the same set of new custom controls that are available in Windows 95. Presently, the only shortcoming of Windows NT relative to Windows 95 is the lack of Windows 95–style shell functionality. Even this shortcoming may not be around much longer; at the time of this writing, a fairly stable "preview" implementation has already been released. (Note, however, that this implementation is unfortunately not yet fully compatible with the Visual C++ development system.)

Of the three platforms, only Windows NT offers Unicode support, advanced security features, and system level support for tape backup. Being a server platform, Windows NT obviously offers a much richer server environment than the other two platforms. Thanks to a fully 32-bit implementation, Windows NT is also the most stable of the three platforms, making it ideally suited as a development environment.

On the downside, Windows NT is by far the slowest, most resource-hungry of the three platforms. The barest minimum on which Windows NT runs at acceptable performance is a 33 MHz 486 system with at least 16MB of memory. The Visual C++ documentation states that at least 20MB of RAM is required for acceptable performance. In practice, a well-equipped NT-based development system would have 32MB of RAM, a 1GB hard disk drive, and at least a 486/66 processor (but preferably a Pentium).

Windows 95

While Windows 95 lacks some of the features Windows NT offers, it more than makes up for it in terms of performance and compatibility with older, lower-end hardware. Most of the features missing from Windows 95 will not be greatly missed by the majority of users.

What is missing? NT's advanced security features, Unicode support, and system-level support for tape backup have already been mentioned. Support for the OpenGL graphics library has become available only recently through the Microsoft Developer Network and is not (yet) part of the standard Windows as distribution.

For graphics programmers coming from the NT environment, there are a few "gotchas"; among these are the lack of GDI support for world transformation functions and the limitation of coordinate spaces to 16-bit coordinate values.

On the other hand, Windows 95 delivers a flexible, stable multithreaded environment comparable to Windows NT in most aspects. It provides a very rich subset of the Win32 API; with the exception of the NT-specific features already mentioned, most API functions are available.

On the performance side, rumor says that most of Windows NT has been developed as relatively high-level portable C/C++ code; in contrast, Windows 95 inherits a fair amount of old Intel-specific Windows 3.1 code, and much of the new code has also been hand-optimized for this environment. It shows. For the functionality it delivers, the memory footprint of Windows 95 is tiny; people have been able to run it successfully on old 4MB 386-based systems. My personal experience with respect to low-end hardware is limited to my 8MB 486SX25 notebook computer; I was quite delighted to find that not only does Windows 95 run on this machine very nicely, even the Visual C++ development system does a more than adequate job compiling large projects.

Speaking of Visual C++, Windows 95 makes an excellent development platform. Its stability, although unlike the rocklike nature of Windows NT, is still fabulous. All 32-bit development tools, including console applications, run remarkably well on this platform. And if my experience with my notebook machine is any indication, even a low-end machine with a 25 MHz 486 CPU, 8MB of RAM, and a 120MB hard disk drive is sufficient for working on small to medium-sized projects.

Still on the performance side, the existence of the newly released Windows 95 Game SDK must also be mentioned. This SDK contains a series of libraries and low-level drivers to provide high-performance graphics and sound APIs facilitating the development of sophisticated action games for Windows 95. For the time being, this SDK is not available for Windows NT.

Win32s

Win32s is by far the most restrictive of the three 32-bit environments. Foremost among its restrictions is its inability to run multithreaded applications.

Like Windows 95, Win32s is also incompatible with NT-specific features like Unicode, security, and tape backup functionality. Win32s does not support the OpenGL graphics library.

Win32s has no support for the long filenames of Windows 95 and Windows NT. It does not support the new common controls. Access to 32-bit MAPI functionality is unsupported.

Win32s does not support overlapped I/O functionality, not even for communication devices. A curious consequence of this fact is that for a communications application to work under all three platforms, it may be necessary to provide both a 16-bit and a 32-bit DLL implementing platform-specific access to communications ports.

Win32s also shares some of the "gotchas" with Windows 95. Like Windows 95, the Win32s GDI implementation is limited to 16-bit coordinates and does not support world transformations.

Win32s cannot be used as a development platform with the 32-bit Visual C++ compiler. A good thing, too; with the dismal stability of Windows 3.1, development using this platform would likely be a frustrating experience.

In short, if your users still run Windows 3.1 with Win32s, urge them to upgrade to Windows 95. The stability improvements alone justify the effort and the expense, and your effort convincing them will be amply rewarded by the reduced number of support calls.

Other Platforms

So far, I have been conspicuously silent about using Visual C++ to develop code for other hardware or software platforms.

The Windows NT implementations on the PowerPC, DEC Alpha, or MIPS CPUs are, for all intents and purposes, compatible with the implementations on the Intel family of CPUs. Well-written applications should be recompilable on these platforms with no modifications. Obviously, you must have the platform-specific version of the Visual C++ development system; cross-platform compilation is not possible.

Visual C++ can also be used to create code for Macintosh computers. In this case, the Intel version of Visual C++ is actually used as a cross-platform development product, after suitable extensions have been purchased and installed. There are many restrictions on what Win32 features applications intended to run on the Macintosh platform can use. (Generally, the Windows Portability Library for the Macintosh has limitations comparable to those of Win32s.)

In addition, there are some promising attempts at porting the MFC library to various UNIX platforms and implementing Win32 compatibility libraries on UNIX.

Summary

Visual C++ applications are said to be targeted for the Win32 environment. This includes the various platform-specific versions of Windows NT, the new Windows 95 operating system, and the 32-bit Win32s extension to Windows 3.1. Additionally, Visual C++ can be used as a cross-platform development environment for the Macintosh.

At the core of every Windows application is its message loop. The Windows operating system delivers information about a variety of events in the form of messages to cooperating applications, which in turn process those messages by dispatching them to the appropriate window procedure. A window is a rectangular area in the screen; it is also an abstract entity that receives and processes messages.

Windows are owned by threads, which are simultaneous paths of execution within an application. Threads, in turn, are owned by processes or applications.

Applications also interact with Windows by calling one of the many operating system functions implemented either in the "core" of Windows or as a variety of add-ons. The core can roughly be divided into three categories: the Kernel module provides memory, file, and process management; the User module manages user-interface elements (specifically, windows) and handles messages; the GDI module provides graphical services.

Other modules implement specific areas of functionality, such as OLE, MAPI, networking, common controls and dialogs, and multimedia.

With some restrictions, Visual C++ applications can also use standard C/C++ library functions.

The three primary Win32 platforms differ in the extent to which the Win32 API is implemented. The most complete implementation is offered by Windows NT. Windows 95 offers a very rich subset, with some NT-specific elements and some advanced components missing. Win32s, on the other hand, offers a very restrictive implementation; most notable among these restrictions is its inability to run multithreaded applications.

The Message Loop

8

It has often been said sarcastically about Windows programming that something must be wrong with an operating system that requires hundreds of lines of code for the simplest program of all, one which displays "Hello, World!" and does nothing else. But is it really true, or is it just another urban legend about the evil company Microsoft and its monstrous operating system contraption called Windows?

The "Real" Hello, World Program

Consider the dialog shown in Figure 8.1. Make a guess: How many lines of C code, how many resource file lines, and so on, were required to create an application that displayed just this dialog, nothing else? How many times longer is this program than the infamous "original" Hello, World program that appeared at the beginning of Chapter 1 of the Kernighan-Ritchie C bible?

FIGURE 8.1.

The simplest Hello, World application under Windows.

You guessed it right. The number of lines (not counting the blank line inserted for cosmetic purposes only) is FIVE in both cases. The Windows version of the Hello, World program is shown in Listing 8.1.

Listing 8.1. Source of the simplest Hello, World program, `hello.c`.

```
#include <windows.h>

int WINAPI WinMain(HINSTANCE d1, HINSTANCE d2, LPSTR d3, int d4)
{
    MessageBox(NULL, "Hello, World!", "", MB_OK);
}
```

Compiling this program is not any more difficult than compiling the original Hello, World program from the command line. (Let this also serve as a little preview on using the Visual C++ compiler from the command line.) In order for the compiler to work from the command line, it is necessary to first run the batch file VCVARS32.BAT, which Visual C++ creates in its binary files directory MSDEV\BIN during installation. (Depending on your operating system and its configuration, you may find it necessary to enlarge the environment space allocation for DOS boxes to avoid any "Out of Environment Space" errors this batch file may cause.)

Afterwards, all you have to do is type `cl hello.c user32.lib` and voilà! The program `hello.exe` is ready to be executed—which you can do by simply typing `hello` at the command line; both Windows 95 and Windows NT can launch Windows applications this way.

For all its simplicity, the behavior of this "application," if it can be thought to deserve that title, is surprisingly complex. Unlike its "plain" C counterpart, this application not only displays the message, it interacts with the user in a complex fashion. After initially displaying its message, the program "stays alive" on the screen—meaning it can be moved around with the mouse. The mouse cursor can be clicked on the OK button to dismiss the program; alternatively, by clicking the mouse over the OK button and keeping the mouse button depressed, you can watch the OK button change its appearance as you move the mouse cursor over it. The window also has a simple menu that can be invoked by pressing Alt+Space or, under Windows 95, clicking its title area with the right mouse button; the single Move command can be used to change the window's position using the clipboard. Finally, the application can also be dismissed by using the Enter or Escape keys.

Remarkably rich behavior from a five-line piece of code, don't you think? But where does all this complexity come from? The secret lies in the magic words *message loop* and *window procedure*; unfortunately, a five-liner is not exactly a very revealing piece of programming excellence when it comes to understanding Windows application behavior. We have to move on to something more complex.

A Simple Message Loop: Sent and Posted Messages

The problem with our first Hello, World program is its simplicity. The MessageBox call at the center of this application encompasses (and hides!) a lot of functionality. In order to better understand what is taking place, we have to make this functionality more visible; in other words, we have to create a window that we manage ourselves, instead of letting the MessageBox function do this for us.

The new version of hello.c is shown in Figure 8.2. This time, the "Hello, World!" text appears as part of a button that occupies the entire client area. (It also appears in the window's title bar.) This is due to the fact that I employed a few unorthodox shortcuts to keep the application as simple as possible; this allows us to focus on the issues at hand instead of getting bogged down with irrelevant details.

FIGURE 8.2.

*Version of Hello,
World with a
simple message loop.*

A "typical" Windows program, during initialization, registers a window class first, and then creates its main window using the newly registered class. For now, I wanted to avoid having to register a new class and all that comes with it (such as writing a window procedure); instead, I decided to use one of the existing window classes, the BUTTON class. The functionality of this class does not enable me to identically reproduce the behavior of the previous version of hello.c, but that is not the purpose anyway; the purpose is to demonstrate the function of a very simple message loop. This new version of the application is shown in Listing 8.2.

Listing 8.2. Source of Hello, World with a simple message loop.

```
#include <windows.h>

int WINAPI WinMain(HINSTANCE hInstance, HINSTANCE d2,
                                LPSTR d3, int d4)
{
    MSG msg;
    HWND hwnd;

    hwnd = CreateWindow("BUTTON", "Hello, World!",
                        WS_VISIBLE | BS_CENTER, 100, 100, 100, 80,
                        NULL, NULL, hInstance, NULL);
    while (GetMessage(&msg, NULL, 0, 0))
    {
        if (msg.message == WM_LBUTTONUP)
        {
            DestroyWindow(hwnd);
            PostQuitMessage(0);
        }
        DispatchMessage(&msg);
    }
    return msg.wParam;
}
```

While not exactly the purpose of this exercise, I cannot help but point out that the application is still far from the legendary hundreds of lines that displaying "Hello, World!" is supposed to take; even with my publisher's formatting requirements, it still fits conveniently in one screen.

This example reveals the infamous message loop. After creating its window, the program enters into a while loop where it makes repeated calls to the GetMessage Windows function. Whenever the application receives a message, GetMessage returns; its return value is FALSE only if the message received was a WM_QUIT message. The special case of a WM_LBUTTONUP message is handled; the call to DestroyWindow causes the application's window to be destroyed, while the call to PostQuitMessage ensures that the GetMessage function receives a WM_QUIT message, which causes the loop to terminate. Messages other than WM_LBUTTONUP are *dispatched* through the DispatchMessage function.

Dispatched through the DispatchMessage function—but dispatched to whom? A good question. These messages are in fact dispatched to the default window procedure of the BUTTON class. As in the case when we called the MessageBox function, this window procedure remains hidden from us, as it is implemented as part of the operating system.

When handling WM_LBUTTONUP messages, a seemingly more elegant solution would be to include the call to PostQuitMessage in another case block that responds to WM_DESTROY messages. The problem is that WM_DESTROY messages are typically not *posted* but *sent* to the application. There is a subtle, but crucial difference.

When a message is posted, the application retrieves it through a GetMessage or PeekMessage call at the time of its own choosing (PeekMessage is used when the application wants to perform some tasks when it has no messages to process). In contrast to posting, sending a message to an application implies a direct, immediate call to the window procedure, bypassing any message loops. So in our case, the WM_DESTROY message that is generated in response to our call to DestroyWindow is never seen by the GetMessage loop; instead, it is passed directly to the window procedure of the BUTTON window class.

This example still failed to show us the innards of the window procedure. Therefore, it is time to move on to yet another, more sophisticated version of our Hello, World program. But do not despair...we are still far from hundreds of lines!

Window Procedures

The new version of hello.c, shown in Listing 8.3, registers its own window class. Done in part for cosmetic reasons (so we can do away with the ugly kludge of using the BUTTON class for our purposes), the most important reason for this is so that we can install our own window procedure.

Listing 8.3. Source of Hello, World with a new window class.

```
#include <windows.h>

void DrawHello(HWND hwnd)
{
    HDC hDC;
    PAINTSTRUCT paintStruct;
    RECT clientRect;

    hDC = BeginPaint(hwnd, &paintStruct);
    if (hDC != NULL)
    {
        GetClientRect(hwnd, &clientRect);
        DPtoLP(hDC, (LPPOINT)&clientRect, 2);
        DrawText(hDC, "Hello, World!", -1, &clientRect,
                DT_CENTER | DT_VCENTER | DT_SINGLELINE);
        EndPaint(hwnd, &paintStruct);
    }
}

LRESULT CALLBACK WndProc(HWND hwnd, UINT uMsg,
                        WPARAM wParam, LPARAM lParam)
{
    switch(uMsg)
    {
        case WM_PAINT:
```

continues

Listing 8.3. continued

```
            DrawHello(hwnd);
            break;
        case WM_DESTROY:
            PostQuitMessage(0);
            break;
        default:
            return DefWindowProc(hwnd, uMsg, wParam, lParam);
    }
    return 0;
}

int WINAPI WinMain(HINSTANCE hInstance, HINSTANCE hPrevInstance,
                                LPSTR d3, int nCmdShow)
{
    MSG msg;
    HWND hwnd;
    WNDCLASS wndClass;

    if (hPrevInstance == NULL)
    {
        memset(&wndClass, 0, sizeof(wndClass));
        wndClass.style = CS_HREDRAW | CS_VREDRAW;
        wndClass.lpfnWndProc = WndProc;
        wndClass.hInstance = hInstance;
        wndClass.hCursor = LoadCursor(NULL, IDC_ARROW);
        wndClass.hbrBackground = (HBRUSH)(COLOR_WINDOW + 1);
        wndClass.lpszClassName = "HELLO";
        if (!RegisterClass(&wndClass)) return FALSE;
    }
    hwnd = CreateWindow("HELLO", "HELLO",
                        WS_OVERLAPPEDWINDOW,
                        CW_USEDEFAULT, 0, CW_USEDEFAULT, 0,
                        NULL, NULL, hInstance, NULL);
    ShowWindow(hwnd, nCmdShow);
    UpdateWindow(hwnd);
    while (GetMessage(&msg, NULL, 0, 0))
        DispatchMessage(&msg);
    return msg.wParam;
}
```

I can almost sense your outrage: What? Sixty-four lines? Worse yet, to compile this program successfully you actually have to specify the gdi32.lib library on the command line? (Compile with cl hello.c user32.lib gdi32.lib.)

Rest assured, this is as far as we go; our text version of Hello, World will not get any more complex at this time. At 64 lines, this is a "full-featured" Windows application (Figure 8.3); it has a system menu, it can be moved, resized, minimized, and maximized, it knows when to redraw itself, and responds to the Close menu item or the Alt+F4 keystroke. Not bad, for an application that still fits easily on a printed page!

FIGURE 8.3.

Version of Hello, World with its own window class.

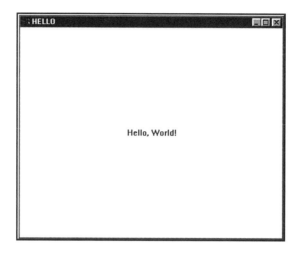

So how does this work? As before, execution starts with the WinMain function. The first thing the application does is checking whether it has any copies already running. If so, there is no need to re-register its window class. Otherwise, the window class is registered, its properties and behavior determined through the WndClass structure. In particular, it is through the WndClass structure that the address of the window procedure, WndProc, is given.

Next, an actual window is created through the CreateWindow system call. Once the window is displayed, WinMain enters the message loop; the message loop exits when GetMessage returns FALSE upon receiving a WM_QUIT message.

Finally, through WndProc, the purpose and structure of the mysterious window procedure are revealed. A typical window procedure is nothing but a giant switch statement. Depending on the message received, different functions are called that perform the necessary action. In our case, we process exactly two messages: WM_PAINT and WM_DESTROY.

WM_PAINT messages indicate that parts or all of the application's window must be redrawn. Sophisticated applications would normally not redraw parts of the application window for which redrawing has not been requested; in our case, we simply don't care, we just redisplay the "Hello, World!" text whenever a WM_PAINT message is received.

WM_DESTROY messages are received in response to user actions that cause the application's window to be destroyed. Our response to this is a call to PostQuitMessage; by doing this, we ensure that the GetMessage function in WinMain receives a WM_QUIT message, causing the main message loop to terminate.

What happens to messages that are not processed by our window procedure? They are instead passed to the *default window procedure*, DefWindowProc. This function determines the behavior of the application's window and many of its nonclient area components (such as its title bar) through the default handling of messages that it provides.

A companion to `DefWindowProc` is `DefDlgProc`. This default window procedure is specifically designed for windows that are dialog windows. This function provides handling for dialog-specific messages and also provides default management of the dialog's controls for cases when the dialog loses or gains focus.

If you have access to the Windows 3.1 SDK (perhaps through a subscription to the Microsoft Developer Network, level 2), it may be an educational exercise to look at the `DEFPROC` sample; this "sample" is nothing else but the source code of the two default window procedures, `DefWindowProc` and `DefDlgProc`.

Comparison with *generic.c*

So if it is this easy to write a Hello, World program with just a few lines of code, what is the explanation for the common myth that even a simple program like this takes several hundred lines of code in Windows?

The explanation to this curious question can be found in how Microsoft presented its Windows Software Development Kit, or SDK, back in the "good old days." The tutorial centerpiece of the old SDK was the *Generic Windows Application*, a program that did nothing other than display a window with standard decorations and provide an About, a Help, and an Exit function. This program successfully served as the skeleton for many well-written Windows applications.

For all its simplicity, the `generic.c` source code was still almost 500 lines long, with another nearly 200 lines in its resource file, `generic.rc`. No wonder programmers in the old days found Windows programming forbidding. Nevertheless, even in the old days it was not necessary to reproduce these hundreds of lines of code "from scratch" every time you embarked upon a new Windows project; on the contrary, `generic.c` was used as a starting point, and it provided a default implementation for all the basic mechanics of a Windows application. It also influenced both the visual appearance and code style of Windows applications; for example, although not strictly necessary, most Windows applications ended up having separate `InitApplication` and `InitInstance` functions.

The task of the Visual C++ programmer is much easier nowadays, although really not that different. Instead of starting from a static skeleton, `generic.c`, MFC programmers start with an application skeleton dynamically created by the Visual C++ AppWizard. But the fact that you start off from a skeleton application that implements a framework for the basic mechanics of your application has not changed. In my opinion, the availability of a well-written skeleton application had a significant positive influence on Windows programming.

Multiple Message Loops and Window Procedures

There was a single message loop in every one of the examples that we have built so far—namely, the three versions of `hello.c`. (Well, in the case of the first one, the presence of the message loop was implicit in the `MessageBox` function call.) Can there be applications with more than one message loop? And if so, why would you want to write an application that way?

The answer to the first question is a sound yes. Applications can have as many message loops as they want. Consider the simplest of these situations, when an application that has its own message loop makes a call to the `MessageBox` function; would this call not imply that, temporarily, the implicit message loop in `MessageBox` takes over the processing of messages while the message is displayed?

This scenario also suggests an answer to the second question. You would implement a second (or third, or fourth) message loop when, during a particular stage of execution of your program, messages must be processed in a fashion that is markedly different from normal processing.

Consider, for example, the case of drawing with *mouse capture*. An application can provide a freehand drawing capability by looking for mouse events and capturing the mouse when the left button is pressed within its client area. While the mouse is captured, the application is informed of every mouse movement through a separate message; thus, the application can draw a freehand line by adding a new segment whenever the user moves the mouse. The mouse is *released* when the user releases the left mouse button.

Our fourth and final version of Hello, World, shown in Figure 8.4, is exactly such an application. This 94-line enormity, which must be compiled with the command line `cl hello.c user32.lib gdi32.lib`, although far less elegant than the Visual C++ "Scribble" tutorial, actually enables you to *draw* the text "Hello, World!" using the mouse cursor.

Even a cursory glance at the application's source code, shown in Listing 8.4, reveals the existence of two `while` loops with calls to the `GetMessage` function. The main message loop found in `WinMain` is not different from before; the new stuff is in the `DrawHello` function.

FIGURE 8.4.

*A graphical version
of Hello, World.*

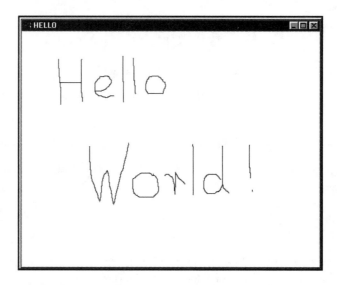

Listing 8.4. Source of the graphical version of Hello, World.

```
#include <windows.h>

void AddSegmentAtMessagePos(HDC hDC, HWND hwnd, BOOL bDraw)
{
    DWORD dwPos;
    POINTS points;
    POINT point;

    dwPos = GetMessagePos();
    points = MAKEPOINTS(dwPos);
    point.x = points.x;
    point.y = points.y;
    ScreenToClient(hwnd, &point);
    DPtoLP(hDC, &point, 1);
    if (bDraw) LineTo(hDC, point.x, point.y);
    else MoveToEx(hDC, point.x, point.y, NULL);
}

void DrawHello(HWND hwnd)
{
    HDC hDC;
    MSG msg;

    if (GetCapture() != NULL) return;
    hDC = GetDC(hwnd);
    if (hDC != NULL)
    {
        SetCapture(hwnd);
        AddSegmentAtMessagePos(hDC, hwnd, FALSE);
        while(GetMessage(&msg, NULL, 0, 0))
        {
```

```
            if (GetCapture() != hwnd) break;
            switch (msg.message)
            {
                case WM_MOUSEMOVE:
                    AddSegmentAtMessagePos(hDC, hwnd, TRUE);
                    break;
                case WM_LBUTTONUP:
                    goto ExitLoop;
        default:
            DispatchMessage(&msg);
            }
        }
ExitLoop:
        ReleaseCapture();
        ReleaseDC(hwnd, hDC);
    }
}

LRESULT CALLBACK WndProc(HWND hwnd, UINT uMsg,
                        WPARAM wParam, LPARAM lParam)
{
    switch(uMsg)
    {
        case WM_LBUTTONDOWN:
            DrawHello(hwnd);
            break;
        case WM_DESTROY:
            PostQuitMessage(0);
            break;
        default:
            return DefWindowProc(hwnd, uMsg, wParam, lParam);
    }
    return 0;
}

int WINAPI WinMain(HINSTANCE hInstance, HINSTANCE hPrevInstance,
                        LPSTR d3, int nCmdShow)
{
    MSG msg;
    HWND hwnd;
    WNDCLASS wndClass;

    if (hPrevInstance == NULL)
    {
        memset(&wndClass, 0, sizeof(wndClass));
        wndClass.style = CS_HREDRAW | CS_VREDRAW;
        wndClass.lpfnWndProc = WndProc;
        wndClass.hInstance = hInstance;
        wndClass.hCursor = LoadCursor(NULL, IDC_ARROW);
        wndClass.hbrBackground = (HBRUSH)(COLOR_WINDOW + 1);
        wndClass.lpszClassName = "HELLO";
        if (!RegisterClass(&wndClass)) return FALSE;
    }
    hwnd = CreateWindow("HELLO", "HELLO",
                        WS_OVERLAPPEDWINDOW,
                        CW_USEDEFAULT, 0, CW_USEDEFAULT, 0,
                        NULL, NULL, hInstance, NULL);
```

continues

Listing 8.4. continued

```
    ShowWindow(hwnd, nCmdShow);
    UpdateWindow(hwnd);
    while (GetMessage(&msg, NULL, 0, 0))
        DispatchMessage(&msg);
    return msg.wParam;
}
```

Previously, DrawHello merely put out a text string with the words "Hello, World!" in it. The new version is much more complex. Its work begins by checking whether any other application is already capturing the mouse or not, and acquiring a device context handle for the main window. Next, it captures the mouse via the SetCapture function, thus instructing Windows to send the application WM_MOUSEMOVE messages.

The DrawHello function also makes a call to the helper function AddSegmentAtMessagePos which, when called with the Boolean value FALSE as its third parameter, simply moves the drawing position to the position of the most recent message. For this, it makes use of the GetMessagePos function, which retrieves the position of the mouse cursor at the time the most recent message was created. AddSegmentAtMessagePos also makes use of coordinate transform functions to translate the screen coordinates of the mouse into logical coordinates in the window.

After the call to AddSegmentAtMessagePos, the DrawHello function enters its new message loop. While the mouse is captured, we expect special behavior from our application; most notably, it is expected to follow mouse movements on the screen by drawing additional freehand segments. This is again accomplished with calls to AddSegmentAtMessagePos with the third parameter set to TRUE, whenever a WM_MOUSEMOVE message is received.

This message loop terminates when the mouse button is released, or when the application loses mouse capture for whatever reason. At that time, DrawHello returns, and the primary message loop resumes processing subsequent messages.

Was it really necessary to implement this application with two message loops? Could we not have handled WM_MOUSEMOVE messages in our window procedure instead, dispatched there through the main message loop? It is certainly possible; however, organizing code the way demonstrated here makes it much more maintainable and helps avoid extremely large and complex window procedures.

Summary

Every Windows application is built around a message loop. A message loop makes repeated calls to the GetMessage or PeekMessage functions and retrieves messages, which it then dispatches to window procedures through DispatchMessage.

Window procedures are defined for window classes at the time the window class is registered through `RegisterClass`. A typical window procedure contains a `switch` statement with `case` blocks for all messages the application is interested in; other messages are dispatched to the default window procedure `DefWindowProc` (or `DefDlgProc` in the case of dialog windows).

Messages can be posted or sent to an application. Posted messages are deposited in a message queue, from which `GetMessage` or `PeekMessage` retrieves them. In contrast, sending a message implies an immediate call to the window procedure, bypassing the message queue and the message loop.

An application can have several message loops, depending on its requirements. Although it is never required to have more than one message loop, this approach can aid in the development of better organized, more maintainable code.

Windows, Dialog Boxes, and Controls

9

A window in Windows can be defined as a rectangular area on the screen. However, this definition, in all its simplicity, hides the volumes of functionality behind the abstract idea of a window as the primary unit through which a user and a Windows application interact.

A window is not only an area through which an application can present its output; it is also a target of events, a target of messages within the Windows environment. Although the window concept in Windows predates the use of object-oriented languages on the PC by several years, the terminology is more than appropriate here: the *properties* of a window determine its appearance, while its *methods* determine how it responds to user input.

A window is identified by a *window handle*. This handle (usually a variable of type HWND) uniquely identifies each window in the system. The list includes the "obvious" application windows and dialog boxes as well as the less obvious ones such as the desktop, certain icons, or buttons. User-interface events are packaged into Windows messages with the appropriate window handle attached and then sent, or queued, to the application (or thread, to be more precise) that owns that window.

Needless to say, Windows offers a lot of functionality covering the creation and management of windows.

The Window Hierarchy

Windows maintains its windows (I wish there were a way to talk about windows within Windows without turning every second sentence into an unintentional joke!) in a hierarchical organization. Each window has a parent and zero or more siblings. At the root of all windows is the *desktop window*, created by Windows at startup time. The parent window for *top-level* windows is the desktop window; the parent window for *child windows* is either a top-level window or another child window higher up in the hierarchy. Figure 9.1 demonstrates this hierarchy by dissecting a typical Windows screen.

Actually, the situation under Windows NT is somewhat more complex. Unlike its simpler cousins, Windows NT has the capability to maintain multiple desktops simultaneously. In fact, Windows NT normally maintains three desktops: one for the Winlogon screen, one for user applications, and one for the screen saver.

The visual window hierarchy normally reflects the logical hierarchy. That is, windows at the same hierarchy level are normally displayed in the *Z-order*, which is essentially the order in which siblings appear. However, this order can be changed for top-level windows. Top-level windows with the extended window style WM_EX_TOPMOST appear on top of any non-topmost top-level windows.

FIGURE 9.1.

The window hierarchy.

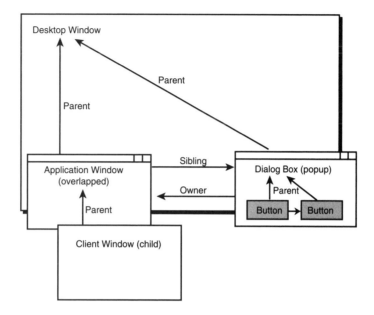

Another relationship exists between top-level windows. A top-level window may have an *owner*, which is another top-level window. An owned window always appears on top of its owner and disappears if its owner is minimized. A typical case of a top-level window owned by another occurs when an application displays a dialog box. The dialog box is not a child window (it is not confined to the client area of the application's main window), but it remains owned by the application window.

Several functions enable applications to traverse the window hierarchy and find a specific window. Here's a review of a few of the more frequently used functions:

- GetDesktopWindow. Through the GetDesktopWindow function, an application can retrieve the handle of the current desktop window.

- EnumWindows. The EnumWindows function enumerates all top-level windows. A user-defined callback function, the address of which is supplied in the call to EnumWindows, is called once for every top-level window. EnumWindows does not enumerate top-level windows that are created after the function has been called, even if it has not yet completed the enumeration when the new window is created.

- EnumChildWindows. The EnumChildWindows function enumerates all child windows of a given window, identified by a handle that is supplied in the call to EnumChildWindows. The enumeration is accomplished by a user-defined callback function, the address of which is also supplied in the call to EnumChildWindows. This function also enumerates descendant windows; that is, child windows that are themselves children (or descendants) of child windows of the window specified in the call to EnumChildWindows.

Child windows that are destroyed before they are enumerated, or child windows that are created after the enumeration process started, will not be enumerated.

■ EnumThreadWindows. The EnumThreadWindows function enumerates all windows owned by a specific thread by calling a user-supplied callback function once for every such window. The handle to the thread and the address of the callback function are supplied by the application in the call to EnumThreadWindows. The enumeration includes top-level windows, child windows, and descendants of child windows.

Windows that are created after the enumeration process began are not enumerated by EnumThreadWindows.

■ FindWindow. The FindWindow function can be used to find a top-level window by its window class name or window title.

■ GetParent. The GetParent function identifies the parent window of the specified window.

■ GetWindow. The GetWindow function offers the most flexible way for manipulating the window hierarchy. Depending on its second parameter, uCmd, this function can be used to retrieve the handle to a window's parent, owner, sibling, or child windows.

Window Management

Typically, an application creates a window in two steps. First, the *window class* is registered; next, the window itself is created through the CreateWindow function. The window class determines the overall behavior of the new window type, including most notably the address of the new *window procedure*. Through CreateWindow the application controls minor aspects of the new window, such as its size, position, and appearance.

The *RegisterClass* Function and the *WNDCLASS* Structure

A new window class is registered when an application calls the following function:

```
ATOM RegisterClass(CONST WNDCLASS *lpwc);
```

The single parameter of this function, lpwc, points to a structure of type WNDCLASS describing the new window type. The return value is a *Windows atom*, a 16-bit value identifying a unique character string in a table maintained by Windows.

The WNDCLASS structure is defined as follows:

```
typedef struct _WNDCLASS {
    UINT    style;
    WNDPROC lpfnWndProc;
    int     cbClsExtra;
    int     cbWndExtra;
    HANDLE  hInstance;
    HICON   hIcon;
```

```
    HCURSOR hCursor;
    HBRUSH  hbrBackground;
    LPCTSTR lpszMenuName;
    LPCTSTR lpszClassName;
} WNDCLASS;
```

The meaning of some of these parameters is fairly straightforward. For example, hIcon is a handle to the icon used to represent minimized windows of this class; hCursor is a handle to the standard mouse cursor that is used when the mouse enters the window rectangle; hbrBackground is a handle to the GDI brush that is used to draw the window's background. The string pointed to by lpszMenuName identifies the menu resource (by name or, through the MAKEINTRESOURCE macro, by an integer identifier) that is used as the standard menu for this class; lpszClassName is the name of the window class.

The parameters cbClsExtra and cbWndExtra can be used to allocate extra memory for the window class or for individual windows. Applications can use this extra memory to store application-specific information pertaining to the window class or individual windows.

I left the explanation of the first two parameters for last, and for good reason. Most of what makes a window such a unique and complex entity is controlled through the window class style and the window procedure.

The parameter lpfnWndProc specifies the address of the window procedure function. This function is responsible for handling any messages the window receives. It can either handle those messages itself, or invoke the default window procedure, DefWindowProc. The messages can be anything: window sizing and moving, mouse events, keyboard events, commands, repaint requests, timer and other hardware-related events, and so on.

A typical window procedure contains a large switch statement block. Inside, case blocks exist for every message the application is interested in. Messages that the application does not handle are passed to DefWindowProc through the default block. The skeleton of such a window procedure is shown in Listing 9.1.

Listing 9.1. Window procedure skeleton.

```
LRESULT CALLBACK WndProc(HWND hwnd, UINT uMsg,
                         WPARAM wParam, LPARAM lParam)
{
    switch(uMsg)
    {
        case WM_DESTROY:
            PostQuitMessage(0);
            break;
        // Other case blocks come here
        default:
            return DefWindowProc(hwnd, uMsg, wParam, lParam);
    }
    return 0;
}
```

Certain global characteristics of the window class are controlled through the class style parameter, `style`. This parameter may be set to a combination of values (using the bitwise OR operator, ¦). For example, `CS_BYTEALIGNCLIENT` specifies that the window's client area is always to be positioned on a byte boundary in the screen display's bitmap to enhance graphics performance (a very useful thing to remember when writing performance-intensive applications intended to run on lower-end graphics hardware). The value `CS_DBLCLKS` specifies that Windows should generate double-click mouse messages when the user double-clicks the mouse within the window. The pair of values `CS_HREDRAW` and `CS_VREDRAW` specify that the window be redrawn in its entirety every time its horizontal or vertical size changes. Or the value `CS_SAVEBITS` specifies that Windows should allocate what UNIX and X programmers often refer to as *backing store*, a copy of the window bitmap in memory, so that it can automatically redraw the window when parts of it become unobscured. (This should be used with caution; the large amounts of memory required for this may cause a significant performance hit.)

> **NOTE**
>
> In 16-bit Windows, it was possible to register an *application global class* through the style `CS_GLOBALCLASS`. An application global class was accessible from all other applications and DLLs. This is not true in Win32. In order for an application global class to work as intended, it must be registered from a DLL that is loaded by every application. Such a DLL can be defined through the Registry.

Creating a Window Through *CreateWindow*

Registering a new window class is the first step in window creation. Next, applications must actually create a window through the `CreateWindow` function:

```
HWND CreateWindow(
    LPCTSTR  lpClassName,
    LPCTSTR  lpWindowName,
    DWORD  dwStyle,
    int  x,
    int  y,
    int  nWidth,
    int  nHeight,
    HWND  hWndParent,
    HMENU  hMenu,
    HANDLE  hInstance,
    LPVOID  lpParam
);
```

The first parameter, `lpClassName`, defines the name of the class that this window inherits its behavior from. The class must either be registered through `RegisterClass` or be one of the *predefined control classes*. The predefined classes include the `BUTTON`, `COMBOBOX`, `EDIT`, `\`, `SCROLLBAR`, and `STATIC` classes. There are also some window classes that are mostly used internally by

Windows and are referenced only through integer identifiers; these include classes for menus, the desktop window, and icon titles, to name but a few.

The dwStyle parameter specifies the window's style. This parameter should not be confused with the class style, passed to RegisterClass through the WNDCLASS structure when the new window class is registered. While the class style determines some of the permanent properties of windows belonging to that class, the window style passed to CreateWindow is used to initialize the more transient properties of the window. For example, dwStyle can be used to determine the window's initial appearance (minimized, maximized, visible or hidden). As is the case with the class style, the window style is also typically a combination of values (combined with the bitwise OR operator). In addition to the generic style values that are common to all types of windows, some values are specific to the predefined window classes; for example, the BS_PUSHBUTTON style can be used for windows of the BUTTON class that are to send WM_COMMAND messages to their parents when clicked.

Some dwStyle values are important enough to deserve a closer look.

The WS_POPUP and WS_OVERLAPPED styles specify top-level windows. The basic difference is that a WS_OVERLAPPED window always has a caption, while a WS_POPUP window does not need to have one. Overlapped windows are typically used as the main window of applications, while popup windows are used for dialog boxes.

When a top-level window is created, the calling application sets its owner window through the hwndParent parameter. The parent window of a top-level window is the desktop window.

Child windows are created with the WS_CHILD style. The major difference between a child window and a top-level window is that a child window is confined to the client area of its parent.

Windows defines some combinations of styles that are most useful when creating "typical" windows. The WS_OVERLAPPEDWINDOW style setting combines the WS_OVERLAPPED style with the WS_CAPTION, WS_SYSMENU, WS_THICKFRAME, WS_MINIMIZEBOX, and WS_MAXIMIZEBOX styles to create a typical top-level application window. The WS_POPUPWINDOW style setting combines WS_POPUP with the WS_BORDER and WS_SYSMENU styles to create a typical dialog box.

Extended Styles and the *CreateWindowEx* Function

The CreateWindowEx function, while otherwise identical to the CreateWindow function, enables you to specify a combination of *extended window styles*. Extended window styles provide finer control over certain aspects of a window's appearance or the way it functions.

For example, through the WS_EX_TOPMOST style applications can make a window a topmost window; that is, a top-level window that is not obscured by other top-level windows. A window created with the WS_EX_TRANSPARENT style does not obscure other windows and only receives a WM_PAINT message when all windows under it have been updated.

Other extended window styles are specific to Windows 95 and versions of Windows NT later than 3.51; for example, Windows NT 3.51 with the beta version of the Windows 95 style shell installed. For example, the WS_EX_TOOLWINDOW style can be used to create a tool window. A tool window is a window with a smaller than usual title bar and other properties that make it useful as a floating toolbar window.

Yet another set of Windows 95 specific extended styles specifies the window's behavior with respect to the selected shell language. For example, the WS_EX_RIGHT, WS_EX_RTLREADING, and WS_EX_LEFTSCROLLBAR extended styles can be used in conjunction with a right-to-left shell language selection such as Hebrew or Arabic.

Painting Window Contents

Painting in a window is performed through the normal set of GDI drawing functions. Applications usually obtain a handle to the display device context through a function such as GetDC, and then call GDI functions such as LineTo, Rectangle, or TextOut.

But even more typically, window painting occurs in response to a specific message, WM_PAINT.

The *WM_PAINT* Message

The WM_PAINT message is sent to a window when parts of it require redrawing by the application and no other message is pending in the message queue of the thread that owns the window. Applications typically respond to this with a set of drawing instructions enclosed between calls to the BeginPaint and EndPaint functions.

The BeginPaint function retrieves a set of parameters that are stored in a PAINTSTRUCT structure:

```
typedef struct tagPAINTSTRUCT {
    HDC  hdc;
    BOOL fErase;
    RECT rcPaint;
    BOOL fRestore;
    BOOL fIncUpdate;
    BYTE rgbReserved[32];
} PAINTSTRUCT;
```

BeginPaint also takes care of erasing the background, if necessary, by sending the application a WM_ERASEBKGND message.

NOTE

The BeginPaint function should only be called in response to a WM_PAINT message. Each call to BeginPaint must be accompanied by a subsequent call to the EndPaint function.

Applications can use the hDC member of the structure to draw into the client area of the window. The rcPaint member represents the smallest rectangle that encloses all areas of the window that require updating. By limiting their activities to this rectangular region, applications can speed up the painting process.

Repainting a Window by Invalidating Its Contents

The functions InvalidateRect and InvalidateRgn can be used to invalidate all or parts of a window. Windows sends a WM_PAINT message to a window if its *update region,* that is, the union of all update regions specified in prior calls to InvalidateRect and InvalidateRgn, is not empty and the thread that owns the window has no more messages in its message queue.

This behavior suggests a very efficient mechanism for applications that need to update parts of their window. Instead of updating the window immediately, they can schedule the update by invalidating the appropriate region. When they process WM_PAINT messages, they can examine the update region (the rcPaint member of the PAINTSTRUCT structure) and update only those elements in the window that fall into this region. Alternatively (or in addition to this), applications can maintain private variables in which they store *hints;* that is, information that assists the window updating procedure in determining the most efficient way of updating the window.

The use of such hints to assist in efficiently updating a window is present throughout the Microsoft Foundation Classes.

Window Management Messages

A typical window responds to many other messages in addition to WM_PAINT messages. Some of the more frequently processed messages are reviewed in this section.

- ■ WM_CREATE. The first message that the window procedure of a newly created window receives is the WM_CREATE message. This message is sent before the window is made visible and before the CreateWindow or CreateWindowEx function returns.

  In response to this message, applications can perform initialization functions that are necessary before the window is made visible.

- ■ WM_DESTROY. The WM_DESTROY message is sent to the window procedure of a window that has already been removed from the screen and is about to be destroyed.

- ■ WM_CLOSE. The WM_CLOSE message is sent to a window indicating that the window should be closed. The default implementation in DefWindowProc calls DestroyWindow when this message is received. Applications can, for example, display a confirmation dialog and call DestroyWindow only if the user confirms closing the window.

- ■ WM_QUIT. The WM_QUIT message is usually the last message an application's main window receives. Receiving this message causes GetMessage to return zero, which terminates the message loop of most applications.

This message indicates a request to terminate the application. It is generated in response to a call to PostQuitMessage.

- WM_QUERYENDSESSION. The WM_QUERYENDSESSION notifies the application that the Windows session is about to be ended. An application may return FALSE in response to this message to prevent the shutdown of Windows. After processing the WM_QUERYENDSESSION message, Windows sends all applications a WM_ENDSESSION message with the results of the WM_QUERYENDSESSION processing.

- WM_ENDSESSION. The WM_ENDSESSION message is sent to applications after the WM_QUERYENDSESSION message has been processed. It indicates whether Windows is about to shut down or whether the shutdown has been aborted.

  If an imminent shutdown is indicated, the Windows session may end at any time after the WM_ENDSESSION message has been processed by all applications. It is important, therefore, that applications perform all tasks pertaining to safe termination.

- WM_ACTIVATE. The WM_ACTIVATE message indicates when a top-level window is about to be activated or deactivated. The message is first sent to the window that is about to be deactivated, then to the window that is about to be activated.

- WM_SHOWWINDOW. The WM_SHOWWINDOW message indicates when a window is about to be hidden or shown. A window can be hidden as a result of a call to the ShowWindow function, or as a result of another window being maximized.

- WM_ENABLE. The WM_ENABLE message is sent to a window when it is enabled or disabled. A window can be enabled or disabled through a call to the EnableWindow function. A window that is disabled cannot receive mouse or keyboard input.

- WM_MOVE. The WM_MOVE message indicates that the window's position has been changed.

- WM_SIZE. The WM_SIZE message indicates that the window's size has been changed.

- WM_SETFOCUS. The WM_SETFOCUS message indicates that the window has gained keyboard focus. An application may, for example, display the caret in response to this message.

- WM_KILLFOCUS. The WM_KILLFOCUS message indicates that the window is about to lose keyboard focus. If the application displays a caret, the caret should be destroyed in response to this message.

- WM_GETTEXT. The WM_GETTEXT message is sent to a window requesting that the window text be copied to a buffer. For most windows, the window text is the window title. For controls like buttons, edit controls, static controls, or combo boxes, the window text is the text displayed in the control. This message is usually handled by the DefWindowProc function.

- WM_SETTEXT. The WM_SETTEXT message requests that the window text be set to the contents of a buffer. The DefWindowProc function sets the window text and displays it in response to this message.

Several messages concern the nonclient area of a window; that is, its title bar, border, menu, and other areas that are typically not updated by the application program. An application can intercept these messages to create a window frame with a customized appearance or behavior.

- ■ WM_NCPAINT. The WM_NCPAINT message indicates that the nonclient area of a window (the window frame) needs to be repainted. The DefWindowProc function handles this message by repainting the window frame.

- ■ WM_NCCREATE. Before the WM_CREATE message is sent to a window, it also receives a WM_NCCREATE message. Applications may intercept this message to perform initializations specific to the nonclient area of the window.

- ■ WM_NCDESTROY. The WM_NCDESTROY message indicates that a window's nonclient area is about to be destroyed. This message is sent to a window after the WM_DESTROY message.

- ■ WM_NCACTIVATE. The WM_NCACTIVATE message is sent to a window to indicate that its nonclient area has been activated or deactivated. The DefWindowProc function changes the color of the window title bar to indicate an active or inactive state in response to this message.

Window Classes

Every window is associated with a window class. A window class is either a class provided by Windows, or a user-defined window class registered through the RegisterClass function.

The Window Procedure

The purpose of a window class is to define the characteristics and behavior of a set of related windows. Perhaps the most notable, but by far not the only property of a window class, is the window procedure.

I have already demonstrated a simple skeleton for a window procedure earlier in Listing 9.1.

The window procedure is called every time a message is sent to the window through the SendMessage function, and every time a posted message is dispatched through the DispatchMessage function. The role of the window procedure is to process messages sent or posted to that window. In doing so, it can rely on the default window procedure (DefWindowProc, or in the case of dialog boxes, DefDlgProc) for the processing of unwanted messages.

It is through the window procedure that the behavior of a window is implemented. By responding to various messages, the window procedure determines how the window reacts to mouse and cursor events and how its appearance changes in reaction to those events. For example, in the case of a button, the window procedure may respond to WM_LBUTTONDOWN messages by repainting the window indicating that the button is pressed. Or in the case of an edit control, the window procedure may respond to a WM_SETFOCUS message by displaying the caret.

Windows supplies two default window procedures: DefWindowProc and DefDlgProc. The DefWindowProc function implements the default behavior for typical top-level windows. It processes nonclient area messages and manages the window frame. It also implements some other aspects of top-level window behavior, such as responding to keyboard events; for example, responding to the Alt key by highlighting the first item in the window's menu bar.

The DefDlgProc function is for the use of dialog boxes. In addition to the default top-level window behavior, it also manages the focus within a dialog box. It implements the behavior of dialogs whereby the focus jumps from one dialog control to the next when the user presses the Tab key.

In addition to the default window procedures, Windows also supplies a set of window classes. These implement the behavior of dialog box controls, such as buttons, edit fields, list and combo boxes, and static text fields. The name for these classes is *system global class*, which is a leftover from the days of 16-bit Windows. In Win32 these classes are no longer global. That is, a change that affects a system global class will only affect windows of that class within the same application and have no effect on windows in another application because Win32 applications run in separate address spaces, and thus they are shielded from one another.

Whether it is a Windows-supplied class, or a class defined by the application, an application can use an existing window class from which to derive a new class and implement new or modified behavior. The mechanisms for accomplishing this are called subclassing and superclassing.

> **WARNING**
>
> An application should not attempt to subclass or superclass a window that belongs to another process.

Subclassing

Subclassing means substituting the window procedure for a window class with another. This is accomplished by calling the SetWindowLong or SetClassLong function.

Calling SetWindowLong with the GWL_WNDPROC index value substitutes the window procedure for a specific window. In contrast, calling SetClassLong with the GCL_WNDPROC index value substitutes the window procedure for all windows of that class that are created after the call to SetClassLong.

Consider the simple example shown in Listing 9.2. (You can compile this code from the command line by typing cl subclass.c user32.lib.) This example displays the "Hello, World!" message. In a somewhat unorthodox fashion, it uses the BUTTON system class for this purpose. However, it subclasses the BUTTON class by providing a replacement window procedure. This replacement procedure implements special behavior when a WM_LBUTTONUP message is received; it destroys the window, effectively ending the application. To ensure proper termination, the WM_DESTROY message also receives special handling: a WM_QUIT message is posted through a call to PostQuitMessage.

Listing 9.2. Subclassing the BUTTON class.

```
#include <windows.h>

WNDPROC OldWndProc;

LRESULT CALLBACK WndProc(HWND hwnd, UINT uMsg,
                         WPARAM wParam, LPARAM lParam)
{
    switch(uMsg)
    {
        case WM_LBUTTONUP:
            DestroyWindow(hwnd);
            break;
        case WM_DESTROY:
            PostQuitMessage(0);
            break;
        default:
            return CallWindowProc(OldWndProc,
                                  hwnd, uMsg, wParam, lParam);
    }
    return 0;
}

int WINAPI WinMain(HINSTANCE hInstance, HINSTANCE d2,
                                 LPSTR d3, int d4)
{
    MSG msg;
    HWND hwnd;

    hwnd = CreateWindow("BUTTON", "Hello, World!",
                    WS_VISIBLE | BS_CENTER, 100, 100, 100, 80,
                    NULL, NULL, hInstance, NULL);
    OldWndProc =
        (WNDPROC)SetWindowLong(hwnd, GWL_WNDPROC, (LONG)WndProc);
    while (GetMessage(&msg, NULL, 0, 0))
        DispatchMessage(&msg);
    return msg.wParam;
}
```

I would like to call your attention to the mechanism used in the new window procedure, WndProc, to reference the old window procedure for the default processing of messages. The old procedure is called through the Win32 function CallWindowProc. In 16-bit Windows, it was possible to call the address obtained by the call to SetWindowLong directly; this was always the address of the old window procedure. In Win32, this is not necessarily so; the value may instead be a handle to the window procedure.

Here, I performed the subclassing through SetWindowLong, meaning it only affected the single button window for which SetWindowLong was called. If I had called SetClassLong instead, I would have altered the behavior of all buttons created subsequently. Consider the example program in Listing 9.3. (To compile this program from the command line, type cl subclass.c user32.lib.)

Listing 9.3. Subclassing the BUTTON class.

```c
#include <windows.h>

WNDPROC OldWndProc;

LRESULT CALLBACK WndProc(HWND hwnd, UINT uMsg,
                         WPARAM wParam, LPARAM lParam)
{
    switch(uMsg)
    {
        case WM_LBUTTONDOWN:
            MessageBeep(0xFFFFFFFF);
        default:
            return CallWindowProc(OldWndProc,
                                  hwnd, uMsg, wParam, lParam);
    }
    return 0;
}

int WINAPI WinMain(HINSTANCE hInstance,
                   HINSTANCE d2, LPSTR d3, int d4)
{
    HWND hwnd;

    hwnd = CreateWindow("BUTTON", "",
                        0, 0, 0, 0, 0,
                        NULL, NULL, hInstance, NULL);
    OldWndProc =
        (WNDPROC)SetClassLong(hwnd, GCL_WNDPROC, (LONG)WndProc);
    DestroyWindow(hwnd);
    MessageBox(NULL, "Hello, World!", "", MB_OK);
}
```

This example creates a button control but never makes it visible; the sole purpose of this control's existence is so that through its handle, the class behavior can be modified. Immediately after the call to SetClassLong, the button control is actually destroyed.

But the effects of SetClassLong linger on! The subsequently displayed message box contains an OK button; and the behavior of this button (namely that when it is clicked by the left mouse button, the PC speaker emits a short beep) reflects the new window procedure. Similarly, if the program displayed other dialogs or message boxes, indeed anything that had button controls in it, all the newly created buttons would exhibit the modified behavior.

Global Subclassing

In 16-bit Windows, a subclassing mechanism similar to that presented in the previous section was often used to change the *system-wide* behavior of certain types of windows such as dialog controls. (This is how the 3-D control library CTL3D.DLL was implemented.) Subclassing the window class affected all newly created windows of that class, regardless of the application that created them. Unfortunately, in Win32 this is no longer the case; only windows of the same application are affected by such a change.

So how can developers influence the global behavior of certain types of windows? The answer is, you have to use a DLL and ensure that it is loaded into every application's address space.

Under Windows NT, this can be accomplished easily by creating a setting in the registry. The following registry value needs to be modified:

\HKEY_LOCAL_MACHINE\Software\Microsoft\Windows NT\CurrentVersion\Windows\APPINIT_DLLS

DLLs that are listed under this registry key are loaded into the address space of every newly created process. If you wish to add several DLLs, separate the pathnames by spaces.

Listing 9.4 shows a DLL that subclasses the BUTTON class just like the example shown in Listing 9.3. If you add the full pathname of this DLL to the above-mentioned registry key, every time a button control is clicked, a short beep will be heard.

Listing 9.4. Subclassing in a DLL.

```
#include <windows.h>

WNDPROC OldWndProc;

LRESULT CALLBACK WndProc(HWND hwnd, UINT uMsg,
                         WPARAM wParam, LPARAM lParam)
{
    switch(uMsg)
    {
        case WM_LBUTTONDOWN:
            MessageBeep(0xFFFFFFFF);
        default:
            return CallWindowProc(OldWndProc,
                             hwnd, uMsg, wParam, lParam);
    }
    return 0;
}

BOOL WINAPI DllMain (HANDLE hModule, DWORD dwReason,
                     LPVOID lpReserved)
{
    HWND hwnd;
```

continues

Listing 9.4. continued

```
switch(dwReason)
{
    case DLL_PROCESS_ATTACH:
        hwnd = CreateWindow("BUTTON", "",
                            0, 0, 0, 0, 0,
                            NULL, NULL, hModule, NULL);
        OldWndProc = (WNDPROC)SetClassLong(hwnd, GCL_WNDPROC,
                                            (LONG)WndProc);
        DestroyWindow(hwnd);
    }
    return TRUE;
}
```

To compile this DLL from the command line, use `cl /LD beepbtn.c user32.lib`. The `/LD` command line flag instructs the compiler to create a DLL instead of an executable file.

> **WARNING**
>
> Be careful to only add a fully tested DLL to the Registry. A faulty DLL may render your system unstable or may prevent it from starting altogether. If that happens, a quick-and-dirty remedy is to boot into MS-DOS and rename the DLL file to prevent it from being loaded. Obviously, if your DLL file sits on an NTFS partition, this may not be so easy to do.

Adding your DLL's pathname to the APPINIT_DLLS Registry key is perhaps the simplest, but certainly not the only technique to inject your DLL's code into another application's address space. This technique also has some drawbacks, not the least of which is the fact that it does not work under Windows 95. (You may find information to the contrary on the Microsoft Developer Library. I tried the technique and it does not work; when I asked Microsoft's product support, they confirmed that this registry setting is not supported under Windows 95.)

Another drawback of this technique includes the fact that a DLL specified this way is loaded into the address space of every application—or, to be more precise, every GUI application that links with USER32.DLL. Even the slightest bug in your DLL may seriously affect the stability of the entire system.

Fortunately, there are other techniques available that enable you to inject your DLL into the address space of another process.

The first such technique requires the use of a Windows hook function. By using the SetWindowsHookEx function, it is possible to install a hook function into the another application's address space. Through this mechanism, you can add a new window function to a window class owned by another application.

The second technique relies on the `CreateRemoteThread` function and its ability to create a thread that runs in the context of another process.

Superclassing

Superclassing means creating a new class based on the behavior of an existing class. An application that wishes to superclass an existing class can use the `GetClassInfo` function to obtain a `WNDCLASS` structure describing that class. After this structure has been suitably modified, it can be used in a call to the `RegisterClass` function that registers the new class for use.

The example shown in Listing 9.5 demonstrates the technique of superclassing. In this example, a new window class, `BEEPBUTTON`, is created, its behavior based on the default `BUTTON` class. This new class is then used to display a simple message. To compile this program from the command line, type `cl supercls.c user32.lib`.

Listing 9.5. Superclassing the BUTTON class.

```
#include <windows.h>

WNDPROC OldWndProc;

LRESULT CALLBACK WndProc(HWND hwnd, UINT uMsg,
                         WPARAM wParam, LPARAM lParam)
{
    switch(uMsg)
    {
        case WM_LBUTTONDOWN:
            MessageBeep(0xFFFFFFFF);
        default:
            return CallWindowProc(OldWndProc,
                                  hwnd, uMsg, wParam, lParam);
    }
    return 0;
}
int WINAPI WinMain(HINSTANCE hInstance, HINSTANCE d2,
                                LPSTR d3, int d4)
{
    MSG msg;
    HWND hwnd;
    WNDCLASS wndClass;

    GetClassInfo(hInstance, "BUTTON", &wndClass);
    wndClass.hInstance = hInstance;
    wndClass.lpszClassName = "BEEPBUTTON";
    OldWndProc = wndClass.lpfnWndProc;
    wndClass.lpfnWndProc = WndProc;
    RegisterClass(&wndClass);
    hwnd = CreateWindow("BEEPBUTTON", "Hello, World!",
                        WS_VISIBLE | BS_CENTER, 100, 100, 100, 80,
                        NULL, NULL, hInstance, NULL);
    while (GetMessage(&msg, NULL, 0, 0))
    {
```

continues

158

Listing 9.5. continued

```
        if (msg.message == WM_LBUTTONUP)
        {
            DestroyWindow(hwnd);
            PostQuitMessage(0);
        }
        DispatchMessage(&msg);
    }
    return msg.wParam;
}
```

We have looked at the difference between the two techniques, subclassing and superclassing, in terms of their implementation. But what is the difference between them in terms of their utility? In other words, when would you use subclassing, and when would you use superclassing?

The difference is simple. Subclassing modifies the behavior of an existing class; superclassing creates a new class based on the behavior of an existing class. In other words, if you use subclassing, you implicitly alter the behavior of every feature in your application that relies on the class that you subclass. In contrast, superclassing only affects windows that are based explicitly on the new class; windows based on the original class are not affected.

Dialog Boxes

In addition to its main application window with its title and menu bar and application-defined contents, an application most commonly uses dialogs to exchange information with the user. Typically, the application's main window exists throughout the life of the application, while its dialogs are more transient in nature, popping up only for the duration of a brief exchange of data; but this is not the key distinguishing characteristics of a main window and a dialog. Indeed, there are applications that use a dialog box as their main window; in other applications, a dialog may remain visible for most of the application's lifetime.

A dialog box usually contains a set of dialog controls, themselves child windows, through which the user and the application exchange data. There are several Win32 functions that assist in constructing, displaying, and managing the contents of a dialog box. Applications developers usually need not be concerned about painting a dialog's controls or handling user-interface events; instead, they can focus on the actual exchange of data between the dialog's controls and the application.

Dialogs represent a versatile capability in Windows. To facilitate their efficient use, Windows provides two types of dialog boxes: modeless and modal.

Modal Dialogs

When an application displays a modal dialog box, the window that owns the dialog box is disabled, effectively suspending the application. The user must complete interaction with the modal dialog before the application can continue.

A modal dialog is usually created and activated through the DialogBox function. This function creates the dialog window from a dialog template resource and displays the dialog as a modal dialog. The application that calls the DialogBox function supplies the address of a callback function; DialogBox does not return until the dialog box is dismissed through a call to EndDialog made from this callback function (possibly in response to a user-interface event, such as a click on the OK button).

Although it is possible to create a modal dialog with no owner, it is not usually recommended. If such a dialog box is used, several issues must be taken into account. As the application's main window is not disabled, steps must be taken to ensure that messages sent or posted to it continue to be processed. Windows does not destroy or hide an ownerless dialog when other windows of the application are destroyed.

Modeless Dialogs

In contrast to modal dialogs, presenting a modeless dialog does not suspend execution of the application by disabling the owner window of the dialog box. However, modeless dialogs remain on top of their owner window even when the owner window gains focus. Modeless dialogs represent an effective way of continuously displaying relevant information to the user.

A modeless dialog is typically created through the CreateDialog function. As there is no equivalent of the DialogBox function for modeless dialogs, applications are responsible for retrieving and dispatching messages for the modeless dialog. Most applications do this in their main message loop; however, to ensure that the dialog responds to keyboard events as expected and enables the user to move between controls using keyboard shortcuts, the application must call the IsDialogMessage function.

A modeless dialog does not return a value to its owner. However, the modeless dialog and its owner can communicate using SendMessage calls.

The dialog box procedure for a modeless dialog must not call the EndDialog function. The dialog is normally destroyed by a call to DestroyWindow. This function can be called in response to a user-interface event from the dialog box procedure.

Applications are responsible for destroying all modeless dialog boxes before terminating.

Message Boxes

Message boxes are special dialogs that display a user-defined message, a title, and a combination of predefined buttons and icons. Their intended use is to display brief informational messages to the user and present the user with a limited set of choices. For example, message boxes can be used to notify the user of an error condition and request instructions whether to retry or cancel the operation.

A message box is created and displayed through the `MessageBox` function. The application that calls this function specifies the text string that is to be displayed and a set of flags indicating the type and appearance of the message box.

In addition to the default *application modal* behavior of a message box, an application can specify two other modes of behavior: *task modal* and *system modal.* Use a task modal message box if you wish to disable interaction with all top-level windows of the application, not just the owner window of the message box. A system modal message box should be used in extreme cases, warning the user of a potential disaster that requires immediate attention. System modal message boxes disable interaction with all other applications until the user deals with the message box.

> **NOTE**
>
> System modal message boxes should be used very carefully. Few things are more annoying than a misbehaving application that displays a system modal message box repeatedly in a loop (perhaps due to a programming error), effectively rendering the entire system useless.

Dialog Templates

Although it is possible to create a dialog in memory, most applications rely on a *dialog template resource* to determine the type and appearance of controls within a dialog.

Dialog templates are typically created as part of the application's resource file. They can be created manually as a set of instructions in the resource file, or they can be created through a visual resource file editor, such as the resource editor of the Developer Studio.

The dialog template defines the style, position, and size of the dialog and lists all controls within it. The style, position, and appearance of controls are also defined as part of the dialog template. The various dialog box functions draw the entire dialog based on the dialog template, except for controls that are marked as owner-drawn.

The Dialog Box Procedure

Dialog box procedure is just another name for the window procedure of a dialog box. There is no fundamental difference between a dialog box procedure and a window procedure, except perhaps the fact that a dialog procedure relies on `DefDlgProc`, rather than `DefWindowProc`, for default processing of messages.

A typical dialog box procedure responds to WM_INITDIALOG and WM_COMMAND messages but little else. In response to WM_INITDIALOG, the dialog box procedure initializes the controls in the dialog. Windows does not send a WM_CREATE message to a dialog box procedure; instead, the WM_INITDIALOG message is sent, but only after all the controls within the dialog have been created, just before the dialog is displayed. This enables the dialog box procedure to properly initialize controls before they are seen by the user.

Most controls send WM_COMMAND messages to their owner window (that is, the dialog box itself). To carry out the function represented by a control, the dialog box procedure responds to WM_COMMAND messages by identifying the control and performing the appropriate action.

Common Dialogs

Win32 implements a series of commonly used dialogs, freeing the programmer from the need to implement these for every application. These *common dialogs* are well known to every Windows user. They include dialogs for opening and saving files, selecting a color or a font, printing and setting up the printer, selecting a page size, and searching and replacing text.

Common dialogs can be used in two ways. Applications can utilize the common dialog "as is" by calling one of the common dialog functions that are part of the Win32 API. Alternatively, applications can customize common dialogs by implementing a special hook function and supplying a custom dialog template.

Windows 95 has introduced several changes to the common dialogs that were known to Windows 3.1 and Windows NT programmers. However, most of these changes are cosmetic and do not affect typical usage of the dialogs. Where the differences are significant, I mention them in the appropriate following sections.

> **NOTE**
>
> The appearance of all common dialog boxes has changed substantially in Windows 95. Applications that supply their own dialog templates must take this fact into account in order to present a visual appearance that is consistent with the rest of the operating system.

When a common dialog function encounters an error, the CommDlgExtendedError function can often be used to obtain additional information about the cause and nature of the problem.

The Open and Save As Dialogs

The File Open and File Save As dialogs are perhaps the most often seen common dialogs. The purpose of these dialogs is to enable the user to browse the file system and select a file to be opened for reading or writing.

The File Open dialog is displayed when the application calls the GetOpenFileName function. The function's single parameter is a pointer to an OPENFILENAME structure. Members of this structure provide initialization values for the dialog box, and, optionally, the address of a hook function and the name of a custom dialog template, which are used for customizing the dialog. When the dialog is dismissed, applications can obtain the user's selection from this structure. A typical File Open dialog is shown in Figure 9.2.

FIGURE 9.2.

The File Open dialog (Explorer-style).

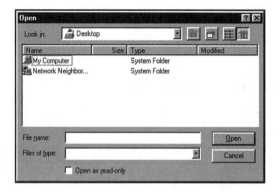

The File Save As dialog is displayed in response to a call to GetSaveFileName. This function also takes a pointer to an OPENFILENAME structure as its single parameter. An example for the File Save As dialog is shown in Figure 9.3.

FIGURE 9.3.

The File Save As dialog (Explorer-style).

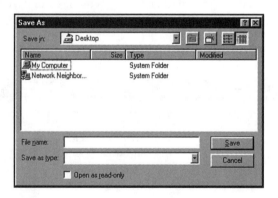

For those familiar with the Windows 3.1 look of the common file dialogs, the difference between that and the new Windows 95 look is striking. Applications that wish to use the new look (and take advantage of the new Explorer-related functionality) must specify the style OFN_EXPLORER in the Flags member of the OPENFILENAME structure.

The Windows 95 versions of the common file dialogs have another new feature. When a file dialog is customized, it is no longer necessary to reproduce the entire dialog template before adding your modifications. Instead, it is possible to create a dialog template containing *only* the controls you wish to add to the dialog and an optional special field, labeled with the ID stc32, indicating where the standard components of the dialog should be placed.

The Choose Color Dialog

The Choose Color dialog box is used when the user is requested to select a color. The dialog can be used to select a color from the system palette, or to specify a custom color.

The Choose Color dialog, shown in Figure 9.4, is presented in response to a call to the ChooseColor function. Applications can control the initialization values of this dialog through the pointer to a CHOOSECOLOR structure, passed to the ChooseColor function as its single parameter. Through this structure, applications can also customize the dialog's behavior by supplying a hook function and the name of a custom dialog template. When the dialog is dismissed, the new color selection is available as the rgbResult member of the CHOOSECOLOR structure.

FIGURE 9.4.

The Choose Color dialog.

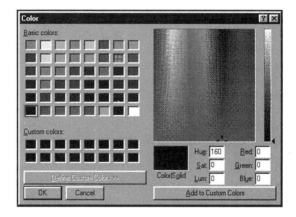

The Font Selection Dialog

Another of the more frequently seen common dialogs is the font selection dialog. Through this dialog, the user can select a typeface, a font style, font size, special effects, text color, and, in the case of Windows 95, a script. The font selection dialog is shown in Figure 9.5.

The font selection dialog is initialized through the CHOOSEFONT structure. This structure can also be used to specify a custom hook function and the name of a custom dialog template. The lpLogFont member of this structure points to a LOGFONT structure that can be used to initialize the dialog and receives information about the newly selected font when the dialog is dismissed. This structure can be used in a call to the GDI function CreateFontIndirect to actually create the font for use.

FIGURE 9.5.

*The Font Selection
dialog.*

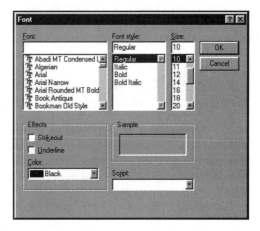

Dialogs for Printing and Print Setup

In the Windows 3.1 version of the Print dialog box, the user selects printing parameters and starts the printing process. The user selects and configures the printer from a separate dialog, the Print Setup dialog.

Under Windows 95, these dialogs look and behave differently. The Print dialog (Figure 9.6) combines the functionality of the Windows 3.1 Print and Print Setup dialogs. Selection of the paper source and paper type, previously a function of the Print Setup dialog, is now available as part of a new dialog, the Page Setup dialog (Figure 9.7).

FIGURE 9.6.

The Print dialog.

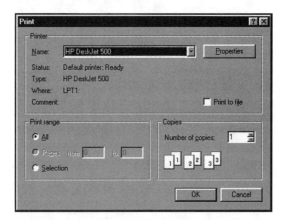

To use the Print dialog, applications must first prepare the contents of a PRINTDLG structure, then call the PrintDlg function with a pointer to this structure as the function's only parameter.

FIGURE 9.7.

The Page Setup dialog.

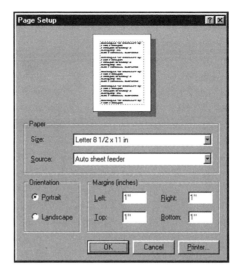

The Page Setup dialog is displayed when applications call the PageSetupDlg function. The function's only parameter is a pointer to a PAGESETUPDLG structure. Through this structure, applications can control the fields of the dialog and possibly specify customization. When the dialog is dismissed, the user's selections are available in this structure.

Text Find and Replace Dialogs

The Find and Find and Replace dialogs present an interface where the user can enter a text search string and, optionally, a replacement string. These dialogs differ fundamentally from the other common dialogs in that they are modeless dialogs; the other common dialogs all operate as modal dialogs. Therefore, the application that creates them is responsible for providing the message loop and dispatching dialog messages through the IsDialogMessage function.

The Find dialog, shown in Figure 9.8, is displayed in response to a call to the FindText function. The function returns a dialog handle that can be used in the application's message loop in a call to IsDialogMessage. The dialog is initialized through a FINDREPLACE structure, which also receives any values the user may enter in the dialog.

The dialog communicates with its owner window through a series of messages. Before calling FindText, applications should register the message string "FINDMSGSTRING" through a call to the RegisterWindowMessage function. The Find dialog will send this message to the application whenever the user enters a new search value.

The Replace dialog (Figure 9.9) is a close cousin to the Find dialog and is initialized through an identical FINDREPLACE structure. This dialog is displayed in response to a call to the ReplaceText function.

FIGURE 9.8.

The Find Text dialog.

FIGURE 9.9.

The Replace dialog.

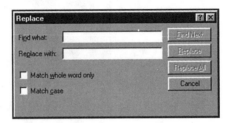

When the application receives a message from a Find or Replace dialog, it can check the `Flags` member of the `FINDREPLACE` structure to determine what action was requested by the user.

> **NOTE**
>
> The Find and Replace dialogs are not destroyed when the `FindText` or `ReplaceText` functions return. For this reason, an application would normally allocate the `FINDREPLACE` structure in global memory. If memory allocated for the `FINDREPLACE` structure is deallocated before the Find or Replace dialogs are destroyed, the application will fail.

Common Dialogs Example

The example program shown in Listing 9.6 creates and displays each of the common dialogs in sequence. This example has little practical value; it simply demonstrates, with a minimum amount of code, how these dialogs can be created and displayed. This sample can be compiled from the command line with `cl commdlgs.c comdlg32.lib user32.lib`.

Listing 9.6. Common dialogs.

```c
#include <windows.h>

LRESULT CALLBACK WndProc(HWND hwnd, UINT uMsg,
                         WPARAM wParam, LPARAM lParam)
{
    switch(uMsg)
    {
        case WM_DESTROY:
            PostQuitMessage(0);
            break;
```

```
            default:
                return DefWindowProc(hwnd, uMsg, wParam, lParam);
        }
        return 0;
}

int WINAPI WinMain(HINSTANCE hInstance, HINSTANCE hPrevInstance,
                                LPSTR d3, int nCmdShow)
{
    MSG msg;
    HWND hwnd;
    WNDCLASS wndClass;

    OPENFILENAME ofn;
    CHOOSECOLOR cc;
    CHOOSEFONT cf;
    PRINTDLG pd;
    PAGESETUPDLG psd;
    FINDREPLACE fr;
    COLORREF crCustColors[16];
    LOGFONT lf;
    char szFindWhat[80];
    char szReplaceWith[80];
    HWND hdlgFt, hdlgFr;

    if (hPrevInstance == NULL)
    {
        memset(&wndClass, 0, sizeof(wndClass));
        wndClass.style = CS_HREDRAW | CS_VREDRAW;
        wndClass.lpfnWndProc = WndProc;
        wndClass.hInstance = hInstance;
        wndClass.hCursor = LoadCursor(NULL, IDC_ARROW);
        wndClass.hbrBackground = (HBRUSH)(COLOR_APPWORKSPACE + 1);
        wndClass.lpszClassName = "COMMDLGS";
        if (!RegisterClass(&wndClass)) return FALSE;
    }
    hwnd = CreateWindow("COMMDLGS", "Common Dialogs Demonstration",
                        WS_OVERLAPPEDWINDOW,
                        CW_USEDEFAULT, 0, CW_USEDEFAULT, 0,
                        NULL, NULL, hInstance, NULL);
    ShowWindow(hwnd, nCmdShow);
    UpdateWindow(hwnd);

    memset(&ofn, 0, sizeof(ofn));
    ofn.lStructSize = sizeof(OPENFILENAME);
    GetOpenFileName(&ofn);
    memset(&ofn, 0, sizeof(ofn));
    ofn.lStructSize = sizeof(OPENFILENAME);
    GetSaveFileName(&ofn);
    memset(&cc, 0, sizeof(cc));
    memset(crCustColors, 0, sizeof(crCustColors));
    cc.lStructSize = sizeof(cc);
    cc.lpCustColors = crCustColors;
    ChooseColor(&cc);
    memset(&cf, 0, sizeof(cf));
    memset(&lf, 0, sizeof(lf));
    cf.lStructSize = sizeof(cf);
    cf.lpLogFont = &lf;
```

continues

Listing 9.6. continued

```
        cf.Flags = CF_SCREENFONTS | CF_EFFECTS;
        ChooseFont(&cf);
        memset(&pd, 0, sizeof(pd));
        pd.lStructSize = sizeof(pd);
        PrintDlg(&pd);
        memset(&psd, 0, sizeof(psd));
        psd.lStructSize = sizeof(psd);
        PageSetupDlg(&psd);
        memset(&fr, 0, sizeof(fr));
        memset(szFindWhat, 0, sizeof(szFindWhat));
        memset(szReplaceWith, 0, sizeof(szReplaceWith));
        fr.lStructSize = sizeof(fr);
        fr.hwndOwner = hwnd;
        fr.lpstrFindWhat = szFindWhat;
        fr.lpstrReplaceWith = szReplaceWith;
        fr.wFindWhatLen = sizeof(szFindWhat);
        fr.wReplaceWithLen = sizeof(szReplaceWith);
        hdlgFt = FindText(&fr);
        hdlgFr = ReplaceText(&fr);

        while (GetMessage(&msg, NULL, 0, 0))
            if(!IsDialogMessage(hdlgFt, &msg))
                if(!IsDialogMessage(hdlgFr, &msg))
                    DispatchMessage(&msg);
        return msg.wParam;
}
```

OLE Common Dialogs

As part of the OLE 2 implementation, the system provides common dialogs for the following set of functions: Insert Object, Paste Special, Change Source, Edit Links, Update Links, Object Properties, Convert, and Change Icon. Most applications do not invoke these dialogs directly, but use the Microsoft Foundation Classes (and, in particular, the wrapper classes for these dialogs) to implement OLE functionality.

Controls

A control is a special window that typically enables the user to perform a simple function and sends messages to this effect to its owner window. For example, a pushbutton control has one simple function, namely that the user can click on it; when that happens, the pushbutton sends a WM_COMMAND message to the window (typically a dialog) that owns it.

Windows offers several built-in control classes for the most commonly used controls. A dialog with a sample collection of these controls is shown in Figure 9.10.

FIGURE 9.10.

A collection of standard controls.

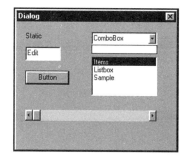

Windows 95 introduced a set of new control classes, collectively referred to as Windows 95 Common Controls. This name is slightly misleading as the new control classes are now also available in Windows NT 3.51 and Win32s 1.3.

Applications can also create their own controls. These can be derived from the standard control classes, or they can be built independently.

The control class and the control style (which defines variations of behavior within a button class) are usually both defined in an application's resource file. Alternatively, applications that create controls programmatically select the button class and specify the button style as parameters to the CreateWindow function.

Static Controls

Static controls are perhaps the simplest of all control types. The sole purpose of their existence is to display a piece of text, such as a label for another control. Static controls do not respond to user-interface events and do not send messages to their owner window.

Buttons

Buttons, as their name implies, are controls that respond to simple mouse clicks. There are several button types. A *pushbutton* is a button that posts a WM_COMMAND message to its owner window when it is clicked. A *check box* indicates one of two states, selected and not selected. A variant of the check box, the *three-state check box*, adds a third, disabled state to the other two. A *radio button* is a control that is typically used in groups, indicating a set of mutually exclusive choices.

There are variants to these control styles that define secondary aspects of their behavior.

Edit Controls

An edit control is a rectangular area where the user can enter unformatted text. The text can be a few characters—such as the name of a file—or an entire text file; for example, the client area of the Windows Notepad application is one large edit control. Applications typically communicate with the edit control through a series of messages that are used to set or retrieve text from the control.

List Boxes

A list box contains a collection of values arranged in rows. Users can use the mouse cursor to select the desired value from the list. If the list box contains more values than can be displayed at ones, a vertical scrollbar is also displayed as part of the list box.

Combo Boxes

A combo box combines the functionality of a list box and an edit control. Users can enter a value in the edit control part of the combo box. Alternatively, they can click the down arrow next to the edit control to display the list box part, where a value can be selected.

Scrollbars

A scrollbar control consists of a rectangular area with two arrows at the end and a sliding pointer. A scrollbar can be vertical or horizontal. Scrollbars are typically used to indicate the position of the visible portion within a larger area. Applications also used scrollbars to implement the functionality of a slide control; however, as one of the new Windows 95 common controls is a slider control, using scrollbars for this purpose is no longer necessary.

Windows 95 Common Controls

Windows 95 defines a new set of common controls.

Tab controls help in implementing multipage dialogs, also known as tabbed dialogs or property sheets. A tab control provides a user-interface where the user can select the dialog page (property page) by clicking on a little tab. The tab gives the visual appearance of several sheets organized on top of each other and clicking on the tab gives the visual impression of bringing the selected sheet to front.

Tree controls present a list of items in a hierarchical organization. Tree controls are ideal for displaying hierarchical lists, such as a list of directories on disk. Tree controls provide an efficient mechanism for displaying a large number of items by providing the ability to expand and collapse higher-level items.

List controls expand the functionality of a list box by providing a means to display a list of items in one of several formats. In a typical list control, items have an icon and some text; the control can display these items in a variety of formats as icons, or as list items arranged in rows.

A slider control provides the functionality similar to the sliding volume control on many stereo systems. The user can position the sliding tab with the mouse to set a specific position in the slider control. Slider controls are ideal in multimedia applications as volume or picture controls, or controls through which the user can set the position during playback of a multimedia data source.

Progress bars are used to indicate the progress of a lengthy process. Progress bars do not accept user input; they are used for informational purposes only.

Spin buttons are used to increment or decrement the value of an associated control, usually an edit control.

The rich-text edit control expands the functionality of the Windows 3.1 edit control by enabling the editing of Microsoft RTF (Rich Text Format) files. Rich-text controls encapsulate the capability of a reasonably sophisticated word processor.

A hot key control accepts a keystroke combination from the user, which the application can use to set up a hot key through the WM_SETHOTKEY message.

Other Windows 95 common controls include the animation control, header control, status bar, toolbar control, and tooltip control. All Windows 95 common controls are also supported in Windows NT beginning with Version 3.51.

Figure 9.11 presents a collection of Windows 95 common controls in a dialog.

FIGURE 9.11.

Some Windows 95 common controls.

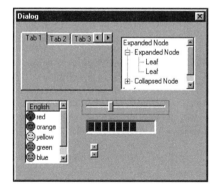

Summary

A window is a rectangular area on the screen through which applications and the user communicate. Applications draw into the window to display information for the user. Applications receive messages on user-interface events through a handle to the window.

Windows are arranged hierarchically. At top is the desktop window. Top-level windows are those whose parent is the desktop window—or those that have no parent window. Child windows are those whose parent is a top-level window or another child window. Windows sharing the same parent are siblings; the order in which sibling windows are displayed is called the Z-order. A special category of windows contains top-level windows that have the topmost attribute; these windows always precede non-topmost windows in the Z-order, even when a non-topmost window is the active window.

A top-level window may have an owner window that is different from its parent window.

Typical windows that users normally interact with include overlapped windows (normal application windows); popup windows (dialog boxes); and controls.

Window messages are handled in the window procedure. A window procedure and other window attributes are associated with the window class from which windows are derived. In addition to the capability of defining their own window classes, applications can also superclass and subclass existing window classes. Subclassing means modifying the behavior of an existing window class; superclassing means creating a new window class based on the behavior of an existing class.

Part of the Win32 API is a set of functions that assist in creating, displaying, and managing dialogs. Windows distinguishes between modal dialogs and modeless dialogs. A modal dialog disables its owner window while it is displayed and does not return control to the application until the user dismisses the dialog. In contrast, modeless dialogs are displayed without disabling their owner window. Applications must provide message loop functionality and dispatch dialog messages through the `IsDialogMessage` function for modeless dialogs.

Windows also provides a set of common dialogs for common tasks. These include dialogs for opening and saving a file, printer and page setup, color and font selection, and text find and replace functions. In addition, a set of common dialogs is available to implement OLE-related functionality.

Controls include buttons, static text, edit boxes, list boxes, combo boxes, and scrollbars. Applications can also implement new control types. In addition, Windows 95 defines a set of new common controls: list views, tree views, tab controls, hot key controls, sliders, progress bars, spin buttons, and rich-text edit controls.

Controls are usually defined through dialog box templates in the application's resource file. Controls communicate with the application by sending messages (such as WM_COMMAND messages) to their owner window, that is, the dialog box.

Resource Files

10

Resource files represent one of the most prominent features of Windows programming. It is through resource files that most applications define the visible elements of their user interface: menus, dialogs, text strings, bitmaps, and other types of resources.

Resource files are created in a form readable by humans and compiled with the *Resource Compiler*. The compiled result is usually linked with the rest of the application to form a single binary image that contains executable code and resource information.

Strictly speaking, use of resource files is not mandatory. However, it would be foolish to write needlessly complex code to implement an application's user-interface elements when resource files provide a convenient way to do the same. Furthermore, the use of resource files makes it much easier to replace language-dependent user-interface elements when working on an application that will be used in multiple language environments.

In the "good old days" programmers used a text editor to edit a resource file. These days, hand-editing of resource files is rare. Instead, graphical resource editors are used, such as the integrated resource editor that is part of the Developer Studio. Nevertheless, the ability to make sense of resource file contents, the ability to hand-edit resource files when necessary, can still prove to be a useful skill. The syntax and the structure of resource files are simple, and understanding what is "under the hood" helps put the features of sophisticated editors in perspective.

This chapter presents a review of the use of resource files and the resource compiler.

NOTE

Often, the term *resource file* is used to apply to files generated by the resource compiler; in other words, files with the .res extensions. However, in this text I use the term exclusively to refer to files containing resource scripts; that is, files with the .rc extension.

Resource File Components

A resource file, or resource script may contain any number of resource script statements and preprocessor directives. For example, consider the sample resource file shown in Listing 10.1.

Listing 10.1. Resource script example.

```
#include <windows.h>

DlgBox DIALOG 20, 20, 90, 64
STYLE DS_MODALFRAME ¦ WS_CAPTION ¦ WS_SYSMENU
CAPTION "Sample Dialog"
BEGIN
```

```
      DEFPUSHBUTTON "Sample Button", IDOK, 19, 44, 52, 14, WS_GROUP
      CTEXT "Sample Message", -1, 0, 8, 90, 8
END
```

This simple script defines a dialog with a button and a static text field (Figure 10.1). The dialog will be referred to by name (DlgBox) from the application using this resource. Although it is not obvious at first sight, some constants (for example, IDOK, DS_MODALFRAME or WS_GROUP) are defined in the file windows.h and not part of the resource script language. The C/C++ style #include directive is used to specify files that contain macro definitions.

FIGURE 10.1.

Sample dialog box.

Generally, a resource file statement consists of an identifier that can either be a text string (DlgBox above) or a numeric value, followed by the statement itself. The statement can be single line (in which case, the statement is followed by one or more parameters) or multiline (in which case the statement is followed by a block of script instructions).

Resource File Preprocessing

Preprocessor syntax and semantics are similar to the syntax and semantics of the C/C++ preprocessor. The resource compiler preprocessor, or RC preprocessor for short, understands the following directives:

- ■ Macro definitions: #define and #undef
- ■ Conditional compilation: #if, #ifdef, #ifndef, #else, #elif, #endif
- ■ Header files: #include
- ■ Compile-time error: #error

The meaning of these directives is familiar to even the novice C programmer.

The preprocessor also understands (and removes) C and C++ style comments; that is, comments enclosed between /* and */ and comment lines that begin with //.

The preprocessor also understands the "stringizing" operator # and the "token-pasting" operator ##.

It is possible to use the same header file from both C source and resource script files. During resource compilation, the resource compiler defines the symbol RC_INVOKED; this symbol can be used in the header file to protect against compiler errors. For example, if the header file contains a class declaration, you may wish to protect it as follows:

```
#ifndef RC_INVOKED
class myclass
{
...
};
#endif // RC_INVOKED
```

Another useful symbol to remember is the symbol APSTUDIO_INVOKED. This symbol is defined when a resource file is loaded by the integrated resource editor in Developer Studio. (In the days of Visual C++ 1.0, resource editing was performed by a separate program, Application Studio. Hence, the name of this constant.)

Resource scripts can also contain constant expressions involving the following operators: addition (+), subtraction (-), multiplication (*), division (/), unary NOT (~), binary AND (&), and binary OR (¦).

Single-Line Statements

Single-line statements define bitmaps, cursors, fonts, icons, message tables, and the language of resource statements.

The BITMAP statement specifies a bitmap file (edited separately with a bitmap editor) that is to define a bitmap resource. For example:

```
MyBitmap BITMAP mybitmap.bmp
```

The CURSOR statement specifies a file that defines the shape of the mouse cursor. The cursor file is a binary file that is edited by a separate editor. Here is an example for this statement:

```
MyCursor CURSOR mycursor.cur
```

The FONT statement specifies a font resource. An example:

```
MyFont FONT myfont.fnt
```

The ICON statement specifies a binary icon file (edited by an icon editor) that defines an icon resource. For example:

```
MyIcon ICON myicon.ico
```

The LANGUAGE statement sets the language of all subsequent resources up to the end of the resource script or until another LANGUAGE statement is encountered. The LANGUAGE statement can also be used to set the language of a specific resource in a multiline resource statement if it appears just before the BEGIN keyword in such a statement. The LANGUAGE statement is followed by a language and a sublanguage identifier, both of which must be constants defined in the file winnls.h.

The MESSAGETABLE statement identifies a message table, which is used primarily in Windows NT event logging. A message table is created by the message compiler, mc.exe.

The BITMAP, CURSOR, FONT, and ICON statements also accept an attribute parameter. The attribute parameter specifies load and memory characteristics of the resource. In 32-bit Windows, only one attribute is used: the DISCARDABLE attribute specifies that a resource can be removed from memory if it is no longer needed. For example:

```
TempBmp BITMAP DISCARDABLE "c:\\bitmaps\\tempbmp.bmp"
```

Multiline Resource Statements

Multiline resource statements define dialogs, string tables, accelerator tables, menus, and version information resources. Multiline statements begin with an identifier, the statement, and optional parameters, followed by a block of instructions enclosed between a BEGIN-END keyword pair:

```
identifier STATEMENT [optional-parameters]
[optional instructions]
BEGIN
    [instructions]
END
```

Optional instructions may include the CHARACTERISTICS instruction (specifies a single 32-bit value used only by resource file management tools), the LANGUAGE instruction, and the VERSION instruction (specifies a 32-bit version number used by resource management tools). Other optional instructions are multiline statement-specific; for example, the CAPTION instruction defines the title of a dialog box.

Because of their relative complexity, we look at multiline statements individually.

Accelerators

Accelerators are keystrokes that represent shortcuts to specific tasks. For example, when you use Ctrl+C to copy an item to the clipboard, you are using an accelerator.

Enclosed between the BEGIN-END keyword pair, an accelerator statement contains an arbitrary number of keyboard events followed by the identifier of the accelerator. Consider the following example:

```
MyAcc ACCELERATOR
BEGIN
    "C", ID_EDIT_COPY, VIRTKEY, CONTROL, NOINVERT
    "V", ID_EDIT_PASTE, VIRTKEY, CONTROL, NOINVERT
    "X", ID_EDIT_CUT, VIRTKEY, CONTROL, NOINVERT
END
```

This example assumes that the symbolic constants ID_EDIT_COPY, ID_EDIT_PASTE, and ID_EDIT_CUT are defined elsewhere (in a header file) and refer to numeric identifiers.

Accelerators are interpreted when an application calls the TranslateAccelerator function after retrieving a message through GetMessage (or PeekMessage). TranslateAccelerator translates

WM_KEYDOWN (or WM_SYSKEYDOWN) messages into WM_COMMAND (or WM_SYSCOMMAND) messages. The identifiers that follow accelerator keys in an accelerator statement will become the command identifiers in the WM_COMMAND messages.

Dialogs

Together with menu statements, dialog statements define what are perhaps the most visible parts of a typical application. A dialog statement defines the layout and appearance of a dialog box.

A sample dialog statement is shown in Listing 10.1. The statement consists of several lines. The first line contains an identifier, the DIALOG keyword, and four numeric parameters that define the position of the dialog's upper-left corner and the size of the dialog box.

All size and position information in a dialog statement is measured in *dialog units*. Dialog units are derived from the size of the font specified for the dialog. *Dialog base units* represent the average height and width of a character in the selected font. Four horizontal dialog units amount to one horizontal dialog base unit; eight vertical dialog units amount to one vertical dialog base unit.

For dialogs that use the system font, applications can obtain the size of dialog base units, in pixels, by calling GetDialogBaseUnits. For dialogs using other fonts, it may be necessary to explicitly calculate the average size of characters to obtain the dialog base units.

Once the dialog base units are known, applications can convert between dialog units and pixels using the following formulae:

```
pixelX = (dialogunitX * baseunitX) / 4
pixelY = (dialogunitY * baseunitY) / 8
dialogunitX = (pixelX * 4) / baseunitX
dialogunitY = (pixelY * 8) / baseunitY
```

Following the line containing the DIALOG keyword, a dialog statement may contain several optional instructions. These may include commonly used optional instructions or dialog-specific optional instructions.

The CAPTION optional instruction is followed by a string specifying the title of the dialog box. The default is a dialog with no title.

The STYLE optional instruction specifies the style of the dialog. Style values are usually predefined in the header file windows.h. Several values can be combined using the logical OR (¦) operator. The default style for dialogs containing no STYLE instruction is WS_POPUP ¦ WS_BORDER ¦ WS_SYSMENU.

The EXSTYLE optional instruction is similar to STYLE and specifies extended styles.

The CLASS optional instruction can be used to specify a special window class for a dialog. The CLASS instruction should be used sparingly, as it redefines the behavior of the dialog.

The FONT statement specifies the font to be used in the dialog. The default is the system font.

The MENU statement identifies the menu resource that defines the menu of the dialog box. In the absence of this statement, the dialog box will be created without a menu bar.

Enclosed between the BEGIN-END keyword pair is a series of control statements specifying the controls within the dialog. There are several types of control statements. Each control statement contains the control type, control text, a control identifier (text or integer), control position, and control style and extended style parameters:

```
CONTROL-STATEMENT control-text, identifier, x, y, width, height
[, style [, extended-style]]
```

An edit control is defined by the EDITTEXT control statement.

A static control is defined by the LTEXT, CTEXT, RTEXT, or ICON control statement. The first three of these control statements define a left-aligned, centered, or right-aligned static control, respectively. The last specifies a static control with the SS_ICON style.

A button control is defined by one of the following keywords: AUTO3STATE, AUTOCHECKBOX, AUTORADIOBUTTON, CHECKBOX, DEFPUSHBUTTON, GROUPBOX, PUSHBOX, PUSHBUTTON, RADIOBUTTON, STATE3, USERBUTTON.

The COMBOBOX control statement defines a combo box control.

The LISTBOX control statement can be used to specify a list box.

The SCROLLBAR control statement defines, what else? A scrollbar.

The CONTROL control statement can be used to define a generic control. The syntax of this statement is somewhat different from the syntax used for other control statements:

```
CONTROL control-text, identifier, class-name, x, y, width, height [, extended-style]
```

The class-name parameter specifies the window class for the control. This can be one of the Windows control classes. Thus, the CONTROL statement can be used as an alternative syntax for all the other control statements.

A variant of the DIALOG statement is the DIALOGEX statement. It extends the syntax of the DIALOG statement in the following ways:

- Help identifiers can be specified for the dialog itself as well as any controls within it.
- Font weight and italic settings can be put in the FONT instruction.
- Control-specific data can be added to control statements (enclosed by the BEGIN-END keyword pair).
- The keywords BEDIT, HEDIT, and IEDIT can be used for pen controls.

Menus

Menu statements in the resource script can be used to specify menu bars or popup menus. Menu statements contain one or more menu definition statements enclosed between a BEGIN-END keyword pair. Consider the following example:

```
MyMenu MENU
BEGIN
    POPUP "&File"
    BEGIN
        MENUITEM "&New\tCtrl+N", ID_FILE_NEW
        MENUITEM SEPARATOR
        MENUITEM "E&xit", ID_FILE_EXIT
    END
    POPUP "&Edit"
    BEGIN
        MENUITEM "Cu&t\tCtrl+X", ID_EDIT_CUT
        MENUITEM "&Copy\tCtrl+C", ID_EDIT_COPY
        MENUITEM "&Paste\tCtrl+V", ID_EDIT_PASTE
    END
    POPUP "&Help"
    BEGIN
        MENUITEM "&About", ID_HELP_ABOUT
    END
END
```

The identifiers (for example, ID_FILE_NEW) in this example are assumed to be defined elsewhere and refer to numeric values.

A menu definition statement can specify a menu item or a submenu. To define a menu item, use the MENUITEM keyword. This is followed either by the text of the menu item and the menu identifier or by the SEPARATOR keyword; the latter specifies a separator that is a vertical line for menu bars or a horizontal line for popup (sub) menus.

A menu item's identifier may be followed by a list of options. Options are separated by commas or spaces and include the following keywords: CHECKED, GRAYED, HELP, INACTIVE, MENUBARBREAK, MENUBREAK.

To specify a submenu, use the POPUP keyword. The POPUP keyword is followed by the title of the submenu, and a set of menu items enclosed between a BEGIN-END keyword pair. A submenu may contain nested submenus.

String Tables

A string table resource defines an arbitrary number of text strings. These text strings can be referred to from within the application by symbolic identifiers. The primary advantage of using a string table resource is that it makes it possible for all language-dependent components of an application to be conveniently located within a resource file and thus renders the task of localization substantially easier.

A string table is defined by the STRINGTABLE keyword, followed by optional instructions, and one or more string definitions enclosed between a BEGIN-END keyword pair. A string definition consists of a string identifier and a string value. For example:

```
STRINGTABLE
BEGIN
    IDS_HELLO "Hello"
    IDS_GOODBYE "Goodbye"
END
```

where IDS_HELLO and IDS_GOODBYE are symbolic identifiers defined elsewhere.

Using a string from a string table resource is straightforward. An application can load a string resource using the LoadString function.

For Microsoft Foundation Class applications, using string table resources is even easier. Many MFC functions that accept a string parameter can also accept a numeric parameter representing a string resource in the application's resource file. For example, an MFC application can display a message box using AfxMessageBox as follows:

```
AfxMessageBox(IDS_ERROR);
```

Here, IDS_ERROR is a symbolic reference to a numeric identifier.

The CString class also offers specific support for string resources. The member function CString::LoadString can be used to initialize a CString object to a value obtained from a string table in the application's resource file.

Toolbars

Toolbar resources are used in MFC applications. A toolbar is defined in a resource file by a TOOLBAR statement. This statement lists the identifiers of the buttons in the toolbar. The size of toolbar buttons is also specified, as in the following example:

```
IDR_MAINFRAME TOOLBAR DISCARDABLE  16, 15
BEGIN
    BUTTON          ID_FILE_NEW
    BUTTON          ID_FILE_OPEN
    BUTTON          ID_FILE_SAVE
        SEPARATOR
    BUTTON          ID_EDIT_CUT
    BUTTON          ID_EDIT_COPY
    BUTTON          ID_EDIT_PASTE
        SEPARATOR
    BUTTON          ID_FILE_PRINT
    BUTTON          ID_APP_ABOUT
END
```

For every toolbar resource, there should be a corresponding bitmap resource that contains the button bitmaps. The button bitmaps should be arranged horizontally, in the same order as the button identifiers appear in the toolbar resource (except for separators). The bitmap resource should have the same identifier as the toolbar resource:

```
IDR_MAINFRAME  BITMAP  MOVEABLE PURE    "res\\Toolbar.bmp"
```

Toolbar resources are accessed through the MFC function `Ctoolbar::LoadToolBar`.

Version Information

The version information resource can be used to identify the version of a binary file (typically, an executable or library file). Version information is used by File Installation Library functions.

The version information resource statement contains several version statements that identify the version number of the file and the product, provide additional version information, and specify the language and the target operating system.

User-Defined and Raw Data Resources

The resource file syntax also allows for the creation of user-defined resource types. A user-defined resource statement can be a single-line or multiline statement. Single-line statements are used to identify user-defined resources that are stored in separate files. The syntax of a single-line statement is as follows:

```
name type [load-memory-options] filename
```

Multiline user-defined resource statements can be used to embed the definition of a user-defined resource within the resource file. The syntax of a multiline user-defined resource statement is this:

```
name type [load-memory-options]
BEGIN
    raw-data
END
```

The *raw-data* block may contain integers in decimal, hexadecimal, or octal notation, or strings enclosed in double quotes. Raw data strings must be explicitly null-terminated. Individual data items are separated by commas.

Raw data can also be specified in the form of an `RCDATA` resource. The syntax of an `RCDATA` statement and the syntax of a multiline user-defined resource statement are nearly identical, except that in the case of raw data statement, the keyword `RCDATA` is used in place of *type*, and the statement may also contain the optional instructions `CHARACTERISTICS`, `LANGUAGE`, and `VERSION`.

> **NOTE**
>
> Strings in all resource statements except raw data and user-defined resource statements are interpreted as null-terminated Unicode strings. If you wish to explicitly specify a Unicode string in an RCDATA or user-defined resource statement, use the L prefix.

Compiling and Using Resource Scripts

Before a resource script can be used by an application, it must be compiled. Although not strictly necessary, in the case of most applications the compiled resource file is also linked with other application components and becomes part of the application's executable file image (.EXE file).

Running the Resource Compiler

A resource file can be compiled from the command line using the resource compiler, rc.exe. For most resource files, this command can be used with no parameters. For example, to compile the resource file shown in Listing 10.1, you would type rc dlg.rc.

In 16-bit versions of Windows, the resource compiler is also used to add resources to the executable file. In Win32, the 32-bit linker is used for this purpose.

Running the Linker

The Visual C++ linker, link.exe, can be used to link a resource file and other components of an application's executable together. In the simplest case, you would specify the name of the compiled resource file on the C/C++ compiler command line just as you would specify any other object file or library file. For example:

```
cl dlg.cpp dlg.res user32.lib
```

In order for the linker to work properly with compiled resource files, the cvtres.exe tool must be present in the same directory as the linker executable, link.exe. This tool converts compiled resource files into the Common Object File Format (COFF), which is understood by the linker.

Resource DLLs

Resources do not need to be linked with your application's executable file. They can also be linked into a separate dynamic-link library. This has the advantage that changing the application's resource file does not require recompiling the entire application, only replacing the DLL. You can also ship your application with multiple DLLs representing resources in various languages. In MFC applications, this approach is made even easier by the

AfxSetResourceHandle call; calling this function with a handle to a resource DLL ensures that subsequently, the MFC loads all resources from that DLL instead of your application's executable file.

Summary

Resource files define the visual appearance of an application. Resources include dialogs, menus, bitmaps, icons, cursors, text strings, and several other types.

While resources are typically created with graphical editors, it is possible (and sometimes necessary) to edit the resource file directly. Resource files (files with the .rc extension) are human readable ASCII text files.

Resource files contain preprocessor directives, single-line, and multiline resource statements. Preprocessor directives are similar in syntax and semantics to their C/C++ counterparts. Single-line resource file statements are used to identify resources stored in separate binary files (edited by specialized editors): bitmaps, icons, cursors, fonts, and generic resources. Single-line statements are also used to specify message table resources (used for Windows NT event logging) and to specify the language of subsequent resource statements.

Multiline statements are used to define menus, dialogs, string tables, accelerator tables, version information resources, and generic resources.

Resource files are compiled using the Resource Compiler, rc.exe. The resulting compiled resource file (usually a file with the .res extension) is suitable for linking with other components of the application. A compiled resource file can also be specified on the cl command line.

Drawing and Device Contexts

11

To say that drawing on the screen, the printer, or another output device is one of the most important aspects of a Windows application is stating the obvious. Throughout their lifetimes, Windows applications continually draw and redraw the contents of their windows in response to user actions or other events.

Needless to say, applications draw to hardware devices using a series of device-independent system functions. Otherwise Windows applications, similar to their MS-DOS counterparts, would be plagued with device incompatibilities and would require device drivers for various video cards, printers, or other graphics hardware. Indeed, device independence is one of the major advantages offered by a graphical operating system like Windows.

The GDI, Device Drivers, and Output Devices

Applications wishing to draw to an output device do so by calling *Graphics Device Interface*, or GDI functions. The GDI library containing these functions, `gdi.dll`, makes calls, in turn, to device-specific function libraries, or *device drivers*. The device drivers perform operations on the actual physical hardware. Device drivers are supplied either as part of Windows or, for less commonly used hardware, as third-party add-ons . The interrelationship between graphical applications, the GDI, device driver software, and hardware devices is schematically illustrated in Figure 11.1.

Most drawing functions take a handle to a *device context* as one of their parameters. In addition to identifying the device on which the drawing should take place, the device context also specifies a number of other characteristics, including

- Mapping of logical coordinates to actual physical coordinates on the device
- Use of drawing objects such as fonts, pens, or brushes to carry out the requested operation
- Clipping of drawing functions to visible areas

FIGURE 11.1.

Interaction between applications, the GDI, device drivers, and output devices.

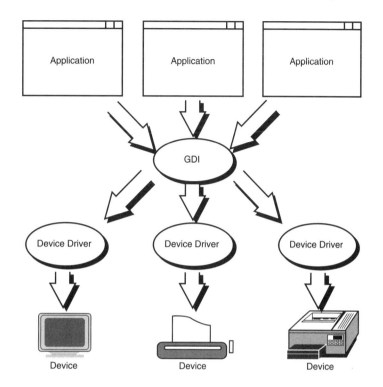

Device Contexts

A device context thoroughly specifies the characteristics of a hardware device. Drawing system functions use this information to translate device-independent drawing calls into a series of device-specific operations carried out with the help of low-level driver code.

Before a device context can be used, it must be created. The most generic function for creating a device context is the CreateDC function. When calling this function, applications specify the device for which the device context is created, the driver software, the physical port to which the device is attached, and device-specific initialization data.

When drawing to the screen, applications need not create a device context using CreateDC. Instead, applications can retrieve a handle to a device context representing the client area of a window through the GetDC function or the entire window (including nonclient areas) through GetWindowDC.

A typical GDI drawing function is the Rectangle function. An application may make the following call to draw a rectangle:

```
Rectangle(hDC, 0, 0, 200, 100);
```

This call draws a rectangle on the device identified by the handle hDC, with its upper-left corner at logical coordinates [0,0], and lower-right corner at [200,100]. Needless to say, a lot takes place behind the scenes before the actual rectangle is formed on the screen. How does the GDI know the physical coordinates corresponding to these logical coordinates? How does it know the color of the rectangle and its interior? The styles used for the rectangle's contours or for filling its interior? The answer is, all this information is available as part of the device context. Coordinate transformations are defined by the mapping mode and any world transformation that may be in effect. The appearance and color of objects drawn are a function of GDI objects which have been selected into the device context. All of this we review shortly.

Device Context Types

In the case of the display, Windows distinguishes between common and private device contexts. Common device contexts represent a shared resource across applications. Private device contexts are created for windows with a window class carrying the CS_OWNDC style. Private device contexts are deleted when the window to which they belong is destroyed.

Memory and Metafile Device Contexts

Device contexts typically represent physical devices, such as the display, the printer, plotters, or FAX modems. However, there are also some special device contexts in Windows. One of them I already mentioned. A *memory device context* is a device context that represents a bitmap. By utilizing this device context, applications can write into a bitmap.

In addition to the obvious use in creating bitmaps (such as in a bitmap editor like the Windows 95 Paint application), memory device contexts have another practical use in graphics-intensive applications. By drawing into a memory device context and transferring the contents only when the drawing is complete, applications can reduce unwanted screen flicker. Through a clever use of multiple memory device contexts, applications can create smooth animation effects. Several functions, which we review shortly, assist in efficiently transferring bitmap data from one device context to another.

A memory device context is created by a call to the CreateCompatibleDC function. This function creates a memory device context that is compatible with a specified physical device.

Another type of a device context is a *metafile device context*. A metafile is essentially a device-independent record of GDI operations. Win32 recognizes two metafile types: standard and enhanced metafiles. Standard metafiles are compatible with Windows 3.1, but they do not implement complete device independence; for this reason, the use of enhanced metafiles for new applications is recommended.

A metafile device context is created by calling the CreateMetaFile function or, in the case of enhanced metafiles, the CreateEnhMetaFile function. When an application is finished drawing into the metafile device context, it closes the metafile using CloseMetaFile (CloseEnhMetaFile).

This call returns a metafile handle that can then be used in calls to `PlayMetaFile` (`PlayEnhMetaFile`) or the various metafile manipulation functions. A metafile handle can also be obtained by a call to `GetMetaFile` (`GetEnhMetaFile`) for metafiles that have been saved to disk previously.

Relatively few applications manipulate metafiles directly. However, most applications use metafiles implicitly through OLE. The device-independent metafile format is used by OLE to graphically represent embedded or linked objects. Applications that display embedded objects thus do not need to call the OLE server application (which may not even be installed on the system) every time an OLE object needs to be rendered; instead, they just play back the recorded metafile.

Information Contexts

Information contexts are used to retrieve information about a specific device. An information context is created by a call to the `CreateIC` function. Creating an information context requires far less overhead than creating a device context and is therefore the preferred method for retrieving information about a device. An information context must be deleted after use by calling `DeleteDC`.

Coordinates

Applications typically specify the position and size of output objects in the form of *logical coordinates*. Before an object appears at a physical location on the screen or printer, a series of calculations takes place to obtain actual physical positions on the device.

Logical and Device Coordinates

The transformation from logical to physical coordinates, although simple in concept, can sometimes trick even the experienced Windows programmer.

The mapping from logical to physical coordinates is accomplished by specifying the characteristics of the *window* and the *viewport*. The window, in this context, represents the logical coordinate space; the viewport represents the physical coordinate space of the device.

For both the window and the viewport, two pairs of values must be supplied. One pair is the horizontal and vertical coordinates of the origin; the other pair is the horizontal and vertical extent.

Figure 11.2 illustrates how the logical coordinates of a set of rectangles are mapped to device-specific physical coordinates. From this illustration, it should be clear that the absolute size of the logical and physical extents should be of no consequence; what matters is their relative sizes— that is, the number of logical units mapped to a physical unit or vice versa.

FIGURE 11.2.

The logical and the physical coordinate system.

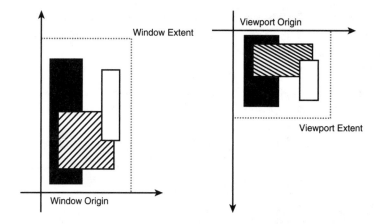

On most devices, the origin of the physical coordinate system is in the upper-left corner and the vertical coordinate grows downward. In contrast, in most logical coordinate systems, the origin is in the lower-left corner and the vertical coordinate grows upward.

The origin and the extent of the logical and physical coordinate systems can be set using the following four functions: SetViewportExtEx, SetViewportOrgEx, SetWindowExtEx, SetWindowOrgEx. (Use of the old functions SetViewportExt, SetViewportOrg, SetWindowExt, and SetWindowOrg is not supported in Win32.)

For reference, here is how the GDI converts from logical to physical coordinates and vice versa:

```
Dx = (Lx - xWO) * xVE/xWE + xVO
Dy = (Ly - yWO) * yVE/yWE + yVO
Lx = (Dx - xVO) * xWE/xVE + xWO
Ly = (Dy - yVO) * yWE/yVE + yWO
```

The meaning of these symbols should be fairly obvious; for example, Dx is the horizontal device coordinate, yWE is the vertical window extent. Figure 11.3 identifies these symbols graphically.

FIGURE 11.3.

Mapping logical to physical coordinates.

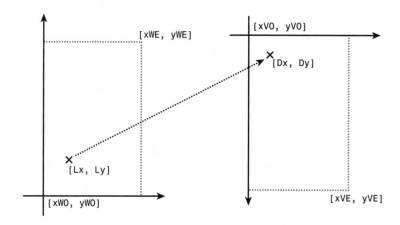

WARNING

Although both Windows 95 and Windows NT use 32-bit coordinate values in GDI function calls, only Windows NT represents coordinates internally as 32-bit values. In the case of Windows 95, 16-bit values are used; the upper 16 bits are simply ignored.

To facilitate easy changes from one mapping to another, Windows offers a few helper functions. These include: `OffsetViewportOrg`, `OffsetWindowOrg`, `ScaleViewportExt`, and `ScaleWindowExt`.

Note that an application can change the horizontal or vertical orientation of the window or viewport by specifying a negative extent value.

To calculate explicitly a set of physical coordinates from logical coordinates, or vice versa, applications can use the `LPtoDP` and `DPtoLP` functions.

Constrained Mapping Modes

What has been said about mapping modes so far is true for the so-called unconstrained mapping mode.

The GDI supports several mapping modes; the unconstrained mapping mode `MM_ANISOTROPIC` is but one. Other mapping modes include the following:

`MM_TEXT`. The origin of the logical coordinate system is the upper-left corner, and vertical coordinates are growing downwards. In other words, `MM_TEXT` is the equivalent of no mapping at all. A logical unit equals one pixel.

`MM_LOENGLISH`. The origin is in the lower-left corner, and vertical coordinates grow upwards. A logical unit is equal to one hundredth of an inch (0.01").

`MM_HIENGLISH`. The origin is in the lower-left corner, and vertical coordinates grow upwards. A logical unit is equal to one thousandth of an inch (0.001").

`MM_LOMETRIC`. The origin is in the lower-left corner, and vertical coordinates grow upwards. A logical unit is equal to one tenth of a millimeter (0.1 mm).

`MM_HIMETRIC`. The origin is in the lower-left corner, and vertical coordinates grow upwards. A logical unit is equal to one hundredth of a millimeter (0.01 mm).

`MM_TWIPS`. The origin is in the lower-left corner, and vertical coordinates grow upwards. A logical unit is one twentieth of a point (1/1440").

`MM_ISOTROPIC`. The only restriction is that horizontal and vertical logical units are of equal length. Applications can freely specify the origin of the logical and physical coordinate systems, as well their horizontal extents. The vertical extents are computed from the horizontal by the GDI.

In the six constrained mapping modes, applications are free to change the viewport and window origin, but attempts to change the viewport or window extent (through `SetViewportExtEx` or `SetWindowExtEx`) are ignored.

World Coordinate Transforms

Flexible as the coordinate mapping capabilities in Windows are, Windows NT further extends these capabilities with the concept of *World Coordinate Transforms*. This capability makes it possible for applications to specify an arbitrary linear transformation as the mapping from the logical to the physical coordinate space.

To understand how world transformations work, it is necessary to delve into coordinate geometry.

Linear transformations fall into the following categories: translation, scaling, rotation, shear, and reflection.

Translation (Figure 11.4) means that constants are added to both the horizontal and vertical coordinates of an object:

$$x' = x + D_x$$

$$y' = y + D_y$$

FIGURE 11.4.
Translation.

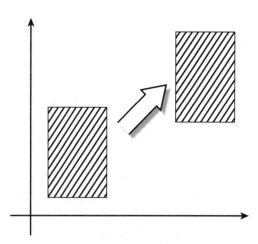

Scaling (Figure 11.5) means stretching or compressing the horizontal or vertical extent of an object:

$$x' = xS_x$$

$$y' = yS_y$$

FIGURE 11.5.

Scaling.

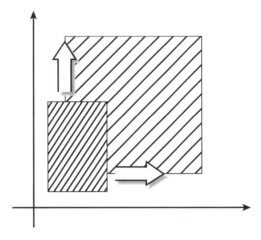

During a rotation (Figure 11.6), points of an object are rotated around the origin. If the angle of the rotation, A, is known, the rotation can be expressed as follows:

$$x' = x \cos \alpha - y \sin \alpha$$

$$y' = x \sin \alpha + y \cos \alpha$$

FIGURE 11.6.

Rotation.

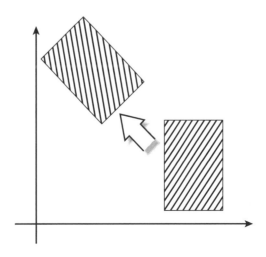

Shearing (Figure 11.7) is a transformation that turns rectangles into parallelograms. Shearing adds a displacement to point's horizontal coordinate that is proportional to the vertical coordinate, and vice versa. Shearing can be expressed by the following formulae:

$$x' = x + S_x y$$

$$y' = y + S_y x$$

FIGURE 11.7.

Shearing.

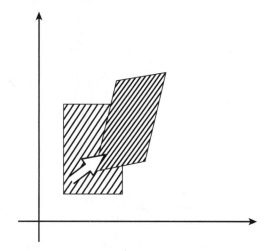

A reflection mirrors an object with respect to either the horizontal or the vertical axis. Figure 11.8 shows a reflection with respect to the horizontal axis. This reflection can be expressed with the following formula:

$$y' = -y$$

A reflection with respect to the vertical axis can in turn be expressed as follows:

$$x' = -x$$

All these transformations can also be expressed in matrix form using 3×3 matrices. The matrix form of a translation is this:

$$[x'\ y'\ 1] = [x\ y\ 1] \begin{bmatrix} 1 & 0 & 0 \\ 0 & 1 & 0 \\ D_x & D_y & 1 \end{bmatrix}$$

FIGURE 11.8.

Reflection with respect to the horizontal axis.

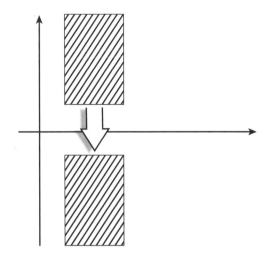

The matrix form of scaling:

$$[x'\ y'\ 1] = [x\ y\ 1] \begin{bmatrix} S_x & 0 & 0 \\ 0 & S_y & 0 \\ 0 & 0 & 1 \end{bmatrix}$$

The matrix form of a rotation, expressed using trigonometric functions of the rotation angle:

$$[x'\ y'\ 1] = [x\ y\ 1] \begin{bmatrix} \cos \alpha & -\sin \alpha & 0 \\ \sin \alpha & \cos \alpha & 0 \\ 0 & 0 & 1 \end{bmatrix}$$

The matrix form of a shearing:

$$[x'\ y'\ 1] = [x\ y\ 1] \begin{bmatrix} 1 & S_x & 0 \\ S_y & 1 & 0 \\ 0 & 0 & 1 \end{bmatrix}$$

A reflection with respect to the horizontal axis is expressed in matrix form as follows:

$$[x'\ y'\ 1] = [x\ y\ 1] \begin{bmatrix} 1 & 0 & 0 \\ 0 & -1 & 0 \\ 0 & 0 & 1 \end{bmatrix}$$

Finally, a reflection with respect to the vertical axis takes the following matrix form:

$$[\, x'\ y'\ 1\,] = [\, x\ y\ 1\,] \begin{bmatrix} -1 & 0 & 0 \\ 0 & 1 & 0 \\ 0 & 0 & 1 \end{bmatrix}$$

Linear transformations can be combined. The result of two linear transformations is a third linear transformation. In matrix formulation, the resulting transformation can be expressed as the product of the matrices representing the original transformation.

> **NOTE**
>
> Linear transformations are not commutative. In other words, the order in which they are performed is important.

While any linear transformation can be expressed in the form of a series of the five basic transformations mentioned here, a generic linear transformation may not be a simple translation, scaling, rotation, shearing, or reflection. A generic linear transformation can be expressed as follows:

$$[\, x'\ y'\ 1\,] = [\, x\ y\ 1\,] \begin{bmatrix} M_{11} & M_{12} & 0 \\ M_{21} & M_{22} & 0 \\ D_x & D_y & 1 \end{bmatrix}$$

This is exactly the type of matrix an application must supply to the SetWorldTransform function. The second parameter of this function is a pointer to an XFORM structure, which is defined as follows:

```
typedef struct  _XFORM
{
    FLOAT eM11;
    FLOAT eM12;
    FLOAT eM21;
    FLOAT eM22;
    FLOAT eDx;
    FLOAT eDy;
} XFORM;
```

Before you start worrying about matrix multiplication, I should tell you about the CombineTransform function. What this function really does is a multiplication of two transformation matrices expressed in the form of XFORM structures.

Once a world transformation has been set for a device context, it will transform logical coordinates from *world space* to *page space*. Page space coordinates are further subject to the transformation specified by the mapping mode, as discussed in the previous section.

Although applications can use the DPtoLP function to obtain the world coordinates for a given set of physical coordinates, it is sometimes useful to explicitly obtain the transformation matrix corresponding to the inverse transform. In order to obtain the inverse matrix, one should first calculate the determinant of the transformation matrix:

$$D = \begin{vmatrix} M_{11} & M_{12} & 0 \\ M_{21} & M_{22} & 0 \\ D_x & D_y & 1 \end{vmatrix} = \begin{vmatrix} M_{11} & M_{12} \\ M_{21} & M_{22} \end{vmatrix} = M_{11}M_{22} - M_{12}M_{21}$$

If this value is zero, the inverse matrix does not exist. This happens when the world transformation is pathological, and maps many points in world space to the same point in page space, for example, when it maps world space onto a line in page space. In this case, a point in page space no longer corresponds to a unique point in world space and thus the inverse transformation is not possible.

Once the determinant has been obtained, the inverse matrix can be calculated easily:

$$A^{-1} = \frac{1}{D} \begin{bmatrix} \begin{vmatrix} M_{22} & 0 \\ D_y & 1 \end{vmatrix} & -\begin{vmatrix} M_{12} & 0 \\ D_y & 1 \end{vmatrix} & \begin{vmatrix} M_{12} & 0 \\ M_{22} & 0 \end{vmatrix} \\ -\begin{vmatrix} M_{21} & 0 \\ D_x & 1 \end{vmatrix} & \begin{vmatrix} M_{11} & 0 \\ D_x & 1 \end{vmatrix} & -\begin{vmatrix} M_{11} & 0 \\ M_{21} & 0 \end{vmatrix} \\ \begin{vmatrix} M_{21} & M_{22} \\ D_x & D_y \end{vmatrix} & -\begin{vmatrix} M_{11} & M_{12} \\ D_x & D_y \end{vmatrix} & \begin{vmatrix} M_{11} & M_{21} \\ M_{12} & M_{22} \end{vmatrix} \end{bmatrix} =$$

$$= \begin{bmatrix} M_{22}/D & -M_{12}/D & 0 \\ -M_{21}/D & M_{11}/D & 0 \\ (M_{21}D_y - M_{22}D_x)/D & (M_{12}D_x - M_{11}D_y)/D & 1 \end{bmatrix}$$

Accordingly, here is a short function (Listing 11.1) that creates the inverse transform of a world transform. If the inverse transform does not exist, the function returns the identity transform. The function's return value is set to FALSE in this case to indicate an error. In keeping with the tradition of other XFORM-related functions, InvertTransform also accepts the same pointer for both the input and the output XFORM structure.

Listing 11.1. Inverting a world transformation.

```
BOOL InvertTransform(LPXFORM lpxformResult, CONST XFORM *lpxform)
{
    XFORM xformTmp;
    FLOAT D;
    D = lpxform->eM11*lpxform->eM22 - lpxform->eM12*lpxform->eM21;
    if (D == 0.0)
    {
        lpxformResult->eM11 = 1.0;
        lpxformResult->eM12 = 0.0;
        lpxformResult->eM21 = 0.0;
        lpxformResult->eM22 = 1.0;
        lpxformResult->eDx = 0.0;
        lpxformResult->eDy = 0.0;
        return FALSE;
    }
    xformTmp.eM11 = lpxform->eM22 / D;
    xformTmp.eM12 = -lpxform->eM12 / D;
    xformTmp.eM21 = -lpxform->eM21 / D;
    xformTmp.eM22 = lpxform->eM11 / D;
    xformTmp.eDx = (lpxform->eM21*lpxform->eDy -
                    lpxform->eM22*lpxform->eDx) / D;
    xformTmp.eDy = (lpxform->eM12*lpxform->eDx -
                    lpxform->eM11*lpxform->eDy) / D;
    *lpxformResult = xformTmp;
    return TRUE;
}
```

On a final note, the SetWorldTransform function will fail unless the graphics mode for the device context has first been set to GM_ADVANCED using the SetGraphicsMode function. In order to reset the graphics mode to GM_COMPATIBLE, applications must first reset the world transformation matrix to the identity matrix.

Drawing Objects

Coordinate transformations define where a drawing is placed on the output device. What the drawing looks like is defined by the use of GDI objects.

GDI offers a variety of drawing objects: pens, brushes, fonts, palettes, and bitmaps. Applications that use such objects must perform the following steps:

1. Create the GDI object.
2. Select the GDI object into the device context.
3. Call GDI output functions.
4. Select the object out of the device context.
5. Destroy the object.

GDI objects are created using any one of a variety of functions that we will acquaint ourselves with in a moment. Once created, a GDI object is referred to by a handle and can be selected into the device context using the `SelectObject` function. (Palettes are selected using `SelectPalette`.) This function also returns a handle to the previously selected pen, brush, font, or bitmap; when drawing is completed, this can be used to restore the device context to its previous state. Unused objects are destroyed using the `DeleteObject` function.

It is not always necessary to create a GDI object from scratch. Applications can also retrieve predefined system objects using the `GetStockObject` function. `GetStockObject` can be used to retrieve a handle to a variety of pens, brushes, fonts, and the system palette. While it is not necessary to call `DeleteObject` for a stock object, it is not harmful either.

Pens

Pens are used to draw lines, curves, and the contours of other shapes. A pen is created using the `CreatePen` function. When calling `CreatePen`, applications specify the pen's width, style, and color.

Pen color is specified as an RGB value; however, if there is matching entry in the logical palette, Windows usually substitutes the nearest palette color. The exception is the case when the width of the pen is greater than one and the style is `PS_INSIDEFRAME`; in this case, Windows uses a dithered color.

Dashed and dotted pen styles are not supported for pens with a width greater than one. However, in the case of Windows NT, such pens can be created using the `ExtCreatePen` function. This function is also available under Windows 95, but its utility is limited.

`ExtCreatePen` also gives greater control over the shapes of joins and end caps.

Another function that can be used to create a pen is the `CreatePenIndirect` function. This function takes a pointer to a `LOGPEN` structure as its parameter. The `LOGPEN` structure defines the pen's width, color, and style.

Drawing with a pen is affected by the *foreground mix mode.* This mode is set using the `SetROP2` function. There are several settings that define various logical operations between the pen color and the pixel color. The current mixing mode can be retrieved using the `GetROP2` function.

Brushes

Brushes are used to fill the interior of drawing shapes. The use of a brush defines the interior color and pattern.

A brush is created by a call to the `CreateBrushIndirect` function. This function accepts a pointer to a `LOGBRUSH` structure, which specifies the brush style, color, and pattern.

A brush pattern can be based on a bitmap. If the brush style is set to the values BS_DIBPATTERN or BS_DIBPATTERNPT, the lbStyle member of the LOGBRUSH structure specifies a handle to a bitmap.

> **NOTE**
>
> Windows 95 only supports 8×8 bitmaps. If a larger bitmap is specified, only a portion of the bitmap is used.

Alternatively, a brush can be hatched; in this case, the lbStyle member of the LOGBRUSH structure specifies the hatch pattern.

The lbColor member specifies the foreground color of a hatched brush. However, the background color and mode are controlled by the SetBkColor and SetBkMode functions, respectively.

A specific problem related to pattern and hatch brushes is the problem of brush origin. In order to provide a smooth appearance, it is necessary to align the origin of a brush bitmap or hatch brush pattern when portions of a shape are drawn at different times. Under Windows 95, this is accomplished by calling UnrealizeObject every time before a brush is selected into a device context. This is not necessary under Windows NT, which tracks brush origins.

Applications can explicitly specify the brush origin through SetBrushOrgEx. The brush origin is a pair of coordinates that specify the displacement of the brush pattern relative to the upper-left corner of the window's client area.

There are several additional functions assisting in the creation and use of brushes. Solid brushes, and pattern brushes, and hatch brushes can be created by calling CreateSolidBrush, CreatePatternBrush, and CreateHatchBrush, respectively. Brushes that are based on device-independent bitmaps can be created with CreateDIBPatternBrushPt.

Drawing the interior of an object is also affected by the foreground mix mode setting as specified by a call to the SetROP2 function.

Fonts

Before an application can output any text, it must select a logical font for text output. Logical fonts are created by calling the CreateFont function.

Users who are accustomed to applications that enable them to explicitly select a font by name, attributes, and size may find using CreateFont confusing at first. Although it is still possible to select a font by name, CreateFont offers a selection of a large number of additional parameters.

However, one has to realize that this method of creating a logical font is yet another feature through which Windows implements complete device-independence. Instead of making applications dependent on the presence of a specific font (which may not be available on all output devices, or may not be available on different computers) fonts are selected on the basis of their characteristics. When an application requests a font through CreateFont, Windows supplies, from the set of available fonts, the font that matches the requested characteristics best.

Nevertheless, it is possible to specify the name and size of a typeface to CreateFont. If this is done, Windows will attempt to select the desired font if it is available on the system.

Applications can also use CreateFontIndirect to obtain a logical font. This function takes a pointer to a LOGFONT structure as its parameter. This function is especially useful when used in conjunction with the Font Selection Common Dialog, which returns the user's choice in the form of a LOGFONT structure.

The EnumFontFamilies function can be used to enumerate all font families, or the fonts in a font family.

Many other font-related functions assist the application programmer. For example, functions such as GetCharABCWidths help determining the width of characters. The function GetTabbedExtent or GetTextExtentPoint32 calculate the width and height of a text string.

Applications can also install and remove fonts using the AddFontResource, CreateScalableFontResource, and RemoveFontResource functions.

Palettes

Palettes would not be necessary if all output devices were capable of displaying the full range of colors defined by a 24-bit RGB value. Unfortunately, most lower cost display devices offer a compromise between color depth and screen resolution. Most PCs nowadays operate using a screen resolution of 800×600, 1024×768, or 1280×1024 using 256 colors.

Whether a given device supports palettes can be determined by calling the GetDeviceCaps function and checking for the RC_PALETTE flag in the RASTERCAPS value. For these devices, a *color palette* defines the colors that are currently available for use by applications.

The *system palette* specifies all colors that can be currently displayed by the device. However, applications cannot directly modify the system palette, although they can view its contents through the GetSystemPaletteEntries function. The system palette contains a number (usually 2–20) of *static colors* that cannot be modified by palette changes. However, applications can set the number of static colors using the SetSystemPaletteUse function.

The *default palette* has typically 20 color entries, although this may vary from device to device. If an application requests a color that is not in the palette, Windows approximates the color by selecting the closest match from the palette or, in the case of solid brushes, by using dithering. However, this may not be sufficient for color-sensitive applications.

What applications can do is specify a *logical palette* to replace the default palette. A logical palette may contain several colors (up to the number of colors defined by the SIZEPALETTE value, returned by GetDeviceCaps). A logical palette is created by a call to CreatePalette, and its colors can later be modified by calling SetPaletteEntries. A palette is selected into a device context using the `SelectPalette` function. A palette that is no longer needed can be deleted by calling `DeleteObject`.

Before use, a palette needs to be *realized* using the `RealizePalette` function. In the case of the display device, depending on whether the palette is a *foreground palette* or a *background palette*, Windows realizes the palette differently. A palette can be selected as the foreground palette if the window for which it is selected is either the active window or a descendant of it. There can be only one foreground palette in the system at any given time. The critical difference is that a foreground palette can overwrite all nonstatic colors in the system palette. This is accomplished by marking all nonstatic entries unused before a foreground palette is realized.

When a palette is realized, Windows fills the unused entries in the system palette with entries from the logical palette. If there are no more unused entries, Windows maps the remaining colors in the logical palette using dithering or using the closest matching color in the physical palette. Windows always realizes the foreground palette first, followed by the remaining background palettes on a first come, first served basis.

It is important to realize that any changes to the system palette are global in nature; that is, they affect the entire display surface, not just the application's window. Changes in the system palette may cause applications to redraw their window contents. Because of this, there is an advantage to specifying a palette as a background palette; this avoids palette changes when the window for which the palette has been realized gains or loses focus.

Windows defines some palette-related messages. A top-level window receives a `WM_PALETTECHANGED` message when Windows changes the system palette. Before a top-level window becomes the active window, it receives a `WM_QUERYNEWPALETTE` message, enabling the application to realize its palette. The application can do this by calling `SelectPalette`, `UnrealizeObject`, and `RealizePalette`.

An interesting feature of palettes is *palette animation*. This technique uses periodic changes in the logical palette to create the impression of animation. Applications can use the `AnimatePalette` function for this purpose.

In order to ensure that a given color from a palette is selected (especially important when palette animation is concerned) applications should use the `PALETTEINDEX` or `PALETTERGB` macros.

An application that implements simple palette animation is shown in Listing 11.2. This application can be compiled from the command line by typing `cl animate.cpp gdi32.lib user32.lib`. Once again, note that this application only works when your video hardware is configured for a 256-color palette-enabled mode.

Listing 11.2. Palette Animation.

```
#include <windows.h>

struct
{
```

```
    WORD palVersion;
    WORD palNumEntries;
    PALETTEENTRY palPalEntry[12];
} palPalette =
{
    0x300,
    12,
    {
        {0xFF, 0x00, 0x00, PC_RESERVED},
        {0xC0, 0x40, 0x00, PC_RESERVED},
        {0x80, 0x80, 0x00, PC_RESERVED},
        {0x40, 0xC0, 0x00, PC_RESERVED},
        {0x00, 0xFF, 0x00, PC_RESERVED},
        {0x00, 0xC0, 0x40, PC_RESERVED},
        {0x00, 0x80, 0x80, PC_RESERVED},
        {0x00, 0x40, 0xC0, PC_RESERVED},
        {0x00, 0x00, 0xFF, PC_RESERVED},
        {0x40, 0x00, 0xC0, PC_RESERVED},
        {0x80, 0x00, 0x80, PC_RESERVED},
        {0xC0, 0x00, 0x40, PC_RESERVED}
    }
};

POINT pt12[12] =
{
    {0, 1000},
    {500, 866},
    {866, 500},
    {1000, 0},
    {866, -500},
    {500, -866},
    {0, -1000},
    {-500, -866},
    {-866, -500},
    {-1000, 0},
    {-866, 500},
    {-500, 866}
};

void Animate(HWND hwnd, HPALETTE hPalette)
{
    HDC hDC;
    PALETTEENTRY pe[12];
    HPALETTE hOldPal;
    static int nIndex;
    int i;

    for (i = 0; i < 12; i++)
        pe[i] = palPalette.palPalEntry[(i + nIndex) % 12];
    hDC = GetDC(hwnd);
    hOldPal = SelectPalette(hDC, hPalette, FALSE);
    RealizePalette(hDC);
    AnimatePalette(hPalette, 0, 12, pe);
    nIndex = (++nIndex) % 12;
    SelectPalette(hDC, hOldPal, FALSE);
    ReleaseDC(hwnd, hDC);
}
```

continues

Listing 11.2. continued

```
void DrawCircle(HWND hwnd, HPALETTE hPalette)
{
    HDC hDC;
    PAINTSTRUCT paintStruct;
    RECT rect;
    SIZE sizeO;
    POINT ptO;
    HPALETTE hOldPal;
    int i;

    hDC = BeginPaint(hwnd, &paintStruct);
    if (hDC != NULL)
    {
        hOldPal = SelectPalette(hDC, hPalette, FALSE);
        RealizePalette(hDC);
        GetClientRect(hwnd, &rect);
        DPtoLP(hDC, (LPPOINT)&rect, 2);
        ptO.x = (rect.left + rect.right) / 2;
        ptO.y = (rect.top + rect.bottom) / 2;
        sizeO.cx = MulDiv((rect.right - rect.left), 2, 3);
        sizeO.cy = MulDiv((rect.bottom - rect.top), 2, 3);
        for (i = 0; i < 12; i++)
        {
            HBRUSH hbr;
            HBRUSH hbrOld;
            hbr = CreateSolidBrush(PALETTEINDEX(i));
            hbrOld = (HBRUSH)SelectObject(hDC, hbr);
            Ellipse(hDC,
                ptO.x + MulDiv(sizeO.cx, pt12[i].x - 259, 2000),
                ptO.y + MulDiv(sizeO.cy, pt12[i].y - 259, 2000),
                ptO.x + MulDiv(sizeO.cx, pt12[i].x + 259, 2000),
                ptO.y + MulDiv(sizeO.cy, pt12[i].y + 259, 2000)
            );
            SelectObject(hDC, hbrOld);
            DeleteObject(hbr);
        }
        SelectPalette(hDC, hOldPal, FALSE);
        EndPaint(hwnd, &paintStruct);
    }
}

LRESULT CALLBACK WndProc(HWND hwnd, UINT uMsg,
                         WPARAM wParam, LPARAM lParam)
{
    static HPALETTE hPalette;

    switch(uMsg)
    {
        case WM_CREATE:
            hPalette = CreatePalette((LPLOGPALETTE)&palPalette);
            break;
        case WM_PAINT:
            DrawCircle(hwnd, hPalette);
            break;
        case WM_TIMER:
            Animate(hwnd, hPalette);
```

```
            break;
        case WM_DESTROY:
            DeleteObject(hPalette);
            hPalette = NULL;
            PostQuitMessage(0);
            break;
        default:
            return DefWindowProc(hwnd, uMsg, wParam, lParam);
    }
    return 0;
}

int WINAPI WinMain(HINSTANCE hInstance, HINSTANCE hPrevInstance,
                                LPSTR d3, int nCmdShow)
{
    MSG msg;
    HWND hwnd;
    WNDCLASS wndClass;

    if (hPrevInstance == NULL)
    {
        memset(&wndClass, 0, sizeof(wndClass));
        wndClass.style = CS_HREDRAW ¦ CS_VREDRAW;
        wndClass.lpfnWndProc = WndProc;
        wndClass.hInstance = hInstance;
        wndClass.hCursor = LoadCursor(NULL, IDC_ARROW);
        wndClass.hbrBackground = (HBRUSH)(COLOR_WINDOW + 1);
        wndClass.lpszClassName = "HELLO";
        if (!RegisterClass(&wndClass)) return FALSE;
    }
    hwnd = CreateWindow("HELLO", "HELLO",
                        WS_OVERLAPPEDWINDOW,
                        CW_USEDEFAULT, 0, CW_USEDEFAULT, 0,
                        NULL, NULL, hInstance, NULL);
    ShowWindow(hwnd, nCmdShow);
    UpdateWindow(hwnd);
    SetTimer(hwnd, 1, 200, NULL);
    while (GetMessage(&msg, NULL, 0, 0))
        DispatchMessage(&msg);
    KillTimer(hwnd, 1);
    return msg.wParam;
}
```

This application draws a series of twelve circles. Each circle has a different color, selected from a logical palette. The application also installs a timer; whenever a WM_TIMER message is received, it makes a call to the AnimatePalette function.

Bitmap Objects

Bitmaps are also treated as GDI objects. Typically, applications either draw into bitmaps, or transfer the contents of a bitmap to an output device.

What exactly is a bitmap? In terms of its visual appearance, it is a rectangular array of *pixels*. Each pixel can have a different color, represented in the form of one or more bits. The actual number of bits depends on the *color depth* of the bitmap. For example, a bitmap with a color depth of 8 bits can represent up to 256 colors; a true color bitmap can represent up to 16,777,216 colors using 24 bits per pixel.

A blank GDI bitmap object is created using the `CreateBitmap` function. Although suitable for creating color bitmaps, it is recommended that `CreateBitmap` be used for monochrome bitmaps only; for color bitmaps, use the `CreateCompatibleBitmap` function.

Bitmap objects are device dependent. Functions exist that enable applications to write into *Device-Independent Bitmaps* (*DIBs*). (This is what is stored in Windows BMP files.)

Applications can draw into a bitmap by selecting the bitmap into a *memory device context.*

To load a bitmap from a resource file, use the `LoadBitmap` function. This function creates a bitmap object and initializes it with the bitmap from the resource file, as specified by the function's second parameter.

Clipping

The technique of *clipping* is of fundamental importance in a multitasking windowing environment. Thanks to this technique, applications do not accidentally write to the display outside the client area of their windows, nor does it present a problem when parts of an application's window are covered or off-screen.

In addition to these uses of clipping by the system, applications are also given explicit access to many clipping functions. They can define a *clipping region* for a device context and limit graphical output to that region.

A clipping region is typically, but not always, a rectangular region. Table 11.1 summarizes the various types of regions and the corresponding functions that can be used to create them.

Table 11.1. Clipping Regions.

Symbolic Identifier	*Description*
Elliptical Region	`CreateEllipticRgn, CreateEllipticRgnIndirect`
Polygonal Region	`CreatePolygonRgn, CreatePolyPolygonRgn`
Rectangular Region	`CreateRectRgn, CreateRectRgnIndirect`
Rounded Rectangular Region	`CreateRoundRectRgn`

NOTE

Using a nonrectangular region for clipping can be inefficient on certain devices.

Applications can select a clipping region into a device context by calling `SelectObject` or `SelectClipRgn`. The effects of these two functions are equivalent. Another function that enables combining a new region with the existing clipping region in the fashion of the `CombineRgn` function is `SelectClipRgnExt`.

Another form of clipping is accomplished by the use of *clip paths*. Clip paths can define complex clipping shapes that could not be defined through clipping regions. A clipping path is a path created through the use of the `BeginPath` and `EndPath` functions, and then selected as the clipping path by calling `SelectClipPath`.

Clip paths can be used to produce interesting special effects. One example is demonstrated in Listing 11.3. This application, shown in Figure 11.9, uses a text string to create a clip path. You can compile this program by typing `cl clippath.c gdi32.lib user32.lib` at the command line.

FIGURE 11.9.

Using clip paths.

Listing 11.3. Using clip paths.

```c
#include <windows.h>
#include <math.h>

void DrawHello(HWND hwnd)
{
    PAINTSTRUCT paintStruct;
    RECT rect;
    HFONT hFont;
    SIZE sizeText;
    POINT ptText;
    HDC hDC;
```

continues

Listing 11.3. continued

```
    double a, d, r;

    hDC = BeginPaint(hwnd, &paintStruct);
    if (hDC != NULL)
    {
        GetClientRect(hwnd, &rect);
        DPtoLP(hDC, (LPPOINT)&rect, 2);
        hFont = CreateFont((rect.bottom - rect.top) / 2,
                            (rect.right - rect.left) / 13, 0, 0,
                            FW_HEAVY, FALSE, FALSE, FALSE,
                            ANSI_CHARSET, OUT_DEFAULT_PRECIS,
                            CLIP_DEFAULT_PRECIS, DEFAULT_QUALITY,
                            DEFAULT_PITCH | FF_DONTCARE, "Arial");
        SelectObject(hDC, hFont);
        GetTextExtentPoint32(hDC, "Hello, World!", 13, &sizeText);
        ptText.x = (rect.left + rect.right - sizeText.cx) / 2;
        ptText.y = (rect.top + rect.bottom - sizeText.cy) / 2;
        SetBkMode(hDC, TRANSPARENT);
        BeginPath(hDC);
        TextOut(hDC, ptText.x, ptText.y, "Hello, World!", 13);
        EndPath(hDC);
        SelectClipPath(hDC, RGN_COPY);
        d = sqrt((double)sizeText.cx * sizeText.cx +
                        sizeText.cy * sizeText.cy);
        for (r = 0; r <= 90; r+= 1)
        {
            a = r / 180 * 3.14159265359;
            MoveToEx(hDC, ptText.x, ptText.y, NULL);
            LineTo(hDC, ptText.x + (int)(d * cos(a)),
                        ptText.y + (int)(d * sin(a)));
        }
        EndPaint(hwnd, &paintStruct);
    }
}

LRESULT CALLBACK WndProc(HWND hwnd, UINT uMsg,
                        WPARAM wParam, LPARAM lParam)
{
    switch(uMsg)
    {
        case WM_PAINT:
            DrawHello(hwnd);
            break;
        case WM_DESTROY:
            PostQuitMessage(0);
            break;
        default:
            return DefWindowProc(hwnd, uMsg, wParam, lParam);
    }
    return 0;
}

int WINAPI WinMain(HINSTANCE hInstance, HINSTANCE hPrevInstance,
                                    LPSTR d3, int nCmdShow)
{
    MSG msg;
```

```
    HWND hwnd;
    WNDCLASS wndClass;

    if (hPrevInstance == NULL)
    {
        memset(&wndClass, 0, sizeof(wndClass));
        wndClass.style = CS_HREDRAW | CS_VREDRAW;
        wndClass.lpfnWndProc = WndProc;
        wndClass.hInstance = hInstance;
        wndClass.hCursor = LoadCursor(NULL, IDC_ARROW);
        wndClass.hbrBackground = (HBRUSH)(COLOR_WINDOW + 1);
        wndClass.lpszClassName = "HELLO";
        if (!RegisterClass(&wndClass)) return FALSE;
    }
    hwnd = CreateWindow("HELLO", "HELLO",
                        WS_OVERLAPPEDWINDOW,
                        CW_USEDEFAULT, 0, CW_USEDEFAULT, 0,
                        NULL, NULL, hInstance, NULL);
    ShowWindow(hwnd, nCmdShow);
    UpdateWindow(hwnd);
    while (GetMessage(&msg, NULL, 0, 0))
        DispatchMessage(&msg);
    return msg.wParam;
}
```

This application draws the text "Hello, World!" using a large Arial font—the actual size is calculated based on the size of the client area. This text forms the clipping path. Next, a series of lines is drawn from the upper-left corner of the text rectangle; due to clipping, only the portions that fall within characters are seen.

Drawing Functions

We have reviewed the idea of a device context as the "canvas" onto which GDI functions paint graphic output; we have reviewed the tools GDI performs the painting with, such as pens, brushes, or fonts. What is left is a review of the actual drawing operations used by the GDI.

The typical steps taken by an application are illustrated in Figure 11.10. They include obtaining a handle to the device context, setting up the device context for drawing, performing drawing operations, restoring the previous state of the device context, and releasing the device context. Naturally, specific applications may elect to perform these steps in a different order, leave out irrelevant steps, or invoke other initialization or drawing functions to satisfy specific requirements.

FIGURE 11.10.

Typical steps of GDI output.

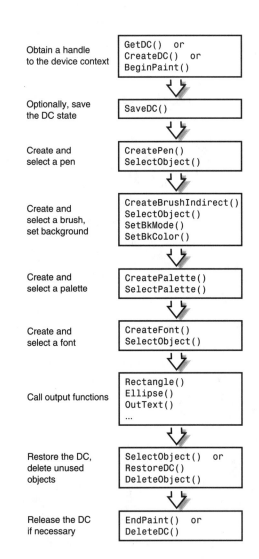

Obtain a handle to the device context	`GetDC()` or `CreateDC()` or `BeginPaint()`
Optionally, save the DC state	`SaveDC()`
Create and select a pen	`CreatePen()` `SelectObject()`
Create and select a brush, set background	`CreateBrushIndirect()` `SelectObject()` `SetBkMode()` `SetBkColor()`
Create and select a palette	`CreatePalette()` `SelectPalette()`
Create and select a font	`CreateFont()` `SelectObject()`
Call output functions	`Rectangle()` `Ellipse()` `OutText()` ...
Restore the DC, delete unused objects	`SelectObject()` or `RestoreDC()` `DeleteObject()`
Release the DC if necessary	`EndPaint()` or `DeleteDC()`

Lines

The simplest drawing function in Windows creates a line. A simple line is created by a call to the MoveToEx function, followed by a call to the LineTo function. The MoveToEx function updates the *current position*, which is a point in the coordinate space of the device context that is used by many drawing functions. The LineTo function creates a line from that position to the position specified through its parameters. The line is drawn using the pen that is currently selected into the device context.

In the case of raster devices, a line is generally drawn using a DDA (Digital Differential Analyzer) algorithm. This algorithm determines which pixels in the drawing surface should be highlighted. Specialized applications that require the use of a nonstandard DDA algorithm can use the LineDDA function.

A polyline is a line consisting of several line segments. A polyline is defined by an array of points, a pointer to which is passed to the Polyline function. Polyline does not use or update the current position; in contrast, PolylineTo begins drawing from the current position, and updates the current position to reflect the last point in the polyline.

The PolyPolyline function can be used to draw a series of polylines using a single function call.

Curves

The simplest function to draw a curve is the Arc function. A curve drawn by this function is actually a segment of an ellipse. The arc is drawn using the current pen. The ArcTo function is identical to the Arc function, except that it also updates the current position.

Win32 applications can also draw *Bézier curves*. Bézier curves represent a cubic interpolation between two endpoints, as defined by two *control points*. An example of a Bézier curve is shown in Figure 11.11.

FIGURE 11.11.

A Bézier curve.

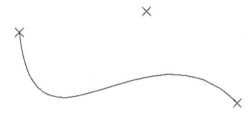

The PolyBezier function draws one or more Bézier curves. One of its parameters is a pointer to an array of points used to define these curves. The endpoint of one curve serves as the starting point of the next curve; consequently, the number of points in this array must be a multiple of three plus one (the first starting point), that is, 4, 7, 10, and so on.

The PolyBezierTo function is identical to the PolyBezier function except that it also updates the current position.

Win32 also provides for combinations of lines and curves. The outline of a pie chart can be drawn using the AngleArc function. More complex combinations of lines and curves can be created using the PolyDraw function.

Filled Shapes

In addition to lines and curves, GDI drawing functions can also be used to create filled shapes. The outline of filled shapes, similar to lines and curves, is drawn using the current pen. The interior of shapes is painted using the current brush.

Perhaps the simplest GDI shape is a rectangle. A rectangle is created by calling the `Rectangle` function. Variants of the `Rectangle` function include `RoundRect` (draws a rectangle with rounded corners), `FillRect` (draws the interior of a rectangle using a specific brush), `FrameRect` (draws the frame of a rectangle using a specific brush), and `InvertRect` (inverts a rectangular area on the screen).

Other shapes can be created using the following functions: `Ellipse`, `Chord`, `Pie`, `Polygon`. A series of polygons can be drawn using the single function call `PolyPolygon`.

Regions

I have already mentioned regions and their role in clipping. However, the GDI offers several other uses for regions.

Regions (summarized in Table 11.1) can be filled (`FillRgn`, `PaintRgn`), framed (`FrameRgn`) or inverted (`InvertRgn`).

Regions can be combined using the `CombineRgn` function. To test whether two regions are identical, use the `EqualRgn` function. A region can be displaced by a specified offset using `OffsetRgn`.

The bounding rectangle of a region can be obtained by calling `GetRgnBox`. To determine whether a specific point or a rectangle falls within the region, call `PtInRegion` or `RectInRegion`, respectively.

Bitmaps

We have already talked about bitmap objects. Windows offers a variety of functions through which these objects can be copied and manipulated.

Individual pixels in a bitmap can be set using the `SetPixel` function. The `GetPixel` function retrieves the color of the specified pixel.

A region in a bitmap bounded by pixels of specific colors can be filled using the `ExtFloodFill` function.

Perhaps the simplest of functions that manipulate whole bitmaps is the `BitBlt` function. This function copies a bitmap from one device context to another. It is often used to copy portions of a bitmap in a memory device context to the screen or vice versa; however, it can also be used to copy a bitmap to a different location within the same device context.

BitBlt returns an error if the source and destination device contexts are not compatible. To ensure that a memory device context is compatible with the display, use the CreateCompatibleDC function to create the device context.

Although BitBlt uses logical coordinates and performs the necessary scaling when copying bitmaps, it fails if a rotation or shear transformation is in effect.

In addition to copying source pixels to the destination, BitBlt can also combine source and destination pixels using a variety of pixel operations.

A variant of the BitBlt function is MaskBlt. This function uses a third bitmap as a mask when performing the operation.

The PatBlt function paints the destination bitmap using the currently selected brush.

The StretchBlt function copies the source bitmap to the destination bitmap, stretching or compressing the bitmap as necessary to fit it into the destination rectangle. The stretching can be controlled by the SetStretchBltMode function.

The PlgBlt function copies the source bitmap into a destination parallelogram. The parallelogram is defined by an array of three points representing three of its vertices; the fourth vertex is calculated using the vector equation $\mathbf{D} = \mathbf{B} + \mathbf{C} - \mathbf{A}$.

The bitmaps discussed so far are associated by a specific device context; hence, they are device-dependent. Windows also handles device-independent bitmaps, which are stored in memory or on disk. A DIB is specified through a BITMAPINFO structure. Applications can create a DIB using the CreateDIBitmap function. The bits in a DIB can be set using SetDIBits; the DIB's color table can be modified using SetDIBColorTable. The SetDIBitsToDevice function copies a DIB to a device; the StretchDIBits function can be used to copy bits from a device to a device-independent bitmap.

Paths

We have already encountered paths in the context of clipping. Paths represent complex shapes created by a series of calls to many GDI output functions, including, for example, the Rectangle, Ellipse, TextOut, LineTo, PolyBezier, Polygon functions.

A path is created by calling the BeginPath function, performing the drawing operations that form part of the path, and calling EndPath. The pair of calls to BeginPath and EndPath is often referred to as a *path bracket*.

Calling EndPath selects the path into the device context. Applications can then do any of the following:

- Draw the outline or interior of the path, or both (StrokePath, FillPath, StrokeAndFillPath)
- Use the path for clipping (SelectClipPath)

- Convert the path into a region (`PathToRegion`)
- Modify the path (`GetPath`, `FlattenPath`, `WidenPath`)

Text Output

The simplest GDI text output function is the `TextOut` function. This function outputs text at the specified coordinates using the currently selected font. The `TabbedTextOut` function is a variant of `TextOut` that also expands tab characters. The `PolyTextOut` function can be used to output a series of text strings using a single function call. The `ExtTextOut` function also accepts a rectangle that can be used for opaquing or clipping.

The `DrawText` and `DrawTextEx` functions can be used to output text with special formatting in a specific rectangle. Text output is affected by formatting attributes, which are set through the `SetTextColor`, `SetTextAlign`, `SetBkColor`, `SetBkMode`, `SetTextCharacterExtra`, and `SetTextJustification` functions. Applications can obtain the size of a block of text before drawing it by calling `GetTabbedTextExtent` or `GetTextExtentPoint32`.

Notes About Printing

The GDI is also responsible for providing hardcopy output on printers, plotters, and outer output devices. In the case of most applications, knowing the details of the printing process is not necessary; creating output to a hardcopy device is no different from creating output to the display, using the standard set of GDI function calls on a printer device context. While sometimes it is necessary to be aware of the physical characteristics of the output page and the limitations of the device (for example, a plotter may not support bitmap operations), WYSIWYG applications can most often reuse, with minimal modifications, the same code for printing that they use for display output.

There are several Windows components involved in printing. The primary component is the *print spooler*, which manages the printing process. The *print processor* converts spooled print jobs into calls to the device driver. The *device driver* generates raw output, which is then processed by the printer device. Finally, the *port monitor* passes raw device commands to the physical device through a specific port or network connection.

There are several Win32 functions for spooling print jobs, retrieving information about jobs and printers, and control the printing process.

Windows 3.1 applications often used *printer escapes* to carry out specific tasks. These have been superseded by new Win32 functions. New applications should not use the `Escape` function to control a printer.

Summary

The Windows GDI provides a device-independent set of functions that applications can use to create graphic output on all Windows-compatible output devices. The GDI is used to create output on the display screen, on printers, plotters, FAX modems, and other specialized graphic devices.

All graphic output is directed to device contexts. A device context provides a description of the output device, its characteristics and parameters, and also acts as an interface between the device-independent GDI routines and the device driver software. In a manner of speaking, the device context is the "canvas" on which GDI drawing operations are performed.

GDI uses a collection of tools for graphic output:

- Pens are used to draw lines or the contours of shapes.
- Brushes are used to fill the interior of shapes.
- Fonts are used for text output.
- Bitmaps are rectangular arrays of pixels that can be drawn to using memory device contexts and manipulated or transferred between device contexts using bitmap manipulation functions.
- Palettes are logical collections of colors that the GDI matches as closely as possible by configuring the color settings of the display device.
- Regions are regular or irregular shapes that can be used, for example, to define clipping.

Clipping is one of the key capabilities on the GDI. Thanks to clipping, applications do not need to confine their output to the visible part of their windows. Applications can also use clipping operations explicitly to create various graphical effects.

The coordinate mapping, drawing tools, and clipping define how the GDI performs its drawing operations. What is actually drawn is specified by a series of graphic functions. Applications can draw lines, curves, and filled shapes; can output text; and can manipulate bitmaps. Applications can also utilize paths for a variety of purposes.

The GDI provides a series of extra functions to facilitate greater control over printing and spooling to the printer. However, unless an application needs to explicitly control the printing process, it is rarely necessary to use these capabilities. Furthermore, in the case of most WYSIWYG applications, you can reuse display output code for printing with minimal modifications.

Threads and
Processes

As is the case with any evolving environment, Windows presents an odd mix of the old and the new, the obsolete, outdated, and the modern, the state-of-the-art. Nowhere is it more evident than in its multitasking capabilities, in particular the differences in those capabilities between the various Win32 platforms.

The old: The cooperative multitasking environment of 16-bit Windows. Its antics and limitations survive intact in Win32s which, although it provides a rich implementation of the Win32 programming interface, nevertheless cannot alter the underlying operating system or eliminate its limitations.

The new: The multithreaded Windows NT operating system. An operating system that was designed fresh from the ground up, Windows NT offers a very robust multitasking capability, suitable for high-reliability applications (such as large corporate servers).

The odd: Windows 95. Here, the goal of the designers was as much to implement the new capabilities as to maintain 100 percent (well, close to 100 percent anyway) compatibility with the old 16-bit Windows environment. The result is an astonishing combination: Windows 95 delivers a surprisingly robust multitasking capability while at the same time doing an excellent job (sometimes better than 16-bit Windows itself) in maintaining compatibility with legacy applications. Naturally, this does not come without a price: Windows 95 suffers from some strange limitations, ever more likely to turn into annoying "gotchas" precisely because the system does such an excellent job delivering elsewhere. With its fluid multitasking capability, it may come as a surprise to the uninitiated that Windows 95 is just as likely to "freeze" because of an ill-behaved 16-bit application as Windows 3.1. (Although admittedly, Windows 95 does a lot better job recovering from such events.)

Multitasking in the Win32 Environment

Because the differences are substantial, it pays to examine the multitasking capabilities of the three Win32 environments separately. But first, we turn our attention to some of the fundamental concepts essential to understanding multitasking in Windows.

Multitasking Concepts

Multitasking in general refers to an operating system's capability to load and execute several applications concurrently. A multitasking operating system is considered a robust and reliable one if it successfully shields concurrent applications from each other, making them believe that they alone "own" the computer and its resources. Furthermore, a well-written multitasking operating system also shields applications from each others' bugs; for example, if one application fails to perform array bounds checking and writes beyond the allocated boundaries of an array, the multitasking operating system should prevent this from overwriting the memory space of another application. To a large extent, multitasking operating systems rely on system hardware to implement these capabilities. For example, without the support of a memory management unit that generates an interrupt when an attempt is made to access memory at an illegal address, the operating system would have no way of knowing that such an attempt took place short of examining every single instruction in an application's code. This would be a very inefficient, time-consuming solution—completely impractical, in fact.

Another important aspect of multitasking is *process scheduling*. As most processors are capable of executing only a single stream of instructions at any given time, multitasking would obviously not be possible without the technique of *context switching*. A context switch, triggered by a specific event (such as an interrupt from a timer circuit or a call by the running application to a specific function), essentially consists of saving the processor context (instruction pointer, stack pointer, register contents) of one running program and loading that of another.

Other no less important aspects of multitasking involve the operating system's capability to provide contention-free access to various system resources (such as the file system, the display device), prevent deadlock situations, and provide mechanisms through which concurrently executing applications can communicate with each other and synchronize their execution.

The degree to which various operating systems provide multitasking support varies greatly. Traditional mainframe operating systems have provided robust support in all aspects of multitasking since decades ago. On the other hand, multitasking on desktop computers is a relatively new phenomenon, largely because these machines only recently became sufficiently powerful to execute several tasks at once efficiently. (That said, many programmers are surprised to learn that even vintage MS-DOS provides rudimentary support for multitasking; this is what enabled developers to write robust Terminate and Stay Resident, or TSR, applications.)

When examining the difference between the multitasking support in the various Win32 environments, we quickly find that the primary emphasis is on the scheduling mechanism employed.

In a *cooperative multitasking* environment (also referred to often as nonpreemptive) the operating system relies explicitly on applications to *yield control* by regularly calling a specified set of operating system functions. Context switching takes place at well-defined points during the execution of a program.

In a *preemptive multitasking* environment, the operating system can interrupt the execution of an application at any time. This usually happens when the operating system responds to a hardware event, such as an interrupt from a timer circuit. An application's flow of execution can be interrupted at any point, not only at predefined spots. This raises the complexity of the system. In particular, in preemptive multitasking environments, the possibility of *reentrancy* becomes a distinct issue; a program may be interrupted while it is executing an operating system function, and while it is suspended, another program may call into the same operating system function, or *reenter* the function before the call to it from the first program was complete.

Another term often heard in the context of multitasking and Windows is *threads*. Perhaps the best way to describe threads is this: While multitasking offers the capability of running several programs concurrently, threads make possible several concurrent paths of execution within the *same* program. The introduction of this mechanism adds a powerful capability to the application programmer's repertoire. The price (you *knew* there was a price to pay for this, didn't you?): problems that were previously the concern of operating system authors only, such as the problems associated with reentrancy and process synchronization, are now something application programmers must also worry about.

Cooperative Multitasking in Win32s

Windows 3.1 is a cooperative multitasking environment. The 32-bit applications that run under Windows 3.1 using Win32s are subject to the same multitasking limitations as ordinary 16-bit applications.

> **NOTE**
>
> A very limited form of preemptive multitasking exists in Windows 3.1. This is what enables the concurrent execution of several MS-DOS programs in separate DOS windows.

In Windows 3.1, applications must regularly yield control to the operating system by calling one of the following functions: GetMessage, PeekMessage (without the PM_NOYIELD flag), and Yield.

It is fortunate that GetMessage is one of the yielding functions; thanks to this fact, applications that rely on a typical message loop for message processing need to do very little else to be well-behaved under the Windows 3.1 environment. However, the nature of the cooperative multitasking environment should never be forgotten; whenever a message triggers the execution of a time-consuming action, such as printing a large document or performing a lengthy calculation, the programmer is well-advised to include regular calls to Yield or PeekMessage in order not to "freeze" the operating system. Better yet, it should make an effort to actually process messages even during the time-consuming procedure; that way, the application's own window will also remain responsive. (For example, it would repaint itself if parts of it were uncovered due to an action of the user.)

Failing to cooperate with the operating system and other applications has more than mere cosmetic effects. As other applications will not have a chance to execute at all, odd things are bound to happen; the buffer of a communication application will overflow, a TCP/IP networking application will lose connection, timing-sensitive application will encounter a time-out condition, and so on. Worse yet, eventually the input buffers of Windows itself will overflow as well; ever heard that ugly rapid-fire beeping that is the response of a very sick Windows to any user-interface event (mouse button clicks, keyboard clicks, even mouse movements)?

There is very little excuse for writing an application that does not abide by the rules of cooperative multitasking. If your application is intended to run in the Win32s environment, abiding by these rules is a must; but, as we see momentarily, these practices are not a bad idea even in the preemptive Windows NT and Windows 95 environments.

Preemptive Multitasking in Windows NT

I must admit, ever since the early versions of Windows NT, and despite some of the compatibility problems associated with it, switching from Windows 3.1 to Windows NT always felt like stepping out from a stuffy, overcrowded room to breathe some fresh mountain air.

This sensation was due in large part to NT's robust multitasking. Gone were the miseries of frozen applications, unresponsive keyboards, unsuccessful attempts to revive a system with the most drastic of methods, hitting Control+Alt+Delete. Instead, here was an operating system that always remained responsive, always offered a way to get rid of a pesky, ill-behaved program.

Windows NT provides preemptive multitasking for concurrent 32-bit processes. The case of 16-bit processes is special. These processes generally appear to Windows NT as a single process (the Windows On Windows, or WOW process), although beginning with Version 3.5, Windows NT enables 16-bit processes to run in a "separate memory space," meaning that a separate WOW process is started for them. Those 16-bit applications that share a WOW process, however, must abide by the rules of cooperative multitasking to enable each other to live. In other words, if a 16-bit process freezes, it will also freeze all other 16-bit processes with which it shares a process; however, it will not have any ill effect on other processes, including 16-bit processes that run as part of another WOW process.

Does preemptive multitasking in Windows NT mean that you can forget everything you learned about well-behaved Windows applications and start writing noncooperative code? Absolutely not, and here is the reason why.

Even though Windows NT is capable of wrestling control away from an uncooperative 32-bit application and thus it can enable other applications to run, it will not be able to process messages aimed at the uncooperative application. Thus, if an application fails to regularly check its message queue, it will still appear unresponsive, buggy to the user. The user will not be able to interact with the application at all. Clicking on the application's window to bring it to the front will fail, and the application will not redraw parts of its window when it is uncovered when another window is moved or closed.

To avoid this, an application should make every effort to regularly check its message queue and dispatch any messages in it, even when it is otherwise busy performing some lengthy task. While failing to do so no longer threatens the integrity of the system as a whole, it certainly serves as a recipe for a very "user-unfriendly" application.

Fortunately, there is another aspect of Windows NT multitasking that makes such lengthy processes much easier to implement. Unlike its 16-bit predecessor, Windows NT is a multithreaded operating system.

A Windows NT program can easily and inexpensively create new threads of execution. For example, if it needs to perform a lengthy calculation, that task can be delegated to a secondary thread, while the primary thread continues processing messages. A secondary thread can even perform user-interface functions; for example, while an application's primary thread continues processing messages sent to its main window, the application can delegate the function of processing messages for a dialog to a secondary thread. (When using the Microsoft Foundation Classes, there is actually special terminology to distinguish threads that own windows and process messages and those that do not; they are referred to as *user-interface threads* and *worker threads*, respectively.)

Windows 95: A Mixed Bag of Multitasking Tricks

Windows 95 combines the best features of both Windows 3.1 and Windows NT and loses surprisingly little in terms of tradeoffs. (I guess you can tell from this that I like Windows 95. Indeed, I like it a lot.)

On the one hand, Windows 95 delivers a Windows NT-like preemptive multitasking and multithreading capability. If anything, Windows 95 is perhaps even more responsive, thanks to code that is more optimized, more specifically tailored to the Intel family of processors than the portable code of Windows NT. On the other hand, Windows 95 delivers a remarkable degree of compatibility with legacy DOS and 16-bit Windows applications. And all this is delivered by an operating system that is only slightly more resource hungry than its predecessor. I witnessed this firsthand, when I successfully installed Windows 95 *and* Visual C++ 2.1 on my 8MB 486SX25 notebook computer.

This compatibility has been accomplished, in part, by incorporating large amounts of legacy code from Windows 3.1 into Windows 95. In other words, although Windows 95 is doubtless a 32-bit operating system, some code at its very heart is old-style 16-bit code. The obvious side effect of this is that some parameters that can have a full range of 32-bit values in Windows NT are restricted to 16 bits in Windows 95 (most notably, graphical coordinates). Another, less than obvious side effect has a direct consequence for multitasking under Windows 95.

Much of the Windows 3.1 legacy code has not been designed with reentrancy in mind. In other words, because 16-bit applications participated in cooperative multitasking, there was never a chance that one was interrupted in the middle of a system call; hence, there was no need to design mechanisms that would make it safe to repeatedly call system functions while a previous call was suspended, unfinished.

Because Windows 95 processes can be interrupted any time, Microsoft had two choices. The first was to rewrite Windows 3.1 system calls completely. Apart from being a monumental task, this approach would result in a loss of the advantage that importing Windows 3.1 legacy code represents, namely a high degree of backward compatibility. In effect, such a rewrite would result in another operating system; and that has been done, the result being Windows NT.

The other, much simpler solution is simply to protect the system while its 16-bit non-reentrant parts are executing. In particular, what the Windows 95 solution means is that while one application is executing 16-bit code, all other applications are prevented from doing so.

This has a very noticeable effect in the case of 16-bit applications. You see, 16-bit applications are *always* running in 16-bit mode. What that means is that as long as a 16-bit application has control of the processor, no other application can execute the 16-bit code.

Which means that an uncooperative 16-bit application (one that fails to yield to the operating system, thus enabling other, 32-bit, processes to gain control) can just as effectively freeze the operating system as it did under Windows 3.1.

Fortunately, Windows 95 does a much better job of recovering. For example, it can kick out the offending process and do a good job cleaning up its mess without struggling with the stability and resource allocation problems that have plagued Windows 3.1.

Programming with Processes and Threads

The Win32 API contains a rich set of functions for accessing all the multitasking and multithreading features of 32-bit Windows. In some cases, these functions supersede or replace traditional UNIX or C library (or, for that matter, MS-DOS) functions. Other functions represent new areas of functionality. Yet another set of functions (for example, the yielding functions) is familiar to Windows 3.1 programmers.

The remainder of this chapter reviews some of the multitasking programming techniques.

Cooperative Multitasking: Yielding in the Message Loop

As I mentioned earlier, authors of most simple Windows applications do not have to worry about cooperative multitasking. The typical message loop, shown in Listing 12.1, takes care of this problem. Every time the application becomes ready to process a new message, it calls the Windows GetMessage function. GetMessage, in turn, may not return immediately; instead, Windows may perform a context switch and pass control to another application.

Listing 12.1. Yielding in the message loop.

```
int WINAPI WinMain(...)
{
    MSG msg;
    ...
    // Application initialization goes here
    ...
```

continues

Listing 12.1. continued

```
    // Entering main message loop
    while (GetMessage(&msg, NULL, 0, 0))     // This call yields!
    {
        // Message dispatching goes here
        ...
    }
}
```

Yielding During Lengthy Processing

As I mentioned earlier, although in the 32-bit environment it is not strictly necessary for an application to yield cooperatively, it is a very good idea to continue doing so. Not only does this make the application more likely to remain compatible with Win32s, but more importantly, it ensures that the application itself remains responsive.

The example program shown in Listing 12.2 (resource file) and 12.3 (source file) demonstrates this technique. This is yet another simple example that can be compiled from the command line with the following instructions:

```
RC LOOP.RC
CL LOOP.C LOOP.RES USER32.LIB
```

Alternatively, you can create a Visual C++ project and add the files LOOP.C and LOOP.RC in order to compile from within the Development Studio.

Listing 12.2. Processing loop example resource file (LOOP.RC).

```
#include "windows.h"

DlgBox DIALOG 20, 20, 90, 64
STYLE DS_MODALFRAME ¦ WS_CAPTION ¦ WS_SYSMENU
CAPTION "LOOP"
BEGIN
    DEFPUSHBUTTON "CANCEL" IDCANCEL, 29, 44, 32, 14, WS_GROUP
    CTEXT "Iterating"      -1,        0,  8, 90,  8
    CTEXT "0"              1000,       0, 23, 90,  8
END
```

Listing 12.3. Processing loop example source file (LOOP.C).

```
#include <windows.h>

HINSTANCE hInstance;
BOOL bDoAbort;
HWND hwnd;
```

```
BOOL CALLBACK DlgProc(HWND hwndDlg, UINT uMsg,
                      WPARAM wParam, LPARAM lParam)
{
    if (uMsg == WM_COMMAND && LOWORD(wParam) == IDCANCEL)
    {
        EnableWindow(hwnd, TRUE);
        DestroyWindow(hwndDlg);
        return (bDoAbort = TRUE);
    }
    return FALSE;
}

void DoIterate(HWND hwndDlg)
{
    MSG msg;
    int i;
    char buf[18];

    i = 0;
    while (!bDoAbort)
    {
        SetWindowText(GetDlgItem(hwndDlg, 1000),
                      _itoa(i++, buf, 10));
        while (PeekMessage(&msg, NULL, 0, 0, PM_REMOVE))
            DispatchMessage(&msg);
    }
}

LRESULT CALLBACK WndProc(HWND hwnd, UINT uMsg,
                         WPARAM wParam, LPARAM lParam)
{
    HWND hwndDlg;

    switch(uMsg)
    {
        case WM_LBUTTONDOWN:
            hwndDlg =
                CreateDialog(hInstance, "DlgBox", hwnd, DlgProc);
            ShowWindow(hwndDlg, SW_NORMAL);
            UpdateWindow(hwndDlg);
            EnableWindow(hwnd, FALSE);
            bDoAbort = FALSE;
            DoIterate(hwndDlg);
            break;
        case WM_DESTROY:
            PostQuitMessage(0);
            break;
        default:
            return DefWindowProc(hwnd, uMsg, wParam, lParam);
    }
    return 0;
}

int WINAPI WinMain(HINSTANCE hThisInstance,
                   HINSTANCE hPrevInstance,
                   LPSTR d3, int nCmdShow)
{
```

continues

Listing 12.3. continued

```
MSG msg;
WNDCLASS wndClass;

hInstance = hThisInstance;
if (hPrevInstance == NULL)
{
    memset(&wndClass, 0, sizeof(wndClass));
    wndClass.style = CS_HREDRAW | CS_VREDRAW;
    wndClass.lpfnWndProc = WndProc;
    wndClass.hInstance = hInstance;
    wndClass.hCursor = LoadCursor(NULL, IDC_ARROW);
    wndClass.hbrBackground = (HBRUSH)(COLOR_WINDOW + 1);
    wndClass.lpszClassName = "LOOP";
    if (!RegisterClass(&wndClass)) return FALSE;
}
hwnd = CreateWindow("LOOP", "LOOP",
                    WS_OVERLAPPEDWINDOW,
                    CW_USEDEFAULT, 0, CW_USEDEFAULT, 0,
                    NULL, NULL, hInstance, NULL);
ShowWindow(hwnd, nCmdShow);
UpdateWindow(hwnd);
while (GetMessage(&msg, NULL, 0, 0))
    DispatchMessage(&msg);
return msg.wParam;
}
```

In this program, a processing-intensive loop is started when the user clicks in the client area of the application's main window. The processing in the DoIterate function is not particularly complex; it is simply incrementing the i variable and displaying the result repeatedly until the user stops the loop.

Before the iteration is started, however, the application displays a modeless dialog box. Moreover, it disables user interaction with the application's main window by calling the EnableWindow function. This has basically the same effect as using a modal dialog box with one crucial difference; we do not need to call the DialogBox function, and thus we retain control while the dialog box is displayed.

Inside the actual iteration loop, the function PeekMessage is called with great frequency. This ensures that the application yields control; but more importantly, it also ensures that the dialog through which the iteration can be aborted responds to user interface events.

NOTE

The PeekMessage call should only be used when the application actually performs background processing. Using PeekMessage instead of GetMessage prevents Windows from performing any "idle-time" processing such as virtual memory optimizations or power management on battery-powered systems. Therefore, PeekMessage should never be used in a general-purpose message loop.

Using a Secondary Thread

While the previous technique can be used in programs intended for all Win32 platforms (including Win32s), it is somewhat cumbersome. For lengthy calculations of this kind, it is much easier to use a secondary thread in which the calculation can proceed uninterrupted, uncluttered with PeekMessage calls. Consider the example shown in Listing 12.4. This example can be compiled with the same resource file as the previous one, using identical command line instructions.

Listing 12.4. Processing in a secondary thread (LOOP.C).

```c
#include <windows.h>

HINSTANCE hInstance;
volatile BOOL bDoAbort;
HWND hwnd;

BOOL CALLBACK DlgProc(HWND hwndDlg, UINT uMsg,
                      WPARAM wParam, LPARAM lParam)
{
    if (uMsg == WM_COMMAND && LOWORD(wParam) == IDCANCEL)
    {
        EnableWindow(hwnd, TRUE);
        DestroyWindow(hwndDlg);
        return (bDoAbort = TRUE);
    }
    return FALSE;
}

DWORD WINAPI DoIterate(LPVOID hwndDlg)
{
    int i;
    char buf[18];

    i = 0;
    while (!bDoAbort)
    {
        SetWindowText(GetDlgItem((HWND)hwndDlg, 1000),
                      _itoa(i++, buf, 10));
    }
}

LRESULT CALLBACK WndProc(HWND hwnd, UINT uMsg,
                         WPARAM wParam, LPARAM lParam)
{
    HWND hwndDlg;
    DWORD dwThreadId;

    switch(uMsg)
    {
        case WM_LBUTTONDOWN:
            hwndDlg =
                CreateDialog(hInstance, "DlgBox", hwnd, DlgProc);
```

continues

Listing 12.4. continued

```c
            ShowWindow(hwndDlg, SW_NORMAL);
            UpdateWindow(hwndDlg);
            EnableWindow(hwnd, FALSE);
            bDoAbort = FALSE;
            CreateThread(NULL, 0, DoIterate, (LPDWORD)hwndDlg, 0,
                         &dwThreadId);
            break;
        case WM_DESTROY:
            PostQuitMessage(0);
            break;
        default:
            return DefWindowProc(hwnd, uMsg, wParam, lParam);
    }
    return 0;
}

int WINAPI WinMain(HINSTANCE hThisInstance,
                   HINSTANCE hPrevInstance,
                   LPSTR d3, int nCmdShow)
{
    MSG msg;
    WNDCLASS wndClass;

    hInstance = hThisInstance;
    if (hPrevInstance == NULL)
    {
        memset(&wndClass, 0, sizeof(wndClass));
        wndClass.style = CS_HREDRAW | CS_VREDRAW;
        wndClass.lpfnWndProc = WndProc;
        wndClass.hInstance = hInstance;
        wndClass.hCursor = LoadCursor(NULL, IDC_ARROW);
        wndClass.hbrBackground = (HBRUSH)(COLOR_WINDOW + 1);
        wndClass.lpszClassName = "LOOP";
        if (!RegisterClass(&wndClass)) return FALSE;
    }
    hwnd = CreateWindow("LOOP", "LOOP",
                        WS_OVERLAPPEDWINDOW,
                        CW_USEDEFAULT, 0, CW_USEDEFAULT, 0,
                        NULL, NULL, hInstance, NULL);
    ShowWindow(hwnd, nCmdShow);
    UpdateWindow(hwnd);
    while (GetMessage(&msg, NULL, 0, 0))
        DispatchMessage(&msg);
    return msg.wParam;
}
```

Perhaps the most significant difference between the two versions of LOOP.C is that in the second version, the iteration loop within the DoIterate function no longer calls PeekMessage and DispatchMessage. It does not have to; for the DoIterate function is now called from within a secondary thread, created by a call to CreateThread in the function WndProc.

Instead, the primary thread of the application continues execution after creating the secondary thread, and returns processing messages in the primary message loop in WinMain. It is this primary loop that now dispatches messages for the dialog as well.

Of particular interest is the changed declaration of the global variable bDoAbort. It is through this variable that the secondary thread is notified that it should stop executing; however, the value of this variable is set in the primary thread when the user dismisses the dialog. Of course, the optimizing compiler is not aware of this fact; so it is quite likely, that the following construct:

```
while (!bDoAbort)
{
    ...
}
```

becomes optimized in such a way that the value of bDoAbort is never reloaded from memory. Why should it be? Nothing inside the while loop modifies its value, so the optimizing compiler can legitimately keep this value in a register, for example, which means that any changes to the value stored in memory by another thread will not be noticed by this thread.

The C keyword volatile comes to our rescue. Declaring a variable volatile essentially tells the compiler that regardless of its optimization rules, the value of such a variable should be written to memory every time it is modified; and the value of such a variable should be reloaded from memory every time it is referenced. Thus, we ensure that when the primary thread sets a bDoAbort to a new value, the secondary thread will actually see this change.

Thread Objects

Our second LOOP.C example contained a call to CreateThread. Calling this function is the preferred method for creating a secondary thread. The return value of this function, which in this simple example we unceremoniously discarded, is a handle to the new *thread object*.

The thread object encapsulates the properties of a thread, including, for example, its security attributes, priority, and other information. Thread manipulation functions refer to threads through thread object handles like the one returned by CreateThread.

Our secondary thread in LOOP.C used the simplest exit mechanism; when the function designated as the thread function in the call to CreateThread returns, the thread is automatically terminated. This is because exiting the thread function amounts to an implicit call to ExitThread.

NOTE

The thread object remains valid even after a thread terminates, unless all handles to it (including the one obtained through CreateThread) have been closed through a call to CloseHandle.

A thread's exit code (the return value of the thread function or the value passed to ExitThread) can be obtained through the GetExitCodeThread function.

A thread's priority can be obtained through GetThreadPriority and set through SetThreadPriority.

A thread can be started in a *suspended* state by specifying CREATE_SUSPENDED as one of the thread's creation flags in the call to CreateThread. A suspended thread can be resumed by calling ResumeThread.

Creating and Managing Processes

Closely related to the creation and management of threads is the creation and management of entire processes.

MS-DOS programmers have long been using the exec family of functions for spawning new processes. Windows programmers have used WinExec, while those from the UNIX world are more familiar with fork. In Win32, this functionality has been consolidated into the CreateProcess function.

The CreateProcess function starts an application specified by name. It returns a handle to a *process object* that can later be used to refer to the newly created process. The process object encapsulates many properties of the new process, such as its security attributes or thread information.

The process can be terminated by a call to the ExitProcess function. A process also terminates if its primary thread terminates.

Synchronization Objects

Our little dance with the bDoAbort variable in the previous multithreaded example represents a simplistic solution to the problem of *synchronizing* two or more independently executing threads. Using a global variable served our purposes well, but may not be adequate in more complex situations.

One such situation arises when one thread has nothing to do while waiting for another thread to complete a particular task. If using a variable accessed from both threads were the only synchronization mechanism available to us, the waiting process would have to enter a loop, repeatedly checking this variable's value. If it is doing that with great frequency, the result is a lot of wasted processing capacity. This problem can be alleviated somewhat by inserting a delay between subsequent checks, for example:

```
while (!bStatus) Sleep(1000);
```

Unfortunately, in many cases this is not a satisfactory solution either; we may not be able to afford to wait tens or hundreds of milliseconds before acting.

The Win32 API provides a set of functions that can be used to wait until a specific object or set of objects becomes *signaled.* There are several types of objects to which these functions apply. Some are dedicated *synchronization objects,* and others are objects for other purposes that nevertheless have signaled and nonsignaled states. Synchronization objects include *semaphores, events,* and *mutexes.*

Semaphore objects can be used to limit the number of concurrent accesses to a shared resource. When a semaphore object is created using the CreateSemaphore function, a maximum count is specified. Each time a thread that is waiting for the semaphore is released, the semaphore's count is decreased by one. The count can be increased again using the ReleaseSemaphore function.

The state of an event object can be explicitly set to signaled or nonsignaled. When an event is created using the CreateEvent function, its initial state is specified, and so is its type. A manual-reset event must be reset to nonsignaled explicitly using the ResetEvent function; an auto-reset event is reset to the nonsignaled state every time a waiting thread is released. The event's state can be set to signaled using the SetEvent function.

A mutex (*mut*ual *ex*clusion) object is nonsignaled when it is owned by a thread. A thread obtains ownership of a mutex object when it specifies the object's handle in a wait function. The mutex object can be released using the ReleaseMutex function.

Threads wait for a single object using the function WaitForSingleObject or the functions WaitForSingleObjectEx; or for multiple objects, using WaitForMultipleObjects, WaitForMultipleObjectsEx, or MsgWaitForMultipleObjects.

Synchronization objects can also be used for interprocess synchronization. Semaphores, events, and mutexes can be named when they are created using the appropriate creation function; another process can then open a handle to these objects using OpenSemaphore, OpenEvent, and OpenMutex.

Critical section objects represent a variation of the mutex object. Critical section objects can only be used by threads of the same process, but they provide a more efficient mutual exclusion mechanism. These objects are typically used to protect critical sections of program code. A thread acquires ownership of the critical section object by calling EnterCriticalSection and releases ownership using LeaveCriticalSection. If the critical section object is owned by another thread at the time EnterCriticalSection is called, this function waits indefinitely until the critical section object is released.

Another simple yet efficient synchronization mechanism is *interlocked variable access.* Using the functions InterlockedIncrement or InterlockedDecrement, a thread can increment or decrement a variable and check the result for zero without fear of being interrupted by another thread (which might also increment or decrement the same variable before the first thread has a chance to check its value). These functions can also be used for interprocess synchronization if the variable is in shared memory.

In addition to dedicated synchronization objects, threads can also wait on certain other objects. The state of a process object becomes signaled when the process terminates; similarly, the state of a thread object becomes signaled when the thread terminates. A *change notification* object, created by FindFirstChangeNotification, becomes signaled when a specified change occurs in the file system. The state of a *console input* object becomes signaled when there is unread input waiting in the console's input buffer.

Programming with Synchronization Objects

The techniques involving multiple threads and synchronization mechanisms are available not only to programs using the graphical interface, but to other programs, such as console applications, as well. In fact, the C++ example in Listing 12.5 is exactly that, a simple console application (compile with cl mutex.cpp).

Listing 12.5. C++ example for the use of a mutex object.

```
#include <iostream.h>
#include <windows.h>

void main()
{
    HANDLE hMutex;

    hMutex = CreateMutex(NULL, FALSE, "MYMUTEX");
    cout << "Attempting to gain control of MYMUTEX object...";
    cout.flush();
    WaitForSingleObject(hMutex, INFINITE);
    cout << '\n' << "MYMUTEX control obtained." << '\n';
    cout << "Press ENTER to release the MYMUTEX object: ";
    cout.flush();
    cin.get();
    ReleaseMutex(hMutex);
}
```

This unremarkable little program creates a mutex object and attempts to gain ownership of it. When only a single copy of it is being executed (in a Windows 95 or Windows NT DOS window), it does not exhibit any revolutionary behavior.

To really see what this application has been designed to demonstrate, open a second DOS window. Run this example in both. You will see that while the first copy successfully gains control of the mutex object, the second copy becomes suspended while attempting to do so. It remains in this suspended state as long as the first copy maintains control of the mutex object; but once the object is released through ReleaseMutex, the second copy's call to WaitForSingleObject returns, and it in turn gains control of the object. In fact, there is no limit of the number of processes that can cooperate through this mechanism; you could launch as many copies of this program in separate DOS windows as you like (or as memory permits).

The reason the two instances of this program were able to refer to the same mutex object is they were both referring to the object by the same name. Using the same name identified the same global object. It is easy to see how named synchronization objects can be used in a similar fashion to synchronize threads and processes, guard access to limited resources, or provide a simple communication mechanism between processes.

Summary

Multitasking represents an operating system's ability to execute several processes concurrently. The operating system accomplishes this task by regularly performing a context switch to switch from one application to another.

In a cooperative multitasking system, applications must explicitly yield control to the operating system. The operating system does not have the capability to interrupt the execution of a noncooperating program.

In a preemptive multitasking system, the operating system can and does interrupt applications based on asynchronous events such as an interrupt from timer hardware. Such an operating system is more complex and has to deal with issues such as reentrancy.

Windows 3.1 and, consequently, Win32s are examples of a cooperative multitasking system. Windows NT and Windows 95 are preemptive multitasking systems, but Windows 95 does inherit some of the limitations of Windows 3.1 through the legacy 16-bit implementation of some of its internal functions.

Both Windows 95 and Windows NT are also multithreaded operating systems. Threads are parallel paths of execution within the same process.

Although programs in Windows 95 and Windows NT are no longer required to yield to the operating system, they should still process messages even while performing lengthy processing. This ensures that these applications remain responsive to user-interface events.

There are several methods for synchronizing the execution of threads and processes. In particular, the Win32 API provides access to special synchronization objects, such as semaphores, mutexes, and events.

Memory Management

13

With the advent of 32-bit Windows, memory management has become a much prettier subject than before. The immense mess of segments, selectors, all the paraphernalia of memory management in 16-bit mode on the segmented Intel processor architecture is completely and irreversibly gone. In fact, memory management has become so greatly simplified that for most applications, `malloc` or `new` are all that are needed; in fact, were this an introductory level book, I would probably be justified to end this chapter right here and move on to a different subject.

That said, Win32 memory management does have its own intricacies. However, programmers are no longer forced to learn about these to perform even the simplest tasks.

Processes and Memory

Win32 provides a sophisticated memory management scheme. The two most distinguishing characteristics of this are the ability to run applications in separate address spaces, and the ability to expand the amount of memory available for allocation through the use of swap files. Both of these capabilities are part of Win32 virtual memory management.

Separate Address Spaces

For programmers familiar with 16-bit Windows, one of the most difficult ideas to adjust to is the notion that an address no longer represents a well-defined spot in physical memory. While one process may find a data item at address `0x10000000`, another process may have a piece of its code running there; yet another process may regard that address as invalid. How is this accomplished?

The addresses Win32 applications use are often referred to as *logical addresses.* Every Win32 process has the entire range of 32-bit addresses available for its use (with some operating system specific restrictions, as we see shortly). When a Win32 process references data at a logical address, the computer's memory management hardware intervenes and translates the address into a *physical address* (more on it later). The same logical address may (and under most circumstances, does) translate into different physical addresses for different processes.

This mechanism has several consequences. Most are beneficial, but some actually render certain programming tasks a bit harder to accomplish.

The most obvious benefit of having separate logical address spaces is that processes can no longer accidentally overwrite code or data belonging to another process. Invalid pointers may still cause the death of the offending process but can no longer mangle data in the address space of other processes or the operating system.

On the other hand, the fact that processes no longer share the same logical address space renders the development of cooperating processes more difficult. It is no longer possible to send the address of an object in memory to another process and expect that process to be able to make use of it. That address only makes sense in the context of the sending application; in the context of the application that receives it, it is meaningless, representing a random spot in memory.

Fortunately, the Win32 API offers a set of new mechanisms for cooperating applications to use. One of these is the capability to use *shared memory*. Essentially, shared memory is a block of physical memory that is mapped into the logical address space of several processes. By writing data into, or reading data from, a block of shared memory, applications can cooperate.

> **NOTE**
>
> Under the simplified memory management regime of Win32s, all Win32 applications share the same address space.

Address Spaces

Earlier I hinted that the use of 32-bit addresses within the logical address space of a process is not entirely unrestricted. Indeed, there are some limitations. Some address ranges are reserved for use by the operating system. Moreover, the restrictions are not the same in the different Win32 environments.

Using 32-bit addresses with byte-addressable memory means a total address space of 4GB (2^{32}=4,294,967,296). Of this, Windows reserves the upper 2GB for its own use, while leaving the lower 2GB available for use by the application.

Windows 95 further reserves the lower 4MB of the address space. This area, often referred to as the *Compatibility Arena* in Microsoft documentation, exists for compatibility with 16-bit DOS and Windows applications.

I mentioned that Win32 applications run in separate address spaces. This is true inasmuch as the nonreserved areas of the logical address space are concerned. However, the situation of the reserved areas is somewhat different.

Under Windows 95, all reserved areas are shared. In other words, if one application finds a particular object at a memory location in one of the two reserved areas (lower 4MB or upper 2GB), all other applications are guaranteed to find the same object there. However, applications should not rely on this behavior; otherwise, the program will be incompatible with Windows NT (and thus not qualify for the new Microsoft logo program). Besides, as we see shortly, there are easy ways for applications to request a shared area in memory explicitly, and that mechanism works well under both Windows NT and Windows 95.

Windows 95 further divides the upper 2GB into two additional arenas. The arena between 2GB and 3GB is the *shared arena* that holds shared memory, memory-mapped files, and some 16-bit components. The *reserved system arena* between 3GB and 4GB is where all of the operating system's privileged code resides. This arena is not addressable by nonprivileged application programs.

Virtual Memory

In the previous sections, I discreetly avoided one question. How exactly are logical addresses mapped to physical memory? After all, most computers do not have enough memory to hold several times the 4GB of memory that each application can address. (Even if they did, the power and heat dissipation requirements of that much memory might represent somewhat of a problem. Or the price.)

The answer is, not all logical addresses of an application are actually mapped to physical storage; and those that are may not be mapped to physical *memory*.

Ever since the introduction of Windows 3.1, Windows has been able to use a *swap file*. The swap mechanism expands the amount of memory that the system can use by storing unused blocks of data on disk and loading them as needed. While swap files are several orders of magnitude slower than RAM, their use enables the system to run more applications or applications that are more resource-intensive.

The reason swap files can be used efficiently is that most applications allocate blocks of memory that are rarely used. For example, if you use a word processor to edit two documents simultaneously, it may happen that while you work on one document, you do not touch the other for extended periods of time. The operating system may free up physical memory in which the other document resides, *swapping* the document to disk; the physical memory then becomes available for other applications. When, after some time, you switch to the other document, you may notice some disk activity and a slight delay before the document is displayed; this is when the operating system loads the relevant portions of the swap file back into memory, possibly swapping out other blocks of recently not used data in the process.

Figure 13.1 shows how the operating system and the computer's hardware accomplish the mapping of logical addresses. A table that is often called the *page table* contains information on all blocks or *pages* of memory. In effect, this table maps blocks in an application's logical address space to blocks in physical memory or portions of the swap file.

When a logical address is mapped to actual physical memory, the mapping is dereferenced and the data is read or written as requested. As the operation is supported by the processor's hardware, it does not require any extra time to resolve memory addresses this way.

When the logical address maps to a block in the system's swap file, a different series of events takes place. The attempt to reference such an invalid address triggers the operating system into action. The operating system loads the requested block of data from the swap file into memory, possibly swapping out other blocks of data from memory to disk to make space. After the requested data is in physical memory and the page table is updated, control is returned to the application. The access to the requested memory location can now be completed successfully. All this is completely transparent to the application; the only sign that would indicate that the requested block of memory was not readily available is the delay caused by the swapping operation.

FIGURE 13.1.

Mapping of logical addresses to physical memory.

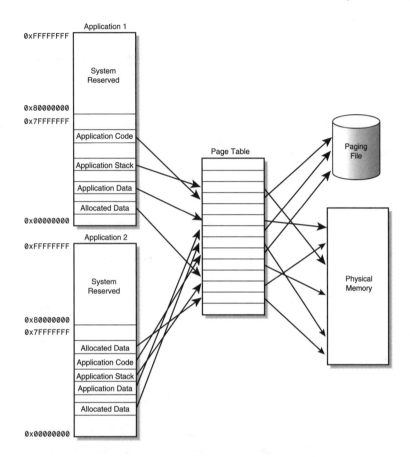

The fact that logical addresses may map to physical memory locations, blocks of the swap file, or nothing at all implies interesting possibilities. Furthermore, the existence of a mechanism that maps the contents of a file (namely, the swap file) to logical addresses also carries the potential for useful features. Indeed, the Win32 API provides the means for applications to explicitly manage virtual memory and to access disk data through *memory-mapped files*. These and other memory management mechanisms are explored in the next section.

32-Bit Programs

Because most Windows programmers have extensive experience in programming 16-bit Windows, it is perhaps helpful to begin our review of 32-bit memory management issues with the differences between 16- and 32-bit programs. A number of issues, such as integer size, the disappearance of the far and near specifiers, or differences in address calculations, affect coding practices.

Integer Size

One of the most striking differences between the 16-bit and 32-bit environments can be demonstrated by the simple example shown in Listing 13.1. This program can be compiled from the command line using `cl intsize.cpp`.

Listing 13.1: Determining integer size.

```
#include <iostream.h>

void main(void)
{
    cout << "sizeof(int) = " << sizeof(int);
}
```

When you run this program, it prints the following result:

```
sizeof(int) = 4
```

UNIX programmers are probably relieved to see this result. Gone is the nightmare of trying to port UNIX programs that implicitly rely on integers and pointers both being of the same size (32 bits). Programmers of 16-bit Windows, on the other hand, are facing the added difficulty of having to review older code for any signs of an explicit dependence on the 16-bit integer size.

One thing that has not changed is the size of types defined by Windows. Specifically, the types WORD and DWORD remain 16 and 32 bits wide, respectively. Use of these types when saving application data to disk ensures that the contents of a disk file remain readable by both the 16-and the 32-bit versions of the same application. In contrast, if an application used the int type when writing to disk, the contents of the disk file would be operating system dependent.

Type Modifiers and Macros

An obvious consequence of 32-bit addressing is that you no longer need to use type modifiers to distinguish between near and far pointers, or to specify huge data. Does this mean that existing programs must be modified and all references to the _near, _far, or _huge keywords must be removed? Fortunately not; the 32-bit C/C++ compiler simply ignores these keywords to ensure backward compatibility.

Similarly, all the types that used to be defined in the windows.h header file, such as LPSTR for a far pointer to characters or LPVOID for a far pointer to a void type, still remain available. In the 32-bit environment, these types are simply defined to be equivalent to their near counterparts; thus, LPSTR is the same as PSTR, and LPVOID is the same as PVOID. To maintain backward compatibility (should you ever need to recompile your code with a 16-bit compiler), it is generally a good idea to continue using the correct types. This is further encouraged by the fact that the published interface to most Windows functions uses the correct (near or far) types.

Address Calculations

Naturally, if your program performs address calculations specific to the segmented Intel architecture, it needs to be modified. (Such calculations would also be in violation of the platform-independent philosophy of the Win32 API, making it difficult to compile your program under Windows NT on the MIPS, Alpha, or other platforms.)

A particular case concerns the use of the LOWORD macro. In Windows 3.1, memory allocated with GlobalAlloc was aligned on a segment boundary, with the offset set to 0. Some programmers used this fact to set addresses by simply modifying the low word of a pointer variable using the LOWORD macro. Under the Win32 API, the assumption that an allocated memory block starts on a segment boundary is no longer valid. The questionable practice of using LOWORD this way will no longer work.

Library Functions

In the 16-bit environment, many functions had two versions: one for near addresses, and one for far addresses. It was often necessary to use both. For example, in medium model programs, one frequently had to use _fstrcpy to copy characters from or to a far memory location. In the 32-bit environment, these functions are obsolete.

The header file windowsx.h defines these obsolete function names to refer to their regular counterparts. By including this file in your program that contains older source code, you can avoid having to manually comb through your source files and remove or change these obsolete function references.

Memory Models

Ever since the introduction of the IBM PC, programmers have learned to hate the multitude of compiler switches and options that control addressing behavior. Tiny, small, compact, medium, large, huge, custom memory models, address conversions, 64KB code and data segments—to make a long story short, in 32-bit Windows, this nightmare is no longer. There is only one memory model, in which both addresses and code reside in a flat 32-bit memory space.

Selector Functions

The Windows 3.1 API contains a set of functions (for example, AllocSelector, FreeSelector) that enable applications to directly manipulate physical memory. These functions are not available in the Win32 API; 32-bit applications should not attempt to manipulate physical memory in any way. Dealing with physical memory is a task best left to device drivers.

Simple Memory Management

As I mention at the beginning of this chapter, memory allocation in the 32-bit environment is greatly simplified. It is no longer necessary to separately allocate memory and lock it for use. The distinction between global and local heaps has disappeared. On the other hand, the 32-bit environment presents a set of new challenges.

Memory Allocation via *malloc* and *new*

The venerable set of memory management functions in Windows versions prior to 3.1, such as GlobalAlloc and GlobalLock, addressed a problem specific to *real mode* programming of the 80×86 processor family. Because applications used actual physical addresses to access objects in memory, there was no other way for the operating system to perform memory management functions. It was necessary for applications to abide by a convoluted mechanism by which they regularly relinquished control of these objects. This enabled the operating system to move these objects around as necessary. In other words, applications had to actively take part in memory management and cooperate with the operating system. Because malloc not only allocated memory but also locked it in place, use of this function caused dangerous fragmentation of available memory.

Windows 3.1 uses Intel processes in *protected mode*. In protected mode, applications no longer have access to physical addresses. The operating system is able to move a memory block around even while applications hold valid addresses to it that they obtained through a call to GlobalLock or LocalLock. Using malloc not only became safe, it became the recommended practice. Several implementations of this function (such as those in Microsoft C/C++ Version 7 and later) also solved another problem. Because of a system-wide limit of 8,192 selectors, the number of times applications could call memory allocation functions without subsequently freeing up memory was limited. By providing a suballocation scheme, the newer malloc implementations greatly helped applications that routinely allocated a large number of small memory blocks.

The 32-bit environment further simplifies memory allocation by eliminating the difference between global and local heaps. (It is actually possible, although definitely not recommended, to allocate memory with GlobalAlloc and free it using LocalFree.)

The bottom line? In a Win32 application, allocate memory with malloc or new, release it with free or delete, and let the operating system worry about all other aspects of memory management. For most applications, this approach is perfectly sufficient.

The Problem of Stray Pointers

Working with a 32-bit linear address space has one unexpected consequence. In the 16-bit environment, every call to GlobalAlloc reserved a new *selector*. In protected mode in the Intel segmented architecture, selectors define blocks of memory; as part of the selector, the length of the block is also specified. Attempting to address memory outside the allocated limits of a selector resulted in a protection violation.

In the 32-bit environment, automatic and static objects, global and local dynamically allocated memory, the stack, and everything else belonging to the same application shares the application's heap and is accessed through flat 32-bit addresses. The operating system is less likely to catch stray pointers. The possibility of memory corruption through such pointers is greater, increasing the programmer's responsibility in ensuring that pointers stay within their intended bounds.

Consider, for example, the following code fragment:

```
HGLOBAL hBuf1, hBuf2;
LPSTR lpszBuf1, lpszBuf2;

hBuf1 = GlobalAlloc(GPTR, 1024);
hBuf2 = GlobalAlloc(GPTR, 1024);
lpszBuf1 = GlobalLock(hBuf1);
lpszBuf2 = GlobalLock(hBuf2);
lpszBuf1[2000] = 'X';   /* Error! */
```

In this code fragment, an attempt is made to write past the boundaries of the first buffer allocated via GlobalAlloc. In the 16-bit environment, this results in a protection violation when the attempt is made to address a memory location outside the limits of the selector reserved by the first GlobalAlloc call. In the 32-bit environment, however, the memory location referenced by lpszBuf1[2000] is probably valid, pointing to somewhere inside the second buffer. An attempt to write to this address will succeed and corrupt the contents of the second buffer.

On the bright side, it is practically impossible for an application to corrupt another application's memory space through stray pointers. This increases the overall stability of the operating system.

Sharing Memory Between Applications

Because each 32-bit application has a private virtual address space, it is no longer possible for such applications to share memory by simply passing pointers to each other in Windows messages. The GMEM_DDESHARE flag is no longer functional. Passing the handle of a 32-bit memory block to another application is meaningless and futile; the handle only refers to a random spot in the private virtual address space of the recipient program.

If it is necessary for two applications to communicate using shared memory, they can do this by using the DDEML library or by using memory-mapped files, which are described later in this chapter.

Virtual Memory and Advanced Memory Management

In the Win32 programming environment, applications have improved control over how they allocate and use memory. An extended set of memory management functions is provided. Figure 13.2 shows the different levels of memory management functions in the Win32 API.

FIGURE 13.2.

Memory management functions in the 32-bit environment.

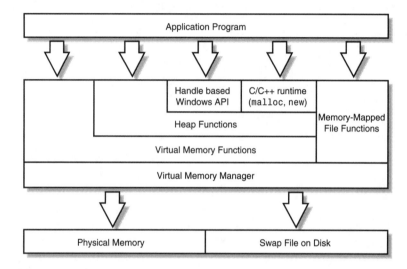

Win32 Virtual Memory Management

Figure 13.1 might appear to suggest that pages of virtual memory must always be mapped to either physical memory or a paging (or swap) file. This is not the case; Win32 memory management makes a distinction between reserved pages and committed pages. A *committed page* of virtual memory is a page that is backed by physical storage, either in physical memory or in the paging file. In contrast, a *reserved page* is not backed by physical storage at all.

Why would you want to reserve addresses without allocating corresponding physical storage? One possibility is that you might not know in advance how much space is needed for a certain operation. This mechanism enables you to reserve a contiguous range of addresses in the virtual memory space of your process, without committing physical resources to it until such resources are actually needed. When a reference to an uncommitted page is made, the operating system generates an exception that your program can catch through structured exception handling. In turn, your program can instruct the operating system to commit the page, and then it can continue the processing that was interrupted by the exception. Incidentally, this is how Windows 95 performs many of its own memory management functions, such as stack allocation or manipulating the page table itself.

One real-life example concerns sparse matrices, which are two-dimensional arrays that have most of their array elements equal to zero. Sparse matrices appear frequently in technical applications. It is possible to reserve memory for the entire matrix but commit only those pages that contain nonzero elements, thus reducing the consumption of physical resources significantly while still keeping the application code simple.

Virtual Memory Functions

An application can reserve memory through the `VirtualAlloc` function. With this function, the application can explicitly specify the address and the size of the memory block about to be reserved. Additional parameters specify the type of the allocation (committed or reserved) and access protection flags. For example, the following code reserves 1MB of memory, starting at address `0x10000000`, for reading and writing:

```
VirtualAlloc(0x10000000, 0x00100000, MEM_RESERVE, PAGE_READWRITE);
```

Later, the application can commit pages of memory by repeated calls to the `VirtualAlloc` function. Memory (reserved or committed) can be freed using `VirtualFree`.

A special use of `VirtualAlloc` concerns the establishment of *guard pages*. Guard pages act as one-shot alarms, raising an exception when the application attempts to access them. Guard pages can thus be used to protect against stray pointers that point past array boundaries, for example.

`VirtualLock` can be used to lock a memory block in physical memory (RAM), preventing the system from swapping out the block to the paging file on disk. This can be used to ensure that critical data can be accessed without disk I/O. This function should be used sparingly because it can severely degrade system performance by restricting the operating system's capability to manage memory. Memory that was locked through `VirtualLock` can be unlocked using the `VirtualUnlock` function.

An application can change the protection flags of committed pages of memory using the `VirtualProtect` function. `VirtualProtectEx` can be used to change the protection flags of a block of memory belonging to another process. Finally, `VirtualQuery` can be used to obtain information about pages of memory; `VirtualQueryEx` obtains information about memory owned by another process.

Listing 13.2 shows another command line application, one that demonstrates the use of virtual memory functions. This program can be compiled with `cl /GX sparse.cpp`.

Listing 13.2. Handling sparse matrices using virtual memory management.

```
#include <iostream.h>
#include <windows.h>

#define PAGESIZE 0x1000
```

continues

Listing 13.2. continued

```c
void main(void)
{
    double (*pdMatrix)[10000];
    double d;
    LPVOID lpvResult;
    int x, y, i, n;

    pdMatrix = (double (*)[10000])VirtualAlloc(NULL,
                            100000000 * sizeof(double),
                            MEM_RESERVE, PAGE_NOACCESS);
    if (pdMatrix == NULL)
    {
        cout << "Failed to reserve memory.\n";
        exit(1);
    }

    n = 0;
    for (i = 0; i < 10; i++)
    {
        x = rand() % 10000;
        y = rand() % 10000;
        d = (double)rand();
        cout << "MATRIX[" << x << ',' << y << "] = " << d << '\n';
        try
        {
            pdMatrix[x][y] = d;
        }
        catch (...)
        {
            if (d != 0.0)
            {
                n++;
                lpvResult = VirtualAlloc((LPVOID)(&pdMatrix[x][y]),
                            PAGESIZE, MEM_COMMIT, PAGE_READWRITE);
                if (lpvResult == NULL)
                {
                    cout << "Cannot commit memory.\n";
                    exit(1);
                }
                pdMatrix[x][y] = d;
            }
        }
    }
    cout << "Matrix populated, " << n << " pages used.\n";
    cout << "Total bytes committed: " << n * PAGESIZE << '\n';

    for(;;)
    {
        cout << "   Enter row: ";
        cout.flush();
        cin >> x;
        cout << "Enter column: ";
        cout.flush();
        cin >> y;

        try
```

```
        {
            d = pdMatrix[x][y];
        }
        catch (...)
        {
            cout << "Exception handler was invoked.\n";
            d = 0.0;
        }
        cout << "MATRIX[" << x << ',' << y << "] = " << d << '\n';
    }
}
```

This program creates a double-precision matrix of 10,000 by 10,000 elements. However, instead of allocating a whopping 800,000,000 bytes of memory, it only allocates memory on an as-needed basis. This mechanism is especially suitable for matrices that have very few nonzero elements; in this example, only 10 out of 100,000,000 elements are set to random nonzero values.

The program first reserves, but does not commit, 800,000,000 bytes of memory for the matrix. Next, it assigns random values to 10 randomly selected elements. If the element falls on a page of virtual memory that is not yet committed (has no backing in physical memory or in the paging file), an exception is raised. The exception is caught using the C++ exception handling mechanism. The exception handler checks whether the value to be assigned is nonzero; if so, it commits the page in question and repeats the assignment.

NOTE

In this simple example, we assumed that the exception we catch is always a Win32 structured exception indicating a memory access violation. In complex programs, this assumption may not always be valid and a more elaborate exception handling mechanism may be necessary to reliably identify exceptions.

In the last part of the program, the user is invited to enter row and column index values. The program then attempts to retrieve the value of the specified matrix element. If the element falls on a page that has not been committed, an exception is raised; this time, it is interpreted as an indication that the selected matrix element is zero.

The rudimentary user-interface loop of this program does not include a halting condition; the program can be stopped using Ctrl+C.

The program's output looks similar to the following:

```
MATRIX[41,8467] = 6334
MATRIX[6500,9169] = 15724
MATRIX[1478,9358] = 26962
MATRIX[4464,5705] = 28145
MATRIX[3281,6827] = 9961
```

```
MATRIX[491,2995] = 11942
MATRIX[4827,5436] = 32391
MATRIX[4604,3902] = 153
MATRIX[292,2382] = 17421
MATRIX[8716,9718] = 19895
Matrix populated, 10 pages used.
Total bytes committed: 40960
   Enter row: 41
Enter column: 8467
MATRIX[41,8467] = 6334
   Enter row: 41
Enter column: 8400
MATRIX[41,8400] = 0
   Enter row: 1
Enter column: 1
Exception handler was invoked.
MATRIX[1,1] = 0
   Enter row:
```

Heap Functions

In addition to their default heap, processes can create additional heaps using the HeapCreate function. Heap management functions can then be used to allocate and free memory blocks in the newly created private heap. A possible use of this mechanism involves the creation of a private heap at startup, specifying a size that is sufficient for the application's memory allocation needs. Failure to create the heap using HeapCreate can cause the process to terminate; however, if HeapCreate succeeds, the process is assured that the memory it requires is present and available.

After a heap is created via HeapCreate, processes can allocate memory from it using HeapAlloc. HeapRealloc can be used to change the size of a previously allocated memory block, and HeapFree deallocates memory blocks and returns them to the heap. The size of a previously allocated block can be obtained using HeapSize.

It is important to note that the memory allocated by HeapAlloc is no different from memory obtained using the standard memory allocation functions such as GlobalAlloc, GlobalLock, or malloc.

Heap management functions can also be used on the default heap of the process. A handle to the default heap can be obtained using GetProcessHeap. The function GetProcessHeaps returns a list of all heap handles owned by the process.

A heap can be destroyed using the function HeapDestroy. This function should not be used on the default heap handle of the process that is returned by GetProcessHeap. (Destroying the default heap would mean destroying the application's stack, global and automatic variables, and so on, with obviously disastrous consequences).

The function HeapCompact attempts to compact the specified heap by coalescing adjacent free blocks of memory and decommitting large free blocks. Note that objects allocated on the heap by HeapAlloc are not movable, so the heap can easily become fragmented. HeapCompact will not unfragment a badly fragmented heap.

Windows API and C Run-time Memory Management

At the top of the hierarchy of memory management functions are the standard Windows and C run-time memory management functions. As noted earlier, these functions are likely to prove adequate for the memory management requirements of most applications. Handle-based memory management functions provided in the Windows API include GlobalAlloc and LocalAlloc, GlobalLock and LocalLock, GlobalFree and LocalFree. The C/C++ run-time library contains the malloc family of functions (malloc, realloc, calloc, free, and other functions). These functions are safe to use and provide compatibility with the 16-bit environment, should it become necessary to build applications that can be compiled as both 16-bit and 32-bit programs.

Miscellaneous and Obsolete Functions

In addition to the API functions already described, a number of miscellaneous functions are also available to the Win32 programmer. Several other functions that were available under Windows 3.1 have been deleted or become obsolete.

Memory manipulation functions include CopyMemory, FillMemory, MoveMemory, and ZeroMemory. These functions are equivalent to their C run-time counterparts such as memcpy, memmove, or memset.

A set of Windows API functions is provided to verify whether a given pointer provides a specific type of access to an address or range of addresses. These functions are IsBadCodePtr, IsBadStringPtr, IsBadReadPtr, and IsBadWritePtr. For the latter pair, huge versions (IsBadHugeReadPtr, IsBadHugeWritePtr) are also provided for backward compatibility with Windows 3.1.

Information about available memory can be obtained using GlobalMemoryStatus. This function replaces the obsolete GetFreeSpace function.

Other obsolete functions include all the functions that manipulate selectors (for example, AllocSelector, ChangeSelector, and FreeSelector); manipulate the processor's stack (SwitchStackBack, SwitchStackTo); manipulate segments (LockSegment, UnlockSegment); or manipulate MS-DOS memory (GlobalDOSAlloc, GlobalDOSFree).

Memory-Mapped Files and Shared Memory

Earlier in this chapter, I mentioned that applications are no longer capable of communicating using global memory created with the GMEM_DDESHARE flag. Instead, they must use memory-mapped files to share memory. What are memory-mapped files?

Normally, the virtual memory mechanism enables an operating system to map nonexistent memory to a disk file, called the paging file. It is possible to look at this the other way around and see the virtual memory mechanism as a method of referring to the contents of a file, namely the paging file, through pointers as if the paging file were a memory object. In other words, the mechanism maps the contents of the paging file to memory addresses. If this can be done with the paging file, why not with other files? Memory-mapped files represent this natural extension to the virtual memory management mechanism.

You can create a file mapping by using the `CreateFileMapping` function. You can also use the `OpenFileMapping` function to enable an application to open an existing named mapping. The `MapViewOfFile` function maps a portion of the file to a block of virtual memory.

The special thing about memory-mapped files is that they are shared between applications. That is, if two applications open the same named file mapping, they will, in effect, create a block of shared memory.

Isn't it a bit of an overkill to be forced to use a disk file when the objective is merely to share a few bytes between two applications? Actually, it is not necessary to explicitly open and use a disk file in order to obtain a mapping in memory. Applications can submit the special handle value of `0xFFFFFFFF` to `CreateFileMapping` in order to obtain a mapping to the system paging file itself. This, in effect, creates a block of shared memory.

Listings 13.3 and 13.4 demonstrate the use of shared memory objects for intertask communication. They implement a very simple mechanism where one program, the client, deposits a simple message (a null-terminated string) in shared memory for the other program. This other program, the server, receives the message and displays it. These programs are written for the Windows 95 or Windows NT command line. To see how they work, start two MS-DOS windows, start the server program first in one of the windows, and then start the client program in the other. The client sends its message to the server; the server, in turn, displays the message it receives and then terminates.

Listing 13.3. Intertask communication using shared memory: the server.

```
#include <iostream.h>
#include <windows.h>

void main(void)
{
    HANDLE hmmf;
    LPSTR lpMsg;

    hmmf = CreateFileMapping((HANDLE)0xFFFFFFFF, NULL,
                          PAGE_READWRITE, 0, 0x1000, "MMFDEMO");
    if (hmmf == NULL)
    {
        cout << "Failed to allocated shared memory.\n";
        exit(1);
```

```
    }
    lpMsg = (LPSTR)MapViewOfFile(hmmf, FILE_MAP_WRITE, 0, 0, 0);
    if (lpMsg == NULL)
    {
        cout << "Failed to map shared memory.\n";
        exit(1);
    }
    lpMsg[0] = '\0';
    while (lpMsg[0] == '\0') Sleep(1000);
    cout << "Message received: " << lpMsg << '\n';
    UnmapViewOfFile(lpMsg);
}
```

Listing 13.4. Intertask communication using shared memory: the client.

```
#include <iostream.h>
#include <windows.h>

void main(void)
{
    HANDLE hmmf;
    LPSTR lpMsg;

    hmmf = CreateFileMapping((HANDLE)0xFFFFFFFF, NULL,
                        PAGE_READWRITE, 0, 0x1000, "MMFDEMO");
    if (hmmf == NULL)
    {
        cout << "Failed to allocated shared memory.\n";
        exit(1);
    }
    lpMsg = (LPSTR)MapViewOfFile(hmmf, FILE_MAP_WRITE, 0, 0, 0);
    if (lpMsg == NULL)
    {
        cout << "Failed to map shared memory.\n";
        exit(1);
    }
    strcpy(lpMsg, "This is my message.");
    cout << "Message sent: " << lpMsg << '\n';
    UnmapViewOfFile(lpMsg);
}
```

These two programs are nearly identical. They both start by creating a file mapping of the system paging file with the name MMFDEMO. After the mapping is successfully created, the server sets the first byte of the mapping to zero and enters a wait loop, checking once a second to see whether the first byte is nonzero. The client, in turn, deposits a message string at the same location and exits. When the server notices that the data is present, it prints the result and also exits.

Both programs can be compiled from the command line: `cl mmfsrvr.cpp` and `cl mmfclnt.cpp`.

Shared Memory and Based Pointers

A shared memory-mapped file object may not necessarily appear at the same address for all processes. While shared memory objects are mapped to identical locations in the address spaces of Windows 95 processes, the same is not true in Windows NT. This can be a problem if applications want to include pointers in the shared data. One solution to this problem is to use based pointers and set them to be relative to the start of the mapping area.

Based pointers are a Microsoft-specific extension of the C/C++ language. A based pointer is declared using the __based keyword, in a fashion similar to the following:

```
void *vpBase;
void __based(vpBase) *vpData;
```

References through the based pointer always point to data relative to the specified base. Their utility extends beyond shared memory; based pointers can also be very useful when saving data that contains pointers to disk.

Threads and Memory Management

The multithreaded nature of 32-bit Windows presents some additional challenges when it comes to memory management. As threads may concurrently access the same objects in memory, it is possible that one thread's operation on a variable is interrupted by another; obviously, a synchronization mechanism is needed to avoid this. In other situations, threads may want private copies of a data object, instead of a shared copy.

Interlocked Variable Access

The first of the two problems I mentioned is solved in many cases by *interlocked variable access.* This mechanism enables a thread to change the value of an integer variable and check the result without the possibility of being interrupted by another thread.

Under normal circumstances, if you increment or decrement a variable within a thread, it is possible that another thread changes the value of this variable once again before the first thread has a change to examine its value. The functions InterlockedIncrement and InterlockedDecrement can be used to atomically increment or decrement a 32-bit value and check the result. A third function, InterlockedExchange, can be used to atomically set a variable's value and retrieve the old value, without the fear of being interrupted by another thread.

Thread-Local Storage

Although automatic variables are always local to the instance of the function in which they are allocated, the same is not true for global or static objects. If your code relies heavily on such objects, it may prove to be very difficult to make your application thread-safe.

Fortunately, the Win32 API offers a mechanism to allocate *thread-local storage*. The TlsAlloc function can be used to reserve a *TLS Index*, which is a DWORD sized space. Threads can use this space, for example, to store a pointer to a private block of memory through the TlsSetValue and TlsGetValue functions. The TlsFree function can be used to release the TLS index.

If this doesn't sound easy, don't despair. The Visual C++ compiler provides an alternative mechanism that is much easier to use. Data objects can be declared thread local using the thread type modifier. For example

```
__declspec(thread) int i;
```

Using __declspec(thread) is problematic in DLLs because of a problem in extending the global memory allocation of a DLL at runtime to accommodate thread-local objects. It is recommended that you use the TLS APIs, such as TlsAlloc, in code that is intended to run in a DLL.

Accessing Physical Memory and I/O Ports

Programmers of 16-bit Windows are used to the idea of accessing physical memory or the input/output ports of Intel processors directly. For example, it is possible to write a 16-bit application that accesses a custom hardware device through memory-mapped I/O. It is natural to expect that those programming practices can be carried over to the 32-bit operating system.

However, this is not the case. Win32 is a *platform-independent* operating system specification. As such, anything that introduces platform (hardware) dependence is fundamentally incompatible with the operating system. This includes all kinds of access to actual physical hardware, such as ports, physical memory addresses, or anything else.

So what can you do if your task is to write an application that communicates directly with hardware? The answer is that you require one of the various DDKs (Device Driver Kits). Through the DDK, it is possible to create a driver library that encapsulates all low-level access to the device and keep your high-level Win32 application free of platform dependencies.

Summary

Memory management in Win32 is markedly different from memory management in 16-bit Windows. Applications need no longer be concerned about issues related to the Intel segmented architecture; on the other hand, new capabilities mean new responsibilities for the programmer.

Win32 applications run in separate address spaces. A pointer in the context of one application is meaningless in the context of another. All applications have access to a 4GB address space through 32-bit addresses (although the different Win32 implementations reserve certain portions of this address space for special purposes).

Win32 operating systems use virtual memory management to map a logical address in an application's address space to a physical address in memory or a block of data in the system's swap or paging file. Applications can explicitly use virtual memory management capabilities to create memory-mapped files, or to reserve, but not commit, huge blocks of virtual memory.

Memory-mapped files offer a very efficient intertask communication mechanism. By gaining access to the same memory-mapped file object, two or more applications can utilize such a file as shared memory.

Special features address the unique problems of memory management in threads. Through interlocked variable access, threads can perform atomic operations on shared objects. Through thread-local storage, threads can allocate privately owned objects in memory.

Many of the old Windows and DOS memory management functions are no longer available. Because of the platform independence of Win32, applications can no longer access physical memory directly. If it is necessary to directly access hardware (as in the case when custom hardware is used), it may be necessary to utilize the appropriate Device Driver Kit.

File Management

14

The Win32 API offers a set of new functions and concepts for accessing and managing disk files. This is in addition to the low-level and stream I/O functions that are available as part of the C and C++ run-time libraries. This chapter reviews all forms of file handling that are available to 32-bit Windows applications.

Figure 14.1 illustrates the relationship between DOS/UNIX-style "low-level" I/O, C/C++ style stream I/O, and the Win32 file I/O functions.

FIGURE 14.1.

I/O functions.

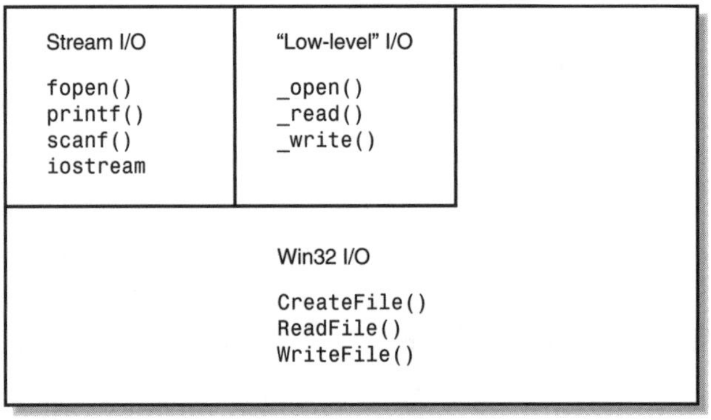

```
┌─────────────────────┬─────────────────────────────┐
│ Stream I/O          │ "Low-level" I/O             │
│                     │                             │
│ fopen()             │ _open()                     │
│ printf()            │ _read()                     │
│ scanf()             │ _write()                    │
│ iostream            │                             │
│         ┌───────────┴─────────────────────────────┤
│         │                                         │
│         │           Win32 I/O                     │
│         │                                         │
│         │           CreateFile()                  │
│         │           ReadFile()                    │
│         │           WriteFile()                   │
└─────────┴─────────────────────────────────────────┘
```

Win32 applications should preferably use Win32 file I/O operations, which provide full access to Win32 security features and other attributes and also enable asynchronous, or *overlapped*, input and output operations.

File System Overview

A typical file is a collection of data stored on nonvolatile media, such as a magnetic disk. Files are organized into *file systems*. File systems implement a particular scheme for storing files on physical media and for representing various file attributes such as filenames, permissions, and ownership information.

File system information can be obtained by calling the function `GetVolumeInformation`. Information about the nature of the storage device can be obtained by a call to `GetDriveType`.

Supported File Systems

Windows NT recognizes four file systems. File Allocation Table (FAT) file systems are compatible with earlier versions of DOS. High Performance File System (HPFS) is the file system used by the OS/2 operating system. New Technology File System (NTFS) is the "native" file system of Windows NT. Finally, an extension of the FAT file system, the Protected Mode FAT file system, supports long filenames on volumes otherwise compatible with earlier versions of MS-DOS.

From an application's point of view, the major difference between the various file systems is the support for special attributes. For example, NTFS volumes support the concept of file ownership and security attributes, which are unavailable in the case of FAT file systems.

> **NOTE**
>
> Windows 95 only recognizes FAT and Protected Mode FAT file systems.

CD-ROM

ISO-9660 CD-ROM volumes appear as regular FAT volumes to applications. There is no support for long filenames or special attributes (for example, "Rock Ridge extensions").

Network Volumes

Windows supports file sharing across a network. Network file systems may appear under local drive letters through network redirection. Alternatively, applications may access files across a network using UNC (Universal Naming Convention) names, such as \\server\vol1\myfile.txt. Different networks may or may not support long filenames.

File and Volume Compression

Starting with Version 3.51, Windows NT now supports per-file compression on NTFS volumes. On the other hand, Windows 95 supports DriveSpace compression of FAT volumes. Unfortunately, the two compression mechanisms are not compatible; at present, only uncompressed FAT volumes can be accessed by both Windows 95 and Windows NT.

Win32 File Objects

In 32-bit Windows, an open file is treated as an operating system object. It is referenced through a Win32 handle; this is not to be confused with the DOS/UNIX style "file handles," which are basically integers assigned by the operating system to represent open files.

Because a file is a kernel object, in addition to file system operations, many other handle-based operations are also possible. For example, it is possible to use the WaitForSingleObject function on a file handle opened for console I/O.

Creating and Opening Files

A file object is created by a call to the CreateFile function. This function can be used to both create a new file and open an existing file. The function name may appear to be a misnomer unless you realize that what the function creates is the *file object*, which represents either a new or an existing file on the storage device.

Parameters to this function specify the access mode (read or write), file sharing mode, security attributes, creation flags, file attributes, and an optional file that serves as an attribute template.

For example, to open the file `C:\README.TXT` for reading, one would issue the following call to `CreateFile`:

```
hReadme = CreateFile("C:\\README.TXT", GENERIC_READ, 0, NULL,
                     OPEN_EXISTING, FILE_ATTRIBUTE_NORMAL, 0);
```

The first parameter is a filename. Applications can also use the UNC name. The length of the filename is limited to the value of the `MAX_PATH` constant. Under Windows NT, this can be circumvented by prepending `"\\?\"` to the path and calling the wide version of `CreateFile`, `CreateFileW`. The prefix `"\\?\"` tells the operating system not to parse the pathname.

Another parameter that deserves special interest is the fourth parameter; this is of type `LPSECURITY_ATTRIBUTES`. Through this parameter, applications request security attributes for the new file object and may also specify the security attributes for newly created files. However, for this parameter to have any effect, it must be supported by the operating system and the file system. In other words, unless the file is on an NTFS volume and the operating system is Windows NT, advanced security features will not be available. Nevertheless, one member of the `SECURITY_ATTRIBUTES` structure, the `bInheritHandle` member, is still useful; it controls whether a handle to the object is inherited by child processes.

Win32 applications should not use the `OpenFile` function for opening files; this function is provided only for compatibility with 16-bit Windows.

An open file object can be closed by calling the `CloseHandle` function.

Simple Input and Output

Input and output are accomplished with the help of the `ReadFile` and `WriteFile` functions. Need I say more? Listing 14.1 contains a simple program (compile with `cl filecopy.c`), which copies the contents of one file to another using the Win32 functions `CreateFile`, `ReadFile`, and `WriteFile`.

Listing 14.1. Copying a file using Win32 file functions.

```
#include <windows.h>
#include <iostream.h>

void main(int argc, char *argv[])
{
    HANDLE hSrc, hDest;
    DWORD dwRead, dwWritten;
```

```
        char pBuffer[1024];

        if (argc != 3)
        {
            cout << "Usage: " << argv[0] << " srcfile destfile\n";
            exit(1);
        }

        hSrc = CreateFile(argv[1], GENERIC_READ, 0, NULL,
                        OPEN_EXISTING, FILE_ATTRIBUTE_NORMAL, 0);
        if (hSrc == INVALID_HANDLE_VALUE)
        {
            cout << "Unable to open " << argv[1] << '\n';
            exit(1);
        }

        hDest = CreateFile(argv[2], GENERIC_WRITE, 0, NULL,
                        CREATE_ALWAYS, FILE_ATTRIBUTE_NORMAL, 0);
        if (hDest == INVALID_HANDLE_VALUE)
        {
            cout << "Unable to create " << argv[2] << '\n';
            CloseHandle(hSrc);
            exit(1);
        }

        do
        {
            ReadFile(hSrc, pBuffer, sizeof(pBuffer), &dwRead, NULL);
            if (dwRead != 0)
                WriteFile(hDest, pBuffer, dwRead, &dwWritten, NULL);
        } while (dwRead != 0);
        CloseHandle(hSrc);
        CloseHandle(hDest);
}
```

For random-access files, Win32 provides the SetFilePointer function to position the *file pointer* before reading or writing. The file pointer is a 64-bit value that determines the position of the next read or write operation within the file. The SetFilePointer function fails if it is called with a handle to a device that cannot perform seek operations, such as the console or a communication port.

SetFilePointer can also be used to retrieve the current value of the file pointer. Call this function as follows:

```
dwPos = SetFilePointer(hFile, 0, NULL, FILE_CURRENT);
```

This call does not move the file pointer but returns its present value.

Asynchronous I/O Operations

A recurring problem when programming interactive applications that perform file I/O is the issue of responsiveness. Typical file system calls are *blocking* calls; for example, a call to scanf may not return until there are enough characters in the operating system's input buffer to complete the call. This is rarely a problem with fast, hard disk-based file systems; however, when the input operation is performed, for example, on a communication port, the problem becomes much more acute.

In 32-bit Windows, there are several solutions to this problem. An obvious solution is to use multiple threads; a dedicated thread may perform the input function and remain blocked indefinitely, without affecting the responsiveness of the application's user interface, managed by another thread. A simple communication program using the multithreaded approach is demonstrated in Listing 14.2. This program can be compiled from the command line by typing `cl commthrd.c`. (I return to the subject of using the console and communication ports in more detail later in this chapter.)

> **NOTE**
>
> Under Windows 95, overlapped I/O operations cannot be used on disk files.

Listing 14.2. Simple communication program using multiple threads.

```c
#include <windows.h>

volatile BOOL bDoRun;

DWORD WINAPI ReadComm(LPVOID hCommPort)
{
    HANDLE hConOut;
    DWORD dwCount;
    char c;

    hConOut = CreateFile("CONOUT$", GENERIC_WRITE,
                         FILE_SHARE_WRITE, NULL, OPEN_EXISTING,
                         FILE_ATTRIBUTE_NORMAL, 0);
    while (bDoRun)
    {
        ReadFile((HANDLE)hCommPort, &c, 1, &dwCount, NULL);
        if (dwCount == 1)
            WriteFile(hConOut, &c, 1, &dwCount, NULL);
    }
    CloseHandle(hConOut);
    return 0;
}

void main(void)
{
    HANDLE hConIn, hCommPort;
    HANDLE hThread;
    DWORD dwThread;
    DWORD dwCount;
    COMMTIMEOUTS ctmoCommPort;
    DCB dcbCommPort;
    char c;
```

```
    hConIn = CreateFile("CONIN$", GENERIC_READ | GENERIC_WRITE,
                        FILE_SHARE_READ, NULL, OPEN_EXISTING,
                        FILE_ATTRIBUTE_NORMAL, 0);
    SetConsoleMode(hConIn, 0);
    hCommPort = CreateFile("COM2", GENERIC_READ | GENERIC_WRITE, 0,
                    NULL, OPEN_EXISTING, FILE_ATTRIBUTE_NORMAL, 0);
    ctmoCommPort.ReadIntervalTimeout = MAXWORD;
    ctmoCommPort.ReadTotalTimeoutMultiplier = MAXDWORD;
    ctmoCommPort.ReadTotalTimeoutConstant = MAXDWORD;
    ctmoCommPort.WriteTotalTimeoutMultiplier = 0;
    ctmoCommPort.WriteTotalTimeoutConstant = 0;
    SetCommTimeouts(hCommPort, &ctmoCommPort);
    dcbCommPort.DCBlength = sizeof(DCB);
    GetCommState(hCommPort, &dcbCommPort);
    SetCommState(hCommPort, &dcbCommPort);
    bDoRun = TRUE;
    hThread = CreateThread(NULL, 0, ReadComm, (LPDWORD)hCommPort,
                        0, &dwThread);
    while (bDoRun)
    {
        ReadFile(hConIn, &c, 1, &dwCount, NULL);
        if (c == 24) bDoRun = FALSE;
        if (dwCount == 1)
            WriteFile(hCommPort, &c, 1, &dwCount, NULL);
    }
    PurgeComm(hCommPort, PURGE_RXABORT);
    if (WaitForSingleObject(hThread, 5000) == WAIT_TIMEOUT)
        TerminateThread(hThread, 1);
    CloseHandle(hConIn);
    CloseHandle(hCommPort);
}
```

This program uses the COM2 port for communications. In order to test it, you should have a modem attached to that port. If your modem is attached to a different port, change the port name in the second CreateFile call and recompile the application.

After opening the communication port COM2 for reading and writing and the console for input, the program proceeds with initializing the port. As part of the initialization, it sets up an infinite timeout for reading; it also initializes communications through a DCB structure. (Yes, the seemingly superfluous GetCommState/SetCommState pair of calls is actually necessary.) After initializing the communication port, the program creates a secondary thread, which opens the console for writing. The purpose of the secondary thread is to perform input on the communication port in a loop, while the primary thread does the same on the console. Whenever the primary thread receives a character on the console, it outputs that character on the communication port. Whenever the secondary thread receives a character from the communication port, it writes that character to the console.

The loops are terminated when a Ctrl+X character is received from the keyboard. The primary thread sets the bDoRun variable (notice that it is declared volatile) to FALSE. It also calls PurgeComm to ensure that any pending ReadFile calls in the secondary thread would be interrupted so the secondary thread can terminate its execution.

While using multiple threads is always a viable option for 32-bit applications, it may not always be the most convenient solution. Another approach available to 32-bit applications is the use of overlapped I/O. Overlapped I/O enables an application to initiate an I/O operation in a nonblocking fashion. For example, if an application uses the ReadFile function for overlapped input, the function will return even if the input operation has not yet been completed. Once the operation is complete, the application can retrieve results using the GetOverlappedResult function. Applications can also use the ReadFileEx and WriteFileEx functions for overlapped I/O operations.

Overlapped input can also be used in combination with a synchronization event. Processes can use the synchronization event to receive notification when the I/O operation has been completed. Using events and the WaitForMultipleObjects function, it is possible to wait for input on several input devices at once. This is exactly the technique demonstrated by the second version of this simple communication program, shown in Listing 14.3. This program can also be compiled by a simple command-line instruction, cl commovio.c.

Listing 14.3. Simple communication program using overlapped I/O.

```
#include <windows.h>

void main(void)
{
    HANDLE hConIn, hConOut, hCommPort;
    HANDLE hEvents[2];
    DWORD dwCount;
    DWORD dwWait;
    COMMTIMEOUTS ctmoCommPort;
    DCB dcbCommPort;
    OVERLAPPED ov;
    INPUT_RECORD irBuffer;
    BOOL fInRead;
    char c;
    int i;

    hConIn = CreateFile("CONIN$", GENERIC_READ | GENERIC_WRITE,
                        FILE_SHARE_READ, NULL, OPEN_EXISTING,
                        FILE_ATTRIBUTE_NORMAL, 0);
    SetConsoleMode(hConIn, 0);
    hConOut = CreateFile("CONOUT$", GENERIC_WRITE,
                        FILE_SHARE_WRITE, NULL, OPEN_EXISTING,
                        FILE_ATTRIBUTE_NORMAL, 0);
    hCommPort = CreateFile("COM2", GENERIC_READ | GENERIC_WRITE, 0,
                    NULL, OPEN_EXISTING, FILE_ATTRIBUTE_NORMAL |
                    FILE_FLAG_OVERLAPPED, 0);
    ctmoCommPort.ReadIntervalTimeout = MAXDWORD;
    ctmoCommPort.ReadTotalTimeoutMultiplier = MAXDWORD;
    ctmoCommPort.ReadTotalTimeoutConstant = MAXDWORD;
    ctmoCommPort.WriteTotalTimeoutMultiplier = 0;
    ctmoCommPort.WriteTotalTimeoutConstant = 0;
    SetCommTimeouts(hCommPort, &ctmoCommPort);
    dcbCommPort.DCBlength = sizeof(DCB);
    GetCommState(hCommPort, &dcbCommPort);
    SetCommState(hCommPort, &dcbCommPort);
    SetCommMask(hCommPort, EV_RXCHAR);
```

```
        ov.Offset = 0;
        ov.OffsetHigh = 0;
        ov.hEvent = CreateEvent(NULL, TRUE, FALSE, NULL);
        hEvents[0] = ov.hEvent;
        hEvents[1] = hConIn;
        fInRead = FALSE;
        while (1)
        {
            if (!fInRead)
                while (ReadFile(hCommPort, &c, 1, &dwCount, &ov))
                    if (dwCount == 1)
                        WriteFile(hConOut, &c, 1, &dwCount, NULL);
            fInRead = TRUE;
            dwWait =
                WaitForMultipleObjects(2, hEvents, FALSE, INFINITE);
            switch (dwWait)
            {
                case WAIT_OBJECT_0:
                    if (GetOverlappedResult(hCommPort, &ov, &dwCount,
                                            FALSE))
                        if (dwCount == 1)
                            WriteFile(hConOut, &c, 1, &dwCount, NULL);
                    fInRead = FALSE;
                    break;
                case WAIT_OBJECT_0 + 1:
                    ReadConsoleInput(hConIn, &irBuffer, 1, &dwCount);
                    if (dwCount == 1 &&
                        irBuffer.EventType == KEY_EVENT &&
                        irBuffer.Event.KeyEvent.bKeyDown)
                      for (i = 0;
                         i < irBuffer.Event.KeyEvent.wRepeatCount; i++)
                    {
                        if (irBuffer.Event.KeyEvent.uChar.AsciiChar)
                        {
                            WriteFile(hCommPort,
                              &irBuffer.Event.KeyEvent.uChar.AsciiChar,
                              1, &dwCount, NULL);
                            if (irBuffer.Event.KeyEvent.uChar.AsciiChar
                                == 24) goto EndLoop;
                        }
                    }
            }
        }
EndLoop:
    CloseHandle(ov.hEvent);
    CloseHandle(hConIn);
    CloseHandle(hConOut);
    CloseHandle(hCommPort);
}
```

As before, if your modem is not attached to COM2, it may be necessary to change the port name in the second CreateFile call and recompile the program before using it.

Like its multithreaded counterpart, this program also begins by opening the console and the communication port and initializing the port. Part of the port initialization is a call to the SetCommMask function, which enables read event notifications for that port.

The communication port is opened with the FILE_FLAG_OVERLAPPED attribute. This enables overlapped I/O operations. When the program's main loop is entered, a call is made to ReadFile, passing to it a pointer to an OVERLAPPED structure.

ReadFile may return data immediately if data is available on the port. If not, ReadFile still returns, but signals an error; GetLastError can be used to check for the error code ERROR_IO_PENDING. (For simplicity, this part has been left out from the code; we just assume that any ReadFile error indicates pending input.)

The heart of this program is the call to WaitForMultipleObjects. The function waits on two objects: an event object that was specified as part of the OVERLAPPED structure used in reading the communication port and the console input object. In the case of the latter, it is not necessary to use overlapped I/O; the console object has its own signaled state indicating that data is waiting in the console's input buffer.

When WaitForMultipleObjects returns, it indicates that data arrived either on the console or on the communication port. It is the subsequent switch statement that distinguishes between the two. Retrieving the console event requires code that is a bit tricky. Unfortunately, a simple ReadFile would not suffice as it leaves the key up event in the console's input buffer, leaving the console object in a signaled state. A subsequent ReadFile would then result in a blocking read, waiting until a key is pressed once again. Because of this behavior, it was necessary to use low-level console functions to retrieve (and discard) all console events, so when WaitForMultipleObjects is called again, the console object would no longer be signaled—at least not until the user presses a key again.

Low-Level I/O

Figure 14.1 makes it obvious that the term "low-level I/O" is somewhat of a misnomer for file descriptor-based I/O operations. Indeed, this term is a relic, a leftover from DOS and UNIX; although Windows NT provides these functions for compatibility with those operating systems, they are effectively implemented using CreateFile, ReadFile, and WriteFile.

File Descriptors

A *file descriptor* is an integer identifying an open file. A file descriptor is obtained when an application uses the _open or _creat functions. Note that throughout the run-time library documentation, file descriptors are often referred to as file handles; once again, this is not to be confused with Win32 handles for file objects. A handle returned by CreateFile and a file descriptor obtained by calling _open are not compatible.

Standard File Descriptors

Win32 console applications have access to the standard input and output file descriptors. These are summarized in Table 14.1.

Table 14.1. Standard file descriptors.

File Descriptor	Stream Name	Description
0	stdin	Standard Input
1	stdout	Standard Output
2	stderr	Standard Error

Note that MS-DOS programs also have access to two additional file descriptors, _stdprn and _stdaux. These file descriptors are not available for Win32 applications.

Low-Level I/O Functions

A file can be opened for low-level I/O using the _open function. A new file can be created for low-level I/O using _creat. Both of these functions have wide character versions; that is, versions that accept a Unicode filename string under Windows NT: _wopen and _wcreat.

Reading and writing can be performed by calling the _read or _write functions. Seeking within the file is accomplished by calling _lseek. The current position within the file can be retrieved by calling _tell.

The contents of any buffers maintained by Windows can be committed to disk by calling _commit. The file can be closed by calling _close. The _eof function can be used to test for an end-of-file condition. All low-level I/O functions use the errno global variable to indicate other error conditions.

The names of all these functions begin with an underscore to indicate that they are not part of the standard ANSI function library. However, for programs that may use the old names of these functions, Microsoft provides the oldnames.lib library.

Stream I/O

C/C++ stream I/O functions are among the most frequently used I/O functions. Not too many programs exist that contain no calls to printf or at least one FILE pointer.

Stream I/O in C

C programs that use stream I/O utilize the FILE structure and related family of functions. A file is opened for stream I/O by calling the fopen function. This function, if successful, returns a pointer to a FILE structure, which can be used in subsequent operations, such as calls to fscanf, fprintf, fread, fwrite, fseek, ftell, or fclose. The Visual C++ run-time library supports all standard stream I/O functions as well as several Microsoft-specific functions.

For applications that mix calls to stream I/O and low-level I/O functions, the `_fileno` function can be used to obtain a file descriptor for a given stream (identified by a `FILE` pointer). The `_fdopen` function can be used to open a stream and associate it with a file descriptor that identifies a previously opened file.

Applications can also access the standard input, standard output, and standard error through the predefined streams `stdin`, `stdout`, and `stderr`.

Stream I/O in C++ (The *iostream* Classes)

The Visual C++ run-time library contains a complete implementation of the C++ `iostream` classes.

The `iostream` class library implements a family of C++ classes, shown in Figure 14.2.

FIGURE 14.2.

The C++ iostream classes.

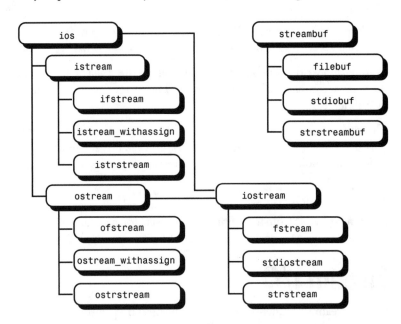

The base class of all `iostream` classes is the `ios` class. Normally, applications do not derive classes from `ios` directly. Instead, they use one of the derived classes, `istream` or `ostream`.

Variants of the `istream` class include `istrstream` (operates on an array of characters stored in memory), `ifstream` (operates on a disk file), and `istream_withassign` (a variant of `istream` that enables assignments to work).

Variants of `ostream` include `ostrstream` (stream output to a character array), `ofstream` (stream output to a file), and `ostream_withassign` (variant of `ostream` that enables assignment).

The predefined stream object `cin`, representing standard input, is of type `istream_withassign`.

The predefined objects cout, cerr, and clog, which represent standard output and standard error, are of type ostream_withassign.

The class iostream combines the functionality of the istream and ostream classes. Derived classes include fstream (for file I/O), strstream (for stream I/O on a character array), and stdiostream (for standard I/O).

All ios-derived objects make use of the streambuf class or the derived classes filebuf, stdiobuf, or strstreambuf for I/O buffering.

Special Devices

In addition to handling disk files, the Win32 file management routines can be used to handle many other types of devices. These include the console, communication ports, named pipes, and mailslots. Functions such as ReadFile or WriteFile may also accept socket handles created by the WinSock functions socket or accept depending on the WinSock implementation.

In the next section, we discuss console and communication port I/O.

Console I/O

Win32 applications can use the CreateFile, ReadFile, and WriteFile functions to perform console input and output. Consoles provide an interface for character-based applications.

Unless its input or output is redirected, an application inherits file handles to the console that can be obtained by calling the function GetStdHandle. However, if the application's standard handles are redirected, GetStdHandle returns the redirected handles. In this case, applications can open the console explicitly by using the special filenames CONIN$ and CONOUT$.

When opening the console for input or output, make sure to specify the FILE_SHARE_READ or FILE_SHARE_WRITE sharing mode, respectively. Also, use the OPEN_EXISTING creation mode. For example:

```
CreateFile("CONIN$", GENERIC_READ, FILE_SHARE_READ, NULL,
           OPEN_EXISTING, FILE_ATTRIBUTE_NORMAL, 0);
```

In order to be able to perform certain operations on a console opened for reading (such as flushing the input buffer or setting the console mode), it may be necessary to open the console for reading and writing (GENERIC_READ ¦ GENERIC_WRITE).

By default, the console is opened for line-oriented input. The SetConsoleMode function can be used to change the input and output mode. For example, to set the console to raw input mode (every character is returned immediately, no control character processing takes place) use the following call:

```
SetConsoleMode(hConsole, 0);
```

The ReadFile function can be used to read keyboard input from the console. However, it is recommended that applications use ReadConsole instead where applicable; unlike ReadFile, ReadConsole can handle both ASCII and Unicode input on Windows NT.

To write to the console, the WriteFile function can be used. WriteConsole has the same functionality, but it can also handle Unicode output on Windows NT, and thus it is the preferred function for console output.

What I have explained so far may give the impression that using the console is just a glorified way of accomplishing what can easily be done using standard C/C++ library functions. This is not so. A console has many capabilities other than providing a facility for keyboard input and character output.

In addition to character input and output, a console also handles mouse input and provides some window management functions for the console window. The low-level console input functions ReadConsoleInput and PeekConsoleInput can be used to retrieve information about keyboard, mouse, and window events. On the output side, the low-level output function WriteConsoleOutputAttribute can be used to write a text and background color attributes to the console.

Graphical Windows applications do not by default have access to a console. These applications can explicitly create a console by calling the AllocConsole function. A process can detach itself from its console by calling the FreeConsole function.

The console window's title and position can be controlled using the SetConsoleTitle and SetConsoleWindowInfo functions, respectively.

Communication Ports

Communication ports are opened and used via the CreateFile, ReadFile, and WriteFile functions. That said, there are several other functions that applications must use to set up the communication ports and control their behavior.

The basic setup of a communication port takes place using a DCB, or *device control block* structure. Members of this structure specify the baud rate, parity, data and stop bits, handshaking, and other aspects of port behavior. The current settings can be obtained using the GetCommState function and can be set by calling the SetCommState function. A helper function, BuildCommDCB, can be used to fill in parts of this structure on the basis of a string formatted in the style of an MS-DOS MODE command.

Read and write timeout behavior is controlled through the COMMTIMEOUTS structure. Current timeouts can be retrieved by calling GetCommTimeouts and set by calling SetCommTimeouts. The helper function BuildCommDCBAndTimeouts can be used to fill in both a DCB structure and a COMMTIMEOUTS structure using command strings.

The size of the input and output buffers can be controlled by calling the SetupComm function.

The WaitCommEvent function can be used to wait for a specific event to occur on the communication port.

The SetCommBreak function places the communication line in a break state. The state can be cleared by calling the ClearCommBreak function.

The ClearCommError function can be used to clear an error condition. This function also reports the status of the communication device.

The PurgeComm function can be used to clear any I/O buffers associated with the communication port, and to interrupt pending I/O operations.

The TransmitCommChar function transmits a character on the communication port ahead of any pending data in the output buffer. This function can be used, for example, to transmit interrupt characters such as Ctrl+C.

The communication port can also be opened for overlapped I/O operations. An event mask, which controls which events set the state of the event object (specified as part of the OVERLAPPED structure), can be set using the SetCommMask function. The current event mask can be retrieved by calling the GetCommMask function.

Low-level access to port functions is provided by the functions EscapeCommFunction and DeviceIoControl.

Further information about the communication port and its status can be obtained by calling the GetCommProperties and GetCommModemStatus functions.

Windows 95 also offers the function CommConfigDialog, which displays a driver-specific configuration dialog for the specified communication port.

Summary

Win32 applications can access files through three distinct sets of file management functions: stream and low-level I/O functions that are part of the C/C++ run-time libraries and Win32 file management functions.

A file is a collection of data on a storage device, such as a disk. Files are organized on the device into file systems. Windows NT recognizes the DOS FAT, protected-mode FAT, NTFS, and HPFS file systems. Windows 95, in contrast, can only deal with FAT and protected-mode FAT file systems. Windows NT supports file-level compression on NTFS file systems; Windows 95, in turn, supports volume compression through DriveSpace. On NTFS volumes, Windows NT also supports advanced security features.

In addition to disks, files may also be accessed on CD-ROM and remote volumes across the network.

The Win32 file management functions treat an open file as an operating system object, referred to by a handle. At the heart of Win32 file management are the functions CreateFile,

ReadFile, and WriteFile. Through file handles, I/O operations can be performed synchronously and asynchronously; for the latter, applications can use the technique of overlapped I/O. Overlapped I/O enables an application to regain control after an I/O call, even before the I/O operation is finished, and do something else until it is notified of the operation's completion.

Win32 file management routines can also be used to perform I/O on the standard input, standard output, and standard error. Handles to these can be obtained by calling the GetStdHandle function.

Applications can also access files through DOS/UNIX style low-level I/O functions. The names of these functions are preceded by an underscore (for example, _open, _read) to indicate that they are not part of the standard ANSI library. However, applications can be linked with the oldnames.lib library file if the use of the old names without underscores is desired.

In addition to low-level I/O, applications can also use stream I/O. This includes C functions such as fopen, fprintf, fscanf, or fclose; it also includes the C++ iostream classes.

The Win32 file management functions can also be used to access special devices. They include the console, communication ports, named pipes and mailslots, and sockets opened by calls to socket or accept. Several special functions provide fine control over console and communication port I/O.

The Windows
Clipboard

15

Not too long ago, the Windows Clipboard represented the only means for applications to exchange data with each other. Before the glorious days of OLE embedding and drag and drop, users had to use clipboard operations such as cutting, copying, and pasting to transfer data from one application to another, or even to move data within the same application.

These days, the clipboard is often forgotten; yet just because it is overshadowed by OLE, it does not mean that applications can stop supporting clipboard operations. Furthermore, various clipboard-related concepts survive even when applications exchange data using more advanced methods.

What exactly is the clipboard? Perhaps it is best defined as a Win32 facility where applications can place data. Such data becomes accessible to all applications. Data can be retrieved in a variety of formats, some of which are supported by the operating system, some by applications.

Clipboard Formats

Applications place data on the clipboard using the `SetClipboardData` function. In addition to providing a handle to the data object, this function also accepts a parameter specifying the format of the data. Applications are encouraged to provide data in a variety of formats; for example, a word processor program may place data on the clipboard using both a private format and a plain text format that is usable by other applications such as the Notepad.

The three types of clipboard formats available to applications include standard formats, registered formats, and private formats.

Standard Clipboard Formats

A multitude of standard clipboard formats exists, identified by symbolic constants. These formats are summarized in Table 15.1. In the cases when the application is supposed to provide a handle of a specific type when calling `SetClipboardData`, the handle type is indicated. In other cases, the handle passed to `SetClipboardData` is typically a handle to a block of memory allocated via the `GlobalAlloc` function.

Table 15.1. Standard clipboard formats.

Format Type	Description
Text Formats	
CF_OEMTEXT	Text containing characters from the OEM character set
CF_TEXT	Text containing characters from the ANSI character set
CF_UNICODETEXT	Text containing Unicode characters

Format Type	Description
Bitmap formats	
CF_BITMAP	Device-dependent bitmap (HBITMAP)
CF_DIB	Device independent bitmap (HBITMAPINFO)
CF_TIFF	Tagged Image File Format
Metafile formats	
CF_ENHMETAFILE	Enhanced metafile (HENHMETAFILE)
CF_METAFILEPICT	Windows Metafile (METAFILEPICT)
Substitute formats for private formats	
CF_DSPBITMAP	Bitmap representation of private data
CF_DSPENHMETAFILE	Enhanced metafile representation of private data
CF_DSPMETAFILEPICT	Metafile representation of private data
CF_DSPTEXT	Text representation of private data
Sound formats	
CF_RIFF	Resource Interchange File Format
CF_WAVE	Standard wave file format audio data
Special formats	
CF_DIF	Data Interchange Format from Software Arts
CF_OWNERDISPLAY	Data displayed by the owner of the clipboard data
CF_PALETTE	Color palette (HPALETTE)
CF_PENDATA	Microsoft Pen Extensions data
CF_PRIVATEFIRST through CF_PRIVATELAST	Private data
CF_SYLK	Microsoft Symbolic Link format
Windows 95-only formats	
CF_GDIOBJFIRST through CF_GDIOBJLAST	Application-defined GDI objects
CF_HDROP	List of files (HDROP)
CF_LOCALE	Locale information for CF_TEXT data

Under certain circumstances, Windows is capable of synthesizing data in formats not explicitly provided by an application. For example, if the application provides data in CF_TEXT format, Windows can render that data in the CF_OEMTEXT format at the request of another application. Windows can perform this conversion of formats between the text formats CF_TEXT, CF_OEMTEXT, and (under Windows NT) CF_UNICODETEXT; the bitmap formats CF_BITMAP and CF_DIB; and the metafile formats CF_ENHMETAFILE and CF_METAFILEPICT. Finally, Windows can also synthesize a CF_PALETTE format from the CF_DIB format.

Registered Formats

Applications that need to place data on the clipboard in a format other than any of the standard formats can register a new clipboard format using the RegisterClipboardFormat function. For example, an application that wishes to place RTF text on the clipboard may make the following call to register this format:

```
cfRTF = RegisterClipboardFormat("Rich Text Format");
```

If several applications call RegisterClipboardFormat with the same format name, the format is only registered once.

There are many clipboard formats registered by Windows. For example, some registered formats are related to OLE, some others to the Windows 95 shell. The name of a registered format can be obtained by calling the GetClipboardFormatName function.

Private Formats

Sometimes it is not necessary for an application to register a new clipboard format. This is the case when the clipboard is used, for example, to transfer data internally within the application and the data is not expected to be used by other applications. For such application-defined private formats, an application can use the CF_PRIVATEFIRST through CF_PRIVATELAST range of values.

In order to enable clipboard viewers to display data stored in a private format, the clipboard owner must provide data in any of the display formats CF_DSPBITMAP, CF_DSPTEXT, CF_DSPMETAFILEPICT, or CF_DSPENHMETAFILE. These formats are identical to their standard counterparts (CF_BITMAP, CF_TEXT, CF_METAFILEPICT, and CF_ENHMETAFILE) except that they are used solely for display purposes and not for pasting.

Clipboard Operations

In order to utilize the clipboard, an application has to perform a variety of operations. These include setting up the clipboard data, obtaining ownership of the clipboard, transferring the data, and responding the clipboard-related events. The application should also provide, as part of its user interface, clipboard-specific user commands (such as commands under its Edit menu).

Transferring Data to the Clipboard

Before data can be transferred to the clipboard, an application has to do two things. First, the data object must be allocated; second, ownership of the clipboard must be obtained.

The data object must be a handle. This handle can refer to a block of memory allocated using GlobalAlloc with the GMEM_MOVEABLE and GMEM_DDESHARE flags (note that the presence of the GMEM_DDESHARE flag does not indicate that the block of memory is shared between applications); or it can be a handle to a GDI object such as a bitmap. It is important to note that once the handle is passed to the clipboard, the application transfers the object's ownership; it should no longer lock the object and should definitely not make an attempt to delete it.

The application obtains ownership of the clipboard by opening the clipboard using OpenClipboard and then emptying the clipboard by calling the EmptyClipboard function. All handles to data that was previously transferred to the clipboard will be freed. Next, the application transfers data to the clipboard using SetClipboardData and closes it by calling CloseClipboard.

The application can call SetClipboardData multiple times if data is available in several formats. For example, an application may call SetClipboardData using the CF_DIB and CF_ENHMETAFILE formats to provide a graphic image in both bitmap and metafile forms.

Delayed Rendering

Delayed rendering is a performance-enhancing technique that are most useful for applications that routinely place large blocks of data on the clipboard.

An application can specify delayed rendering by passing NULL as the second parameter of SetClipboardData. The system informs the application that data in a specific format must be rendered by sending the application a WM_RENDERFORMAT message. In response to this message, the application must call SetClipboardData and place the requested data on the clipboard.

An application that placed data on the clipboard using delayed rendering may also receive a WM_RENDERALLFORMATS message. This message is sent to the clipboard owner before it is destroyed to ensure that the data on the clipboard remains available to other applications.

When processing a WM_RENDERFORMAT or WM_RENDERALLFORMATS message, the application must not open the clipboard before calling SetClipboardData or close it afterwards.

Pasting Data from the Clipboard

An application can use the IsClipboardFormatAvailable function to determine if data in a specific format is available on the clipboard. If it wishes to obtain a copy of the data on the clipboard, the application can call OpenClipboard, followed by a call to GetClipboardData. The handle obtained by calling GetClipboardData will not be assumed to remain persistent; applications should immediately copy any data associated with that handle, preferably before calling CloseClipboard. After the call to CloseClipboard, it is possible for other applications to empty the clipboard, rendering the handle obtained through GetClipboardData useless.

The IsClipboardFormatAvailable function can also be used to update the application's Edit menu items. For example, if IsClipboardFormatAvailable indicates that no clipboard data is available in a format that the application understands, the application should disable its Paste command.

Applications can also obtain information about the data formats available in the clipboard by calling CountClipboardFormats or EnumClipboardFormats.

Controls and the Clipboard

Edit controls have built-in clipboard support (also supported by the edit control in combo boxes). Edit controls respond to a series of messages by performing clipboard operations. When receiving a WM_COPY message, edit controls copy the current selection to the clipboard using the CF_TEXT format. When receiving a WM_CUT message, edit controls transfer the current selection to the clipboard using the CF_TEXT format and erase the selection from the control. In response to a WM_PASTE message, edit controls take the clipboard contents (if anything is available in the CF_TEXT format) and use it to replace the current selection. Finally, edit controls also process the WM_CLEAR message (erasing the current selection).

Clipboard Messages

There are several Windows messages associated with the clipboard.

Applications that use delayed rendering must process the WM_RENDERFORMAT and WM_RENDERALLFORMATS messages.

The WM_DESTROYCLIPBOARD message is sent to the clipboard owner when the contents of the clipboard are destroyed. In response to this message, an application may free up any resources associated with rendering or drawing clipboard items.

A series of messages is sent to applications that place data on the clipboard using the CF_OWNERDISPLAY format. These include WM_ASKCBFORMATNAME, WM_DRAWCLIPBOARD, WM_HSCROLLCLIPBOARD, WM_VSCROLLCLIPBOARD, and WM_PAINTCLIPBOARD.

Another set of messages is sent to or used by clipboard viewer applications.

Clipboard Viewers

A *clipboard viewer* is an application that displays the current contents of the clipboard. An example of a clipboard viewer is the Windows Clipboard Viewer application.

A clipboard viewer merely exists for the user's convenience and does not disrupt or alter clipboard operations.

There can be several clipboard viewers in operation. An application inserts a window in the chain of clipboard viewers by calling the SetClipboardViewer function with the handle of the window. Once added to the chain, the clipboard viewer will receive WM_CHANGECBCHAIN and WM_DRAWCLIPBOARD messages. The clipboard viewer can remove itself from the chain by calling the ChangeClipboardChain function.

A Simple Implementation

The program shown in Listing 15.1 (yes; yet another Hello, World program) puts all this nice theory into practice. This very simple application provides an implementation for the four basic clipboard commands: Cut, Copy, Paste, and Delete. The program's resource file is shown in Listing 15.2, and its header file in Listing 15.3. To compile this application from the command line, you need to enter the following two commands in a DOS window (still not complex enough to warrant a make file):

```
rc hellocf.rc
cl hellocf.c hellocf.res user32.lib gdi32.lib
```

Listing 15.1. A simple clipboard-aware application.

```
#include <windows.h>
#include "hellocf.h"

HINSTANCE hInstance;
char *pszData;

void DrawHello(HWND hwnd)
{
    HDC hDC;
    PAINTSTRUCT paintStruct;
    RECT clientRect;

    if (pszData != NULL)
    {
        hDC = BeginPaint(hwnd, &paintStruct);
        if (hDC != NULL)
        {
            GetClientRect(hwnd, &clientRect);
            DPtoLP(hDC, (LPPOINT)&clientRect, 2);
            DrawText(hDC, pszData, -1, &clientRect,
                    DT_CENTER ¦ DT_VCENTER ¦ DT_SINGLELINE);
            EndPaint(hwnd, &paintStruct);
        }
    }
}

void CopyData(HWND hwnd)
```

continues

Listing 15.1. continued

```
{
    HGLOBAL hData;
    LPVOID pData;

    OpenClipboard(hwnd);
    EmptyClipboard();
    hData = GlobalAlloc(GMEM_DDESHARE | GMEM_MOVEABLE,
                        strlen(pszData) + 1);
    pData = GlobalLock(hData);
    strcpy((LPSTR)pData, pszData);
    GlobalUnlock(hData);
    SetClipboardData(CF_TEXT, hData);
    CloseClipboard();
}

void DeleteData(HWND hwnd)
{
    free(pszData);
    pszData = NULL;
    InvalidateRect(hwnd, NULL, TRUE);
}

void PasteData(HWND hwnd)
{
    HANDLE hData;
    LPVOID pData;

    if (!IsClipboardFormatAvailable(CF_TEXT)) return;
    OpenClipboard(hwnd);
    hData = GetClipboardData(CF_TEXT);
    pData = GlobalLock(hData);
    if (pszData) DeleteData(hwnd);
    pszData = malloc(strlen(pData) + 1);
    strcpy(pszData, (LPSTR)pData);
    GlobalUnlock(hData);
    CloseClipboard();
    InvalidateRect(hwnd, NULL, TRUE);
}

void SetMenus(HWND hwnd)
{
    EnableMenuItem(GetMenu(hwnd), ID_EDIT_CUT,
                   pszData ? MF_ENABLED : MF_GRAYED);
    EnableMenuItem(GetMenu(hwnd), ID_EDIT_COPY,
                   pszData ? MF_ENABLED : MF_GRAYED);
    EnableMenuItem(GetMenu(hwnd), ID_EDIT_PASTE,
                   IsClipboardFormatAvailable(CF_TEXT) ?
                                       MF_ENABLED : MF_GRAYED);
    EnableMenuItem(GetMenu(hwnd), ID_EDIT_DELETE,
                   pszData ? MF_ENABLED : MF_GRAYED);
}

LRESULT CALLBACK WndProc(HWND hwnd, UINT uMsg,
                         WPARAM wParam, LPARAM lParam)
{
    switch(uMsg)
```

```
    {
        case WM_COMMAND:
            switch (LOWORD(wParam))
            {
                case ID_FILE_EXIT:
                    DestroyWindow(hwnd);
                    break;
                case ID_EDIT_CUT:
                    CopyData(hwnd);
                    DeleteData(hwnd);
                    break;
                case ID_EDIT_COPY:
                    CopyData(hwnd);
                    break;
                case ID_EDIT_PASTE:
                    PasteData(hwnd);
                    break;
                case ID_EDIT_DELETE:
                    DeleteData(hwnd);
                    break;
            }
            break;
        case WM_PAINT:
            DrawHello(hwnd);
            break;
        case WM_DESTROY:
            PostQuitMessage(0);
            break;
        case WM_INITMENUPOPUP:
            if (LOWORD(lParam) == 1)
            {
                SetMenus(hwnd);
                break;
            }
        default:
            return DefWindowProc(hwnd, uMsg, wParam, lParam);
    }
    return 0;
}

int WINAPI WinMain(HINSTANCE hThisInstance,
                   HINSTANCE hPrevInstance,
                   LPSTR d3, int nCmdShow)
{
    HWND hwnd;
    MSG msg;
    WNDCLASS wndClass;
    HANDLE hAccTbl;

    pszData = malloc(14);
    strcpy(pszData, "Hello, World!");
    hInstance = hThisInstance;
    if (hPrevInstance == NULL)
    {
        memset(&wndClass, 0, sizeof(wndClass));
        wndClass.style = CS_HREDRAW | CS_VREDRAW;
        wndClass.lpfnWndProc = WndProc;
```

continues

Listing 15.1. continued

```
            wndClass.hInstance = hInstance;
            wndClass.hCursor = LoadCursor(NULL, IDC_ARROW);
            wndClass.hbrBackground = (HBRUSH)(COLOR_WINDOW + 1);
            wndClass.lpszMenuName = "HelloMenu";
            wndClass.lpszClassName = "Hello";
            if (!RegisterClass(&wndClass)) return FALSE;
    }
    hwnd = CreateWindow("Hello", "Hello",
                            WS_OVERLAPPEDWINDOW,
                            CW_USEDEFAULT, 0, CW_USEDEFAULT, 0,
                            NULL, NULL, hInstance, NULL);
    ShowWindow(hwnd, nCmdShow);
    hAccTbl = LoadAccelerators(hInstance, "HelloMenu");
    UpdateWindow(hwnd);
    while (GetMessage(&msg, NULL, 0, 0))
    {
        if (!TranslateAccelerator(hwnd, hAccTbl, &msg))
        {
            TranslateMessage(&msg);
            DispatchMessage(&msg);
        }
    }
    return msg.wParam;
}
```

Listing 15.2. Resource file for the sample clipboard-aware application.

```
#include "windows.h"
#include "hellocf.h"

HelloMenu MENU
BEGIN
    POPUP       "&File"
    BEGIN
        MENUITEM "E&xit",               ID_FILE_EXIT
    END
    POPUP       "&Edit"
    BEGIN
        MENUITEM "Cu&t\tCtrl+X",        ID_EDIT_CUT, GRAYED
        MENUITEM "&Copy\tCtrl+C",       ID_EDIT_COPY, GRAYED
        MENUITEM "&Paste\tCtrl+V",      ID_EDIT_PASTE, GRAYED
        MENUITEM "&Delete\tDel",        ID_EDIT_DELETE, GRAYED
    END
END

HelloMenu ACCELERATORS
BEGIN
        "X", ID_EDIT_CUT, VIRTKEY, CONTROL
        "C", ID_EDIT_COPY, VIRTKEY, CONTROL
        "V", ID_EDIT_PASTE, VIRTKEY, CONTROL
        VK_DELETE, ID_EDIT_DELETE, VIRTKEY
END
```

Listing 15.3. Header file for the sample clipboard-aware application.

```
#define ID_FILE_EXIT   1000
#define ID_EDIT_CUT    1001
#define ID_EDIT_COPY   1002
#define ID_EDIT_PASTE  1003
#define ID_EDIT_DELETE 1004
```

To see how this application works, try using its clipboard functions. You can use the Cut or Copy functions to copy the text it displays to the clipboard; you can also use another application (for example, the Windows Notepad) to create a block of text, copy it to the clipboard, and then paste it into this application.

This program has a simple data object; a pointer that is initially set to point to the character string "Hello, World!" The application also has a simple set of menus containing an Edit menu with the clipboard functions Cut, Copy, Paste, and Delete.

Clipboard operations are performed in response to the user selecting these Edit menu commands. The function CopyData copies the current string to the clipboard by first gaining ownership of it through EmptyClipboard and then performing a SetClipboardData call. The function PasteData copies data from the clipboard; it does so by first freeing any current data, and then obtaining clipboard data by calling GetClipboardData.

The function SetMenus updates the enabled state of menu items in the Edit menu based on the availability of data in the CF_TEXT format on the clipboard. If no such data is available, the Paste command is disabled. The state of the Cut, Copy, and Delete menu items is also updated to reflect whether the application has any data that can be placed on the clipboard.

To ensure that the application's window is properly updated when the data changes, both the DeleteData and the PasteData functions call InvalidateRect.

Note that the data handle allocated in CopyData is never freed by the application. After this handle has been passed to the clipboard, freeing it (when the clipboard is emptied) is no longer the responsibility of the application. Similarly, the application never frees the handle obtained through GetClipboardData (in PasteData); after the clipboard data has been obtained and the clipboard is closed, this handle is simply discarded.

Summary

The Windows clipboard represents one of the oldest mechanisms for transferring data between applications. The clipboard is a Windows facility where applications can place data in a variety of formats, to be retrieved later by other applications.

Windows defines several standard clipboard formats. Applications can also register additional clipboard formats or use private clipboard formats.

An application transfers data to the clipboard by first gaining ownership of it calling the function EmptyClipboard. It may transfer data immediately or choose to use delayed rendering by passing a NULL handle to the SetClipboardData function. When using delayed rendering, applications must process the WM_RENDERFORMAT and WM_RENDERALLFORMATS messages.

Edit controls (and the edit control parts of combo boxes) have built-in clipboard support. They respond the WM_CUT, WM_COPY, WM_PASTE, and WM_CLEAR messages by performing a cut, copy, paste, or delete operation using data in the CF_TEXT format.

Clipboard viewers are programs that show the current contents of the clipboard. These programs merely serve the user's convenience and do not alter the clipboard's contents or affect clipboard operations.

The Registry

16

Ah, the Registry. This mysterious object that appeared with the introduction of OLE under Windows 3.1. No matter how hard we programmer types were trying to ignore it, it is here to stay; in fact, while we were looking the other way it quietly took over the role of initialization, or INI files, among other things.

But what is it? Perhaps more importantly, what should you, the Win32 programmer, know about it? How can you access and manipulate it from within your applications? These are the questions that I attempt to answer in this chapter.

Registry Structure

The Registry is a hierarchically organized store of information. Each entry in this tree-like information structure is called a *key*. A key may contain any number of subkeys; it can also contain data entries called *values*. In this form, the Registry stores information about the system, its configuration, hardware devices, and software applications. It also assumes the role of the ubiquitous INI files by providing a place where application-specific settings can be stored.

A Registry key is identified by its name. Keynames consist of printable ASCII characters except the backslash (\), space, and wildcard (* or ?) characters. The use of keynames that begin with a period (.) is reserved. Keynames are not case sensitive.

Registry Values

A value in the Registry is identified by its name. Value names consist of the same characters as keynames. The value itself can be a string, binary data, or a 32-bit unsigned value.

There are some apparent differences between the behavior of the Windows 95 and the Windows NT Registries. The Windows 95 Registry appears to allow for the assignment of a value to a Registry key (as opposed to a value name); this appears as the default value for that key. Upon closer examination, however, one finds that this is a superficial difference. The default value for a key is really a value with an empty name; empty names are also permitted in the Windows NT Registry. Perhaps the only difference is that the value with the empty name appears to be always defined for a key in the Windows 95 Registry, while it must be explicitly created in the Windows NT Registry.

Another apparent difference between the two Registries is the existence of a variety of string types in the Windows NT Registry, whereas Windows 95 appears to support only one string type. But is this really the case? Jumping a bit ahead of myself here, let me show you some of the output created by the Registry reader program that we examine later in this chapter. For example, look at the following output:

```
Enter key: HKEY_CURRENT_USER\Environment\include
Expandable string: f:\msvc20\include;f:\msvc20\mfc\include
```

However, if you examine the same value using the Windows 95 Registry Editor, it will appear as a binary value. But this is a shortcoming of the Registry Editor, not the Registry itself.

Table 16.1 contains a list of all value types that can go into the Windows 95 and Windows NT Registries.

Table 16.1. Registry value types.

Symbolic Identifier	Description
REG_BINARY	Raw binary data
REG_DWORD	Double word in machine format (low-endian on Intel)
REG_DWORD_LITTLE_ENDIAN	Double word in little-endian format
REG_DWORD_BIG_ENDIAN	Double word in big-endian format
REG_EXPAND_SZ	String with unexpanded environment variables
REG_LINK	Unicode symbolic link
REG_MULTI_SZ	Multiple strings ended by two null characters
REG_NONE	Undefined type
REG_RESOURCE_LIST	Device-driver resource list
REG_SZ	Null-terminated string

Registry Capacity

Generally, it is not recommended to store items larger than a kilobyte or two in the Registry. For larger items, use a separate file, and use the Registry for storing the filename.

Under Windows 95, Registry values are limited to 64KB in size.

Another consideration when using the Registry is that storing a key generally requires substantially more storage space than storing a value. Whenever possible, organize values under a common key rather than using several keys for the same purpose.

Predefined Registry Keys

The Registry contains several predefined keys.

The HKEY_LOCAL_MACHINE key contains entries that describe the computer and its configuration. This includes information about the processor, system board, memory, and installed hardware and software.

The HKEY_CLASSES_ROOT key is the root key for information relating to document types and OLE types. This key is a subordinate key to HKEY_LOCAL_MACHINE. (It is equivalent to HKEY_LOCAL_MACHINE\SOFTWARE\Classes.) Information stored here is used by shell applications such as the Program Manager, File Manager, or the Explorer, and by OLE applications.

The HKEY_USERS key serves as the root key for the default user preference settings as well as individual user preferences.

The HKEY_CLASSES_USER key is the root key for information relating to the preferences of the current (logged in) user.

Under Windows 95, there are two additional predefined keys. The HKEY_CURRENT_CONFIG key contains information about the current system configuration settings. This key is equivalent to a subkey (such as 0001) of the key HKEY_LOCAL_MACHINE\Config.

The HKEY_DYN_DATA key provides access to dynamic status information, such as information about plug and play devices.

The predefined keys and their relationships are illustrated in Figure 16.1.

FIGURE 16.1.

*Predefined
Registry keys.*

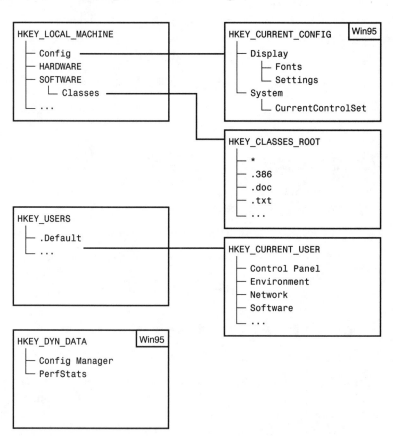

Manually Editing the Registry

The Registry can be manually edited using the Registry Editor. This program is named `regedt32.exe` under Windows NT and `regedit.exe` under Windows 95. The Windows NT program `regedit.exe` is a version of the Registry Editor that offers behavior similar to the 16-bit Windows Registry Editor. This program is not very useful when editing the Registry as it only sees a subset of Registry keys.

Figure 16.2 shows the Windows 95 Registry Editor in operation.

FIGURE 16.2.

The Windows 95 Registry Editor.

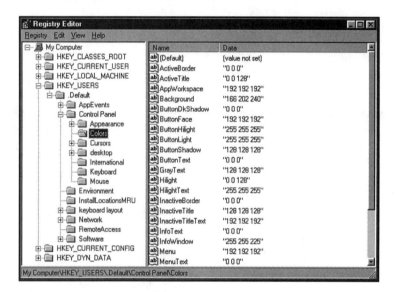

Needless to say, using the Registry Editor is a last resort solution. Programmers may need to frequently access the Registry this way (for example, to remove keys that have been placed there by misbehaving applications that are under development). However, end users should never be required to manually change Registry settings.

Many Registry settings are controlled implicitly through configuration applications such as the Control Panel. Other Registry settings are created during application installation. OLE applications that have been created using AppWizard update their Registry settings every time they run.

Commonly Used Registry Keys

Information about Registry keys is often difficult to find. For this reason, I decided to collect information on some frequently used Registry keys here that are of interest to the programmer.

Subtrees in *HKEY_LOCAL_MACHINE*

Keys in HKEY_LOCAL_MACHINE contain information about the computer's software and hardware configuration. Of these, the Config and Enum subkeys are specific to Windows 95 and its plug and play capabilities. The Config subkey is where Windows 95 stores various hardware configurations; the Enum subkey contains Windows 95 bus enumerators that build the tree of hardware devices.

Both Windows 95 and Windows NT maintain the System subkey under HKEY_LOCAL_MACHINE. The System\CurrentControlSet subkey contains configuration information for services and device drivers.

Other subkeys in HKEY_LOCAL_MACHINE include Software and Classes. The Software subkey is where information about installed software packages can be found. The Classes subkey is where HKEY_CLASSES_ROOT points to.

The Software subtree is of peculiar interest to application programmers. This is where you should store configuration and installation information specific to your application. Microsoft recommends that you build a series of subtrees under HKEY_LOCAL_MACHINE\Software. These subkeys should represent your company name, the name of your product, and the product's version number:

```
HKEY_LOCAL_MACHINE\Software\CompanyName\ProductName\1.0
```

For example, configuration information pertaining to the version of Microsoft Bookshelf that is installed on my computer can be found under the following key:

```
HKEY_LOCAL_MACHINE\Software\Microsoft\Bookshelf '95\95.0.0.39
```

What you store under such a key is entirely application-dependent. Note that you should not store anything here that is user-specific; user-specific information pertinent to your application should be organized under a subkey of HKEY_CURRENT_USER.

Of particular interest is the key

```
HKEY_LOCAL_MACHINE\Software\Microsoft\Windows\CurrentVersion
```

which describes the current Windows configuration. Another important key is

```
HKEY_LOCAL_MACHINE\Software\Microsoft\Windows NT\CurrentVersion
```

This key actually has a curious, unexpected role under Windows 95. I presume the reason is to maintain compatibility with 32-bit debuggers originally written for Windows NT, but debugger information stored under the key

```
HKEY_LOCAL_MACHINE\Software\Microsoft\Windows NT\CurrentVersion\Aedebug
```

will affect debugger behavior under Windows 95.

Subtrees in *HKEY_CLASSES_ROOT*

The HKEY_CLASSES_ROOT key contains two types of subkeys: subkeys that correspond to filename extensions and class definition subkeys.

A filename extension subkey has a name that corresponds to the filename extension (such as .doc). The key typically contains one unnamed value, which holds the name of the class definition subkey.

A class definition subkey describes the behavior of a document class. The information stored here includes data on shell and OLE-related properties.

A subkey under HKEY_CLASSES_ROOT is CLSID. This is the place where OLE class identifiers are stored.

When you create an MFC application using the Visual C++ AppWizard, a series of subkeys that are to be installed under HKEY_CLASSES_ROOT are also created. These identify the document type and filename extension of your new application and also its OLE properties such as the OLE class identifier. For example, creating an MFC application named Test with a file extension .tst for its document files yielded the following Registry entries under HKEY_CLASSES_ROOT:

```
.TST = Test.Document
Test.Document\shell\open\command = TEST.EXE %1
Test.Document\shell\open\ddeexec = [open("%1")]
Test.Document\shell\open\ddeexec\application = TEST
Test.Document = Test Document
Test.Document\protocol\StdFileEditing\server = TEST.EXE
Test.Document\protocol\StdFileEditing\verb\0 = &Edit
Test.Document\Insertable =
Test.Document\CLSID = {FC168A60-F1EA-11CE-87C3-00403321BFAC}
```

The following entries were also created under HKEY_CLASSES_ROOT\CLSID:

```
{FC168A60-F1EA-11CE-87C3-00403321BFAC} = Test Document
{FC168A60-F1EA-11CE-87C3-00403321BFAC}\DefaultIcon = TEST.EXE,1
{FC168A60-F1EA-11CE-87C3-00403321BFAC}\LocalServer32 = TEST.EXE
{FC168A60-F1EA-11CE-87C3-00403321BFAC}\ProgId = Test.Document
{FC168A60-F1EA-11CE-87C3-00403321BFAC}\MiscStatus = 32
{FC168A60-F1EA-11CE-87C3-00403321BFAC}\AuxUserType\3 = test
{FC168A60-F1EA-11CE-87C3-00403321BFAC}\AuxUserType\2 = Test
{FC168A60-F1EA-11CE-87C3-00403321BFAC}\Insertable =
{FC168A60-F1EA-11CE-87C3-00403321BFAC}\verb\1 = &Open,0,2
{FC168A60-F1EA-11CE-87C3-00403321BFAC}\verb\0 = &Edit,0,2
{FC168A60-F1EA-11CE-87C3-00403321BFAC}\InprocHandler32 = ole32.dll
```

Subtrees in *HKEY_USERS*

The key HKEY_USERS contains a subkey named .Default and zero or more subkeys corresponding to users on the system. The .Default subkey corresponds to the default user profile. Other entries correspond to profiles of existing users.

Subtrees in *HKEY_CURRENT_USER*

The HKEY_CURRENT_USER key corresponds to the profile of the currently logged in user. This key has several subkeys, some common to both Windows 95 and Windows NT, some specific to one or the other.

Application configuration information specific to the current user should be stored under the subkey Software. Information should be organized by keys corresponding to company name, product name, and product version number. For example, user settings for Microsoft Excel 5.0 can be found under the key

HKEY_CURRENT_USER\Software\Microsoft\Excel\5.0

The user's settings and preferences for Windows, its components, and applets can be found under the key

HKEY_CURRENT_USER\Software\Microsoft\Windows\CurrentVersion

and its subkeys.

The Registry and INI Files

In new applications, the Registry should be used instead of INI files. This is obvious; but what about old applications, how would they behave under 32-bit Windows?

As it turns out, their behavior is different under Windows NT and Windows 95. In order to maintain maximum backward compatibility, Windows 95 still maintains INI files, such as a win.ini file or a system.ini file. These files do not exist under Windows NT. Instead, Windows NT maps these files to the Registry.

Which files are mapped and which are not is determined by the settings under the key

SOFTWARE\Microsoft\Windows NT\CurrentVersion\IniFileMapping

This key contains a subkey for every mapped INI file. Values under such a subkey correspond to sections in the INI file and typically point to other keys in the Registry.

The mapping of INI files affects the operation of functions such as ReadProfileString or WriteProfileString. If a mapping exists for the specified INI file, these functions will read from and write to the Registry as opposed to an actual INI file.

Application Programs and the Registry

The Win32 API offers a variety of functions for manipulating the Registry.

Opening a Registry Key

All access to the Registry is performed through handles. In order to access a key in the Registry, applications must use a handle to an existing, open key. There are several predefined key handles that are assumed to be always open. These handles include the following: HKEY_LOCAL_MACHINE, HKEY_CLASSES_ROOT, HKEY_USERS, HKEY_CURRENT_USER.

A Registry key is accessed through the function RegOpenKeyEx. For example, in order to obtain a handle to the Registry key HKEY_LOCAL_MACHINE\Software, one would issue the following call:

```
RegOpenKeyEx(HKEY_LOCAL_MACHINE, "Software", 0, KEY_READ, &hKey);
```

To access a subkey under the key HKEY_LOCAL_MACHINE\Software, it is necessary to call RegOpenKeyEx again. For example, to obtain a handle to HKEY_LOCAL_MACHINE\Software\Classes, one would have to issue the following two calls:

```
RegOpenKeyEx(HKEY_LOCAL_MACHINE, "Software", 0, KEY_READ, &hKey);
RegOpenKeyEx(hKey, "Classes", 0, KEY_READ, &hSubKey);
```

Logical as it may appear, it is not possible to use concatenated key values delimited by a backslash as the keyname parameter to RegOpenKeyEx. Thus, the following call is an error:

```
RegOpenKeyEx(hKey, "Key\\Subkey", 0, KEY_READ, &hSubKey); // ERROR!
```

When an application is finished using a Registry key, it should close the key by calling RegCloseKey.

Querying a Value

A Registry value can be retrieved by calling the RegQueryValueEx function. Before this function can be called, the appropriate subkey must be opened using RegOpenKey.

RegQueryValueEx offers a mechanism that enables applications to find out the memory requirements for storing a value before the value is actually retrieved. If you call this function with a NULL pointer passed as the data buffer pointer, the function will return the requested length of the data buffer without actually copying any data. Thus, it is possible to call RegQueryValueEx twice: first to obtain the length of the buffer, and next to actually copy the data, as in the following example:

```
RegQueryValueEx(hKey, "MyValue", NULL, &dwType, NULL, &dwSize);
pData = malloc(dwSize);
RegQueryValueEx(hKey, "MyValue", NULL, &dwType, pData, &dwSize);
```

Setting a Value

A value in the Registry can be set using the RegSetValueEx function. Before this function can be used, the appropriate subkey must be opened with KEY_SET_VALUE access using RegOpenKeyEx.

Creating a New Key

Applications can also create a new subkey in the Registry. The `RegCreateKeyEx` function creates the new key, opens it, and obtains a key handle. This function can also be used to open existing keys; thus it is ideal in situations when the application wishes to access a key whether it already exists or not—during an installation procedure, for example.

Under Windows NT, when creating a new key, the application also assigns security attributes to it. The key's security attributes determine who can access the key for reading and writing. Security information can be obtained about an open key using `RegGetKeySecurity` and set using `RegSetKeySecurity` (that is, if the application has the necessary privileges).

Other Registry Functions

There are several other functions that assist in dealing with the Registry efficiently. For example, the `RegEnumKeyEx` and `RegEnumValue` functions can be used to enumerate the subkeys and values under a specific Registry key. Registry keys can be deleted using the `RegDeleteKey` function. Several other functions exist to deal with saving and loading subkeys, connecting to remote Registries, and performing other administrative functions.

A Working Example

To demonstrate the use of the Registry from application programs, I decided to create a simple command-line program to read Registry settings. This program is shown in Listing 16.1. To compile this program from the command line, you must specify the advanced API library: `cl readreg.cpp advapi32.lib`.

Listing 16.1. A simple Registry reader.

```
#include <windows.h>
#include <iostream.h>
#include <iomanip.h>
#include <string.h>

#define STR_HKEY_LOCAL_MACHINE "HKEY_LOCAL_MACHINE"
#define STR_HKEY_CLASSES_ROOT "HKEY_CLASSES_ROOT"
#define STR_HKEY_USERS "HKEY_USERS"
#define STR_HKEY_CURRENT_USER "HKEY_CURRENT_USER"

#define LEN_HKEY_LOCAL_MACHINE (sizeof(STR_HKEY_LOCAL_MACHINE)-1)
#define LEN_HKEY_CLASSES_ROOT (sizeof(STR_HKEY_CLASSES_ROOT)-1)
#define LEN_HKEY_USERS (sizeof(STR_HKEY_USERS)-1)
#define LEN_HKEY_CURRENT_USER (sizeof(STR_HKEY_CURRENT_USER)-1)

#define SWAP_ENDIAN(x) (((x<<24)&0xFF000000)¦((x<<8)&0xFF0000)¦\
                       ((x>>8)&0xFF00)¦((x>>24)¦0xFF))

void printval(unsigned char *pBuffer, DWORD dwType, DWORD dwSize)
```

```
{
    switch (dwType)
    {
        case REG_BINARY:
            cout << "Binary data:";
            {
                for (unsigned int i = 0; i < dwSize; i++)
                {
                    if (i % 16 == 0) cout << '\n';
                    cout.fill('0');
                    cout << hex << setw(2) <<
                            (unsigned int)(pBuffer[i]) << ' ';
                }
            }
            cout << '\n';
            break;
        case REG_DWORD:
            cout.fill('0');
            cout << "Double word: " << hex << setw(8) <<
                    *((unsigned int *)pBuffer) << '\n';
            break;
        case REG_DWORD_BIG_ENDIAN:  // Intel specific!
            cout.fill('0');
            cout << "Big-endian double word: " << hex << setw(8) <<
                    SWAP_ENDIAN(*((unsigned int *)pBuffer)) << '\n';
            break;
        case REG_EXPAND_SZ:
            cout << "Expandable string: " << pBuffer << '\n';
            break;
        case REG_LINK:
            cout << "Unicode link.";
            break;
        case REG_MULTI_SZ:
            cout << "Multiple strings:\n";
            {
                char *pStr;
                int i;
                for (i = 0, pStr = (char *)pBuffer; *pStr != '\0';
                     i++, pStr += strlen((char *)pStr) + 1)
                {
                    cout << "String " << i << ": " << pStr << '\n';
                }
            }
            break;
        case REG_NONE:
            cout << "Undefined value type.\n";
            break;
        case REG_RESOURCE_LIST:
            cout << "Resource list.\n";
            break;
        case REG_SZ:
            cout << "String: " << pBuffer << '\n';
            break;
        default:
            cout << "Invalid type code.\n";
            break;
    }
```

continues

Listing 16.1. continued

```c
}

void main(void)
{
    char szKey[1000];
    char *pKey;
    HKEY hKey, hSubKey;
    DWORD dwType;
    DWORD dwSize;
    unsigned char *pBuffer;
    int nKey;

    while (1)
    {
        cout << "Enter key: ";
        cin.getline(szKey, 1000);
        nKey = strcspn(szKey, "\\");
        hKey = NULL;
        if (!strncmp(szKey, STR_HKEY_LOCAL_MACHINE, nKey) &&
                nKey == LEN_HKEY_LOCAL_MACHINE)
            hKey = HKEY_LOCAL_MACHINE;
        if (!strncmp(szKey, STR_HKEY_CLASSES_ROOT, nKey) &&
                nKey == LEN_HKEY_CLASSES_ROOT)
            hKey = HKEY_CLASSES_ROOT;
        if (!strncmp(szKey, STR_HKEY_USERS, nKey) &&
                nKey == LEN_HKEY_USERS)
            hKey = HKEY_USERS;
        if (!strncmp(szKey, STR_HKEY_CURRENT_USER, nKey) &&
                nKey == LEN_HKEY_CURRENT_USER)
            hKey = HKEY_CURRENT_USER;
        if (hKey == NULL || szKey[nKey] != '\\')
        {
            cout << "Invalid key.\n";
            continue;
        }
        pKey = szKey + nKey + 1;
        nKey = strcspn(pKey, "\\");
        while (pKey[nKey] == '\\')
        {
            pKey[nKey] = '\0';
            if (RegOpenKeyEx(hKey, pKey, NULL, KEY_READ,&hSubKey)
                == ERROR_SUCCESS)
            {
                RegCloseKey(hKey);
                hKey = hSubKey;
            }
            else
            {
                RegCloseKey(hKey);
                hKey = NULL;
                break;
            }
            pKey += nKey + 1;
            nKey = strcspn(pKey, "\\");
        }
        if (hKey == NULL)
        {
```

```
            cout << "Invalid key.\n";
            continue;
        }
        if (RegQueryValueEx(hKey, pKey, NULL, &dwType, NULL,
                            &dwSize) == ERROR_SUCCESS)
        {
            pBuffer = (unsigned char *)malloc(dwSize);
            if (pBuffer == NULL)
            {
                cout << "Insufficient memory.\n";
                break;
            }
            if (RegQueryValueEx(hKey, pKey, NULL, &dwType, pBuffer,
                                &dwSize) == ERROR_SUCCESS)
                printval(pBuffer, dwType, dwSize);
            else
                cout << "Error reading key.\n";
            free(pBuffer);
        }
        else
            cout << "Error reading key.\n";
        RegCloseKey(hKey);
    }
}
```

This program demonstrates many aspects of handling the Registry. Execution begins in the main function where the program immediately enters an endless loop (terminate the program by hitting Ctrl+C). After displaying a prompt and reading in a Registry key typed by the user, the program first checks for the presence of the name of any of the top-level keys in the string the user typed. If such a keyname is found, the program begins an iteration.

The string typed by the user is expected to contain backslash characters as key delimiters. In the iteration part, subsequent strings are extracted from the input string using the strcspn function. The iteration proceeds until the last string is extracted, which is assumed to be a value name. The iteration allows for empty (zero-length) names for both keys and values.

During the iteration, a key handle is obtained through RegOpenKeyEx for every string extracted from the user input. If obtaining the key handle fails (presumably because the user specified an invalid key) the iteration stops with an error. However, if the iteration succeeds, the value corresponding to the last extracted string is retrieved by calling RegQueryValueEx. This function is in fact called twice: once to determine the amount of memory required to store the data and a second time to actually retrieve the data.

The value is printed in the printval function. This function takes a pointer to the value and takes the value's type and its length, from which it produces formatted output.

Here is some sample output produced by this program:

```
Enter key: HKEY_CURRENT_USER\Software\Microsoft\Hover!\HighScoreNames
Multiple strings:
String 0: Viktor
```

```
String 1: Steve
String 2: John
String 3: Patrick
String 4: Jennifer
String 5: Julie
String 6: Jon
String 7: Tony
String 8: Larry
String 9: Harley
Enter key: HKEY_LOCAL_MACHINE\Enum\Monitor\Default_Monitor\0001\ConfigFlags
Binary data:
00 00 00 00
Enter key: HKEY_CURRENT_USER\Environment\include
Expandable string: f:\msvc20\include;f:\msvc20\mfc\include
```

You may even find this program useful when trying to determine the exact type of a value in the Registry, above and beyond the information provided by the Registry Editor. With some work, the program could be modified to have the capability to actually write to the Registry as well.

Summary

The Registry is a place where Windows and applications can store configuration data. The Registry is a tree-like, hierarchically organized information store. Registry entries, or keys, are identified by a name and may contain any number of subkeys or values.

At the top level of the Registry are the root keys HKEY_USERS and HKEY_LOCAL_MACHINE. Other predefined keys include HKEY_CLASSES_ROOT, HKEY_CURRENT_USER, HKEY_CURRENT_CONFIG, and HKEY_DYN_DATA.

A Registry value can be a 4-byte integer, a string or a series of strings, or arbitrary binary data. Registry values are usually created by application programs, installation procedures, or configuration utilities such as the Control Panel. However, the Registry can also be manually edited using the Registry Editor.

Applications typically store configuration information under HKEY_LOCAL_MACHINE\Software, and user-specific data under HKEY_CURRENT_USER\Software. In both cases, subkeys should be created to correspond to a company name, product name, and product version number.

Additionally, applications that manage specific document types create a filename extension and a class definition entry under HKEY_CLASSES_ROOT. OLE applications also store OLE information here.

The Win32 API provides a series of functions for applications to access the Registry. Using one of the predefined Registry keys, applications can access any subkey for reading and writing, query values, and set values. Applications can also create new keys or delete existing keys.

Exception Handling

17

The Win32 API supports *structured exception handling*. Through this mechanism, applications can handle various hardware- and software-related conditions. Structured exception handling is not to be confused with the concept of exceptions in the C++ language, which is a feature of that language. The Win32 exception handling mechanism is not dependent on its implementation in a specific language. To avoid confusion, I decided to follow the conventions used in Microsoft documentation and use the term "C exception" to refer to Win32 structured exceptions, and "C++ exception" to refer to the typed exception handling mechanism of the C++ language.

Exception Handling in C and C++

Microsoft provides a set of extensions to the C language, which enable C programs to handle Win32 structured exceptions. This exception handling mechanism is markedly different from the typed exceptions in the C++ language. This section offers a review of both mechanisms in the context of exceptions in the Win32 environment.

C Exceptions

What is, indeed, an exception? How do exceptions work? In order to understand the exception handling mechanism, first take a look at the program shown in Listing 17.1.

Listing 17.1. A program that generates an exception.

```
void main(void)
{
    int x, y;
    x = 5;
    y = 0;
    x = x / y;
}
```

Needless to say, an integer division by zero is likely to cause a program to terminate abnormally. If you compile the above program and run it under Windows 95, it generates the dialog shown in Figure 17.1.

FIGURE 17.1.

Division by zero error.

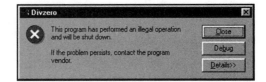

What exactly happened here? Obviously, when you attempt to divide by zero, the processor will generate an error condition (the actual mechanism is hardware dependent and not of our concern). This error condition is detected by the operating system, which looks for an *exception handler* for the specific error condition. As no such handler was detected, the default exception handling mechanism took over, displaying the dialog.

Using the C exception handling mechanism, it is possible for us to *catch* this exception and handle the divide by zero condition gracefully. Consider the program shown in Listing 17.2.

Listing 17.2. Handling the divide by zero exception.

```c
#include "windows.h"

void main(void)
{
    int x, y;
    __try
    {
        x = 5;
        y = 0;
        x = x / y;
    }
    __except (GetExceptionCode() == EXCEPTION_INT_DIVIDE_BY_ZERO ?
              EXCEPTION_EXECUTE_HANDLER :
              EXCEPTION_CONTINUE_SEARCH)
    {
        printf("Divide by zero error.\n");
    }
}
```

Running this program no longer produces the dialog shown in Figure 17.1; instead, the message "Divide by zero error" is printed and the program terminates gracefully.

The block of statements following the __try instruction is often called a *guard block*. This block of statements is executed unconditionally. When an exception is raised within the guard block, the expression following the __except statement (often called the *filter expression*) is evaluated. This expression should be an integer expression yielding one of the following values:

Table 17.1. Filter expression values.

Symbolic constant	Value	Description
EXCEPTION_CONTINUE_EXECUTION	-1	Continue execution at the location where exception was raised
EXCEPTION_CONTINUE_SEARCH	0	Pass control to next exception handler
EXCEPTION_EXECUTE_HANDLER	1	Execute exception handler

If the filter expression's value is -1 (EXCEPTION_CONTINUE_EXECUTION), execution continues at the location where the exception was raised. That is, *at* the location, not *after*—which means that the offending piece of code may get executed again. Whether it actually does get executed or not depends on the type of the exception. For example, in the case of an integer division by zero, it does; in the case of a floating-point division by zero, it does not. In any case, care should be taken to avoid creating an infinite loop by returning control to the point where the error occurs without eliminating the conditions which caused the exception in the first place.

In the other two cases, the first thing that happens is that the guard block goes out of scope. Any function calls that might have been interrupted by the exception are terminated and the stack is unwound.

If the filter expression evaluates to 1 (EXCEPTION_EXECUTE_HANDLER), control is transferred to the statement block following the __except statement.

The third filter value, 0 (EXCEPTION_CONTINUE_SEARCH), hints at the possibility of nested exceptions. Indeed, consider the program shown in Listing 17.3. In this program, two exceptions are generated, one for a floating-point division by zero, one for an integer division by zero. The two exceptions are handled very differently.

Listing 17.3. Nesting exception handlers.

```
#include <stdio.h>
#include <float.h>
#include <windows.h>

int divzerofilter(unsigned int code, int *j)
{
    printf("Inside divzerofilter\n");
    if (code == EXCEPTION_INT_DIVIDE_BY_ZERO)
    {
        *j = 2;
        printf("Handling an integer division error.\n");
        return EXCEPTION_CONTINUE_EXECUTION;
    }
    else return EXCEPTION_CONTINUE_SEARCH;
}

void divzero()
{
    double x, y;
    int i, j;

    __try
    {
        x = 10.0;
        y = 0.0;
        i = 10;
        j = 0;
        i = i / j;
        printf("i = %d\n", i);
        x = x / y;
```

```
        printf("x = %f\n", x);
    }
    __except (divzerofilter(GetExceptionCode(), &j))
    {
    }
}

void main(void)
{
    _controlfp(_EM_OVERFLOW, _MCW_EM);
    __try
    {
        divzero();
    }
    __except (GetExceptionCode() == EXCEPTION_FLT_DIVIDE_BY_ZERO ?
            EXCEPTION_EXECUTE_HANDLER :
            EXCEPTION_CONTINUE_SEARCH)
    {
        printf("Floating point divide by zero error.\n");
    }
}
```

When an exception is raised inside the divzero function, the filter expression is evaluated. This results in a call to the divzerofilter function. The function checks if the exception was an integer division by zero exception; if so, it corrects the value of the divisor (j) and returns the EXCEPTION_CONTINUE_EXECUTION value, which causes the exception handling mechanism to return control to the point where the exception was raised. In the case of any other exceptions, divzerofilter returns EXCEPTION_CONTINUE_SEARCH; this causes the exception handling mechanism to seek another exception handler.

This other exception handler has been installed in the main function. This handler handles floating-point division by zero exceptions. Instead of returning to the point where execution was interrupted, it simply prints an error message.

Running this program produces the following output:

```
Inside divzerofilter
Handling an integer division error.
i = 5
Inside divzerofilter
Floating point divide by zero error.
```

As you can see, both times an exception is raised, the exception filter installed in the function divzero is activated. However, in the case of the floating-point division, the exception remains unhandled; therefore, the exception is propagated to the next level, the exception handler installed in the main function.

NOTE

To handle floating-point exceptions, it was necessary to call the _controlfp function.

This function can be used to enable floating-point exceptions. By default, floating-point exceptions on the Intel architecture are disabled; instead, the floating-point library generates IEEE-compatible infinite results.

A discussion of C exception handling would not be complete without a list of some of the commonly occurring C exceptions. These exceptions are shown in Table 17.2.

Table 17.2. Filter expression values.

Symbolic constant	Description
EXCEPTION_ACCESS_VIOLATION	Reference to invalid memory location
EXCEPTION_PRIV_INSTRUCTION	Attempt to execute privileged instruction
EXCEPTION_STACK_OVERFLOW	Stack overflow
EXCEPTION_FLT_DIVIDE_BY_ZERO	Floating-point division
EXCEPTION_FLT_OVERFLOW	Floating point result too large
EXCEPTION_FLT_UNDERFLOW	Floating point result too small
EXCEPTION_INT_DIVIDE_BY_ZERO	Integer division
EXCEPTION_INT_OVERFLOW	Integer result too large

In addition to system-generated exceptions, applications can raise software exceptions using the RaiseException function. Windows reserves exception values with bit 29 set for user-defined software exceptions.

C Termination Handling

Closely related to the handling of C exceptions is the topic of C termination handling. To better understand the problem of which termination handling provides a solution, consider the program shown in Listing 17.4.

Listing 17.4. Resource allocation problem.

```
#include <stdio.h>
#include <windows.h>

void badmem()
{
    char *p;

    printf("allocating p\n");
    p = malloc(1000);
```

```
        printf("p[1000000] = %c\n", p[1000000]);
        printf("freeing p\n");
        free(p);
}

void main(void)
{
    __try
    {
        badmem();
    }
    __except (GetExceptionCode() == EXCEPTION_ACCESS_VIOLATION ?
                EXCEPTION_EXECUTE_HANDLER :
                EXCEPTION_CONTINUE_SEARCH)
    {
        printf("An access violation has occurred.");
    }
}
```

In this program, the function badmem allocates the p character array. However, its execution is interrupted when it refers to an invalid array element. Because of this, the function never has a chance to free up the allocated array, as demonstrated by its output:

```
allocating p
An access violation has occurred.
```

This problem can be solved by installing a termination handler in the badmem function, as shown in Listing 17.5.

Listing 17.5. A termination handler.

```
#include <stdio.h>
#include <windows.h>

void badmem()
{
    char *p;

    __try
    {
        printf("allocating p\n");
        p = malloc(1000);
        printf("p[1000000] = %c\n", p[1000000]);
    }
    __finally
    {
        printf("freeing p\n");
        free(p);
    }
}

void main(void)
{
    __try
```

Listing 17.5. continued

```
    {
        badmem();
    }
    __except (GetExceptionCode() == EXCEPTION_ACCESS_VIOLATION ?
            EXCEPTION_EXECUTE_HANDLER :
            EXCEPTION_CONTINUE_SEARCH)
    {
        printf("An access violation has occurred.");
    }
}
```

Running this program produces the desired result:

```
allocating p
freeing p
An access violation has occurred.
```

As you can see, the instructions in the badmem function are now enclosed in a __try block, which is now followed by the __finally keyword. The __finally keyword is special in that the instruction block that follows it is *always* executed, no matter under what circumstances the function terminates. So when badmem goes out of scope due to the exception, the instructions in the __finally block are given a chance to clean up any resources that might have been allocated within this function.

C++ Exception Handling

The Win32 exception handling mechanism uses the GetExceptionCode function to determine the nature of the exception. In contrast, C++ exception handling is type-based; the nature of the exception is determined by its type.

Most examples that demonstrate C++ exception handling do so in the context of a class declaration. This is not necessary, and in my opinion often hides the simplicity of C++ exception handling. Consider the simple example in Listing 17.6. (When you compile this example or any other program that uses C++ exceptions, do not forget to add the /GX switch to the cl command line.)

Listing 17.6. C++ Exception handling.

```
#include <iostream.h>

int divide(int x, int y)
{
    if (y == 0) throw int();
    return x / y;
}

void main(void)
{
```

```
    int x, y;

    try
    {
        x = 5;
        y = 0;
        x = divide(x, y);
    }
    catch (int)
    {
        cout << "A division by zero was attempted.\n";
    }
}
```

In this example, the function `divide` raises an exception of type `int` when a division by zero is attempted. This exception is caught by the exception handler in `main`.

Termination Handling in C++

C++ exceptions can also be used for termination handling. For termination handling, a C++ program can wrap a block of code using a "catchall" exception handler, and perform resource cleanup before propagating all exceptions to a higher level handler by using `throw`. Consider the example in Listing 17.7, which is a C++ variant of the program shown in Listing 17.5.

Listing 17.7. Termination handling with C++ exceptions.

```
#include <stdio.h>
#include <windows.h>

void badmem()
{
    char *p;

    try
    {
        printf("allocating p\n");
        p = (char *)malloc(1000);
        printf("p[1000000] = %c\n", p[1000000]);
    }
    catch(...)
    {
        printf("freeing p\n");
        free(p);
        throw;
    }
}

void main(void)
{
    try
    {
```

continues

Listing 17.7. continued

```
        badmem();
    }
    catch(...)
    {
        printf("An exception was raised.");
    }
}
```

Running this program produces the following output:

```
allocating p
freeing p
An exception was raised.
```

The exception handler in the function badmem plays the role of the __finally block in the C exception handling mechanism.

Although these examples demonstrate the power of C++ exception handling with C-style code, the use of classes in exception handling has some obvious advantages. For example, when the exception is thrown, an object of the type of the exception is actually created; thus it is possible to provide additional information about the exception in the form of member variables. Also, appropriate use of constructors and destructors can replace the relatively inelegant resource cleanup mechanism shown in Listing 17.7.

C++ Exception Classes

Visual C++ Version 4 provides an implementation of the exception class hierarchy, as put forward in the draft ANSI C++ standard. This hierarchy consists of the exception class and derived classes representing various conditions, such as run-time errors. The exception class and derived classes are declared in the header file stdexcpt.h. Because these classes are based on an evolving draft standard, it is possible that they will change with future releases of Visual C++.

Mixing C and C++ Exceptions

While the C compiler does not support C++ exceptions, the C++ compiler supports both C++ exceptions and the Microsoft extensions for C exceptions. Sometimes it is necessary to mix these two in order to use the C++ exception syntax while catching Win32 structured exceptions. There are basically two methods for this: You can use an ellipsis handler, or you can use a translator function.

The Ellipsis Handler

In the termination handling example shown in Listing 17.7, we already made use of the *ellipsis handler*. This catchall handler, which has the form

```
catch(...)
{
}
```

can be used to catch exceptions of any type, including C exceptions. This offers a simple exception handling mechanism like the one used in Listing 17.7. Unfortunately, the ellipsis handler does not have any information about the actual type of the structured exception.

This should be easy, you say. (Well, I certainly said that when I first read about the differences between C and C++ exception handling.) Why not just catch an exception of type unsigned int (after all, the Microsoft Visual C++ documentation states that this is the type of C exceptions) and examine its value? Consider the program in Listing 17.8:

Listing 17.8. Failed attempt to catch C exceptions as C++ exceptions of type unsigned int.

```
#include <windows.h>
#include <iostream.h>

void main(void)
{
    int x, y;

    try
    {
        x = 5;
        y = 0;
        x = x / y;
    }
    catch (unsigned int e)
    {
        if (e == EXCEPTION_INT_DIVIDE_BY_ZERO)
        {
            cout << "Division by zero.\n";
        }
        else throw;
    }
}
```

Alas, this elegant solution is no solution at all. C exceptions can only be caught by an ellipsis handler. But not all is lost just yet; could we not simply use the GetExceptionCode function in the C++ catch block and obtain the structured exception type? For example, consider the program in Listing 17.9.

Listing 17.9. C++ exception handlers cannot call `GetExceptionCode`.

```
#include <windows.h>
#include <iostream.h>

void main(void)
{
    int x, y;

    try
    {
        x = 5;
        y = 0;
        x = x / y;
    }
    catch (...)
    {
        // The following line results in a compiler error
        if (GetExceptionCode() == EXCEPTION_INT_DIVIDE_BY_ZERO)
        {
            cout << "Division by zero.\n";
        }
        else throw;
    }
}
```

As they say, nice try but no cigar. The function `GetExceptionCode` is implemented as an intrinsic function and can only be called as part of the filter expression in a C __except statement. It seems that some other mechanism is necessary to differentiate between C exceptions in C++ code.

There is yet another possible solution. We could create a C exception handler to catch all C exceptions and throw a C++ exception of type `unsigned int` with the value of the C exception code. An example program for this is shown in Listing 17.10.

Listing 17.10. Raising C++ exceptions in a C exception filter.

```
#include <windows.h>
#include <iostream.h>

int divide(int x, int y)
{
    try
    {
        x = x / y;
    }
    catch(unsigned int e)
    {
        cout << "Inside C++ exception.\n";
        if (e == EXCEPTION_INT_DIVIDE_BY_ZERO)
        {
            cout << "Division by zero.\n";
        }
```

```
        else throw;
    }
    return x;
}

unsigned int catchall(unsigned int code)
{
    cout << "inside catchall: " << code << '\n';
    if (code != 0xE06D7363) throw (unsigned int)code;
    return EXCEPTION_CONTINUE_SEARCH;
}

void main(void)
{
    int x, y;

    __try
    {
        x = 10;
        y = 0;
        x = divide(x, y);
    }
    __except(catchall(GetExceptionCode())) {}
}
```

This approach has but one problem. When the `catchall` function throws a C++ exception that is *not* handled by a C++ exception handler, it is treated as yet another C exception, resulting in another call to `catchall`. This would go on forever, were it not for the test for the value `0xE06D7363`, which appears to be a magic value associated with C++ exceptions. But we are getting into seriously undocumented stuff here; there has to be another solution!

At this point, you might ask the obvious question: if C++ programs can use the Microsoft C exception handling mechanism, why go through this dance at all? Why not just use `__try` and `__except` and get it over with? Indeed, this is a valid solution; however, to improve code portability, you may want to use the C++ exception handling mechanism when possible, and localize and dependence on Microsoft extensions as much as possible.

Translating C Exceptions

Fortunately, the Win32 API provides a function that allows a much more elegant solution for translating a C exception into a C++ exception. The name of the function is `_set_se_translator`. Using this function, one can finally obtain an elegant, satisfactory solution for translating C exceptions to C++ exceptions. An example for this is shown in Listing 17.11.

Listing 17.11. Using `_set_se_translator` to translate C exceptions.

```
#include <windows.h>
#include <iostream.h>
#include <eh.h>
```

continues

Listing 17.11. continued

```c
int divide(int x, int y)
{
    try
    {
        x = x / y;
    }
    catch(unsigned int e)
    {
        cout << "Inside C++ exception.\n";
        if (e == EXCEPTION_INT_DIVIDE_BY_ZERO)
        {
            cout << "Division by zero.\n";
        }
        else throw;
    }
    return x;
}

void se_translator(unsigned int e, _EXCEPTION_POINTERS* p)
{
    throw (unsigned int)(e);
}

void main(void)
{
    int x, y;

    _set_se_translator(se_translator);
    x = 10;
    y = 0;
    x = divide(x, y);
}
```

Summary

Win32 programmers using the C++ language must face two separate, only partially compatible exception handling mechanisms. Win32-structured exceptions are often generated by the operating system. These exceptions are not dependent on any language-specific implementation and are used to communicate a condition to the application's exception handler using a 32-bit unsigned value.

In contrast, C++ exceptions are typed expressions; the nature of the exception is often derived from the type of the object that is used when the expression is thrown.

C programs can use the __try and __except keywords (which are Microsoft extensions to the C language) to handle structured exceptions. Exception handlers can be nested. The type of the expression is obtained by calling the GetExceptionCode function in the __except filter expression. Depending on the value of the filter expression, an exception may be handled by the exception handler, execution may continue at the point where the exception occurred, or control can be transferred to the next exception handler. An unhandled exception causes an application error.

C programs can also use termination handlers. These handlers, installed using the __try and __finally keywords, can ensure that a function which is abnormally terminated by an exception is given a chance to perform cleanup.

C++ programs use the C++ try and catch keywords to handle exceptions. The type of the exception is declared following the catch keyword. The catch keyword with an ellipsis declaration (...) can be used to catch all exceptions; one possible use of this construct is to act as a termination handler, analogous to the __finally block in C exception handling.

As C++ programs can also use C exceptions, it is possible to mix the two exception handling mechanisms. C++ programs can catch C exceptions using an ellipsis handler. Unfortunately, this method does not allow C++ programs to obtain the exception code. However, C++ programs can install an exception translator function, which can be used to translate C structured exceptions into C++ typed exceptions.

PART

III

IN THIS PART

Microsoft Foundation Classes

Microsoft Foundation Classes: An Overview

18

The Microsoft Foundation Classes Library is arguably the most distinguishing component of the Visual C++ development system. This vast collection of C++ classes encapsulates most of the Win32 API and provides a powerful framework for typical (and not so typical) applications.

MFC and Applications

A typical MFC application is one that is created using the Visual C++ AppWizard. However, it is not necessary to use the AppWizard to create an MFC application, nor is the use of MFC restricted to such AppWizard-generated programs. Many simple MFC classes can be used in simple programs including, to the surprise of many programmers, command-line (console) applications.

In fact, consider the simple program shown in Listing 18.1. This MFC program can be compiled from the command line (cl /MT hellomfc.cpp).

Listing 18.1. A simple MFC console application.

```
#include <afx.h>

CFile& operator<<(CFile& file, const CString& string)
{
    file.Write(string, string.GetLength());
    return file;
}
void main(void)
{
        CFile file((int)GetStdHandle(STD_OUTPUT_HANDLE));
        CString string = "Hello, MFC!";
        file << string;
}
```

That said, the primary goal of the MFC is to provide an encapsulation for the Windows API. Its major classes, such as CWnd, CDialog, or CGdiObject, represent the results of this design philosophy. Ideally, an MFC application never has to call Windows API functions directly; instead, it constructs an object of the appropriate type and utilizes the object's member functions. The object's constructor and destructor take care of any initialization and cleanup that is necessary.

For example, an application that needs to draw into a window can do so by constructing a CClientDC object and calling the object's member functions (which closely map GDI drawing functions). The CClientDC constructor makes the appropriate calls to create a device context, set up the mapping mode, and perform other initializations. When the object goes out of scope or is destroyed using the delete operator, the destructor automatically releases the device context. This kind of encapsulation would make writing application programs easier even without the benefit of the Developer Studio, its AppWizard, and other powerful features.

The problem many programmers new to MFC must face is the steep learning curve. I remember well that when I first got my hands on MFC 1.0 (which was, needless to say, significantly less complex than MFC 4 is today), I felt at first completely overwhelmed. It seemed that to accomplish even the simplest task took days of browsing through the thick paper manuals. True, it is simple to write a few lines of code like this:

```
CClientDC *pDC;
pDC = new CClientDC(this);
pDC->Rectangle(0, 0, 100, 100);
delete pDC;
```

but only if you know exactly what you are doing! Otherwise, you have to first find out that there is indeed a class that encapsulates the functionality of a device context associated with a window's client area. Next, you must explore the member functions of the CClientDC class and its parent classes, to find out that there is indeed a CDC::Rectangle member function. (After all, a different design approach might have placed such a member function into the CWnd class.) Third, you may wish to double-check to ensure that no other initialization work is needed. With paper manuals and no other guidance, these steps may consume many valuable hours.

That said, the programmer today is not without guidance anymore. Apart from this splendid book you are holding in your hands, there are online references, help files, excellent tutorials, valuable example programs, and most importantly, the AppWizard.

I always found that a high-level overview, "getting the big picture," helps tremendously when trying to understand a complex subject. So before we get bogged down in the details, allow me to devote the rest of this chapter to presenting just such an overview of MFC.

Foundation Class Fundamentals

The classes in MFC are loosely organized into several major categories. Of these, the two major categories are *Application Architecture* classes and *Window Support* classes. Other categories contain classes that encapsulate a variety of system, GDI, or miscellaneous services.

Most classes in MFC are derived from a common root, the CObject class. The CObject class implements two important features: *serialization* and *run-time type information*. (Note that the CObject class predates RTTI, the new C++ run-time type information mechanism; the CObject class does not use RTTI.) However, there are several simple support classes that are not derived from CObject.

The major MFC categories are illustrated in Figure 18.1.

Because of the importance of CObject, we take a look at that class first.

FIGURE 18.1.
Overview of MFC.

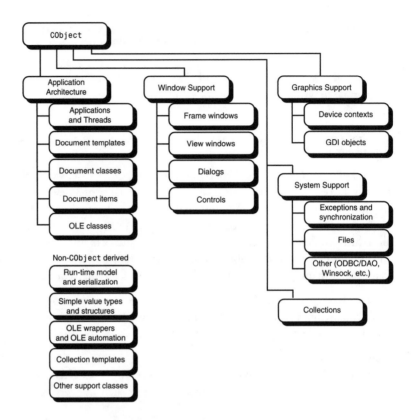

The *CObject* Class and Serialization

As I mentioned, the CObject class, the "mother of all classes" (well, almost) implements serialization and run-time type information. But what do these concepts mean?

Serialization is the conversion of an object to and from a persistent form. Or, in simpler terms, it means writing an object to disk or reading it from the disk or any other forms of persistent storage.

Why is serialization necessary? Why not just write

```
cout << myObject;
```

and get it over with? For one thing, everybody knows that writing anything to disk that involves pointers can be tricky. When you later read that disk file, chances are that whatever your pointer pointed to has either been moved or is no longer present in memory at all. But this is not the end of the story.

MFC objects are not only written to disk files. Serialization is also used to place an object on the clipboard or to prepare the object for OLE embedding.

The MFC Library uses CArchive objects for serialization. A CArchive object represents persistent storage of some kind. When an object is about to be serialized, CArchive calls the object's Serialize member function, one of the overridable functions in CObject. Thus, the underlying philosophy is that it is the object that knows best how to prepare itself for persistent storage, while it is the CArchive object that knows how to transfer the resulting data stream to persistent media.

But let an example do the talking. This example implements something simple, a string class CMyString. (Note that this has nothing to do with the sophisticated MFC CString class; the sole purpose of this exercise is to demonstrate CObject serialization.)

CMyString has two data members; one represents the length of the string, the other is a pointer to the string data. Unlike C strings, a CMyString can contain embedded null characters and does not require a terminating null character. The declaration of the CMyString class would thus look like this (only the data members and the Serialize member function are shown):

```
class CMyString
{
private:
    WORD m_nLength;
    LPSTR m_pString;
public:
    virtual void Serialize(CArchive &ar);
};
```

Why am I using the Windows type WORD instead of declaring m_nLength an integer? There is a very important reason. Windows guarantees that the WORD type will represent a 16-bit integer on all present and future versions of Windows. This is important when it comes to storing data on persistent storage; it ensures that data files written under one operating system specific version of our application remain readable under another. Had we used int instead, we would be facing the problem that an int is a 16-bit type under Windows 3.1, a 32-bit type under Windows 95 and Windows NT, and who knows what under future versions of Windows. Thus, data files created under these different operating systems would be incompatible.

The Serialize member function is responsible for actually writing data to, and reading data from, a CArchive object. However, we cannot simply just write m_nLength and m_pString to the archive. Instead, we have to write the data m_pString points to, that is, the string itself. When it comes to reading the data, we must first determine the length of the string, allocate memory for it, and then read the string itself:

```
CMyString::Serialize(CArchive &ar)
{
    if (ar.IsStoring())
    {
        ar << m_nLength;
        ar.Write(m_pString, m_nLength);
    }
    else
    {
        ar >> m_nLength;
```

```
        m_pString = new char[m_nLength];
        ar.Read(m_pString, m_nLength);
    }
}
```

In order for this code to compile and run correctly, it is also necessary to use a few helper macros. For a class to be serializable, one must use the DECLARE_SERIAL macro in the class declaration and the IMPLEMENT_SERIAL macro somewhere in the class's implementation file. One specific feature that these macros add to a class is MFC run-time type information.

Why is type information necessary for successful serialization? Well, consider what happens when data is read from persistent storage. Before reading an object, we know nothing about it other than the fact that it is CObject derived. Run-time type information that has been serialized together with the object helps to determine the actual type of the object. Once type information has been obtained, the CArchive object can create an object of the new type and call its Serialize member function to read in object-specific data. Without run-time type information this would not be possible.

Run-Time Type Information

MFC maintains run-time type information with the help of the CRuntimeClass class and several helper macros.

The CRuntimeClass class has member variables holding the name of the class and the size of an object belonging to that class. This information not only identifies the class but also assists in serialization.

Applications rarely use CRuntimeClass directly. Instead, they rely on a series of macros that embed a CRuntimeClass object in the declaration of a CObject-derived class and provide an implementation.

There are three pairs of macros, summarized in Table 18.1.

Table 18.1. Helper macros.

Symbolic constant	Description
DECLARE_DYNAMIC and IMPLEMENT_DYNAMIC	Adds run-time information to the class. Enables the use of the IsKindOf member function.
DECLARE_DYNCREATE and IMPLEMENT_DYNCREATE	Renders the class dynamically creatable through CRuntimeClass::CreateObject.
DECLARE_SERIAL and IMPLEMENT_SERIAL	Adds serialization capability to the class; enables the use of << and >> operators with a CArchive.

You only need to use one set of these macros at any time. The functionality of DECLARE_DYNCREATE/ IMPLEMENT_DYNCREATE is a superset of the functionality of DECLARE_DYNAMIC/IMPLEMENT_DYNAMIC; and the functionality of DECLARE_SERIAL/IMPLEMENT_SERIAL is a superset of the functionality of DECLARE_DYNAMIC/IMPLEMENT_DYNAMIC.

To use these macros, you embed the DECLARE_ macro in the declaration of your class and you add the IMPLEMENT_ macro to your implementation file. To create a CMyString class that is CObject-derived and supports serialization, you would therefore declare the class as follows:

```
class CMyString : public CObject
{
    DECLARE_SERIAL(CMyString)
    ...
};
```

In the implementation file, you would add the following macro (outside any member functions):

```
IMPLEMENT_SERIAL(CMyString, CObject, 0)
```

MFC and Multiple Inheritance

A frequently asked question with respect to MFC concerns the use of the classes of MFC with multiple inheritance. Generally, the answer is that although using multiple inheritance with MFC is possible, doing so is not recommended.

In particular, the CRuntimeClass class does not support multiple inheritance. As CRuntimeClass is used by CObject for run-time class information, dynamic object creation, and serialization, this limitation has a serious effect on any attempt to use multiple inheritance in an MFC program.

If your project requires the use of multiple inheritance with MFC, I recommend MFC Technical Note 16 (*Using C++ Multiple Inheritance with MFC*), supplied as part of the Visual C++ on-line documentation. This technical note provides an excellent in-depth review of the issues concerning MFC and multiple inheritance.

MFC and Windows Objects

Many MFC classes represent objects in Windows, such as a window, a device context, or a GDI object. It is important to realize that an object of such an MFC class (for example, a CWnd object) is not the same as the Windows object. The CWnd object only *represents* a window; the same goes for other MFC classes. The existence of a Windows object does not automatically imply the existence of a corresponding MFC object, nor does the existence of an MFC object automatically imply that a corresponding Windows object also exists. In many situations, an unattached MFC object is created, only to be attached later to an existing or newly created

322

Windows object. In other situations, temporary MFC objects are created to briefly represent long-lived Windows objects (for example, a temporary CWnd object may be used to represent the desktop window).

Window Support Classes

Window Support classes provide encapsulation for common types of windows. These include frame and view windows, dialog windows, and controls. All window support classes are derived from the class CWnd, which itself is derived from CObject. The CWnd class encapsulates the functionality common to all windows. Its large number of member functions can be organized into several categories, which are summarized in Table 18.2.

Table 18.2. CWnd **member function categories.**

Category	Description
Initialization	Window initialization and creation
Window state functions	Set or retrieve window settings
Size and position	Retrieve or change size and position
Window access	Window identification
Update and painting	Drawing functions
Coordinate mapping	Mapping between logical and physical coordinates
Window text	Manipulate window text or alter its appearance
Scrolling	Manipulate scrollbars
Drag and drop	Accept drag and drop files
Caret	Manipulate the caret
Dialog box	Manipulate dialog box items
Menu	Manipulate menus
Tooltips	Manipulate tooltips
Timer	Set and kill timers
Alert	Window flashing and message boxes
Window message	Manage messages
Clipboard	Manipulate clipboard contents
OLE controls	Handle OLE controls
Overridables	Handle messages and other conditions

Frame Windows

Frame windows are typically used in the context of MFC framework applications. They encapsulate the functionality of the application's main window and manage the application's menu bar, toolbar buttons, and status bar.

The different types of frame windows are shown in Figure 18.2. They are used in the context of SDI and MDI applications and OLE in-place editing as appropriate. All frame windows are derived from the CFrameWnd class, itself a descendant of CWnd.

FIGURE 18.2.

Frame window classes.

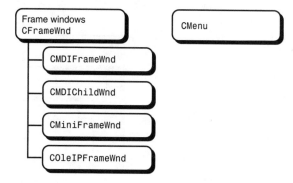

These frame window classes are typically used as the base classes for user-defined frame window classes.

Closely related to frame windows are control bars such as toolbars and status bars. Control bar classes are derived from CControlBar, which in turn is derived from CWnd. These classes are shown in Figure 18.3.

FIGURE 18.3.

Control bar classes.

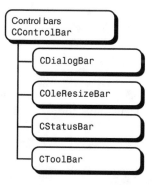

One additional class, CSplitterWnd, is used to create *splitter windows*, windows that have multiple panes. Typical use of CSplitterWnd involves embedding a CSplitterWnd object inside a frame window object.

View Windows

View windows are also specific to the MFC framework. An MFC application uses view windows to present the contents of its document to the user for interaction.

There are several view window types representing the different forms in which a document's view can be presented. View window classes exist that support scrolling, text editing, list and tree controls, and dialog-like forms.

All view window classes are derived from the CView class, which is a descendant of CWnd. The hierarchy of view window classes is shown in Figure 18.4.

FIGURE 18.4.

View window classes.

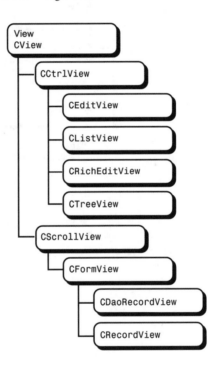

Like frame window classes, view window classes also typically serve as base classes for user-defined classes that implement application-specific view functionality.

Dialogs

Dialog classes encapsulate the functionality of both user-defined and common dialogs. The hierarchy of dialog classes is shown in Figure 18.5.

FIGURE 18.5.

Dialog classes.

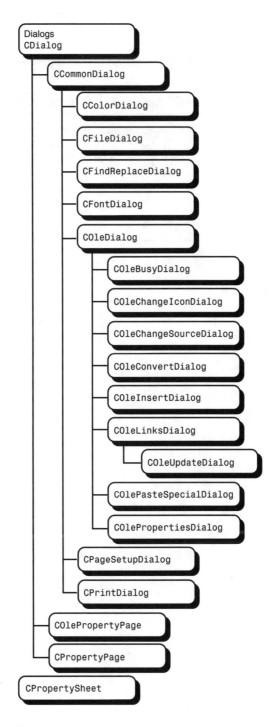

Dialog classes can be used outside MFC framework applications. For example, the program in Listing 18.2 displays a color selection common dialog using the CColorDialog class. You can compile this program from the command line by typing cl /MT colors.cpp.

Listing 18.2. Using an MFC dialog class in a non-MFC application.

```
#include <afx.h>
#include <afxdlgs.h>

int WINAPI WinMain(HINSTANCE d1, HINSTANCE d2, LPSTR d3, int d4)
{
    CColorDialog dlg;

    dlg.DoModal();
    return 0;
}
```

Controls

Control classes encapsulate the functionality of standard Windows controls, Windows 95 common controls, and OLE controls (OCXs). The hierarchy of control classes is shown in Figure 18.6.

FIGURE 18.6.

Control classes.

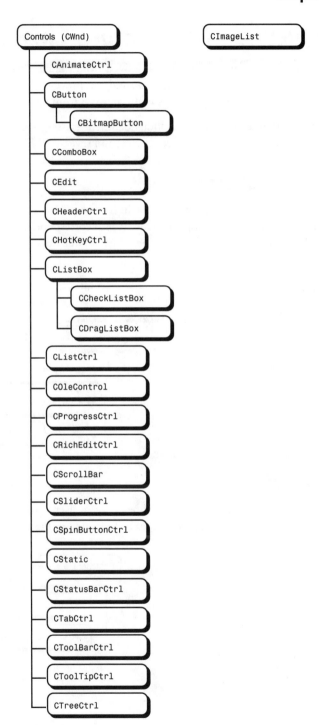

Application Architecture Classes

Application architecture classes are all derived from the base class `CCmdTarget`. A `CCmdTarget` object is an object that has a *message map* and can process messages. As windows are obvious recipients of messages, the `CWnd` class is also derived from `CCmdTarget`.

Application architecture classes include document classes, document template classes, document item classes, application object classes, and several OLE related classes.

Document Classes

Documents are entities that represent a unit of data that the user opens and manipulates. Document objects usually cooperate closely with corresponding view objects that handle presentation of the data and user interaction. The hierarchy of document classes is shown in Figure 18.7.

FIGURE 18.7.

Document classes.

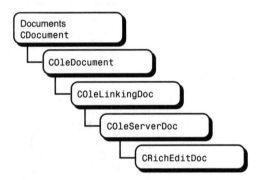

Document Templates

Document templates describe the basic behavior of user-defined document and view classes. The family of document template classes is illustrated in Figure 18.8.

FIGURE 18.8.

Document template classes.

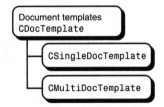

Application Objects

Application object classes represent threads and processes (Figure 18.9).

FIGURE 18.9.

Application object classes.

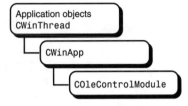

Every MFC framework application has a `CWinApp`-derived object, which supplies your application's main message loop.

Document Items

Document items are objects that comprise a document. For example, the document of a drawing application may consist of objects that represent drawing shapes. MFC uses its document item classes for OLE server and client items. The hierarchy of document item classes is shown in Figure 18.10.

FIGURE 18.10.

Document item classes.

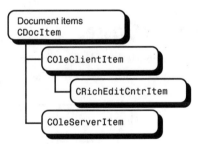

Other Application Architecture Classes

Several other Application Architecture classes exist that contribute to the implementation of OLE within the MFC framework. These classes are shown in Figure 18.11.

FIGURE 18.11.

*OLE-related
Application
Architecture classes.*

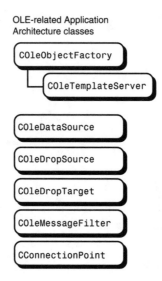

OLE-related Application
Architecture classes

Miscellaneous Classes

For lack of a better term, I called class families that support system and graphic services, collections, and other `CObject`-derived classes miscellaneous classes.

Graphic Support Classes

GDI functionality is supported by device-context classes and GDI object classes, which are illustrated in Figure 18.12. Both class families are derived from `CObject`.

FIGURE 18.12.

*Graphic support
classes.*

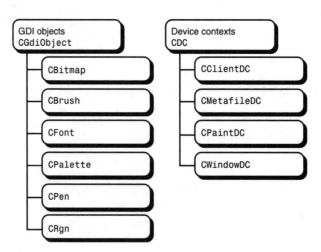

System Support Classes

System support classes encapsulate the functionality of system objects such as exceptions, synchronization objects, and files. Other system support classes provide support for ODBC, DAO, and WinSock. The hierarchy of these classes is shown in Figure 18.13.

FIGURE 18.13.

System support classes.

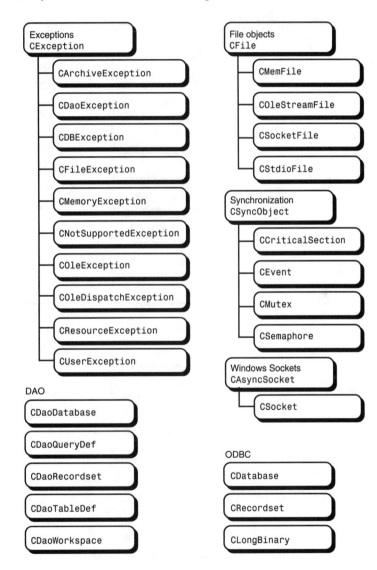

Collection Classes

Collection classes include arrays, lists, and maps. Arrays are dynamically allocated collections of objects organized by an integer index. Lists are ordered collections. Maps are collections organized by a key.

The hierarchy of collection classes is shown in Figure 18.14.

FIGURE 18.14.

Collection classes.

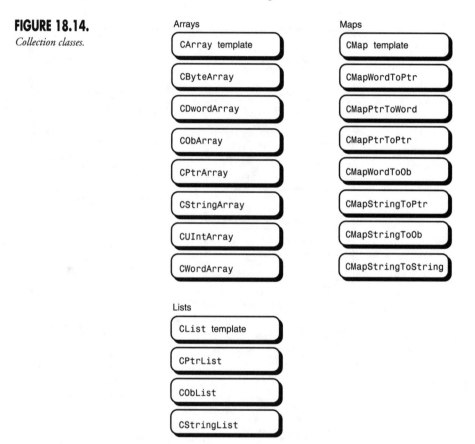

Arrays

CArray template
CByteArray
CDwordArray
CObArray
CPtrArray
CStringArray
CUIntArray
CWordArray

Maps

CMap template
CMapWordToPtr
CMapPtrToWord
CMapPtrToPtr
CMapWordToOb
CMapStringToPtr
CMapStringToOb
CMapStringToString

Lists

CList template
CPtrList
CObList
CStringList

Non-*CObject*-derived Classes

The MFC also contains several support classes that are not derived from the CObject class. These include simple value types (for example, CRect or CString), typed template collections, and many other support classes. Non CObject-derived classes are shown in Figure 18.15.

FIGURE 18.15.

Non-CObject-derived classes.

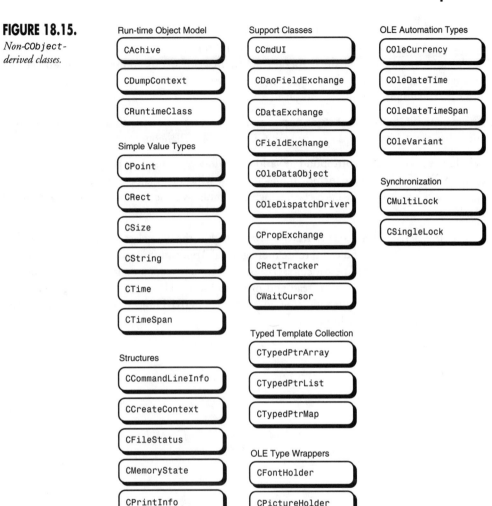

Run-time Object Model
- CArchive
- CDumpContext
- CRuntimeClass

Simple Value Types
- CPoint
- CRect
- CSize
- CString
- CTime
- CTimeSpan

Structures
- CCommandLineInfo
- CCreateContext
- CFileStatus
- CMemoryState
- CPrintInfo

Support Classes
- CCmdUI
- CDaoFieldExchange
- CDataExchange
- CFieldExchange
- COleDataObject
- COleDispatchDriver
- CPropExchange
- CRectTracker
- CWaitCursor

Typed Template Collection
- CTypedPtrArray
- CTypedPtrList
- CTypedPtrMap

OLE Type Wrappers
- CFontHolder
- CPictureHolder

OLE Automation Types
- COleCurrency
- COleDateTime
- COleDateTimeSpan
- COleVariant

Synchronization
- CMultiLock
- CSingleLock

Summary

The MFC Library represents a powerful framework for constructing Windows applications. Classes in MFC encapsulate most Windows functionality, including functionality related to applications, threads, windows, dialogs, controls, graphic objects, device contexts, and much, much more. However, the use of MFC is not restricted to so-called MFC framework applications; other Windows programs and even some console applications can benefit from this library.

The root of most MFC classes is the `CObject` class. This class implements run-time type checking (distinct from the new C++ RTTI feature) and serialization. Serialization is a powerful, platform-independent mechanism for creating an image of an object on persistent storage and loading object data from such storage to memory. Serialization is not limited to disk files; it is also used in clipboard transfers and OLE.

The major MFC categories include Application Architecture classes, Window Support classes, and other classes that encapsulate system, GDI, and miscellaneous services.

Window support classes correspond to various window types used by the system or provided by the MFC Library. These include frame and view windows, dialogs, and controls. All such classes are derived from the `CWnd` class, which encapsulates basic functionality common to all windows.

`CWnd` itself is derived from the `CCmdTarget` class, which is the base class for all classes that have message maps and can handle and route messages. All Application Architecture classes are also derived from `CCmdTarget`. These include classes for documents, document templates, document items, OLE functionality, and thread and process objects. The latter type is called `CWinApp`; every MFC framework application contains a `CWinApp`-derived object, which implements the application's main message loop.

Exploring an MFC Skeleton Application

19

What is a typical MFC framework application like? How does it utilize the application, document template, and document classes? How do you create and build such an application? These are the questions that I attempt to answer in this chapter.

A Simple MFC Application Skeleton

Have you not guessed it yet? We are going to build a YAHWA! No, I am not swearing in Yiddish; it is short for Yet Another Hello World Application.

But this time, it is going to be a framework application built using the MFC AppWizard. We will use this application to experiment with MFC features and to explore the relationships between the application's various classes.

Creating the YAH Project

I would have liked to name my project YAHWA but with a 5-character project name, AppWizard would have generated filenames that are longer than 8 characters. Alas, such filenames would have been mangled when put on an ISO9660 CD-ROM. Instead of getting into that mess, I figured it is easier to just use a shorter name.

The YAH project is created through AppWizard. From the Developer Studio, select the New command under the File menu; select Project Workspace in the New dialog; and select MFC AppWizard (exe). Type in the name of the project ("YAH") and select a directory where the new project would be placed. Click on the Create button.

YAH should be a single document interface (SDI) project; set this option in the first AppWizard dialog step that appears. Most other default settings should be accepted, except for a few settings that can be accessed by clicking the Advanced button in AppWizard Step 4. In this advanced dialog, enter YAH as the file extension and change the main frame caption to "Hello, World!" (or whatever you find suitable). See Figure 19.1.

After these changes, you can let AppWizard create the project. Once the project has been created, the Developer Studio opens the project and displays the project workspace in ClassView (see Figure 19.2).

FIGURE 19.1.

AppWizard advanced options for the YAH project.

FIGURE 19.2.

YAH classes.

Exploring the Application Object

As you can see, AppWizard created five classes for the YAH project. Take a look at CYAHApp. This class is derived from CWinApp and represents the application itself.

The CYAHApp class is declared in YAH.h; this file can be opened either by double-clicking on the CYAHApp class in ClassView or double-clicking the filename in FileView. A look at the declaration (Listing 19.1) reveals three member functions: a constructor, an override of the virtual function InitInstance, and a member function CAppAbout. How do these functions relate to a typical WinMain function in a non-MFC application?

Listing 19.1. CYAHApp **class declaration.**

```
class CYAHApp : public CWinApp
{
public:
    CYAHApp();

// Overrides
    // ClassWizard generated virtual function overrides
    //{{AFX_VIRTUAL(CYAHApp)
    public:
    virtual BOOL InitInstance();
    //}}AFX_VIRTUAL

// Implementation

    //{{AFX_MSG(CYAHApp)
    afx_msg void OnAppAbout();
        // NOTE - the ClassWizard will add and remove member
        // functions here. DO NOT EDIT what you see in these blocks
        // of generated code !
    //}}AFX_MSG
    DECLARE_MESSAGE_MAP()
};
```

A look at the implementation of AfxWinMain in the MFC source file winmain.cpp reveals the answer. The major initialization steps performed here are shown in Figure 19.3.

How can the application object be constructed before AfxWinMain is executed? Simple; in YAH.cpp, a global object of type CYAHApp named theApp is declared. By the time execution begins, this object will have been constructed (which implies that its constructor will have been called).

The member functions InitApplication and InitInstance can be overridden. They correspond to one-time and instance-specific initializations. These functions are called explicitly by AfxWinMain before the message loop is entered.

Look at the file YAH.cpp, the implementation file for the CYAHApp class (if you wish to open this file from ClassView, you may have to expand the CYAHApp class and double-click on one of the member functions). Actually, to be precise, look at the first half of this file; the second half contains a declaration and the implementation of the CAboutDlg class, which is the skeleton application's About dialog; this does not concern us at the moment. The relevant parts of YAH.cpp are shown in Listing 19.2.

FIGURE 19.3.

Major initializa-
tion steps.

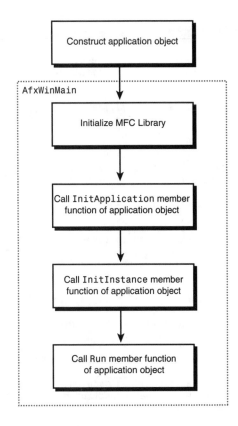

Listing 19.2. CYAHApp **class implementation.**

```
//////////////////////////////////////////////////////////////////
// CYAHApp

BEGIN_MESSAGE_MAP(CYAHApp, CWinApp)
    //{{AFX_MSG_MAP(CYAHApp)
    ON_COMMAND(ID_APP_ABOUT, OnAppAbout)
 // NOTE - the ClassWizard will add and remove mapping macros here.
 // DO NOT EDIT what you see in these blocks of generated code!
    //}}AFX_MSG_MAP
    // Standard file based document commands
    ON_COMMAND(ID_FILE_NEW, CWinApp::OnFileNew)
    ON_COMMAND(ID_FILE_OPEN, CWinApp::OnFileOpen)
    // Standard print setup command
    ON_COMMAND(ID_FILE_PRINT_SETUP, CWinApp::OnFilePrintSetup)
END_MESSAGE_MAP()

//////////////////////////////////////////////////////////////////
// CYAHApp construction

CYAHApp::CYAHApp()
```

continues

Listing 19.2. continued

```
{
    // TODO: add construction code here,
    // Place all significant initialization in InitInstance
}


///////////////////////////////////////////////////////////////////
// The one and only CYAHApp object

CYAHApp theApp;

///////////////////////////////////////////////////////////////////
// CYAHApp initialization

BOOL CYAHApp::InitInstance()
{
  // Standard initialization
  // If you are not using these features and wish to reduce the size
  //  of your final executable, you should remove from the following
  //  the specific initialization routines you do not need.

#ifdef _AFXDLL
    Enable3dControls();  // Call this when using MFC in a shared DLL
#else
    Enable3dControlsStatic();   // Call this when linking statically
#endif

    LoadStdProfileSettings();      // Load standard INI file options

    // Register the application's document templates.  Document
    // templates serve as the connection between documents, frame
    // windows and views.

    CSingleDocTemplate* pDocTemplate;
    pDocTemplate = new CSingleDocTemplate(
        IDR_MAINFRAME,
        RUNTIME_CLASS(CYAHDoc),
        RUNTIME_CLASS(CMainFrame),          // main SDI frame window
        RUNTIME_CLASS(CYAHView));
    AddDocTemplate(pDocTemplate);

    // Enable DDE Execute open
    EnableShellOpen();
    RegisterShellFileTypes(TRUE);

  // Parse command line for standard shell commands, DDE, file open
    CCommandLineInfo cmdInfo;
    ParseCommandLine(cmdInfo);

    // Dispatch commands specified on the command line
    if (!ProcessShellCommand(cmdInfo))
        return FALSE;

    // Enable drag/drop open
    m_pMainWnd->DragAcceptFiles();

    return TRUE;
}
```

The framework only created an override version of InitInstance, not InitApplication. Because Win32 applications run in separate memory spaces, application-specific (as opposed to instance-specific) initializations are now rare (as they would normally affect only the current instance of the application anyway).

In InitInstance, a number of initializations take place. These initialization steps reflect many of the choices you select when you create the project through AppWizard. For example, we selected the default 3-D look for the YAH application; correspondingly, the 3-D look is enabled here in InitInstance.

Perhaps the most important initialization step is the creation of a document template. An object of type CSingleDocTemplate (because we selected an SDI application) is created and added to the application's document templates using the AddDocTemplate member function.

The information stored in document templates is used when the user selects the New command from the File menu. The default implementation of this command is in the function CWinApp::OnFileNew. This function uses the template information to decide what kind of objects it must create to represent the new document object and its corresponding view.

There are applications that can handle many kinds of documents. For example, a graphics application may be able to handle both bitmap and vector graphic files. A programmer's editor may handle source (text) files and provide graphical editing for resource files. How can an MFC application accommodate multiple document types?

Well, first of all, you need to create a Multiple Document Interface (MDI) application. SDI applications created with AppWizard do not support multiple document types. Afterwards, it takes little effort to add additional document types. After declaring and implementing a new document class and a corresponding view class, make sure that these classes are added in the form of a new document template to the application object by calling AddDocTemplate in your application object's InitInstance member function. Subsequently, when the user selects the File New command, the framework automatically presents a dialog where the user can select the desired document type.

The Message Map

In the files YAH.h and YAH.cpp, we encountered the macros DECLARE_MESSAGE_MAP, BEGIN_MESSAGE_MAP, and END_MESSAGE_MAP. What do these macros represent and how do they connect to the application's main message loop in the application object's Run member function?

The Run member function dispatches messages to their target windows much like any non-MFC application would in its message loop. In fact, it calls the very same function, ::DispatchMessage, for this purpose. Thus, the first recipient of a message is always a window.

The message handler function in an object capable of receiving messages (that is, a command target object, including window objects) generally dispatches, or routes, messages in the following order:

1. To any currently active child command target objects
2. To itself
3. To other command target objects

For example, a command message that is ultimately processed by the application's document class may be routed through its frame window and view window first before eventually reaching the message handler in the document class.

Table 19.1 summarizes how messages are handled by the major MFC command target classes.

Table 19.1. Message routing.

Class	Routing order
MDI frame windows (`CMDIFrameWnd`)	1. Active MDI child window 2. This window 3. Application object
Document frame windows (`CMDIChildWnd, CFrameWnd`)	1. Active view 2. This window 3. Application object
View	1. This window 2. Attached document object
Document	1. This document 2. Document template
Dialog box	1. This window 2. Owner window 3. Application object

So how do those message map macros relate to message processing? Simple. The `DECLARE_MESSAGE_MAP` macro declares an array of message map entries as part of your class declaration. The `BEGIN_MESSAGE_MAP` and `END_MESSAGE_MAP` macros enclose a series of initializers for this array that represent the individual messages that your class can respond to.

Look at the message map entries in `YAH.cpp`. These default entries connect a few standard commands in the File menu to default implementations supplied as part of the `CWinApp` class.

ON_COMMAND is one of several macros that make creating message map entries easier. Normally, message map entries are created automatically by the ClassWizard; however, sometimes it is necessary to manually add entries (for example, when processing an application-specific message).

The Frame, the Document, and the View

In a simple non-MFC Windows application, you would typically create one window and use its client area to present your application's output. MFC applications, on the other hand, use at least two windows: a *frame window* and a *view window.*

The frame window manages the application's menus, toolbars, and other user-interface components. The view window, in turn, is dedicated to presenting data from the application's document.

The document object is not a visual object. It is an object that represents the application's data; it typically corresponds to the contents of a file. The document object closely interacts with the view window for presenting the data and for user interaction.

The relationship between the frame and view windows and the document object is depicted in Figure 19.4.

FIGURE 19.4.

Frames, views, and documents.

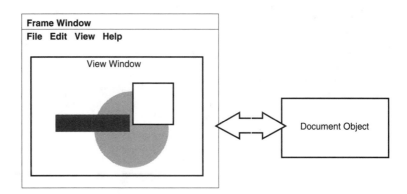

The next sections present a look at the declaration and implementation of these three classes.

The Frame Window Class

The application's frame window is supported by the CMainFrame class, which is declared in MainFrm.h (Listing 19.3).

Listing 19.3. `CMainFrame` class declaration.

```
class CMainFrame : public CFrameWnd
{
protected: // create from serialization only
    CMainFrame();
    DECLARE_DYNCREATE(CMainFrame)

// Attributes
public:

// Operations
public:

// Overrides
    // ClassWizard generated virtual function overrides
    //{{AFX_VIRTUAL(CMainFrame)
    virtual BOOL PreCreateWindow(CREATESTRUCT& cs);
    //}}AFX_VIRTUAL

// Implementation
public:
    virtual ~CMainFrame();
#ifdef _DEBUG
    virtual void AssertValid() const;
    virtual void Dump(CDumpContext& dc) const;
#endif

protected:  // control bar embedded members
    CStatusBar  m_wndStatusBar;
    CToolBar    m_wndToolBar;

// Generated message map functions
protected:
    //{{AFX_MSG(CMainFrame)
    afx_msg int OnCreate(LPCREATESTRUCT lpCreateStruct);
        // NOTE - the ClassWizard will add and remove member
        // functions here. DO NOT EDIT what you see in these blocks
        // of generated code!
    //}}AFX_MSG
    DECLARE_MESSAGE_MAP()
};
```

Nothing surprising here. A constructor, a destructor, an overridden PreCreateWindow, an overridden OnCreate, and some debug member functions. However, I would like to call your attention to the two member variables m_wndStatusBar and m_wndToolBar. These correspond to the application's single toolbar and status bar. For any control bars that you may wish to add to your program, this is the preferred way to do it; declare them as member variables of the frame window class and add supporting code in the frame window class's implementation file.

The implementation of CMainFrame (Listing 19.4) can be found in MainFrm.cpp. In this file it is the OnCreate member function that deserves a closer look. It is here in this function that the toolbar and status bar are initialized.

Listing 19.4. CMainFrame class implementation.

```
/////////////////////////////////////////////////////////////////
// CMainFrame

IMPLEMENT_DYNCREATE(CMainFrame, CFrameWnd)

BEGIN_MESSAGE_MAP(CMainFrame, CFrameWnd)
    //{{AFX_MSG_MAP(CMainFrame)
 // NOTE - the ClassWizard will add and remove mapping macros here.
 //     DO NOT EDIT what you see in these blocks of generated code !
    ON_WM_CREATE()
    //}}AFX_MSG_MAP
END_MESSAGE_MAP()

static UINT indicators[] =
{
    ID_SEPARATOR,            // status line indicator
    ID_INDICATOR_CAPS,
    ID_INDICATOR_NUM,
    ID_INDICATOR_SCRL,
};

/////////////////////////////////////////////////////////////////
// CMainFrame construction/destruction

CMainFrame::CMainFrame()
{
    // TODO: add member initialization code here

}

CMainFrame::~CMainFrame()
{
}

int CMainFrame::OnCreate(LPCREATESTRUCT lpCreateStruct)
{
    if (CFrameWnd::OnCreate(lpCreateStruct) == -1)
        return -1;

    if (!m_wndToolBar.Create(this) ¦¦
        !m_wndToolBar.LoadToolBar(IDR_MAINFRAME))
    {
        TRACE0("Failed to create toolbar\n");
        return -1;      // fail to create
    }

    if (!m_wndStatusBar.Create(this) ¦¦
        !m_wndStatusBar.SetIndicators(indicators,
          sizeof(indicators)/sizeof(UINT)))
    {
        TRACE0("Failed to create status bar\n");
        return -1;      // fail to create
    }

    // TODO: Remove this if you don't want tool tips or a
    //   resizeable toolbar
```

continues

Listing 19.4. continued

```
    m_wndToolBar.SetBarStyle(m_wndToolBar.GetBarStyle() |
        CBRS_TOOLTIPS | CBRS_FLYBY | CBRS_SIZE_DYNAMIC);

    // TODO: Delete these three lines if you don't want the toolbar
    //   to be dockable
    m_wndToolBar.EnableDocking(CBRS_ALIGN_ANY);
    EnableDocking(CBRS_ALIGN_ANY);
    DockControlBar(&m_wndToolBar);

    return 0;
}

BOOL CMainFrame::PreCreateWindow(CREATESTRUCT& cs)
{
    // TODO: Modify the Window class or styles here by modifying
    //   the CREATESTRUCT cs

    return CFrameWnd::PreCreateWindow(cs);
}
```

For those familiar with earlier versions of Visual C++, there is a notable difference here. Although there is still a global array called indicators that specifies the indicators that go into the status bar, there is no corresponding global array which would specify toolbar buttons. Where did it go? As it turns out, Visual C++ Version 4 now supports a toolbar resource type in its resource files. This resource is editable with the Developer Studio resource editor; thus it is no longer necessary to manually set up and maintain an array of button command identifiers that correspond to buttons in the toolbar bitmap.

The Document Class

The declaration of the document class in YAHDoc.h (Listing 19.5) provides overrides for two functions: OnNewDocument and Serialize. OnNewDocument is called when the user selects the File New command; this member function is especially important for SDI applications in which the same document object is used over and over again. OnNewDocument is the place where the document object should be reinitialized; for this reason, many initialization operations that would normally go into the constructor really belong here instead.

Listing 19.5. CYAHDoc class declaration.

```
class CYAHDoc : public CDocument
{
protected: // create from serialization only
    CYAHDoc();
    DECLARE_DYNCREATE(CYAHDoc)

// Attributes
public:
```

```
// Operations
public:

// Overrides
    // ClassWizard generated virtual function overrides
    //{{AFX_VIRTUAL(CYAHDoc)
    public:
    virtual BOOL OnNewDocument();
    virtual void Serialize(CArchive& ar);
    //}}AFX_VIRTUAL

// Implementation
public:
    virtual ~CYAHDoc();
#ifdef _DEBUG
    virtual void AssertValid() const;
    virtual void Dump(CDumpContext& dc) const;
#endif

protected:

// Generated message map functions
protected:
    //{{AFX_MSG(CYAHDoc)
        // NOTE - the ClassWizard will add and remove member
        // functions here. DO NOT EDIT what you see in these blocks
        // of generated code !
    //}}AFX_MSG
    DECLARE_MESSAGE_MAP()
};
```

The Serialize member function is called when the document is loaded or saved. This member function must be overridden; you must write your own saving and loading code in the override version in order to save and load your document data.

Apropos serialization—isn't there a glaring inconsistency here? Why is the DECLARE_DYNCREATE macro used in the class declaration when this class obviously supports serialization? Shouldn't it be DECLARE_SERIAL instead?

The reason using DECLARE_SERIAL is unnecessary is that although the class has a Serialize member function, the operator >> is never used to retrieve a document from a CArchive. The Serialize member function is called explicitly, from CDocument::OnOpenDocument. The use of DECLARE_SERIAL (and IMPLEMENT_SERIAL) is only necessary for classes that are loaded from a CArchive object using the >> operator.

Both CYAHDoc override functions are implemented in the file YAHDoc.cpp (Listing 19.6). Their default implementations do nothing; you must supply the code to initialize your document type, and save and load document data.

Listing 19.6. CYAHDoc class implementation.

```
/////////////////////////////////////////////////////////////////
// CYAHDoc

IMPLEMENT_DYNCREATE(CYAHDoc, CDocument)

BEGIN_MESSAGE_MAP(CYAHDoc, CDocument)
    //{{AFX_MSG_MAP(CYAHDoc)
 // NOTE - the ClassWizard will add and remove mapping macros here.
 //    DO NOT EDIT what you see in these blocks of generated code!
    //}}AFX_MSG_MAP
END_MESSAGE_MAP()

/////////////////////////////////////////////////////////////////
// CYAHDoc construction/destruction

CYAHDoc::CYAHDoc()
{
    // TODO: add one-time construction code here
}

CYAHDoc::~CYAHDoc()
{
}

BOOL CYAHDoc::OnNewDocument()
{
    if (!CDocument::OnNewDocument())
        return FALSE;

    // TODO: add reinitialization code here
    // (SDI documents will reuse this document)

    return TRUE;
}

/////////////////////////////////////////////////////////////////////
// CYAHDoc serialization

void CYAHDoc::Serialize(CArchive& ar)
{
    if (ar.IsStoring())
    {
        // TODO: add storing code here
    }
    else
    {
        // TODO: add loading code here
    }
}
```

The View Class

The default declaration of the view class in YAHView.h (Listing 19.7) includes several function overrides. Perhaps the most significant of these is OnDraw; it is this function that is responsible for presenting a visual representation of the data of the document that corresponds to this view.

Listing 19.7. CYAHView class declaration.

```
class CYAHView : public CView
{
protected: // create from serialization only
    CYAHView();
    DECLARE_DYNCREATE(CYAHView)

// Attributes
public:
    CYAHDoc* GetDocument();

// Operations
public:

// Overrides
    // ClassWizard generated virtual function overrides
    //{{AFX_VIRTUAL(CYAHView)
    public:
    virtual void OnDraw(CDC* pDC);  // overridden to draw this view
    virtual BOOL PreCreateWindow(CREATESTRUCT& cs);
    protected:
    virtual BOOL OnPreparePrinting(CPrintInfo* pInfo);
    virtual void OnBeginPrinting(CDC* pDC, CPrintInfo* pInfo);
    virtual void OnEndPrinting(CDC* pDC, CPrintInfo* pInfo);
    //}}AFX_VIRTUAL

// Implementation
public:
    virtual ~CYAHView();
#ifdef _DEBUG
    virtual void AssertValid() const;
    virtual void Dump(CDumpContext& dc) const;
#endif

protected:

// Generated message map functions
protected:
    //{{AFX_MSG(CYAHView)
        // NOTE - the ClassWizard will add and remove member
        // functions here. DO NOT EDIT what you see in these blocks
        // of generated code !
    //}}AFX_MSG
    DECLARE_MESSAGE_MAP()
};
```

Notice that this class, like the document class, is also declared with the DECLARE_DYNCREATE macro. Use of this macro is necessary because when a new document is created, the view object is created dynamically.

The implementation of the view class in YAHView.cpp (Listing 19.8) contains few surprises. The override functions are only skeletons; you must supply your own implementation. However, only the OnDraw member function must be edited in order to obtain a functional application. In order to have printing capability, it is not necessary to adjust any of the printing-related member functions here, although you would probably want to do so because the default printing behavior may not be satisfactory.

Listing 19.8. CYAHView class implementation.

```
/////////////////////////////////////////////////////////////////
// CYAHView

IMPLEMENT_DYNCREATE(CYAHView, CView)

BEGIN_MESSAGE_MAP(CYAHView, CView)
    //{{AFX_MSG_MAP(CYAHView)
 // NOTE - the ClassWizard will add and remove mapping macros here.
 //    DO NOT EDIT what you see in these blocks of generated code!
    //}}AFX_MSG_MAP
    // Standard printing commands
    ON_COMMAND(ID_FILE_PRINT, CView::OnFilePrint)
    ON_COMMAND(ID_FILE_PRINT_DIRECT, CView::OnFilePrint)
    ON_COMMAND(ID_FILE_PRINT_PREVIEW, CView::OnFilePrintPreview)
END_MESSAGE_MAP()

/////////////////////////////////////////////////////////////////
// CYAHView construction/destruction

CYAHView::CYAHView()
{
    // TODO: add construction code here

}

CYAHView::~CYAHView()
{
}

BOOL CYAHView::PreCreateWindow(CREATESTRUCT& cs)
{
    // TODO: Modify the Window class or styles here by modifying
    //   the CREATESTRUCT cs

    return CView::PreCreateWindow(cs);
}

/////////////////////////////////////////////////////////////////
// CYAHView drawing

void CYAHView::OnDraw(CDC* pDC)
{
```

```
    CYAHDoc* pDoc = GetDocument();
    ASSERT_VALID(pDoc);

    // TODO: add draw code for native data here
}

/////////////////////////////////////////////////////////////////////////
// CYAHView printing

BOOL CYAHView::OnPreparePrinting(CPrintInfo* pInfo)
{
    // default preparation
    return DoPreparePrinting(pInfo);
}

void CYAHView::OnBeginPrinting(CDC* /*pDC*/, CPrintInfo* /*pInfo*/)
{
    // TODO: add extra initialization before printing
}

void CYAHView::OnEndPrinting(CDC* /*pDC*/, CPrintInfo* /*pInfo*/)
{
    // TODO: add cleanup after printing
}
```

Notice that there are several message map entries here that are related to printing. They call the base class functions that implement default printing and print preview behavior.

Skeleton Application Resources

To complete our tour of the skeleton MFC application, here is a brief look at the resources that were generated by AppWizard. To see the list of resources, open the project in ResourceView and expand the single item seen in this view.

The accelerator resource requires little explanation; it contains the keyboard shortcuts to many standard menu functions. The menu bar itself is defined in the application's single menu resource.

AppWizard created one dialog resource, an About dialog. This dialog is displayed when the user selects the About command from the Help menu.

Two icons have been generated; IDR_MAINFRAME is the application icon, and IDR_YAHTYPE is the icon representing the application's document type.

The string table contains numerous strings. Many of these correspond to MFC framework messages; others represent status bar messages, tooltips, and other text items specific to this application. Of particular interest is the string resource IDR_MAINFRAME, also referred to as the *document template string*. This string contains up to nine substrings, separated by the newline (\n) character. Here is what it has been set to by AppWizard:

```
Hello, World!\n\nYAH\nYAH Files (*.yah)\n.YAH\nYAH.Document\nYAH Document
```

The substrings of the document template string are described in Table 19.2. The general syntax for this string is the following:

```
<windowTitle>\n<docName>\n<fileNewName>\n<filterName>\n
<filterExt>\n<regFileTypeID>\n<regFileTypeName>\n
<filterMacExt(filterWinExt)>\n<filterMacName(filterWinName)>
```

Table 19.2. Substrings of the document template string.

Substring	Description
`<windowTitle>`	The title of the application's main frame window
`<docName>`	Root document name for document windows (this name plus a number will be used as window titles)
`<fileNewName>`	Document type displayed in the File New dialog when the application supports multiple types
`<filterName>`	Filter used in the file dialogs
`<filterExt>`	Extension used in the file dialogs
`<regFileTypeID>`	File type registered in the Registry
`<regFileTypeName>`	Visible name of the file type registered in the Registry
`<filterMacExt>`	Filename filter for Macintosh version
`<filterMacName>`	Filename filter for Macintosh version

The resource file also contains a toolbar resource and a version resource.

Note how several resources share the same identifier, `IDR_MAINFRAME`. Such common identifiers are used when the application calls the `CSingleDocTemplate` (or `CMultiDocTemplate`) constructor. It identifies the menu, icon, accelerator table, and document template string corresponding to a specific document type.

Adding Code to the Application

Now that we have seen the basic elements of an MFC skeleton, it is time to look at actually modifying the skeleton by adding some of our own code. We'll try something simple this time. In the document class, we will add a string member variable and initialize it from a resource; in the view class, we will add code to display this string in the middle of the application's view window.

Adding a String Resource

To add a string resource, open the project workspace in ResourceView and open the string table. Add a string named `IDS_HELLO` and set its value to "Hello, World!" (or whatever else may suit your taste).

Modifying the Document

The first step in modifying our application is to add a member variable to the document class. To do this, edit the YAHDoc.h file. In the Attributes section, add a declaration for a member variable of type CString as follows:

```
// Attributes
public:
    CString m_sData;
```

Obviously, m_sData must be initialized somewhere. We must also add this member to the Serialize member function to enable it to be saved to, and loaded from, a file. These changes are carried out in the YAHDoc.cpp file.

We will initialize the string in the OnNewDocument member function to ensure that it is reinitialized every time the user selects the New command from the File menu. Here is the modified OnNewDocument:

```
BOOL CYAHDoc::OnNewDocument()
{
    if (!CDocument::OnNewDocument())
        return FALSE;

    // TODO: add reinitialization code here
    // (SDI documents will reuse this document)
    m_sData.LoadString(IDS_HELLO);
    return TRUE;
}
```

And here is the modified Serialize member function:

```
void CYAHDoc::Serialize(CArchive& ar)
{
    if (ar.IsStoring())
    {
        // TODO: add storing code here
        ar << m_sData;
    }
    else
    {
        // TODO: add loading code here
        ar >> m_sData;
    }
}
```

We are almost done! All that is left is to actually display the string; this must be implemented as part of our view class.

Modifying the View

To display our string, we must modify the view class's OnDraw member function. As AppWizard already provided us with an empty implementation for this function, it is not necessary to modify the class declaration; we only add code to the existing function skeleton in YAHView.cpp:

```
void CYAHView::OnDraw(CDC* pDC)
{
    CYAHDoc* pDoc = GetDocument();
    ASSERT_VALID(pDoc);

    // TODO: add draw code for native data here
    CRect rect;
    GetClientRect(&rect);
    pDC->DPtoLP(&rect);
    pDC->DrawText(pDoc->m_sData, &rect,
                  DT_CENTER | DT_VCENTER | DT_SINGLELINE);
}
```

All that is left is to recompile and run the application. If all goes well, the application window should look similar to that shown in Figure 19.5.

FIGURE 19.5.

The Yet Another Hello World Application.

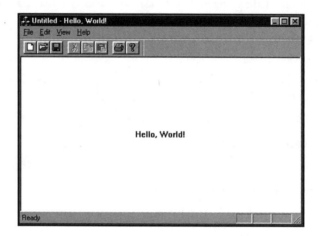

Summary

MFC applications are created through AppWizard. At the heart of every MFC application is a `CWinApp`-derived object, which implements application initialization and the application's main message loop.

Messages are dispatched and routed through message maps, which are a feature of command handler objects (such as windows). The `CWinApp::Run` member function dispatches messages through `::DispatchMessage`; further routing takes place according to MFC's message routing rules. Generally, a command handler object routes a message first to any child command handler objects; next, to itself; and finally, to additional command handler objects.

Visual presentation of an application and management of the application's data are a result of cooperation between a frame window, a view window, and a document object. The document object holds the application's data and generally corresponds to a disk file. The view window is used to present the contents of a document to the user and accept user interaction. The view window works hand-in-hand with the frame window, which manages other elements of the application's user interface, such as its menu bar, toolbars, or status bar.

When implementing an MFC application, one typically edits the document and view classes simultaneously. Representations of new document objects are declared as members of the document class; the visual interfaces corresponding to the new elements are implemented as part of the view class.

Working with Documents and Views

20

At the core of an MFC application is the concept of a *document object* and a corresponding *view window.* The document object represents (usually) a file opened by the application; the view window provides a visual presentation of the document's data and accepts user interaction. The relationship between documents and views is a *one-to-many* relationship; a view can be associated with only one document, but a document may have many views associated with it.

Document objects are represented by a class derived from CDocument. View window classes are derived from CView. In this chapter, we review these two classes, the most common ways of utilizing their capabilities to build a versatile representation of your data, and an efficient user interface.

The *CDocument* Class

The CDocument class provides the basic functionality for your application's document objects. This includes the ability to create a new document, serialize document data, and provide basic cooperation between a document and a view window. MFC also provides a series of CDocument-derived classes that implement functionality specific to OLE applications.

Declaring a Document Class in Your Application

In the case of an AppWizard-created application, you often don't have to worry about declaring your document class; the AppWizard does it for you. However, it is still useful to know more about the behavior of CDocument. Not only does this knowledge enable you to enhance the AppWizard-provided application skeleton, it may also help you easily add additional document types that your application supports. The AppWizard, in contrast, only creates application skeletons that support a single document type.

When you are building a simple MFC application, it is often enough to make relatively minor modifications to your application's AppWizard-supplied document class. Often no more is needed that a few member variables and perhaps a couple of member functions that provide access to those variables.

For example, consider a simple communication program (terminal emulator). Its document object is a series of settings (telephone number, speed, parity, and so on) that correspond to a connection. These can easily be represented by a set of simple data items in the document class, something similar to the following:

```
class CTerminalDoc : public CDocument
{
protected: // create from serialization only
    CTerminalDoc();
    DECLARE_DYNCREATE(CTerminalDoc)

// Attributes
public:
```

```
    CString m_sPhone;
    DWORD m_dwSpeed;
    WORD m_nParity;
    WORD m_nBits;
    ...
```

In addition to the declaration of member variables, all you need to do is to initialize them to reasonable defaults in your document class's OnNewDocument member function, and ensure that they are properly serialized:

```
...
BOOL CTerminalDoc::OnNewDocument
{
    if (!CDocument::OnNewDocument())
        return FALSE;
    m_sPhone = "555-1212";
    m_dwSpeed = 2400;
    m_nParity = 0;
    m_nBits = 8;
    return TRUE;
}
...
void CTerminalDoc::Serialize(CArchive &ar)
{
    if (ar.IsStoring())
    {
        ar << m_sPhone;
        ar << m_dwSpeed;
        ar << m_nParity;
        ar << m_nBits;
    }
    else
    {
        ar >> m_sPhone;
        ar >> m_dwSpeed;
        ar >> m_nParity;
        ar >> m_nBits;
    }
}
```

For a simple application, nothing else needs to be done to have a complete, fully functional document class.

CDocument Member Functions

The CDocument class has several member functions that are frequently used by applications.

The first set of member functions provides access to the associated view objects. Every document object has a list of view objects associated with it. An iterator to this list, in the form of a variable of type POSITION, can be obtained by calling the GetFirstViewPosition member function.

Values of type POSITION are used throughout the MFC, primarily in association with collection classes. Applications that need to traverse a list usually obtain an iterator that is associated with the first object on the list, and then use an iterator function to access the list's elements one by one. The case of CDocument and its associated views is no different; after obtaining a list iterator using GetFirstViewPosition, the elements of the list can be obtained by repeatedly calling GetNextView.

Thus, to process all the views associated with a document, your code would typically look like this:

```
POSITION pos = GetFirstViewPosition();
while (pos != NULL)
{
    CView *pView = GetNextView(pos);
    // Do something with pView
}
```

If all you want to accomplish is to notify the views for this document that the document has changed, it may not be necessary to use an iteration at all. Instead, you can call the UpdateAllViews member function. When calling this member function, you can also specify application-specific data that enables the view objects to selectively update only portions of the view windows. We take another look at this issue later, when we discuss the CView::OnUpdate member function.

Much less frequently used view-related functions are AddView and RemoveView. These functions let you manually add views to and remove views from your document's list of views. The reason these functions are not used that often is that most applications rely on the default MFC implementation with little or no modification for managing their windows.

Whenever the document's data changes, you should call the SetModifiedFlag member function. Consistent use of this function ensures that the framework prompts the user before destroying an unsaved, changed document. The status of this flag can be obtained by calling the IsModified member function.

The SetTitle member function can be used to set the document's title. This title is displayed as the document's title in the frame window (the main frame window in the case of an SDI application or the child frame in the case of an MDI application).

The fully qualified pathname for the document can be set by calling SetPathName and obtained through GetPathName.

The document template object associated with the current document can be obtained by calling GetDocTemplate.

Documents, Events, and Overridable Functions

Although a CDocument object is not directly associated with a window, it is nevertheless a command target object that can receive messages. Messages are routed to CDocument objects by the associated view objects.

While it is up to you to decide which messages will be handled by your document object and which should be left to the view window (or perhaps the frame window) for processing, there are a few sensible rules of thumb to follow.

Always keep in mind that the document is an abstract representation of your data, independent of the visual representation provided by the view window. Moreover, a document may have several views attached to it (or possibly none at all). Any messages the document responds to should be global in nature, having an immediate effect on the document data itself that should be reflected in all the views. In contrast, views should respond to messages that are specific to that window only.

How does this translate into practical terms? Take, for example, the command message that is generated when the user selects the Save command from the File menu. What you are saving is the document as a whole, not a visual representation of it; thus, this command is best handled by the document class.

Take, in contrast, the Cut command in the Edit menu. If you ask yourself what it is you are cutting, you come to the quick conclusion that whatever it is, it is selected through a view of the document. In fact, if multiple views exist for the same document, chances are that different selections are active in them; thus the meaning of the Cut command changes from one view to the next. Conclusion: This command should likely be handled by the view class.

Then there are some borderline cases. Is the Paste command best handled by the document class or the view class? True, this command affects the entire document, not just a single view. However, it may have particular effects in the current view—for example, it may cause the current selection to be replaced by the pasted data. Therefore, the decision regarding which class should handle this command is dependent on your application's design.

I should also mention that there are commands that should not be handled by either the view class or the document class, but by the frame window instead. Commands that hide and show toolbars are good examples. The presence or absence of a toolbar is not a feature of a document or one of its views; instead, this is a configuration issue with an effect that's global to the entire application.

Now to return our attention to the CDocument class. The MFC framework provides default implementations for many commands; these implementations, in turn, call overridable member functions in CDocument. (These functions are overridable because they are declared virtual; thus, you can provide your overrides in a class derived from CDocument and expect the override version to be called instead of the base class version.)

The OnNewDocument member function is called during the initialization of a new document object (or when an existing document is reused in an SDI application). Call to this function is typically part of handling the File New command.

The OnCloseDocument member function is called when a document is about to be closed. You should override this function if it is necessary to perform any cleanup operations before your document is destroyed.

The `OnOpenDocument` and `OnSaveDocument` functions are called to read a document from disk or save the document to a disk file. You should override these functions only if the default implementation (which calls your document class's `Serialize` member function) is not sufficient for your purposes.

The `DeleteContents` function is called from the default implementations of `OnCloseDocument` and `OnOpenDocument` to delete the document's previous contents before opening the new file. This function deletes the document's data without actually destroying the document object.

The `OnFileSendMail` member function sends the document object as an attachment to a mail message. It calls `OnSaveDocument` to save a copy of the document to a temporary disk file, which it then attaches to a MAPI mail message. The `OnUpdateFileSendMail` member function is used to enable the command identified by `ID_FILE_SEND_MAIL` in the application's menu or remove it altogether if MAPI support is not available. Both `OnFileSendMail` and `OnUpdateFileSendMail` are overridable functions, which enables you to implement customized messaging behavior.

Document Data

I already mentioned simple `CDocument`-derived classes, where the document's data can be implemented in the form of simple member variables. However, real-world applications tend to be more demanding, their data requirements far beyond what can be reasonably represented by a few variables of simple data types.

Perhaps the best approach to implement an application with a complex series of data elements is to use a set of `CObject`-derived classes to represent the data elements themselves, while relying on a standard or custom collection class to embed these elements in your document class. For example, in one application I created I used classes like this:

```
class CMyObject : public CObject
{
// ...
};
class CMyFirstSubObject : public CObject
{
// ...
};

class CMySecondSubObject : public CObject
{
// ...
};
```

In the declaration of the document class, I included a `CObList` member:

```
class CMyDocument : public CDocument
{
// ...
// Attributes
public:
    CObList m_obList;
```

```
// ...
};
```

In a complex situation like this, it is often not sufficient to just declare member variables. Member functions are also needed that provide methods to access the document's data. For example, in the above case you may not want to allow other classes (such as the view class) to manipulate the m_obList member variable directly; instead, you may wish to provide member functions that add data to or remove data from this list.

Such member functions should also ensure that all the document's views are updated properly. They should also call the document's SetModified member function to indicate that a change to the document's data has been made. If your application supports an undo capability, this is where you should update your buffered undo data.

As a simple example, consider the following function, which updates the document's object list by adding a new object:

```
BOOL CMyDocument::AddObject(CMyObject *pObject)
{
    try
    {
        m_obList.AddTail((CObject *)pObject);
        SetModifiedFlag(TRUE);
        UpdateAllViews(NULL, UPDATE_OBJECT, pObject);
        return TRUE;
    }
    catch(CMemoryException *e)
    {
        TRACE("CMyDocument::AddObject memory allocation error.\n");
        e->Delete();
        return FALSE;
    }
}
```

Consider, for a moment, how control is passed back and forth between the document and its views. First, the user interacts with the view, which results in a new object being added. The view object than calls the document object's AddObject member. Once the new object has been added successfully, the document object calls UpdateAllViews, which, in turn, calls the OnUpdate member function of each view associated with the document. The hint passed to UpdateAllViews (in the form of the application-defined constant UPDATE_OBJECT and a pointer to a CObject) assists views in implementing an efficient window update by only repainting those regions that are affected by the appearance of the new object. This control-passing mechanism is illustrated in Figure 20.1.

Another advantage of using MFC collection classes is that they support serialization. For example, to load and save your document's data that is stored in the form of a CObList collection, all you need to do in the document's Serialize member function is this:

```
void CTerminalDoc::Serialize(CArchive &ar)
{
    if (ar.IsStoring())
    {
```

```
        // Serialize any non CObject-derived data
    }
    else
    {
        // Serialize any non CObject-derived data
    }
    m_obList.Serialize(ar);
}
```

FIGURE 20.1.

Passing control.

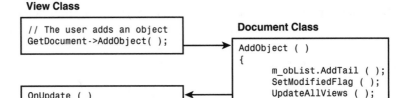

Be warned, though, that for this to work you must implement the `Serialize` member function for all your object classes. A `CObject`-derived class will not magically serialize itself.

If you decide to use one of the collection templates, serialization is an issue that requires special attention. The collection templates `CArray`, `CList`, and `CMap` rely on the `SerializeElements` function to serialize the objects in the collection. This function is declared as follows:

```
template <class TYPE> void
    SerializeElements(CArchive &ar, TYPE *pElements, int nCount);
```

Because the collection class templates do not require TYPE to be derived from `CObject`, they do not call the `Serialize` member function of their elements (simply because this member function is not guaranteed to exist). Instead, the default implementation of `SerializeElements` performs a *bitwise read or write*. This is definitely not what we want in most cases! (Arguably, it might have been better if the MFC provided no default implementation at all, thus forcing the programmer to write `SerializeElements` rather than fall prey to a subtle trap.) Here is an example of how you would implement `SerializeElements` for an object type you define that supports a `Serialize` member function:

```
void SerializeElements(CArchive &ar, CMyObject **pObs, int nCount)
{
    for (int i = 0; i < nCount; i++, pObs++)
        (*pObs)->Serialize(ar);
}
```

CCmdTarget and CDocItem

Often it is not sufficient to derive your document's objects from the `CObject` class. A prime example for this is when you wish to support OLE automation. OLE automation support requires that your objects be command targets; something that CObject does not support. For this reason, it may be beneficial to use CCmdTarget as the base class for your objects.

Better yet, you should consider the CDocItem class. You can either create a collection of CDocItem objects yourself or rely on the COleDocument class for this purpose; that is, derive your document class from COleDocument instead of CDocument. COleDocument is used in OLE applications where either this class or a class derived from it serves as the base class for the OLE application's document class. COleDocument supports a collection of CDocItem objects; these are objects of type COleServerItem and COleClientItem. However, the support for a list of CDocItem objects in COleDocument is generic. You can add your own CDocItem-derived objects to the collection maintained by COleDocument and not fear that it would interfere with normal OLE behavior.

How do you declare additional CDocItem members in a COleDocument? Funny thing is, you don't have to! All you need to do is use COleDocument member functions such as AddItem, RemoveItem, GetStartPosition, and GetNextItem to add, remove, and retrieve document items. The rest (such as serialization) comes for free.

There is a catch, though. Because of how your document items and the OLE COleClientItem and COleServerItem objects are derived, it may be necessary to add some magic to implement certain functions. For example, consider that you declared your objects as follows:

```
class CMyDocItem : public CDocItem
{
    // ...
    CRect m_rect;
};
```

Further suppose that you also support the m_rect member variable in your OLE client items:

```
class CMyClientItem : public COleClientItem
{
    // ...
    CRect m_rect;
};
```

Given these class declarations, how would you create a function that can take an item from your document and utilize its m_rect member?

The obvious answer is also the wrong one:

```
MyFunc(CDocItem *pItem)
{
    AnotherFunc(pItem->m_rect);  // Error!
}
```

This will not compile because the CDocItem class has no member variable named m_rect. Using a pointer to your own CDocItem-derived class does not help either:

```
MyFunc(CMyDocItem *pItem)
{
    AnotherFunc(pItem->m_rect);
}
```

This version of MyFunc does not support OLE client items. Obviously, you could simply create two override versions of MyFunc, but it is a real pain having to maintain two identical versions because of this problem. So the solution that remains is to create a wrapper function that takes a pointer to a CDocItem object and uses MFC run-time type information to obtain the member variable:

```
CRect GetRect(CDocItem *pDocItem)
{
    if (pDocItem->IsKindOf(RUNTIME_CLASS(CMyDocItem)))
        return ((CMyDocItem *)pDocItem)->m_rect;
    else if (pDocItem->IsKindOf(RUNTIME_CLASS(CMyClientItem)))
        return ((CMyClientItem *)pDocItem)->m_rect;
    ASSERT(FALSE);
    return CRect(0, 0, 0, 0);
}

MyFunc(CDocItem *pItem)
{
    AnotherFunc(GetRect(pItem));
}
```

Note that this solution requires that both CMyDocItem and CMyClientItem be declared and implemented using the DECLARE_DYNAMIC/IMPLEMENT_DYNAMIC macros. This is usually not a problem as your application probably supports serializing these items, and thus the items are declared and implemented using DECLARE_SERIAL/IMPLEMENT_SERIAL (which imply DECLARE_DYNAMIC/IMPLEMENT_DYNAMIC).

The *CView* Class

For every CDocument-derived class, there is a CView-derived class that provides the visual presentation of your document's data and handles user interaction through the view window.

The view window is a child of a frame window. In the case of SDI applications, this is the main frame window. For MDI applications, this is the MDI child frame. Additionally, it can be the in-place frame window during OLE in-place editing (if your application supports it).

A frame window may contain several view windows (for example, splitter windows).

Declaring a View Class

All data that is part of a document should be declared as part of the document class. That said, there are many data elements that pertain to a specific view and, more importantly, are transient in nature, not saved as part of the document.

Consider, for example, an application that is capable of presenting its data at different zoom factors. The zoom factor is specific to an individual view. (Different views may use different zoom factors even when they present parts of the same application.) The zoom factor is also transient; it is not saved as part of the document.

Under these conditions, the zoom factor would best be declared as a member variable of your view class:

```
class CZoomView : public CView
{
protected: // create from serialization only
    CZoomView();
    DECLARE_DYNCREATE(CZoomView)

// Attributes
public:
    CZoomDoc* GetDocument();
    double m_dZoom;
...
```

Much more important than any member variables representing a setting is a member variable that represents the *current selection*. This is the collection of objects in your document that the user selected for manipulation. The nature and type of that manipulation are entirely application-dependent, but may include such interapplication operations as clipboard cut and copy or OLE drag and drop.

Perhaps the easiest way to implement a selection is to use a collection class just as you would in the document class. For example, you may declare the collection representing the current selection like this:

```
class CMyView : public CView
{
    // ...
    CList<CDocItem *, CDocItem *> m_selList;
    // ...
```

In addition to modifying the declaration of the view class, you must write at least one member function to give your view class some functionality. The function in question is the OnDraw member function. The default implementation does nothing; you must write code here that displays your document's data items.

For example, if your document class is derived from COleDocument and you rely on CDocItem objects for your document's data, your OnDraw member function implementation may look like this:

```
void CMyView::OnDraw(CDC *pDC)
{
    CMyDoc *pDoc = GetDocument();
    ASSERT_VALID(pDoc);

    POSITION pos = pDoc->GetStartPosition();
    while (pos != NULL)
    {
        CDocItem *pObject = pDoc->GetNextItem(pos);
        if (pObject->IsKindOf(RUNTIME_CLASS(CMyDocItem)))
        {
            ((CMyDocItem *)pObject)->Draw(pDC);
        }
        else if (pObject->IsKindOf(RUNTIME_CLASS(CMyClientItem)))
```

```
        {
            ((CMyClientItem *)pObject)->Draw(pDC);
        }
        else
            ASSERT(FALSE);
    }
}
```

CView Member Functions

The CView class offers a rich selection of member functions.

Among the most commonly used member functions is GetDocument, which returns a pointer to the document object associated with the view. Another member function is DoPreparePrinting; this function displays the Print dialog and creates a printer device context in accordance with the user's selections.

The remaining CView member functions are overridables. They supplement the large number of overridable functions available as part of the CWnd class (the base class of CView) and handle most types of user-interface events. These functions are far too numerous to be listed here; among them are message handlers for keyboard, mouse, timer, system and other messages, clipboard and MDI events, and initialization and termination messages. Your application should provide overrides for these as appropriate; for example, if your application enables the user to place an object in a document by clicking and dragging the mouse, you should provide an override for the CWnd::OnLButtonDown member function. As most of these overrides are recognized by the ClassWizard, adding and manipulating them is easy.

There are some notable CView overridables. One, I already mentioned; overriding OnDraw is a must for a CView-derived object to display anything.

The IsSelected member function must be implemented for OLE applications. This function returns TRUE if the object that is pointed to by its argument is part of the view's current selection. If you implemented your selection using the CList template collection as a list of CDocItem objects, here is how you could implement IsSelected:

```
BOOL CMyView::IsSelected(const CObject* pDocItem) const
{
        return (m_selList.Find((CDocItem *)pDocItem) != NULL);
}
```

Another notable overridable is the OnUpdate member function. This function is called by the UpdateAllViews member function of the document class associated with the view. The default implementation simply invalidates the entire client area of the view window. To improve your application's performance, you may wish to override this function and invalidate only those areas that need updating. For example, you may implement OnUpdate as follows:

```
void CMyView::OnUpdate(CView *pView, LPARAM lHint, CObject *pObj)
{
```

```
    if (lHint == UPDATE_OBJECT)
        InvalidateRect((((CMyObject *)pObj)->m_rect);
    else
        Invalidate();
}
```

Normally you should not do any drawing in `OnUpdate`. Use your view's `OnDraw` member function for that purpose.

The `OnPrepareDC` member function acquires special significance if your view supports nonstandard mapping modes like zooming. It is in this function that you can set the view window's mapping mode before any actual drawing takes place. Make sure that if you create a device context for your view window, you call `OnPrepareDC` yourself to ensure that the proper settings are applied to the device context.

Sometimes it is necessary to create a device context just to retrieve the current mapping using `OnPrepareDC`. For example, your view's `OnLButtonDown` member function may need to convert the position of the mouse click from physical to logical coordinates:

```
void CMyView::OnLButtonDown(UITN nFlags, CPoint point)
{
    CClientDC dc(this);
    OnPrepareDC(&dc);
    dc.DPtoLP(&point);
    // ...
```

Other `CView` overridables deal with initialization and termination, OLE drag and drop support, scrolling, view activation and deactivation, and printing. Whether these functions require overriding or not depends on whether you support the particular feature, and whether the default implementation (if it exists) is sufficient for your purposes or not.

Views and Messages

In addition to messages for which default handlers already exist in `CView` or its parent, `CWnd`, a typical view class handles many other messages. These are typically command messages representing the user's selection of a menu command, toolbar button, or other user-interface object.

As I explained earlier, when deciding whether it is the view or the document (or the frame) that should handle a particular message, the prevailing criteria is the scope and the effect of the message or command. If the command affects the entire document, it is best handled by the document class (unless the command's effect is through a specific view, as in some implementations of the Paste command). If the command only affects a particular view (such as setting a zoom factor), it should be handled by that view object.

Variants of *CView*

In addition to the basic CView class, the MFC Library provides several derived classes that serve specific purposes. These classes are summarized in Table 20.1.

Table 20.1. CView variants.

Class Name	Description
CCtrlView	This view class supports views that are based on a control (such as a tree or edit control).
CDaoRecordView	This view class displays database records using dialog controls.
CEditView	This view class provides a multiline text editor window using an edit control.
CFormView	This view class is based on a dialog template and displays dialog box controls.
CListView	This view class displays a list control.
CRecordView	This view class displays database records using dialog controls.
CRichEditView	This view class displays a rich-text edit control.
CScrollView	This view class enables the use of scrollbars.
CTreeView	This view class displays a tree control.

A rarely overridden variant of CView is CPreviewView; this class is used by the MFC framework to provide print preview support.

All these classes provide member functions that are specific to their function. Member functions of view classes derived from CCtrlView encapsulate Windows messages that are specific to the control class they represent.

CFormView and classes derived from it (CDaoRecordView and CRecordView) support Dialog Data Exchange. You can use these classes in a fashion similar to the way CDialog-derived classes would be used.

Dialog-Based Applications

Dialog-based applications represent an exception from the standard MFC document-view model. If you create a dialog-based application using the AppWizard, the resulting program will not have a document or a view class (nor a frame window class, for that matter). Instead, all functionality will be implemented by a single dialog class, derived from CDialog.

While this is sufficient for many simple applications, it also means a loss of support for many MFC features that you have come to like. A dialog-based application will have no menu, toolbar, or status bar; it will not support OLE or MAPI; it will not have printing capabilities.

An alternative to using a dialog-based application is to build your application using the CFormView class as the base class for your view window and utilize the SDI application model. This enables you to retain all the advantages of a full-featured MFC application, yet present the same dialog-like appearance, utilize a dialog box template for defining the view's contents, and use Dialog Data Exchange.

Summary

Most MFC applications are based on the *document-view model.* The document, an abstract object, represents the application's data and typically corresponds to the contents of a file. The view, in turn, provides presentation of the data and accepts user-interface events. The relationship is one-to-many; a document may have several associated views, but a view is always associated with exactly one document.

Document classes are derived from CDocument. This class encapsulates much of the basic functionality of a document object. In the simplest case, applications need only add member variables representing application-specific data and provide overrides for the OnNewDocument (initialization) and Serialize (saving and loading) member functions to obtain a fully functional document class.

More sophisticated applications often rely on collection classes to implement the set of objects that comprise a document. In particular, applications can use the COleDocument class and rely on its capability to manage a list of CDocItem objects that is not restricted to OLE client and server objects.

View classes are derived from CView. View windows that are represented by CView objects are child windows of frame windows; a frame window may have several child view windows, as is the case when splitter windows are used.

A view object, in addition to containing member variables representing view-specific settings, often implements a current selection. The current selection is the set of document objects that the user designated in the current view for further manipulation. As with documents, applications can use collection classes for this purpose.

At the very least, a view class must provide an implementation for the OnDraw member function to draw the objects of the associated document. OLE applications must also provide an implementation for the IsSelected member function. Other, frequently overridden, member functions include OnPrepareDC and OnUpdate.

The CView class has several variants specifically designed to handle scrolling views, views based on dialogs, controls, and views representing database records. You should select the class that is most appropriate for your application as the base class for your view class.

Both documents and views (as well as frame objects) handle messages. A decision about which of these three classes should handle a particular message is based upon the effects of the message. If the message affects the entire document, it is the document class that should handle the message, unless the effect takes place through a specific view. In that case, or in the case when the effect is specific to a view, it is the view class that should provide handling. Lastly, messages that have a global effect on the application are best handled by the frame class.

Dialogs and Property Sheets

21

Applications use dialogs in many situations. The MFC Library supports dialogs through the CDialog class and derived classes.

A CDialog object corresponds to a dialog window, the content of which is based on a dialog template resource. The dialog template resource can be edited using any dialog editor; typically, however, you would use the dialog editor that is part of the Developer Studio for this purpose.

Perhaps the most important feature of CDialog is its support for Dialog Data Exchange, a mechanism that facilitates the easy and efficient exchange of data between controls in a dialog and member variables in the dialog class.

The CDialog class is derived from CWnd; thus, you can use many CWnd member functions to enhance your dialog. Furthermore, your dialog classes can have message maps; indeed, except for the most simple dialogs, it is often necessary to add message map entries to handle specific control messages.

Newer applications often support tabbed dialogs, or *property sheets*. A property sheet is really several dialogs merged into one; the user uses tab controls to pick any one of the *property pages* that comprise a property sheet.

Our tour of MFC dialog support starts with a review of how simple dialogs are constructed in an MFC application.

Constructing Dialogs

The basic steps in constructing a dialog and making it part of your application include creating the dialog template resource, creating a CDialog-derived class that corresponds to this resource, and constructing an object of this class at the appropriate location in your application.

For our experiments with dialogs, we use a simple AppWizard-created SDI application named DLG. Other than selecting the Single document application type, this application should be created with AppWizard's defaults.

The next section shows you how to create a simple dialog that has an editable text field and make it part of the DLG application by connecting it to a new menu item, View Dialog. The dialog, as displayed by DLG, is shown in Figure 21.1.

Adding a Dialog Template

The first step in constructing a dialog is to create the dialog template resource. This resource can be built using the integrated dialog editor that is part of the Developer Studio. Figure 21.2 shows the dialog under construction. The OK and Cancel buttons are supplied by the dialog editor when a blank dialog is created; to that, we should add a static control and an edit control. The edit control will have the identifier IDC_EDIT; the dialog itself will be identified as IDD_DIALOG.

FIGURE 21.1.

A simple dialog.

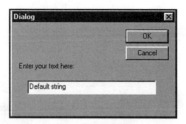

FIGURE 21.2.

Constructing a simple dialog.

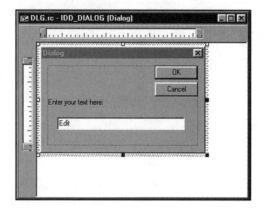

While the dialog template is open for editing in the dialog editor, you can directly invoke the ClassWizard to construct the dialog class corresponding to this template.

Constructing the Dialog Class

Although it is possible to create a dialog class by hand, in many cases it is easier to rely on the ClassWizard for this purpose. To create a dialog class corresponding to the dialog shown in Figure 21.2, use the right mouse button anywhere in the dialog editor window to bring up a popup menu; from this popup menu, select the ClassWizard command.

The ClassWizard, after detecting that it has been invoked for a newly constructed resource, presents the Adding a Class dialog that is shown in Figure 21.3. Select the Create a new class radio button and click OK.

At this time, the ClassWizard displays the Create New Class dialog (Figure 21.4). Here, you can enter the dialog's name and set other options, such as the filename, the resource identifier, or OLE automation settings. You can also add this class to the Component Gallery for later reuse in other applications.

Add a suitable name for the new class, for example, CMyDialog. It may also be a good idea to uncheck the Add to Component Gallery check box; after all, it is not necessary to clutter the component gallery with code that is used for demonstration purposes only.

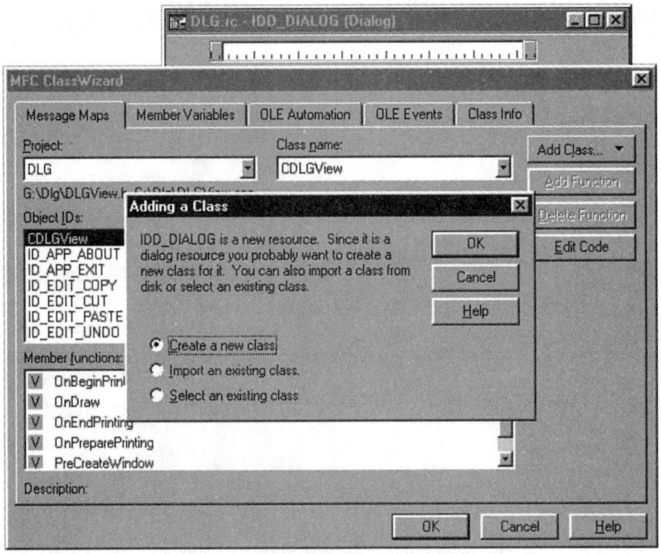

FIGURE 21.3.

The Adding a Class dialog.

FIGURE 21.4.

The Create New Class dialog.

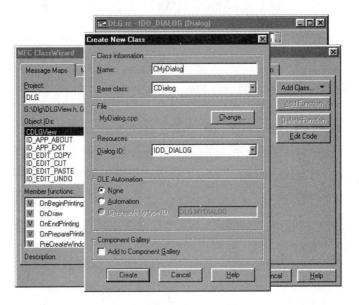

Should you change the filenames that the ClassWizard suggests for your new class's header and implementation files? Should you use a separate header and implementation file for every new dialog you create? This is an interesting question. At the surface, the answer would appear to be a yes; then again, even the AppWizard itself violates this "rule" when it places both the declaration and implementation of your application's About dialog into the application object's implementation file. Thus, I believe that in the end, it is best left to the judgment of the programmer. I often grouped dialog classes together if they were small, simple, and related.

Leaving them in separate files tended to clutter the application workspace. However, this is less of a concern with Visual C++ 4 where you no longer have to use FileView to access your source code; also, using separate files makes it easier to use the Component Gallery.

For now, leave the filenames at the ClassWizard-generated defaults: `MyDialog.h` and `MyDialog.cpp`. Clicking on the Create button actually creates the new class and leaves the ClassWizard main dialog open.

The next step is to add a member variable that corresponds to the edit field in the dialog template.

Adding Member Variables

To add a new member variable, select the Member Variables tab in ClassWizard (Figure 21.5).

FIGURE 21.5.

Member variables in ClassWizard.

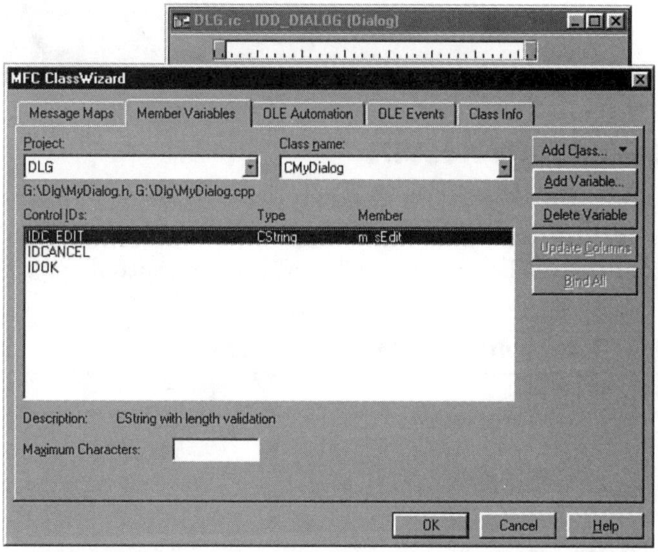

The member variable for the `IDC_EDIT` control can be added by double-clicking this identifier in the Control IDs column. This invokes yet another dialog, shown in Figure 21.6. Type in the new variable's name (`m_sEdit`) and click on the OK button. Once the member variable has been added, you can dismiss the ClassWizard altogether by clicking on the OK button in the ClassWizard dialog.

If you still have the dialog template resource open for editing, dismiss that window as well. In a moment, we'll begin creating the code that will invoke our new dialog. Before we do that, however, take a look at the code that the ClassWizard has generated for us so far.

FIGURE 21.6.

*The Add Member
Variable dialog.*

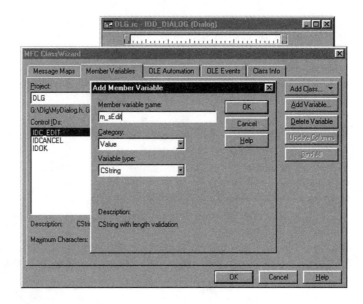

ClassWizard Results

The declaration of `CMyDialog` (in `MyDialog.h`) is shown in Listing 21.1. Part of the class declaration is the declaration of `IDD`, which identifies the dialog template. The class declaration also
contains the member variable `m_sEdit`, which we created through ClassWizard.

Listing 21.1. `CMyDialog` class declaration.

```
class CMyDialog : public CDialog
{
// Construction
public:
    CMyDialog(CWnd* pParent = NULL);    // standard constructor

// Dialog Data
    //{{AFX_DATA(CMyDialog)
    enum { IDD = IDD_DIALOG };
    CString m_sEdit;
    //}}AFX_DATA


// Overrides
    // ClassWizard generated virtual function overrides
    //{{AFX_VIRTUAL(CMyDialog)
    protected:
    virtual void DoDataExchange(CDataExchange* pDX);
    //}}AFX_VIRTUAL

// Implementation
protected:
```

```
        // Generated message map functions
        //{{AFX_MSG(CMyDialog)
            // NOTE: the ClassWizard will add member functions here
        //}}AFX_MSG
        DECLARE_MESSAGE_MAP()
};
```

Declarations for the constructor function and an override for the DoDataExchange member function are also provided here.

These two functions are defined in MyDialog.cpp (Listing 21.2). Notice that the ClassWizard inserted code into both of them; the member variable m_sEdit is initialized in the constructor and also referred to in DoDataExchange.

Listing 21.2. CMyDialog member functions.

```
CMyDialog::CMyDialog(CWnd* pParent /*=NULL*/)
    : CDialog(CMyDialog::IDD, pParent)
{
    //{{AFX_DATA_INIT(CMyDialog)
    m_sEdit = _T("");
    //}}AFX_DATA_INIT
}


void CMyDialog::DoDataExchange(CDataExchange* pDX)
{
    CDialog::DoDataExchange(pDX);
    //{{AFX_DATA_MAP(CMyDialog)
    DDX_Text(pDX, IDC_EDIT, m_sEdit);
    //}}AFX_DATA_MAP
}


BEGIN_MESSAGE_MAP(CMyDialog, CDialog)
    //{{AFX_MSG_MAP(CMyDialog)
        // NOTE: the ClassWizard will add message map macros here
    //}}AFX_MSG_MAP
END_MESSAGE_MAP()
```

DoDataExchange is the function that facilitates data exchange between member variables and dialog controls. It is invoked both when the dialog is constructed and when it is dismissed. The macros inserted by ClassWizard (such as the DDX_Text macro) facilitate data exchange in both directions; the direction is determined by the m_bSaveAndValidate member of the CDataExchange object, pointed to by the pDX parameter. We revisit this function and the various data exchange helper macros shortly.

Invoking the Dialog

Construction of our dialog object is now complete. How are we going to invoke this dialog from our DLG application?

First, we must make a "design decision," if it can be dignified with that phrase: The new dialog will be invoked when the user selects a new menu item, Dialog, from the View menu.

This menu item must first be added to the application's menu using the resource editor (see Figure 21.7).

FIGURE 21.7.

Adding the View Dialog menu item.

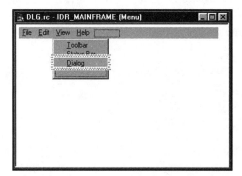

To add code that handles the new menu item, invoke the ClassWizard, and add a command handler function for `ID_VIEW_DIALOG` to the `CMainFrame` class. (Why `CMainFrame`? Displaying this dialog has nothing to do with a specific document or any of its views, so `CMainFrame` appears to be the most logical choice.) This is accomplished most easily by right-clicking on the new Dialog menu item to invoke the ClassWizard, selecting ClassWizard's Message tab, selecting the `ID_VIEW_DIALOG` identifier, and using the Add Function button.

The implementation of `CMainFrame::OnViewDialog` is shown in Listing 21.3. After constructing the dialog object, we assign an initial value to the member variable `m_sEdit`. Next, we invoke the dialog via the `DoModal` function. After the dialog is dismissed by the user, we examine the new value of `m_sEdit` by simply displaying it in a message box.

Listing 21.3. The `CMainFrame::OnViewDialog` member function.

```
void CMainFrame::OnViewDialog()
{
    // TODO: Add your command handler code here
    CMyDialog myDialog;

    myDialog.m_sEdit = "Default string";
    myDialog.DoModal();
    MessageBox(myDialog.m_sEdit);
}
```

Note that in order to be able to declare an object of type `CMyDialog` in `CMainFrame::OnViewDialog`, it is necessary to include the `MyDialog.h` header file in `MainFrm.cpp`.

That's it. The application is ready to be recompiled and run.

Modeless Dialogs

Invoking a dialog through the `DoModal` member function invokes the dialog as a modal dialog. However, sometimes applications require the use of modeless dialogs. The steps of creating and displaying a modeless dialog are different from the steps taken for modal dialogs.

To convert our dialog in DLG to a modeless dialog, we must first modify the dialog's constructor function. In the constructor, we must make a call to the `Create` member function in order to construct the dialog box object. We must also call a different version of the base class constructor, as shown in Listing 21.4.

Listing 21.4. Modeless version of `CMyDialog::CMyDialog`.

```
CMyDialog::CMyDialog(CWnd* pParent /*=NULL*/)
    : CDialog()
{
    Create(CMyDialog::IDD, pParent);
    //{{AFX_DATA_INIT(CMyDialog)
    m_sEdit = _T("");
    //}}AFX_DATA_INIT
}
```

Invocation of the dialog from `CMainFrame::OnViewDialog` is also different. Instead of calling the dialog's `DoModal` member function, we just construct the dialog object; the call to `Create` within the constructor takes care of the rest.

Note that we can no longer construct the dialog box on the stack. Because a modeless dialog box is long lived and continues to exist even after `CMainFrame::OnViewDialog` returns, we have to allocate the `CDialog` object differently. This new version of `CMainFrame::OnViewDialog` is shown in Listing 21.5 (`MainFrm.cpp`).

Listing 21.5. Constructing a modeless dialog in `CMainFrame::OnViewDialog`.

```
void CMainFrame::OnViewDialog()
{
    // TODO: Add your command handler code here
    CMyDialog *pMyDialog;

    pMyDialog = new CMyDialog;
    pMyDialog->m_sEdit = "Default string";
    pMyDialog->UpdateData(FALSE);
    pMyDialog->ShowWindow(SW_SHOW);
}
```

Why was it necessary to call UpdateData in this function? Because we set the value of m_sEdit *after* the dialog box object has been constructed and initial Dialog Data Exchange took place. By calling UpdateData, we ensure that the controls in the dialog box object are updated to reflect the settings in the member variables of the CDialog object. This is yet another example that should remind us that the C++ object and the Windows object are two different entities.

We must also call the ShowWindow member function to make the new dialog visible. Alternatively, we could have created the dialog box template resource with the WS_VISIBLE style.

How long will this dialog exist? As long as the user does not dismiss it by clicking on the OK or Cancel button. At that time, the default implementations of CDialog::OnOK and CDialog::OnCancel hide the dialog box but do not destroy it. Obviously, we must override these functions to properly destroy the dialog. In both of these functions, a call must be made to the DestroyWindow member function.

We must also override the dialog's OnOK function to ensure that we process whatever the user entered in the dialog. We can no longer rely on the function calling DoModal for this purpose, for the simple reason that DoModal is never called.

Calling the DestroyWindow member function from OnOK and OnCancel ensures that the Windows dialog box object is destroyed; but how will the C++ object be destroyed? The answer to that question is yet another override. You must override the PostNcDestroy member function and delete the CDialog-derived object from within it.

To override the default implementations of OnOK, OnCancel, and PostNCDestroy, you must first add these functions to the CMyDialog class through ClassWizard. Perhaps the simplest way to do this is to open the implementation file, MyDialog.cpp, and use the WizardBar to add the functions.

Implementations of CMyDialog::OnOK, CMyDialog::OnCancel, and CMyDialog::PostNcDestroy are shown in Listing 21.6 (MyDialog.cpp).

Listing 21.6. Member functions in the modeless version of CMyDialog.

```
void CMyDialog::OnCancel()
{
    // TODO: Add extra cleanup here

    CDialog::OnCancel();
    DestroyWindow();
}

void CMyDialog::OnOK()
{
    // TODO: Add extra validation here
    MessageBox(m_sEdit);
    CDialog::OnOK();
    DestroyWindow();
}
```

```
void CMyDialog::PostNcDestroy()
{
    // TODO: Add your specialized code here and/or call the base class

    CDialog::PostNcDestroy();
    delete this;
}
```

If your modeless dialog must notify the frame, document, or view, it can do so by calling a member function. The dialog class can have a member variable that stores a pointer to the frame, document, or view object from within which the dialog has been created. Other mechanisms for communication between the modeless dialog and other parts of your application are also conceivable; for example, the dialog may post a message to the application.

More on Dialog Data Exchange

In the preceding example, we have used Dialog Data Exchange to map the contents of an edit control to the contents of a CString member variable in the dialog class. The Dialog Data Exchange mechanism offers many other capabilities for mapping simple variables or control objects to controls in a dialog box.

> **NOTE**
>
> Although Dialog Data Exchange and Dialog Data Validation are described in the context of dialog boxes, they are not limited in use to dialog boxes only. The member functions discussed, such as DoDataExchange and UpdateData, are actually member functions of CWnd, not CDialog. Dialog Data Exchange is also used outside the context of a dialog box; CFormView and classes derived from it are one example.

Dialog Data Exchange

Dialog Data Exchange takes place in the dialog class's DoDataExchange member function. In this function, calls are made for all member variables that are mapped to controls. The calls that are made are to a family of MFC functions with names that begin with DDX_. These functions are responsible for performing the actual data exchange.

For example, to perform data exchange between an edit control and a member variable of type CString, the following call is made:

```
DDX_Text(pDX, IDC_EDIT, m_sEdit);
```

Dialog Data Validation

In addition to the simple exchange of data between member variables and dialog controls, MFC also offers a data validation mechanism. Data validation is accomplished through calls to functions with names that begin with DDV_. These functions perform the necessary validation and if a validation error is encountered, display a standard error message box and raise an exception of type CUserException. They also call the Fail member function of the CDataExchange object that is passed to DoDataExchange; this object, in turn, sets the focus to the offending control.

An example for a data validation function is DDV_MaxChars, which is used to validate the length of a string typed into an edit control. To validate that a string in an edit control is no longer than 100 characters, you would make the following call:

```
DDV_MaxChars(pDX, m_sEdit, 100);
```

Data validation calls for a given control must immediately follow the data exchange function call for the same control.

Using Simple Types

Dialog Data Exchange with simple types is supported for edit controls, scrollbars, check boxes, radio buttons, list boxes, and combo boxes.

Table 21.1 summarizes the types supported by Dialog Data Exchange for edit controls.

Table 21.1. Dialog Data Exchange and validation for edit controls.

Control	Data Type	DDX function	DDV function
edit control	BYTE	DDX_Text	DDV_MinMaxByte
edit control	short	DDX_Text	DDV_MinMaxInt
edit control	int	DDX_Text	DDV_MinMaxInt
edit control	UINT	DDX_Text	DDV_MinMaxUnsigned
edit control	long	DDX_Text	DDV_MinMaxLong
edit control	DWORD	DDX_Text	DDV_MinMaxDWord
edit control	float	DDX_Text	DDV_MinMaxFloat
edit control	double	DDX_Text	DDV_MinMaxDouble
edit control	CString	DDX_Text	DDV_MaxChars
edit control	COleDateTime	DDX_Text	
edit control	COleCurrency	DDX_Text	
check box	BOOL	DDX_Check	

Control	Data Type	DDX function	DDV function
radio button	int	DDX_Radio	
list box	int	DDX_LBIndex	
list box	CString	DDX_LBString	
list box	Cstring	DDX_LBStringExact	
combo box	int	DDX_CBIndex	
combo box	CString	DDX_CBString	DDV_MaxChars
combo box	Cstring	DDX_CBStringExact	
scrollbar	int	DDX_Scroll	

The MFC Library provides additional versions of the DDX functions to facilitate data exchange between a dialog box and records in a database. These functions have names that begin with DDX_Field; for example, the database variant of DDX_Text would be named DDX_FieldText.

Using Control Data Types

In addition to assigning a member variable to a control representing the control's value, it is also possible to assign member variables that represent the control object itself. For example, it is possible to assign a variable of type CEdit to an edit control.

The Dialog Data Exchange mechanism uses the DDX_Control function to exchange data between a dialog control and a CWnd-derived control object.

A control object can be used concurrently with a member variable representing the control's value. For example, it is possible to assign both a CString object representing the control's value and a CEdit object representing the control itself to an edit control in a dialog.

Why would you use a control object? Through such an object, you can implement much greater control over the appearance and behavior of dialog controls. For example, as control objects are CWnd-derived, your application can use CWnd member functions to change the control's size and position. Through the control object, it is also possible to send messages to the control.

In the case of many control types (including the new common controls) you must use a control object for Dialog Data Exchange. The use of a simple data type is meaningless and not supported.

Implementing Custom Data Types

Versatile as the Dialog Data Exchange mechanism is, it would not be sufficient in many situations were it not for the capability to extend it for custom data types. Fortunately, the ClassWizard offers the capability to handle custom DDX and DDV routines.

The steps required to implement custom DDX/DDV support are time consuming and may only be beneficial for data types that you frequently reuse. That said, it is possible to add custom DDX/DDV support to a specific project, or to all projects, by modifying either your project's CLW file, or the ddx.clw file in your msdev\bin subdirectory.

The exact steps to be taken for custom DDX/DDV support are described in MFC Technical Note 26 that is part of your Visual C++ on-line documentation.

Dialogs and Message Handling

CDialog-derived objects are, as you might expect from CWnd-derived objects, capable of handling messages. In fact, in all but the simplest cases, it is necessary to add message handlers to your CDialog-derived dialog class.

Message handling in a dialog is no different from message handling in a view or frame window. Message handler functions can be easily added to the dialog class's message map using ClassWizard. In the earlier examples we have already done that when we added override versions of the OnOK and OnCancel member functions. These member functions are handlers of WM_COMMAND messages. (The third override function we implemented, PostNcDestroy, is not a message handler; however, it is called from within the handler for WM_NCDESTROY messages, OnNcDestroy.)

The most frequently used message handlers in a dialog class correspond to messages sent to the dialog window by one of its controls. These include BN_CLICKED messages sent by a button; the variety of CBN_ messages sent by a combo box; EN_ messages sent by an edit control; and so on. Another set of message that dialog classes often handle consists of WM_DRAWITEM and WM_MEASUREITEM for owner-draw controls.

Owner-draw controls bring up an interesting issue. Should you handle such a situation from within your dialog class, or should you assign an object of a class derived from a control class to the control and handle it there? For example, if you have an owner-draw button, you have the choice of adding a handler for WM_DRAWITEM messages to your dialog class, or deriving a class from CButton and overriding its DrawItem member function.

I suppose there is no definite answer to this question. Perhaps the best rule of thumb is that you should derive your own control class if you expect the control to be reused in many dialogs; otherwise, handling WM_DRAWITEM within the dialog class may be sufficient (and also simpler).

Property Sheets

Property sheets are several overlapping dialogs in one. The user selects one of the dialogs, or property pages, by clicking on the corresponding tab in a tab control.

MFC supports property sheets through two classes: CPropertySheet and CPropertyPage. CPropertySheet corresponds to the property sheet; CPropertyPage-derived classes correspond to the individual property pages within the property sheet.

Using a property sheet requires several steps. First, the property pages must be constructed; next, the property sheet must be created.

The following simple example reviews this process. A new application, PRP, is used to display a property sheet, as shown in Figure 21.8. Like our earlier application, DLG, PRP is also a standard SDI application created by AppWizard.

FIGURE 21.8.

A sample property sheet.

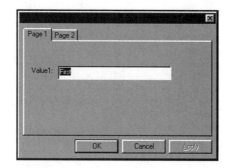

Constructing Property Pages

Constructing a property page is very similar to constructing dialogs. The first step is to construct the dialog template resource for every property page that you wish to add to the property sheet.

There are a few special considerations when constructing a dialog template resource for a property page object:

1. The dialog's caption should be set to the text that you wish to see appear in the tab corresponding to the dialog.
2. The dialog's style should be set to child.
3. The dialog's border style should be set to thin.
4. The Titlebar style should be checked.
5. The Disabled style should be checked.

Although the property pages in a property sheet will overlap, it is not necessary to create them with the same size. The MFC Library will automatically adjust the size of property pages to match the size of the largest property page.

In this example we construct two property pages for our application—nothing fancy, just a simple text field in both of them. The first property page, titled "Page 1," is shown in Figure 21.9. To insert a blank property page template similar to the one shown here, use the IDR_PROPPAGE_SMALL subtype of the Dialog resource type in the Insert Resource dialog. Afterwards, you can add the controls as shown.

FIGURE 21.9.

Constructing a property page.

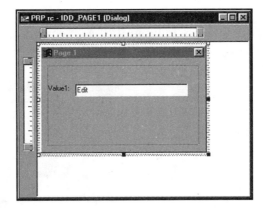

The identifier of the dialog template resource should be set to IDD_PAGE1; the identifier of the edit control should be set to IDC_EDIT1. Make sure that the dialog template's properties are set correctly. To set the dialog's caption, double click on the dialog to invoke the Dialog Properties property sheet (Figure 21.10).

FIGURE 21.10.

Property page dialog resource caption setting.

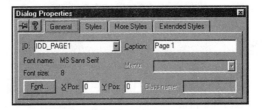

To set the style, border style, and titlebar setting, select the Styles tab in the property sheet of the dialog resource (Figure 21.11).

FIGURE 21.11.

Property page dialog resource styles.

To set the Disabled style of the dialog resource, use the More Styles tab in the dialog resource property sheet (Figure 21.12).

FIGURE 21.12.

Setting the property page dialog resource to Disabled.

The second property page in our simple example is, for the sake of simplicity, nearly identical to the first. In fact, you can create the dialog resource for this second property page by simply making a copy of the first. Make sure that the identifier of the new dialog resource is set to IDD_PAGE2 and that the identifier of the edit control within it is IDC_EDIT2. (It would be perfectly legal to use the same identifier for controls in separate property pages; they act and behave like separate dialogs. Nevertheless, I prefer to use distinct identifiers; this helps reduce the possibility for errors.)

Once both property page dialog resources have been constructed, it is time to invoke the ClassWizard and construct classes that correspond to these property pages. To do so, invoke the ClassWizard while the focus is on the first property page dialog resource while it is open for editing. As with dialogs, the ClassWizard will recognize that the dialog template has no corresponding class and offer you the opportunity to create a new class.

In the Create New Class dialog, specify a name for the class corresponding to the dialog template (for example, CMyPage1). More importantly, make sure that this new class is based on CPropertyPage (and not the default CDialog). Once the correct settings have been entered, create the class.

While in ClassWizard, you should also add a member variable that corresponds to the edit control in the property page. Name this variable m_sEdit1.

These steps should be repeated for the second property page. The class for this property page should be named CMyPage2, and the member variable corresponding to its edit control should be named m_sEdit2.

Construction of our property pages is now complete. Take a brief look at the code generated by ClassWizard. The declaration of CMyPage1 is shown in Listing 21.7. (The declaration of CMyPage2 is virtually identical.)

Listing 21.7. CMyPage1 declaration.

```
class CMyPage1 : public CPropertyPage
{
    DECLARE_DYNCREATE(CMyPage1)

// Construction
public:
    CMyPage1();
    ~CMyPage1();

// Dialog Data
    //{{AFX_DATA(CMyPage1)
    enum { IDD = IDD_PAGE1 };
    CString m_sEdit1;
    //}}AFX_DATA


// Overrides
    // ClassWizard generate virtual function overrides
    //{{AFX_VIRTUAL(CMyPage1)
    protected:
    virtual void DoDataExchange(CDataExchange* pDX);
    //}}AFX_VIRTUAL

// Implementation
protected:
    // Generated message map functions
    //{{AFX_MSG(CMyPage1)
        // NOTE: the ClassWizard will add member functions here
    //}}AFX_MSG
    DECLARE_MESSAGE_MAP()

};
```

As you can see, there is very little difference between this declaration and the ClassWizard-generated declaration of a CDialog-derived dialog class. Most importantly, CPropertyPage-derived classes can use Dialog Data Exchange functions just as classes derived from CDialog.

The implementation of CMyPage1 member functions (Listing 21.8) is also no different from the implementation of similar functions in a CDialog-derived class. Perhaps the one notable difference is that this class has been declared as dynamically creatable with the help of the DECLARE_DYNCREATE and IMPLEMENT_DYNCREATE macros.

Listing 21.8. CMyPage1 implementation.

```
IMPLEMENT_DYNCREATE(CMyPage1, CPropertyPage)

CMyPage1::CMyPage1() : CPropertyPage(CMyPage1::IDD)
{
    //{{AFX_DATA_INIT(CMyPage1)
    m_sEdit1 = _T("");
    //}}AFX_DATA_INIT
}
```

```
CMyPage1::~CMyPage1()
{
}

void CMyPage1::DoDataExchange(CDataExchange* pDX)
{
    CPropertyPage::DoDataExchange(pDX);
    //{{AFX_DATA_MAP(CMyPage1)
    DDX_Text(pDX, IDC_EDIT1, m_sEdit1);
    //}}AFX_DATA_MAP
}


BEGIN_MESSAGE_MAP(CMyPage1, CPropertyPage)
    //{{AFX_MSG_MAP(CMyPage1)
        // NOTE: the ClassWizard will add message map macros here
    //}}AFX_MSG_MAP
END_MESSAGE_MAP()
```

As its declaration, the implementation of CMyPage2 is virtually identical to that of CMyPage1.

Adding a Property Sheet Object

Now that the property pages have been constructed, the one remaining task is to create the property sheet. Again, we need to invoke the new property sheet when the user selects a new menu command, Property Sheet, from the application's View menu. Add this command to the menu using the resource editor, and invoke the ClassWizard to add a corresponding member function, CMainFrame::OnViewPropertysheet, to the CMainFrame class.

In this member function, we have to perform a series of tasks. First, a property sheet object must be constructed. Next, the property pages must be added to it using the AddPage member function; and finally, the property sheet must be invoked using the DoModal member function.

Listing 21.9 contains the implementation of CMainFrame::OnViewPropertysheet that performs all these tasks.

Listing 21.9. The CMainFrame::OnViewPropertysheet function.

```
void CMainFrame::OnViewPropertysheet()
{
    // TODO: Add your command handler code here
    CPropertySheet myPropSheet;
    CMyPage1 myPage1;
    CMyPage2 myPage2;

    myPage1.m_sEdit1 = "First";
    myPage2.m_sEdit2 = "Second";
    myPropSheet.AddPage(&myPage1);
    myPropSheet.AddPage(&myPage2);
    myPropSheet.DoModal();
}
```

Do not forget to include the header files `MyPage1.h` and `MyPage2.h` in `MainFrm.cpp`; otherwise, you will not be able to declare objects of type `CMyPage1` or `CMyPage2` and the function in Listing 21.9 will not compile.

At this time, the application is ready to be compiled and run.

Although in this example we made no use of the property page member variables after the property sheet is dismissed, we could access them simply through the property page objects `myPage1` and `myPage2`.

CPropertyPage Member Functions

Our simple example did not utilize many of the advanced capabilities of the `CPropertyPage` class.

For example, in a more realistic application, you may wish to override the `CancelToClose` member function whenever a change is made to a property page. This member function changes the OK button to Close and disables the Cancel button in the property sheet. This function is best used after an irreversible change has been made in a property page.

Another frequently used property page function is the `SetModified` function. This function can be used to enable the Apply Now button in the property sheet.

Other property page overridables include `OnOK` (called when the OK, Apply Now, or Close button is clicked in the property sheet), `OnCancel` (called when the cancel button is clicked in the property sheet), and `OnApply` (called when the Apply Now button is clicked in the property sheet).

Property sheets can also be used to implement wizard-like behavior; that is, behavior similar to the behavior of the ubiquitous wizards that can be found in many Microsoft applications. Wizard mode can be enabled by calling the `SetWizardMode` member function of the property sheet; in the property pages, override the `OnWizardBack`, `OnWizardNext`, and `OnWizardFinish` member functions.

Modeless Property Sheets

Using the `DoModal` member function of a property sheet implies modal behavior. As is the case with dialogs, it is also possible to implement a modeless property sheet.

To accomplish this, it is first of all necessary to derive our own property sheet class. This is important because at the very least, we must override its `PostNcDestroy` member function to ensure that objects of this class are destroyed when the modeless property sheet is dismissed.

The new property sheet class can be created using ClassWizard. Create a new class derived from `CPropertySheet`, and name it `CMySheet`. While in ClassWizard, add the `PostNcDestroy` member function.

The declaration of CMySheet (in the file MySheet.h), as generated by ClassWizard, is shown in Listing 21.10.

Listing 21.10. CMySheet **declaration.**

```
class CMySheet : public CPropertySheet
{
    DECLARE_DYNAMIC(CMySheet)

// Construction
public:
    CMySheet(UINT nIDCaption, CWnd* pParentWnd = NULL,
            UINT iSelectPage = 0);
    CMySheet(LPCTSTR pszCaption, CWnd* pParentWnd = NULL,
            UINT iSelectPage = 0);

// Attributes
public:

// Operations
public:

// Overrides
    // ClassWizard generated virtual function overrides
    //{{AFX_VIRTUAL(CMySheet)
    protected:
    virtual void PostNcDestroy();
    //}}AFX_VIRTUAL

// Implementation
public:
    virtual ~CMySheet();

    // Generated message map functions
protected:
    //{{AFX_MSG(CMySheet)
        // NOTE - the ClassWizard will add and remove member
        // functions here.
    //}}AFX_MSG
    DECLARE_MESSAGE_MAP()
};
```

In the implementation file, MySheet.cpp, it is necessary to modify the PostNcDestroy member function to destroy not only the property sheet object, but also any property pages associated with it. The implementation of this function, together with other, ClassWizard-supplied member function implementations for the CMySheet class, is shown in Listing 21.11.

Listing 21.11. CMySheet **declaration.**

```
/////////////////////////////////////////////////////////////////
// CMySheet

IMPLEMENT_DYNAMIC(CMySheet, CPropertySheet)

CMySheet::CMySheet(UINT nIDCaption, CWnd* pParentWnd,
                   UINT iSelectPage)
    :CPropertySheet(nIDCaption, pParentWnd, iSelectPage)
{
}

CMySheet::CMySheet(LPCTSTR pszCaption, CWnd* pParentWnd,
                   UINT iSelectPage)
    :CPropertySheet(pszCaption, pParentWnd, iSelectPage)
{
}

CMySheet::~CMySheet()
{
}


BEGIN_MESSAGE_MAP(CMySheet, CPropertySheet)
    //{{AFX_MSG_MAP(CMySheet)
 // NOTE - the ClassWizard will add and remove mapping macros here.
    //}}AFX_MSG_MAP
END_MESSAGE_MAP()

/////////////////////////////////////////////////////////////////
// CMySheet message handlers

void CMySheet::PostNcDestroy()
{
    // TODO: Add your specialized code here and/or call the base class

    CPropertySheet::PostNcDestroy();
    for (int i = 0; i < GetPageCount(); i++)
        delete GetPage(i);
    delete this;
}
```

A modeless property sheet does not have OK, Cancel, and Apply Now buttons by default. If any buttons are required, these must be added by hand. We are not going to worry about these now; the modeless property sheet can still be dismissed by closing it through its control menu.

How is the modeless property sheet invoked? Obviously, we have to modify the OnViewPropertysheet member function in our CMainFrame class, as using DoModal is no longer appropriate. Nor is it appropriate to create the property sheet or any of its property pages on the stack, as we do not want them destroyed when the OnViewPropertysheet function returns. The new OnViewPropertysheet function is shown in Listing 21.12.

Listing 21.12. Invoking a modeless property sheet.

```
void CMainFrame::OnViewPropertysheet()
{
    // TODO: Add your command handler code here
    CMySheet *pMyPropSheet;
    CMyPage1 *pMyPage1;
    CMyPage2 *pMyPage2;

    pMyPropSheet = new CMySheet("");
    pMyPage1 = new CMyPage1;
    pMyPage2 = new CMyPage2;

    pMyPage1->m_sEdit1 = "First";
    pMyPage2->m_sEdit2 = "Second";
    pMyPropSheet->AddPage(pMyPage1);
    pMyPropSheet->AddPage(pMyPage2);
    pMyPropSheet->Create();
}
```

In order for `CMainFrame::OnViewPropertysheet` to compile in its new form, it is necessary to add the include file `MySheet.h` to `MainFrm.cpp`; otherwise, the attempt to declare an object of type `CMySheet` will fail.

The application is now ready to be recompiled and run.

Summary

In MFC, dialogs are represented by classes derived from `CDialog`.

The steps of constructing a dialog that is part of an MFC application are as follows:

1. Create the dialog template resource.
2. Invoke ClassWizard and create the dialog class corresponding to the resource.
3. Through ClassWizard, add member variables corresponding to controls.
4. Still using ClassWizard, add message handlers if necessary.
5. Add code to your application that constructs a dialog object, invokes it (through the `DoModal` member function), and retrieves results.

MFC applications can also have modeless dialogs. These dialogs are constructed differently. The constructor function in your dialog class should call the `Create` member function; it should also call the modeless version of the constructor of the `CDialog` base class. The modeless dialog must also explicitly be made visible by calling the `ShowWindow` member function.

Classes that correspond to modeless dialogs should override the `OnOK` and `OnCancel` member functions and call the `DestroyWindow` member function from within them. They should also override `PostNcDestroy` and destroy the C++ object (using `delete this`, for example).

Controls in a dialog are often represented by member variables in the corresponding dialog class. To facilitate the exchange of data between controls in the dialog box object and member variables in the dialog class, the Dialog Data Exchange mechanism can be used. This mechanism provides a simple method for matching member variables to controls. Member variables can be of simple value types or can represent control objects. It is possible to simultaneously use a member variable of a simple type to obtain the value of a control while using a control object to manage other aspects of the control. The Dialog Data Exchange mechanism also offers data validation capabilities.

For frequently used nonstandard types, it is possible to extend the ClassWizard's ability to handle Dialog Data Exchange. New data exchange and validation routines can be added either on a per project basis or to your overall Visual C++ configuration.

Property sheets represent several overlapping dialogs, or property pages, which the user can choose by clicking on corresponding tabs in a tab control.

Creating a property sheet is a two-phase process. First, property pages must be created; second, a property sheet object must be constructed, the property pages must be added to it, and the property sheet must be displayed.

Construction of property pages involves the same steps as construction of a dialog:

1. Create the dialog template resource for every property page; ensure that the resources have the Child style, Thin border style, Titlebar style, Disabled style, and that their caption is set to the text that is desired in the corresponding tab.
2. Invoke ClassWizard and create a class derived from `CPropertyPage` corresponding to every dialog template resource.
3. Through ClassWizard, add member variables corresponding to controls in each property page.
4. Still using ClassWizard, add message handlers if necessary.

Once the property pages have been constructed, you can proceed with the second phase:

1. Construct a `CPropertySheet` object or an object of a class derived from `CPropertySheet`.
2. Construct a property page object for every property page you wish to add to the property sheet.
3. Add the property pages to the property sheet by calling `AddPage`.
4. Invoke the property sheet by calling `DoModal`.

It is also possible to create modeless property sheets. To implement modeless property sheets, it is necessary to derive a class from `CPropertySheet` and override its `PostNcDestroy` member function to delete not only the property sheet object, but also all of its property pages. The modeless property sheet should be invoked via the `Create` member function instead of `DoModal`.

MFC Support for
Common Dialogs and
Common Controls

22

The Microsoft Foundation Classes Library provides extensive support for common dialogs and the new Windows 95 common controls.

Common dialogs have been a feature of Microsoft Windows since Version 3.1. They are used for opening and closing files, selecting colors and fonts, performing text searches, and setting up and using the printer. Use of these dialogs has never been particularly difficult; unless extensive customization was required, it usually involved populating the members of a C structure, invoking the common dialog, and processing the user's selection. The MFC Library makes it even easier by automating the construction of the necessary structures. The common dialog classes of MFC also make customization easier.

Windows has always provided support for a small selection of standard controls, such as edit controls, static controls, or buttons. The new Windows 95 common controls represent a powerful new set of controls that can be used to enhance the appearance of applications. MFC 4 now provides complete class support for these new controls and integrates them with other MFC framework features where applicable.

Common Dialogs

MFC support for common dialogs is provided through classes derived from the class `CCommonDialog`, which is itself derived from `CDialog`. You would never derive a class from `CCommonDialog` directly or create a `CCommonDialog` object. Instead, to use a common dialog, you create an object of the appropriate dialog class; or, if you use a customized common dialog template, you derive a class from that dialog class.

The set of classes in MFC that provide common dialog support is shown in Figure 22.1.

FIGURE 22.1.

Common dialog support in MFC.

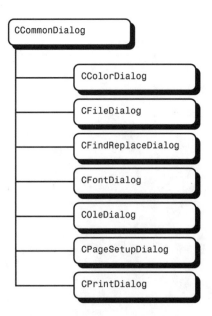

In case of an error, many common dialogs provide extended error information. This information can be retrieved by calling CommDlgExtendedError.

In the following sections, we take a brief look at every one of the common dialog classes provided by the MFC Library. In order to do this, we are going to use an AppWizard-generated application skeleton. This application, CDLG, can be created as an SDI application with AppWizard defaults. We use its View menu for additional commands that invoke the various dialogs. However, to avoid being repetitive, I do not mention separately the creation of a menu command in CDLG's View menu for every common dialog.

CColorDialog

The CColorDialog class supports the Windows color selection common dialog.

To display a color dialog, construct a CColorDialog object and call its DoModal function. Before calling DoModal, you can initialize the dialog by setting up the m_cc member of CColorDialog, which is a Win32 structure of type CHOOSECOLOR. Once the dialog has been dismissed, the user's color selection can be retrieved by calling the GetColor member function.

Listing 22.1 shows a possible implementation of a color selection dialog using the CColorDialog class.

Listing 22.1. Use of CColorDialog in CDLG.

```
void CMainFrame::OnViewColordialog()
{
    // TODO: Add your command handler code here
    CColorDialog dlg;
    if (dlg.DoModal() == IDOK)
    {
        char temp[100];
        wsprintf(temp, "Color selected: %#8.8X", dlg.GetColor());
        AfxMessageBox(temp);
    }
}
```

You can also customize the color selection dialog. To do so, derive your own class from CColorDialog and supply a custom dialog template. The Windows color selection dialog template can be found in the file color.dlg in your msdev\include directory. If you add any new controls, you may wish to add a message map to your new class to process notification messages from the new controls.

CFileDialog

The CFileDialog class provides support for the Windows Open and Save As dialogs.

To use a file dialog in an MFC application, you should first construct a CFileDialog object. The constructor takes several parameters; the first parameter is a mandatory Boolean value that determines whether the dialog is an Open or a Save As dialog. Once the dialog has been constructed, call its DoModal member function to display it.

Most common initialization settings for this dialog can be specified in the CFileDialog constructor. You may also set the values of the m_ofn structure; this is a Win32 OPENFILENAME structure. When the dialog terminates, the user's filename selection can be retrieved by calling the GetPathName member function. If the selection of multiple filenames was allowed, an iterator to the filename list can be obtained by calling GetStartPosition; individual filenames can be retrieved by repeatedly calling GetNextPathName with the iterator.

Listing 22.2 demonstrates the use of the Open dialog.

Listing 22.2. Use of CFileDialog in CDLG.

```
void CMainFrame::OnViewFiledialog()
{
    // TODO: Add your command handler code here
    CFileDialog dlg(TRUE);
    if (dlg.DoModal() == IDOK)
    {
        CString temp = "File selected: " + dlg.GetPathName();
        AfxMessageBox(temp);
    }
}
```

If you derive a class from CFileDialog, you can provide customized handling for conditions such as sharing violation, filename validation, and list box change notifications.

The file dialog can also be customized. To do so, derive a class from CFileDialog, add a custom dialog template, and add your message map to handle notifications from any new controls. The original file dialog template can be found in the file fileopen.dlg in your msdev\include directory.

CFindReplaceDialog

The CFindReplaceDialog class supports the use of the Windows Find and Replace dialog in MFC applications.

Use of the Find and Replace dialog is fundamentally different from the user of other common dialogs. While other common dialogs are modal, the Find and Replace dialog is modeless and must be constructed and used accordingly.

To use the Find and Replace dialog, first construct a CFindReplaceDialog object. This object cannot be constructed on the stack; it must be created using the new operator to ensure its persistence after the function in which it is created returns.

The Find and Replace dialog communicates with its owner window using special messages. To enable use of these messages, use the ::RegisterWindowMessage function. The value obtained upon registering Find and Replace dialog messages can be used in a window's message map using the ON_REGISTERED_MESSAGE macro.

The actual dialog is created by calling the Create member function. Make sure to specify the window that should receive messages from the dialog in the call to CFindReplaceDialog::Create.

Now you're ready to put all this into practice. Listing 22.3 shows how the use of the Find and Replace dialog is implemented in the CDLG application. All the code shown here is part of the MainFrm.cpp source file.

Listing 22.3. Use of CFindReplaceDialog in CDLG.

```cpp
// MainFrm.cpp : implementation of the CMainFrame class
//

...

static UINT WM_FINDREPLACE = RegisterWindowMessage(FINDMSGSTRING);

/////////////////////////////////////////////////////////////////
// CMainFrame

IMPLEMENT_DYNCREATE(CMainFrame, CFrameWnd)

BEGIN_MESSAGE_MAP(CMainFrame, CFrameWnd)
    //{{AFX_MSG_MAP(CMainFrame)
    ...
    //}}AFX_MSG_MAP
    ON_REGISTERED_MESSAGE(WM_FINDREPLACE, OnFindReplace)
END_MESSAGE_MAP()

...

void CMainFrame::OnViewFindreplacedialog()
{
    // TODO: Add your command handler code here
    CFindReplaceDialog *pDlg = new CFindReplaceDialog;
    pDlg->Create(TRUE, "Findme", NULL, FR_DOWN, this);
}

LRESULT CMainFrame::OnFindReplace(WPARAM wParam, LPARAM lParam)
{
    if (((LPFINDREPLACE)lParam)->Flags & FR_FINDNEXT)
    {
        CString temp = "Search string: ";
        temp = temp + ((LPFINDREPLACE)lParam)->lpstrFindWhat;
        AfxMessageBox(temp);
```

continues

Listing 22.3. continued

```
    }
    return 0;
}
```

The function `OnFindReplace` must also be declared in `MainFrm.h`. Towards the end of the class declaration, after the ClassWizard-generated message map, but before the `DECLARE_MESSAGE_MAP` macro call, insert the following line:

```
afx_msg LRESULT OnFindReplace(WPARAM wParam, LPARAM lParam);
```

Customization of the Find and Replace dialog involves deriving a class from `CFindReplaceDialog`, providing a custom dialog template, and adding your own message map to process notification messages from any extra controls you added. The original dialog template can be found in the file `findtext.dlg` in your `\msdev\include` directory.

CFontDialog

The `CFontDialog` class supports font selection in MFC applications through the Windows font selection common dialog.

To use the font selection dialog, create a `CFontDialog` object and call its `DoModal` member function. Before calling `DoModal`, you can initialize the dialog by setting the values of the `m_cf` member of `CFontDialog`. This member is a structure of type `CHOOSEFONT`.

When the dialog returns, you can use `CFontDialog` member functions such as `GetFaceName`, `GetSize`, or `GetColor` to obtain information about the font selected by the user. Alternatively, you can examine the values of the `m_cf` structure. Of specific interest is `m_cf.lpLogFont`; upon return of `CFontDialog::DoModal`, this pointer points to a `LOGFONT` structure, which can be used in subsequent calls to `::CreateFontIndirect` or `CFont::CreateFontIndirect` to create a logical font.

The use of `CFontDialog` is demonstrated in Listing 22.4.

Listing 22.4. Use of `CFontDialog` in CDLG.

```
void CMainFrame::OnViewFontdialog()
{
    // TODO: Add your command handler code here
    CFontDialog dlg;
    if (dlg.DoModal() == IDOK)
    {
        CString temp = "Font selected: " + dlg.GetFaceName();
        AfxMessageBox(temp);
    }
}
```

To use a customized font selection dialog, derive your own class from CFontDialog and create a custom dialog template. Add a message map to the new class to process notification messages from any new controls you might have created. As the basis of the dialog template, use the font selection dialog template font.dlg that can be found in your msdev\include directory.

CPageSetupDialog

The Page Setup dialog is used under Windows 95 and Windows NT 3.51 to set up the printed page. This dialog replaces the Print Setup dialog.

To use the Page Setup dialog, create an object of type CPageSetupDialog and call its DoModal member function. Information about the user's page setup preferences can be obtained through a variety of member functions, such as GetDeviceName, GetMargins, or GetPaperSize. Alternatively, you can examine the m_psd member variable (which is of type PAGESETUPDLG). It is also possible to modify members of this structure prior to calling DoModal in order to override default behavior.

Listing 22.5 shows an example of using the Page Setup dialog.

Listing 22.5. Use of CPageSetupDialog in CDLG.

```
void CMainFrame::OnViewPagesetupdialog()
{
    // TODO: Add your command handler code here
    CPageSetupDialog dlg;
    if (dlg.DoModal() == IDOK)
    {
        char temp[100];
        sprintf(temp, "Paper size: %g\" x %g\".",
                (double)dlg.m_psd.ptPaperSize.x / 1000.0,
                (double)dlg.m_psd.ptPaperSize.y / 1000.0);
        AfxMessageBox(temp);
    }
}
```

It is possible to create a customized page setup dialog. To do so, derive a class from CPageSetupDialog, supply your own dialog template, and supply a message map to process notifications from any controls you might have added. The original dialog template for the Page Setup dialog can be found in the file prnsetup.dlg in your msdev\include directory.

If you derive your own class from CPageSetupDialog, you can override the member functions OnDrawPage and PreDrawPage to draw a customized version of the image of the printed page in the dialog. You can utilize this capability to render an image of a printed page that closely resembles a page printed by your application.

CPrintDialog

Although AppWizard-generated application skeletons provide printing and page setup capabilities, sometimes it is not possible to rely on AppWizard-generated code for this purpose. In this case, applications must explicitly utilize the Print, Print Setup, and Page Setup dialogs.

The CPrintDialog class supports the use of the Print and Print Setup dialogs in MFC applications. However, applications written for Windows 95, or Windows NT 3.51 or later should refrain from using the Print Setup dialog; they should instead use the new Page Setup dialog.

To create a Print dialog, construct a CPrintDialog object and call its DoModal member function. The first parameter of the constructor, a Boolean value, determines whether the dialog is a Print or Print Setup dialog; you should set this parameter to TRUE if you wish to use the Print Setup dialog.

The dialog can be initialized by setting the values in the m_pd member structure, which is a structure of type PRINTDLG. The user's printing preferences can be obtained through member functions such as GetDeviceName or GetPrinterDC.

The CPrintDialog class can also be used to obtain a printer device context corresponding to the default printer without displaying a dialog. Use the CreatePrinterDC function for this purpose. Note that this function overwrites any previously stored device context handles in m_pd.hDC without actually deleting the device context object.

The device context object must be deleted not only when it has been created by a call to CreatePrinterDC, but also when CPrintDialog has been constructed for a Print dialog (with the first parameter of the constructor set to FALSE). Applications must also delete any DEVMODE and DEVNAMES structures supplied by CPrintDialog by calling the Windows function GlobalFree for the handles m_pd.hDevMode and m_pd.hDevNames.

Listing 22.6 shows how a Print dialog is created in the CDLG application.

Listing 22.6. Use of CPrintDialog in CDLG.

```
void CMainFrame::OnViewPrintdialog()
{
    // TODO: Add your command handler code here
    CPrintDialog dlg(FALSE);
    if (dlg.DoModal() == IDOK)
    {
        CString temp = "Device selected: " + dlg.GetDeviceName();
        AfxMessageBox(temp);
    }
    GlobalFree(dlg.m_pd.hDevMode);
    GlobalFree(dlg.m_pd.hDevNames);
    DeleteDC(dlg.GetPrinterDC());
}
```

It is possible to customize the Print and Print Setup dialogs. To do so, derive a class from CPrintDialog, create a custom dialog template, and add a message map to process notification messages from any new controls. Use the dialog templates in the file prnsetup.dlg in your msdev\include directory as the basis for any new dialog template you create.

Note that if you want different class behavior depending on whether the Print or Print Setup dialog is displayed, you may have to derive to separate classes from CPrintDialog.

COleDialog

OLE supports several additional common dialogs. These common dialogs are also supported by the MFC Library through a series of dialog classes. The class COleDialog serves as the base class for all OLE common dialog classes.

Figure 22.2 shows the set of OLE common dialogs.

FIGURE 22.2.

OLE Common dialogs in MFC.

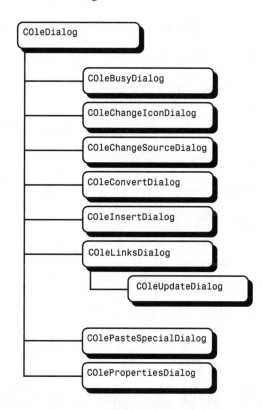

Common Controls

The MFC provides a wrapper class for each of the new Windows 95 style common controls. Many of these controls can now be constructed using the dialog editor within the Developer Studio. Assigning an object of the appropriate control class to a newly created control is often simply a matter of creating a member variable through ClassWizard.

In our tour of Windows 95 controls, we are going to use a simple application to demonstrate control usage where applicable. This application, which I named CTRL, is based on an AppWizard-generated application skeleton (dialog-based) with all the standard settings. This application demonstrates the use of sliders, progress bars, hot keys, spin buttons, list controls, tree controls, animation controls, and tab controls. The tab control is used to implement a tabbed dialog by hand; something you would not normally do when you can use property sheets, but it serves as a perfect demonstration of the tab control's capabilities.

Animation Control

The animation control is a control that can display simple AVI format video files. You can create an animation control in a dialog using the dialog editor in Developer Studio. You can then use the ClassWizard to assign a member variable of type CAnimateCtrl. It is typically not necessary to derive your own class from CAnimateCtrl.

To load a video clip into an animation control you should call the CAnimateCtrl::Load member function. This function accepts either a filename or a resource identifier as its parameter. For example, in the CTRL application, I added an AVI file as a custom resource in an external file, and assigned to it the text identifier "VIDEO". Afterwards, in the CTRL dialog's OnInitDialog member function, I made the following function call:

```
m_cAnimate.Open("VIDEO");
```

Unless the animation control has been created with the auto play style, you have to start playback by calling the CAnimateCtrl::Play member function. By setting the appropriate parameters of this function, you can specify the starting and ending frame, and the number of times the clip should be replayed. To play back the entire clip and repeat playback continuously, I used the following call to this function in CTRL:

```
m_cAnimate.Play(0, -1, -1);
```

Figure 22.3 illustrates the animation control in the CTRL application.

> **NOTE**
>
> The animation control is not designed as a general-purpose video clip playback facility. It serves the specific purpose of displaying simple animations, such as an animated icon during a lengthy operation.

FIGURE 22.3.

Animation control in the CTRL application.

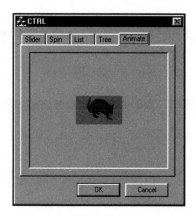

Header Control

The header control is used to create column headers for columnized lists. This control is most frequently encountered as part of list controls in report view. For example, the list control in Figure 22.5 contains a header control.

If you wish to create a header control on its own, you can use the CHeaderCtrl class for this purpose. To create the actual control, call this class's Create member function. To add items to the header control, call CHeaderCtrl::InsertItem.

If the header control is placed inside a view window, you would typically perform these initializations in the view object's OnInitialUpdate member function.

A header control cannot be added to a dialog using the dialog editor in Developer Studio. If you wish to use a header control in your dialog, add a member variable of type CHeaderCtrl to your dialog class manually, and initialize the header control in your dialog's OnInitDialog member function.

Hot Key Control

A hot key control is a special edit control; it accepts single keystrokes, displays a symbolic representation of the keystroke (for example, Alt+Shift+F1), and returns the virtual key code and shift codes corresponding to the key. It is typically used in conjunction with the WM_SETHOTKEY message to associate a hot key with a window.

The use of the hot key control is demonstrated in the CTRL application (Figure 22.4). When the user selects a hot key and clicks the Set button, a WM_SETHOTKEY message is sent to the dialog window; subsequently, any time the user types the selected key, the CTRL dialog is activated.

A hot key control can be added to a dialog using the Developer Studio dialog editor, and a corresponding object of type CHotKeyCtrl can be created as a member variable of the dialog class using ClassWizard.

FIGURE 22.4.

A hot key control and a spin button in CTRL.

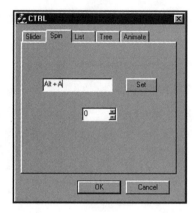

The hot key's current setting is usually retrieved when the user indicates that the selection is complete, for example, by clicking on a button. In the CTRL application, the Set button serves this purpose. The value of the hot key can be retrieved by calling the member function CHotKey::GetHotKey; the DWORD value returned by this function can be used in a subsequent call to SendMessage as the WPARAM parameter of a WM_SETHOTKEY message. Listing 22.7 illustrates this usage in the CTRL application.

Listing 22.7. Processing a hot key in CTRL.

```
void CCTRLDlg::OnButton()
{
    // TODO: Add your control notification handler code here
    SendMessage(WM_SETHOTKEY, m_cHotKey.GetHotKey());
}
```

The hot key control can also be used in conjunction with the Win32 function RegisterHotKey to set up thread-specific hot keys.

List Control

A list control presents a collection of items, each identified by an icon and a label. Items in a list control can be arranged in a variety of ways. In Icon View, items appear as large icons with text underneath and can be dragged anywhere in the control. In Small Icon View, items are displayed as small icons with text to the right and can be dragged to any position. In List View, items appear in columnar form as small icons with text to the right, and their position cannot be altered. In Report View, items are presented in multiple columns, with subitems occupying the columns right of the first columns.

The MFC supports list controls in two ways. The CListView class can be used to create a view window with a list control occupying the entire client area. For other uses of list controls, including use of list controls in dialogs, you can use the `CListCtrl` class. If you wish to add a list control to a dialog, you can do so using the Developer Studio dialog editor.

Construction of a list control is a multiple step process. It involves the creation of the list control, the setting up of its columns by calling the `InsertColumn` member function, and the insertion of list control items by calling `InsertItem`.

The icons associated with items must be supplied in the form of an *image list*. Image lists represent a collection of small graphic items of identical size. Support for image lists in MFC is provided in the form of the `CImageList` class.

Figure 22.5 shows the use of a list control in the CTRL application. The list control in the dialog template has been configured for Report View and single selection.

FIGURE 22.5.

A list control in CTRL.

The bitmap that is used in the list control consists of four images, 16 by 16 pixels each. This bitmap is shown in Figure 22.6.

FIGURE 22.6.

Bitmap of list control icons.

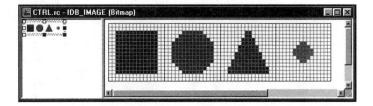

To manage the list control in CTRL, I used the ClassWizard to create a member variable of type `CListCtrl` in my dialog. The list control is then initialized in `OnInitDialog`, as show in Listing 22.8.

Listing 22.8. Setting up a list control in CTRL.

```
m_cImageList.Create(IDB_IMAGE, 16, 10, 0);
m_cList.InsertColumn(0, "Shape", LVCFMT_LEFT, 200);
m_cList.SetImageList(&m_cImageList, LVSIL_SMALL);
PSTR pszListItems[] = {"Square", "Rectangle", "Rounded Rectangle",
                        "Circle", "Ellipse", "Equilateral Triangle",
                        "Right Triangle", NULL};
int nListTypes[] = {0, 0, 0, 1, 1, 2, 2};
for (int i = 0; pszListItems[i] != NULL; i++)
m_cList.InsertItem(i, pszListItems[i], nListTypes[i]);
```

When processing the results of the user's selection in a list control, the state of an item can be obtained by calling the member function `CListCtrl::GetItemState`.

Progress Bar

A progress bar is used to provide graphical feedback to the user about progress during a lengthy operation. It is different from other controls inasmuch as its sole purpose is to provide information to the user; it does not accept input of any kind.

To use a progress bar in a dialog, insert a progress bar control using the Developer Studio and assign a member variable of type `CProgressCtrl` to it using ClassWizard. Initialization of the control consists of setting up the minimum and maximum value and, optionally, the control's current position. When using the control in a dialog, this can be done in the dialog class's `OnInitDialog` member function.

Figure 22.7 shows the use of a progress bar in conjunction with a slider control in CTRL.

FIGURE 22.7.

A progress bar and a slider control in CTRL.

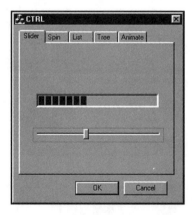

Listing 22.9 shows the initialization of the progress bar in CTRL's `CCTRLDlg::OnInitDialog`.

Listing 22.9. Initializing a progress bar in CTRL.

```
m_cProgress.SetRange(1, 100);
m_cProgress.SetPos(1);
```

The position of the progress bar can be set by calling the `SetPos` member function.

Rich-Text Edit Control

The rich-text edit control, or RTF control, vastly enhances the capabilities of the standard Windows edit control. RTF controls display and manage formatted text.

Rich-text edit controls present a complex programming interface, which is reflected in the numerous member functions of the classes supporting this type of control. In fact, the MFC Library offers a total of four classes in connection with this control.

Simple support for rich-text edit controls is provided via the `CRichEditCtrl` class. However, the MFC Library also supports applications with documents based on rich-text control capabilities. Such support is provided through the classes `CRichEditDoc`, `CRichEditView`, and `CRichEditCntrItem`.

Rich edit controls can be viewed as controls providing a superset of the capabilities of multiline edit controls.

Text in a rich edit control can be assigned character and paragraph formatting. Formatting of text within a rich edit control represented by a `CRichEditCntr` object can be accomplished by calling the `SetSelectionCharFormat`, `SetWordCharFormat`, and `SetParaFormat` member functions of the control class. The rich edit control does not provide a user interface for text formatting; the application must implement the user interface in the form of menus, toolbars, and other user-interface controls.

Rich edit controls can also support clipboard, OLE, printing, and file operations. Rich edit controls can load and save text in both text (ASCII) and rich text format.

Use of a rich edit control in an MFC application is demonstrated by the Windows 95 WordPad application. As a minor miracle, Microsoft decided to release the source code for this application in its entirety to developers. (We are talking about production quality source code here, not some small implementation like my three-liner examples!) This application provides an excellent reference for anyone wishing to utilize a rich edit control in an MFC application.

Slider Control

Slider controls, also called trackbars, are often compared to the sliding volume controls on stereo equipment. In this facility, they provide a replacement for the dubious practice of using scrollbars for this purpose (for lack of anything better).

Slider controls are supported in MFC through the `CSliderCtrl` class. If used in a dialog, a slider control can be inserted into the dialog template using the Developer Studio dialog editor. Next, create a corresponding member variable in your dialog class using ClassWizard. Through this member variable, the slider control can be initialized in your dialog class's `OnInitDialog` member function. Initialization includes setting up minimum and maximum values for the slider and optionally setting its initial position and changing its appearance.

The use of a slider control in the CTRL application was shown in Figure 22.7. This slider control in CTRL is used to control the position of the progress bar. Initialization of the slider control consists of a single function call:

```
m_cSlider.SetRange(1, 100);
```

Slider controls send WM_HSCROLL messages to their parent window whenever the position of the slider changes. Handlers for these messages can be installed in an MFC application using ClassWizard. In CTRL, a handler function has been installed that takes the position of the slider control and uses it to update the position of the progress bar. This handler function is shown in Listing 22.10.

Listing 22.10. Handling WM_HSCROLL messages from a slider control.

```
void CCTRLDlg::OnHScroll(UINT nSBCode, UINT nPos,
                         CScrollBar* pScrollBar)
{
    // TODO: Add your message handler code here and/or call default
    if ((CSliderCtrl *)pScrollBar == &m_cSlider)
    {
        m_cProgress.SetPos(m_cSlider.GetPos());
    }
    else
        CDialog::OnHScroll(nSBCode, nPos, pScrollBar);
}
```

Spin Button

A spin button, also known as an up-down control, consists of a pair of arrows that is typically used to increment or decrement a value. Spin buttons are most often used in conjunction with edit controls that contain a numerical value.

Spin buttons can be inserted into a dialog using the Developer Studio dialog editor. A spin button automatically adjusts the value of an edit control if such a control is set to be its "buddy" control. Alternatively, you can create a spin button with the auto-buddy style set; such a spin button automatically selects the control preceding it in the dialog's tab order as its buddy control.

Often nothing else is needed; by setting up a spin control with the auto-buddy style, you may eliminate the need to write a single line of additional code in your application. However, should you need to manipulate the spin button, you can create a member variable of type CSpinButtonCtrl in your dialog class.

The CTRL application demonstrates the use of a spin control (Figure 22.4). A member variable for the spin control has been created for the sole purpose of showing or hiding the control.

Status Window

Anyone who is used to the standard appearance of MFC applications must be familiar with status windows, or status bars. MFC applications display a status bar in the bottom of their main frame window.

The Windows 95 style status window control is supported in MFC by the CStatusBarCtrl class. Applications can utilize this class if there is a need to create status bars above and beyond what is offered by the MFC framework.

In order to create a status bar object, you must first create a CStatusBarCtrl object and next use its Create member function to create the actual control. Status bar controls are not supported by the Developer Studio dialog editor (nor are they typically part of dialogs).

The CStatusBar class is used to integrate status bars with MFC frame windows.

Tab Control

Tab controls are used to present a series of overlapping items using a more compact visual interface. The typical use of tab controls is in property sheets (tabbed dialogs).

Tab controls can be created in a dialog template by using the Developer Studio dialog editor. Next, a dialog class member variable of type CTabCtrl can be created using ClassWizard. Through such a member variable, the labels and appearance of the tab control can be set.

Tab controls send notification messages to their parent window. Handlers for these messages can be installed using ClassWizard.

In the CTRL application, a tab control is used to simulate the appearance of a tabbed dialog (property sheet). Refer to Figure 22.3 and subsequent illustrations to see this tab control in action.

The member variable assigned to the tab control, m_cTab, is initialized in the CCTRLDlg::OnInitDialog member function. This initialization is shown in Listing 22.11.

Listing 22.11. Tab control initialization in CTRL.

```
TC_ITEM tcItem;
PSTR pszTabItems[] = {"Slider", "Spin", "List", "Tree",
                      "Animate", NULL};
for (i = 0; pszTabItems[i] != NULL; i++)
```

continues

Listing 22.11. continued

```
{
    tcItem.mask = TCIF_TEXT;
    tcItem.pszText = pszTabItems[i];
    tcItem.cchTextMax = strlen(pszTabItems[i]);
    m_cTab.InsertItem(i, &tcItem);
}
```

A handler for messages of type TCN_SELCHANGE has been installed (using ClassWizard) to respond to the user's selection of a tab in the tab control. In this handler, shown in Listing 22.12, other controls in the dialog are enabled and disabled in accordance with the newly selected tab. The function also sets the focus to the appropriate control, and restarts video playback in CTRL's animation control if that control is made visible as a result of selecting the Animate tab.

Listing 22.12. Handling of TCN_SELCHANGE messages in CTRL.

```
void CCTRLDlg::OnSelchangeTab(NMHDR* pNMHDR, LRESULT* pResult)
{
    // TODO: Add your control notification handler code here
    m_cSlider.ShowWindow(m_cTab.GetCurSel() == 0 ? SW_SHOW :
                                                   SW_HIDE);
    m_cProgress.ShowWindow(m_cTab.GetCurSel() == 0 ? SW_SHOW :
                                                     SW_HIDE);
    m_cEdit.ShowWindow(m_cTab.GetCurSel() == 1 ? SW_SHOW :
                                                 SW_HIDE);
    m_cSpin.ShowWindow(m_cTab.GetCurSel() == 1 ? SW_SHOW :
                                                 SW_HIDE);
    m_cHotKey.ShowWindow(m_cTab.GetCurSel() == 1 ? SW_SHOW :
                                                   SW_HIDE);
    m_cButton.ShowWindow(m_cTab.GetCurSel() == 1 ? SW_SHOW :
                                                   SW_HIDE);
    m_cList.ShowWindow(m_cTab.GetCurSel() == 2 ? SW_SHOW :
                                                 SW_HIDE);
    m_cTree.ShowWindow(m_cTab.GetCurSel() == 3 ? SW_SHOW :
                                                 SW_HIDE);
    switch (m_cTab.GetCurSel())
    {
        case 0: m_cSlider.SetFocus(); break;
        case 1: m_cEdit.SetFocus(); break;
        case 2: m_cList.SetFocus(); break;
        case 3: m_cTree.SetFocus(); break;
        case 4: m_cAnimate.SetFocus(); break;
    }
    if (m_cTab.GetCurSel() == 4)
    {
        m_cAnimate.ShowWindow(SW_SHOW);
        m_cAnimate.Play(0, (UINT)-1, (UINT)-1);
    }
    else
    {
        m_cAnimate.Stop();
        m_cAnimate.ShowWindow(SW_HIDE);
    }
```

```
    *pResult = 0;
}
```

Toolbar

Toolbars are windows containing a set of buttons. If the user clicks on a button, the toolbar sends a command message to its parent window. Toolbars are used in MFC applications extensively.

Support for toolbar controls is provided in MFC through the CToolBarCtrl class. A toolbar control is created by first creating an object of type CToolBarCtrl, and then calling its Create member function to create the control. The control supports buttons containing bitmaps, text strings, or both; these can be added by calling the AddBitmap or AddString member functions of CToolBarCtrl. Toolbar buttons can be created by calling the AddButtons member function.

Toolbars work in conjunction with tooltips. If you create a toolbar with the TBSTYLE_TOOLTIPS style, the toolbar will send tooltip notification messages to its parent window. These notifications are requests for tooltip text, which is then used in tooltip controls that are created and managed by the toolbar control.

Toolbars support extensive customization through a system-defined dialog box that enables the user to add, delete, and rearrange toolbar buttons. During toolbar customization, the toolbar sends notification messages to its parent window.

The state of a toolbar can be saved to the Registry using the CToolBarCtrl::SaveState member function. The saved state of the toolbar can be retrieved using CToolBarCtrl::RestoreState.

MFC supports toolbars that are integrated with frame windows through the CToolBar class.

Tooltip Control

Tooltips are small popup windows that display a single line of text. Tooltips are typically used as a visual aid in identifying the function of a control, or tool, in an application.

Tooltips are automatically created and managed by toolbar controls. Tooltip support is also provided in the CWnd class through the functions EnableToolTips, CancelToolTips, FilterToolTipMessage, and OnToolHitTest.

To create a tooltip, first create an object of type CToolTipCtrl, then call its Create member function to create the control. Use the AddTool member function to register a tool with the tooltip. Registering consists of identifying a window and a rectangular area within it; if the mouse cursor rests within that area for more than one second, the tooltip will appear. You can register several tools with the same tooltip control.

To activate a tooltip, call the member function CToolTipCtrl::Activate.

Tooltips send notification messages to their parent windows. In particular, if a tooltip needs information on the text that is to be displayed, it will send `TTN_NEEDTEXT` notifications to its parent window.

Tree Control

A tree control displays a list of items in a hierarchical form. Three controls are supported in MFC by the `CTreeView` and `CTreeCtrl` classes. `CTreeView` is used by applications that use views that consist entirely of a single tree control.

Tree controls can be added to a dialog template using the Developer Studio dialog editor. For every tree control, a corresponding object of type `CTreeCtrl` should be created using ClassWizard. It is through this object that the tree control is initialized.

The items in a tree control are set using the `CTreeCtrl::InsertItem` member function. Tree controls, like their list control cousins, use image lists for displaying icons associated with items. To create an image list, use the class `CImageList`.

Tree controls send notification messages to their parent window. For example, when an item in a tree control is selected, the tree control sends a `TVN_SELCHANGED` notification.

Figure 22.8 demonstrates the use of a tree control in the CTRL application. This control was added to the application's dialog using the Developer Studio dialog editor. Three style settings (Has buttons, Has lines, Lines at root) were set to enable the display of lines and expand buttons within the control.

FIGURE 22.8.

A tree control in CTRL.

The control is initialized in the `CCTRLDlg::OnInitDialog` member function (Listing 22.13).

Listing 22.13. Initialization of a tree control in CTRL.

```
PSTR pszTreeRoots[] = {"Rectangles", "Ellipses", "Triangles"};
m_cTree.SetImageList(&m_cImageList, TVSIL_NORMAL);
```

```
HTREEITEM rootitems[3];
for (i = 0; i < 3; i++)
    rootitems[i] = m_cTree.InsertItem(TVIF_PARAM | TVIF_TEXT |
                                      TVIF_IMAGE |
                                      TVIF_SELECTEDIMAGE,
                                      pszTreeRoots[i], i, i, 0, 0,
                                      -1, TVI_ROOT, TVI_LAST);
for(i = 0; pszListItems[i] != NULL; i++)
    m_cTree.InsertItem(TVIF_PARAM | TVIF_TEXT | TVIF_IMAGE |
                       TVIF_SELECTEDIMAGE, pszListItems[i], 3, 3,
                       0, 0, i, rootitems[nListTypes[i]], TVI_LAST);
```

The CTRL application handles notification messages from this tree control. When an item in the tree control is selected, the handler for TVN_SELCHANGED messages sets the selection state of the corresponding item in the application's list control. This handler function is shown in Listing 22.14.

Listing 22.14. Handling of TVN_SELCHANGED messages in CTRL.

```
void CCTRLDlg::OnSelchangedTree(NMHDR* pNMHDR, LRESULT* pResult)
{
    NM_TREEVIEW* pNMTreeView = (NM_TREEVIEW*)pNMHDR;
    // TODO: Add your control notification handler code here
    int i = m_cTree.GetItemData(m_cTree.GetSelectedItem());
    if (i != -1)
        m_cList.SetItemState(i, LVIS_SELECTED, LVIS_SELECTED);
    *pResult = 0;
}
```

Summary

The Microsoft Foundation Classes Library provides extensive support for the common dialogs and common controls that are available in Windows.

Common dialog support is available through a series of classes that are derived from CCommonDialog. These classes encapsulate the functionality of the Windows common dialogs, and provide easy ways to set up, display, and process such dialogs. Specifically, the following dialogs are supported:

- Color selection dialogs are supported through the CColorDialog class.
- File Open and File Save As dialogs are supported through the CFileDialog class.
- Find and Replace dialogs are supported through CFindReplaceDialog.
- Font selection dialogs are supported through the class CFontDialog.
- Page setup dialogs are supported through CPageSetupDialog.
- Print and Print Setup dialogs are supported through CPrintDialog.

In addition, a variety of classes derived from `COleDialog` support OLE-related common dialogs.

Common controls are a new feature of Windows, introduced with Windows 95. Common controls drastically enrich the set of controls available for application programmers for use in dialogs and views.

The type of common controls and the form of support MFC and the Developer Studio dialog editor offer for these controls are summarized in Table 22.1.

Table 22.1. MFC and Developer Studio support for common controls.

Control Type	*Control Class*	*View Class*	*In Dialog Editor?*
Animation control	`CAnimateCtrl`		Yes
Header control	`CHeaderCtrl`		No
Hot key control	`CHotKeyCtrl`		Yes
List control	`CListCtrl`	`CListView`	Yes
Progress Bar	`CProgressCtrl`		Yes
Rich-text edit control	`CRichEditCtrl`	`CRichEditView`	No
Slider control	`CSliderCtrl`		Yes
Spin button	`CSpinButtonCtrl`		Yes
Status window	`CStatusBarCtrl`		No
Tab control	`CTabCtrl`		Yes
Toolbar	`CToolBarCtrl`		No
Tooltip	`CToolTipCtrl`		No
Tree control	`CTreeCtrl`	`CTreeView`	Yes

Additional rich-text edit control support is provided in the form of the `CRichEditDoc` and `CRichEditCntrItem` classes. Through these classes and `CRichEditView`, applications can be constructed that manage rich-text documents.

More integrated support for toolbars and status windows is provided in the form of the `CToolBar` and `CStatusBar` classes. These classes integrate toolbars and status bars with MFC frame windows.

Using OLE Controls

23

Microsoft's Visual Basic programming environment introduced a new style of software development. Visual Basic Custom Controls, or VBXs, provided the basis for component-based programming.

While VBXs were not exactly revolutionary (they represented just another form of a dynamic link library), they fulfilled the promise of reusability to a degree not previously thought possible. Novice programmers who may not even have heard the acronym DLL manipulated VBXs with ease and created near-professional quality Visual Basic applications in days.

Although VBX technology was developed as a technology specific to Visual Basic, its unprecedented success prompted Microsoft to add VBX support to the Visual C++ development system. Interfacing C programs and a VBX library is not as hard as it sounds; after all, the VBX is also written in the C language. The difficulty lies in the fact that the data types used were tailored towards the Basic language, not C.

Unfortunately, the good days of VBX support in C programs were too good to last. Shortly after VBX support was introduced, ongoing development of the 16-bit version of Visual C++ ceased. The 32-bit version, which represented the development environment of choice for Windows NT and now Windows 95, was fundamentally incompatible with 16-bit VBX libraries.

Microsoft decided to address this issue and design a new custom control mechanism that also promised to resolve other VBX limitations. No longer a technology specific to a single programming environment, the new OLE Custom Controls use OLE technology for communicating with a *control container* application and promise the same ease of use as VBX technology.

In the rest of this chapter, we examine OLE controls from the perspective of the *control user*; that is, the application programmer who takes an OLE control as some kind of a black box and incorporates it as a component into his or her application. This perspective markedly differs from that of the *control developer*, who creates the OLE control in the form of an OCX library; and that of the *end user*, who is the recipient of the application created by the control user.

For the purposes of demonstration, I developed a very simple OLE control with the uninspired name OCTL. OCTL is a button that can have a rectangular, elliptical, or triangular shape; when the button is clicked with the mouse, it changes color from green to red or back to indicate its selected or deselected state (Figure 23.1).

FIGURE 23.1.
*The OCTL control
in action.*

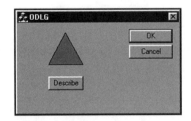

What exactly is an OLE custom control? It can be viewed as an object that presents itself to the application programmer in the form of a series of properties, methods, and events. *Control properties* can be set or retrieved and are represented by values of various types, such as integers or character strings. *Control methods* are procedures that you can call in order for the control to perform a function. *Events* are messages that the control sends to its parent window indicating an occurrence of some kind, such as a mouse click.

Although many controls present a visual interface, a control does not necessarily have to be visible in order to be functional. It is possible to create controls that offer properties, respond to methods, and send event notifications without ever presenting a visual interface to the end user.

Adding OLE Custom Controls to Your Application

Follow these steps to add custom control support to an application:

1. Ensure that your application supports custom controls by calling `AfxEnableControlContainer`.
2. Add the custom control to a dialog template.
3. Set the control's initial properties.
4. Add member variables to represent the control or its properties as appropriate.
5. Add message handlers to handle messages from the control as appropriate.

To demonstrate custom control usage, I built an application named ODLG, which uses a dialog with my OCTL control in it. ODLG is an AppWizard-generated, dialog-based application; the only nondefault option when creating this application with AppWizard was OLE custom control support.

Although I describe OLE custom control use in the context of dialogs, custom control use is no more restricted to dialog boxes than is the use of standard Windows controls.

Creating a Control Container

In order to be capable of using OLE custom controls, an application must be a control container. This is accomplished by calling `AfxEnableControlContainer` during application initialization. Applications created by AppWizard and marked to support OLE custom controls have this call placed into the `InitInstance` member function of their application objects. If you created an application with AppWizard and did not include OLE custom control support, you can add this call manually any time.

422

Adding a Custom Control to a Dialog Template

Custom controls can be added to a dialog template just like other controls, using the dialog editor in Developer Studio. However, custom controls, at least initially, may not appear in the palette of controls. Therefore, it is necessary to use the right mouse button to invoke a popup menu with the option of inserting a custom control (Figure 23.2).

FIGURE 23.2.

*Inserting an OLE
custom control.*

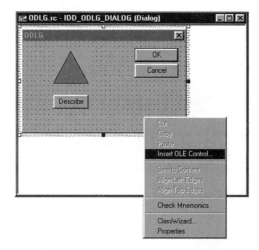

When you select the Insert OLE Control option, the Developer Studio responds with a dialog listing all OLE controls that are installed on your system (Figure 23.3). Select a control and click on the OK button to have it placed in your dialog at a default location in the upper-left corner.

FIGURE 23.3.

*Installed OLE
controls.*

Once the control has been placed in the dialog, you can move it around and resize it just as you would move and resize any other control.

In the ODLG application, I added a button in addition to the OCTL control. This button will be used by the end user to retrieve and display the control's Shape property. This button is identified as IDC_BUTTON; the OCTL control itself is identified as IDC_OCTLCTRL.

Setting Control Properties

Although it may not be obvious at first sight, as soon as you insert a control in your dialog template, the code comprising the control becomes active. The Developer Studio actually loads the library code in the OCX file and activates the control in *design mode*. The behavior of many controls varies according to whether the control has been activated in this mode or in *user mode* when an application using the control is running.

The significance of this is that most OLE custom controls offer a property page interface where the control's properties can be set. Many control properties are *persistent*; settings configured at design time define the run-time appearance and behavior of the control.

The OCTL control has exactly two properties. IsSelected, a Boolean property, tells whether the control is in a selected or deselected state. This property is read-only (and so obviously cannot be set at design time). The other property, Shape, determines whether the control acquires an elliptical, rectangular, or triangular shape, and is meant to be used as a design-time property. (In fact, attempting to set this property at runtime results in an error.)

A control's properties can be set by right-clicking on the control in the dialog editor to invoke the control's property sheet interface (Figure 23.4).

FIGURE 23.4.

OLE custom control properties.

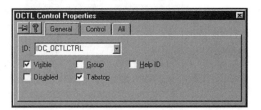

Of the three or more property pages that form part of this property sheet, the first and the last are supplied by Developer Studio; the ones in the middle are supplied by the control itself. For example, the OCTL control supplies a single property page where the value of its Shape property can be set (Figure 23.5).

FIGURE 23.5.

OCTL property page: Control.

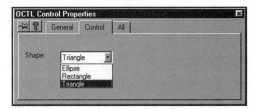

The last property page (Figure 23.6) in this property sheet offers an interface to all control properties. This includes read-only properties as well, whose values cannot be modified.

FIGURE 23.6.

All OCTL control properties.

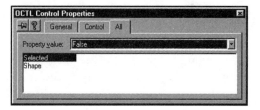

Adding Member Variables

The procedure for adding member variables for an OLE custom control is like the one for adding member variables for other types of controls. Select the control in the dialog editor and invoke the ClassWizard, select the Member Variables tab in ClassWizard, and double-click on the line containing the control's identifier to add a member variable.

However, at this point, something strange takes place. The ClassWizard responds with the dialog shown in Figure 23.7. In order to create variables corresponding to the OLE control, it is necessary to first create a CWnd-derived class representing the control. This is done automatically by ClassWizard when you first attempt to add a member variable for the control.

FIGURE 23.7.

Creation of class for OLE custom control.

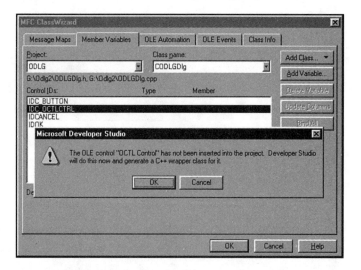

If you click OK, Developer Studio responds with yet another dialog (Figure 23.8) where you can modify any default class and file names that the ClassWizard generated for you.

After the new classes, you can add a member variable (m_cOCTL) for the OLE custom control. This procedure occurs only once; subsequently, you can add member variables for the control normally.

FIGURE 23.8.

*Confirm OLE
custom control
classes.*

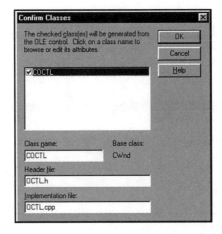

Now we take a brief look at the code generated by ClassWizard. When I added a member variable for the OCTL control to my ODLG application, ClassWizard created the COCTL class; the header file was octl.h, the implementation file octl.cpp.

The declaration of class COCTL, shown in Listing 23.1, includes all member functions necessary to create the control, adjust its properties, and invoke its methods.

Listing 23.1. COCTL class declaration.

```
class COCTL : public CWnd
{
protected:
    DECLARE_DYNCREATE(COCTL)
public:
    CLSID const& GetClsid()
    {
        static CLSID const clsid
            = { 0x677600e7, 0xf6c5, 0x11ce,
                { 0x87, 0xc3, 0x0, 0x40, 0x33, 0x21, 0xbf, 0xac } };
        return clsid;
    }
    virtual BOOL Create(LPCTSTR lpszClassName,
        LPCTSTR lpszWindowName, DWORD dwStyle,
        const RECT& rect,
        CWnd* pParentWnd, UINT nID,
        CCreateContext* pContext = NULL)
    { return CreateControl(GetClsid(), lpszWindowName, dwStyle,
        rect, pParentWnd, nID); }

    BOOL Create(LPCTSTR lpszWindowName, DWORD dwStyle,
        const RECT& rect, CWnd* pParentWnd, UINT nID,
        CFile* pPersist = NULL, BOOL bStorage = FALSE,
        BSTR bstrLicKey = NULL)
```

continues

Listing 23.1. continued

```
    { return CreateControl(GetClsid(), lpszWindowName, dwStyle,
        rect, pParentWnd, nID,
        pPersist, bStorage, bstrLicKey); }

// Attributes
public:
    short GetShape();
    void SetShape(short);
    BOOL GetSelected();
    void SetSelected(BOOL);

// Operations
public:
    void AboutBox();
};
```

There is nothing surprising in the implementation file (Listing 23.2) either. However, consider yourself strongly advised to heed the warnings at the top of these files. These pieces of code are machine-generated for the sole purpose of providing an interface to a control *written by somebody else.* It is not your job as the application programmer to attempt to modify the control's behavior (nor are you able to do that without having access to the control's source code).

Listing 23.2. COCTL class implementation.

```
/////////////////////////////////////////////////////////////////
// COCTL

IMPLEMENT_DYNCREATE(COCTL, CWnd)

/////////////////////////////////////////////////////////////////
// COCTL properties

short COCTL::GetShape()
{
    short result;
    GetProperty(0x1, VT_I2, (void*)&result);
    return result;
}

void COCTL::SetShape(short propVal)
{
    SetProperty(0x1, VT_I2, propVal);
}

BOOL COCTL::GetSelected()
{
    BOOL result;
    GetProperty(0x2, VT_BOOL, (void*)&result);
    return result;
}
```

```
void COCTL::SetSelected(BOOL propVal)
{
    SetProperty(0x2, VT_BOOL, propVal);
}


////////////////////////////////////////////////////////////////
// COCTL operations

void COCTL::AboutBox()
{
    InvokeHelper(0xfffffdd8, DISPATCH_METHOD, VT_EMPTY, NULL, NULL);
}
```

Back to my ODLG sample application. I added a single member variable of type COCTL, which I named m_cOCTL. To utilize this variable, I added a message handler function for the Describe button. In this function, shown in Listing 23.3, I retrieve the control's Shape property by calling the COCTL::GetShape member function and display the result in a message box.

Listing 23.3. Accessing a control's properties.

```
void CODLGDlg::OnButton()
{
    // TODO: Add your control notification handler code here
    CString shape;
    switch (m_cOCTL.GetShape())
    {
        case 0: shape = "Ellipse"; break;
        case 1: shape = "Rectangle"; break;
        case 2: shape = "Triangle"; break;
    }
    AfxMessageBox("The control's shape is " + shape + ".");
}
```

Handling Messages

Handling messages from an OLE custom control is perhaps even simpler than handling properties. You can add handlers for any event the control supports via ClassWizard. For example, Figure 23.9 demonstrates adding a message handler for the single event that the OCTL control can generate, a Select event.

Depending on the type of the event, the event handler may receive parameters. In the case of OCTL, a handler for the Select event received a Boolean parameter specifying whether the control has just been selected or deselected. The sample handler function in ODLG simply displays a message box to this effect, as shown in Listing 23.4.

FIGURE 23.9.

Adding a message map entry for an OLE custom control event.

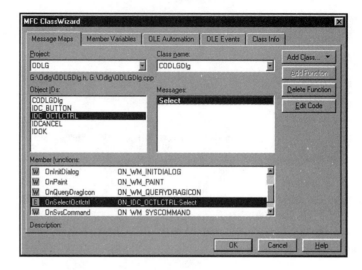

Listing 23.4. Handling an OLE custom control event.

```
void CODLGDlg::OnSelectOctlctrl(BOOL IsSelected)
{
    // TODO: Add your control notification handler code here
    if (IsSelected)
        AfxMessageBox("The control has been selected.");
    else
        AfxMessageBox("The control has been deselected.");
}
```

That's all there is to it! All that remains is recompiling and running your application.

As you can see, the procedure for inserting an OLE custom control is no more complex than the procedure for inserting other types of controls. Moreover, in order to efficiently use an OLE custom control, you need not know the details of its implementation (or even how OLE custom controls are implemented in the first place). All you need is documentation on the control's purpose and behavior, its properties, methods, and events.

I believe Microsoft really delivered on its promise of providing a 32-bit custom control technology that is superior to VBX technology. All we need now is a variety of wonderful third-party custom controls.

Custom Controls Supplied with Visual C++

Microsoft supplies several OLE custom controls with Visual C++. These controls are similar in function and appearance to VBX controls found in earlier versions (for example, Version 3.0) of Visual Basic.

Among these controls is the Animated Button Control; this flexible control can be used to implement multistate or animated buttons.

The Grid Control presents a two-dimensional array of cells organized into rows and columns in a spreadsheet-like interface.

The Key State Control can be used to display the state of the Num Lock, Caps Lock, or Scroll Lock keys or the Insert/Overwrite status.

The Microsoft Comm control is an example of a control that is not visible at runtime. This control provides a communication port interface.

The Microsoft Masked Edit Control provides an edit control with customized, formatted editing capabilities.

The Microsoft Multimedia Control provides a programmatic multimedia interface.

The PicClip control is yet another control that is not visible at runtime; this control provides an efficient mechanism for organizing a large number of small icons or bitmaps.

Some of these controls (the Animated Button Control, the Grid Control, the Key State Control, and the Microsoft Multimedia Control) are demonstrated in a dialog box shown in Figure 23.10.

FIGURE 23.10.

Some custom controls supplied with Visual C++.

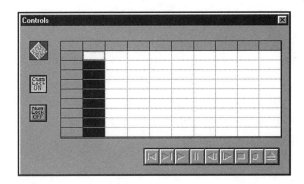

Summary

OLE custom controls represent a technology that is a 32-bit successor to the Visual Basic custom control (VBX) technology.

In order for an application to act as an OLE control container, it is necessary to call the `AfxEnableControlContainer` function when the application is being initialized.

OLE custom controls can be used in applications just like ordinary controls. They can be inserted into a dialog template using the Developer Studio dialog editor. The control can be configured through a set of property page interfaces that appear in the control's property sheet in the dialog editor.

The control's properties can be accessed from within the application by using the ClassWizard to add member variables that correspond to the control. When adding a member variable for a certain type of control for the first time, ClassWizard creates a wrapper class for the control and adds it to the project.

The ClassWizard can also be used to add handler functions for control events.

Microsoft supplies several custom controls as part of the Visual C++ development environment.

Device Context and
GDI Objects

24

Drawing and graphics have special significance in almost every Windows application; MFC applications are no exception to this rule.

The Windows Graphics Device Interface (GDI) capabilities are encapsulated in two families of MFC classes. Device context classes provide an encapsulation of GDI device contexts and most drawing functions; GDI object classes encapsulate GDI objects such as pens, brushes, bitmaps, or fonts.

As in non-MFC Windows applications, drawing to an output device consists of obtaining the appropriate device context, setting up GDI drawing objects, performing drawing operations, and cleaning up. The MFC framework greatly simplifies these steps by assuming many of the more mundane responsibilities that used to befall the application developer. For example, you can construct a pen object by passing the appropriate parameters to the Cpen constructor function:

```
Cpen myPen(PS_SOLID, 0, RGB(255, 0, 0));
```

and never worry about it afterwards; the GDI pen object is destroyed automatically by the Cpen destructor when the Cpen object goes out of scope.

As is the case with windows and CWnd objects, there is a distinction between the MFC (CDC- or CGdiObject-derived) object and the actual device context or GDI object in Windows. Constructing the MFC object does not automatically imply construction of an underlying Windows object. On the contrary, it is a legitimate practice to construct a blank MFC object first and later associate it with the Windows object as the need arises.

In this chapter, we first focus our attention on device contexts, which serve as the "canvas" onto which drawing takes place. Actual drawing operations (functions such as Rectangle, Ellipse, or DrawText) are also encapsulated in the CDC class and are discussed here. In the second part of this chapter, we shift our focus to classes that encapsulate GDI objects, which represent drawing tools.

Device Contexts

Although constructing a device context using MFC is easy, often trivial, there are many situations where it is not even necessary. Typical drawing functions (such as the OnDraw member function in a view class) are called by the MFC framework with a pointer to a device context object representing a device context that is already created and configured for use.

MFC classes that represent device contexts are all derived from the CDC base class. Figure 24.1 illustrates the hierarchy of device context classes.

Although there are several classes derived from CDC, the CDC class itself is frequently used as a wrapper class for device contexts. The other CDC-derived classes differ from CDC primarily in their constructor function and offer no extra functionality. If you need to construct an MFC object that is attached to an existing device context handle, you should always use the base CDC class instead of any of the derived classes.

FIGURE 24.1.

Hierarchy of device context classes.

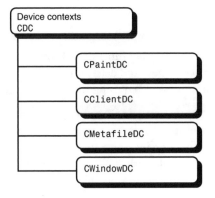

The Basic CDC Class

The CDC class encapsulates the functionality of the Windows device context. And there is a lot of functionality to encapsulate! The CDC class not only maps functions that are directly related to configuring and managing a device context, it also maps all GDI drawing functions. Last time I counted, there were approximately 180 documented member functions.

With such a large and complex interface, where should we begin? With the simplest. First, we review how a CDC object is created and attached to a GDI device context.

Creating a Device Context

When a CDC object is created through its constructor function, a GDI device context is not automatically created. Instead, it is necessary to create a device context through the CreateDC function or attach the CDC object to a device context that has been created earlier.

The CreateDC member function takes several parameters that specify the device, the device driver software, and the port the device is attached to. These parameters correspond to the parameters of the GDI ::CreateDC function.

A CDC object has not one, but two member variables that are GDI device context handles. These are m_hDC and m_hAttribDC. Usually, these two handles point to the same device context object. The m_hDC handle, or output device context handle, is used for all output operations; the m_hAttribDC handle, or attribute device context handle, is used, in turn, for operations that request information from the device context.

To attach a CDC object to a device context handle that has been created earlier, use the Attach member function. To detach a CDC object from a device handle, use the Detach member function. Note that neither Detach, nor the member functions ReleaseOutputDC and ReleaseAttributeDC (which reset the values of m_hDC and m_hAttribDC to NULL) actually delete the GDI device context object. In this case, if the device context object was created using the GDI function ::CreateDC, it may be necessary to manually call ::DeleteDC. Calling ::DeleteDC is not required if you do not detach the CDC object from the device context; the CDC destructor function makes this call automatically.

The CDC class also has a member function DeleteDC, which can be used to detach the CDC object from the GDI device context and delete the device context. This function should only be used if the device context was created using the CreateDC member function.

Another function that creates a device context object is CreateCompatibleDC. This function creates a memory device context that is compatible with a given device context. For example, applications may use this function in conjunction with the CClientDC class to create a memory device context that is compatible with the device context representing the current window's client area:

```
CClientDC clientDC(&myWnd);
CDC memDC;
memDC.CreateCompatibleDC(&clientDC);
```

Subsequently, operations such as CDC::BitBlt can be used to transfer blocks of pixels between the two device contexts. Similar techniques are often used in programs that perform smooth animation; by constructing the next animation frame in a memory device context and transferring only completed frames to the display, you can create animations that are free of jerkiness.

A static CDC member function is CDC::FromHandle. This function enables you to retrieve the address of a CDC object (if such an object exists) that corresponds to a device context handle. If no such CDC object exists, a temporary CDC object is created. This function may be called as follows:

```
CDC *pDC = CDC::FromHandle(hDC);
```

Be warned that the pointer returned by this function is not be stored beyond immediate use. As it points to a CDC object that may be under the control of another part of your application, you do not usually know when the CDC object may be destroyed, rendering the pointer returned by CDC::FromHandle invalid. Temporary CDC objects returned by CDC::FromHandle are also deleted by the CDC::DeleteTempMap function, which is typically called from by the idle-time handler in your application's CWinApp object.

One more function worth mentioning is the GetSafeHdc function. This function returns the m_hDC member of the CDC object. This is a "safe" function inasmuch as it can also be used with NULL pointers; that is, the following code would be valid and not cause an exception:

```
CDC *pDC = NULL;
HDC hDC = pDC->GetSafeHdc();
```

Paint-Time Device Contexts

The CPaintDC class encapsulates the calls to the BeginPaint and EndPaint in its constructor and destructor. This class is designed to be used when responding to WM_PAINT messages.

Note that most applications do not need to create a CPaintDC object directly. The default implementation of the Cview::OnPaint member function creates such a device context and passes it to the class's OnDraw member function (which is usually overridden to provide application-specific drawing of a view).

Client-Area Device Contexts

The CClientDC class is used to create a device context object corresponding to the client area of a given window. The constructor and destructor of CClientDC encapsulate calls to the GetDC and ReleaseDC functions. CClientDC objects are most often used when drawing into a device context is required outside an OnDraw function.

A particular use of CClientDC objects concerns mapping modes. Sometimes, it is necessary for an application to translate logical coordinates into physical coordinates or vice versa even when no actual drawing is performed. In these situations, it is a frequently used practice to create a CClientDC object for the sole purpose of being able to use one of its coordinate transformation functions. For example:

```
CClientDC dc(myView);
myView->OnPrepareDC(&dc);
dc.LPtoDP(&point);
```

Window Device Contexts

Similar to client-area device contexts are window device contexts, represented by the CWindowDC class. The constructor and destructor of CWindowDC encapsulate calls to GetWindowDC and ReleaseDC, respectively.

Metafile Device Contexts

The CMetaFileDC class represents metafile device contexts. Metafile device contexts provide a means to draw into Windows metafiles or the new enhanced metafiles.

Metafile device contexts differ from other device contexts in a variety of ways. Most importantly, the m_hAttribDC member of a metafile device context, which would normally be set to refer to the same device as m_hDC, is set to NULL instead. Thus, calls that would retrieve information about the device context would typically fail for an object of type CMetaFileDC.

It is possible to assign a value to the m_hAttribDC member. For example, you can assign it the value of another device context that you created, which represents the screen, the printer, or another output device.

Constructing a metafile device context is a two-step process. First, the CMetaFileDC object is created; next, its Create or CreateEnhanced member functions are called.

Depending on whether you supply a filename to the Create or CreateEnhanced member functions or not, the metafile will be either file-based or memory-based. A memory-based metafile exists only temporarily.

When you are finished with drawing into the metafile, you close the metafile object by calling CMetaFileDC::Close or CMetaFileDC::CloseEnhanced (depending on the type of the metafile). These functions return a handle to a metafile object. This handle can be used, for example, in a call to CDC::PlayMetafile to play back the metafile into another device context. It can also be passed to the Windows function ::CopyMetaFile (or ::CopyEnhMetaFile) to copy the metafile to a disk file.

As soon as you call its Close or CloseEnhanced member function, you can delete the CMetaFileDC object. When you are done with using the metafile handle obtained through calling Close or CloseEnhanced, you should delete the Windows metafile object by calling DeleteMetaFile or DeleteEnhMetaFile.

CDC Attributes

A device context object has many attributes that can be set or retrieved through CDC member functions. Of these, we review attributes that relate to mapping modes and coordinate transformations in the next section. This section focuses on other attributes.

The background color, used to fill the gaps in styled lines, hatched brushes, and in character cells, is set by the SetBkColor member function. The current background color can be retrieved by calling GetBkColor. The background mode, which determines whether the background is transparent or opaque, is set by calling SetBkMode; GetBkMode retrieves the current background mode.

The SetROP2 member function can be used to set the drawing mode. The drawing mode determines how bits in the drawing tool and bits on the device surface are combined. The default drawing mode is R2_COPYPEN; in this mode, pixels from the drawing tool are copied over pixels in the device bitmap. This is what you would expect as normal behavior; as you draw with a specific pen or brush, the pen or brush will simply overwrite what may already be on the device context surface.

There are several other commonly used drawing modes that can be set with SetROP2. These include, for example, R2_BLACK (the target pixels turn always black), R2_NOTCOPYPEN (the target pixel acquires a color that is the inverse of the drawing tool's color), or R2_XORPEN (the target pixel's color is formed by performing an exclusive OR operation between the target pixel and the pixel in the drawing tool).

Drawing modes are not restricted to these preset values; the drawing mode setting can specify an arbitrary binary operation between pixels of the device surface and pixels of the drawing tool.

The current drawing mode setting can be acquired by calling GetROP2. Note that drawing mode settings are specific to raster devices and have no effect on vector devices, like plotters.

The SetPolyFillMode function determines the polygon filling mode. The difference between the ALTERNATE and WINDING filling modes is illustrated in Figure 24.2. The current filling mode can be retrieved by calling GetPolyFillMode.

FIGURE 24.2.

Filling modes.

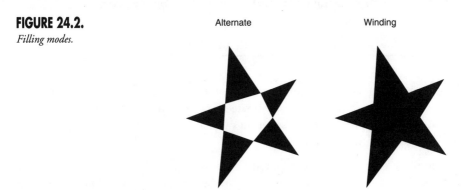

Alternate

Winding

Coordinate Mapping and Views

The coordinates for most graphical operations are provided in the form of logical coordinates. Logical coordinates are translated into device coordinates through what is called coordinate mapping.

Mapping defines a linear relationship between the logical and the physical coordinate space. Mapping matches the origin of the logical coordinate space to the origin of the physical coordinate space, and also matches logical and physical coordinate units. Mapping in the horizontal and vertical directions may be independent of each other.

Windows defines a set of mapping modes. These mapping modes can be set using the SetMapMode member function.

On a raster device such as the screen or printer, device coordinates represent pixel coordinates. The upper-left corner is assigned the coordinates [0,0]; the horizontal coordinate increases from left to right, the vertical coordinate increases from top to bottom.

Of the many predefined mapping modes, MM_TEXT matches logical coordinates to physical coordinates. Other predefined mapping modes reverse the direction of the horizontal coordinate, so it grows from bottom to top. These mapping modes are listed in Table 24.1.

Table 24.1. Mapping modes.

Mapping mode	Description
MM_LOENGLISH	100 logical units equal one inch on the device
MM_HIENGLISH	1,000 logical units equal one inch on the device
MM_LOMETRIC	100 logical units equal one centimeter on the device
MM_HIMETRIC	1,000 logical units equal one centimeter on the device
MM_TWIPS	One logical unit is one twentieth of a point (1/1440")

In all of these mapping modes, applications can use the SetWindowOrg and SetViewportOrg functions to set the origin of the logical coordinate space (window) and physical coordinate space (viewport). The significance of these settings is that the two origins are mapped onto each other when coordinates are transformed.

In addition to MM_TEXT and the mapping modes in Table 24.1, Windows also defines the MM_ISOTROPIC and MM_ANISOTROPIC mapping modes. In these mapping modes, applications can not only specify the origin, but also the extent of the window and viewport coordinate space. By specifying the extent, applications define how many logical units are mapped to how many physical units. The difference between MM_ISOTROPIC and MM_ANISOTROPIC is that in the former mode, applications only define extents in the horizontal direction, while Windows calculates the vertical extent preserving the device aspect ratio. In the latter mode, applications can freely define any extents in both directions.

Figure 24.3 illustrates the effects of a typical mapping from logical to physical coordinates.

FIGURE 24.3.

Coordinate mapping.

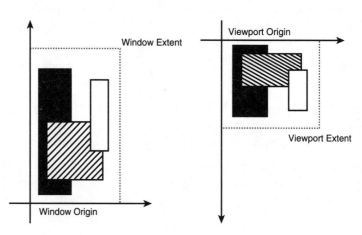

For those who prefer to think in terms of formulae, here is how device coordinates (Dx and Dy) are derived from logical coordinates (Lx and Ly) and vice versa, using the window and viewport origin (xWO and yWO, xVO and yVO), and window and viewport extent (xWE and yWE, xVE and yVE) values:

```
Dx = (Lx - xWO) * xVE/xWE + xVO
Dy = (Ly - yWO) * yVE/yWE + yVO
Lx = (Dx - xVO) * xWE/xVE + xWO
Ly = (Dy - yVO) * yWE/yVE + yWO
```

The CDC class does not directly support world coordinate transformations that are available in Windows NT. To use world coordinate transforms, applications may need to call the Windows function SetWorldTransform directly.

The CDC class provides a set of coordinate transformation functions that can be used to obtain logical coordinates from physical coordinates or vice versa. These functions are DPtoLP and LPtoDP; both of these functions have several overloaded versions that enable them to be used on points, rectangles, and SIZE objects, or MFC classes that encapsulate these objects (CPoint, CRect, CSize).

Additional transformation functions include DPtoHIMETRIC, HIMETRICtoDP, LPtoHIMETRIC, and HIMETRICtoLP. These functions are particularly useful for OLE applications. OLE objects are usually measured in HIMETRIC units; these functions provide a direct means of transforming those units directly into physical or logical coordinates or vice versa.

Coordinate mapping is used extensively in views (that is, classes derived from CView). In these classes, the member function OnPrepareDC is used to set up coordinate mapping that appropriately reflects the view and its current state. For example, in scroll views, OnPrepareDC is used by the framework to displace the window and/or viewport origin to reflect the amount by which the view client area is scrolled. Applications that wish to implement features such as zooming can do so, for example, by overriding CView::OnPrepareDC and changing the window or viewport extent.

Simple Drawing Functions

The CDC class offers a series of member functions that correspond to low-level GDI drawing operations. Among these is the function FillRect (fills a rectangle with a specific brush), FillSolidRect (fills a rectangle with a specific color), FrameRect (draws the borders of a rectangle), and InvertRect (inverts the interior of a rectangle). Analogous functions that accept regions as their parameters are FillRgn, FrameRgn, and InvertRgn.

Additional functions include DrawIcon (draws an icon) and DrawDragRect (erases and draws a dragging rectangle). Other simple drawing functions assist in drawing controls in various (selected, deselected) states and with various border settings.

Selecting GDI Objects

Many drawing functions that operate on device contexts require that you select a GDI object into the device context first. To select a GDI object into a device context, use the

`CDC::SelectObject` member function. This member function has several overloaded versions that enable you to select an object of type `CPen`, `CBrush`, `CFont`, `CBitmap`, or `CRgn` into the device context.

Selecting a pen into a device context is required for functions that draw lines. These include simple line drawing functions (such as `Line`, `Arc`) as well as functions that draw shapes, as the contour of shapes is drawn using the current pen.

Selecting a brush is required when a shape (for example, `Ellipse`, `Rectangle`) is drawn. The brush will be used to fill the interior of the shape.

Select an object of type `CFont` into a device context if you wish to draw text using a specific font.

To use memory device contexts, you must select a `CBitmap` object into them. The `CBitmap` object must represent either a monochrome bitmap or a bitmap that is compatible with the device context.

Selecting a `CRgn` object into a device context sets the clipping region of the device context to the specified region. Doing this is equivalent to calling the `CDC::SelectClipRgn` member function.

In many situations, it is expected that when you are finished using a device context, you restore its previous state including any previous GDI object selections. There are two ways of doing this. You can save the return value of `SelectObject` (which is usually a pointer to a `CPen`, `CBrush`, `CFont`, or `CBitmap` object representing the previous selection) and use it in a subsequent call to `SelectObject`. Alternatively, you can use the `SaveDC` and `RestoreDC` member functions. In either case, it is your responsibility to delete any GDI objects you created once they are no longer in use.

A variant of `SelectObject` is `SelectStockObject`; this `CDC` member function enables you to select a GDI stock object into the device context.

Basic Lines and Shapes

The `CDC` class provides a series of drawing functions that correspond to Windows GDI drawing functions. Basic drawing functions include those that draw various (straight and curved) lines and those that draw shapes.

Many line drawing functions make use of the concept of the current position in the device context. The current position is a pair of coordinates that usually represents the endpoint of the last drawing operation. The current position can be set using the `MoveTo` member function and can be retrieved using the `GetCurrentPosition` member function.

Line drawing functions use the current pen for drawing the line. To draw a straight line, use the `MoveTo` and `LineTo` member functions. To draw an elliptical arc, use the `Arc` or `ArcTo` functions. The direction of the arc can be controlled using the `SetArcDirection` member function; (use `GetArcDirection` to retrieve the current setting).

The `Polyline` and `PolylineTo` functions can be used to draw a series of connected line segments; `PolyPolyline` is a function to draw several polylines in a single operation. Windows can also draw Bézier curves; use the `PolyBezier` or `PolyBezierTo` member functions. Finally, a series of line segments and Bézier curves can be drawn in a single operation using `PolyDraw`.

Shape functions include `Rectangle`, `RoundRect`, `Ellipse`, `Chord`, `Pie`, and `Polygon`. The shapes generated by these functions are shown in Figure 24.4. One additional function, `PolyPolygon`, enables the drawing of multiple polygons in a single operation.

FIGURE 24.4.

Some basic shapes.

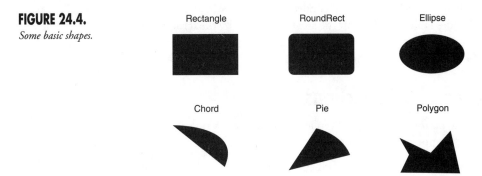

The `PaintRgn` function draws a region using the current brush. The `DrawFocusRect` function is used to draw a rectangle around an object to indicate that the object has the focus. The focus rectangle is drawn using the exclusive `OR` logical function, so calling `DrawFocusRect` for the second time effectively removes the focus rectangle. Note that if you scroll an area containing a focus rectangle, it is necessary to remove the focus rectangle first, scroll the area, and then redraw the focus rectangle.

Bitmaps and Scrolling

Many member functions in the `CDC` class are used to perform bitwise operations on pixel maps, or bitmaps.

Perhaps the simplest pixel operation is `SetPixel`, which sets a pixel, specified by its logical coordinates, to a specific color. The current color of a pixel can be retrieved by calling `GetPixel`. A somewhat faster variant of `SetPixel` is `SetPixelV`; this version of the function does not return the actual color of the pixel.

The `BitBlt` member function can be used to transfer a rectangular area from one location to another. `BitBlt` can also be used to transfer blocks of pixels between device contexts. Thus, `BitBlt` is the operation of choice when, for example, you are transferring blocks of pixels from the screen to a compatible memory bitmap or vice versa.

A variant of BitBlt, StretchBlt, also transfers blocks of pixels from one location to another, but it also compresses and stretches the pixel block to fit the destination rectangle. The stretching mode (the method used to eliminate and/or add pixels) is controlled by SetStretchMode (GetStretchMode) and SetColorAdjustment (GetColorAdjustment).

The PatBlt member function combines the pixels on the device with the pixels of the selected brush in a bitwise logical operation. The MaskBlt operation combines the source and destination bitmaps and a mask bitmap in a bitwise logical operation.

To fill an area in a bitmap using the current brush, call the FloodFill or ExtFloodFill member functions.

To scroll an area within a device context, use the ScrollDC member function. This function also provides information about the areas uncovered by the scrolling operation, which you can use for repainting purposes. However, if you wish to scroll the entire client area of a window, you should instead utilize the CWnd::ScrollWindow function.

Text and Font Functions

In order to perform text output, applications can use any one of a wide selection of text output and font manipulation functions.

The simplest text output function is CDC::TextOut. This function places a character string at a specified location using the currently selected font. A variant, CDC::ExtTextOut, outputs a character string into a specified rectangle.

Yet another variant is TabbedTextOut; this function expands tabs in the text that is to be outputted in accordance with an array specifying tab stop positions.

The color of the text is determined by SetTextColor (use GetTextColor to retrieve the current setting). The horizontal and vertical text alignment are determined by SetTextAlign (GetTextAlign). This function can also be used to specify that text output functions use the current position (as specified by functions such as MoveTo) rather than any coordinates specified in the function call as the location of the text.

It is possible to obtain the size of a block of text without actually drawing the text. The function GetTextExtent calculates the width and height of a line of text using the attribute device context. To perform the same calculation using the output device context, use GetOutputTextExtent. The functions GetTabbedTextExtent and GetOutputTabbedTextExtent perform the same calculations for text that contains tab characters that are to be expanded.

The function SetTextJustification can be used in conjunction with the function GetTextExtent to create justified text. SetTextJustification evenly distributes an amount of space among the break characters (usually spaces) in the text. A related function is SetTextCharacterSpacing, which can be used to set the amount of intercharacter spacing. (Use GetTextCharacterSpacing to retrieve the current setting.)

A more sophisticated text output function is `DrawText`. This function can be used to output multiline text. Note that the `DrawText` function is not recorded in standard Windows metafiles. (It is recorded in enhanced metafiles.)

The `GrayString` function can be used to create grayed (dimmed) text.

Information about the current font can be obtained using `GetTextFace` (retrieves the name of the font), `GetTextMetrics` (retrieves a `TEXTMETRICS` structure containing information about the font currently selected in the attribute device context), and `GetOutputTextMetrics` (same, for the output device context).

Several other `CDC` member functions deal with scalable (TrueType) fonts and information that can be retrieved from such font files.

Clipping Operations

A particularly important GDI capability is the ability to clip output to a specified rectangle or region. This capability is used by Windows throughout; for example, clipping is used to only repaint portions of a window that are not covered by other windows.

Applications can make explicit use of clipping through a series of `CDC` member functions that act as wrappers for similar GDI functions. These include `SelectClipRgn`, `ExcludeClipRect`, `ExcludeUpdateRgn`, `IntersectClipRect`, and `OffsetClipRgn`. To obtain the smallest rectangle that encloses the entire clipping region, call `GetClipBox`. To determine whether a point or any parts of a rectangle are inside the clipping region, use the `PtVisible` or `RectVisible` member functions.

Windows can also maintain a bounding rectangle in which bounding information about the bounds of subsequent drawing operations is accumulated. To access the bounding rectangle, use the `SetBoundsRect` and `GetBoundsRect` member functions.

Printing

Although printing is essentially no different from drawing into any other kind of device contexts, the `CDC` class offers a series of printer escape member functions that control specific aspects of printing.

Printing a document and individual pages is controlled by the `StartDoc`, `StartPage`, `EndPage`, and `EndDoc` member functions. To abort the printing process (and effectively erase everything that has been sent to the printer device context since the last call to `StartDoc`), call the `AbortDoc` member function. Note that if printing is canceled or the printer device driver returns any other error, your application should not call the `EndDoc` or `AbortDoc` member functions.

Use the `SetAbortDoc` member function to create a callback function that Windows calls when the print job is canceled or must be terminated. The `QueryAbort` member function can be used to query this callback function to determine whether printing should be aborted.

444

Device driver specific features can be accessed through the Escape member function. However, because Win32 provides many more printer control functions, the utility of this function relative to earlier Windows implementations has greatly diminished.

Path Functions

The CDC class also offers member functions that encapsulate path functionality. A path is a complex shape created by a series of GDI function calls. A path is created by calling the BeginPath member function, calling the appropriate drawing functions, and calling EndPath. Calling EndPath automatically selects the path into the device context for subsequent manipulation.

Functions that manipulate paths include CloseFigure, FlattenPath, StrokePath, and WidenPath. The path can be rendered into the device context using StrokePath. To render the path's interior, use FillPath; or you can use StrokeAndFillPath to render both the path's contours and its interior at the same time using the current pen and brush.

A path can be turned into a clipping region by calling SelectClipPath.

GDI Object Support in MFC

Many GDI drawing operations are accomplished using a series of GDI objects, such as pens, brushes, or fonts. The Microsoft Foundation Classes Library provides a series of wrapper classes that encapsulate the functionality of these GDI objects.

All GDI object classes are derived from the class CGdiObject. Figure 24.5 illustrates GDI object classes in MFC.

FIGURE 24.5.

GDI object classes.

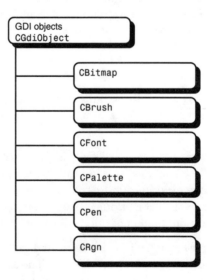

The CGdiObject class provides generic support for GDI objects in the form of a series of member functions. The Attach and Detach member functions can be used to attach a CGdiObject-derived MFC object to a GDI object or detach it from the GDI object. The handle of the object, stored in the m_hObject member variable, can be retrieved through the "safe" function GetSafeHandle. (This function can also be used with null CGdiObject pointers.) A pointer to a CGdiObject that corresponds to a Windows GDI object handle can be obtained by calling the static member function FromHandle. To obtain a GDI object's type, use the GetObjectType member function.

The CreateStockObject member function can be used to crate a stock pen, brush, font, or palette. Note that this function should be called with a CGdiObject-derived object that is of the appropriate class (CPen, CBrush, CFont, or CPalette).

The UnrealizeObject member function can be used to reset the origin of a brush or reset a palette. Do not use this member function for objects of any other type.

The DeleteObject member function deletes the GDI object that the CGdiObject-derived MFC object is attached to. The DeleteTempMap function, called usually from the idle-time handler of your application's CWinApp object, is used to delete any temporary CGdiObject objects that were created by the FromHandle member function.

Pens

Support for GDI pen objects in MFC is provided through the CPen class. A pen can be created either in a single step or in two steps. If you wish to create a pen in a single step, you can utilize overloaded versions the CPen constructor for this purpose. For example, to create a dashed black pen, you can declare the pen object as follows:

```
CPen myPen(PS_DASH, 0, RGB(0, 0, 0));
```

Alternatively, pens can be created in a two-step operation, by creating first the MFC CPen object using a parameterless constructor, and then calling the CreatePen or CreatePenIndirect member functions to create a corresponding GDI pen object. For example:

```
CPen *pPen;
pPen = new CPen;
pPen->CreatePen(PS_SOLID, 3, RGB(255, 0, 0));
```

To obtain a LOGPEN structure from a CPen object, use the GetLogPen function. You can also use a CPen object in any GDI function calls that require a pen handle of type HPEN because the CPen class defines the operator HPEN operator function.

Brushes

The MFC supports GDI brushes through the CBrush class. Like pens, brushes can also be created in either a single step or a two-step process.

To create a GDI brush while constructing the `CBrush` object, use one of the overloaded versions of the `CBrush` constructor. For example, to create a solid yellow brush, you could construct the `CBrush` object as follows:

```
CBrush *pBrush;
pBrush = new CBrush(RGB(255, 255, 0));
```

Alternatively, you can first create the `CBrush` MFC object through the parameterless constructor and then create the GDI brush object by calling the `CreateSolidBrush`, `CreateHatchBrush`, `CreatePatternBrush`, `CreateDIBPatternBrush`, `CreateSysColorBrush`, or `CreateBrushIndirect` member functions. For example:

```
CBrush cyanBrush;
cyanBrush.CreateSolidBrush(RGB(0, 255, 255));
```

To obtain a `LOGBRUSH` structure from a `CBrush` object, use the `GetLogBrush` member function. You can also use `CBrush` objects in place of handles of type `HBRUSH` in GDI function calls because the `CBrush` class defines the `operator HBRUSH` operator function.

Bitmaps

GDI bitmaps are supported in MFC by the `CBitmap` class. Constructing a bitmap is a two-step process. First, the MFC `CBitmap` object must be created; next, one of the initialization functions must be called to create the GDI bitmap object.

The initialization functions include `LoadBitmap`, `LoadOEMBitmap`, `LoadMappedBitmap`, `CreateBitmap`, `CreateBitmapIndirect`, `CreateCompatibleBitmap`, and `CreateDiscardableBitmap`.

To obtain a pointer to a `BITMAP` structure representing the GDI bitmap the `CBitmap` object is attached to, call the `GetBitmap` member function. You can also use `CBitmap` objects in place of handles of type `HBITMAP` in GDI function calls, thanks to the presence of the `operator HBITMAP` operator function.

The bits in a bitmap can be set or read using the `SetBitmapBits` and `GetBitmapBits` member functions. You can also assign a width and a height to the bitmap (in `LOMETRIC` units) using `SetBitmapDimension`. However, these values are only used as return values with `GetBitmapDimension` and serve no other purpose.

Fonts

Support for GDI logical fonts is encapsulated in MFC in the `CFont` class. Creation of a font in MFC is a two-step process; first, the `CFont` MFC object is created; next, an initialization function is called to create the underlying GDI logical font.

The initialization functions include `CreateFont`, `CreateFontIndirect`, `CreatePointFont`, and `CreatePointFontIndirect`.

A pointer to a LOGFONT structure can be obtained by calling the GetLogFont member function. CFont objects can also be used in place of HFONT handles in GDI function calls thanks to the presence of the operator HFONT operator function.

Palettes

Logical palette support in MFC is provided through the CPalette class. Palettes, like fonts and bitmaps, are constructed in a two-step operation. First, the CPalette object is created; next, an initialization function is called to create the underlying GDI palette object.

The two palette initialization functions are CreatePalette and CreateHalftonePalette.

Palette operations include AnimatePalette, GetNearestPaletteIndex, GetEntryCount, GetPaletteEntries, SetPaletteEntries, and ResizePalette.

CPalette objects can be used in GDI function calls that require a palette handle of type HPALETTE because the CPalette class defines the operator function operator HPALETTE.

Regions

Support for GDI regions is provided in MFC through the CRgn class. A region is created by first creating the CRgn object, and then calling an initialization function.

There are a large number of CRgn initialization functions. These are summarized in Table 24.2.

Table 24.2. CRgn initialization functions.

Member Function	Creates
CreateRectRgn	A rectangular region
CreateRectRgnIndirect	A region from a RECT structure
CreateEllipticRgn	An elliptical region
CreateEllipticRgnIndirect	An elliptical region from a RECT structure
CreatePolygonRgn	A polygonal region
CreatePolyPolygonRgn	A region of several (possibly disjoint) polygons
CreateRoundRectRgn	A region in the shape of a rounded rectangle
CombineRgn	A region that is the union of two existing regions
CopyRgn	A region that is the copy of another region
CreateFromPath	A region from a path
CreateFromData	A region from a RGNDATA structure and an XFORM matrix

To compare two CRgn objects and check if they are equivalent, use the EqualRgn member function. To obtain a RGNDATA structure for a CRgn object, call GetRegionData. To obtain a region's bounding rectangle (that is, the tightest rectangle that encloses the region), call GetRgnBox.

To set a region to a specific rectangle, call SetRectRgn. To move a region by a specific offset, use OffsetRgn.

You can determine whether a given point or parts of a given rectangle fall within the region; use the PtInRegion or RectInRegion member functions.

A CRgn object can be used in place of an HRGN handle in GDI function calls, thanks to the presence of the operator function operator HRGN.

Summary

Windows Graphics Device Interface (GDI) functionality is encapsulated by the CDC class (representing device contexts), the CGdiObject class (representing GDI objects), and classes derived from both.

CDC-derived classes include CClientDC (representing a window's interior), CWindowDC (representing a window), and CPaintDC (representing a device context while processing a WM_PAINT message). These derived classes only differ from the base class inasmuch as their constructor and destructor encapsulate calls that create and destroy the appropriate GDI device context (for example, by calling GetDC and ReleaseDC, or BeginPaint/EndPaint). In contrast, a base CDC object is not automatically attached to a GDI device context; the device context must be explicitly created through the CreateDC member function (or attached to through the Attach member function).

Another class derived from CDC is CMetafileDC, which represents metafile device contexts.

A CDC object maintains two GDI device context handles. The output device context handle is used for drawing operations; the attribute device context handle is used for operations obtaining information about the device context. The two handles are usually identical, except for the case of CMetafileDC objects, in which case the attribute device context is set to NULL.

The CDC class encapsulates most GDI drawing functionality. This includes basic drawing functions, simple lines and shapes, text and font functions, clipping functions, bitmap and scrolling functions, and region and path-related functions. The CDC class also provides functionality related to mapping modes. Note that encapsulation of the Windows NT world coordinate transformation functions is not provided as part of the CDC class.

Most drawing operations utilize drawing tools that are selected into a device context using the SelectObject or SelectStockObject functions. These tools are GDI objects such as pens, brushes, palettes, bitmaps, fonts, and regions. Support for these GDI objects in MFC is provided through a series of classes derived from CGdiObject. The CPen, CBrush, CFont, CBitmap, CPalette, and CRgn classes encapsulate the functionality of pens, brushes, fonts, bitmaps, palettes, and regions, respectively.

Serialization: File and Archive Objects

25

A concept of central importance in the Microsoft Foundation Class Library is serialization.

Through serialization, objects derived from CObject obtain persistence. Before you begin wondering why such glorified terminology is used for what is essentially saving and loading data to or from a file, let me point out that serialization can take place with a target other than a disk file. It is also through serialization that a CObject-derived object is copied to or from the clipboard or passed to other applications through OLE.

Serialization represents a relationship between objects derived from the CObject class, the CArchive class representing an archive, and the CFile class that represents physical storage (Figure 25.1).

FIGURE 25.1.

Relationship of
CObject,
CArchive, and
CFile.

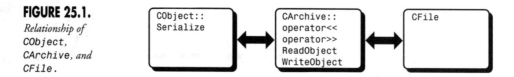

This relationship notwithstanding, the utility of the CFile class transcends CObject serialization. The next section presents an examination of the CFile class and shows how it can be utilized in simple scenarios.

The *CFile* Class

CFile is the base class for MFC file services. As is, CFile supports unbuffered binary input/output for disk files. Through derived classes, it supports text files, memory files, and Windows sockets. The hierarchy of CFile and its derived classes is shown in Figure 25.2.

FIGURE 25.2.

CFile class
hierarchy.

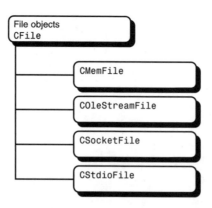

A recurring theme with MFC classes that act as wrapper classes for Windows objects is the duality of the C++ object versus the Windows object itself. Briefly, a CFile object is not identical to a file object in Windows; it merely represents one. Construction of the CFile object does not necessarily ensure construction of a file object (that is, constructing a CFile object may or may not mean that a file is actually opened).

In a CFile object, the member variable m_hFile contains (usually) the handle of the file that the CFile object represents. This handle may be initialized in the CFile constructor or through an explicitly called initialization function.

> **NOTE**
>
> The file handle m_hFile is a Win32 file handle; this is not to be confused with the file handles or file descriptors used in the C/C++ low-level file I/O libraries.

CFile Initialization

Construction of a CFile object may be done in either one or two steps. To construct a CFile object in a single step, use the form of the constructor that accepts a handle to an already open file or the name of file that is to be opened with the CFile object.

Alternatively, you can use a parameterless constructor and call the Open member function.

When you are opening a file through the CFile constructor or the Open member function, several flags can be specified. Files can be opened for reading or writing, in text or binary mode. Both the constructor and the Open member function can also create files. Additional mode flags specify file sharing and other attributes.

An open file can be closed by calling the Close member function. The Abort member function can also be used for this purpose; unlike Close, Abort will close the file under all circumstances, ignoring any errors.

Reading from and Writing to a CFile Object

Quite unsurprisingly, reading and writing to/from a CFile object can be accomplished by calling the Read or Write member functions. Needless to say, the file must be opened with the appropriate mode in order for the reading or writing operation to be successful.

The Flush member function can be used to force any buffered data to be written to the file.

Random access to files is provided through the Seek member function. This function is used to set the position within the file for the next read or write operation. Two variants, SeekToBegin and SeekToEnd, set the position to the beginning or the end of the file, respectively. The current position can be obtained by calling GetPosition.

The length of the file can be obtained through GetLength. The SetLength function can be used to set the length of the file; the file will be extended with uninitialized data or truncated as applicable.

File Management

Two static CFile member functions can be used without constructing a CFile object. CFile::Rename can be used to rename a file; CFile::Remove can be used to delete a file.

The status of a file can be obtained by calling the GetStatus member function. This function sets the values of a CFileStatus object. GetStatus also has a static variant that can be used to obtain the status of a file that was not opened previously.

To set the status of a file from a CFileStatus object, call the SetStatus member function.

Error Handling

Many file operations can fail. While some CFile member functions (for example, Open) indicate such failures in their return values, many other member functions throw an exception to indicate such conditions. The exception is always of type CFileException. To handle error conditions, you would write code similar to the following:

```
CFile myFile("filename.txt", CFile::modeWrite)
try
{
    CFile.Write("Data", 4);
    CFile.Close();
}
catch (CFileException *e)
{
    if (e->m_cause == CFileException::diskFull)
        cout << "The disk is full!";
    else
    {
        // Handle other errors
    }
    e->Delete();
}
```

Locking

The CFile class also supports locking. A region of a file, as determined by the starting position and the number of bytes that are part of the region, can be locked using the LockRange member function. To unlock the region, use the UnlockRange member function.

Simultaneous locking of several regions is allowed; however, locking of overlapping regions is not. Calls to UnlockRange must match exactly earlier calls to LockRange; for example, if you lock two regions of the file using LockRange, you must use two separate calls to UnlockRange even if the regions are adjacent.

An attempt to lock a region of a file that is already locked results in an error.

Using a *CFile* in a Simple Application

The CFile class can be used in many situations, including console applications. Such a simple application is demonstrated in Listing 25.1. You can compile this program from the command line by typing cl /MT hello.cpp.

Listing 25.1. Using CFile in a console application.

```
#include <afx.h>

#define HELLOSTR "Hello, World!\n"
#define HELLOLEN (sizeof(HELLOSTR)-1)

void main(void)
{
        CFile file((int)GetStdHandle(STD_OUTPUT_HANDLE));
        file.Write(HELLOSTR, HELLOLEN);
}
```

As this example also illustrates, there is little advantage to using CFile in this fashion. The real advantages of the CFile class come to light when it is used in conjunction with CArchive for MFC object serialization.

The *CStdioFile* Class

The CStdioFile class is used to associate a CFile-derived object with a standard C stream (that is, a FILE pointer). Its use is demonstrated with yet another simple program in Listing 25.2.

Listing 25.2. Using CStdioFile.

```
#include <afx.h>

#define HELLOSTR "Hello, World!\n"
#define HELLOLEN (sizeof(HELLOSTR)-1)

void main(void)
{
    CStdioFile file(stdout);
    file.Write(HELLOSTR, HELLOLEN);
}
```

The stream pointer that a CStdioFile object is associated with is stored in the m_pStream member variable.

CStdioFile objects are intended primarily for text I/O. Two additional member functions, ReadString and WriteString, support the input and output of CString objects and null-terminated text strings.

The CStdioFile class does not support the CFile member functions Duplicate, LockRange, and UnlockRange. Attempts to use these functions result in a CNotSupportedException being thrown.

The *CMemFile* Class

The CMemFile class supports CFile functionality in memory. One possible use of CMemFile objects is to provide fast temporary storage.

When a CMemFile object is created, you can specify a parameter that defines the amount by which the CMemFile object grows its storage at every subsequent allocation. The CMemFile class uses the standard C library functions malloc, realloc, free, and memcpy to allocate and deallocate memory and to transfer data to or from allocated memory blocks.

It is possible to derive a class from CMemFile and override the default memory allocation behavior. Overridable member functions include Alloc, Free, Realloc, Memcpy, and GrowFile.

A CMemFile object can also be attached to a previously allocated memory block. Use the Attach member function or the three-parameter version of the CMemFile constructor for this purpose. Note that in order to make the CMemFile object use the contents of the attached memory block, you must set the parameter controlling the growth of memory allocation to zero; in other words, a memory block attached in this fashion cannot be grown.

Use the Detach member function to detach the memory block from a CMemFile object and obtain a pointer to it. To determine the size of the memory block, use the GetLength member function prior to calling Detach.

CMemFile does not support the CFile member functions Duplicate, LockRange, and UnlockRange. Attempts to use these functions result in a CNotSupportedException being thrown.

The *COleStreamFile* Class

The COleStreamFile class is associated with the OLE IStream interface. It provides CFile-like functionality on OLE streams.

To construct a COleStreamFile object, pass to its constructor the pointer to an IStream interface. Alternatively, you can create a COleStreamFile object using the default constructor, and then call one of the initialization member functions.

Initialization member functions include Attach (attaches the COleStreamFile object to an IStream interface), CreateMemoryStream, CreateStream, and OpenStream. To detach the COleStreamFile object from the IStream interface and obtain a pointer to that interface, call the Detach member function.

The *CSocketFile* Class

The CSocketFile class provides a CFile-like interface on Windows socket (CSocket) objects. A CSocketFile object can be attached to a CArchive object to support serialization through a socket; it can also be used as a stand-alone file object.

Note that CSocketFile does not support several CFile member functions (such as Seek and related functions) and thus any use that assumes availability of these functions will fail. In particular, this renders the CEditView member function SerializeRaw unusable with CSocketFile objects.

CArchive

What is a CArchive object? What is its significance? Why can CObject objects not be written directly to CFile objects?

While the CFile class is a generic wrapper class for Win32 file objects, CArchive creates the link between permanent storage and the serialization functions in a CObject. In other words, CArchive enables the objects to serialize themselves. While in some cases (for example, when you are serializing an array of integers) it is enough to simply write out the memory image of the objects to permanent storage, in many other cases (for example, when the objects contain pointers) this is clearly not sufficient. By delegating the actual task of creating a persistent image to the objects themselves, the CArchive class provides an elegant solution to this problem.

A CArchive object must be thought of as a "one-shot" or "single pass" entity. A CArchive is used for the sole purpose of either writing or reading a series of objects to/from permanent storage. You cannot perform random reads or writes, nor can you use the same CArchive object for both reading and writing. For example, if you wish to read back a series of objects after they have been written to permanent storage, you need to create a separate CArchive object for this purpose. Furthermore, you will have to read back the objects in the same order in which they were written to the archive originally.

Creating a *CArchive*

Creating and using a CArchive object is a multistep process. Before the CArchive can be created, you must have a CFile object representing a file that was opened with permissions appropriate for what you are planning to do.

Once the CFile object has been created, the CArchive object can be created by passing a pointer to the CFile object to its constructor.

In the constructor, you also specify whether the archive is used for reading or writing.

Every CArchive object has a member variable m_pDocument that is a pointer to a CDocument object. Common use of this pointer is to refer to the document that is being serialized in MFC framework applications. However, it is not necessary to use this member variable for this purpose (or indeed, for any purpose at all) if the objects you serialize do not depend on the presence of a valid m_pDocument.

If you wish to obtain a pointer to the CFile object that a CArchive is associated with, call the GetFile member function.

The CFile can be closed and the archive disconnected from it by calling the Close member function. Calling this function is usually not necessary, as the CFile is closed automatically when the archive is destroyed. If you do call Close, note that no further operations on the archive are permitted.

Reading and Writing Objects

The CArchive class can be used to read and write simple data types as well as CObject-derived objects.

You can determine whether a CArchive object has been created for reading or writing by calling the IsLoading or IsStoring member functions.

To read or write raw binary data, use the Read or Write member functions. To read or write null-terminated strings, use the ReadString or WriteString member functions.

To write a CObject-derived object to the archive, call the WriteObject function. The ReadObject function creates and reads a CObject-derived object from the archive. This function uses runtime type information when creating the CObject; therefore, it is necessary that the CObject-derived class be declared and implemented using the DECLARE_DYNCREATE and IMPLEMENT_DYNCREATE macros.

CArchive supports the concept of a *schema number* through the GetObjectSchema and SetObjectSchema member functions. Schema numbers enable an application to distinguish between different versions of the same archive. Using schema numbers, you can implement upward compatibility.

The Overloaded >> and << Operators

In many situations, applications do not call CArchive member functions directly in order to read or write an object to/from an archive. Instead, they rely on the overloaded input and output operators for this purpose.

These overloaded operators have been defined for many simple types as well as the CObject type. The simple types include BYTE, WORD, LONG, DWORD, float, and double. An obvious question is, why haven't these operators been defined for basic C types, such as int, short, or long? The answer is that the size of these types is implementation dependent; using them in CArchive operations would render the resulting storage object also dependent on the operating system version under which it was created. For example, in a 16-bit Windows application, the size of an `int` variable is 2 bytes; in contrast, the size of an `int` in 32-bit Windows is 4 bytes.

> **NOTE**
>
> Do not define your own versions of the operators << and >> to archive basic C types in a `CArchive`. Use type casting instead and rely on the existing operators instead to avoid a dependence on the operating system version.

When a simple type is being archived, the data is simply copied to or from the archive. The situation is very different when a `CObject` is being archived. The operators << and >> refer to the `CObject`'s `Serialize` member function, passing to it a reference to the archive object. Thus, the object is responsible for serializing itself.

The *CObject::Serialize* Member Function

The `Serialize` member function in objects of type `CObject` is used to write an object to, or read an object from, a `CArchive`.

This function is called with a reference to the `CArchive` object. The implementation of `Serialize` should use the `CArchive::IsLoading` or `CArchive::IsStoring` member function to determine whether the archive is used for reading or writing. A typical `Serialize` member function implementation looks like this skeleton:

```
void CMyClass::Serialize(CArchive &ar)
{
    if (ar.IsLoading())
    {
        // Load the data
    }
    else
    {
        // Save the data
    }
}
```

In the `Serialize` member function, calls are often made to the >> or << operators or to the `Serialize` member functions of other objects. For example, if your class `CMyClass` contains a member variable `m_other` of type `COtherClass` (and this is also a class derived from `CObject`), your serialize member function may look like this:

```
void CMyClass::Serialize(CArchive &ar)
{
    m_other.Serialize(ar);
    if (ar.IsLoading())
    {
        // Load the data
    }
```

```
    else
    {
        // Save the data
    }
}
```

Error Handling

During the course of archive operations, many types of errors can occur. There can be a file operation error; there can be an inconsistency in the archive; there can be memory allocation problems. Most CArchive member functions use exceptions to communicate the fact that an error occurred.

CArchive member functions can throw three types of exceptions: CFileException exceptions are thrown in case of file errors; CArchiveException exceptions are thrown in case of archive problems (for example, when an object of the wrong type is being read); and CMemoryException exceptions indicate memory allocation problems (for example, when the CArchive is attempting to allocate memory for an object it is about to read).

Using CArchive in Simple Applications

Before we proceed exploring the use of CArchive in MFC framework applications, I believe that an example that demonstrates the use of CArchive in simple situations is probably in order.

The program shown in Listing 25.3 uses a CArchive object to write the contents of a list to permanent storage. The list is built using the template class CList. Because CList is derived from CObject, it provides support for a Serialize member function. However, it does not support the operators << and >>. We can add this support, though, by explicitly declaring an operator<< function. This is exactly what we do for objects of type CList<WORD, WORD>.

Listing 25.3. Saving a list using a CArchive.

```
#include <afx.h>
#include <afxtempl.h>
#include <iostream.h>

CArchive& operator<<(CArchive& ar, CList<WORD, WORD> &lst)
{
    lst.Serialize(ar);
    return ar;
}

void main(void)
{
    CList<WORD, WORD> myList;

    cout << "Creating list: ";
    for (int i = 0; i < 10; i++)
```

```
    {
        int n = rand();
        cout << n << ' ';
        myList.AddTail(n);
    }
    CFile myFile("mylist.dat", CFile::modeCreate ¦ CFile::modeWrite);
    CArchive ar(&myFile, CArchive::store);
    ar << myList;
}
```

The real power of CArchive becomes apparent when you consider that most of this code is about building a sample list; two lines are used to construct the archive object, and the entire list is written out using a single line of code. Similarly, the entire list can be read in a single line, as demonstrated by the reading program shown in Listing 25.4.

Listing 25.4. Loading a list from a CArchive.

```
#include <afx.h>
#include <afxtempl.h>
#include <iostream.h>

CArchive& operator>>(CArchive& ar, CList<WORD, WORD> &lst)
{
    lst.Serialize(ar);
    return ar;
}

void main(void)
{
    CList<WORD, WORD> myList;

    CFile myFile("mylist.dat", CFile::modeRead);
    CArchive ar(&myFile, CArchive::load);
    ar >> myList;
    POSITION pos = myList.GetHeadPosition();
    cout << "Reading list: ";
    while (pos)
    {
        int n = myList.GetNext(pos);
        cout << n << ' ';
    }
}
```

Both of these programs can be compiled from the command line. (For example, type cl /MT readlst.cpp).

Note that this simple example may be a little misleading. When using a collection template such as CList, it may be necessary to implement the SerializeElements helper function. The default implementation simply performs a bitwise read or write on elements of the collection; while this is adequate when the elements are of type WORD, it falls short of what is required in case of more complex types (such as types derived from CObject). (Why do the collection templates not rely on the Serialize member function of objects that comprise the collection? For the simple reason that these collection classes are not restricted to CObject-derived objects only.)

Serialization in MFC Framework Applications

CFile and CArchive are the building blocks; CObject::Serialize is the glue that connects objects and archives. But it is in MFC framework applications where the concepts behind archives and serialization realize their full potential.

Serialization in Documents

In an MFC framework application, classes derived from CDocument play a central role. These classes represent the entities your applications manipulate. CDocument-derived objects achieve persistence through the serialization mechanism that we reviewed in this chapter.

When AppWizard creates a skeleton framework application, it already supplies implementations for the File Open and File Save (and Save As) menu commands. These implementations create a CArchive object and call the document class's Serialize member function. It is your responsibility to supply an implementation of this member function that serializes all persistent data members of your document class.

Helper Macros

The MFC provides several helper macros that make serialization CObject-derived classes possible.

When the CArchive reads data for a new object from a file, it is necessary for it to have a mechanism whereby an object of the given type can be created. This is accomplished by adding a static member function named CreateObject to the class in question. However, you do not need to declare or implement this function by hand; instead, you can use the DECLARE_DYNCREATE and IMPLEMENT_DYNCREATE macros for this purpose.

How does the CArchive know the type of the object that is about to be created? Simple: Together with the object, run-time type information is also saved. In order for a CObject-derived class to support run-time type information (through CRuntimeClass), you can use the DECLARE_DYNAMIC and IMPLEMENT_DYNAMIC macros; however, as the functionality of these macros is implied by DECLARE_DYNCREATE and IMPLEMENT_DYNCREATE, it is not necessary to explicitly add these to the class declaration.

Yet another pair of macros is DECLARE_SERIAL and IMPLEMENT_SERIAL. Although the documentation states that these macros are required to enable serialization, you may find that in an

AppWizard-generated skeleton, the obviously serializable CDocument-derived class of your application does not use these macros. The reason for this is that DECLARE_SERIAL and IMPLEMENT_SERIAL are really only needed if you intend to use the << and >> operators with your class and a CArchive. (DECLARE_SERIAL and IMPLEMENT_SERIAL declare and implement the overloaded >> operator for your class.)

DECLARE_SERIAL and IMPLEMENT_SERIAL encompass the functionality of DECLARE_DYNCREATE and IMPLEMENT_DYNCREATE, so you do not need to use those macros if DECLARE_SERIAL and IMPLEMENT_SERIAL are used.

Serialization, OLE, and the Clipboard

So far, we have discussed serialization in the context of file load and save operations. However, MFC applications also use serialization for OLE-related operations.

MFC framework applications that act as OLE servers use the COleServerItem-derived class to provide a server interface. The Serialize member function of this class provides the mechanism whereas application specific data is stored for embedded or linked OLE objects.

In the simplest implementation, this Serialize function delegates the task of serializing the document to the Serialize member function of the CDocument-derived document class. However, if the application supports serializing only portions of a document, a separate implementation may be required.

Serialization of portions of a document can happen under two circumstances. First, it may happen for linked items. Second, the COleServerItem-derived class is also used for clipboard operations. If the application supports copying the user's selection to the clipboard (as opposed to the entire document), the Serialize member function of the COleServerItem-derived class must provide an implementation where only the user's selection is serialized.

Summary

Serialization in MFC applications represents a relationship of CObject-derived objects (those that need to be serialized), CFile-derived objects that represent persistent storage such as a disk file, and CArchive objects that provide the serialization interface.

The CFile class encapsulates the functionality of a Win32 file object. Its member functions provide the means to open, read, write, and otherwise manipulate disk files.

Variants of the CFile class include CStdioFile, CMemFile, COleStreamFile, and CSocketFile. These classes provide I/O functionality through C-style stream objects (FILE pointers), memory blocks, OLE IStream interfaces, and Windows sockets.

The CArchive class provides the basic interface for serialization. Serialization is a mechanism that enables CObject-derived classes to assume responsibility for writing or reading their own data to/from persistent storage. CArchive accomplishes this by calling the Serialize member function for CObject-derived objects whenever data transfer takes place.

The CObject::Serialize member function must be implemented for classes derived from CObject. In this function, data is written to, or read from a CArchive object, a reference to which is passed to the function as its sole parameter. The direction of the operation, namely whether it is a save to, or load from the archive, can be determined by calling the CArchive object's IsLoading member function.

Inside Serialize, member variables of the class are transferred to or from the archive. This can be accomplished by using the << or >> operators, by calling the member variable's Serialize member function (if the member variable is of a type derived from CObject), or calling the CArchive::Read or CArchive::Write functions for bitwise transfer of data.

Serialization is used throughout in MFC framework applications. The framework provides a default implementation for the File Open and File Save commands. These default implementations call your document class's Serialize member function. This function, which you must implement yourself, should serialize all your document's persistent data.

In order for a CObject-derived class to be serializable, it must be declared using the DECLARE_SERIAL macro and implemented using IMPLEMENT_SERIAL. If you do not plan to use the overloaded >> operator with your class, you may declare it using DECLARE_DYNCREATE and IMPLEMENT_DYNCREATE. For an example of a class with this behavior, take a look at any document class created by AppWizard.

Collection Classes

26

The Microsoft Foundation Classes Library implements a number of collection classes. These collection classes include a variety of lists, arrays, and mappings.

Collections have been supported by the MFC Library since its early versions. In the days of Visual C++ 1.5 and earlier versions, template support was not yet available in the compiler; correspondingly, there are several non-template-based collection classes in the Library.

Newer, 32-bit versions of the compiler obviously provide full template support. Accordingly, starting with MFC 3.0, a series of new *type-safe* collection classes was introduced. However, they do not render the old classes obsolete; if you have been using the non-template-based collection classes in your code, there is no reason why you should not continue to do so. In new code, it is recommended that you try to use the new, template-based classes, as their type-safe nature provides for safer, more robust code.

Throughout the MFC Library, the most commonly used collections are collections of CObject items. This fact, plus the relative simplicity of the CObject collection classes, provides a good reason for starting our review of collection classes with CObList, and CObArray.

CObject Collections

The MFC Library provides two ordered collections of CObject items. The CObList collection is a list of CObject items; the CObArray collection is an array of CObject items. But, you may ask, what exactly is the difference between the two? What are the advantages of using one or the other?

The CObList class organizes CObject pointers in a linked list. Due to the nature of such a list, insertion and removal of elements are very fast operations. On the other hand, the list is not indexed; retrieving an element by a numerical index is a slow process. List collections are meant to be used in situations where the list is "walked" with the help of an iterator. Consider, for example, a typical use of a CObList collection, namely to organize all items in a document. When the items are accessed in order to serialize or to draw the document, elements in the list are accessed sequentially.

The CObArray class, in contrast, indexes elements by an integer index value. Inserting or removing elements are slow operations, as they involve moving potentially large blocks of data. However, retrieving data by the integer index is fast.

While both classes are nominally collections of CObject pointers, you will probably never use them with the CObject class. While technically not an abstract class, the CObject class is pretty useless by itself. Instead, CObList and CObArray are used as collections of CObject-derived classes, such as collections of items of type CWnd, CView, or CDocItem. In the following sections, I present several small examples of code in which objects of type CObject are declared; note that these code fragments will not compile "as is," as creation of a CObject is prevented by the declaration of a protected constructor in the MFC library. When applying these examples to concrete situations, just substitute a CObject-derived class in these examples and assume any required typecasts.

The *CObList* Class and the *POSITION* Type

Using a CObList collection involves creating the collection, adding items to the collection, and accessing items through iterator functions.

A CObList can be created either by declaring a variable of type CObList or using the new operator to obtain a pointer to a new CObList collection.

Items can be added to a CObList by calling the AddHead or AddTail functions. As their names imply, these functions add an element at the beginning and at the end of the list, respectively. Items do not need to be unique; the same CObject pointer can occur any number of times in the list.

To obtain the first or the last element on the list, use the GetHead or GetTail member functions.

It is also possible to add a new element to the list at a specific position. The InsertBefore and InsertAfter member functions can be used to insert a new element before or after a specific element. The element position is identified by a variable of type POSITION. This type is used throughout collection classes as a general-purpose iterator type.

A value of type POSITION can be obtained by calling either the GetHeadPosition or the GetTailPosition member functions. The returned POSITION value can be used in subsequent calls to GetNext or GetTail to access elements of the list sequentially. For example, to walk the elements in a CObList from the beginning to the end of the list, you would use code similar to the following:

```
CObList myList;
...
// Populate the list
...
POSITION pos = myList.GetHeadPosition();
while (pos != NULL)
{
    CObject *pObject = myList.GetNext(pos);
    ...
    // Do something nasty to *pObject
    ...
}
```

Similarly, you can walk the elements of a CObList backwards as follows:

```
CObList myList;
...
// Populate the list
...
POSITION pos = myList.GetTailPosition();
while (pos != NULL)
{
    CObject *pObject = myList.GetPrev(pos);
    ...
    // Do something nasty to *pObject
    ...
}
```

As you can see from these two examples, the names of the GetNext and GetPrev functions can be slightly misleading. What these functions do is return the *current* element pointed to by the POSITION parameter, while at the same time advancing this parameter to refer to the next (or previous) element.

A POSITION value can also be used with the GetAt, SetAt, and RemoveAt member functions. All three of these functions take a parameter of type POSITION; GetAt retrieves a CObject pointer corresponding to that position, SetAt sets the element at the given position to a new value, and RemoveAt removes the element from the list altogether.

Removing an element during an iteration may cause problems. In order to ensure that you always maintain a valid POSITION value for GetNext, you should use a method similar to the following:

```
POSITION pos = myList.GetHeadPosition();
while (pos != NULL)
{
    POSITION pos2 = pos;
    CObject *pObject = GetNext(pos);
    if ( /* pObject is to be removed */ )
    {
        myList.RemoveAt(pos2);
    }
}
```

Additional functions that can be used to remove elements are RemoveHead and RemoveTail. The RemoveAll function can be used to remove all elements (empty the list).

Removing an element does not destroy the element; the program that created the element is responsible for its destruction. For example:

```
CObject *pObject;
CObList myList;
...
pObject = new CObject;
myList.AddTail(pObject);
...
// some time later
...
pObject = myList.RemoveTail();
delete pObject;
```

To determine if a list is empty, use the IsEmpty member function. To obtain the number of elements in the list, call GetCount.

You can also search for a specific element in the list. The Find member function determines whether a particular CObject pointer is in the list; if so, it returns a value of type POSITION indicating its first occurrence. The FindIndex member function returns the POSITION value that corresponds to a given numerical index. Note that as the CObList class does not maintain an index of any kind, these operations can be slow if the list is large.

The CObList type is itself derived from CObject. As such, the CObList class supports serialization. If its Serialize member function is called, it in turn serializes every CObject element in the list using the << and >> operators. In order to ensure that the list is serialized correctly, elements added to it should be of a CObject-derived type that is declared and implemented using the DECLARE_SERIAL and IMPLEMENT_SERIAL macros.

CObList objects can be used in conjunction with the CArchive class and the << and >> operators, as in the following example:

```
class CMyDocument : public CDocument
{
    CObList m_List;
    // rest of the class declaration follows
    ...
}

void CMyDocument::Serialize(CArchive &ar)
{
    if (ar.IsStoring())
    {
        ar << m_List;
    }
    else
    {
        ar >> m_List;
    }
}
```

Because CObList is also CObject-derived, it is possible to use a CObList collection to refer to items of type CObList, in effect creating a list of lists.

The *CObArray* Class

CObArray objects are arrays of CObject pointers. These arrays are similar in function and behavior to C arrays, with one crucial difference: a CObArray can grow or shrink dynamically.

Using a CObArray involves constructing the CObArray object, populating it with CObject pointer elements, and retrieving array elements (possibly by using the overloaded [] operator).

You can create a CObArray like you would create any other variable, either on the stack as an automatic variable or through the new operator.

At the heart of the CObArray class are the SetAt, GetAt, and SetAtGrow member functions. SetAt and GetAt behave as you would expect, setting and retrieving an element at the specified location. SetAtGrow also sets an element at the specified location; however, this function causes the array to grow if the location is past the current array bounds.

Neither SetAt nor GetAt report an error if an invalid index is specified. However, they do cause an assertion in the debug version of the MFC Library.

Elements can also be added to the array using the Add member function. This member function appends a new element to the array, growing the array as necessary.

The current number of elements in the array can be obtained by calling GetSize. The largest valid array index (which is equal to the number of array elements minus one, as array indexes are zero based) can be obtained by calling GetUpperBound.

The SetSize function can be used to set the number of elements in the array, allocating additional memory if necessary. If SetSize is used to shrink the array, unused memory will be freed.

Whenever the array is grown as a result of a call to SetAtGrow, Add, or SetSize, a memory allocation error may occur. These errors are indicated by an exception of type CMemoryException being thrown.

The SetSize function can also be used to specify the amount by which memory allocated by CObArray is grown. Whenever new memory needs to be allocated, the amount allocated will hold as many CObject pointers as specified in the second parameter of SetSize. If this parameter is not set, the CObArray class attempts to determine the optimum amount of memory that it should allocate to avoid heap fragmentation.

Any extra memory allocated when the array was grown can be released by calling FreeExtra. The entire array can be emptied and all memory released by calling RemoveAll.

The CObArray class provides and override version of the [] operator. Through this operator, array elements can be accessed. The operator can be used in situations where an lvalue is needed (for example, on the left side of an assignment operation). This behavior is implemented with the help of the ElementAt member function, which returns a reference to the CObject pointer at the specified location. Thus, the following line:

```
myArray[10] = &myObject;
```

is equivalent to

```
myArray.ElementAt(10) = &myObject;
```

Two member functions, InsertAt and RemoveAt, can be used to insert elements into the array or to remove an element at a specific index. Note that these operations are slow; in the case of large arrays, they potentially require the moving of large blocks of data.

As with CObList, the CObArray class does not destroy any elements when they are removed from the array. You are responsible for freeing such items yourself. For example:

```
CObject *pObject;
CObArray myList;
...
pObject = new CObject;
myArray.Add(pObject);
...
// some time later
...
pObject = myArray[myArray.GetUpperBound()];
myArray.SetSize(myArray.GetUpperBound());
delete pObject;
```

The CObArray type is derived from CObject. One advantage of this fact is that CObArray collections can also be serialized. When the CObArray::Serialize member function is called, it in turn serializes array elements using the << and >> operators. To support serialization, elements added to the array must be of a CObject-derived type that is declared and implemented using the DECLARE_SERIAL and IMPLEMENT_SERIAL macros.

CObArray collections can be used with the CArchive class and the << and >> operators.

Other List Collections

There are several other list collections with features and behavior very similar to that of CObList.

The *CPtrList* Class

The CPtrList class implements identical behavior to that of CObList, but for elements that are void pointers. The features and member functions of this class are otherwise identical to the features and member functions of CObList.

Note that the CPtrList class does not support serialization.

The *CStringList* Class

The CStringList class is also similar in behavior and implementation to CObList. However, there is one crucial difference; instead of storing pointers to items of type CString, a CStringList stores copies of the actual CString objects themselves.

As a consequence, the application is no longer required to explicitly delete a CString object after removing it from the CStringList. Nor is it necessary to allocate an element using new or malloc to ensure that an object remains valid after the function in which it was declared terminates. For example, consider the following (incorrect) function implementation:

```
void MyAddElement(CObList *pList)
{
    CObject myObject;
    pList->AddTail(&myObject);  // WRONG!
}
```

This is obviously wrong as the address &myObject becomes meaningless when the function returns. Instead, the following implementation should have been used:

```
void MyAddElement(CObList *pList)
{
    CObject *pObject;
    pObject = new CObject;
    pList->AddTail(pObject);
}
```

The same problem does not present itself when using a CStringList. The following implementation is correct:

```
void MyAddElement(CStringList *pList)
{
    CString myString;
    pList->AddTail(myString);
}
```

Serialization of CStringList collections is supported.

Other Array Collections

In addition to CObArray, the MFC Library provides a series of additional ready-to-use array collections. Analogous to the list collections CPtrList and CStringList are the array collections CPtrArray and CStringArray; however, there are also a series of additional array collections that hold integral types.

The *CPtrArray* Class

The CPtrArray class implements the same behavior as CObArray but for void pointer elements. The behavior of member functions and the features of the class are identical to the features and member function behavior of CObArray.

Serialization is not supported by CPtrArray.

Integral Array Classes

There are several array classes in MFC that store elements of integral types. These are summarized in Table 26.1.

Table 26.1. Integral array collection classes.

Class Name	Element Type
CByteArray	BYTE
CWordArray	WORD
CDWordArray	DWORD
CUIntArray	UINT

The type CUIntArray differs from the other three types in that the size of a UINT is implementation-dependent. Under 16-bit Windows, a UINT as 16 bits wide; under Windows NT or Windows 95, it is a 32-bit type. Consequently, unlike the other three types, CUIntArray does not support serialization.

The other three collection classes use element types that are guaranteed to be of the same size on different implementations. A BYTE is always 8 bits wide; a WORD, 16 bits, and a DWORD is always 32 bits.

With the exception of the difference in serialization support by CUIntArray, the features and behavior of these classes is identical to the features and behavior of CObArray.

The *CStringArray* Class

The CStringArray class represents an array of CString objects. As in the case of CStringList, CStringArray stores copies of the CString objects themselves, not just pointers to them. Consequently, application programmers are not responsible for destroying CString objects that are removed from the array.

The features and behavior of CStringArray are otherwise similar to the features and behavior of CObArray. In particular, CStringArray supports serialization.

Mappings

Mappings represent a type of a collection that is markedly different from lists or arrays. Lists and arrays are ordered collections; in contrast, mappings represent unordered mappings of key objects to value objects. Because of the obvious similarity, mappings are sometimes also referred to as dictionaries (and indeed, implementing the functionality of a dictionary of words is a trivial task using, for example, the mapping collection CMapStringToString).

Mappings are tailored towards fast searches by key value. In all the mapping classes, key values are expected to be unique. An attempt to set a value with an existing key will overwrite the current entry in the mapping as opposed to creating an entry with a duplicate key value.

The MFC Library offers several map collections. Keys that are pointers, strings, or 16-bit words are used to index items that are pointers to CObject, pointer to void, strings, or 16-bit words. Because not all combinations of these types are implemented in the form of a mapping collection, and because there are minor variations and differences in the behavior of these classes, I review them individually.

The *CMapStringToString* Class

The CMapStringToString class maps keys of type CString to values of the same type.

To construct a CMapStringToString collection, simply declare an object of this type or use the new operator. Once the collection has been constructed, key-value pairs can be added to it using the SetAt member function. A convenient shorthand for using SetAt is the overloaded [ ] operator. Curiously, this operator can *only* be used in the place of an lvalue; it cannot be used for looking up keys for the simple reason that key values are often not found in the collection.

To look up data by key value, use instead the Lookup member function. The Boolean return value of this function indicates whether the key was found or not.

I suppose it would be possible to implement an overloaded form of the [ ] operator that can be used on the right-hand side of assignments and use an exception to communicate a lookup failure. However, an unhandled exception would cause your application to terminate even though the failure to find a key in an index is "normal" behavior.

To remove a key-value pair from the collection, use the RemoveKey member function. You can also remove all key-value pairs and thus empty the collection using RemoveAll.

You can find out if a collection is empty by calling the IsEmpty member function. The GetCount member function returns the number of key-value pairs in the collection.

It is also possible to iterate through a collection. The GetStartPosition member function yields an iterator of type POSITION that can be used in subsequent calls to GetNextAssoc to obtain key-value pairs. Note that the order in which elements are returned is arbitrary and has no significance. In particular, these functions are not guaranteed to yield elements in ascending key order.

CMapStringToString collections can be serialized. They can be used in conjunction with the CArchive class and the << and >> operators.

Listing 26.1 shows a simple, yet functional program that implements a word vocabulary. This command-line application can be compiled from the command line (cl /MT vocab.cpp).

Listing 26.1. Using CMapStringToString in a console application.

```
#include <afx.h>
#include <iostream.h>
#include <stdio.h>

void main(void)
{
    CString wrd, def;
    CMapStringToString map;
    CStdioFile inf(stdin);

    cout << "Populating the dictionary\n";
    while (TRUE)
    {
        cout << "Enter word: ";
        cout.flush();
        inf.ReadString(wrd);
        if (wrd == "Q") break;
        cout << "Definition: ";
        cout.flush();
        inf.ReadString(def);
        map[wrd] = def;
    }
    if (map.IsEmpty())
    {
```

```
            cout << "Empty vocabulary!\n";
            exit(0);
        }
    cout << "Vocabulary populated with ";
    cout << map.GetCount() << " elements.\n";
    cout << "Looking up words in the dictionary\n";
    while (TRUE)
    {
        cout << "Enter word: ";
        cout.flush();
        inf.ReadString(wrd);
        if (wrd == "Q") break;
        if (map.Lookup(wrd, def))
            cout << def << '\n';
        else
            cout << "not found!\n";
    }
}
```

This program allocates a CMapStringToString collection and then enters an input loop. In this loop, corresponding word-definition pairs are entered by the user and added to the collection. The loop terminates when the user enters a capital *Q* for the word. At this time, after displaying the size of the collection, the program enters a second loop. In this loop, the user enters words that are to be looked up in the vocabulary. Here is a sample session with this program:

```
Populating the dictionary
Enter word: mouse
Definition: small, nocturnal rodent
Enter word: cat
Definition: small, domesticated carnivore
Enter word: dog
Definition: large, supposedly domesticated ugly animal that barks
Enter word: Q
Vocabulary populated with 3 elements.
Looking up words in the dictionary
Enter word: cat
small, domesticated carnivore
Enter word: mouse
small, nocturnal rodent
Enter word: rat
not found!
Enter word:
```

As I said, implementing a dictionary with these dictionary collections is indeed a trivially simple task.

The *CMapStringToOb* Class

The CMapStringToOb class maps objects of type CString to CObject pointers. That is, it uses string indexes to maintain a collection of CObject items. The obvious use of this class is to create a named set of CObject items.

The features and behavior of this class are almost identical to the features and behavior of CMapStringToString, with one crucial difference. As this class stores CObject pointers, it is the programmer's responsibility that any CObject items that are removed from the collection are destroyed. For example:

```
CObject *pObject;
CMapStringToOb myMap;
...
pObject = new CObject;
myMap["myObject"] = pObject;
...
// some time later
...
if (myMap.Lookup("myObject", pObject))
{
    myMap.RemoveKey("myObject");
    delete pObject;
};
```

CMapStringToOb can also be serialized and used with the CArchive class, and the << and >> operators.

The *CMapStringToPtr* Class

The CMapStringToPtr class maps objects of type CString to pointers to void. This class can be used to provide a collection of named items of arbitrary type.

Like the CMapStringToOb class, this class also stores pointers to items and does not free the items when the pointers are removed from the collection. It is the application programmer's responsibility to destroy the items the pointers point to.

Unlike the CMapStringToOb class, CMapStringToPtr collections cannot be serialized.

In all other respects, the features and behavior of CMapStringToPtr are identical to the features and behavior of CMapStringToOb.

The *CMapPtrToPtr* Class

The CMapPtrToPtr class maps void pointers to void pointers. Note that it is the pointer value that serves as a key to this collection, not the entities that these pointers refer. Thus, two pointers that refer to two identical but distinct objects will be treated as unequal keys by CMapPtrToPtr. For example, consider the following code:

```
CMapPtrToPtr myMap;
int a, b, x, y;
a = b = 123;
myMap[&a] = &x;
myMap[&b] = &y;
```

Although a and b are equal, &a and &b are not; consequently, this code adds two distinct key-value pairs to the collection.

When a key-value pair is removed from a CMapPtrToPtr collection, the application is responsible for destroying both entities that the two pointers (the key and the value) refer to.

The *CMapPtrToWord* Class

The CMapPtrToWord class maps void pointers to values of type WORD. Note that as with CMapPtrToPtr, it is the pointer value, not the entity it points to, that serves as the key to this collection.

When removing a key-value pair from this collection, applications should ensure that the entities the keys point to are appropriately destroyed.

The *CMapWordToOb* Class

The CMapWordToOb class maps an index of type WORD to items that are CObject pointers.

What is the difference between this class and a CObArray? In an array collection, indexes are assumed to start at zero and be consecutive. In contrast, the WORD indexes in a CMapWordToOb collection can be arbitrary. For example, to use the indexes 1 and 100 in a CObArray collection requires allocating memory for 101 elements; the same two indexes in a CMapWordToOb only occupy two slots in the collection.

Collections of type CMapWordToOb support serialization and work in conjunction with the CArchive class, and the << and >> operators.

The *CMapWordToPtr* Class

The CMapWordToPtr class maps an index of type WORD to items that are void pointers. The features and behavior of this class are identical to the features and behavior of CMapWordToOb with one exception: CMapWordToPtr does not support serialization.

Template-Based Object Collections

The collection classes that we have reviewed thus far are not type safe. Allow me to elaborate on this point.

Consider, for example, how a collection of CWnd objects would be implemented using CObList. Items that are CWnd pointers would be added to the list in a fashion similar to the following:

```
CWnd *pWnd;
CObList myList;
...
myList.AddTail((CObject *)pWnd);
...
pWnd = (CWnd *)(myList.GetHead());
```

Because of the typecast in the call to AddTail, the collection has no way of verifying that the object passed to it is indeed of the correct type. Similarly, when the item is retrieved from the collection, it is always a pointer to the CObject type. If, due to a programming error, a pointer of another CObject-derived type is passed to the collection, there will be no errors, no compiler warnings, but the application will silently fail. For example, you can add a pointer of type CDocument to the collection:

```
CDocument *pDoc;
...
myList.AddTail((CObject *)pDoc);
```

and not notice a thing; only later, when you retrieve this pointer assuming it is a pointer to a CWnd object, will your program show hard-to-analyze signs of misbehavior.

Type-safe collection templates provide a solution to this problem. By declaring the collection as follows:

```
CTypedPtrList<CObList, CWnd *> myList;
```

one can eliminate the need for typecasts and thus ensure that if anything other than a CWnd pointer is added to the collection, the compiler will indicate an error.

> **NOTE**
>
> It is also possible to derive type-safe versions from non-template collection classes by adding properly typed wrapper functions. However, the templates discussed here represent a more general approach.

There are two types of template collections. The first category consists of simple arrays, lists, and mappings; the second category consists of arrays, lists, and maps of typed pointers. Members of the first category are the CList, CArray, and CMap templates; members of the second category include CTypedPtrList, CTypedPtrArray, and CTypedPtrMap.

Collection Class Helper Functions

The simple collection templates CList, CArray, and CMap use seven collection class helper functions. Implementing these functions may be necessary in order for these classes to provide expected behavior.

For construction of elements, the collection classes use the ConstructElements helper function. ConstructElements is called after memory has been allocated for the new elements. The default implementation uses the constructor of type TYPE to create the elements. This function is used by all three simple collection templates when memory for new elements is allocated.

The function DestructElements is called before memory allocated for elements in the collection is deallocated. The default implementation of this function uses the destructor of type

TYPE to deinitialize collection elements. This function is also used by all three simple collection templates.

The CompareElements function compares two elements for equality. The default implementation uses the == operator for this purpose. This function is used by the function CList::Find and by CMap-based collections.

The CopyElements function copies elements. The default implementation performs a bitwise copy (hardly adequate in many situations). This function is used by the CArray::Append and CArray::Copy member functions.

The SerializeElements helper function serializes elements in the collection. The default implementation performs bitwise serialization (again, this is hardly adequate in many cases). Override this function, for example, when you wish to call the Serialize member function of your collection elements instead.

The HashKey helper function is used by CMap-based collections to create a hash key. The default implementation creates a hash key by right-shifting the key value by four bit positions. Override this member function if you wish to use a hash key that is more appropriate for your application.

Finally, the DumpElements member function is used to create a diagnostic dump of collection elements. The default implementation of this function does nothing. Override this function, for example, if you wish to call the Dump member function of the collection elements instead.

The *CList* Template

The CList template is used to create lists of a given element type. A list is an ordered collection of items; it supports access to these items using an iterator.

The CList template takes two parameters. It is declared as follows:

```
template<class TYPE, class ARG_TYPE> class CList : public CObject
{
...
};
```

Of the two parameters, TYPE represents the type of elements that the list consists of; ARG_TYPE represents the type used in function arguments. ARG_TYPE is often a reference to TYPE. For example, a list of CString objects could be declared as follows:

```
CList<CString, CString&> myList;
```

Although the behavior of a CList and a CObList are similar, note one fundamental difference: A CList stores objects of type TYPE, not pointers to those objects. In the previous example, for every CString that is added to the list, a copy of the item is created.

A `CList` collection is constructed when it is declared. Elements of type `TYPE` are added to the collection using the `AddHead` or `AddTail` member functions. You can also add elements at a given position, identified by a `POSITION` value using `InsertBefore` and `InsertAfter`.

An iterator of type `POSITION` can be obtained by calling `GetHeadPosition` or `GetTailPosition`. Iterating through elements in the collection can be done by repeatedly calling `GetNext` or `GetPrev`, as in the following example:

```
CList<CString, CString&> myList;
...
// Populate the list
...
POSITION pos = myList.GetHeadPosition();
while (pos != NULL)
{
    CString str = GetNext(pos);
    ...
    // Do something ugly with str
    ...
}
```

The head and tail element of the list can be obtained using the `GetHead` and `GetTail` member functions.

A `POSITION` value can also be used in calls to `GetAt`, `SetAt`, and `RemoveAt`. These member functions obtain an element at a given position, set the element at a given position to a new value, and remove an element at a given position.

The head or tail of the list can be removed by calling `RemoveHead` or `RemoveTail`. The entire list can be emptied by calling `RemoveAll`. To find out if the list is empty, call the `IsEmpty` member function; `GetCount` can be used to obtain the number of elements in the list.

Elements can be searched for by numerical index using the `FindIndex` function; and by value, using the `Find` function. Note that you may need to provide an override version of `CompareElements` in order for the `Find` member function to work correctly.

The `CList` template supports serialization. In order for serialization to work properly, it may be necessary to provide an override version of the `SerializeElements` helper function.

The CArray Template

The `CArray` template is used to create a dynamically allocated array of a given element type. An array is a collection of elements accessed through a zero-based integer index. The function and behavior of `CArray` are identical to the function and behavior of C arrays, with the important exception that a `CArray` can dynamically grow and shrink.

The `CArray` template takes two parameters. It is declared as follows:

```
template<class TYPE, class ARG_TYPE> class CArray : public CObject
{
...
};
```

The `TYPE` parameter represents the type of items that this collection consists of; the `ARG_TYPE` represents the argument type passed to functions. Often, `ARG_TYPE` is a reference to type. For example:

```
CArray<CString, CString&> myArray;
```

Despite the many similarities, there is a fundamental difference between the behavior of `CArray` and the non-template-based array collection `CObArray`. `CArray` stores copies the items themselves as opposed to pointers to items, as is the case with `CObArray`.

After declaring and thus constructing a `CArray` object, you can use the `SetSize` member function to set its size. To set an element at a given index, use the `SetAt` member function; to obtain an element at a given index, use `GetAt`. `SetAt` will not grow the array if an index is specified that is out of bounds. However, you can use `SetAtGrow` for this purpose. You can also add elements to the array and grow the array as necessary by calling the `Add` member function.

The `[]` operator is a shortcut for the `SetAt` and `GetAt` member functions. It can be used on both sides of an assignment operation. When used as an lvalue, it utilizes the `ElementAt` member function that retrieves a reference to the specified element.

The `SetSize` function can also be used to define the amount by which memory allocated for the array grows when additional memory is allocated. The default implementation attempts to use an optimal value to minimize heap fragmentation. Any extra memory thus allocated can be freed by calling the `FreeExtra` member function.

The current size of the array can be obtained by calling `GetSize`. The `GetUpperBound` function returns the maximum allowable index in the array (which is one less than the array's size).

It is possible to insert elements at a given location or remove an element at a given location using the `InsertAt` and `RemoveAt` functions. However, these operations may involve moving large chunks of data and thus tend to be slow.

Elements from another array (of the same type) can be copied into the array at a specified index position using the `Copy` member function, or appended to the end of the array using the `Append` member function. Proper operation of these functions may require that you provide an overloaded version of the `CopyElements` helper function.

The `CArray` class supports serialization. Proper serialization behavior may require that you provide an overloaded implementation of `SerializeElements`.

The *CMap* Template

The CMap collection template provides an indexed collection of key-value pairs. CMap is declared as follows:

```
template<class KEY, class ARG_KEY, class VALUE, class ARG_VALUE>
        class CMap : public CObject
{
    ...
};
```

KEY and VALUE represent the types of keys and values; ARG_KEY and ARG_VALUE represent types passed as function arguments. Often, ARG_KEY is a reference to KEY and ARG_TYPE is a reference to TYPE, as in the following example:

```
CMap<CString, CString&, CString, CString&> myMap;
```

An efficient implementation of a CMap-based collection may require that you provide a version of the HashKey function overloaded for your KEY type.

To use a CMap-based collection, construct it by declaring it. Key-value pairs can be added to the collection by calling the SetAt member function. The [] operator is a shortcut for this function. It can only be used in this situation; because not every key value is expected to be found in the collection, the [] operator cannot be used on the right-hand side of assignment expressions (in other words, as something other than an lvalue).

Elements in the collection can be found using the LookUp member function. An element identified by a given key can be removed using the RemoveKey member function; to remove all elements (empty the collection), call RemoveAll.

It is possible to iterate through the collection. An iterator of type POSITION can be obtained by calling GetStartPosition; elements can be obtained one by one by repeatedly calling GetNextAssoc. The order in which the elements are returned is arbitrary and is not expected to match the key order.

To obtain the number of elements, call GetCount. Call IsEmpty to determine whether the collection has any elements.

Two additional functions, InitHashTable and GetHashTable, can be used to initialize the collection's hashing table to a given size and to retrieve the hashing table's size.

The *CTypedPtrList* Template

The CTypedPtrList template provides a type-safe list of pointers by implementing a template wrapper for the non-template-based classes CObList and CPtrList. CTypedPtrList is declared as follows:

```
template<class BASE_CLASS, class TYPE>
        CTypedPtrList : public BASE_CLASS
```

```
{
...
};
```

The type `BASE_CLASS` should be either `CObList` or `CPtrList`. If `CObList` is used, `TYPE` must represent a pointer to `CObject`-derived class; if `CPtrList` is used, `TYPE` can be any kind of a pointer.

`CTypedPtrList` works by providing wrapper functions for all `CObList` or `CPtrList` member functions that refer to the collection elements by type. The wrapper functions perform any necessary type casting. Otherwise, the behavior of `CTypedPtrList` is identical to that of `CObList` or `CPtrList`. In particular, `CTypedPtrList` supports serialization of it is used in conjunction with `CObList`; however, serialization is not supported when `CPtrList` is used.

The *CTypedPtrArray* Template

The `CTypedPtrArray` collection template provides a type-safe array of pointers. This template is a wrapper for the non-template-based collections `CObArray` and `CPtrArray`. It is declared as follows:

```
template<class BASE_CLASS, class TYPE>
       CTypedPtrArray : public BASE_CLASS
{
...
};
```

The `BASE_CLASS` type should be either `CObArray` or `CPtrArray`. `TYPE` represents a pointer type; this must be a pointer to a `CObject`-derived type if `CObArray` is used as the `BASE_CLASS` but can be any pointer type if `CPtrArray` is used.

`CTypedPtrArray` works by providing a wrapper function for every `CObArray` or `CPtrArray` function that refers to collection elements by type. The wrapper functions also perform all necessary type casting.

Serialization is supported by `CTypedPtrArray`-derived classes if they are based on `CObArray`.

The *CTypedPtrMap* Template

The `CTypedPtrMap` template provides type-safe mappings. It is a wrapper template for the mapping collection classes `CMapPtrToPtr`, `CMapPtrToWord`, `CMapWordToPtr`, and `CMapStringToPtr`.

Type-safe behavior is provided by implementing wrapper functions for base class member functions that reference the type of elements.

`CTypedPtrMap`-based classes do not support serialization.

Summary

The Microsoft Foundation Classes Library provides a series of collection classes. There are several non-template-based collections, and also several type-safe collection templates.

Perhaps the most widely used collection classes are collections of CObject pointers. The CObList collection represents an ordered list (linked list) of CObject pointers and is used frequently for storing, for example, lists of windows in the MFC. Elements in the collection are accessed through an iterator of the special type POSITION. The other CObject pointer collection is CObArray; the function and behavior of this type of collection are similar to the function and behavior of C arrays with one crucial difference: a CObArray can dynamically grow and shrink. Both CObArray and CObList are serializable collections.

Other list collections include CPtrList (a list of void pointers) and CStringList (a list of CString items). Of these two, CPtrList does not support serialization.

Other array collections include CPtrArray, CStringArray, and a variety of integral array types. The CPtrArray class does not support serialization.

In addition to lists and arrays, the MFC Library also supports mappings. Mappings are unordered collections of key-value pairs indexed by the key. A variety of mapping classes provides support for keys of type CString, WORD, and pointers to void; values can be of type CString, WORD, pointers to void, and CObject pointers (not all combinations are supported). With the exception of mappings where either the key or the value (or both) are void pointers, mapping classes also support serialization.

Ever since template support was introduced in Visual C++, the MFC Library supports type-safe collection templates. Two types of collection templates exist; simple templates support collections of a specific type, and typed pointer templates support type-safe collections of pointers.

The simple collection templates rely on several overridable helper functions to work correctly. These include SerializeElements, which is used when collection items are serialized, and CompareElements, which is used when collection items are searched for by value. Other helper functions are used for construction and destruction, element copy, diagnostic dumping, and hashing.

The simple collection templates include CList (linked list collection), CArray (dynamically allocated array), and CMap (key-value mappings). The pointer-based collection templates include CTypedPtrList, CTypedPtrArray, and CTypedPtrMap.

The simple collection templates can be used with any type. They support serialization through the helper function SerializeElements.

The pointer-based collection templates rely on non-template collections for their behavior. Specifically, they build upon the behavior of CObList and CPtrList, CObArray and CPtrArray, and any of the pointer-based mapping classes (CMapPtrToPtr, CMapPtrToWord, CMapWordToPtr, and CMapStringToPtr). Serialization is supported by CTypedPtrList and CTypedPtrArray if they are used in conjunction with CObList and CObArray, but not when they are used in conjunction with CPtrList or CPtrArray. Serialization of pointer-based mapping templates is not supported.

Exceptions, Multithreading, and Other MFC Classes

27

Many MFC functions use C++ exceptions for reporting errors. We begin this chapter by looking at exception handling in MFC, with particular emphasis on C++ style exception handling and the CException class.

The MFC Library fully supports multithreading. Specific support for Win32 multithreading is available in the form of synchronization classes that wrap Win32 synchronization objects. MFC multithreading support and the CSyncObject class are the subject of the second half of this chapter.

Finally, we take a brief look at a series of miscellaneous MFC classes including simple data types, support classes for OLE and databases, and other classes and structures.

Using Exceptions in MFC Applications

The Microsoft Foundation Classes Library provides two different forms of exception handling. It supports C++ style typed expressions, and it also supports exception handling through old-style MFC macros.

Exception Handling with Macros

New applications should not use MFC exception processing macros. That said, as there are probably many applications out there that rely on the old, macro-based exception handling mechanism, it is probably helpful to have a brief summary of how those macros can be converted into code following the C++ exception syntax.

The first and most obvious step is to replace the macro names with C++ keywords. The macros TRY, CATCH and AND_CATCH, and THROW and THROW_LAST should be replaced with the C++ keywords try, catch, and throw. The END_CATCH macro has no C++ equivalent and should simply be deleted.

The syntax of the CATCH macro and the C++ catch keyword are different. What used to look like this:

```
CATCH(CException, e)
```

should be replaced with:

```
catch(CException *e)
```

An important difference between the two forms of exception handling is that when you are using the C++ exception handling mechanism, you are supposed to delete the exception object yourself. You can delete objects of type CException by calling their Delete member function. For example, if you used to catch an exception like this:

```
TRY
{
    // Do something nasty here
```

```
}
CATCH(CException, e)
{
    // Process the exception here
}
END_CATCH
```

should be translated into code similar to this:

```
try
{
    // Do something nasty here
}
catch (CException *e)
{
    // Process the exception here
    e->Delete();
}
```

> **NOTE**
>
> Do not attempt to delete an exception object in a catch block using the delete operator. The delete operator will fail if the exception object was not allocated on the heap.

C++ Exceptions and the *CException* Class

The C++ language provides support for the reporting and detection of abnormal conditions through typed exceptions. The MFC Library utilizes this support through a series of exception types that are derived from the class CException.

> **NOTE**
>
> The MFC Library does not directly support Win32 structured exceptions. If you wish to process structured exceptions, you may have to use the C style structured exception handling mechanism or write your own translator function that translates structured exceptions into C++ exceptions.

The primary function of the CException class is to provide a distinct type for MFC Library exceptions. It could fulfill that function even as an empty class. It does, however, provide several member functions that can be utilized when processing an exception.

The member function GetErrorMessage can be used to retrieve a textual description of the error. The member function ReportError can be used to retrieve this error message and display it in a standard message box. Note that not all exceptions caught by a CException handler have a valid error message associated with them.

The third member function that is important to know about is the Delete function. Use this function to delete an exception in a catch block if you process the exception. (Do not delete the exception if you use throw to pass it to another exception handler.)

There are several classes derived from CException (Figure 27.1). These classes are used to indicate errors and abnormal conditions relating to memory, file management, serialization, resource management, data access objects (DAO), database functions, OLE, and other categories. In the following sections, we review these exception classes individually.

FIGURE 27.1.

Exception classes in MFC.

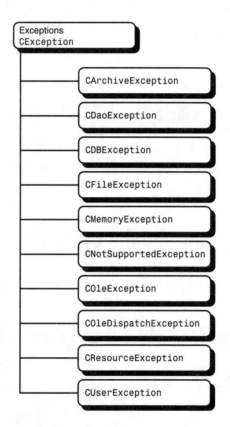

The *CMemoryException* Class

Exceptions of type CMemoryException are thrown to indicate a memory allocation failure. These exceptions are thrown automatically in MFC applications by the new operator. If you write your own memory allocation functions, you are responsible for throwing such exceptions yourself; for example:

```
char *p = malloc(1000);
if (p == NULL) AfxThrowMemoryException();
```

```
else
{
    // Populate p with data
}
```

The *CFileException* Class

Exceptions of type CFileException indicate one of many file-related failures. To determine the cause of the exception, examine the m_cause member variable. For example:

```
try
{
    CFile myFile("myfile.txt", CFile::modeRead);
    // Read the contents of the file
}
catch(CFileException *e)
{
    if (e->m_cause == CFileException::fileNotFound)
        cout << "File not found!\n";
    else
        cout << "A disk error has occurred.\n";
    e->Delete();
}
```

Table 27.1 lists the possible values of m_cause.

Table 27.1. CFileException::m_cause values.

Value	Description
none	No error.
generic	Unspecified error.
fileNotFound	File could not be located.
badPath	Part of the path name is invalid.
tooManyOpenFiles	Maximum number of open files exceeded.
accessDenied	Attempt to open file with insufficient privileges.
invalidFile	Attempt to use an invalid file handle.
removeCurrentDir	Attempt to remove current directory
directoryFull	Maximum number of directory entries reached.
badSeek	Could not set file pointer to specified location.
hardIO	Hardware error.
sharingViolation	Attempt to access a locked region.
lockViolation	Attempt to lock a previously locked region.
diskFull	The disk is full.
endOfFile	The end of the file was reached.

These m_cause values are operating system independent. If you wish to retrieve an operating system specific error code, examine the member variable m_lOsError.

Two member functions, OsErrorToException and ErrnoToException, can be used to translate operating system specific error codes and C run-time library error numbers into exception codes. Two helper member functions, ThrowOsError and ThrowErrno, can be used to throw exceptions using these error codes.

The *CArchiveException* Class

The CArchiveException class is used in exceptions indicating serialization errors. These exceptions are thrown by member functions of the CArchive class.

To determine the cause of the exception, examine the m_cause member variable. For example:

```
CMyDocument::Serialize(CArchive &ar)
{
    try
    {
        if (ar.IsLoading())
        {
            // Load from the archive here
        }
        else
        {
            // Store in the archive here
        }
    }
    catch (CArchiveException *e)
    {
        if (e->m_cause == CArchiveException::badSchema)
        {
            AfxMessageBox("Invalid file version");
            e->Delete();
        }
        else
            throw;
    }
}
```

Table 27.2 lists the possible values of m_cause.

Table 27.2. CArchiveException::m_cause **values.**

Value	Description
none	No error.
generic	Unspecified error.
readOnly	Attempt to store into an archive opened for loading.

Value	Description
endOfFile	The end of the file was reached.
writeOnly	Attempt to load from an archive opened for storing.
badIndex	Invalid file format.
badClass	Attempt to read an object of the wrong type.
badSchema	Incompatible schema number in class.

The *CNotSupportedException* Class

Exceptions of type CNotSupportedException are thrown when a feature is requested that is not supported. No further information is available on this error.

This exception is frequently used in overridden versions of member functions in derived classes when the derived class does not support a base class feature. For example, the class CStdioFile does not support the base class feature LockRange:

```
try
{
    CStdioFile myFile(stdin);
    myFile.LockRange(0, 1024);
    ...
}
catch (CNotSupportedException *e)
{
    cout << "Unsupported feature requested.\n";
    e->Delete();
}
```

The *CResourceException* Class

Exceptions of type CResourceException are thrown when a resource allocation fails or when a resource is not found. No further information is available on this error.

Exceptions of this type are used in conjunction with GDI resources. For example:

```
try
{
    CPen myPen(PS_SOLID, 0, RGB(255, 0, 0));
}
catch (CResourceException *e)
{
    AfxMessageBox("Failed to create GDI pen resource\n");
    e->Delete();
}
```

The *CDaoException* Class

CDaoException exceptions are used to indicate errors that occur when MFC database classes are used in conjunction with data access objects (DAO). All DAO errors are expressed in the form of DAO exceptions of the type CDaoException.

To obtain detailed information about the error, examine members of the CDaoErrorInfo structure pointed to by m_pErrorInfo. Further OLE and extended MFC error codes can be obtained by examining the member variables m_scode and m_nAfxDaoError.

To obtain information about a specific DAO error code, use the GetErrorInfo member function. To find out the number of error codes for which error information can be obtained, call GetErrorCount.

The *CDBException* Class

Exceptions of type CDBException are used to indicate errors that occur when using MFC ODBC database classes.

To obtain information about the error, examine the m_nRetCode member variable, that contains an ODBC error code. To obtain a textual description of the error, examine the m_strError member variable. More detailed information is available in the member variable m_strStateNativeOrigin, which provides a textual description of the error in the following format:

```
"State: %s,Native: %ld,Origin: %s"
```

In this string, the format codes are replaced as follows. The first code (%s) is replaced by a five character ODBC error code corresponding to the *szSqlState* parameter of the ::SQLError function. The second code corresponds to the *pfNativeError* parameter of ::SQLError and represents a native error code specific to the data source. Finally, the third code corresponds to error message text returned in the *szErrorMsg* parameter of ::SQLError.

The *COleException* Class

The COleException class is used in exceptions indicating general OLE errors. To obtain information about the error, examine the m_sc member variable, which contains an OLE status code.

The static member function Process can be used to turn any caught exception into an OLE status code. For example, this function, when passed an object of type CMemoryException, returns the OLE status code E_OUTOFMEMORY.

The *COleDispatchException* Class

Exceptions of type COleDispatchException are used to indicate OLE errors related to the OLE IDispatch interface. This interface is used in conjunction with OLE automation and OLE controls.

An error code specific to IDispatch can be obtained by examining the m_wCode member variable. The member variable m_strDescription contains a textual description of the error.

Additional member variables identify a help context (m_dwHelpContext), the name of the applicable help file (m_strHelpFile), and the name of the application that threw the exception (m_strSource).

The *CUserException* Class

Exceptions of type CUserException are meant to be used by application programs to indicate an error caused by the user. Typically, these exceptions are thrown after the user has been notified of the error condition through a message box.

Throwing an MFC Exception

If you wish to throw an MFC exception from your own code, you can do so by using one of the helper functions that are available in the MFC Library for this purpose. These helper functions are summarized in Table 27.3.

Table 27.3. Exception helper functions.

Function Name	*Action*
AfxThrowArchiveException	Throws a CArchiveException
AfxThrowDaoException	Throws a CDaoException
AfxThrowDBException	Throws a CDBException
AfxThrowFileException	Throws a CFileException
AfxThrowMemoryException	Throws a CMemoryException
AfxThrowNotSupportedException	Throws a CNotSupportedException
AfxThrowOleDispatchException	Throws a COleDispatchException
AfxThrowOleException	Throws a COleException
AfxThrowResourceException	Throws a CResourceException
AfxThrowUserException	Throws a CUserException

These functions take a varying number of parameters in accordance with the type of the exception being thrown.

These functions construct an exception object of the specified type, initialize it using the supplied parameters, and then throw the exception.

Naturally, you can also elect to construct an exception object and throw the exception manually. This may be necessary if you derive a class from CException yourself.

MFC and Multithreading

MFC support for multithreading has two aspects. First, the MFC Library is thread-safe; it can be used in the context of multithreading applications. Second, the library provides a series of classes that provide explicit support for multithreading-related synchronization objects in Win32.

Thread-Safe MFC

A curious, frequently seen phrase in the MFC documentation states that "MFC objects are not thread safe at the object level, only at the class level." I believe that this sentence requires more elaboration than what is provided in the pages of various MFC manuals.

If read at face value, this would mean that it is patently unsafe to use separate threads in your application to manipulate two member variables in, say, a CDocument-derived class of your application. If this were indeed the case, it would mean a very severe restriction on multithreading usage, almost to the point where it would render multithreading and the MFC fundamentally incompatible in most real-life situations. Fortunately, this is not so.

When you define member variables in an MFC-derived class of your own, you are responsible for making them thread-safe if necessary. This can be accomplished, for example, by providing wrapper functions that restrict access to these variables and by the judicious use of synchronization techniques inside those wrapper functions.

In view of this, what the sentence I quoted above really means is that for reasons of performance and simplicity, this was not done in the MFC Library. For this reason, accessing the same object from two different threads may fail because no synchronization mechanism is used.

Consider, for example, the case of a CString. When you assign a value to a CString object, it frees any memory previously allocated for it, allocates the necessary memory for the new string data, and copies the data to this memory block. These operations are not protected by synchronization techniques, which means that if another thread attempts to obtain the value of the CString, the object will be in an inconsistent transitory state. When the attempt is made to retrieve its value, only parts of the string may be returned, garbage information may be returned, or worse yet, an access violation may occur.

On the other hand, if you add a CString member variable to your own CDocument-derived class, you can make this a protected or private member variable and restrict access to it through wrapper functions. In the wrapper functions, you can use, for example, mutex objects to provide exclusive access to the CString. This way, different threads in your application will be able to safely access the same object.

In fact, notwithstanding the blanket statement quoted above, many MFC objects are actually safely accessible from separate threads *assuming that you know what you are doing*. For example, you can access a CString object through the operator LPCSTR operator from as many threads as you wish, but do not try to modify the same `CString` object from two different threads simultaneously!

The rule of thumb: Unless you *know* that what you are doing is safe, do not do it. By default, accessing an object from two different threads should be considered unsafe, unless you know explicitly that the particular access mechanism you intend to use has no harmful consequences.

Creating Threads in MFC

The MFC Library differentiates between two types of threads. *User-interface threads* are threads that have a message loop and process messages; *worker threads* are everything else.

The typical use of a user-interface thread is to create a message loop for a window that runs independently of your application's main message loop. The typical use of a worker thread is to perform some background processing (for example, background printing).

Creating a user-interface thread involves deriving a class from `CWinThread` and calling `AfxBeginThread` to create the thread object. In the class derived from `CWinThread`, you must override several `CWinThread` member functions. As a minimum, you must provide an override version of `InitInstance`, the member function that is called when the thread is initialized.

The creation of worker threads is simpler. Worker threads do not require a separate `CWinThread`-derived class; instead, `AfxBeginThread` is called with the address of the thread function.

Note that MFC objects should not be used in conjunction with threads not created using `AfxBeginThread`.

As an example for creating a worker thread, consider the following code:

```
UINT MyWorkerThread(LPVOID pParam)
{
    // Do something lengthy with pParam
    return 0; // Terminate the thread
}
...
    // elsewhere
    AfxBeginThread(MyWorkerThread, myParam);
```

Thread Synchronization

The Win32 API provides a series of synchronization objects that support the synchronization of concurrently executing threads. Of these, events, mutexes, critical sections, and semaphores are supported by MFC class wrappers.

The base class for all MFC synchronization classes is `CSyncObject`, which is a pure virtual base class. The hierarchy of MFC synchronization classes is shown in Figure 27.2.

FIGURE 27.2.
Synchronization classes.

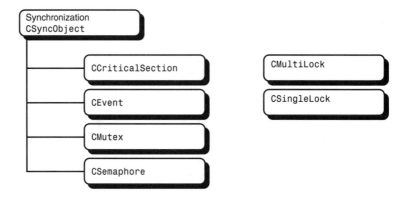

The `CSyncObject` class supports creation of a synchronization object by name through its constructor. Subsequently, the `Lock` and `Unlock` member functions can be used to gain access to, and release, the synchronization object. The specific meaning of these functions depends on the synchronization class being used.

`CSyncObject`-derived objects can be used in conjunction with the `CSingleLock` or `CMultiLock` classes. These classes provide an access control mechanism to the objects. After examining the synchronization classes, we return our attention to these synchronization access classes.

The *CEvent* Class

The `CEvent` class encapsulates the functionality of a Win32 event. An event's state is set to signaled by calling the `CEvent::SetEvent` function.

An event can be either a manual-reset event or an automatic event. A manual-reset event must be explicitly reset to its nonsignaled state; an automatic event is reset to nonsignaled when a waiting thread is released.

An event can be waited upon by calling the `Lock` member function. The `Unlock` member function is not used for `CEvent` objects.

The `PulseEvent` member function sets the event's state to signaled, releases waiting threads (if any), and resets the event's state to nonsignaled. In case of a manual-reset event, all waiting threads are released; in case of an automatic event, only a single thread is released.

The *CMutex* Class

Mutex objects, represented by the `CMutex` class, are used to gain mutually exclusive access to a resource. While one thread owns a mutex, other threads cannot gain access to it.

When you construct a `CMutex` object, you can specify in the call to the constructor whether you wish to initially own the mutex object. If yes, the constructor will not return until it gains ownership of the mutex object.

To otherwise gain ownership to a mutex object, call the Lock member function. To release the mutex object, call Unlock.

The *CCriticalSection* Class

Critical section objects have functionality similar to that of mutexes; however, critical sections are slightly more efficient but cannot be used across process boundaries. A critical section object is typically used to prevent multiple threads from executing the same piece of code simultaneously.

The critical section object is initialized by the CCriticalSection constructor. Subsequently, you can use the Lock and Unlock member functions to access the critical section. To access the underlying critical section object, you can use the operator CRITICAL_SECTION* operator.

Note that objects of type CCriticalSection cannot be used in conjunction with the classes CSingleLock and CMultiLock.

The *CSemaphore* Class

Semaphores are used to limit the number of accesses to a resource. Semaphore objects are represented by the CSemaphore class.

When a semaphore is object created through the CSemaphore constructor, you can specify the initial and maximum usage count. The usage count can be increased by calling CSemaphore::Lock; if the usage count exceeds the maximum usage count, this function will wait until the semaphore object becomes available. The usage count can be decreased by calling Unlock.

Synchronization with *CSingleLock* and *CMultiLock*

Synchronization objects of type CEvent, CMutex, and CSemaphore can be accessed through the synchronization access classes CSingleLock and CMultiLock.

To create an access object of type CSingleLock, create the synchronization object first, then pass a pointer to this object to the CSingleLock constructor. Subsequently, you can gain access to the object by calling CSingleLock::Lock and release the object using CSingleLock::Unlock. To determine if an object has been locked, use the CSingleLock::IsLocked member function.

The functionality of the CMultiLock class is similar to that of CSingleLock; however, CMultiLock makes it possible for you to wait on several synchronization objects at the same time.

To construct a CMultiLock object, pass an array of CSyncObject-derived objects to its constructor. Later, you can wait for any or all of these objects to become signaled by calling the Lock member function. The return value of this function identifies the object that was signaled. You can release that object by calling CMultiLock::Unlock. The CMultilock::IsLocked function can be used to determine the locked state of a specific synchronization object.

Note that objects of type `CCriticalSection` cannot be used in conjunction with `CSingleLock` and `CMultiLock`.

Miscellaneous MFC Classes

The Microsoft Foundation Classes Library provides a series of miscellaneous classes. Some of these are general purpose (for example, `CString`) while others are used in specific contexts. In the remainder of this chapter, we take a brief tour exploring these classes.

Simple Value Types

The MFC Library provides a series of classes that represent simple data types.

The `CPoint` class is an MFC wrapper for the Win32 `POINT` structure. A pointer to a `CPoint` object can be used every time when a pointer to a `POINT` structure is expected. The `CPoint` class supports a series of operators including addition and subtraction, testing for equality and in-equality, and the `+=` and `-=` operators. The `Offset` member function can be used to offset a `CPoint` by a given pair of values in the horizontal and vertical direction.

The `CRect` class wraps the functionality of the Win32 `RECT` structure. Pointers to objects of this class and pointers to structures of type `RECT` can be used interchangeably.

`CRect` supports a variety of member functions and overloaded operators to compare, copy, off-set, inflate, or deflate rectangles; calculate the union and intersection of two rectangles; and perform other operations.

The `CSize` class is an MFC wrapper for the Win32 `SIZE` structure. Pointers to type `CSize` and pointers to `SIZE` structures can be used interchangeably. The `CSize` class defines a series of operators for comparing, adding, and subtracting `CSize` objects.

The addition and subtraction operators can also be used with mixed types. Objects of type `CPoint` and `CRect` can be offset by an object of type `CSize` or `CPoint` using the addition or sub-traction operator.

The `CString` type represents a variable-length string. Memory for the string in a `CString` object is dynamically allocated and released as appropriate. Objects of type `CString` can be used to store ANSI and OEM strings, and on systems supporting Unicode (such as Windows NT), Unicode strings as well. The `CString` class defines a large variety of functions and operations that can be used for manipulating the string.

In particular, `CString` objects can be concatenated using the addition operator. They can be compared using the equality, less than, and greater than operators. The `Mid`, `Left`, and `Right` member functions can be used to perform operations similar to those available in the BASIC language. Other functions can be used to extract parts of a string, change the case of a string, find substrings in the string, and collate and compare strings.

The CString class supports loading a string value directly from a Windows resource file via the LoadString function.

The CString class also supports serialization and the use of the << and >> operators with CString objects in conjunction with the CArchive class.

CString objects can be used in many situations in place of pointers to type char, thanks to the existence of the operator LPCSTR operator.

The CTime class represents an absolute time; the CTimeSpan class represents the difference between two time values. Both of these classes support a variety of member functions to set, compare, and manipulate time values and to extract various elements (for example, seconds, minutes, hours) from time values. The CTime class also supports time zones and the conversion of a CTime value into a formatted string representing date and time. Both CTime and CTimeSpan support serialization and the use of the << and >> operators in conjunction with a CArchive.

Much of the functionality of these two classes has been superseded by the COleDateTime class.

Structures and Support Classes

There is a series of miscellaneous structures and classes in MFC that support specific areas of functionality.

The CCommandLineInfo encapsulates command line information in an MFC application. An object of type CCommandLineInfo or an object of a derived class can be used in conjunction with CWinApp::ParseCommandLine to parse the command line. The default implementation of CCommandLineInfo supports a filename on the command line and a variety of flags that specify printing, DDE, OLE automation, and editing an OLE-embedded item. If other command-line flags or parameters are needed, derive a class from CCommandLineInfo and override its ParseParam member function.

The CCreateContext class is used when the framework creates frame windows and views associated with a document in an MFC framework application. Member variables of CCreateContext are pointers identifying the view class, the document, and the view and the frame windows.

The CFileStatus structure is used by the functions CFile::GetStatus and CFile::SetStatus to retrieve and set a file's attributes (such as creation date, permissions, or the filename).

The CMemoryState class is used for detecting memory leaks. By creating CMemoryState objects and calling their Checkpoint member functions at various stages during program execution, you can verify that all allocated memory has been correctly released and dump the contents of unreleased objects.

The CPrintInfo class is used to store information about a print job. Objects of this type are used by the framework when calling printing relating member functions of the CView class.

The CCmdUI class is used in ON_UPDATE_COMMAND_UI handler functions of classes derived from CCmdTarget. Through objects of this type, applications can enable, disable, or otherwise manipulate user-interface items.

The CDataExchange class is used to support dialog data exchange. Objects of this type store context information that is used by dialog data exchange (DDX) and dialog data validation (DDV) functions. Classes of similar functionality include CPropExchange (used to exchange data on persistent properties of OLE controls), CFieldExchange (used for exchanging data between ODBC records and dialog controls), and CDaoFieldExchange (used for exchanging data between DAO records and dialog controls).

The CRectTracker class implements a tracking rectangle for on-screen objects. It is used by the framework in conjunction with embedded OLE objects, but can also be used by applications for application-specific objects.

The CWaitCursor class provides a one-line mechanism for displaying an hourglass cursor. When the object is constructed, the hourglass cursor is displayed; when the object is destroyed, the original cursor is restored. Declare an object of this class in functions that perform lengthy operations.

Additional support classes and structures provide support for OLE, OLE automation, ODBC, and DAO.

Summary

The MFC Library uses C++ style exceptions to communicate error conditions. Exceptions that are of a type derived from CException are thrown using a variety of helper functions and caught by your application.

Older MFC applications that predate C++ exception support in Visual C++ used a series of macros for this purpose. These macros can be easily translated into the C++ keywords try, throw, and catch.

The CException-derived classes that are used by MFC functions are summarized in Table 27.4.

Table 27.4. Exception helper functions.

Function Name	Action
CArchiveException	Serialization errors
CDaoException	Errors occurring with data access objects
CDBException	Errors occurring during ODBC usage
CFileException	File system errors
CMemoryException	Memory allocation failure

Function Name	Action
CNotSupportedException	Notification of unsupported feature request
COleDispatchException	OLE IDispatch errors (automation, controls)
COleException	Generic OLE errors
CResourceException	Resource allocation failure (GDI)
CUserException	Errors caused by the user

For every one of these exception types, there is a corresponding helper function (for example, AfxThrowArchiveException). You can also construct a CException-derived object and throw an exception manually.

In the exception handler, you are responsible for deleting the CException-derived object by calling its Delete member function.

You can also derive your own exception class from CException.

Multithreading support in MFC can be considered from two aspects. First, the MFC Library is thread-safe at the class level. Second, it provides multithreading support in the form of CWinThread and a series of synchronization classes derived from CSyncObject.

The MFC distinguishes between threads that maintain a message loop (user-interface threads) and threads that do not (worker threads). User-interface threads are created by deriving a type from CWinThread, while work threads only require a worker thread function. Both types of threads are created by calling AfxBeginThread.

CSyncObject-derived synchronization classes include CEvent, CMutex, CCriticalSection, and CSemaphore. All of these classes with the exception of CCriticalSection can be used in conjunction with the classes CSingleLock and CMultiLock.

The MFC Library defines a series of support classes that encapsulate various Win32 structures or provide support for various operations. Simple data types include CPoint, CSize, CRect, CString, CTime, and CTimeSpan. Other support classes and structures include CCommandLineInfo, CCreateContext, CFileStatus, CMemoryState, CPrintInfo, and CCmdUI. Dialog data exchange is supported by CDataExchange, and the specific classes CPropExchange, CFieldExchange, and CDaoFieldExchange. The CRectTracker class implements a tracking rectangle; the CWaitCursor class can be used to easily display an hourglass cursor. Additional support classes and structures exist for OLE, ODBC, and DAO.

PART

OLE in MFC Applications

Object Linking and Embedding: An Overview

28

Object linking and embedding is at the core of most modern Windows applications. It is also a very complex technology that would be difficult to master without the help of MFC.

However, in order to use the MFC Library efficiently for OLE applications, it is helpful to have a solid understanding of OLE fundamentals. While not strictly needed if you are satisfied with the "stock" implementation of basic OLE features in your application (provided by AppWizard), this understanding becomes essential if you wish to implement more advanced features, such as OLE drag and drop, linked OLE objects, or OLE-based clipboard operations.

OLE Basics and the Component Object Model

At the heart of OLE is a technology known as the *Component Object Model* (COM). COM is a binary standard that specifies how OLE components, or objects, interact with each other. It is important to note that COM is a language-independent standard; the only requirement is that the language used must support the concept of pointers and calling functions through pointers. Naturally, it is easier to develop OLE applications in object-oriented language environments.

Interfaces and Methods

A COM object is accessed exclusively through one or more sets of *interfaces*. An interface is a set of functions, also referred to as *methods*.

The COM standard not only specifies the binary object standard, it also defines a series of standard interfaces that provide common functionality.

Let me attempt to translate this into different terms. An OLE interface should best be thought of as a table of function pointers and information relating to those function pointers that define the parameters and return values of those functions. For example, methods of an OLE automation object are exposed through a METHODDATA structure, which is defined as follows:

```
typedef struct FARSTRUCT tagMETHODDATA {
    OLECHAR FAR* szName;
    PARAMDATA FAR* ppdata;
    DISPID dispid;
    UINT iMeth;
    CALLCONV cc;
    UINT cArgs;
    WORD wFlags;
    VARTYPE vtReturn;
} METHODDATA, FAR* LPMETHODDATA;
```

Of particular interest in this structure is the iMeth member. This member is an index into a table of function pointers. In C++ implementations, it is used in conjunction with the virtual function table of a C++ class.

Virtual function tables are not often on the C++ programmer's mind. While we accept and use the benefits of virtual functions, we rarely think of the specifics of their implementation. Allow me to present a quick reminder as to the whys and hows of virtual function implementation.

Virtual functions in C++ have been introduced to answer a common problem: namely, how to refer to member functions in a derived class when all you have is a pointer of base class type. By referring to derived functions through a table of function pointers, the compiler ensures that the function appropriate to the object in question is called, even when it lacks type information on the object otherwise.

A recommendation found in Stroustrup's *The Annotated C++ Reference Manual* suggests a table of function pointers preceding the object data. It is this table of functions that is also utilized through the indexes in the OLE METHODDATA structure.

Naturally, if you implement OLE in C or another language that does not automatically build virtual function tables, it may become necessary to construct those tables by hand.

An obvious consequence of this is that all OLE methods, if declared as C++ member functions, must be declared with the virtual keyword. This is accomplished by using a standard set of macros; more about it later in this chapter.

It is important to realize that a COM interface is not the same as the C++ class, object, or C structure that is used to implement the interface. The COM standard specifies how interfaces are exposed; it does not specify the implementation of methods. In other words, we know through the COM standard how to interpret tables that reference function addresses; however, the standard says nothing about how those functions implement the expected behavior.

Interfaces are strongly typed. Furthermore, an interface cannot be changed or altered. It is not possible to add methods to, or remove methods from, an interface; doing so creates a new interface. (Of course, COM objects can implement multiple interfaces.)

Methods and Memory Allocation

Of particular interest when implementing methods is the issue of memory allocation. OLE defines specific rules for cases when it becomes necessary for the caller to pass a pointer to the called method, or for the method to return data in the form of a pointer to the caller.

When memory is allocated by the caller, it must be freed by the caller.

When memory is allocated by the method, it must be freed by the caller. The exception is error conditions; in such cases, the method must ensure that memory allocated by it will be reliably freed and furthermore, that all returned pointers are explicitly set to NULL as appropriate.

When a pointer is passed to the method, the method may free the memory associated with it and reallocate. The caller is responsible for freeing the final value. However, if an error occurs, the method is responsible for releasing any memory allocations it made.

OLE provides a memory allocation interface (the IMalloc interface) that provides thread-safe memory allocation methods. A pointer to this allocator can be obtained by calling the CoGetMalloc OLE function.

Inheritance and Reusing Objects

Inheritance and reusability are terms with specific meanings for the developer of object-oriented code. These terms imply the capability of deriving your own classes from base classes, replacing methods with customized versions, and adding methods of your own. None of this is available with respect to COM objects. Although it is possible to inherit an interface, that does not mean inheritance of functionality; the interface contains no implementation.

Instead, COM objects are treated as black boxes. Nothing is known about the details of the implementation of the interface, only the specifications of the interface itself. In other words, what we know is the object's behavior, not how that behavior is implemented.

OLE offers two specific mechanisms for reusability. Containment/delegation is a mechanism whereas "outer" objects act as clients to "inner" objects acting as servers. Sounds familiar? Think of an OLE drawing embedded in a Word document. The other mechanism, aggregation, enables outer objects to expose interfaces from inner objects, making it appear as if the outer object implemented those interfaces itself.

Interface Identifiers

Interfaces are identified through *globally unique identifiers*, or GUIDs. GUIDs are 128-bit identifiers that are unique (hopefully) throughout the world. Thus, a programmer assigning a GUID to an interface can reasonably expect that no other interface, no matter who develops it, would conflict with this one with an identical identifier.

The Visual C++ development system provides two utilities that help you generate globally unique identifiers. Both the command-line utility uuidgen.exe and the Windows utility guidgen.exe can be used for this purpose. The guidgen.exe utility can create identifiers in a form suitable for pasting into source code.

These programs rely on the OLE API function CoCreateGuid, which in turn uses the RPC function UuidCreate to create an identifier that is globally unique to a high degree of certainty.

Interface Definition Through *IUnknown*

All COM objects must implement the interface known as IUnknown. This interface defines three essential methods: QueryInterface, AddRef, and Release.

The AddRef and Release methods are used to manage the lifetime of an object. They are typically implemented as functions that increase or decrease a reference count. When the reference count in Release reaches zero, the object should be destroyed.

`QueryInterface` is used to query the object about specific interfaces. This method receives a unique identifier for the interface requested; upon return, it should supply an indirect pointer to the interface, or an error if the requested interface is not supported by the object.

To add support for the `IUnknown` interface in a C++ class, you can derive the class from the class `IUnknown`, which is declared in `unknwn.h`. The member functions `QueryInterface`, `AddRef`, and `Release` are declared as pure virtual functions; you must supply your own implementation.

OLE Class Objects and Registration

An OLE class object should not be confused with the concept of a class in object-oriented languages. It is merely another COM object, one that specifically implements the `IClassFactory` interface. This interface is the key to a fundamental OLE capability. Through the `IClassFactory` interface, applications that were written without any knowledge as to the particular class can still create objects for that class.

This is accomplished in part by *registering* the class, and in part by specific methods within the class.

A class is identified through a CLSID, which is just another GUID. The operating system maintains a database of all registered CLSIDs in the system. What this means in the Windows environment is a set of entries in the Windows Registry. Registration entries are made in the form of a subkey under `HKEY_CLASSES_ROOT\CLSID`, identified by the CLSID in string form.

Applications that are aware of a CLSID can use the OLE API functions `CoGetClassObject` and `CoCreateInstance` to create a class object, or create an uninitialized object of the kind associated with the CLSID.

Inter-Object Communication

Once you have obtained a pointer to an interface, you can call the methods in that interface. If the interface is within the same process as the caller, the call is made directly to the functions implementing the methods of the interface, with no intervening operating system code. However, if the interface is outside the boundaries of the current process, an intervening infrastructure becomes essential. (Remember that Win32 processes run in their own private memory space and do not see each others' processes or data.)

In order for a call to reach a server across process boundaries, it is necessary for a mechanism to exist that packages the call's parameters in the client side, and unpackages them on the server side. The process of packaging parameters for transmission across process boundaries is called *marshaling*; the process of unpackaging them on the server side is called *unmarshaling*. OLE provides a useful and efficient marshaling mechanism (standard marshaling) but also enables developers to implement customized marshaling techniques (custom marshaling).

Marshaling is always performed by a *proxy object*, an object which, from the client's point of view, looks, feels, and smells like the real thing. The only difference is that the table of function pointers representing the object's methods point to stub implementations instead of actual ones. The stub implementations translate a call on the client side into a call on the server side using a communication mechanism such as Remote Procedure Calls (RPCs). Neither the client nor the server sees any difference between calls made in-process, and calls made across process boundaries.

Monikers

Monikers are COM objects that implement the IMoniker interface. Through this interface, applications can obtain a pointer to an object identified by the moniker. They can do so by calling the IMoniker method BindToObject.

OLE identifies several types of monikers. File monikers are those that identify objects stored in their own files. Item monikers identify objects contained within another object; for example, an embedded object in an OLE container document or a user selection such as a range of cells in a spreadsheet. Composite monikers are concatenations of monikers; you can think of them, for example, as concatenated partial pathnames that form a complete pathname. Finally, anti-monikers serve the same role in composite monikers as the ".." symbol does in pathnames, effectively removing parts of a composite moniker just like using ".." removes parts of a path from a pathname.

Monikers are used as a method of naming COM objects. Monikers can be saved so the naming is persistent. A special, rarely used moniker type, the pointer moniker, provides a moniker-like wrapping of interface pointers that can be passed whenever a moniker is expected. However, pointer monikers are not persistent; they cannot be saved.

OLE and Threads

OLE defines a specific approach for thread-safe implementation. This *apartment model* defines a set of rules applications must follow if they wish to create and access objects from within separate threads of the same process.

The apartment model groups objects by owner thread. Objects can only live in a single thread (an *apartment*). Within the same thread, methods can be called directly; however, when calls are made across thread boundaries, the same marshaling technique must be used as with calls across process boundaries. The OLE libraries provide a set of helper functions for this purpose.

OLE and Compound Documents

The most commonly known use of OLE technology is in the form of OLE containers and servers. Together, container and server applications enable users to manipulate, within a single application, data coming from different sources and several applications.

Compound document technology is based, in addition to the Component Object Model, on OLE Structured Storage and OLE Uniform Data Transfer.

Structured Storage

OLE provides two interfaces that closely mimic traditional functions found in most disk-based file systems.

The IStorage interface provides functionality analogous to that of file systems (directories). Just like disk-based directories, a storage object can contain hierarchical references to other storage objects. It also tracks the locations and sizes of other objects stored within.

The IStream interface is analogous to a file. As its name implies, a stream object contains data as a contiguous sequence of bytes.

OLE compound files consist of a root storage object with at least one stream object representing native data. Additional storage objects can represent linked or embedded items. File-based storage is implemented with the help of the IRootStorage interface.

Objects that can be embedded within container application documents must implement the IPersistStorage interface, which enables the object to be saved in a storage object. Other persistent storage-related interfaces include IPersistStream and IPersistFile.

Structured storage has many benefits other than providing the means to treat a hierarchical set of objects as a single file. As in the case of real file systems, replacing a single object does not require that the entire compound file be rewritten. Objects can be accessed individually, without having to load the entire file. Structured storage also provides facilities for concurrent access by several processes and for transaction-based processing (commit and reverse functionality).

The OLE compound file implementation is operating system and file system independent. A compound file created, for example, on a FAT file system under Windows 95 can be reused from within a Windows NT application on an NTFS file system or by a Macintosh application using the Macintosh file system.

Storage and stream objects are named according to a set of conventions. The root storage object is named as the underlying file, with the same restrictions on naming as applicable for the file system. Names of nested elements that are up to 32 characters in length (including any terminating null characters) must be supported by implementations. Whether a case conversion is applied to names or not is an implementation-defined behavior.

Data Transfer

Transferring data between applications is accomplished through the IDataObject interface. This interface provides a mechanism for transferring data and also for notifications of changes in the data.

Data transfer occurs with the help of two structures: FORMATETC and STGMEDIUM. The FORMATETC structure is defined as follows:

```
typedef struct tagFORMATETC
{
    CLIPFORMAT  cfFormat;
    DVTARGETDEVICE  *ptd;
    DWORD  dwAspect;
    LONG  lindex;
    DWORD  tymed;
}FORMATETC;  *LPFORMATETC;
```

This structure generalizes the idea of clipboard formats, providing, in addition to the cfFormat parameter, parameters that identify the target device for which the data was composed and information on how the data should be rendered.

The STGMEDIUM structure generalizes the idea of global memory handles used in traditional Windows clipboard operations. This structure is defined as follows:

```
typedef struct tagSTGMEDIUM
{
    DWORD tymed;
    union {
        HBITMAP hBitmap;
        HMETAFILEPICT hMetafilePict;
        HENHMETAFILE hEnhMetaFile;
        HGLOBAL hGlobal;
        LPOLESTR lpszFileName;
        IStream *pstm;
        IStorage *pstg;
    };
    IUnknown *pUnkForRelease;
}STGMEDIUM;
```

Through these two structures, providers and recipients of data can negotiate the types of data they can send and accept along with the most efficient storage mechanism used in transmitting the data.

Compound Documents

OLE compound documents may, in addition to native data, contain two types of items: *linked objects* and *embedded objects*.

Linked objects represent objects that continue to reside where they were originally created (for example, in a file). The compound document contains a reference to this item (a *link*) and information on how the item should be presented. The container can present the linked item without activating the link—indeed, it can present the item even if the application that created the item is not available on a particular system. Activating the link means invoking the server application for editing and manipulating link data. The use of links results in small container documents and is also beneficial if the linked item is routinely maintained by a user other than the owner of the container document.

Embedded objects reside physically within the container document. The advantage of using embedded objects is that documents can be manipulated as single files; in contrast, when linked items are used, several files may need to be exchanged between users. Furthermore, links are easily broken if linked items are moved. (Windows currently does not implement a tracking mechanism for linked items.)

Servers for objects in a container document are implemented either as *in-process servers* or as *local servers.* An in-process server is essentially a DLL running in the process space of the container application. The major advantage of an in-process server is performance; methods in such a server are called directly, without the associated OLE overhead. However, local servers offer several benefits also. They can support links (in-process servers cannot); they provide compatibility with OLE1; and they provide the added benefits of running in a separate process space (increased robustness, ability to serve multiple concurrent clients).

Compound documents also support *in-place activation.* The in-place activation mechanism enables embedded items to be edited within the container application's window.

Basic support for compound document containers and servers comes in the form of the `IOleClientSite` and `IOleObject` interfaces. Servers also implement the `IDataObject` and `IPersistStorage` interface; furthermore, in-process servers implement `IViewObject2` and `IOleCache2`. In-place activation is accomplished via the `IOleInPlaceSite`, `IOleInPlaceObject`, `IOleInPlaceFrame`, and `IOleInPlaceActiveObject` interfaces.

Applications of OLE

Calling OLE Object Linking and Embedding is somewhat of a misnomer. As the discussion to this point should have made obvious, OLE is a set of specifications going far beyond mere object linking and embedding capability. Indeed, compound documents are just one of the many applications of OLE; other uses include OLE automation, OLE drag and drop, and OLE controls, which we review shortly. OLE also finds its way into specialized areas; for example, much of MAPI, the Messaging Application Programming Interface, is based on OLE.

Most OLE applications require specific registration entries. Entries in the Windows Registry are typically made under the keys `HKEY_CLASSES_ROOT\CLSID` and `HKEY_CLASSES_ROOT\Interface`.

OLE Document Containers and Servers

OLE containers and servers together implement compound document technology. OLE containers maintain compound documents consisting of linked and embedded items; the OLE servers provide such linked and embedded items and the functionality required for their activation.

OLE Automation

OLE automation enables an OLE automation server application to expose automation objects through a series of properties and methods. Information about properties and methods is published through the IDispatch interface. By querying this interface, automation clients can obtain information about the properties and methods identified by name.

OLE automation objects need not be visible objects. For example, an OLE automation server may perform scientific calculations, do spell checking, or supply physical constants identified by name, without ever presenting a visual interface on its own.

OLE automation clients, also known as automation controllers, are applications that manipulate OLE automation objects. Automation controllers can be generic (for instance a programming environment, such as Visual Basic) or can be developed to control specific automation objects.

OLE Drag and Drop

OLE drag and drop provides a powerful mechanism for implementing drag and drop functionality.

OLE drag and drop capabilities are implemented through the IDropSource and IDropTarget interfaces and the DoDragDrop function. After receiving the data item that is the object of the drag and drop operation and a pointer to an IDropSource interface, DoDragDrop enters a loop during which it tracks mouse events. If the mouse is over a window, DoDragDrop checks whether that window is registered as a valid drop target. DoDragDrop calls various methods of IDropTarget and IDropSource to carry out its operation.

Drag and drop functionality and clipboard cut and paste are very similar. Often it is beneficial to implement these two areas of functionality together, reusing code as much as possible.

OLE Controls

OLE controls represent a 32-bit replacement technology for Visual Basic controls. OLE controls are OLE objects that provide an extended interface, which implements the behavior of a Windows control. OLE control servers are typically implemented as in-process servers (an OCX file is simply a dynamic link library with a special filename extension). OLE control containers are applications that support OLE controls in their windows or dialogs.

OLE Custom Interfaces

For specialized applications, you can also develop your own OLE custom interfaces. Custom interfaces are developed using the tools available in the Microsoft Windows Software Development Kit, including the Microsoft Interface Definition Language (MIDL) compiler.

A Simple Example

Before I began writing this chapter, I did not think that including a meaningful example was possible. While programs with OLE capabilities are simple to write through the MFC Library, use of MFC frequently obscures the underlying technology. Presenting a set of instructions that tell you which buttons to push in the Developer Studio would have helped little in furthering your understanding of the underlying concepts and principles. Pasting a large, complex piece of AppWizard-generated code into my manuscript would have helped even less.

However, after spending some time thinking on this issue, I realized that it is possible to write an OLE program that is small, compact, yet demonstrates some of the OLE fundamentals. The application I am going to present in the remainder of this chapter is little more than 300 lines in length, is contained within a single file, yet provides all the capabilities of an OLE automation server.

Why an automation server? In a sense, OLE automation exposes the underlying mechanisms in their purest form. Were I to implement, for example, an OLE container, it would require dealing with formats, visual presentation of the data, management of windows, and other issues. The same applies for OLE drag and drop. The complexity of these applications would have ruled out their utility in demonstrating fundamental concepts in any meaningful manner.

In contrast, an automation server can be implemented with a minimum of fuss, and its use can be easily demonstrated with a few lines of script in an automation client, such as Visual Basic.

Functional Description

What should the simplest automation server do? The venerable traditions of C and C++ programming dictate the only reasonable answer: Obviously, it should present the string "Hello, World!"

The automation server that I set out to write does exactly that; it presents a string containing this text in the middle of its window, while also exposing the string as an OLE automation property through a pair of get and put methods.

Assuming that the server has been properly installed, it can be used from any OLE automation client. To exercise the server from Visual Basic, create a form with a single button, and attach the code shown in Listing 28.1 to the button. This code activates the server and changes the default text of the server to the text specified in the Visual Basic code.

Listing 28.1. Using the HELLO automation server from Visual Basic.

```
Sub Command1_Click ()
Dim hello As object
Set hello = CreateObject("HELLO.Application")
```

continues

Listing 28.1. continued

```
hello.text = "Hello from Visual Basic!"
End Sub
```

As this Visual Basic code demonstrates, the Hello application exposes exactly one property that is a property of the application object. This `text` property determines what text is shown in the middle of the application's window and can be both read from and written to. Figure 28.1 shows the Hello application after its text has been changed from within Visual Basic.

FIGURE 28.1.

Manipulating the Hello server from Visual Basic.

Hello from Visual Basic!

> **NOTE**
>
> Visual Basic is an excellent tool for testing OLE Automation servers. As this example demonstrates, you can test a server by adding a button to a Visual Basic form and writing a few lines of code in mere seconds. However, if you do not have Visual Basic installed on your system, do not despair; Microsoft has included the program `disptest.exe`, a simplified version of Visual Basic 3.0, for the express purpose of aiding OLE automation server development.

The Hello Server Application

Listing 28.2 shows the complete Hello server application. We begin our review of its operations at the `WinMain` function. But first, a note: For the sake of compactness, this application contains no error checking code. If it works, it works; if it doesn't, strange things are bound to happen.

Listing 28.2. An OLE automation server.

```
#include <windows.h>
#include <initguid.h>
```

```
#ifndef INITGUID
#define INITGUID
#endif

DEFINE_GUID(CLSID_CHello, 0xfeb8c280, 0xfd2d, 0x11ce, 0x87, 0xc3,
                          0x0, 0x40, 0x33, 0x21, 0xbf, 0xac);

static PARAMDATA rgpDataTEXT = { OLESTR("TEXT"), VT_BSTR };

enum IMETH_CTEXT
{
    IMETH_SET = 0,
    IMETH_GET,
};

enum IDMEMBER_CTEXT
{
    IDMEMBER_TEXT = DISPID_VALUE
};

static METHODDATA rgmdataCHello[] =
{
    { OLESTR("TEXT"), &rgpDataTEXT, IDMEMBER_TEXT, IMETH_SET,
      CC_CDECL, 1, DISPATCH_PROPERTYPUT, VT_EMPTY },
    { OLESTR("TEXT"), NULL, IDMEMBER_TEXT, IMETH_GET,
      CC_CDECL, 0, DISPATCH_PROPERTYGET, VT_BSTR }
};

INTERFACEDATA idataCHello =
{
    rgmdataCHello, 2
};

class CHello;

class CText
{
public:
    STDMETHOD_(void, Set)(BSTR text);
    STDMETHOD_(BSTR, Get)(void);
    CText(CHello *pHello, char *p = NULL);
    ~CText();
    void Paint();
    HWND m_hwnd;
private:
    char *m_text;
    CHello *m_pHello;
};

class CHello : public IUnknown
{
public:
    static CHello *Create(char *p);
    STDMETHOD(QueryInterface)(REFIID riid, void **ppv);
    STDMETHOD_(unsigned long, AddRef)(void);
    STDMETHOD_(unsigned long, Release)(void);
```

continues

Listing 28.2. continued

```
    CHello(char *p = NULL);
    CText m_text;
private:
    IUnknown *m_punkStdDisp;
    unsigned long m_refs;
};

class CHelloCF : public IClassFactory
{
public:
    static IClassFactory *Create();
    STDMETHOD(QueryInterface)(REFIID riid, void **ppv);
    STDMETHOD_(unsigned long, AddRef)(void);
    STDMETHOD_(unsigned long, Release)(void);
    STDMETHOD(CreateInstance)(IUnknown *punkOuter,
                              REFIID riid, void **ppv);
    STDMETHOD(LockServer)(BOOL fLock);
    CHelloCF() { m_refs = 1; }
private:
    unsigned long m_refs;
};

CHello *pHello;

CText::CText(CHello *pHello, char *p)
{
    m_pHello = pHello;
    if (p != NULL)
    {
        m_text = new char[strlen(p) + 1];
        strcpy(m_text, p);
    }
    else m_text = NULL;
    m_hwnd = NULL;
}

CText::~CText()
{
    delete[] m_text;
}

STDMETHODIMP_(void) CText::Set(BSTR p)
{
    char *bf;
    int size;
    size =
     WideCharToMultiByte(CP_ACP, NULL, p, -1, NULL, 0, NULL, NULL);
    bf = new char[size];
    WideCharToMultiByte(CP_ACP, NULL, p, -1, bf, size, NULL, NULL);

    delete[] m_text;
    if (p != NULL)
    {
        m_text = new char[strlen(bf) + 1];
        strcpy(m_text, bf);
    }
```

```
        else m_text = NULL;
        if (m_hwnd != NULL) InvalidateRect(m_hwnd, NULL, TRUE);
}

STDMETHODIMP_(BSTR) CText::Get()
{
    static WCHAR *wbf;
    BSTR bbf;
    int size;
    size = MultiByteToWideChar(CP_ACP, 0, m_text, -1, NULL, 0);
    wbf = new WCHAR[size];
    MultiByteToWideChar(CP_ACP, 0, m_text, -1, wbf, size);
    bbf = SysAllocString(wbf);
    delete[] wbf;
    return bbf;
}

void CText::Paint()
{
    HDC hDC;
    PAINTSTRUCT paintStruct;
    RECT clientRect;

    if (m_text != NULL)
    {
        hDC = BeginPaint(m_hwnd, &paintStruct);
        if (hDC != NULL)
        {
            GetClientRect(m_hwnd, &clientRect);
            DPtoLP(hDC, (LPPOINT)&clientRect, 2);
            DrawText(hDC, m_text, -1, &clientRect,
                    DT_CENTER | DT_VCENTER | DT_SINGLELINE);
            EndPaint(m_hwnd, &paintStruct);
        }
    }
}

CHello *CHello::Create(char *p)
{
    ITypeInfo *pTI;
    IUnknown *pUnk;
    CHello *pHello = new CHello(p);
    pHello->AddRef();
    CreateDispTypeInfo(&idataCHello, LOCALE_SYSTEM_DEFAULT, &pTI);
    CreateStdDispatch(pHello, &(pHello->m_text), pTI, &pUnk);
    pTI->Release();
    pHello->m_punkStdDisp = pUnk;
    return pHello;
}

STDMETHODIMP CHello::QueryInterface(REFIID riid, void **ppv)
{
    if (IsEqualIID(riid, IID_IUnknown))
        *ppv = this;
    else
    if (IsEqualIID(riid, IID_IDispatch))
        return m_punkStdDisp->QueryInterface(riid, ppv);
    else
```

continues

Listing 28.2. continued

```
    {
        *ppv = NULL;
        return ResultFromScode(E_NOINTERFACE);
    }
    AddRef();
    return NOERROR;
}

STDMETHODIMP_(unsigned long) CHello::AddRef()
{
    return ++m_refs;
}

STDMETHODIMP_(unsigned long) CHello::Release()
{
    if (--m_refs == 0)
    {
        if(m_punkStdDisp != NULL) m_punkStdDisp->Release();
        PostQuitMessage(0);
        delete this;
        return 0;
    }
    return m_refs;
}

#pragma warning(disable:4355)
CHello::CHello(char *p) : m_text(this, p)
{
    m_refs = 0;
}

IClassFactory *CHelloCF::Create()
{
    return new CHelloCF;
}

STDMETHODIMP CHelloCF::QueryInterface(REFIID riid, void **ppv)
{
    if(IsEqualIID(riid, IID_IUnknown) ||
       IsEqualIID(riid, IID_IClassFactory))
    {
        AddRef();
        *ppv = this;
        return NOERROR;
    }
    *ppv = NULL;
    return ResultFromScode(E_NOINTERFACE);
}

STDMETHODIMP_(unsigned long) CHelloCF::AddRef()
{
    return m_refs++;
}

STDMETHODIMP_(unsigned long) CHelloCF::Release()
{
```

```
        if (--m_refs == 0)
        {
            delete this;
            return 0;
        }
        return m_refs;
}

STDMETHODIMP CHelloCF::CreateInstance(IUnknown *punkOuter,
                                      REFIID riid, void **ppv)
{
    if(punkOuter != NULL)
        return ResultFromScode(CLASS_E_NOAGGREGATION);
    return pHello->QueryInterface(riid, ppv);
}

STDMETHODIMP CHelloCF::LockServer(BOOL fLock)
{
    return NOERROR;
}

LRESULT CALLBACK WndProc(HWND hwnd, UINT uMsg,
                         WPARAM wParam, LPARAM lParam)
{
    switch(uMsg)
    {
        case WM_PAINT:
            pHello->m_text.Paint();
            break;
        case WM_DESTROY:
            PostQuitMessage(0);
            break;
        default:
            return DefWindowProc(hwnd, uMsg, wParam, lParam);
    }
    return 0;
}

int WINAPI WinMain(HINSTANCE hInstance, HINSTANCE hPrevInstance,
                   LPSTR d3, int nCmdShow)
{
    MSG msg;
    HWND hwnd;
    WNDCLASS wndClass;
    IClassFactory *pHelloCF;
    unsigned long dwHelloCF = 0;
    unsigned long dwRegHello = 0;

    OleInitialize(NULL);
    pHello = CHello::Create("Hello, World!");
    pHelloCF = CHelloCF::Create();
    CoRegisterClassObject(CLSID_CHello, pHelloCF,
        CLSCTX_LOCAL_SERVER, REGCLS_MULTIPLEUSE, &dwHelloCF);
    RegisterActiveObject(pHello, CLSID_CHello, NULL, &dwRegHello);
    pHelloCF->Release();

    if (hPrevInstance == NULL)
    {
```

continues

Listing 28.2. continued

```
        memset(&wndClass, 0, sizeof(wndClass));
        wndClass.style = CS_HREDRAW | CS_VREDRAW;
        wndClass.lpfnWndProc = WndProc;
        wndClass.hInstance = hInstance;
        wndClass.hCursor = LoadCursor(NULL, IDC_ARROW);
        wndClass.hbrBackground = (HBRUSH)(COLOR_WINDOW + 1);
        wndClass.lpszClassName = "HELLO";
        if (!RegisterClass(&wndClass)) return FALSE;
    }
    hwnd = CreateWindow("HELLO", "HELLO",
                        WS_OVERLAPPEDWINDOW,
                        CW_USEDEFAULT, 0, CW_USEDEFAULT, 0,
                        NULL, NULL, hInstance, NULL);
    pHello->m_text.m_hwnd = hwnd;
    ShowWindow(hwnd, nCmdShow);
    UpdateWindow(hwnd);
    while (GetMessage(&msg, NULL, 0, 0))
        DispatchMessage(&msg);
    RevokeActiveObject(dwRegHello, NULL);
    CoRevokeClassObject(dwHelloCF);
    pHello->Release();
    OleUninitialize();
    return msg.wParam;
}
```

WinMain begins with a call to OleInitialize. Calling this function is necessary to initialize the OLE libraries.

Next, two objects are created; an object of type CHello and an object of type CHelloCF. The first represents the interfaces of the application object; the second provides an IClassFactory interface. More about this in a moment.

The availability of the class object is published through the call to CoRegisterClassObject. The active object that the class represents is registered through the call to RegisterActiveObject. Subsequently, the class object can be released.

The rest of WinMain simply implements a plain window in which the application's text will be displayed and a standard message loop. When the application is about to terminate, calls are made to revoke the OLE registrations, the application object is destroyed, and the OLE library is uninitialized.

Before we start exploring the CHello and CHelloCF classes, we should take a brief peek at the WndProc function. This function processes two messages. When a WM_PAINT message is received, the content of the application's window is refreshed with data taken from the application's one and only CHello object. When a WM_DESTROY message is received, the application terminates.

At the heart of the OLE automation implementation are the classes CHello and CHelloCF. Both classes implement the IUnknown interface. The implementations of the AddRef and Release functions are trivial and require little explanation. In the implementations of QueryInterface, CHello responds to requests for IUnknown and IDispatch; CHelloCF responds to requests for IUnknown and IClassFactory.

CHelloCF provides a simple implementation of CreateInstance, in which it returns a pointer to the appropriate interface provided by CHello.

Both CHello and CHelloCF objects are created through a static member function named Create. The creation of CHelloCF is trivial. However, in CHello::Create some odd things are taking place. In order to provide an IDispatch interface, CHello relies on a standard implementation; this implementation is created through the calls to CreateDispTypeInfo and CreateStdDispatch. The information used by the standard implementation is encoded in the form of structures at the top of the file.

The actual implementations of the get and set methods that implement the text property are contained in a third class, CText. The first two member functions of this class, Get and Set, retrieve the value of its m_text member variable and set the value of that variable, respectively. An additional member function, Paint, is used to display the text within the window identified by the m_hwnd member variable. The Set member function causes this window to be redrawn (thus ensuring that the modified text is displayed) by calling InvalidateRect.

Notice how the CText::Get and CText::Set functions handle strings; in particular, the conversion between OLE strings and plain ASCII strings that can be displayed by the application. Also notice how, in accordance with memory allocation rules, CText::Set does not free the memory allocated for its BSTR parameter. Nor does CText::Get free the memory it allocates for its return value; that will be freed by the caller (the OLE library).

The CLSID for this server has been obtained using the guidgen.exe application.

Finally, here comes the horror of horrors: This application can simply be compiled from the command line! (If you abhor so-called examples in which the make file alone exceeds the length of this simple program here, you are not alone.) To compile this program, type the following:

```
cl hello.cpp user32.lib gdi32.lib ole32.lib oleaut32.lib uuid.lib
```

Of course, if you plan to experiment with OLE using this application as a basis and wish to use the debugging features of Developer Studio, you can easily create a Visual C++ project file for this program.

Registering and Running the Server

Although as soon as it is compiled, the Hello server can be run stand-alone, in order for it to work as an automation server, entries must be made in the Registry. (Well, you didn't really expect a 300-line example program to do that for you, did you?)

In the Registry, the following entries must be made:

Listing 28.3. Registry entries.

```
HKEY_CLASSES_ROOT\
  HELLO.Application = HELLO Application
HKEY_CLASSES_ROOT\
  HELLO.Application\CLSID = {FEB8C280-FD2D-11ce-87C3-00403321BFAC}

HKEY_CLASSES_ROOT\
  CLSID\{FEB8C280-FD2D-11ce-87C3-00403321BFAC} = HELLO Application
HKEY_CLASSES_ROOT\
  CLSID\{FEB8C280-FD2D-11ce-87C3-00403321BFAC}\LocalServer32 =
    HELLO.EXE /Automation
HKEY_CLASSES_ROOT\
  CLSID\{FEB8C280-FD2D-11ce-87C3-00403321BFAC}\ProgId =
    HELLO.Application
```

Note that unless the location of the Hello executable is in your path, it may be necessary to change the `LocalServer32` key to reflect the complete pathname of the executable.

Adding these entries to the Registry manually can be error-prone. To avoid potentially corrupting the Registry, you can add the entries using the Registry Editor's import feature. Copy the entries in Listing 28.3 into an ASCII file (for example, `hello.reg`). Note that the entries cannot be broken up as they appear here on the printed page; each of the five entries must be presented in a single line. This file can then be added to the Registry using the import feature of either the Windows 95 or the Windows NT version of the Registry Editor.

Summary

The complex technology behind OLE is at the core of many modern Windows applications.

At the heart of OLE is the Component Object Model (COM). COM objects are accessed through a set of interfaces, each consisting of a set of methods. The standard defines the interface, but does not define the implementation of the interface, which is completely at the discretion of the programmer providing that implementation (to the point of choosing a programming language for the implementation).

COM objects are black boxes. Although they represent reusable components, reusability is not possible in the fashion of object-oriented languages. COM objects can contain other COM objects and delegate the implementation of specific interfaces to other COM objects; however, you cannot derive an object from an existing object in the fashion of deriving a class from a base class in C++.

COM objects are identified through GUIDs, globally unique interface identifiers. GUIDs are 128-byte numbers that are statistically unique; programmers need not worry about anyone else using the same GUID that has been generated through tools or functions provided for this purpose.

All COM objects implement a specific interface, IUnknown. Through this interface, information about other interfaces a COM object may support can be obtained.

Through the IClassFactory interface, implemented by COM class objects, applications that were written with no prior knowledge of an object can create such an object. Class objects are registered in a system-wide registration database (in Windows, the Registry) through their CLSID, which is just another GUID.

Objects communicate with each other in one of two ways. If the method called is within the process space of the caller, the function implementing that method is called directly, with no overhead. However, if the method is outside the process space of the calling process, the call is made through an intervening infrastructure. This interface makes use of proxy objects and the techniques of marshaling and unmarshaling, which is used to render the parameters of a method for transmission and unpackaging those parameters at the receiving end.

COM objects can also be identified by name through monikers. Various types of monikers can be used to identify objects stored in files, or objects stored within other objects. Monikers can also be concatenated and used in conjunction with antimonikers to create new monikers.

Using OLE for linking and embedding objects is based on the OLE compound document technology. This technology relies, in addition to COM, on OLE Structured Storage and OLE Uniform Data Transfer. The former provides a means whereby compound data can be stored in a single file in a hierarchical form reminiscent of directories and files in a file system. The latter represents a mechanism for communicating objects between applications.

Other uses of OLE include OLE automation, OLE controls, and OLE drag and drop. Specialized applications can also implement custom OLE interfaces using the Microsoft Windows Software Development Kit.

OLE Servers

29

OLE servers or OLE component applications are applications that provide OLE components for use within OLE container applications. MFC and Visual C++ support the development of servers, containers, and server-containers in a variety of ways.

Server Concepts

This section offers a review of a few server-related concepts before we begin exploring how MFC supports the construction of OLE servers.

Full-Servers and Mini-Servers

There is a distinction between full-servers and mini-servers. A full-server is an OLE component application that can also be run stand-alone. A mini-server can only operate when launched from within a container application.

Note that a mini-server should not be confused with the concept of an in-process server. An in-process server runs in the process space of the client application. A typical example of an OLE in-process server is an OLE control. Mini-servers are executable applications; however, they do not offer facilities that would make their execution in a stand-alone configuration meaningful. For example, a mini-server typically does not offer functions to save a file to disk, nor does it have printing capabilities on its own.

In-Place Editing

In-place editing represents the capability of presenting a server item within the container application's window. As simple as it sounds, it requires a complex series of interactions between the server and the container application.

In addition to presenting the server item in a rectangular area within the container application's window, servers also take over the container application's toolbars and parts of their menu bars.

Server Activation

Servers are activated through *verbs*. Executing a verb means calling the method `DoVerb` of the `IOleObject` interface. A series of predefined verb values corresponds to editing the object in-place or within its own window, activating or hiding an object.

Creating a Server Application with MFC

OLE component server applications can be created using the Visual C++ AppWizard. Server capabilities can be easily added or modified through the ClassWizard.

Using AppWizard to Create an Application Skeleton

To create an OLE server application through AppWizard, first of all you must specify an application that is either single-document-based or multiple-document-based. Server capabilities are not supported for dialog-based applications. If you wish to develop a server using a dialog-like interface (such a server would typically not support visual editing and in-place sessions), you can still use a view class based on CFormView.

Regardless of whether your new program is an SDI or MDI application, you specify OLE server capabilities in Step 3 of AppWizard (Figure 29.1). Three forms of support are available. You can select mini-server, full-server, or container-server support for your application.

FIGURE 29.1.

Creating an OLE server through AppWizard.

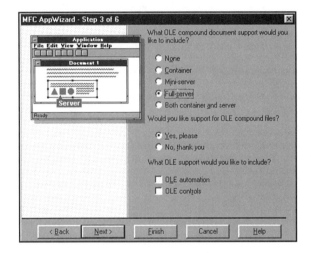

On this page, you can also specify whether your application should use OLE compound files. Using OLE files requires more disk space, but it offers the advantages of improved performance and a standardized file structure.

On this page of AppWizard, there are also check boxes for OLE automation and OLE controls. These options are not connected to OLE container and OLE component server support and are of no concern to us at this moment.

The OLE Server Skeleton Application

This section examines a full-server skeleton application that was created by AppWizard.

The OSRV application was created with default AppWizard settings as a multiple-document interface full-server application. Figure 29.2 shows the classes created by AppWizard for this application.

FIGURE 29.2.

Classes created by AppWizard for an OLE server.

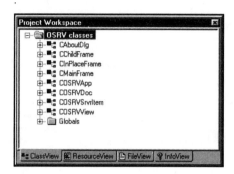

In what way do these classes differ from the classes that AppWizard creates for a non-OLE application? There are two readily visible differences: two new classes, CInPlaceFrame and COSRVSrvrItem. Another difference is less obvious; if you double-click on the class name COSRVDoc, you may notice that this class is not derived from CDocument as would be the case for a non-OLE application. Instead, this class is derived from COleServerDoc.

The reason for these changes is easy to explain. First of all, the application's document class is now derived from COleServerDoc because it is this base class that provides a number of services that implement the application's document in a server environment. Among other things, this class implements interaction with an in-place frame, provides container notification functions, and has helper functions that assist in positioning items (possibly zoomed) within a container application's window during in-place editing.

The role of the new class CInPlaceFrame is closely related. This class, derived from COleIPFrameWnd, represents the in-place frame window. During an in-place editing session, it is this window that takes over the role of the child frame window (or, in the case of SDI applications, the application's frame window). Figure 29.3 compares the relationship between frame windows and views during stand-alone and in-place sessions.

FIGURE 29.3.

Comparing in-place and stand-alone sessions.

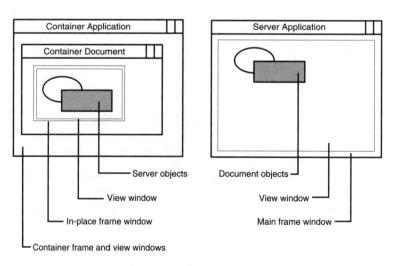

The other new class, COSRVSrvrItem, is a class that represents the OLE interface during a session with a container application.

The Server Item

The COleServerItem-derived class representing the server item has a very special role. This class, among other things, implements the OLE interfaces IOleObject and IDataObject, which facilitate its role in representing an OLE server item.

COleServerItem-derived server items are closely linked with COleDocument-derived documents. Their purpose is to represent all or part of a document in an OLE data transfer context. However, their role is not limited to OLE linking or embedding; other roles of COleServerItem-derived objects include facilitating clipboard transfers and OLE drag and drop.

Among the overridable member functions of COleServerItem are OnDraw and Serialize. Both of these functions play a very important role in OLE. COleServerItem::Serialize is used to serialize an embedded item for storage in the container application. COleServerItem::OnDraw is called to render the item's appearance; typically, this function is called to render the embedded item into a metafile device context. The resulting metafile object will be stored by the container application, thus avoiding the need to activate the server whenever the item needs to be redrawn.

The default, AppWizard-supplied implementation of COleServerItem::Serialize (Listing 29.1) relies on the document class's Serialize member function to accomplish its task. While satisfactory in simple situations, this implementation needs to be revised if a COleServerItem-derived object is used to represent only parts of a document. This is the case when the server enables OLE links, and also if COleServerItem is used, for example, to transfer portions of a document (the current selection) to the clipboard.

Listing 29.1. AppWizard-supplied implementation of the `Serialize` member function of a server item class.

```
void COSRVSrvrItem::Serialize(CArchive& ar)
{
    // COSRVSrvrItem::Serialize will be called by the framework if
    //  the item is copied to the clipboard.  This can happen
    //  automatically through the OLE callback OnGetClipboardData.
    //  A good default for the embedded item is simply to delegate
    //  to the document's Serialize function.  If you support
    //  links, then you will want to serialize just a portion of
    //  the document.

    if (!IsLinkedItem())
    {
        COSRVDoc* pDoc = GetDocument();
        ASSERT_VALID(pDoc);
        pDoc->Serialize(ar);
    }
}
```

The default implementation of COleServerItem::OnDraw (Listing 29.2) does not perform any drawing. You must provide your own implementation of this function. In simple situations, the drawing function here may be a replica of the OnDraw member function of your application's view class.

Listing 29.2. AppWizard-supplied implementation of the OnDraw member function of a server item class.

```
BOOL COSRVSrvrItem::OnDraw(CDC* pDC, CSize& rSize)
{
    COSRVDoc* pDoc = GetDocument();
    ASSERT_VALID(pDoc);

    // TODO: set mapping mode and extent  (The extent is usually
    //   the same as the size returned from OnGetExtent)
    pDC->SetMapMode(MM_ANISOTROPIC);
    pDC->SetWindowOrg(0,0);
    pDC->SetWindowExt(3000, 3000);

    // TODO: add drawing code here.  Optionally, fill in the
    //   HIMETRIC extent.  All drawing takes place in the metafile
    //   device context (pDC).

    return TRUE;
}
```

COleDocument and Document Items

The class COleDocument, which is the base class of COleServerDoc, offers a very useful capability. It can maintain a list of document items of type CDocItem. The CDocItem class is used, among other things, as the base class for COleServerItem; however, you can also use it to implement application-specific document items. Thus, it is possible to create a simple OLE server application without adding any code to the application's COleDocument-derived document class; the code provided by AppWizard already manages the list of CDocItem objects.

The In-Place Frame Window

The in-place frame window essentially has the same functionality as the frame window in SDI applications. It is the parent window for the current view; it also manages menus and toolbars. However, it does so by cooperating with the container application's frame window, replacing the menus and toolbars of that frame window for the duration of the in-place session.

Modes of Operation and Resources

When you work with an OLE server, you must never forget about this dual role of the application. Did I say dual? Actually, a full OLE server has three basic modes of operation. It can operate in stand-alone mode, it can be used to edit an OLE item in its own window, and it can be used for in-place editing. This fact is also reflected in the AppWizard-generated resource file (Figure 29.4). As you can see, the application has three accelerators, four menus, and two different toolbars.

FIGURE 29.4.

Duplicate resources in an OLE server application.

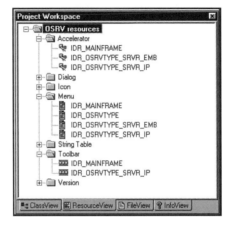

Of the four menus, two are found in every multiple document application; one is displayed when the application has no documents open, the other one is used otherwise. An OLE server, however, has to provide a third menu reflecting the state when it is used to edit an embedded item. The basic difference between this and the regular menu bar is that the File menu contains the choices Update and Save Copy As, instead of Save and Save As. This is to reflect the fact that "saving" an embedded item implies serializing it into the container application; saving it under a different filename creates a stand-alone copy of the embedded item.

The fourth menu is a very special one. This menu (Figure 29.5) is displayed when the server is used for in-place editing. What makes this menu so special is that it is incomplete; in place of two of its top-level menu items there are only separate bars.

FIGURE 29.5.

The incomplete menu used during in-place editing.

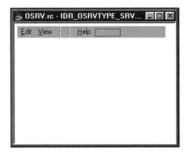

During an in-place session, this menu and a similarly incomplete menu provided by the server are "combed" together, forming the menu seen by the user. This combing reflects the fact that during the in-place session, various functions are carried out by the server application, while other functions (for example, window management) remain the responsibility of the container application. Figure 29.6 shows how the complete menu is formed from the incomplete menus provided by the server and the container.

FIGURE 29.6.

How server and container menus are combined during in-place editing.

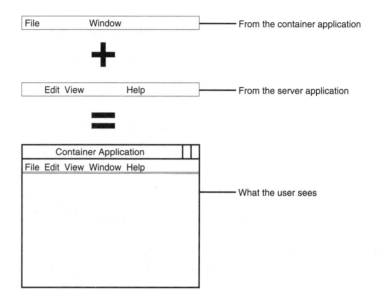

If you know that there are separate menus, the need for separate acceleration tables is easy to understand. As for the toolbars, a brief look at them (Figure 29.7) quickly reveals that the toolbar used during in-place editing simply lacks those file-related functions that the server does not offer during such sessions.

FIGURE 29.7.

Toolbars in an OLE server skeleton.

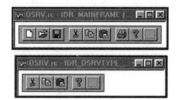

Running the Server Skeleton

As is, the server skeleton supplied by AppWizard can be compiled and run. Although it does not perform any useful function, the interaction between the server and the container works and can be demonstrated. For example, you can use the Windows 95 WordPad application to invoke the new server. Note that you must run the server stand-alone first in order for it to create the appropriate entries in the Registry. Afterwards, when running WordPad, you can insert a new object of type "OSRV Document" by selecting the Object command from its Insert menu. Figure 29.8 shows an in-place editing session using the OSRV server with WordPad.

FIGURE 29.8.

In-place editing session.

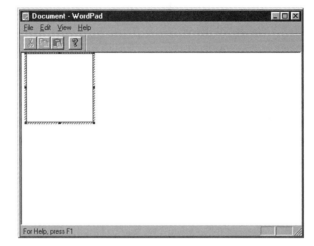

Notice how the Edit and View menus, the toolbar, and the status bar have been taken over by the server application; WordPad's toolbar, ruler, and menus that are normally visible disappear for the session's duration.

Customizing a Skeleton Server

Now to add some very simple functionality to our skeleton server. The new OSRV server will do a very simple task: it will display a string in the middle of view windows. The string will be stored in the form of a member variable of the server's document class and will be serialized by that class.

In order to make modification of the string possible, we must add a dialog. The dialog will be invoked when the user clicks within a view using the left mouse button.

Although this is clearly a very simple example, it nevertheless demonstrates all the key aspects that one must pay attention to while developing a server. Although a real-life OLE server application is significantly more complex, the basic steps and principles remain the same.

Modifying the Document

The first thing to do to implement the new behavior is to add a member variable to the document class, COSRVDoc. A member variable of type CString should be added in the Attributes section of the declaration of COSRVDoc:

```
// Attributes
public:
```

```
COSRVSrvrItem* GetEmbeddedItem()
    { return (COSRVSrvrItem*)COleServerDoc::GetEmbeddedItem(); }
CString m_sData;
```

This member variable should also be initialized to some meaningful value. In the implementation file of COSRVDoc, modify COSRVDoc::OnNewDocument as follows:

```
BOOL COSRVDoc::OnNewDocument()
{
    if (!COleServerDoc::OnNewDocument())
        return FALSE;

    // TODO: add reinitialization code here
    // (SDI documents will reuse this document)

    m_sData = "Hello, World!";
    return TRUE;
}
```

Adding Drawing Code

In the case of nonserver applications, we had to add drawing code to the appropriate view class. In the case of a server application, we also have to add drawing code to the OnDraw member function of the OLE server item class.

To add drawing code to the view class, modify the implementation of COSRVView::OnDraw function as follows:

```
void COSRVView::OnDraw(CDC* pDC)
{
    COSRVDoc* pDoc = GetDocument();
    ASSERT_VALID(pDoc);

    // TODO: add draw code for native data here
    CRect rect;
    CFont font, *pOldFont;
    GetClientRect(&rect);
    font.CreateStockObject(SYSTEM_FONT);
    pOldFont = pDC->SelectObject(&font);
    pDC->DPtoLP(&rect);
    pDC->DrawText(pDoc->m_sData, &rect,
                DT_CENTER | DT_VCENTER | DT_SINGLELINE);
    pDC->SelectObject(pOldFont);
}
```

A similar modification must be made to COSRVSrvrItem::OnDraw:

```
BOOL COSRVSrvrItem::OnDraw(CDC* pDC, CSize& rSize)
{
    COSRVDoc* pDoc = GetDocument();
    ASSERT_VALID(pDoc);

    // TODO: set mapping mode and extent  (The extent is usually
    //  the same as the size returned from OnGetExtent)
    pDC->SetMapMode(MM_ANISOTROPIC);
```

```
        pDC->SetWindowOrg(0,0);
        pDC->SetWindowExt(3000, 3000);

        // TODO: add drawing code here.  Optionally, fill in the
        //  HIMETRIC extent.  All drawing takes place in the metafile
        //  device context (pDC).

        CRect rect;
        CFont font, *pOldFont;
        rect.TopLeft() = pDC->GetWindowOrg();
        rect.BottomRight() = rect.TopLeft() + pDC->GetWindowExt();
        font.CreateStockObject(SYSTEM_FONT);
        pOldFont = pDC->SelectObject(&font);
        pDC->DrawText(pDoc->m_sData, &rect,
                    DT_CENTER ¦ DT_VCENTER ¦ DT_SINGLELINE);
        pDC->SelectObject(pOldFont);
        return TRUE;
}
```

In a more sophisticated application, the first part of this function would also be modified, reflecting the true size of the item (as opposed to the rather arbitrary size chosen here). Similarly, the COSRVSrvrItem::OnGetExtent function would also use a more sophisticated mechanism for determining the size of the embedded item.

At this time, you can recompile and run the application. To test it from within an OLE container application, use the container's Insert Object function, and insert on OSRV document. Figure 29.9 shows the new OSRV application during an in-place session with the Windows 95 WordPad.

FIGURE 29.9.

OSRV and the Windows 95 WordPad.

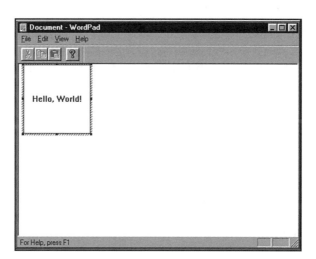

If you play around with OSRV, you may notice an odd behavior. While the string is normally centered during an in-place session, after the session has been terminated, this is no longer so. Instead, the string's upper-left corner appears to be positioned at the center of the item's rectangle.

This odd behavior is specific to CDC::DrawText in a metafile device context. We are not going to be concerned about this right now (consider it a documented bug); however, let this serve as a warning that the two OnDraw functions (one in the view class, the other in the OLE server item class) are invoked under very different circumstances and must be tested separately.

Adding a Dialog

In order to make the text displayed by OSRV changeable, we need to add a dialog where the user can enter or modify the text item. Adding the dialog is easy using the built-in dialog editor. The dialog, as shown in Figure 29.10, should contain a single edit field, IDC_TEXT, where the new text can be entered.

FIGURE 29.10.

The Window Text dialog in OSRV.

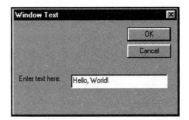

To complete creation of this dialog, invoke the ClassWizard. Let the ClassWizard create a new class representing this dialog (CTextDlg), and add a member variable m_sText, representing the edit field IDC_TEXT.

How will this dialog be invoked? To avoid having to mess with menus or toolbars, I decided to use the simplest possible method. The dialog will be invoked whenever a view window receives a WM_LBUTTONDOWN message; that is, whenever the user clicks within the view using the left mouse button.

The simplest way to add a handler to the view class for these messages is to open the implementation file for the OSRV view class (OSRVView.cpp) and use the WizardBar. In the WizardBar, select the WM_LBUTTONDOWN item in the Messages combo box, and answer affirmatively when you are asked if a new handler should be created for this message.

The handler function is shown in Listing 29.3. Nothing mysterious here; the function simply creates and invokes the dialog, and transfers the data between the dialog and the document. Note that in order for this function to compile successfully, you must also include the TextDlg.h header file at the top of the file OSRVView.cpp.

Listing 29.3. Implementation of COSRVView::OnLButtonDown.

```
void COSRVView::OnLButtonDown(UINT nFlags, CPoint point)
{
    // TODO: Add your message handler code here and/or call default
```

```
//  CView::OnLButtonDown(nFlags, point);
    CTextDlg dlg;
    COSRVDoc* pDoc = GetDocument();
    ASSERT_VALID(pDoc);
    dlg.m_sText = pDoc->m_sData;
    if ((dlg.DoModal() == IDOK) && (dlg.m_sText != pDoc->m_sData))
    {
        pDoc->m_sData = dlg.m_sText;
        pDoc->UpdateAllViews(NULL);
        pDoc->UpdateAllItems(NULL);
        pDoc->SetModifiedFlag();
    }
}
```

In addition to calling the document class member functions UpdateAllViews (to reflect the user's entry in all views of the document) and SetModifiedFlag (to notify the document class that its contents changed and may need to be saved), the function also calls UpdateAllItems. Through UpdateAllItems, it notifies containers that the contents of the embedded item have changed and may need to be redrawn.

Serialization

There is one thing missing before we can call our application complete: Its data must be saved. Namely, the m_sData member variable of the document class needs to be serialized in COSRVDoc::Serialize. This is very easily done:

```
void COSRVDoc::Serialize(CArchive& ar)
{
    if (ar.IsStoring())
    {
        // TODO: add storing code here
        ar << m_sData;
    }
    else
    {
        // TODO: add loading code here
        ar >> m_sData;
    }
}
```

At this time, our simple server application is complete and can be recompiled.

Registering the New Application

You might have noticed that we have run the OSRV application without ever attempting to enter anything into the Windows Registry. How do clients, such as the Windows 95 WordPad, know about our application?

The reason it was not necessary to update the Registry manually is because AppWizard-generated applications register themselves. Every time such an application is run stand-alone, it creates or updates the appropriate entries in the Registry. This also applies to mini-servers; although a mini-server would not typically be run stand-alone, you can do so for the purpose of registering.

However, AppWizard also creates a file that contains all relevant Registry entries. In the case of OSRV, this file is called OSRV.reg. It contains the following Registry entries (all under the key HKEY_CLASSES_ROOT):

```
OSRV.Document = OSRV Document
OSRV.Document\protocol\StdFileEditing\server = OSRV.EXE
OSRV.Document\protocol\StdFileEditing\verb\0 = &Edit
OSRV.Document\Insertable =
OSRV.Document\CLSID = {494CDF20-FE4B-11CE-87C3-00403321BFAC}
```

It is through these items that an OLE container can identify OSRV documents as insertable objects. The last of these items identifies the CLSID under which additional information about the server can be found (note that your CLSID may be different from mine). A further set of Registry entries is made using this CLSID, under the key HKEY_CLASSES_ROOT\CLSID:

```
{494CDF20-FE4B-11CE-87C3-00403321BFAC} = OSRV Document
{494CDF20-FE4B-11CE-87C3-00403321BFAC}\DefaultIcon = OSRV.EXE,1
{494CDF20-FE4B-11CE-87C3-00403321BFAC}\LocalServer32 = OSRV.EXE
{494CDF20-FE4B-11CE-87C3-00403321BFAC}\ProgId = OSRV.Document
{494CDF20-FE4B-11CE-87C3-00403321BFAC}\MiscStatus = 32
{494CDF20-FE4B-11CE-87C3-00403321BFAC}\AuxUserType\3 = OSRV
{494CDF20-FE4B-11CE-87C3-00403321BFAC}\AuxUserType\2 = OSRV
{494CDF20-FE4B-11CE-87C3-00403321BFAC}\Insertable =
{494CDF20-FE4B-11CE-87C3-00403321BFAC}\verb\1 = &Open,0,2
{494CDF20-FE4B-11CE-87C3-00403321BFAC}\verb\0 = &Edit,0,2
{494CDF20-FE4B-11CE-87C3-00403321BFAC}\InprocHandler32 = ole32.dll
```

Summary

OLE servers, or OLE component servers, are applications that maintain OLE component items that can be used from within OLE container applications.

Creating an MFC-based OLE server application is easy using the Visual C++ AppWizard. All you need to do is to specify server support during AppWizard Step 3.

OLE server capability is supported only for single- or multiple-document-based applications (not for dialog-based programs). However, you can develop an OLE server with a dialog-like interface using the CFormView class.

The MFC distinguishes between mini-servers, full-servers, and container-servers. A mini-server is an application that can only be used in conjunction with embedded objects; a full-server is a program that can also operate in a stand-alone mode and can save its data to files. A container server is an OLE server that also offers container functionality.

To create an OLE server with AppWizard, specify the desired server behavior in AppWizard Step 2. When compared to applications that do not support OLE, an OLE server offers two new classes. The server item class, derived from COleServerItem, represents an embedded item in the container application and offers the IOleObject OLE interface through which the container application can communicate with the server. The in-place frame window class, derived from COleIPFrameWnd, represents the frame window during in-place sessions, and manages the interaction between the server and the frame window of the container.

The in-place frame window provides the functionality that is necessary for the menus and toolbars of the container and the server application to coexist. During an in-place session, the server application takes over the container's toolbar and status bars. The menu bar that is visible during such a session is created from a combination of menus provided by the container and the server.

The server item class provides two member functions of fundamental importance. Its OnDraw member function is used to draw an image of the OLE item into a metafile device context; this image is used later by the container to display the item without invoking the server. The Serialize member function is used to serialize the item for storage in the container document.

Customizing an AppWizard-generated server skeleton consists of the following steps:

1. After having created the server skeleton, implement basic functionality by adding member variables and code to the application's document and view classes. Add other elements (resources, dialogs) as appropriate.

2. Modify the server item's OnDraw member function to draw the item into a metafile device context. This is the image that will be displayed by containers when there is no active session with the server.

3. Modify the server item's Serialize member function to serialize the item for embedding. If your application supports only embedded items, you can use the default implementation that relies on your document class's serialization function. If you support links, or if you use the server item class to facilitate clipboard transfers, add code here that serializes selected items only.

Your application does not have to be registered; it registers itself (or updates the appropriate registry entries) whenever it is run as a stand-alone application. However, AppWizard also emits a file that can be used for registering the application manually or from within an installation program.

OLE Containers

OLE containers are applications that manage, in addition to native data, a set of OLE server items.

The MFC Library provides a high level of support for creating OLE containers. Using an AppWizard-generated container application skeleton, it is possible to build, with a minimal amount of added code, a decently working container application.

In this chapter, we first review the AppWizard-generated skeleton for a container application. Subsequently, we add the necessary code for this application to handle the selection and editing of multiple-embedded objects.

Creating a Container Application Through AppWizard

The Visual C++ AppWizard supports the creation of skeleton applications for two types of containers: simple containers and container-servers. The latter term refers to applications that offer both OLE container and OLE component server functionality. However, since the two areas of functionality are quite distinct, we focus on simple containers in the rest of this chapter.

Creating the Skeleton Application

To create a container application through AppWizard, first of all you must specify a single-document-based or multiple-document-based application. Container capabilities are not supported for dialog-based applications. While it is possible to create a container application based on the view class CFormView, I do not see how the dialog template-based view class and the visual embedding and in-place editing associated with OLE components can coexist.

OLE container support in the new application skeleton must be specified in AppWizard Step 3 (Figure 30.1). You can either specify a container application or a container-server.

Other than setting the container application option, I used the default settings when I created the OCON application skeleton through AppWizard. Throughout the rest of this chapter, it is this OCON application that we review and modify.

The OLE Container Skeleton Application

By looking at the set of classes created by AppWizard (Figure 30.2), we can see that AppWizard created one extra class when compared to a skeleton application with no OLE container support. This extra class is named COCONCntrItem and represents OLE components that are contained within the container application's documents.

FIGURE 30.1.

Creating an OLE container through AppWizard.

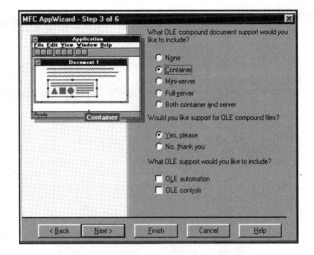

FIGURE 30.2.

AppWizard-generated classes for an OLE container.

Of course, the appearance of a new class is not the only difference between an OLE container and other applications. There are also noticeable differences between the implementations of other classes.

Running the Skeleton Container

Before we begin analyzing how the skeleton container works, running it may be a good idea. It will give us a picture as to how the container works and what functionality we need to add to enhance its usefulness.

To explore the container capabilities of the OCON application, compile and run this application, and then select the Insert New Object command from its Edit menu. This command displays the dialog shown in Figure 30.3, where you can select the type of object you wish to insert into the document.

Now to insert a Bitmap Image object. This object type is available on all Windows 95 systems that have the Windows 95 Paint application installed. Figure 30.4 shows a session while the bitmap object is being edited inside the OCON container.

FIGURE 30.3.

The Insert Object dialog.

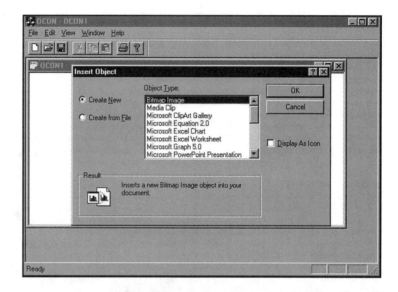

FIGURE 30.4.

In-place editing of a bitmap object.

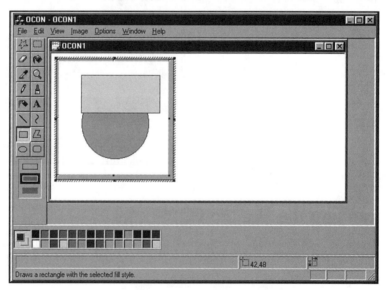

You may notice a few peculiarities right here, pointing out areas of code that must be improved.

First of all, there does not seem to be a way to terminate the in-place session. Normally you would expect that clicking outside the in-place editing area would terminate the session; however, this does not seem to happen. The reason is simple: As we see shortly, the OCON skeleton application does not provide a handler function for mouse clicks, so it is no wonder that nothing happens.

Another peculiarity can be noticed if you attempt to move or resize the in-place area. This area can be resized by dragging any of the eight resize handles (small black squares) around its border; it can also be moved by dragging the shaded border area. But look what happens (Figure 30.5): After moving the in-place area, another image of our drawing appears at the original location!

FIGURE 30.5.

Discrepancy between in-place frame and embedded item positions.

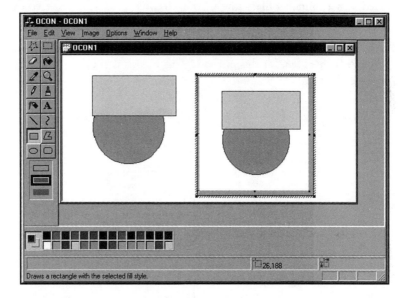

As it turns out, that image is at the position where the container application thinks the image should be drawn. Code that would properly update this location to reflect any changes made during an in-place editing session does not yet exist.

Although there is no trivial way to end an in-place editing session, you can actually save the container file even while an in-place session is active. After saving the file using the File Save command, you can terminate the in-place session by simply closing the document window altogether. Upon reopening the file, you can see that the embedded object was saved correctly and is redisplayed at its original location. At this stage it is possible to either edit this object again, or insert a new object, both through commands in the Edit menu.

If you insert a new object, it will be positioned on top of the first object in the container. For this reason, it is not possible to see at this stage the third oddity concerning AppWizard-generated container skeletons; namely, that the skeleton application only displays one object at a time. As we shall see, this is a cosmetic problem only; the application is actually capable of saving container files with more than one object, it is the OnDraw member function of its view class that requires modification.

The Skeleton Container Code

It is time to stop playing with our new container application and start looking at how its functions are implemented.

How are new objects inserted into the document? How are the new objects represented and saved with a container file? How are they drawn? How are in-place editing sessions managed? These are the questions that we seek answers for in this section.

First, take a look at how items in a container are represented. The AppWizard generated a new class, COCONCntrItem, for this purpose. This class is derived from COleClientItem and comes with a default implementation of several member functions (Figure 30.6).

FIGURE 30.6.

Container item class member functions.

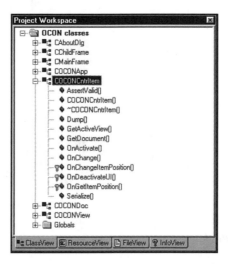

On the one hand, this class implements the necessary OLE interfaces for in-place editing. On the other hand, it provides a series of member functions (such as `Serialize`) that enable it to exist within the MFC application framework.

Looking at the implementation of this class, we can notice a few shortcomings. In particular, look at the implementations of the `OnChangeItemPosition` and `OnGetItemPosition` member functions (Listing 30.1). As you can see, `OnGetItemPosition` always returns an arbitrary, fixed position; on the other hand, `OnChangeItemPosition`, although it calls the base class implementation, does not make note of the new position in any way. (No wonder that `OnGetItemPosition` cannot return a meaningful value!)

Listing 30.1. The default implementations of COCONCntrItem member functions OnChangeItemPosition and OnGetItemPosition.

```
BOOL COCONCntrItem::OnChangeItemPosition(const CRect& rectPos)
{
    ASSERT_VALID(this);
```

```
// During in-place activation COCONCntrItem::OnChangeItemPosition
//   is called by the server to change the position of the in-place
//   window.  Usually, this is a result of the data in the server
//   document changing such that the extent has changed or as a
//   result of in-place resizing.
//
// The default here is to call the base class, which will call
// COleClientItem::SetItemRects to move the item
//   to the new position.

    if (!COleClientItem::OnChangeItemPosition(rectPos))
        return FALSE;

    // TODO: update any cache you may have of the item's
    //   rectangle/extent

    return TRUE;
}

void COCONCntrItem::OnGetItemPosition(CRect& rPosition)
{
    ASSERT_VALID(this);

// During in-place activation, COCONCntrItem::OnGetItemPosition
//   will be called to determine the location of this item.  The
//   default implementation created from AppWizard simply returns a
//   hard-coded rectangle.  Usually, this rectangle would reflect
//   the current position of the item relative to the view used for
//   activation.
//   You can obtain the view by calling
//   COCONCntrItem::GetActiveView.

    // TODO: return correct rectangle (in pixels) in rPosition

    rPosition.SetRect(10, 10, 210, 210);
}
```

As the AppWizard-generated comments also imply, we will have to revisit this class shortly to manage these position changes.

How are COCONCntrItem objects represented in our document class? Strangely enough, there is no additional code in our skeleton application for this purpose. The only change relative to a noncontainer application is that our application's document class, COCONDoc, is now derived from COleDocument as opposed to CDocument. COleDocument has the wonderful capability of managing and storing a list of CDocItem-derived items. When a new item of class COCONCntrItem (derived from COleClientItem which, in turn, is derived from CDocItem) is created, it is automatically added to the container document's list of items. The container document, in turn, can serialize itself, including this list of CDocItem-derived objects without any additional code.

If you add items of your own design to an OLE container application, you can rely on this capability. You can add your own CDocItem-derived items to the container, and the container will handle them correctly. The only catch is that in your application code, you will have to be careful in your handling of application-specific items, container items, and (if the application also acts as an OLE server) server items. One possible solution is to create a series of wrapper functions that determine a particular object's type using MFC run-time type information.

The differences between the implementations of the document classes in a container and a noncontainer application were relatively minor (although the effects of the difference in the base class from which the document classes are derived are rather significant). In contrast, the difference between the implementations of view classes in the two cases is very significant. The implementation file of the container application's view class is nearly twice as long, with several additional member functions (Figure 30.7).

FIGURE 30.7.

Container view class member functions.

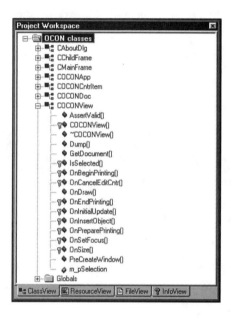

The implementation of these member functions will, in fact, answer our questions concerning the peculiar behavior of the skeleton container.

The first thing to notice in the declaration of COCONView is the presence of a new member variable, m_pSelection:

```
class COCONView : public CView
{
protected: // create from serialization only
    COCONView();
    DECLARE_DYNCREATE(COCONView)

// Attributes
public:
    COCONDoc* GetDocument();
    COCONCntrItem* m_pSelection;
```

This member variable represents a very simple item selection mechanism; the mechanism only allows a single document item to be selected at any given time. While in many sophisticated applications such a selection mechanism would be completely inadequate, in our effort to build a simple container application, it is going to be sufficient.

The m_pSelection member variable plays a role in the implementation of the OnDraw member function, answering our question with respect to why only a single item is drawn when a document with more than one embedded item is loaded. The implementation of this function (Listing 30.2) simply does not draw any other items.

Listing 30.2. The default implementation of COCONView::OnDraw.

```
void COCONView::OnDraw(CDC* pDC)
{
    COCONDoc* pDoc = GetDocument();
    ASSERT_VALID(pDoc);

    // TODO: add draw code for native data here
    // TODO: also draw all OLE items in the document

    // Draw the selection at an arbitrary position.  This code
    //  should be removed once your real drawing code is
    //  implemented.  This position corresponds exactly to the
    //  rectangle returned by COCONCntrItem, to give the effect of
    //  in-place editing.

    // TODO: remove this code when final draw code is complete.

    if (m_pSelection == NULL)
    {
        POSITION pos = pDoc->GetStartPosition();
        m_pSelection = (COCONCntrItem*)pDoc->GetNextClientItem(pos);
    }
    if (m_pSelection != NULL)
        m_pSelection->Draw(pDC, CRect(10, 10, 210, 210));
}
```

The other shortcoming of this default implementation is made obvious by the comment embedded in this AppWizard-generated code. The selection item is drawn at an arbitrary, fixed position; it does not reflect in any way any positional changes that may happen during an in-place editing session. Clearly, a modified implementation must be made in conjunction with changes to COCONCntrItem::OnChangeItemPosition and COCONCntrItem::OnGetItemPosition.

The AppWizard-generated view class implementation contains five additional member functions that are completely new (Listing 30.3). These member functions implement the insertion of new objects and also manage the in-place session. We are going to look at these functions one by one.

Listing 30.3. New view class member functions.

```
BOOL COCONView::IsSelected(const CObject* pDocItem) const
{
 // The implementation below is adequate if your selection consists
 //  of only COCONCntrItem objects.  To handle different selection
 //  mechanisms, the implementation here should be replaced.

    // TODO: implement this function that tests for a selected OLE
    //  client item

    return pDocItem == m_pSelection;
}

void COCONView::OnInsertObject()
{
    // Invoke the standard Insert Object dialog box to obtain
    //  information for new COCONCntrItem object.
    COleInsertDialog dlg;
    if (dlg.DoModal() != IDOK)
        return;

    BeginWaitCursor();

    COCONCntrItem* pItem = NULL;
    TRY
    {
        // Create new item connected to this document.
        COCONDoc* pDoc = GetDocument();
        ASSERT_VALID(pDoc);
        pItem = new COCONCntrItem(pDoc);
        ASSERT_VALID(pItem);

        // Initialize the item from the dialog data.
        if (!dlg.CreateItem(pItem))
            AfxThrowMemoryException();   // any exception will do
        ASSERT_VALID(pItem);

        // If item created from class list (not from file) then
        //  launch the server to edit the item.
        if (dlg.GetSelectionType() ==
            COleInsertDialog::createNewItem)
                pItem->DoVerb(OLEIVERB_SHOW, this);

        ASSERT_VALID(pItem);

        // As an arbitrary user interface design, this sets the
        //  selection to the last item inserted.

        // TODO: reimplement selection as appropriate for your
        //  application

        m_pSelection = pItem; //set selection to last inserted item
        pDoc->UpdateAllViews(NULL);
    }
    CATCH(CException, e)
    {
        if (pItem != NULL)
```

```
        {
            ASSERT_VALID(pItem);
            pItem->Delete();
        }
        AfxMessageBox(IDP_FAILED_TO_CREATE);
    }
    END_CATCH

    EndWaitCursor();
}


// The following command handler provides the standard keyboard
//   user interface to cancel an in-place editing session.  Here,
//   the container (not the server) causes the deactivation.
void COCONView::OnCancelEditCntr()
{
    // Close any in-place active item on this view.
    COleClientItem* pActiveItem =
        GetDocument()->GetInPlaceActiveItem(this);
    if (pActiveItem != NULL)
    {
        pActiveItem->Close();
    }
    ASSERT(GetDocument()->GetInPlaceActiveItem(this) == NULL);
}

// Special handling of OnSetFocus and OnSize are required for a
//   container when an object is being edited in-place.
void COCONView::OnSetFocus(CWnd* pOldWnd)
{
    COleClientItem* pActiveItem =
        GetDocument()->GetInPlaceActiveItem(this);
    if (pActiveItem != NULL &&
      pActiveItem->GetItemState() == COleClientItem::activeUIState)
    {
        // need to set focus to this item if it is in the same view
        CWnd* pWnd = pActiveItem->GetInPlaceWindow();
        if (pWnd != NULL)
        {
            pWnd->SetFocus();    // don't call the base class
            return;
        }
    }

    CView::OnSetFocus(pOldWnd);
}


void COCONView::OnSize(UINT nType, int cx, int cy)
{
    CView::OnSize(nType, cx, cy);
    COleClientItem* pActiveItem =
        GetDocument()->GetInPlaceActiveItem(this);
    if (pActiveItem != NULL)
        pActiveItem->SetItemRects();
}
```

The IsSelected member function is called by the framework to determine whether a particular item is selected within the view. Its implementation is straightforward and obvious.

The OnInsertObject member function implements the Insert New Object command in the Edit menu. This function relies on the capabilities of one of the OLE common dialog classes, COleInsertDialog. This common dialog can be used not only to display the list of insertable OLE items that are available on your system, but its member function CreateItem can actually be used to create a new item of the type selected by the user. If the item is freshly created, OnInsertObject launches the server application; items created from a file are simply inserted into the container document. The implementation of this function utilizes MFC exception-handling macros to catch any errors that may occur during the creation of the new item.

The member function OnCancelEditCntr terminates an in-place editing session. This function is called by the framework when the user hits the Escape key.

The OnSetFocus member function is used to ensure that when a view with an active in-place session receives the focus, the focus is actually set to the in-place item's frame window.

The implementation of the OnSize member function ensures that if the view window changes, the in-place session has a chance to reflect such a change.

While there are additional, minor differences between an OLE container and a non-OLE application, this concludes our review of the significant changes. The one thing that we have not looked at yet is the container application's resource file.

Container Menus

Looking at the AppWizard-generated resource file created for our OCON application (Figure 30.8), we can notice two obvious differences: a new accelerator table and a new menu.

FIGURE 30.8.

Container resources.

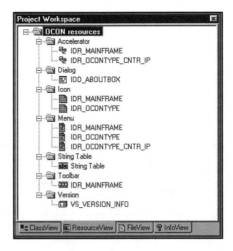

The new menu, IDR_OCONTYPE_CNTR_IP (Figure 30.9), is very obviously incomplete. The reason? This menu, during an in-place editing session, is combined with a similarly incomplete menu provided by the OLE component server application.

FIGURE 30.9.

Container menu for in-place editing session.

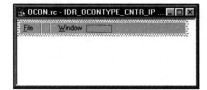

This "combing" of container and server menus, shown in Figure 30.10, ensures that commands that are the responsibility of the container are executed by the container application, and server-related commands are executed by the server.

FIGURE 30.10.

How server and container menus are combined during in-place editing.

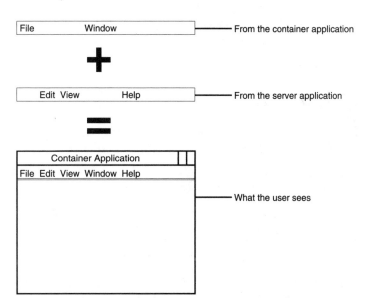

Understanding the need for a separate acceleration table during in-place editing is easy in view of the mechanism used to construct the menu for such a session.

This concludes our review of the differences between container and noncontainer applications. The next section shows how to modify this skeleton application to implement some useful container functionality.

Customizing the Application

Before we start writing code blindly, we should look at the changes we wish to add to the OLE container skeleton. In addition to the skeleton application's capabilities, our OCON application should

1. Reflect any changes in size and position made during an in-place session to an item
2. Save size and position information in document files
3. Display all container items in a document
4. Implement a simple selection mechanism using the mouse
5. Indicate the current selection visually

There are additional capabilities that one may reasonably expect from a container application, but which we do not implement at this time. These are

1. Selection of multiple items
2. Sizing and positioning of nonactive items using the mouse
3. Application-specific custom objects

Object Positions

When you look at the skeleton implementation of COCONCntrItem::OnChangeItemPosition, the need for a member variable holding the object's position becomes obvious. For this purpose, we can add a member variable of type CRect to the COCONCntrItem class:

```
class COCONCntrItem : public COleClientItem
{
    ...
// Attributes
public:
    ...
    CRect m_rect;
```

This member variable obviously needs to be initialized. In the constructor of COCONCntrItem (Listing 30.4), we can set this item to represent a fixed rectangle.

Listing 30.4. Initialization of m_rect in the constructor of COCONCntrItem.

```
COCONCntrItem::COCONCntrItem(COCONDoc* pContainer)
    : COleClientItem(pContainer)
{
    // TODO: add one-time construction code here
    m_rect = CRect(10, 10, 210, 210);
}
```

A more sophisticated application may make an attempt to initialize m_rect to reflect a server-supplied size. To do this, one could set m_rect to a null rectangle to indicate an uninitialized state and make an attempt to update it from the server when the first call is made to COCONCntrItem::OnGetItemPosition. For now, we are going to stick with this simple implementation of a fixed default size.

Where is the rectangle m_rect updated? Obviously, we need to change the implementation of COCONCntrItem::OnChangeItemPosition. In order to reflect the updated position, the function COCONCntrItem::OnGetItemPosition must also be altered.

The change in the member function OnChangeItemPosition requires only two lines of new code (Listing 30.5). First, the rectangle must be updated; second, because the item's position has changed, views must be updated to reflect the change.

Listing 30.5. Modified version of COCONCntrItem::OnChangeItemPosition.

```
BOOL COCONCntrItem::OnChangeItemPosition(const CRect& rectPos)
{
    ASSERT_VALID(this);

    if (!COleClientItem::OnChangeItemPosition(rectPos))
        return FALSE;

    // TODO: update any cache you may have of the item's
    //   rectangle/extent
    m_rect = rectPos;
    GetDocument()->UpdateAllViews(NULL);
    return TRUE;
}
```

The change to COCONCntrItem::OnGetItemPosition is equally simple. All we need to do is replace the default action that sets the rPosition parameter to a constant rectangle to a line, which sets it to the value of m_rect. This modified function is shown in Listing 30.6.

Listing 30.6. Modified version of COCONCntrItem::OnGetItemPosition.

```
void COCONCntrItem::OnGetItemPosition(CRect& rPosition)
{
    ASSERT_VALID(this);
    // TODO: return correct rectangle (in pixels) in rPosition

//  rPosition.SetRect(10, 10, 210, 210);
    rPosition = m_rect;
}
```

All that is left to be done to COCONCntrItem is a change to its Serialize member function. In order for the item positions to be persistent, they must be serialized. This is implemented by adding two lines to the COCONCntrItem::Serialize, as shown in Listing 30.7.

Listing 30.7. Modified version of `COCONCntrItem::Serialize`.

```
void COCONCntrItem::Serialize(CArchive& ar)
{
    ASSERT_VALID(this);

    COleClientItem::Serialize(ar);

    // now store/retrieve data specific to COCONCntrItem
    if (ar.IsStoring())
    {
        // TODO: add storing code here
        ar << m_rect;
    }
    else
    {
        // TODO: add loading code here
        ar >> m_rect;
    }
}
```

Now that we have implemented position and size information for objects in the container, it is time to turn our attention to the view class and reflect the new positions when the objects are drawn.

Drawing All Objects

We have identified two shortcomings of default skeleton implementation of the view class `COCONView`. First, only the item representing the current selection was drawn; second, the item was drawn at a fixed position, not reflecting any changes in size and position that might have occurred during an in-place editing session.

The solution to these problems is shown in Listing 30.8. Instead of drawing a single item, this version of the `COCONView::OnDraw` function iterates through the list of all items in the document. As individual items are drawn, they are placed at the position indicated by their `m_rect` member variable, which reflects their current size and position.

Listing 30.8. Modified version of `COCONView::OnDraw`.

```
void COCONView::OnDraw(CDC* pDC)
{
    COCONDoc* pDoc = GetDocument();
    ASSERT_VALID(pDoc);

    // TODO: remove this code when final draw code is complete.

//  if (m_pSelection == NULL)
//  {
//      POSITION pos = pDoc->GetStartPosition();
//      m_pSelection = (COCONCntrItem*)pDoc->GetNextClientItem(pos);
//  }
//  if (m_pSelection != NULL)
```

```
//      m_pSelection->Draw(pDC, CRect(10, 10, 210, 210));

    POSITION pos = pDoc->GetStartPosition();
    while (pos)
    {
        COCONCntrItem *pItem =
            (COCONCntrItem*)pDoc->GetNextClientItem(pos);
        pItem->Draw(pDC, pItem->m_rect);
    }
}
```

Note that this code must be changed if your application also has application-specific objects (that is, objects other than those representing embedded items). Instead of using `COleDocument::GetNextClientItem`, you may wish to use `COleDocument::GetNextItem` for iteration and use run-time type information to determine the drawing action appropriate for the type of object retrieved.

Object Selection

To implement a simple object selection mechanism, we must do two things. First, a handler for the mouse event `WM_LBUTTONDOWN` must be added; second, the current selection must be reflected when the object is drawn in `COCONView::OnDraw`.

To add a handler for the mouse event, use ClassWizard. The handler function should be added to the `COCONView` class; after all, selection of items is specific to the current view (and indeed, separate views may have different selections).

The handler function is shown in Listing 30.9. This function begins by closing any active in-place item. Next, it calls `InvalidateRect` to invalidate the rectangle of the current selection; the significance of this becomes evident shortly, when we look at the code that implements the drawing of a selection rectangle indicating the selection.

Listing 30.9. Handler function for WM_LBUTTONDOWN messages.

```
void COCONView::OnLButtonDown(UINT nFlags, CPoint point)
{
    // TODO: Add your message handler code here and/or call default

//  CView::OnLButtonDown(nFlags, point);
    COCONDoc* pDoc = GetDocument();
    ASSERT_VALID(pDoc);

    COCONCntrItem *pItem =
        (COCONCntrItem *)pDoc->GetInPlaceActiveItem(this);
    if (pItem != NULL) pItem->Close();
    if (m_pSelection != NULL)
    {
        CRect rect = m_pSelection->m_rect;
```

continues

Listing 30.9. continued

```
        rect.InflateRect(1, 1);
        InvalidateRect(rect);
        m_pSelection = NULL;
    }
    POSITION pos = pDoc->GetStartPosition();
    while (pos)
    {
        pItem = (COCONCntrItem*)pDoc->GetNextClientItem(pos);
        if (pItem->m_rect.PtInRect(point))
            m_pSelection = pItem;
    }
    if (m_pSelection != NULL)
    {
        CRect rect = m_pSelection->m_rect;
        rect.InflateRect(1, 1);
        InvalidateRect(rect);
    }
}
```

In the second half of this function, an iteration is made to identify the item on which the user clicked with the mouse. If such an item is found, it is set to become the current selection. However, the iteration continues, to ensure that eventually, the item we pick as the current selection is actually the topmost item. This is important in case the mouse is clicked at a position that is covered by multiple items. Once a new selection is found, its rectangle is also invalidated.

While this code implements selecting individual items with the mouse, we must also modify COCONView::OnDraw to provide a visual feedback of the new selection. Listing 30.10 shows this final version of COCONView::OnDraw.

Listing 30.10. Final version of COCONView::OnDraw.

```
void COCONView::OnDraw(CDC* pDC)
{
    COCONDoc* pDoc = GetDocument();
    ASSERT_VALID(pDoc);

    // TODO: remove this code when final draw code is complete.

//   if (m_pSelection == NULL)
//   {
//       POSITION pos = pDoc->GetStartPosition();
//       m_pSelection = (COCONCntrItem*)pDoc->GetNextClientItem(pos);
//   }
//   if (m_pSelection != NULL)
//       m_pSelection->Draw(pDC, CRect(10, 10, 210, 210));

    POSITION pos = pDoc->GetStartPosition();
    while (pos)
    {
```

```
        COCONCntrItem *pItem =
            (COCONCntrItem*)pDoc->GetNextClientItem(pos);
        pItem->Draw(pDC, pItem->m_rect);
        if (pItem == m_pSelection)
        {
            CRectTracker tracker;
            tracker.m_rect = pItem->m_rect;
            tracker.m_nStyle = CRectTracker::resizeInside |
                               CRectTracker::solidLine;
            if (pItem->GetItemState() == COleClientItem::openState
         || pItem->GetItemState() == COleClientItem::activeUIState)
                    tracker.m_nStyle |= CRectTracker::hatchInside;
            tracker.Draw(pDC);
        }
    }
}
```

In this version of the OnDraw member function, we use the CRectTracker class to create a *tracking rectangle* around the selection. While we do not make use of all its features, this class could also be used to facilitate moving and resizing the object. In our implementation, we simply utilize this class to provide visual feedback.

A notable shortcoming of this implementation is that the tracker will be drawn by the OnDraw member function every time. This includes, unfortunately, the cases when the framework uses OnDraw for printing or print preview. In a more realistic implementation, we would surround the code drawing the tracker with conditionals that determine whether this is a "normal" drawing situation and if not, would prevent the drawing of the tracking rectangle.

This concludes our changes to the OCON application. After recompiling and running the application, you can explore its ability to manage multiple embedded objects, and save and load documents while retaining object positions (Figure 30.11).

Other Features

There are several other container application features that can be added easily to the OCON application.

In the current version of the application, in order to edit an embedded object, you must first select it with the mouse and then invoke the Edit menu, select the object's submenu (for example, "Bitmap Image Object"), and use the Edit command. To provide an easier way to activate an embedded object, implement a handler for the WM_LBUTTONDBLCLK function. In it, you can utilize the DoVerb member function of the COCONCntrItem class to activate an item for in-place editing.

In the handler for WM_LBUTTONDOWN, you can utilize the capabilities of the CRectTracker class to implement moving and sizing.

FIGURE 30.11.

*Final version
of the OCON
application.*

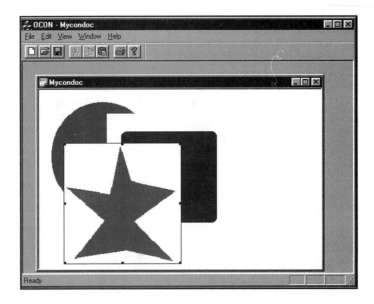

The selection does not need to be restricted to a single item. Instead of a single pointer, you can implement the selection as a list of COCONCntrItem objects using a collection class such as CObList. Multiple selection can be implemented by either monitoring the Shift and Control keys in the handler for WM_LBUTTONDOWN or by adding a rubberbanding capability.

While these capabilities are doubtless important in real-life applications, I believe that the OCON application serves the purpose of demonstrating basic container functions.

Summary

OLE containers are applications that handle embedded or linked items. Container applications can be created through the AppWizard. All you need to do is specify container support in AppWizard Step 3. OLE containers must be single-document-based or multiple-document-based applications; container capability for dialog-based applications is not supported.

An AppWizard-generated container application skeleton supports the insertion of a single component object at a fixed position. The item is inserted through the Insert Object command in the Edit menu. The application does not reflect changes in the item's size or position during an in-place editing session.

The container application represents component objects with a class derived from COleClientItem. Other differences between a container and a noncontainer application include new code in the container application's view class that implements object insertion and a simple selection mechanism, and a new, partially complete menu that represents container-provided portions of the menu that is visible during an in-place editing session.

Customizing a skeleton application may involve the following steps:

1. To add support for the proper positioning of container objects, modify the OnChangeItemPosition and OnGetItemPosition member functions of the container item class. Add a member variable reflecting the current size and position of the item. Make sure that this member variable is serialized.

2. To draw items at their correct position, modify the OnDraw member function of the view class.

3. To draw items other than the current selection, modify the OnDraw member function of the view class.

4. To provide visual feedback reflecting the current selection, modify the OnDraw member function of the view class. Utilize the CRectTracker class for drawing a rectangle around your selection.

5. To implement a mouse-driven selection mechanism, add a handler function to your view class for WM_LBUTTONDOWN events.

6. To invoke an object for in-place editing by double-clicking it, add a handler function to your view class for WM_LBUTTONDBLCLK events.

7. To implement the selection of multiple items, replace the m_pSelection member variable in your view class. Modify the WM_LBUTTONDOWN handler to implement a multiple selection mechanism.

8. In your WM_LBUTTONDOWN handler, you can utilize the capabilities of the CRectTracker class to implement sizing and positioning.

9. To add application-specific items to the document, consider deriving the class that represents these items from CDocItem. Utilize the capabilities of COleDocument for handling and serializing CDocItem objects. Revise the OnDraw member function in your view class to draw objects that are not container items. Revise your mouse event handlers as appropriate.

OLE Drag and Drop

31

OLE provides an elegant, simple, standardized way to implement drag and drop capability in applications.

To explore drag and drop support in this chapter, we build an OLE container application. This simple application is able to hold a series of container objects. Through the OLE drag and drop mechanism, this application supports dragging items between its view and another application, between its own view windows, and within a single view window.

Drag and Drop Basics

Drag and drop represents a technique of sharing data between applications that act as *drag sources* and applications that act as *drop targets*. Drag sources are applications that enable their items to be dragged from their windows to the windows of other applications. Drop targets are applications that accept items dragged from drag sources and released within their window (Figure 31.1).

FIGURE 31.1.

Drag and Drop.

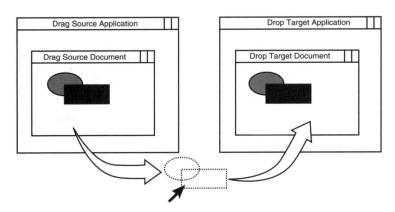

Implementing a drag source using MFC is very simple. Implementing a drop target is somewhat more difficult, but it is still not an overwhelmingly complex task.

The simple implementations presented in this chapter are based on the drag and drop support in the class COleClientItem. In applications that support drag and drop of native data or drag and drop of multiple items, you may decide to utilize the drag and drop support in COleServerItem instead.

Drag and drop functionality and clipboard functionality have many things in common. If you wish to implement clipboard cut, copy, and paste functions using OLE, you can share most of the clipboard support code and drag and drop code.

Creating a Container Application

The container application required for our purposes is based on the AppWizard-generated container application default, with a few modifications that make it possible to select items using the mouse and that support persistent storage of item positions.

Creating the Application

To create the application, use AppWizard's defaults, except for specifying container application support in AppWizard Step 3. I named the application OCON for the simple reason that it is based on the example I present in Chapter 30. First, here's a brief review of the changes that need to be made to the AppWizard-generated skeleton to support persistent storage of embedded object positions and to support item selection using the mouse.

Adding Positioning Support

The default AppWizard-supplied implementation of a container application positions inserted objects using a fixed rectangle. To make it possible for inserted items to be positioned anywhere in the drawing surface, a member variable of type CRect must be added to the class COCONCntrItem. This variable must also be serialized. The Draw member function of the view class must utilize this variable when drawing objects.

This variable should also be utilized in the COCONCntrItem member functions OnChangeItemPosition and OnGetItemPosition. Another change to COCONCntrItem is the addition of a new helper function, Invalidate; this function, taking a CWnd pointer as its parameter, invalidates the item's rectangle in the specified window.

To add the new member variable to the COCONCntrItem class and to declare the new helper function, Invalidate, use the following code:

```
class COCONCntrItem : public COleClientItem
{
    ...
// Attributes
public:
    ...
    CRect m_rect;
    ...
// Operations
public:
    void Invalidate(CWnd *pWnd);

// Implementation
    ...
```

This member variable must be initialized in the COCONCntrItem constructor (Listing 31.1).

Listing 31.1. Initialization of m_rect in the constructor of COCONCntrItem.

```
COCONCntrItem::COCONCntrItem(COCONDoc* pContainer)
    : COleClientItem(pContainer)
{
    // TODO: add one-time construction code here
    m_rect = CRect(0, 0, 0, 0);
}
```

The modified versions of COCONCntrItem::OnChangeItemPosition and COCONCntrItem::OnGetItemPosition (Listing 31.2) are used to reflect any changes in the item's size or position that were made during an in-place session. It also makes use of the GetCachedExtent member function to update the item's size and position if it has not yet been initialized.

Listing 31.2. COCONCntrItem::OnChangeItemPosition and COCONCntrItem::OnGetItemPosition.

```
BOOL COCONCntrItem::OnChangeItemPosition(const CRect& rectPos)
{
    ASSERT_VALID(this);

    if (!COleClientItem::OnChangeItemPosition(rectPos))
        return FALSE;

    // TODO: update any cache you may have of the item's
    //   rectangle/extent
    m_rect = rectPos;
    GetDocument()->UpdateAllViews(NULL);

    return TRUE;
}

void COCONCntrItem::OnGetItemPosition(CRect& rPosition)
{
    ASSERT_VALID(this);

//  rPosition.SetRect(10, 10, 210, 210);
    if (m_rect.IsRectNull())
    {
        CSize size;
        CClientDC dc(NULL);
        GetCachedExtent(&size, GetDrawAspect());
        dc.HIMETRICtoDP(&size);
        m_rect = CRect(CPoint(10, 10), size);
    }
    rPosition = m_rect;
}
```

Listing 31.3 shows how COCONCntrItem::Serialize must be modified to support serialization of the new member variable.

Listing 31.3. Modified version of COCONCntrItem::Serialize.

```
void COCONCntrItem::Serialize(CArchive& ar)
{
    ASSERT_VALID(this);

    COleClientItem::Serialize(ar);

    if (ar.IsStoring())
    {
        // TODO: add storing code here
        ar << m_rect;
    }
    else
    {
        // TODO: add loading code here
        ar >> m_rect;
    }
}
```

Finally, the addition of the new Invalidate helper function (Listing 31.4) concludes changes to the implementation of COCONCntrItem.

Listing 31.4. The helper function COCONCntrItem::Invalidate.

```
void COCONCntrItem::Invalidate(CWnd *pWnd)
{
    CRect rect = m_rect;
    rect.InflateRect(1, 1);
    pWnd->InvalidateRect(rect);
}
```

Listing 31.5 shows the changes to COCONView::OnDraw; the new version takes into account the items' stored positions and draws them accordingly. It also draws all items (as opposed to just the current selection). Furthermore, this version of the function uses a CRectTracker object to highlight the currently selected item.

Listing 31.5. Modified version of COCONCntrItem::OnDraw.

```
void COCONView::OnDraw(CDC* pDC)
{
    COCONDoc* pDoc = GetDocument();
    ASSERT_VALID(pDoc);

    POSITION pos = pDoc->GetStartPosition();
    while (pos)
```

continues

Listing 31.5. continued

```
    {
        COCONCntrItem *pItem =
            (COCONCntrItem*)pDoc->GetNextClientItem(pos);
        pItem->Draw(pDC, pItem->m_rect);
        if (pItem == m_pSelection)
        {
            CRectTracker tracker;
            tracker.m_rect = pItem->m_rect;
            tracker.m_nStyle = CRectTracker::resizeInside ¦
                                CRectTracker::solidLine;
            if (pItem->GetItemState() == COleClientItem::openState
         ¦¦ pItem->GetItemState() == COleClientItem::activeUIState)
                    tracker.m_nStyle ¦= CRectTracker::hatchInside;
            tracker.Draw(pDC);
        }
    }
}
```

Adding Selection Support

In the previous section, we already implemented highlighting the current selection. Adding support for selection of items using the mouse requires adding a handler for WM_LBUTTONDOWN events to the view class. This handler, shown in Listing 31.6, can be added using the ClassWizard.

Listing 31.6. Handler function for WM_LBUTTONDOWN messages.

```
void COCONView::OnLButtonDown(UINT nFlags, CPoint point)
{
    // TODO: Add your message handler code here and/or call default

//  CView::OnLButtonDown(nFlags, point);
    COCONDoc* pDoc = GetDocument();
    ASSERT_VALID(pDoc);

    COCONCntrItem *pSelection = NULL;
    COCONCntrItem *pItem =
        (COCONCntrItem *)pDoc->GetInPlaceActiveItem(this);

    if (pItem != NULL) pItem->Close();
    POSITION pos = pDoc->GetStartPosition();
    while (pos)
    {
        pItem = (COCONCntrItem*)pDoc->GetNextClientItem(pos);
        if (pItem->m_rect.PtInRect(point))
            pSelection = pItem;
    }
    if (pSelection != m_pSelection)
    {
        if (m_pSelection != NULL)
            m_pSelection->Invalidate(this);
```

```
            m_pSelection = pSelection;
            if (m_pSelection != NULL)
                m_pSelection->Invalidate(this);
        }
    }
```

Adding Drag and Drop Support

Although the two areas of functionality are usually mentioned together, the requirements for a drag source application and for a drop target application are quite distinct. Of the two, implementation of a drag source is the easier task. However, both tasks are supported extensively in part by the OLE architecture, in part by the MFC.

The support for implementing a drag source comes in the form of the DoDragDrop member function of several classes, namely COleClientItem, COleServerItem, and COleDataSource.

Drop target functionality is supported through a series of member functions of the CView class; namely, its member functions OnDrop, OnDragEnter, OnDragOver, and OnDragLeave. However, unlike the DoDragDrop function, which can be called as is, these functions require customized implementations in your application.

Implementing a Drag Source

With the help of the COleClientItem::DoDragDrop member function, adding drag source capability to an OLE container is almost embarrassingly simple. All we need to do is modify the handler function for WM_LBUTTONDOWN events, COCONView::OnLButtonDown. If and when a valid object is selected by the user using the mouse, we must call the object's DoDragDrop member function to perform the drag and drop operation. We must also perform a minor housekeeping chore: If the object was moved from our application to another, we must delete it from the list of objects maintained by our document class. However, with CDocItem-derived objects, this is also a very simple task; it is sufficient to simply delete the object using the delete operator. The CDocItem destructor function ensures that the object is properly removed from the document's list of objects.

The modified version of COCONView::OnLButtonDown is shown in Listing 31.7.

Listing 31.7. COCONView::OnLButtonDown with drag source support.

```
void COCONView::OnLButtonDown(UINT nFlags, CPoint point)
{
    // TODO: Add your message handler code here and/or call default

//  CView::OnLButtonDown(nFlags, point);
    COCONDoc* pDoc = GetDocument();
    ASSERT_VALID(pDoc);
```

continues

Listing 31.7. continued

```
COCONCntrItem *pSelection = NULL;
COCONCntrItem *pItem =
    (COCONCntrItem *)pDoc->GetInPlaceActiveItem(this);

if (pItem != NULL) pItem->Close();
POSITION pos = pDoc->GetStartPosition();
while (pos)
{
    pItem = (COCONCntrItem*)pDoc->GetNextClientItem(pos);
    if (pItem->m_rect.PtInRect(point))
        pSelection = pItem;
}
if (pSelection != m_pSelection)
{
    if (m_pSelection != NULL)
        m_pSelection->Invalidate(this);
    m_pSelection = pSelection;
    if (m_pSelection != NULL)
        m_pSelection->Invalidate(this);
}

if (m_pSelection != NULL)
{
    m_dragRect = m_pSelection->m_rect;
    if (m_pSelection->DoDragDrop(m_pSelection->m_rect,
        (CPoint)(point - m_pSelection->m_rect.TopLeft())) ==
            DROPEFFECT_MOVE)
    {
        m_pSelection->Invalidate(this);
        delete m_pSelection;
        m_pSelection = NULL;
    }
}
}
```

Before we move onto the implementation of drop target functionality, I want to add a few notes concerning this drag source implementation.

Obviously, most applications have functionality above and beyond being an OLE container (if they implement container functionality at all). How would you implement drag source capabilities for those applications?

One possibility is to utilize the DoDragDrop member function of COleServerItem. If your application is an OLE server, it already has a COleServerItem-derived class defined to represent your application's document in an embedded item. Modify this class to support representation of only the current selection (as opposed to the entire document). This modification is easy; you need only to change the Serialize and OnDraw member functions and create a constructor that takes a parameter representing the current selection. The utility of this class goes beyond drag source functionality; it can also be used to represent linked items and to facilitate the transfer of the current selection to the clipboard.

Once your `COleServerItem`-derived class is complete, you can create an item of this type in your `WM_LBUTTONDOWN` handler (or wherever you wish to implement drag source functionality). Subsequently, you can utilize the member function `COleServerItem::DoDragDrop` to implement drag source capability just as simply as we did for OLE client items.

If you do not wish to use a `COleServerItem`-derived class for this purpose (for example, if your application is not an OLE server), you can also utilize the `COleDataSource` class. This class can be used to represent a selection for drag and drop and clipboard transfers. `COleDataSource` also has a `DoDragDrop` member function, so implementing drag source functionality using this class is equally simple.

Implementing a Drop Target

Implementing an OLE drop target requires a lot more work than implementing a drag source. Several member functions of your view class require override versions. The view class must be registered as a drop target. Special considerations must be made to ensure that objects originating from within the application itself are handled properly and efficiently; for example, if the drag and drop operation effectively reduces to a move within the same window, it should be treated that way.

The set of `CView` member functions that require overrides is listed in Table 31.1.

Table 31.1. Drag and drop related overridables in `CView`.

Member Function	Description
OnDragEnter	Called when an item is dragged into the window
OnDragLeave	Called when a dragged item leaves the window
OnDragOver	Called while an item is dragged within the window
OnDrop	Called when an item is released in the window

Before we start writing code madly, here's a summary of exactly what we would like to see in our drop target application.

First, the obvious: If an object is released over our application's view window, we would like the object to appear at that location, preferably preserving its original size.

We would also like to see a tracking rectangle while the mouse is inside the view window. The rectangle will reflect the size of the object that is about to be dropped in the window.

Lastly, we would like to ensure that a drag and drop operation that reduces to merely moving an object within the same window is treated accordingly.

The implementation of the `OnDragEnter`, `OnDragLeave`, and `OnDragOver` function overrides requires a few additional member variables. These variables will be used to remember the drag rectangle's size and position and other drag characteristics during a drag operation. In addition, a member variable of type COleDropTarget is also required in order to register the view window as a drop target. The declaration of these variables should be added to the declaration of the view class as follows:

```
class COCONView : public CView
{
    ...
// Attributes
public:
    ...
    COCONCntrItem* m_pSelection;
    COleDropTarget m_dropTarget;
    BOOL m_bInDrag;
    DROPEFFECT m_prevDropEffect;
    CRect m_dragRect;
    CPoint m_dragPoint;
    CSize m_dragSize;
    CSize m_dragOffset;
    ...
```

The declarations for the overrides of OnDragEnter, OnDragLeave, OnDragOver, and OnDrop should be added using the ClassWizard.

Our first task in making the application work as a drop target is to register it as one. This is accomplished by adding a member variable of type COleDropTarget and calling its Register member function at the appropriate moment of time. The most appropriate place for this is in the view class's OnCreate member function. To implement this registration, create a handler for WM_CREATE messages using the ClassWizard, and add the code shown in Listing 31.8.

Listing 31.8. The COCONView::OnCreate member function.

```
int COCONView::OnCreate(LPCREATESTRUCT lpCreateStruct)
{
    if (CView::OnCreate(lpCreateStruct) == -1)
        return -1;

    // TODO: Add your specialized creation code here
    m_dropTarget.Register(this);

    return 0;
}
```

The OnDragEnter, OnDragLeave, and OnDragOver member functions are used to manage visual feedback during a drag operation. OnDragEnter (Listing 31.9) attempts to retrieve the item's size by querying the item for the Object Descriptor clipboard type. This data type, when supplied, contains information about the transfer item including its size and the offset of the mouse pointer relative to the item's upper-left corner.

Listing 31.9. The `COCONView::OnDragEnter` member function.

```
DROPEFFECT COCONView::OnDragEnter(COleDataObject* pDataObject,
                                  DWORD dwKeyState, CPoint point)
{
 // TODO: Add your specialized code here and/or call the base class

//   return CView::OnDragEnter(pDataObject, dwKeyState, point);
     ASSERT(m_prevDropEffect == DROPEFFECT_NONE);

     m_dragSize = CSize(0, 0);
     m_dragOffset = CSize(0, 0);
     HGLOBAL hObjDesc =
         pDataObject->GetGlobalData(cfObjectDescriptor);
     if (hObjDesc != NULL)
     {
         LPOBJECTDESCRIPTOR pObjDesc =
             (LPOBJECTDESCRIPTOR)GlobalLock(hObjDesc);
         ASSERT(pObjDesc != NULL);
         m_dragSize.cx = (int)pObjDesc->sizel.cx;
         m_dragSize.cy = (int)pObjDesc->sizel.cy;
         m_dragOffset.cx = (int)pObjDesc->pointl.x;
         m_dragOffset.cy = (int)pObjDesc->pointl.y;
         GlobalUnlock(hObjDesc);
         GlobalFree(hObjDesc);
     }
     CClientDC dc(NULL);
     dc.HIMETRICtoDP(&m_dragSize);
     dc.HIMETRICtoDP(&m_dragOffset);
     m_dragPoint = point - CSize(1, 1);
     return OnDragOver(pDataObject, dwKeyState, point);
}
```

This function makes use of the global variable `cfObjectDescriptor`. Declare this variable at the top of your view class's implementation file as follows:

```
static cfObjectDescriptor =
    (CLIPFORMAT)::RegisterClipboardFormat(_T("Object Descriptor"));
```

The next member function is `OnDragOver` (Listing 31.10). This function is called every time the mouse moves while within the view window's client area. This function plays a dual role. First, it determines the currently applicable *drop effect*; based on the state of the Control, Shift, and Alt keys it determines whether the item, were it dropped in the window at this moment, should be copied, linked, or moved to this window.

Listing 31.10. The `COCONView::OnDragOver` member function.

```
DROPEFFECT COCONView::OnDragOver(COleDataObject* pDataObject,
                                 DWORD dwKeyState, CPoint point)
{
 // TODO: Add your specialized code here and/or call the base class
```

continues

Listing 31.10. continued

```
//  return CView::OnDragOver(pDataObject, dwKeyState, point);
    DROPEFFECT de = DROPEFFECT_NONE;

    point -= m_dragOffset;

    if ((dwKeyState & (MK_CONTROL¦MK_SHIFT)) ==
        (MK_CONTROL¦MK_SHIFT))
        de = DROPEFFECT_LINK;
    else if ((dwKeyState & MK_CONTROL) == MK_CONTROL)
        de = DROPEFFECT_COPY;
    else if ((dwKeyState & MK_ALT) == MK_ALT)
        de = DROPEFFECT_MOVE;
    else
        de = DROPEFFECT_MOVE;

    if (point == m_dragPoint)
        return de;

    CClientDC dc(this);
    if (m_prevDropEffect != DROPEFFECT_NONE)
        dc.DrawFocusRect(CRect(m_dragPoint, m_dragSize));
    m_prevDropEffect = de;
    if (m_prevDropEffect != DROPEFFECT_NONE)
    {
        m_dragPoint = point;
        dc.DrawFocusRect(CRect(point, m_dragSize));
    }
    return de;
}
```

The other role of this function is to actually draw visual feedback. This is accomplished by drawing a rectangle using the CDC::DrawFocusRect function.

The third function in this group is OnDragLeave (Listing 31.11). This function, the simplest of the three, is called to mark the end of a dragging operation.

Listing 31.11. The COCONView::OnDragLeave member function.

```
void COCONView::OnDragLeave()
{
 // TODO: Add your specialized code here and/or call the base class

//  CView::OnDragLeave();
    CClientDC dc(this);
    if (m_prevDropEffect != DROPEFFECT_NONE)
    {
        dc.DrawFocusRect(CRect(m_dragPoint, m_dragSize));
        m_prevDropEffect = DROPEFFECT_NONE;
    }
}
```

Now it's time to turn our attention to the `OnDrop` member function (Listing 31.12). This function is by far the most important one in our implementation of drop target functionality. As its
name implies, it is this function where the actual insertion of a dropped item takes place.

Listing 31.12. The `COCONView::OnDrop` member function.

```
BOOL COCONView::OnDrop(COleDataObject* pDataObject,
                       DROPEFFECT dropEffect, CPoint point)
{
 // TODO: Add your specialized code here and/or call the base class

//   return CView::OnDrop(pDataObject, dropEffect, point);
     ASSERT_VALID(this);
     COCONDoc* pDoc = GetDocument();
     ASSERT_VALID(pDoc);
     CSize size;

     OnDragLeave();
     CClientDC dc(NULL);
     point -= m_dragOffset;

     pDoc->SetModifiedFlag(TRUE);
     if ((dropEffect & DROPEFFECT_MOVE) && m_bInDrag)
     {
         ASSERT(m_pSelection != NULL);
         m_pSelection->Invalidate(this);
         m_pSelection->m_rect =
             m_dragRect + point - m_dragRect.TopLeft();
         m_bInDrag = FALSE;
         return TRUE;
     }

     COCONCntrItem* pItem = NULL;
     TRY
     {
         pItem = new COCONCntrItem(pDoc);
         ASSERT_VALID(pItem);
         if (dropEffect & DROPEFFECT_LINK)
         {
             if (!pItem->CreateLinkFromData(pDataObject))
                 AfxThrowMemoryException();
         }
         else
         {
             if (!pItem->CreateFromData(pDataObject))
                 AfxThrowMemoryException();
         }
         ASSERT_VALID(pItem);
         pItem->GetExtent(&size, pItem->GetDrawAspect());
         dc.HIMETRICtoDP(&size);
         pItem->m_rect = CRect(point, size);
         if (m_pSelection != NULL)
             m_pSelection->Invalidate(this);
         m_pSelection = pItem;
         if (m_pSelection != NULL)
             m_pSelection->Invalidate(this);
```

continues

Listing 31.12. continued

```
}
CATCH(CException, e)
{
    if( pItem != NULL ) delete pItem;
    AfxMessageBox(IDP_FAILED_TO_CREATE);
}
END_CATCH

return pItem != NULL;
}
```

This function first terminates the drag operation by calling OnDragLeave and notifies the document that the contents are changing by calling CDocument::SetModifiedFlag.

Next, it makes an attempt to determine if the drag and drop operation actually represents moving an object within the same window. For this, we make use of the m_bInDrag member variable; this variable is set in COCONView::OnLButtonDown when a drag operation begins, as we see momentarily. If the operation is a move, the function simply updates the affected item's rectangle and returns.

In the case of a genuine drop operation, an attempt is made to create a new item of type COCONCntrItem using the drop data. If the attempt is successful, the item's size is determined and the item's rectangle is updated.

As I mentioned, the key to determining whether a drag and drop operation reduces to a mere move is the m_bInDrag member variable. To set this variable, we have to implement yet another modification to COCONView::OnLButtonDown. This final version of this function is shown in Listing 31.13.

Listing 31.13. Final version of COCONView::OnLButtonDown.

```
void COCONView::OnLButtonDown(UINT nFlags, CPoint point)
{
    // TODO: Add your message handler code here and/or call default

//  CView::OnLButtonDown(nFlags, point);
    COCONDoc* pDoc = GetDocument();
    ASSERT_VALID(pDoc);

    COCONCntrItem *pSelection = NULL;
    COCONCntrItem *pItem =
        (COCONCntrItem *)pDoc->GetInPlaceActiveItem(this);

    if (pItem != NULL) pItem->Close();
    POSITION pos = pDoc->GetStartPosition();
    while (pos)
    {
        pItem = (COCONCntrItem*)pDoc->GetNextClientItem(pos);
        if (pItem->m_rect.PtInRect(point))
            pSelection = pItem;
```

```
    }
    if (pSelection != m_pSelection)
    {
        if (m_pSelection != NULL)
            m_pSelection->Invalidate(this);
        m_pSelection = pSelection;
        if (m_pSelection != NULL)
            m_pSelection->Invalidate(this);
    }

    if (m_pSelection != NULL)
    {
        m_bInDrag = TRUE;
        m_dragRect = m_pSelection->m_rect;
        DROPEFFECT dropEffect =
            m_pSelection->DoDragDrop(m_pSelection->m_rect,
                (CPoint)(point - m_pSelection->m_rect.TopLeft()));
        m_pSelection->Invalidate(this);
        if (m_bInDrag == TRUE && dropEffect == DROPEFFECT_MOVE)
        {
            delete m_pSelection;
            m_pSelection = NULL;
        }
        m_bInDrag = FALSE;
    }
}
```

As you can see, the `m_bInDrag` member variable is set to `TRUE` just before calling `COCONCntrItem::DoDragDrop`. If, during the drag, a callback is made to the same view object, by looking at `m_bInDrag`, we can determine that the source of the drag operation is the same view window.

The `OnDrop` member function resets `m_bInDrag` to `FALSE` if a drag operation is successfully reduced to a move. In this case, `OnLButtonDown` will not delete the selected item. That deletion is necessary otherwise, if the item was moved to a different window.

Finally, we need to initialize two of the member variables to ensure proper functioning of the view class. Listing 31.14 shows the initialization of `m_bInDrag` and `m_prevDropEffect` in the view class's constructor.

Listing 31.14. Member variable initialization in the constructor of `COCONView`.

```
COCONView::COCONView()
{
    // TODO: add construction code here
    m_pSelection = NULL;
    m_bInDrag = FALSE;
    m_prevDropEffect = DROPEFFECT_NONE;
}
```

This concludes our construction of an OLE container supporting drag and drop. The completed application, shown in Figure 31.2, can serve as a drop target (or drag source) for word processor objects, spreadsheet cells, drawings, and many other types of OLE objects.

FIGURE 31.2.

The OCON drag and drop application.

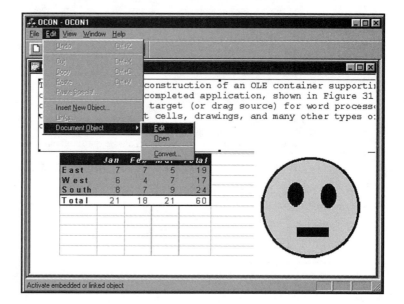

Summary

Drag and drop represents the capability to select items in one application (the drag source) and, using the mouse, drag the items and drop them in the window of another application (the drop target). Drag and drop, from the user's perspective, is a simpler mechanism for sharing data between applications than using the clipboard.

OLE provides extensive drag and drop support. This support is encapsulated in the MFC Library in the form of a series of drag and drop related classes and functions.

The implementation of a drag source is relatively easy. For this purpose, you can utilize the member functions of COleClientItem, COleServerItem, and COleDataSource.

Use of COleClientItem::DoDragDrop is recommended if the drag item is an embedded or linked OLE item represented by a COleClientItem-derived class. In this case, simply call the DoDragDrop function for the object that the user selected for dragging, and the framework does the rest. Remember to delete the object if the return value of DoDragDrop indicates that the selection has been moved (as opposed to copied or linked) to another application.

Use of COleServerItem::DoDragDrop is recommended for applications that are OLE servers. This function is most useful if your COleServerItem-derived class is already capable of representing a selection (as opposed to the entire contents of a document). Just create a

COleServerItem-derived object representing the drag selection and use its DoDragDrop member function to perform the drag operation.

In applications that are not OLE servers, you can also consider using COleDataSource for implementing a drag source.

Implementing a drop target is a more involved operation. In addition to providing an override version of the OnDrop member function of your view class, you must also override the OnDragEnter, OnDragLeave, and OnDragOver member functions. The purpose of these functions, called by the framework while the mouse is over the view window during a drag and drop operation, is twofold: first, they are used to provide visual feedback during the drag; and second, they are used to inform the framework regarding the allowable drop operations.

In the simplest implementation of OnDrop, you can create a COleClientItem-derived object representing the drop item. In more involved implementations, you may consider inspecting the item and identify native data originating from within your own application, or data available in formats that your application can recognize.

In an application that acts both as a drag source and drop target, you should improve the application's efficiency by recognizing operations that reduce to a simple move. In this case, instead of removing the dragged item or items and creating new items, you can implement the operation as a simple position change.

OLE Automation

32

582

OLE automation represents a communication mechanism between cooperating applications. Applications that are *OLE automation servers* have the capability to expose their objects through a series of *properties* and *methods*. Applications that are OLE clients or *OLE controllers* can access these exposed properties and methods through the OLE IDispatch interface.

One of the most popular uses of OLE automation is to expose the capabilities of your application to the extent that your application becomes fully controllable from a general purpose OLE controller, such as Microsoft's Visual Basic. In this fashion, Visual Basic can act as a powerful macro language for your application.

The MFC Library and the Visual C++ Developer Studio provide extensive support for developing OLE automation servers. In this chapter, we first explore these capabilities by constructing a simple server application; later, we review other issues that concern OLE automation development.

Building an Automation Server

The OLE automation server that we build in this chapter is simple indeed; this tiny program performs one task only, and that is the multiplication of two numbers. The program is capable of running stand-alone using a simple dialog-based user interface. It also supports invocation from within an OLE controller.

Figure 32.1 shows the user interface of this application, ASRV. To use this application, first enter the two multiplicands in the two edit fields on the left side, then click on the = button to calculate the result.

FIGURE 32.1.

The user interface of the ASRV server.

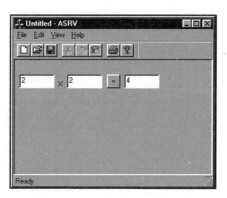

The OLE automation methods and properties closely correspond to these user-interface elements. Two properties, `Multi1` and `Multi2`, correspond to the two multiplicands; these properties are read and write. The `Result` property, representing the result of the multiplication, is a read-only property. Finally, the `Set` method corresponds to the function of the = button; this method carries out the actual multiplication.

We construct this application in three steps. First, the application's skeleton is created. Next, the user interface is edited and the functions performing the calculations are added. Finally, OLE automation capabilities are implemented.

Constructing the ASRV Application Skeleton

The ASRV application skeleton should be constructed using the AppWizard. The application should be a single-document-based application with default settings.

Support for OLE automation is specified in Step 3 of AppWizard (Figure 32.2). Make sure the OLE automation check box is marked before proceeding from this step.

FIGURE 32.2.

Adding OLE automation support.

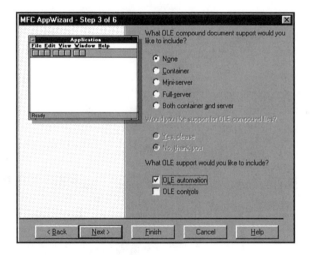

We should also change the base class of the new application's view class before dismissing AppWizard. In AppWizard Step 6 (Figure 32.3), select the class `CASRVView` and select `CFormView` as its base class. As a `CFormView`-based class, our new view class uses a dialog template to provide its visual appearance.

At this point, you can click on the Finish button to complete construction of the skeleton application.

FIGURE 32.3.

*Changing the base
class for the view.*

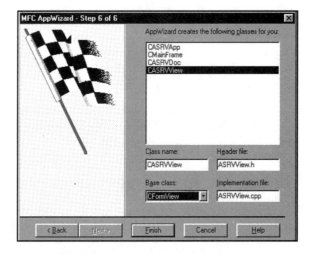

Implementing the Calculation

I almost used the term "Calculator Engine" in the title, but I figured that such a term might cause some of you to burst out in hysterical laughter. After all, calling a simple multiplication operation an "engine" may be too much, even in this day and age of hype, pomp, and circumstance!

The first step in implementing the calculator is to create its user interface. AppWizard created for us a dialog corresponding to the `CFormView`-derived view class; however, the dialog is spartan, to say the least (Figure 32.4). Edit this dialog by removing the default TODO field and adding three edit fields, a button, and a static field as shown earlier in Figure 32.1.

FIGURE 32.4.

*"Spartan" default
dialog supplied by
AppWizard.*

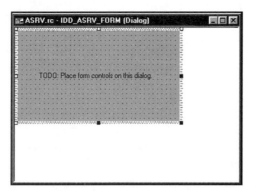

The two edit fields on the left side should be called `IDC_MULTI1` and `IDC_MULTI2`, respectively. The edit field on the right-hand side should be called `IDC_RESULT`. You may consider making this field a read-only field. The button, with a caption set to a single equal sign, should be called

IDC_CALCULATE. You may consider setting the Default property for this button to enable using the Enter key to perform the calculation.

While the dialog is open for editing, invoke the ClassWizard. Using the ClassWizard, add a member function to the view class corresponding to a mouse click on the IDC_CALCULATE button (Figure 32.5).

FIGURE 32.5.

Adding a member function to handle clicks on the Calculate button.

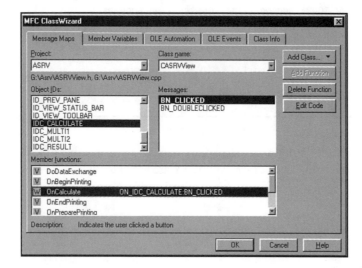

At this point, you are probably expecting us to add member variables corresponding to the edit fields. However, this is not how we are going to proceed at this time. The member variables that represent the multiplicands and the result are added to the document class instead; correspondingly, we have to modify the DoDataExchange member function of the view class manually.

After dismissing the ClassWizard, open the header file for the document class for editing. In the Attributes section of the CASRVDoc class declaration, add declarations for three new member variables as follows:

```
class CASRVDoc : public CDocument
{
protected: // create from serialization only
    CASRVDoc();
    DECLARE_DYNCREATE(CASRVDoc)

// Attributes
public:
    long m_lMulti1;
    long m_lMulti2;
    long m_lResult;
...
```

These variables must also be initialized. Initialization can take place in the constructor (Listing 32.1).

Listing 32.1. Variable initialization in the CASRVDoc constructor.

```
CASRVDoc::CASRVDoc()
{
    // TODO: add one-time construction code here
    m_lMulti1 = 0;
    m_lMulti2 = 0;
    m_lResult = 0;

    EnableAutomation();

    AfxOleLockApp();
}
```

To actually perform the calculation, we need a new member function in CASRVDoc. This member function, DoCalculate, will be declared as follows:

```
class CASRVDoc : public CDocument
{
    ...
// Operations
public:
    void DoCalculate();
...
```

The implementation of DoCalculate is shown in Listing 32.2.

Listing 32.2. Implementation of CASRVDoc::DoCalculate.

```
void CASRVDoc::DoCalculate()
{
    m_lResult = m_lMulti1 * m_lMulti2;
}
```

Two things remain to be done. First, we need to connect the member variables in CASRVDoc with the CFormView-based dialog. Second, we must add a call to CASRVDoc::DoCalculate from within the handler function for mouse clicks on the IDC_CALCULATE button.

The modified version of CASRVView::DoDataExchange is shown in Listing 32.3. Basically, we do what ClassWizard would have done, if only the variables were local to this class.

Listing 32.3. Modified version of CASRVDoc::DoDataExchange.

```
void CASRVView::DoDataExchange(CDataExchange* pDX)
{
    CFormView::DoDataExchange(pDX);
    //{{AFX_DATA_MAP(CASRVView)
```

```
//}}AFX_DATA_MAP
CASRVDoc *pDoc = GetDocument();
ASSERT_VALID(pDoc);
DDX_Text(pDX, IDC_MULTI1, pDoc->m_lMulti1);
DDX_Text(pDX, IDC_MULTI2, pDoc->m_lMulti2);
DDX_Text(pDX, IDC_RESULT, pDoc->m_lResult);
}
```

In the implementation of CASRVView::OnCalculate (Listing 32.4), we call the document class's member function DoCalculate to perform the actual calculation. We also utilize the UpdateData function to ensure that the member variables and the dialog fields are properly updated before and after the calculation.

Listing 32.4. Implementation of CASRVView::OnCalculate.

```
void CASRVView::OnCalculate()
{
    // TODO: Add your control notification handler code here
    CASRVDoc *pDoc = GetDocument();
    ASSERT_VALID(pDoc);
    UpdateData(TRUE);
    pDoc->DoCalculate();
    UpdateData(FALSE);
}
```

At this point, the application can be recompiled and should operate normally as a stand-alone application.

Adding Automation Support

The first step in adding automation support is through the ClassWizard. To add properties and methods to the CASRVDoc class, invoke the ClassWizard, select the OLE Automation tab, and select the CASRVDoc class (Figure 32.6).

First, add two properties corresponding to the two multiplicands. Click on the Add Property button to invoke the Add Property dialog. In this dialog, specify Multi1 as the external name of the new property and long as the property's type. Modify the default variable name supplied by ClassWizard to read m_lMulti1 (Figure 32.7). Click on the OK button to dismiss this dialog.

Next, use the ClassWizard to add another property, Multi2, in a similar fashion.

The third property, Result, differs from the previous two. Because this is a read-only property, we choose Get/Set methods as the property's implementation. Or, to be more precise, we use a Get method, for implementing a read-only property is accomplished simply by erasing the ClassWizard-generated name for the Set function (Figure 32.8).

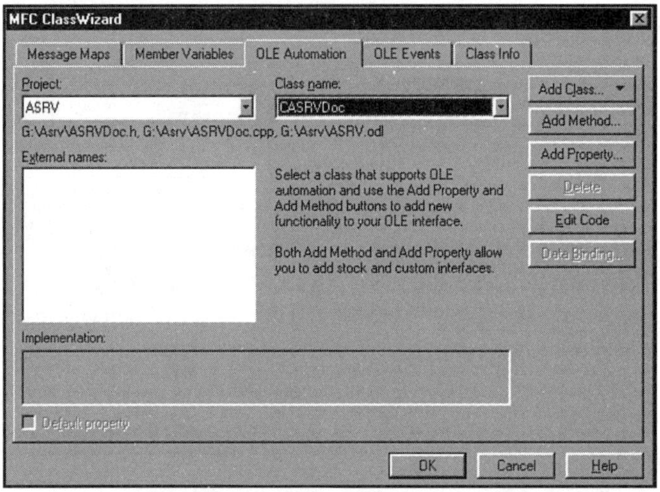

FIGURE 32.6.

Using the ClassWizard to add automation support.

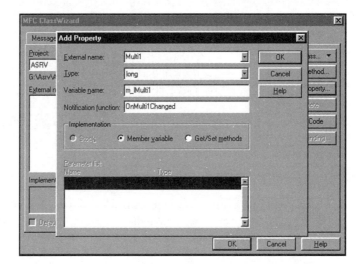

FIGURE 32.7.

Adding a new property.

The one thing that remains is adding the `Calculate` method that performs the actual calculation. To add this method, click on the Add Method button. In the Add Method dialog, type `Calculate` as both the External and Internal name of the new method, and select `void` as the method's return type (Figure 32.9).

At this point, we are finished with ClassWizard; it can be dismissed by clicking on the OK button.

Chapter 32

FIGURE 32.8.

Adding a read-only property.

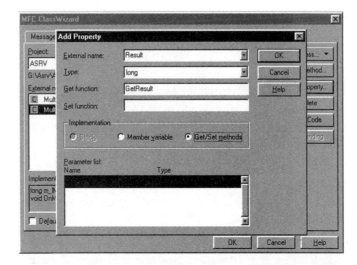

FIGURE 32.9.

Adding a new method.

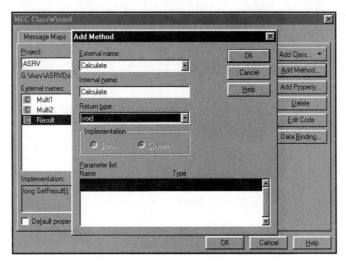

Take a brief look at the header file of CASRVDoc. Towards the end of the class declaration, the ClassWizard added a series of items to the class's dispatch map:

```
class CASRVDoc : public CDocument
{
    ...
protected:
    ...
    // Generated OLE dispatch map functions
    //{{AFX_DISPATCH(CASRVDoc)
    long m_lMulti1;
    afx_msg void OnMulti1Changed();
    long m_lMulti2;
```

```
    afx_msg void OnMulti2Changed();
    afx_msg long GetResult();
    afx_msg void Calculate();
    //}}AFX_DISPATCH
    DECLARE_DISPATCH_MAP()
    DECLARE_INTERFACE_MAP()
};
```

There are several things that should be noticed here. First, as you can see, the ClassWizard generated declarations for the member variables m_lMulti1 and m_lMulti2; therefore, the declarations we added by hand earlier are no longer needed and should be removed from the Attributes section.

Second, the ClassWizard created the method function Calculate; as there is no need for this and a separate DoCalculate, these two functions can be consolidated into one and we can get rid of DoCalculate.

Third, you should notice that the variables m_lMulti1 and m_lMulti2 are in a section of the class declaration that is marked protected. However, we access these variables from CASRVView::DoDataExchange. The simplest way to ensure that the program can be compiled is to add CASRVView as a friend class to CASRVDoc.

Because of these numerous changes, I have listed the final form of the CASRVDoc class declaration in its entirety (see Listing 32.5).

Listing 32.5. CASRVDoc class declaration with automation support.

```
class CASRVDoc : public CDocument
{
friend class CASRVView;

protected: // create from serialization only
    CASRVDoc();
    DECLARE_DYNCREATE(CASRVDoc)

// Attributes
public:
    long m_lResult;

// Operations
public:

// Overrides
    // ClassWizard generated virtual function overrides
    //{{AFX_VIRTUAL(CASRVDoc)
    public:
    virtual BOOL OnNewDocument();
    virtual void Serialize(CArchive& ar);
    //}}AFX_VIRTUAL

// Implementation
public:
    virtual ~CASRVDoc();
#ifdef _DEBUG
```

```
    virtual void AssertValid() const;
    virtual void Dump(CDumpContext& dc) const;
#endif

protected:

// Generated message map functions
protected:
    //{{AFX_MSG(CASRVDoc)
        // NOTE - the ClassWizard will add and remove member
        //   functions here.  DO NOT EDIT what you see in these
        //   blocks of generated code !
    //}}AFX_MSG
    DECLARE_MESSAGE_MAP()

    // Generated OLE dispatch map functions
    //{{AFX_DISPATCH(CASRVDoc)
    long m_lMulti1;
    afx_msg void OnMulti1Changed();
    long m_lMulti2;
    afx_msg void OnMulti2Changed();
    afx_msg long GetResult();
    afx_msg void Calculate();
    //}}AFX_DISPATCH
    DECLARE_DISPATCH_MAP()
    DECLARE_INTERFACE_MAP()
};
```

The ClassWizard added two notification handlers and two method functions to the implementation of CASRVDoc. After removing the DoCalculate member function from the implementation file, modify CASRVDoc::GetResult and CASRVDoc::Calculate as shown in Listing 32.6. The notification handler functions do not need to be altered.

Listing 32.6. CASRVDoc::GetResult **and** CASRVDoc::Calculate.

```
long CASRVDoc::GetResult()
{
    // TODO: Add your property handler here

    return m_lResult;
}

void CASRVDoc::Calculate()
{
    // TODO: Add your dispatch handler code here
    m_lResult = m_lMulti1 * m_lMulti2;
}
```

One thing remains to be done before we can recompile the application. In the function CASRVView::OnCalculate there is a now obsolete reference to the DoCalculate member function of the document class. Change this reference to Calculate instead, and now you can recompile the program.

The Type Library

Before we test our application, let's take a quick peek at one of the files generated and maintained by ClassWizard. The `ASRV.odl` file (Listing 32.7) is a script file created in Microsoft's *Object Definition Language*. It is compiled using the `MkTypLib.exe` tool; the resulting type library (TLB) file is an OLE compound document that can be accessed by automation clients using the `ITypeComp`, `ITypeInfo`, and `ITypeLib` OLE interfaces.

Listing 32.7. The `ASRV.odl` type library source file.

```
// ASRV.odl : type library source for ASRV.exe

// This file will be processed by the Make Type Library (mktyplib)
// tool to produce the type library (ASRV.tlb).

[ uuid(603E9429-01C6-11CF-87C3-00403321BFAC), version(1.0) ]
library ASRV
{
    importlib("stdole32.tlb");

    //  Primary dispatch interface for CASRVDoc

    [ uuid(603E942A-01C6-11CF-87C3-00403321BFAC) ]
    dispinterface IASRV
    {
        properties:
      // NOTE - ClassWizard will maintain property information here.
      //     Use extreme caution when editing this section.
            //{{AFX_ODL_PROP(CASRVDoc)
            [id(1)] long Multi1;
            [id(2)] long Multi2;
            [id(3)] long Result;
            //}}AFX_ODL_PROP

        methods:
      // NOTE - ClassWizard will maintain method information here.
      //     Use extreme caution when editing this section.
            //{{AFX_ODL_METHOD(CASRVDoc)
            [id(4)] void Calculate();
            //}}AFX_ODL_METHOD
    };

    //  Class information for CASRVDoc

    [ uuid(82F6E8E9-01BD-11CF-87C3-00403321BFAC) ]
    coclass CASRVDoc
    {
        [default] dispinterface IASRV;
    };

    //{{AFX_APPEND_ODL}}
};
```

The interfaces `ICreateTypeInfo` and `ICreateTypeLib` are used by the tools themselves (such as `MkTypLib.exe`).

Testing the Application

OLE automation servers can best be tested from within a general-purpose automation controller. If you have Visual Basic installed on your system, you can use it as an ideal OLE automation testing tool. (Both 16- and 32-bit versions should work fine together with 32-bit automation servers created using Visual C++.)

To test the ASRV server from within Visual Basic 3.0, I created the simple form shown in Figure 32.10.

FIGURE 32.10.

Visual Basic form used for testing ASRV.

The three edit fields in this form are called `Multi1`, `Multi2`, and `Result`, respectively. The button with the equal sign in it is called `Calculate`.

To perform the test, I attached the code shown in Listing 32.8 to the Form. The declaration (`Dim` statement) of `ASRV` is performed in the `(general)` section; the `Form_Load` subroutine is attached to the `Load` event of the `Form` object; the `Calculate_Click` subroutine is attached to the `Click` event of the `Calculate` button. By implementing the test application this way, we can avoid reloading the ASRV server every time a calculation is performed.

Listing 32.8. Visual Basic code used for testing ASRV.

```
Dim ASRV As object

Sub Form_Load ()
    Set ASRV = CreateObject("ASRV.Document")
End Sub

Sub Calculate_Click ()
    ASRV.Multi1 = Val(Multi1.Text)
    ASRV.Multi2 = Val(Multi2.Text)
    ASRV.Calculate
    Result.Text = Str(ASRV.Result)
End Sub
```

Note that during the test, the ASRV application never becomes visible. This is because when launched with the `/Automation` command-line parameter (and this is how Visual Basic launches it), the AppWizard-generated application never displays its main application window. If it were a multiple-document interface application that was already running, the behavior would be slightly different: The application window would remain visible, but no new frame window would be displayed to represent the new document. Either way, it should be kept in mind that a document launched using OLE automation may not have an associated view window.

This Visual Basic application is identical in functionality and nearly identical in appearance to the original user interface of ASRV. The difference, of course, is that the ASRV application now performs as a black-box module. Not only does even this simple server application show the power of OLE automation, it also demonstrates the potential of OLE automation controllers such as Visual Basic to act as highly powerful system integration applications.

Standard Methods and Properties

When building the ASRV server, I intentionally used a very simple set of methods and properties in order to keep the example program simple and focused. However, Microsoft actually provides a recommended set of properties and methods that production applications should implement:

- Every application should implement at least one object, an Application object, with its standard set of methods and properties.

- Applications should also implement, if applicable, collections of documents, document objects, and object collections within documents.

This brings up an interesting issue that we have not had an opportunity to address during the construction of ASRV. ASRV's simple properties were merely long integers. The use of string properties is relatively straightforward, but what if the value of a property or the result of a method is another object? This is the case, for example, when an OLE controller requests a particular item from an application's document collection. How is the document item passed to the controller?

The answer is simple, but far from obvious. A method that returns another object should in fact return a pointer to an IDispatch OLE interface. Such a pointer can be obtained for any CCmdTarget-derived object by calling the CCmdTarget member function GetIDispatch. For example, if your application object has a method that returns the active document, this method may be implemented similarly to the following:

```
LPDISPATCH GetActiveDocument()
{
    CFrameWnd *pWnd = (CFrameWnd *)AfxGetMainWnd();
    ASSERT_VALID(pWnd);
    CMyDocument *pDoc = pWnd->GetActiveDocument();
    ASSERT_VALID(pDoc);
    return pDoc->GetIDispatch(TRUE);
}
```

The hierarchy of standard objects that OLE automation servers should support is shown in Figure 32.11.

FIGURE 32.11.
*Standard OLE
automation objects.*

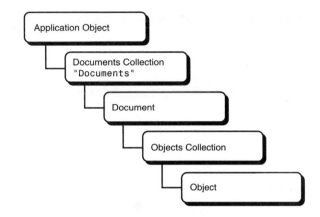

All objects must support two standard properties, shown in Table 32.1.

Table 32.1. Properties common to all standard objects.

Property/Method	Mandatory	Read/Write	Description
P: Application	Yes	Read-only	The application object
P: Parent	Yes	Read-only	The parent of the current object

All collection objects (for example, the documents collection) must support an additional set of properties and methods, shown in Table 32.2.

Table 32.2. Properties and methods for collection objects.

Property/Method	Mandatory	Read/Write	Description
P: Count	Yes	Read-only	Number of items in collection
P: _NewEnum	Yes	Read-only	Enumerator for iteration
M: Add	No		Adds an item to the collection
M: Item	Yes		Retrieves a collection item
M: Remove	No		Removes a collection item

The Application Object

The application object represents the application itself. This object should support the set of properties and methods listed in Table 32.3.

Table 32.3. Properties and methods for application objects.

Property/Method	Mandatory	Read/Write	Description
P: ActiveDocument	No	Read-only	Active document object
P: Caption	No	Read-write	Application window title
P: DefaultFilePath	No	Read-write	Default directory path
P: Documents	No	Read-only	The documents collection
P: FullName	Yes	Read-only	Executable full filename
P: Height	No	Read-write	Height of application window
P: Interactive	No	Read-write	User interaction allowed
P: Left	No	Read-write	Application window left side
P: Name	Yes	Read-only	Application name
P: Path	No	Read-only	Executable file path
P: StatusBar	No	Read-write	Status bar text
P: Top	No	Read-write	Application window top
P: Visible	Yes	Read-write	Application window visible
P: Width	No	Read-write	Width of application window
M: Help	No		Display online help
M: Quit	Yes		Exit the application
M: Repeat	No		Repeat last action
M: Undo	No		Undo last action

The Documents Collection

The documents collection represents all the application's currently active documents in a collection. This collection object should implement, in addition to properties and methods common to all objects and to all collections, an additional two methods, shown in Table 32.4.

Table 32.4. Methods of the documents collection.

Property/Method	Mandatory	Read/Write	Description
M: Close	Yes		
M: Open	Yes		Opens a new document

The Document Object

The document object represents an individual document. In addition to standard properties and methods, document objects should support the properties and methods shown in Table 32.5.

Table 32.5. Properties and methods of document objects.

Property/Method	Mandatory	Read/Write	Description
P: Author	No	Read-write	Author of the document
P: Comments	No	Read-write	Document comments
P: FullName	Yes	Read-only	Document full filename
P: Keywords	No	Read-write	Document keywords
P: Name	No	Read-only	Document filename
P: Path	Yes	Read-only	Document filepath
P: ReadOnly	No	Read-only	Read-only document
P: Saved	Yes	Read-write	Changes were saved
P: Subject	No	Read-write	Subject of document
P: Title	No	Read-write	Document title
M: Activate	Yes		Activates first document window
M: Close	Yes		Closes the document
M: NewWindow	No		Creates new window for document
M: Print	Yes		Prints the document
M: PrintOut	No		Same as Print
M: PrintPreview	No		Activates Print Preview
M: RevertToSaved	No		Reloads last saved version
M: Save	Yes		Saves the document
M: SaveAs	Yes		Saves using filename

The Objects Collection

The objects collection is offered by document objects as applicable. This collection contains application-specific items. For example, in the case of a graphics application, the objects collection may represent a series of shapes that together comprise a drawing (a document). In the case of a word processor, the objects collection may represent paragraphs of text. Or, in the case of a spreadsheet application, this collection may represent the collection of spreadsheet cells.

The implementation of the objects collection and that of individual objects (and indeed, whether these are implemented at all) is implementation-dependent. If you choose to implement these items, remember to add the methods and properties common to all objects, and those common to all collections.

Summary

OLE automation is a means of communication between OLE automation servers and OLE automation controllers using the OLE IDispatch interface. The MFC Library and the Developer Studio provide extensive support for the development of OLE automation servers.

Constructing an automation server through AppWizard requires that you select the OLE automation check box in AppWizard Step 3. This adds automation support to your application and enables your application's document class for automation.

Automation methods and properties are added through the ClassWizard. Methods are represented by member functions. Properties are either represented by member variables or by Get/Set methods. If you wish to implement a read-only (or write-only) property, use Get/Set methods as the property's implementation, and erase the unwanted method while still in ClassWizard.

ClassWizard also creates a type library source file, which is a script written using the Object Description Language. When a type library is generated from this script using the MkTypLib.exe tool, it can be utilized by other applications for finding out about the server's automation interface.

OLE automation servers can be tested and used from automation controllers. General purpose automation controllers include programming environments such as Visual Basic. The ability to use automation servers as black box components shows the power of OLE automation as well as the power of Visual Basic and similar development systems as system integration tools.

Microsoft recommends that OLE automation applications expose a series of standard objects through properties and methods. These objects include the Application object, the application's documents collection, individual document objects, the collection of objects within a document, and, if applicable, objects (items) that comprise a document. A set of standard properties and methods is defined for these that other applications may attempt to utilize.

V

PART

Advanced Programming Topics

Database Programming Through ODBC

33

ODBC, or Open Database Connectivity, represents a vendor-independent mechanism for accessing data in a variety of data sources.

ODBC drivers are available for many different types of data sources. You can use ODBC to retrieve data from text files, dBase tables, Excel spreadsheets, SQL Server databases, and many other sources.

Many ODBC drivers are redistributable. You can package your application for installation with the appropriate ODBC drivers and software for driver installation and management.

At the heart of ODBC is its capability to execute SQL (Structured Query Language) statements against data sources. In addition to reviewing ODBC in this chapter, we also take a (very) brief look at SQL itself. If you plan to perform extensive development work using ODBC, I recommend a reference manual on SQL, such as Date's *The SQL Standard.*

The MFC Library provides extensive support for ODBC applications. A series of classes exists encapsulating ODBC databases, tables, and records. The AppWizard supports the creation of ODBC applications, and further support for ODBC is provided by ClassWizard.

ODBC in Action

This section presents a review of some of the fundamental concepts of ODBC that we need to cover before we can begin an attempt to create an ODBC application.

The ODBC Setup Applet

Invoked through the Control Panel or as a stand-alone application, the ODBC setup applet is used to register data sources.

What exactly is a data source? That depends on the driver. In the case of a driver such as the SQL Server driver, the data source can be a database on a server. In the case of a driver such as the Microsoft Access or Microsoft Excel drivers, the database is a file (an MDB or XLS file). In the case of the Microsoft Text driver, the database is a disk directory that contains text files, which serve as tables in the database from the driver's perspective.

To add a data source, invoke the ODBC setup applet and select the Add button. In the resulting dialog (Figure 33.1), pick a driver and click OK.

Next, a driver-specific dialog is displayed (Figure 33.2), where you can select the database and adjust the desired characteristics of the driver.

The ODBC setup applet's main dialog (Figure 33.3) lists all installed data sources. You can add or delete data sources, or you can modify the setup of existing data sources using this dialog.

FIGURE 33.1.

*ODBC Add Data
Source dialog.*

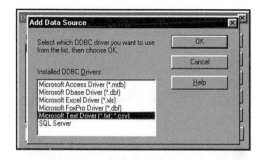

FIGURE 33.2.

*ODBC driver setup
(Microsoft Text
driver).*

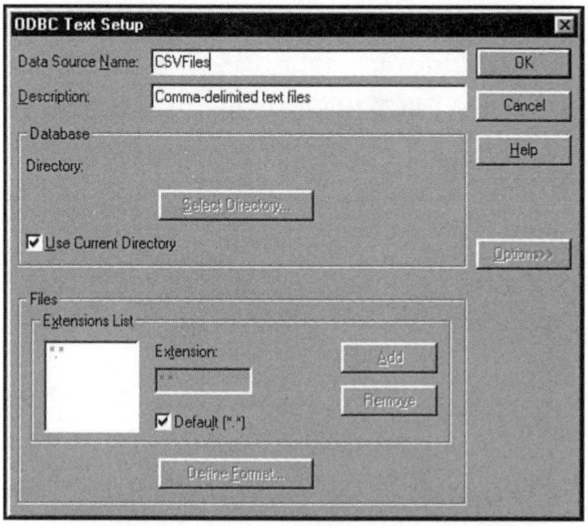

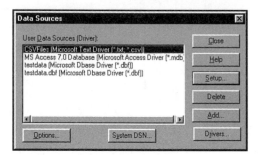

FIGURE 33.3.

*ODBC Setup
Applet.*

ODBC API Concepts

Applications that use ODBC rely on ODBC drivers for data access. Drivers can be single-tier
or multiple-tier. Single-tier drivers process ODBC calls and SQL statements. Multiple-tier
drivers process ODBC calls and pass SQL statements to the data source (potentially a server
residing elsewhere on the network).

The ODBC standard defines three conformance levels. The Core API includes those fundamental ODBC calls that are required to access a data source and execute SQL commands. The Level 1 API contains a set of additional calls used to retrieve information about data sources and the driver itself. The Level 2 API contains additional calls, such as calls that operate using parameter and result arrays. As some drivers may not support Level 2 calls (although most support Level 1), it is important to know whether a particular command is available or not; ODBC references clearly mark each command with the API level that it conforms to.

With respect to the SQL grammar, ODBC defines a core grammar and two variants: a minimum SQL grammar and an extended grammar.

Note that ODBC is not equivalent to Embedded SQL. Embedded SQL uses SQL statements in source programs written in another language. Such a hybrid program is processed by a precompiler before it is passed to the compiler of the host programming language.

In contrast, ODBC interprets SQL statements at run-time. The host program does not need to be recompiled to execute different SQL statements, nor is it necessary to compile separate versions of a host program for different data sources.

An ODBC application has to perform a series of steps to connect to a data source before it can execute SQL statements. These steps are illustrated in Figure 33.4.

FIGURE 33.4.

Typical set of ODBC calls.

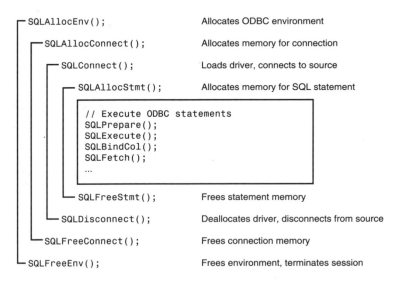

SQLAllocEnv();	Allocates ODBC environment
SQLAllocConnect();	Allocates memory for connection
SQLConnect();	Loads driver, connects to source
SQLAllocStmt();	Allocates memory for SQL statement

```
// Execute ODBC statements
SQLPrepare();
SQLExecute();
SQLBindCol();
SQLFetch();
...
```

SQLFreeStmt();	Frees statement memory
SQLDisconnect();	Deallocates driver, disconnects from source
SQLFreeConnect();	Frees connection memory
SQLFreeEnv();	Frees environment, terminates session

The first of the calls in Figure 33.1, SQLAllocEnv, allocates an ODBC environment. In effect, this call initializes the ODBC library and returns an environment handle of type SQLENVH.

The second call, SQLAllocConnect, allocates memory for a connection. The handle that is returned by this function, of type SQLHDBC, is used in subsequent ODBC function calls to refer to a specific connection. One application can maintain several open connections.

The third call, `SQLConnect`, establishes a connection by loading the driver and connecting to the data source. This call has alternatives; for example, the `SQLDriverConnect` call can be utilized to connect to data sources that are not set up via the ODBC setup applet.

Memory for an SQL statement is allocated through a call to `SQLAllocStmt`. By allocating memory for statements in a separate step, ODBC offers a mechanism whereas statements can be constructed, used, and reused before the memory allocated for them is released.

After these four calls, a typical ODBC application performs a series of calls to execute SQL statements against a database. It can use `SQLPrepare` to prepare (compile) an SQL statement for execution and `SQLExecute` to actually execute it. It can use a variety of calls to bind variables to statements and to retrieve the results of a statement.

When its work is finished, the application should free the ODBC resources it has allocated. The statement handle is freed by calling `SQLFreeStmt`. The connection is terminated by calling `SQLDisconnect`; the memory allocated for the collection is released by a call to `SQLFreeConnect`. Finally, the ODBC environment is released by calling `SQLFreeEnv`.

A Simple ODBC Example

To put this into practice, I developed a very simple ODBC application that reads rows stored in an Excel spreadsheet. When an Excel spreadsheet is accessed using the Microsoft Excel ODBC driver, worksheets play the role of database tables; and rows in a worksheet play the role of records in a table.

The spreadsheet is shown in Figure 33.5. It is a simple table of people's last names, first names, and ages.

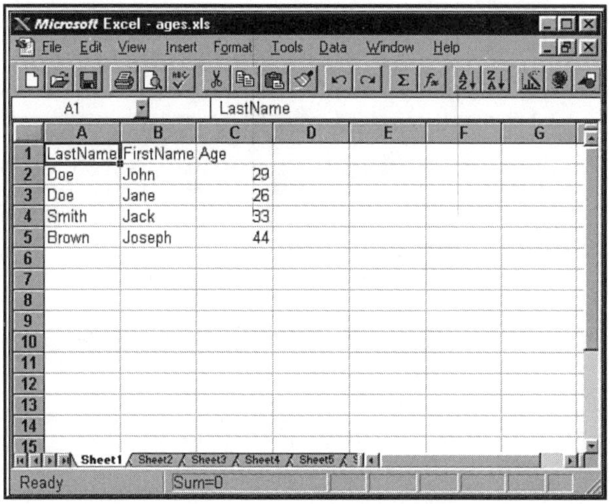

FIGURE 33.5.

A simple Excel spreadsheet to be accessed through ODBC.

Instead of installing this Excel spreadsheet as a data source through the ODBC setup applet, I opted to utilize the capabilities of the SQLDriverConnect function. This function enables you to connect to a data source even if it has not been previously installed through the ODBC setup applet.

At first, I was thinking of developing a command line-based example (a console application). Unfortunately, the beta version of Visual C++ that I was using at the time failed to link the command line ODBC applications properly.

Therefore, I decided to write a simple Windows application in which I utilize calls to MessageBox to display data retrieved from the ODBC source.

The application is shown in Listing 33.1. This program can be compiled from the command line by typing cl ages.c odbc32.lib user32.lib. Using this program requires the file ages.xls to be available in the current directory.

Listing 33.1. Simple ODBC application.

```c
#include <windows.h>
#include <sql.h>
#include <sqlext.h>
#include <string.h>

#define CONNSTR \
        "DBQ=AGES.XLS;DRIVER={Microsoft Excel Driver (*.xls)}"
#define CONNLEN (sizeof(CONNSTR)-1)
#define SQLTRY(x,y) \
        { \
          rc = y; \
          if (rc != SQL_SUCCESS) \
          { \
            char buf[255]; \
            char szState[6]; \
            char szMsg[255]; \
            SDWORD sdwNative; \
            SWORD swMsgLen; \
            SQLError(hEnv, hDBC, hStmt, szState, &sdwNative, \
                    szMsg, sizeof(szMsg), &swMsgLen); \
            wsprintf(buf, "Error %d performing %s\nSQLState = %s" \
                    "\nSQL message = %s", rc, x, szState, szMsg); \
            MessageBox(NULL, buf, "Error", MB_OK | MB_ICONSTOP); \
            goto Terminate; \
          } \
        }

int WINAPI WinMain(HINSTANCE d1, HINSTANCE d2, LPSTR d3, int d4)
{
    SQLHENV hEnv = 0;
    SQLHDBC hDBC = 0;
    SQLHSTMT hStmt = 0;
```

```
        SQLCHAR szConnStr[255];
        SQLCHAR szStmt[255];
        SQLCHAR szFirstName[255];
        SQLCHAR szLastName[255];
        long nAge;
        SWORD cbConnStr;
        RETCODE rc;
        SDWORD sdwLNLen;
        SDWORD sdwFNLen;
        SDWORD sdwALen;
        int i;
        char szResult[1000];

        SQLTRY("SQLAllocEnv", SQLAllocEnv(&hEnv))
        SQLTRY("SQLAllocConnect", SQLAllocConnect(hEnv, &hDBC))
        SQLTRY("SQLDriverConnect", SQLDriverConnect(hDBC, NULL,
                                    CONNSTR, CONNLEN, szConnStr,
                                    sizeof(szConnStr), &cbConnStr,
                                    SQL_DRIVER_NOPROMPT))
        SQLTRY("SQLAllocStmt", SQLAllocStmt(hDBC, &hStmt))

        wsprintf(szStmt, "SELECT * FROM [Sheet1$]");
        SQLTRY("SQLPrepare", SQLPrepare(hStmt, szStmt, strlen(szStmt)))

        SQLTRY("SQLBindCol", SQLBindCol(hStmt, 1, SQL_C_CHAR,
                    (PTR)szLastName, sizeof(szLastName), &sdwLNLen))
        SQLTRY("SQLBindCol", SQLBindCol(hStmt, 2, SQL_C_CHAR,
                    (PTR)szFirstName, sizeof(szFirstName), &sdwFNLen))
        SQLTRY("SQLBindCol", SQLBindCol(hStmt, 3, SQL_C_SLONG,
                    (PTR)&nAge, sizeof(nAge), &sdwALen))

        SQLTRY("SQLExecute", SQLExecute(hStmt))

        for (i = 1; (rc = SQLFetch(hStmt)) == SQL_SUCCESS; i++)
        {
            wsprintf(szResult, "Record #%d\nLast Name: %s\nFirst Name:"
                    " %s\nAge: %d", i, szLastName, szFirstName, nAge);
            MessageBox(NULL, szResult, "Data", MB_OK);
        }
        if (rc != SQL_NO_DATA_FOUND)
        {
            SQLTRY("SQLFetch", rc)
        }

        MessageBox(NULL, "Successfully completed.", "Success", MB_OK);
    Terminate:
        if (hStmt) SQLFreeStmt(hStmt, SQL_CLOSE);
        if (hDBC) SQLDisconnect(hDBC);
        if (hDBC) SQLFreeConnect(hDBC);
        if (hEnv) SQLFreeEnv(hEnv);
}
```

Because there are so many things that can go wrong during an ODBC call, I did not think that I could get away with an example that has no error checking. Fortunately, ODBC calls use a uniform error reporting mechanism; thus, it was easy to create a simple macro, SQLTRY, and use that for simple error reporting. In a more sophisticated application you may utilize, for example, exception processing for this purpose (instead of that nasty goto).

The rest is fairly simple. After the obligatory calls to SQLAllocEnv and SQLAllocConnect, the program calls SQLDriverConnect. This call enables it to open a table that has not been set up using the ODBC setup applet, and do it (optionally) without presenting a user interface. This is exactly what we are doing here; note the constants CONNSTR and CONNLEN that are used for this purpose. In CONNSTR, the driver's name must be specified *exactly*; otherwise, the call will fail.

Once the database (spreadsheet) has been successfully connected to, a single SQL statement is executed:

```
SELECT * FROM [Sheet1$]
```

The name Sheet1$ (enclosed in square brackets because it contains a character, '$', not recognized by SQL) is the driver-supplied name for the first spreadsheet in an Excel workbook. The SELECT SQL statement is used to retrieve a record or set of records; in its present form, it is used to simply retrieve all fields in all records.

The next three calls *bind* C variables to table columns. This is the purpose of the SQLBindCol function. When records are subsequently retrieved, field values are deposited into these variables.

The records themselves are retrieved by SQLFetch and displayed, in a rather pedestrian fashion, using MessageBox. SQLFetch is called repeatedly until its return value is something other than SQL_SUCCESS. A return value of SQL_NO_DATA_FOUND indicates that the last record has been retrieved; anything else is an error and treated accordingly.

The program ends with the obligatory calls to SQLFreeStmt, SQLDisconnect, SQLFreeConnect, and SQLFreeEnv to free up resources and terminate the connection to the data source.

If you run this program, it displays a series of dialogs like the one shown in Figure 33.6.

FIGURE 33.6.

Dialog displayed by
ages.exe.

Other ODBC calls

The example program in Listing 33.1 demonstrated some of the basic features of ODBC. Needless to say, there are many other ODBC function calls that application can utilize.

In addition to SQLConnect and SQLDriverConnect, the SQLBrowseConnect provides a third alternative for connecting to a data source. This function enables applications to iteratively browse data sources.

Several connection options related to transaction processing, character set translation, time-outs, tracing, and other features can be set using SQLSetConnectOption. Current settings can be retrieved through SQLGetConnectOption.

Information about drivers, data sources, and other options can be retrieved through a variety of functions, including SQLDataSources, SQLDrivers, SQLGetFunctions, SQLGetInfo, and SQLGetTypeInfo.

Statement-level options can be specified by calling SQLSetStmtOption.

As an alternative to calling SQLPrepare and SQLExecute, applications can utilize the SQLExecDirect function to execute SQL statements in a single step. The advantages of using SQLPrepare include the capability to execute a prepared statement more than once and to retrieve information about the result set prior to executing the statement.

The driver's translated version of an SQL statement can be retrieved by calling SQLNativeSql.

Some SQL statements require parameters. You can use SQLBindParameter to match variables in your program with question marks in an SQL statement. For example, you can use an SQL statement like this one:

```
INSERT INTO [Sheet1$] (LastName, FirstName, Age) VALUES (?, ?, ?)
```

Prior to executing this statement, you can use three SQLBindParameter calls to match program variables to question marks in the SQL statement. This function is used in conjunction with SQLParamData and SQLPutData, which are used in response to an SQL_NEED_DATA return value from SQLExecute.

SQLParamOptions, which is a Level 2 ODBC extension, enables an application to set multiple values. Another Level 2 extension, SQLExtendedFetch, can be used to return data on several rows in an array form.

Information about a statement's parameters can be retrieved by calling SQLDescribeParam and SQLNumParams.

Information about a statement's results can be obtained by calls to SQLNumResultCols, SQLColAttributes, and SQLDescribeCol. The SQLRowCount function returns the number of rows affected by an SQL UPDATE, INSERT, or DELETE operation; it, however, is not guaranteed to return the number of rows in a result set, and few SQL drivers support that functionality.

As an alternative to using SQLBindCol to bind columns, an application can rely on SQLGetData to retrieve data from unbound columns.

ODBC supports positioning of SQL cursors. A Level 2 extension function, SQLSetPos, can be used to position the cursor to a specific row and to update, delete, or add data to the row set.

Transaction processing is supported by the SQLTransact function.

Information about a data source can be retrieved by calling the functions `SQLTables`, `SQLTablePrivileges`, `SQLColumns`, `SQLColumnPrivileges`, `SQLPrimaryKeys`, `SQLForeignKeys`, `SQLSpecialColumns`, `SQLStatistics`, `SQLProcedures`, and `SQLProcedureColumns`. The information is returned by these functions as a result set, accessible by calling `SQLBindCol` and `SQLFetch`.

ODBC enables the asynchronous execution of functions. Asynchronous execution is enabled by calling `SQLSetStmtOption` or `SQLSetConnectOption` with `SQL_ASYNC_ENABLE`. When, afterwards, a function that supports asynchronous execution is called, it returns immediately with the return value `SQL_STILL_EXECUTING`. Repeated calls to the same function (with parameters that must be valid but are ignored, except for the first, *hStmt* parameter) can be used to determine whether the function's execution has completed.

Information about ODBC errors can be retrieved in a standardized form using `SQLError`.

The SQL Standard and ODBC

SQL, or Structured Query Language, is an official (ANSI) standard for relational database processing. In this section, I present a very brief overview of SQL, with special emphasis on the use of its statements in the context of ODBC. Hopefully, this brief summary will prove to be helpful in carrying out simple ODBC SQL operations in your applications without having to surround yourself with SQL reference works.

At the heart of SQL are *data manipulation statements* and *schema definition statements*. Data manipulation statements retrieve, add, delete, or change data in a recordset (row set). Schema definition statements define the layout of a database.

Data Manipulation Statements

There are four basic data manipulation statements: `SELECT`, `INSERT`, `UPDATE`, and `DELETE`.

`SELECT` operations have a general form of `"SELECT-FROM-WHERE"`. For example, a `SELECT` statement may look like the following:

```
SELECT FirstName, LastName FROM EMPLOYEES WHERE EMPLOYEES.Age<30
```

Many other clauses and qualifiers can be used to refine a `SELECT` statement.

One of the most distinguishing features of relational databases is the ability to perform *join* operations. Loosely speaking, join operations means combining two or more tables into a single result set. For example, consider the following statement:

```
SELECT EMPLOYEES.FirstName, EMPLOYEES.LastName, PLANS.Name
FROM EMPLOYEES, PLANS
WHERE EMPLOYEES.Age < PLANS.MaxAge
```

This statement operates on two tables, `EMPLOYEES` and `PLANS`; the former represents the employees of a corporation, the latter the set of benefit packages the corporation offers. This `SELECT` statement retrieves, for each employee, the name of the employee and the name of all the plans the employee qualifies for by age. Note that if the employee qualifies for more than one plan, his or her name will appear more than once in the result set.

If you wish to use a SELECT statement to retrieve all the fields in a row, you can use a single asterisk as a shorthand. For example, for an EMPLOYEES table that has three fields, FirstName, LastName, and Age, the following two statements are equivalent:

```
SELECT FirstName, LastName, Age FROM EMPLOYEE
SELECT * FROM EMPLOYEE
```

SQL also offers a series of *aggregate functions.* These functions include COUNT, MIN, MAX, AVG, and SUM. For example, to count, in the EMPLOYEES table, the number of employees whose last names are distinct, you would use the following statement:

```
SELECT COUNT (DISTINCT EMPLOYEES.LastName) FROM EMPLOYEES
```

Or, to calculate the combined life experience of the corporation's work force, you would issue the following statement:

```
SELECT SUM (EMPLOYEES.AGE) FROM EMPLOYEES
```

Obviously, many forms of the SELECT statement operate on multiple rows and return row sets as results. The SQL standard defines the concept of a *cursor* that is used to iteratively fetch the rows from a result set. The ODBC SQLBindCol and SQLFetch functions are based on the same principle.

The INSERT statement is used to add rows to a table. The UPDATE statement is used to modify existing rows. The DELETE statement is used to remove rows. The syntax of these commands is similar to the syntax of the SELECT command. In particular, these commands have cursor-based and noncursor variants. For example, consider the following command that you would execute on December 31 every year to update the corporate employee database (naturally, nobody ages after 30):

```
UPDATE EMPLOYEES
SET EMPLOYEES.AGE = EMPLOYEES.AGE + 1
WHERE EMPLOYEES.AGE < 30
```

This *searched update* operates on all rows specified by the WHERE clause and does not require a cursor to execute. Other forms of these statements are cursor based; ODBC supports such operations via SQLBindParameter and related functions.

Views

A view, loosely speaking, is a kind of "virtual" table. Not backed by physical storage, a view represents a row set created dynamically using the CREATE VIEW statement.

A view can be created with the help of a SELECT statement. For example, to create a view containing all employees younger than 30, you would use the following statement:

```
CREATE VIEW YOUNGEMPLOYEES (LastName, FirstName, Age)
AS SELECT EMPLOYEES.LastName, EMPLOYEES.FirstName, EMPLOYEES.Age
   FROM EMPLOYEES
   WHERE EMPLOYEES.Age < 30
```

In subsequent operations, you can use this view just like you would use any other table. For example, you can use the following SELECT statement:

```
SELECT * FROM YOUNGEMPLOYEES
```

Data Definition Statements

Data definition statements are used to create and update tables and indexes in a database.

The CREATE TABLE statement can be used for, what else? To create a table, of course. To create the EMPLOYEES table that we used in the preceding sections, you could use the following statement:

```
CREATE TABLE EMPLOYEES
  ( LastName   CHAR(30)  NOT NULL,
    FirstName CHAR(30),
    Age        INTEGER
  )
```

The CREATE TABLE statement supports constraint clauses. These include UNIQUE clauses (specifying that a field's value must be unique) and CHECK clauses (specifying a condition). For example, our EMPLOYEES table definition may look like this:

```
CREATE TABLE EMPLOYEES
  ( LastName   CHAR(30) NOT NULL,
    FirstName CHAR(30) NOT NULL,
    Age INTEGER,
    UNIQUE (LastName, FirstName),
    CHECK (Age < 30)
  )
```

Tables can also be created with indexes. For example, to create an EMPLOYEES table indexed by last name, use the following syntax:

```
CREATE TABLE EMPLOYEES
  ( LastName   CHAR(30)  NOT NULL,
    FirstName CHAR(30),
    Age        INTEGER,
    PRIMARY KEY (LastName)
  )
```

The CREATE INDEX statement can be used to create an index on an existing table.

The ALTER TABLE statement can be used to modify the structure of an existing table.

The DROP statement can be used to delete an existing table or index from the database.

Finally, the GRANT and REVOKE commands can be used to grant and revoke security privileges on specific tables.

ODBC in MFC Applications

The use of ODBC is greatly simplified by the Microsoft Foundation Classes Library. Simple applications that access tables through ODBC can be created with only a few mouse clicks using the AppWizard and ClassWizard. Several MFC classes exist that support accessing databases and recordsets.

Our discussion of ODBC-related features in the MFC Library starts with the construction of a simple example.

Setting Up a Data Source

Before an MFC ODBC application can be constructed using AppWizard, it is necessary to identify a data source on which the application will operate. The data source must be identified and set up through the ODBC setup applet.

The data source used in our example application is a text file. To access this file, we need the Microsoft Text ODBC driver. (If you did not install this driver when you set up Visual C++, rerun the Visual C++ setup program.)

The data file, ages.txt, will contain a set of records with first names, last names, and ages. The first row in the file will be used as a header row. The file will be a comma-separated file, with the following contents:

```
LastName,FirstName,Age
Doe,John,29
Doe,Jane,26
Smith,Joe,44
Brown,Joseph,27
```

After creating this file, we must identify the data source through the 32-bit ODBC setup applet. Invoke this applet and click on the Add button; select the Microsoft Text Driver in the dialog shown in Figure 33.7.

FIGURE 33.7.

Adding a text data source.

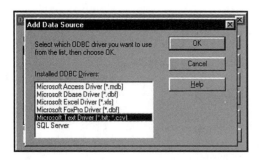

Clicking on this dialog's OK button invokes the ODBC Text Setup dialog (Figure 33.8), which is a dialog specific to the selected driver. The Microsoft Text driver views disk directories as databases and individual text files as tables in the database. The driver can be set up to use either the current directory or a specific directory as the data source.

FIGURE 33.8.

ODBC Text Setup.

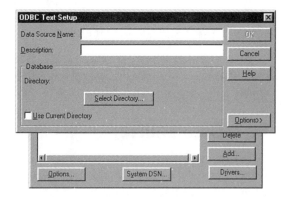

If you select a specific directory, the driver enables, through the Options extension of its dialog, setting up individual tables (text files). For example, I specified g:\amfc as the directory where the new application will be placed and created ages.txt in that directory. After specifying this directory name by clicking on the Select Directory button, the Define Format button became active in the ODBC Text Setup dialog (Figure 33.9).

FIGURE 33.9.

*ODBC Text
Setup options.*

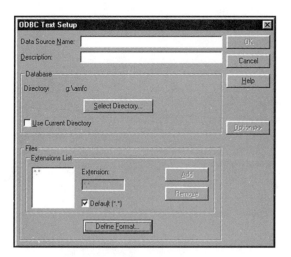

Clicking on the Define Format button brings up yet another dialog (Figure 33.10) where the format of individual tables (text files) can be specified. In the case of the ages.txt table, setting the Column Name Header check box enables the Guess button to work correctly and retrieve the names of fields and correctly guess their type.

FIGURE 33.10.

Defining the format of a text table.

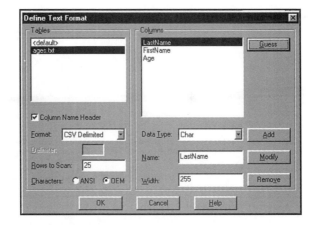

Dismiss this dialog by clicking on the OK button. When the ODBC Text Setup dialog reappears, add a name to this data source. I decided to name this data source "CSV Files in AMFC." Dismiss this dialog, too, by clicking on its OK button, and dismiss the Data Sources dialog by clicking on its Close button.

At this point, a look at the `amfc` directory where the `ages.txt` file resides reveals that the ODBC setup applet created another file, one named `schema.ini`. This file, shown in Listing 33.2, contains information on the characteristics of the ODBC data source that we just specified.

Listing 33.2. The `schema.ini` file created by the ODBC setup applet.

```
[ages.txt]
ColNameHeader=True
Format=CSVDelimited
MaxScanRows=25
CharacterSet=OEM
Col1=LASTNAME Char Width 255
Col2=FIRSTNAME Char Width 255
Col3=AGE Integer
```

Now that our data source has been set up and identified, we can turn to the AppWizard to construct a skeleton for our application.

Creating an ODBC Application Skeleton Through AppWizard

To begin creating the ODBC skeleton application, fire up AppWizard and create a project named AMFC. The project should be single-document-based (AppWizard Step 1). Database options are specified in AppWizard Step 2 (Figure 33.11), where you should specify the Database view without file support option.

FIGURE 33.11.

Specifying database support in AppWizard.

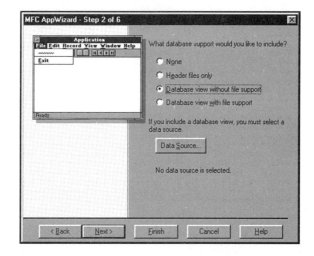

Once you have specified this option, you must click the Data Source button and define a data source for this application before proceeding. Specify the recently created data source, CSV Files in AMFC, as the ODBC data source in this Database Options dialog (Figure 33.12).

FIGURE 33.12.

Specifying a data source.

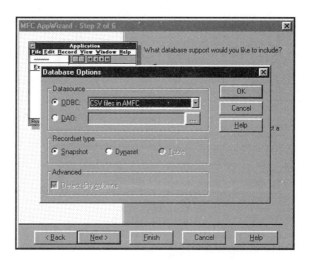

When you click the OK button in the Database Options dialog, AppWizard responds by showing yet another dialog (Figure 33.13) where you can select database tables. Select the ages.txt file as the database table and click the OK button.

Clicking the OK button returns you to the AppWizard main dialog and enables you to proceed from Step 2.

FIGURE 33.13.

Specifying a table.

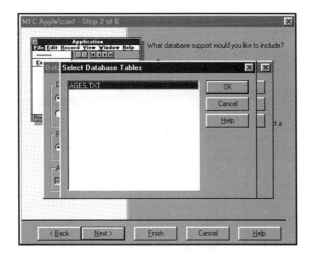

For our test application, we do not need to change any other options, so you might as well proceed by clicking the Finish button. The AMFC test application will be created by AppWizard at this time.

Take a look at the classes created by AppWizard (Figure 33.14). When compared with applications that have no database support, you may notice a new class and a few new member variables in the application's document and view classes.

FIGURE 33.14.

ODBC application classes.

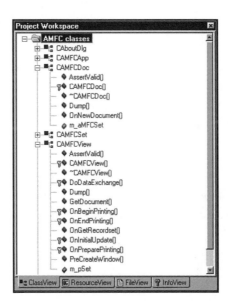

The new class, CAMFCSet, is a class derived from CRecordset. Looking at this class's declaration (shown in Listing 33.3), we can see that AppWizard not only created the class, it also added member variables that reflect the fields of the database table that we specified.

Listing 33.3. Declaration of CAMFCSet.

```
class CAMFCSet : public CRecordset
{
public:
    CAMFCSet(CDatabase* pDatabase = NULL);
    DECLARE_DYNAMIC(CAMFCSet)

// Field/Param Data
    //{{AFX_FIELD(CAMFCSet, CRecordset)
    CString m_LastName;
    CString m_FirstName;
    long    m_Age;
    //}}AFX_FIELD

// Overrides
    // ClassWizard generated virtual function overrides
    //{{AFX_VIRTUAL(CAMFCSet)
    public:
  virtual CString GetDefaultConnect(); // Default connection string
  virtual CString GetDefaultSQL();     // default SQL for Recordset
  virtual void DoFieldExchange(CFieldExchange* pFX); // RFX support
    //}}AFX_VIRTUAL

// Implementation
#ifdef _DEBUG
    virtual void AssertValid() const;
    virtual void Dump(CDumpContext& dc) const;
#endif
};
```

These member variables are also reflected in the class's implementation file (Listing 33.4), in the constructor function, and also in the function DoFieldExchange. The latter is called by the MFC framework to exchange data between the recordset's member variables and corresponding columns in the database table.

Listing 33.4. Implementation of CAMFCSet.

```
IMPLEMENT_DYNAMIC(CAMFCSet, CRecordset)

CAMFCSet::CAMFCSet(CDatabase* pdb)
    : CRecordset(pdb)
{
    //{{AFX_FIELD_INIT(CAMFCSet)
    m_LastName = _T("");
    m_FirstName = _T("");
    m_Age = 0;
    m_nFields = 3;
```

```
    //}}AFX_FIELD_INIT
    m_nDefaultType = snapshot;
}

CString CAMFCSet::GetDefaultConnect()
{
    return _T("ODBC;DSN=CSV files in AMFC");
}

CString CAMFCSet::GetDefaultSQL()
{
    return _T("[AGES].[TXT]");
}

void CAMFCSet::DoFieldExchange(CFieldExchange* pFX)
{
    //{{AFX_FIELD_MAP(CAMFCSet)
    pFX->SetFieldType(CFieldExchange::outputColumn);
    RFX_Text(pFX, _T("[LastName]"), m_LastName);
    RFX_Text(pFX, _T("[FirstName]"), m_FirstName);
    RFX_Long(pFX, _T("[Age]"), m_Age);
    //}}AFX_FIELD_MAP
}
```

Before we proceed, let me call your attention to a subtle yet deadly bug present in Visual C++ Version 4. Notice that the GetDefault member function returns the string value "[AGES].[TXT]". This, unfortunately, is wrong, and will result in an SQL syntax error if you attempt to run the application. The correct string should be "[AGES.TXT]"; you must change the implementation of this function to reflect the correct value.

The changes in the application's document and view classes are minor. The document class acquired a new member variable, m_aMFCSet, which is of type CAMFCSet and, rather unsurprisingly, represents the table that the application's document is associated with. The view class also acquired a member variable, m_pSet, which is set by default to point to the document class's m_aMFCSet member. The view class also has a new function, OnGetRecordset; the default implementation simply returns the value of m_pSet.

Although the skeleton application can be built at this time, it is not very useful in its present state. As shown in Figure 33.15, it merely displays a blank dialog; and although the record selection commands work, their only visible effect is the enabling and disabling of command items and buttons as one end or the other of the table is reached. Clearly, we must modify the application's dialog before the application is of any practical use.

Customizing the ODBC Application

As it turns out, customizing our ODBC application is laughably simple. In fact, the customization that enables us to browse records in our table *does not require adding a single line of code by hand.* All that is required is the addition of controls to the application's main dialog and the use of ClassWizard to add the appropriate member variables.

FIGURE 33.15.

The skeleton application in action.

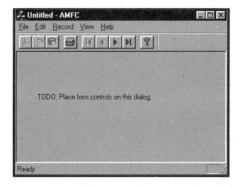

To begin, open the IDD_AMFC_FORM dialog for editing. Remove the static "TODO" control, then add three static controls and three edit controls as shown in Figure 33.16. Name the edit controls IDC_LASTNAME, IDC_FIRSTNAME, and IDC_AGE, respectively.

FIGURE 33.16.

Adding controls to AMFC's main dialog.

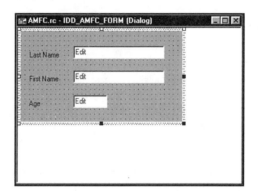

Now comes the tricky part. In order to have ClassWizard assign member variables, hold down the Control key, and double-click on one of the edit fields. The result is a ClassWizard Add Member Variable dialog that is already filled with values that represent ClassWizard's guess as to the proper recordset member variable (Figure 33.17). The ClassWizard guesses the proper variable name by looking at the static fields in the dialog.

Repeat this action for the other two dialog fields. When done, recompile the application.

Surprise! This was all that needed to be done to turn AMFC into a functional application. In its present form (Figure 33.18), it is a functional browser of records in the ages.txt file.

Needless to say, as a simple browser, AMFC barely scratches the surface of the ODBC capabilities of MFC. Before we conclude this chapter, we take a look at what else is supported by the ODBC classes in the MFC Library.

FIGURE 33.17.

Assigning recordset member variables to dialog fields.

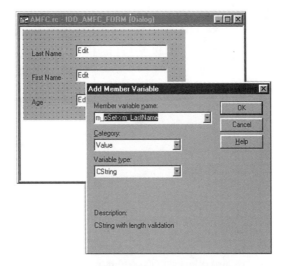

FIGURE 33.18.

The AMFC application in action.

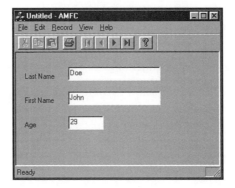

ODBC Classes in MFC

The set of classes that the MFC Library offers in support of ODBC applications is shown in Figure 33.19. Among these classes, the two important ones are CDatabase and CRecordset.

The CDatabase class represents a connection to a data source. Its member variable m_hdbc represents an ODBC connection handle. The member functions Open and Close can be used to establish a connection to the data source or to terminate the connection.

Other member functions are used to set or retrieve connection settings. These functions include GetConnect (returns the ODBC connection string), IsOpen, GetDatabaseName, CanUpdate, CanTransact, InWaitForDataSource, SetLoginTimeout, SetQueryTimeout, and SetSynchronousMode. By default, the CDatabase class uses asynchronous mode for accessing the data source. An asynchronous operation that is in progress can be canceled by calling the Cancel member function.

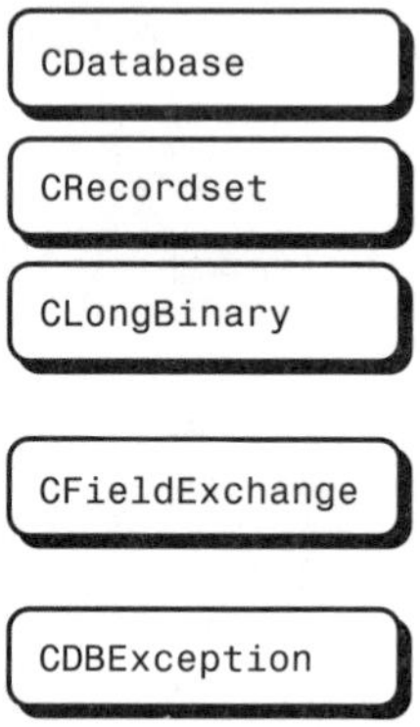

FIGURE 33.19.

ODBC support classes in MFC.

CDatabase

CRecordset

CLongBinary

CFieldExchange

CDBException

Transaction processing is supported through the member functions BeginTrans, CommitTrans, and Rollback.

The CDatabase class also offers two overridable functions. OnSetOptions is used to set standard connection options. OnWaitForDataSource is called by the framework to yield processing time while performing a lengthy operation.

The ExecuteSQL member function can be used to directly execute an SQL statement. This statement cannot be used in conjunction with SQL statements that return data records.

The CRecordset class encapsulates the functionality of an ODBC SQL statement and the row set returned by the statement. Member variables of this class identify the ODBC statement handle, the number of fields and parameters in the recordset, the CDatabase object through which this recordset is connected to the data source, and two strings that correspond to SQL WHERE and ORDER BY clauses.

The two principal types of recordsets are *dynasets* and *snapshots*. The type of a recordset is specified when calling the CRecordset::Open member function. Snapshots represent a static view of the data as it existed at the time the snapshot was created. This is most useful for tasks such as report generation. Dynasets present a dynamic view of the data, reflecting changes to it made by other users or through other recordsets in your application.

When the recordset is opened through its Open member function, the table is accessed and the query that the recordset represents is performed. The recordset and the associated statement handle can be closed by calling the Close member function.

Attributes of the recordset can be retrieved by calling the member functions CanAppend, CanRestart, CanScroll, CanTransact, CanUpdate, GetRecordCount, GetStatus, GetTableName, GetSQL, IsOpen, IsBOF, IsEOF, and IsDeleted.

The recordset can be navigated through the functions Move, MoveFirst, MoveLast, MoveNext, and MovePrev.

Operations on the recordset can be carried out by calling AddNew, Delete, Edit, or Update.

Other recordset functions carry out miscellaneous housekeeping functions.

You never use an object of type CRecordset directly. Rather, you should derive a class from CRecordset and add member variables that correspond to the fields (columns) of the table that the recordset represents. Next, override the recordset's DoFieldExchange member function; this function should facilitate the exchange of data between member variables and fields in the database through RFX_ functions. These functions, similar in syntax and concept to the dialog data exchange (DDX_) functions, are summarized in Table 33.1.

Table 33.1. RFX_ functions.

Function Name	Field Type	ODBC SQL Type
RFX_Binary	CByteArray	SQL_BINARY, SQL_LONGVARBINARY, SQL_VARBINARY
RFX_Bool	BOOL	SQL_BIT
RFX_Byte	BYTE	SQL_TINYINT
RFX_Date	CTime	SQL_DATE, SQL_TIME, SQL_TIMESTAMP
RFX_Double	double	SQL_DOUBLE
RFX_Int	int	SQL_SMALLINT
RFX_Long	LONG	SQL_INTEGER
RFX_LongBinary	CLongBinary	SQL_LONGVARCHAR
RFX_Single	float	SQL_REAL
RFX_Text	CString	SQL_CHAR, SQL_DECIMAL, SQL_LONGVARCHAR, SQL_NUMERIC, SQL_VARCHAR

Field exchange is facilitated through the CFieldExchange class. An object of this class contains information about the field that is being exchanged when the recordset's DoFieldExchange member function is called.

The CRecordView class is a view class derived from CFormView that is designed specifically to display database records in forms. Objects of type CRecordView utilize dialog data exchange (DDX) and record field exchange (RFX) functions to facilitate the movement of data between the form and the data source. CRecordView-derived objects are used in conjunction with CRecordset-derived objects.

ODBC operations utilize the CDBException class for reporting errors via the MFC exception mechanism.

Summary

ODBC is a powerful, SQL-based, vendor-independent mechanism for accessing data in various data sources.

At the heart of ODBC are ODBC drivers, which are often redistributable DLLs that implement access to data sources of various types. Single-tier drivers implement both the connection to the data source and the processing SQL statements. Multiple-tier drivers connect to data sources and pass on the SQL statements. ODBC data sources can be local files (for example, text files, dBase files, Excel files) and remote data servers (for example, SQL Server, Oracle).

Data sources are usually specified through the ODBC setup applet (invoked through the Control Panel), although the SQLDriverConnect call makes it possible to connect to a data source that has not been set up this way.

An ODBC session involves calls that build up a connection to the data source, construct and submit SQL statements, and process the results. The ODBC API defines a series of function calls that facilitate these sessions. The API defines a set of conformance levels (Core, Level 1, and Level 2); most drivers support at least Level 1 ODBC functions.

ODBC supports a variation of the standard SQL syntax. Data manipulation statements such as SELECT, INSERT, UPDATE, and DELETE—as well as data definition statements such as CREATE TABLE, DROP TABLE, CREATE INDEX, DROP INDEX, and ALTER TABLE—are supported. ODBC also supports the CREATE VIEW SQL statement.

The Microsoft Foundation Classes Library provides two classes for ODBC support. The CDatabase class represents an ODBC connection; the CRecordset class represents an ODBC SQL statement and the row set the statement returns. Applications typically derive a class from CRecordset and add member variables corresponding to table columns. The CRecordset class offers member functions that facilitate browsing and editing the row set.

Data Access Objects

34

Data Access Objects, or DAOs, are Microsoft's latest invention in database access technology. This technology is used for database access in Microsoft's Visual Basic 4, Microsoft Access, and Visual Basic for Applications; and now, with the help of a set of specialized MFC classes, it is also available to the Visual C++ programmer.

DAO is supplied in the form of redistributable components. Redistributable DAO files can be found in the msdev\redist\dao directory on your Visual C++ 4 CD-ROM. You may either utilize the setup program provided in this directory or incorporate the DAO components found here into your application's setup utility.

DAO Overview

Data Access Objects enable you to access and manipulate databases through the Microsoft Jet database engine. Through this engine, you can access data in Microsoft Access database files (MDB files). The technology also enables you to access local and remote databases through ODBC drivers.

Data Access Object technology is based on OLE. Figure 34.1 depicts the hierarchy of Data Access Objects. This hierarchy is greatly simplified by the DAO classes in MFC.

Many DAO functions utilize Structured Query Language (SQL) statements. You can use the SQL SELECT statement to retrieve data from a database, or the SQL UPDATE, INSERT, and DELETE statements to modify the contents of the database. An easy way to create SQL statements for use with DAO objects is to create the query from within Microsoft Access, save the query in the database, and access the query through a QueryDef object.

Visual C++ provides extensive support for building DAO applications through the AppWizard. In addition to ODBC, AppWizard enables you to create applications that are based on DAO Classes. Our tour of DAO begins with the creation of a simple DAO application and exploration of its behavior.

FIGURE 34.1.

DAO object hierarchy.

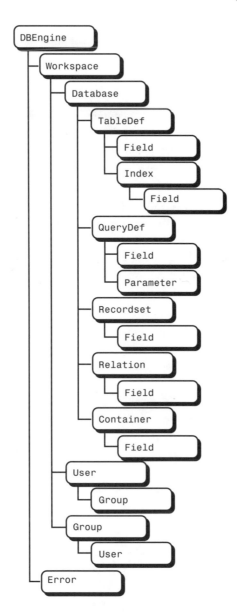

Building a DAO Application

Building a DAO application is quite simple. First, if it does not exist yet, we must create a data source. For the application demonstrated here, the data source is a simple Access database of two tables. Next, the skeleton application must be created using AppWizard; and finally, we must customize this application as appropriate.

The application is a simple browser; it browses a row set that is created as a relational join of two tables.

The Database

The database used in this example contains two tables. One table contains the first names, last names, and and ages of employees; the other table contains the names of benefit packages offered to employees and the maximum qualifying age for each package. The purpose of our application, which I decided to call ADAO, is simple: display, for each employee, all benefit packages he or she qualifies for.

The database, adao.mdb, is constructed using Microsoft Access. To construct the database, start Access and create a blank database named adao.mdb in the directory of your choice. Upon successful creation, select the Table tab in the Database window, and click the New button. Select New Table. (Note that the database file used to create the sample code in this chapter was itself created using Access 2.0; if you are using a later version of Access, your database file, and hence the code generated by AppWizard, may differ slightly from what is shown here.)

Figure 34.2 shows the newly constructed Employees table just before it is saved. As you can see, three fields were added (LastName, FirstName, and Age) of which the first two are 50-character-wide text fields, the third is a number field. The table's primary key was set to the combination of the LastName and FirstName fields.

FIGURE 34.2.

Creating the
Employees table.

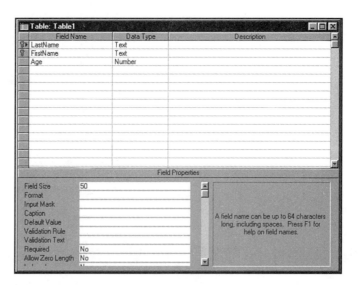

Save the new table under the name Employees and repeat this procedure to create a second table (Figure 34.3). This table contains information about benefit packages. It contains two fields, the first of which, Name, serves as the table's primary key. This table should be saved under the name Plans.

FIGURE 34.3.

Creating the
Plans table.

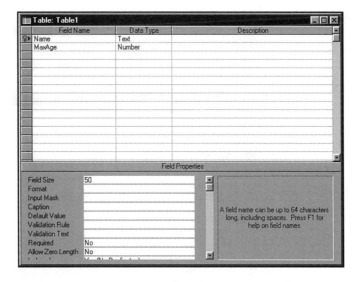

When your work creating these tables is done, the Database window should show two tables, as seen in Figure 34.4.

FIGURE 34.4.

Tables in
adao.mdb.

The next step is to add data to these tables. You can do so by simply double-clicking the table's name in the Database window.

Figure 34.5 shows the four records I added to Employees. Figure 34.6 shows the three records I added to the Plans table.

FIGURE 34.5.

Records in the
`Employees` *table.*

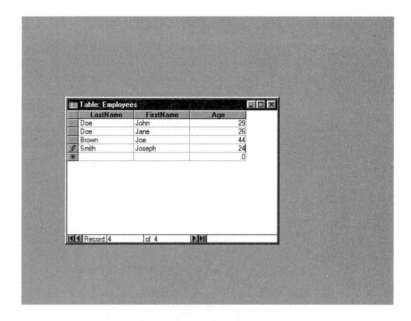

FIGURE 34.6.

Records in the
`Plans` *table.*

This is all we need to do with Microsoft Access. Our MDB file is now ready for use from within a C++ DAO application.

Creating the Skeleton Application

To create the ADAO application, launch the AppWizard and start creating a single-document-based project. Database support is specified in AppWizard Step 2; select the Database view without file support option (Figure 34.7).

FIGURE 34.7.

Adding database support to a skeleton application.

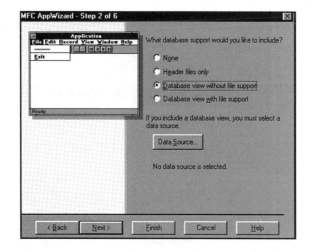

Before you can proceed from this step, you must specify a data source. To do so, click on the Data Source button. In the Database Options dialog that appears, select DAO as the data source (Figure 34.8).

FIGURE 34.8.

Adding a DAO data source.

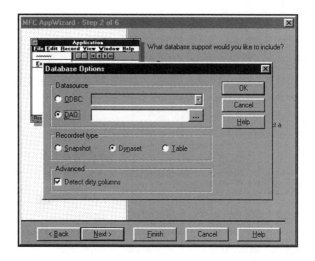

Clicking on the ellipsis button next to the DAO field enables you to specify the actual database file. It brings up a standard File Open dialog, where you can select the file adao.mdb. Select this file and when the Database Options dialog reappears, click the OK button. This should display another dialog where the tables of the database can be selected. Select both the Employees and the Plans table and click OK (Figure 34.9).

FIGURE 34.9.

Selecting tables.

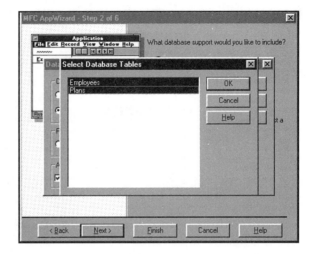

At this time, all dialogs should disappear except for the AppWizard Step 2 dialog; this dialog should now display our data source selection.

All other AppWizard settings can remain at their default values; therefore, you can quickly complete creating the skeleton application by clicking on the Finish button.

Exploring the DAO Application Skeleton

The classes of the skeleton application created by AppWizard are shown in Figure 34.10. When compared to an application with no database support, this application offers one extra class and a few additional member variables and functions in its document and view classes. Not evidently visible, but also a notable difference, is the fact that the view class is derived from CDaoRecordView.

If you are experienced with MFC ODBC programming, you may note that the structure of this application is very similar to that of ODBC applications created by AppWizard.

The new class, CADAOSet, is derived from CDaoRecordset and represents the row set that we will select from the join of the Employees and Plans table. Looking at this class's declaration (Listing 34.1), you can see that the AppWizard already inserted member variables that correspond to the columns (fields) in the two tables.

FIGURE 34.10.

*Skeleton
application
classes.*

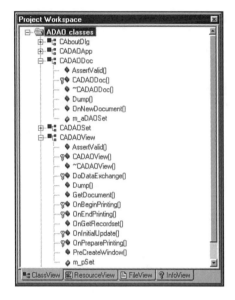

Listing 34.1. CDAOSet **class declaration.**

```
class CADAOSet : public CDaoRecordset
{
public:
    CADAOSet(CDaoDatabase* pDatabase = NULL);
    DECLARE_DYNAMIC(CADAOSet)

// Field/Param Data
    //{{AFX_FIELD(CADAOSet, CDaoRecordset)
    CString m_LastName;
    CString m_FirstName;
    double  m_Age;
    CString m_Name;
    double  m_MaxAge;
    //}}AFX_FIELD

// Overrides
    // ClassWizard generated virtual function overrides
    //{{AFX_VIRTUAL(CADAOSet)
    public:
    virtual CString GetDefaultDBName();
    virtual CString GetDefaultSQL();
    virtual void DoFieldExchange(CDaoFieldExchange* pFX);
    //}}AFX_VIRTUAL

// Implementation
#ifdef _DEBUG
    virtual void AssertValid() const;
    virtual void Dump(CDumpContext& dc) const;
#endif

};
```

A look at the implementation of CADAOSet shows that AppWizard created the CADAOSet::Get DefaultDBName member function with an explicit pathname reference (e.g., "C:\\ADAO\\adao.mdb"). In order to ensure that the code compiles on your system, I removed the explicit path, so that the program will look for the data source in the current directory. Listing 34.2 reflects this modification and also reveals how the CADAOSet member variables are initialized in the class's constructor. The variables are also referred to in the AppWizard-generated implementation of the DoFieldExchange member function. This function exchanges data between member variables in the class and fields in the database.

Listing 34.2. CADAOSet class implementation.

```
IMPLEMENT_DYNAMIC(CADAOSet, CDaoRecordset)

CADAOSet::CADAOSet(CDaoDatabase* pdb)
    : CDaoRecordset(pdb)
{
    //{{AFX_FIELD_INIT(CADAOSet)
    m_LastName = _T("");
    m_FirstName = _T("");
    m_Age = 0.0;
    m_Name = _T("");
    m_MaxAge = 0.0;
    m_nFields = 5;
    //}}AFX_FIELD_INIT
    m_nDefaultType = dbOpenDynaset;
}

CString CADAOSet::GetDefaultDBName()
{
    return _T("adao.mdb");
}


CString CADAOSet::GetDefaultSQL()
{
    return _T("[Employees],[Plans]");
}

void CADAOSet::DoFieldExchange(CDaoFieldExchange* pFX)
{
    //{{AFX_FIELD_MAP(CADAOSet)
    pFX->SetFieldType(CDaoFieldExchange::outputColumn);
    DFX_Text(pFX, _T("[LastName]"), m_LastName);
    DFX_Text(pFX, _T("[FirstName]"), m_FirstName);
    DFX_Double(pFX, _T("[Age]"), m_Age);
    DFX_Text(pFX, _T("[Name]"), m_Name);
    DFX_Double(pFX, _T("[MaxAge]"), m_MaxAge);
    //}}AFX_FIELD_MAP
}
```

To do its work, DoFieldExchange makes use of DFX_ functions. These functions are the DAO cousins of the RFX_ functions used for ODBC field exchange. The set of DFX_ functions available for use in DoFieldExchange is summarized in Table 34.1.

Table 34.1. DFX_ functions.

Function Name	Field Type	ODBC SQL Type
DFX_Binary	CByteArray	DAO_BYTES
DFX_Bool	BOOL	DAO_BOOL
DFX_Byte	BYTE	DAO_BYTES
DFX_Currency	COleCurrency	DAO_CURRENCY
DFX_DateTime	COleDateTime	DAO_DATE
DFX_Double	double	DAO_R8
DFX_Long	long	DAO_I4
DFX_LongBinary	CLongBinary	DAO_BYTES
DFX_Short	short	DAO_I2
DFX_Single	float	DAO_R4
DFX_Text	CString	DAO_CHAR, DAO_WCHAR

NOTE

It is recommended that applications not use the DFX_LongBinary function but use DFX_Binary instead. DFX_LongBinary is provided for compatibility with ODBC.

The new member variables and functions in our application's view and document classes are a simple business. The document class, CADAODoc, contains a new member variable of type CADAOSet, m_aDAOSet. Very obviously, this variable represents the recordset that the document is associated with.

The view class contains a pointer of type CADAOSet (m_pSet); in the default implementation, this pointer is set to point to the document object's m_aDAOSet member. The view class also has a new member function, OnGetRecordset, which in the default implementation simply returns m_pSet.

Although you can recompile the ADAO application at this time, as Figure 34.11 illustrates, it is not yet a very useful application. We need to customize its dialog, and we also need to add the necessary operations that will restrict the rows selected to rows that we wish to see.

FIGURE 34.11.

*Running the
ADAO application
skeleton.*

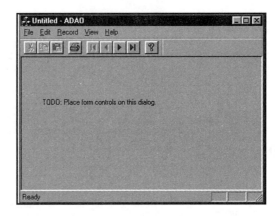

Customizing the Application

The first step in customizing the ADAO application is changing its main dialog. Open the IDD_ADAO_FORM dialog for editing, remove the default "TODO" static control, and add static controls and edit controls as shown in Figure 34.12.

FIGURE 34.12.

*Customizing the
ADAO dialog.*

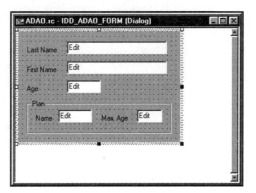

Name the five edit fields IDC_LASTNAME, IDC_FIRSTNAME, IDC_AGE, IDC_NAME, and IDC_MAXAGE as appropriate. Before dismissing this dialog, you can also use the ClassWizard to identify dialog fields with corresponding recordset member variables.

To do so, hold down the Control key, and double-click on the IDC_LASTNAME edit field. The ClassWizard Add Member Variable dialog appears, with ClassWizard's guess as to the name of the member variable (Figure 34.13). ClassWizard derives its guess by looking at the static fields in the dialog.

FIGURE 34.13.

Adding a recordset member variable.

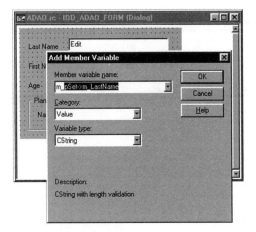

ClassWizard's guess is appropriate for the first three fields in our dialog; however, for the plan name and plan maximum age fields, it is necessary to manually change ClassWizard's selection. This can be done by selecting the proper m_pSet member variable from the drop-down list in the Add Member Variable dialog.

After you specified the member variables for all five edit fields, you can dismiss the dialog. However, we are not done yet; we have not yet specified anywhere the selection criteria that would make our application display only the rows representing valid plans for each employee.

To change the selection criteria, open the CADAOSet::GetDefaultSQL function for editing. The default implementation of this function simply returns the table names that form the recordset. What we wish to do is add additional criteria that would restrict the selections from the tables to only those rows that we wish to see.

In SQL, our desired selection can be expressed in the form of a SELECT statement:

```
SELECT Employees.LastName, Employees.FirstName, Employees.Age,
       Plans.Name, Plans.MaxAge
FROM Employees, Plans
WHERE Employees.Age < Plans.MaxAge
ORDER BY Employees.LastName, Employees.FirstName, Plans.Name
```

Indeed, one way to specify our selection would be to change GetDefaultSQL to return a string representing the above SQL SELECT statement. However, there is another way; and that is to utilize the member variables of the CDaoRecordset class.

In particular, CDaoRecordset offers two member variables, one of which corresponds to the SQL WHERE clause, the other, to the SQL ORDER_BY clause. Our new version of CADAOSet::GetDefaultSQL (Listing 34.3) utilizes these member variables to create the desired selection of rows.

Listing 34.3. Updated version of `CADAOSet::GetDefaultSQL`.

```
CString CADAOSet::GetDefaultSQL()
{
    m_strFilter = "[Employees].[Age] < [Plans].[MaxAge]";
    m_strSort =
    "[Employees].[LastName],[Employees].[FirstName],[Plans].[Name]";
    return _T("[Employees],[Plans]");
}
```

This completes our work on the ADAO project. Recompiling and running the application (Figure 34.14) shows that it indeed behaves as expected, displaying benefit plans that employees qualify for, ordered by the name of the employee and the name of the benefit package.

FIGURE 34.14.

*Running the
ADAO application.*

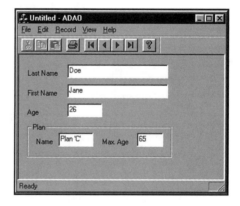

DAO Classes

Although the ADAO application demonstrates how a simple DAO program can be created, it fails to demonstrate many DAO features. To remedy this deficiency, in the remainder of this chapter we take a brief tour of MFC DAO classes and their capabilities.

The set of DAO classes offered by MFC is shown in Figure 34.15. In addition to the CDaoRecordset class that we have encountered while constructing ADAO, there are four other major classes and two helper classes related to DAO. Still, this is a significant improvement over the multitude of raw DAO objects (Figure 34.1).

Before we review the role and features of each of these classes one by one, this section presents a brief overview of how DAO works. For this, it might be helpful to take another look at Figure 34.1, at the beginning of this chapter.

All DAO objects are derived from the DBEngine object; furthermore, all database objects are derived from DAO workspace objects. However, unless you need to manipulate secure databases, you typically do not need to reference either of these; instead, a default workspace object is assumed for all transactions.

FIGURE 34.15.
DAO Classes.

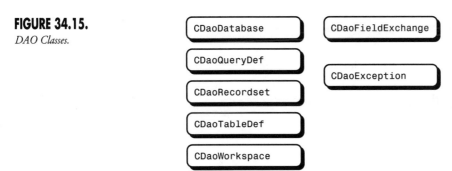

The database and recordset objects very obviously represent databases and selection sets (tables, recordsets, or dynasets) in those databases.

Query definition (QueryDef) objects are used to execute specific SQL queries against a database. Query definitions are normally used in conjunction with recordsets to access data in a database using a specific query.

Table definition (TableDef) objects represent the structure of tables in the database. Through table definition objects, it is possible to create new tables and to modify the structure and characteristics of existing tables.

There are several other DAO object types. These object types (Field objects, Parameter objects, Index objects, User objects, Group objects, and Error objects) are not represented by specific MFC classes. Instead, DAO objects of this type are accessed through the other DAO MFC classes as appropriate.

The *CDaoRecordset* Class

CDaoRecordset objects represent recordsets. A recordset can represent records in a table, a dynaset, and a snapshot. A table-type recordset is updatable and represents the records in a single table. A dynaset-type recordset represents records from one or more tables as a result of a query; dynaset records are also updatable. A snapshot, on the other hand, can also contain fields from one or more tables, but these fields are not updatable; the snapshot is a static copy of records used to find data or generate reports.

A recordset is created by calling the CDaoRecordset::Open member function. The three forms of this function enable you to create a recordset using an SQL query string, a CDaoTableDef object, or a CDaoQueryDef object.

The CDaoRecordset class offers a large number of member functions. Perhaps the most important among these are recordset navigation functions and data update functions. The navigation functions include Find, FindFirst, FindLast, FindNext, and FindPrev; and Move, MoveFirst, MoveLast, MoveNext, and MovePrev. Data update functions include AddNew, CancelUpdate, Delete, Edit, and Update.

Other navigation-related functions include GetAbsolutePosition, GetBookmark, GetPercentPosition, and SetAbsolutePosition, SetBookmark, and SetPercentPosition.

The CDaoRecordset class offers a variety of attribute functions to set and retrieve recordset attributes. For example, the CanUpdate function can be used to determine whether a recordset is updatable; the SetCurrentIndex function can be used to set the current index on a table-type recordset.

Normally, you use the CDaoRecordset class by deriving your own recordset class from it, adding member variables that represent fields, and overriding the DoFieldExchange member function to facilitate the exchange of data between the database and the member variables. However, several member functions exist that provide an alternative. These include GetFieldValue and SetFieldValue, which enable you to directly access the value of a field by name. This method is referred to as *dynamic binding*, as opposed to the static binding accomplished through DoFieldExchange.

Other recordset operations can be used to control the locally maintained cache of records and to manipulate recordset indexes.

The *CDaoDatabase* Class

The CDaoDatabase class represents a connection to a database. A connection is created by calling CDaoDatabase::Open and terminated by calling CDaoDatabase::Close. A new database can be created by calling CDaoDatabase::Create.

The CDaoDatabase class offers a series of attribute member functions; for example, the GetName member function can be used to retrieve the name of the database, or the IsOpen member function can be used to determine if the connection represented by the CDaoDatabase object is open.

Other member functions can be used to manipulate the collections of table definition and query definition objects that are defined for this database. In particular, you can use the DeleteTableDef member function to delete not only a DAO TableDef object but also the underlying table and all its data from the database.

The *CDaoWorkspace* Class

The CDaoWorkspace class represents database sessions. Typically, you do not need to create objects of type CDaoWorkspace, unless you wish to utilize specific functionality available through this class or to access password-protected databases.

A DAO workspace can be created by calling CDaoWorkspace::Create. Arguments to this function specify the name of the workspace, the user name, and password. An existing workspace object can be opened by calling CDaoWorkspace::Open; by passing a NULL parameter to this function, you can explicitly open the default workspace.

Several member functions exist that manipulate databases and the database engine itself. For example, you can compact or repair a database by calling the CompactDatabase or RepairDatabase member functions. Other functions can be used to manipulate user names, passwords, and other database attributes.

The *CDaoQueryDef* Class

The CDaoQueryDef class represents query definitions. To create a new query definition, use the CQueryDef::Create member function; to access a query definition that was saved into a database, use CQueryDef::Open. A newly created query can be added to the database by calling the CQueryDef::Append member function.

CQueryDef objects can be used in conjunction with CRecordSet objects to retrieve data from the database. CQueryDef objects can also be used directly; to execute an action query that modifies the data in the database, use the CQueryDef::Execute member function.

Other CQueryDef member functions can be used to set and retrieve query definition attributes and to manipulate query fields and parameters.

The *CDaoTableDef* Class

The CDaoTableDef class represents table definitions. A table definition describes the structure and attributes of a table in a database.

You can open an existing table definition in a database by calling CDaoTableDef::Open. A new table definition can be created by calling CDaoTableDef::Create. To add a table corresponding to a new definition to the database, call the Append member function.

Fields can be created and deleted by calling the CreateField and DeleteField member functions. Indexes for the table can be created or deleted by calling CreateIndex and DeleteIndex. Other member functions can be used to set or retrieve various table attributes; for example, GetFieldCount returns the number of fields in the table, and SetValidationRule can be used to assign a validation rule to a field.

Miscellaneous DAO Classes

In addition to the five fundamental DAO classes, DAO operations make use of two additional classes: CDaoFieldExchange and CDaoException.

CDaoFieldExchange is used in calls to CDaoRecordset::DoFieldExchange. An object of type CDaoFieldExchange defines the field that is affected by the field exchange operation and provides other parameters that characterize the field exchange.

All DAO classes utilize exception objects of type CDaoException to report errors.

Summary

Data Access Objects represent an OLE-based technology used in Visual Basic 4, Visual Basic for Applications, and Microsoft Access to access databases through the Microsoft Jet database engine. The Microsoft Foundation Classes Library and the Visual C++ AppWizard and ClassWizard provide extensive support for developing DAO-based applications in Visual C++. DAO libraries are supplied in the form of redistributable components that you can freely distribute with your Visual C++ applications.

Constructing a DAO application through AppWizard is simple. The steps to construct a simple application include specifying the data source, modifying the application's main dialog, and adding recordset member variables to the dialog.

The DAO object hierarchy is a complex hierarchy of several objects. The MFC provides a greatly simplified view of DAO, through a set of five core DAO classes and two supplementary classes. Of the core classes, CDaoQueryDef and CDaoRecordset represent queries against a database and the query results; databases themselves are represented by CDaoDatabase. A class used more rarely is CDaoWorkspace; unless you need to access secure databases, you can normally rely on the implied default workspace rather than create an object of type CDaoWorkspace explicitly. Finally, CDaoTableDef is used to represent table structures; through this class, you can add tables to your database and manipulate existing tables.

Writing Messaging Applications with MAPI

35

Writing messaging-enabled applications is no longer the task of a few corporate programmers working on enterprise-wide system integration projects. Microsoft Exchange and MAPI services are now available on every Windows 95 desktop; and with the recent phenomenal growth of the Internet, users in increasing numbers demand messaging features in end-user applications. Solutions that were developed for corporate networks yesterday are used on home computers today; if this sounds like an outrageous claim, consider the fact that I am submitting the very pages of this manuscript by dragging the files into Microsoft Exchange and letting them go.

Microsoft recognized this fact when it decided to add the requirement for some level of MAPI support to its Windows 95 Logo Program. For applications to qualify under this program, it is now necessary for them to support, at the very minimum, a Send command that enables them to send a document to a MAPI recipient. (Obviously, if your application is conceptually different, such as a game program, MAPI support is not required.)

The MAPI acronym stands for Messaging Applications Programming Interface. But what exactly is MAPI? How is MAPI implemented? And, most importantly, in what way can applications utilize MAPI services most efficiently? These are the questions that I attempt to answer in the present chapter.

Be aware that the purpose of this chapter is *not* to provide an introduction to MAPI at the level required to develop MAPI providers. Such discussion would itself warrant a book. Instead, I am trying to present an overview of MAPI as an application interface, with special emphasis on MAPI usage from within MFC framework applications.

> **NOTE**
>
> Throughout this chapter, the MAPI architecture I describe corresponds to MAPI in Windows 95 or in upcoming versions of Windows NT. Earlier versions of Microsoft Mail, although they provide limited support for Simple MAPI and CMC, do not provide full Extended MAPI support, nor are they compatible with the architecture described in this chapter.

The MAPI Architecture

What exactly is MAPI? Is it the Microsoft Exchange Client that is supplied with Windows 95? Is it the much anticipated Exchange Server? Is it the MAPI spooler that is quietly running in the background whenever Exchange is started?

The answer is, none of the above. MAPI is not an application, a DLL, or a system service; rather, it is a series of specifications. Although Microsoft is the prime supplier of MAPI components, it is by no means necessary to have a single Microsoft component in order to use MAPI (nor is it necessary to use a Windows or Win32 platform, actually). You can have a MAPI-compliant system with third party message store, address book, and transport providers on a non-Windows operating system. MAPI is part of what Microsoft calls WOSA, the Windows Open Services Architecture, that consists of a common set of APIs for distributed computing.

MAPI, in fact, can be viewed as two independent sets of APIs that link client applications on the one hand with service providers on the other (Figure 35.1).

FIGURE 35.1.

The MAPI architecture.

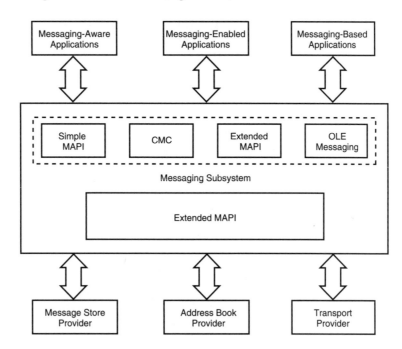

Why several APIs? The reasons are partly historical. First, Microsoft released the specifications for Simple MAPI, which included about a dozen fundamental calls that enabled applications to use messaging. The Common Messaging Calls (CMC)API has been developed as a platform-independent replacement for Simple MAPI. It also contains about 10 fundamental calls that provide access to basic messaging services. In contrast, Extended MAPI is a large, complex, evolving specification that not only provides an application programming interface for client applications but for service providers as well. OLE Messaging, an API specifically developed for Visual Basic and Visual C++ applications, uses the OLE automation architecture.

Before we plunge into exploring the APIs, the next section gives us a closer look at the MAPI architecture itself.

Types of MAPI Support

There are three distinct levels of MAPI support that applications can provide.

The simplest MAPI applications are *messaging-aware* applications. These applications do not depend on the presence of MAPI to perform their functions; they merely provide some simple MAPI functionality. The Windows 95 WordPad, which provides a Send command in its File menu, is a good example for a messaging-aware application. In contrast, *messaging-enabled* applications require MAPI to be present in order to offer full functionality. While these applications may function when MAPI is not present, they cannot offer the full range of their services under these conditions. A perfect example for a messaging-enabled application is Microsoft Schedule+; while this program can be used as a stand-alone personal information manager, many of its capabilities do not make sense unless it is running on a system with MAPI installed.

At the top of the hierarchy are *messaging-based* applications. Running these applications requires that the full range of MAPI services (message store, address book, transport) be present and available. These applications are also often referred to as workgroup applications. A good example for a workgroup application is the Microsoft Exchange client; I will spare you the explanation why this application cannot be run on a stand-alone system with no MAPI support.

The next section presents a brief tour of MAPI service providers; then we can examine how the various APIs are used in applications that provide these different levels of support

Service Providers

MAPI service providers are the components that collectively implement MAPI service on a system. There are three distinct types of service providers: *message stores*, *address books*, and *transports*.

Address books contain one or more lists of recipients. An address book provider implements a specific set of interfaces through which messaging applications or other providers can gain access to address entries or lists of addresses.

Message stores are hierarchical depositories of MAPI messages. A message consists of a multitude of properties that include the sender of the message, the recipient, the date, subject, message body, and many other items. Message store providers implement some form of persistent storage for messages (for example, a local disk file) and provide a set of interfaces through which messaging applications and other providers can enumerate messages in the message store, retrieve specific message properties, or retrieve a set of messages.

Transport providers represent the link between the local system and remote systems. Transport providers take outgoing messages, establish connections to remote systems, and transmit messages in a format that the remote system can comprehend. Transport providers also accept incoming messages from the remote system, translate these into MAPI message objects as necessary, and place them into the local message store. A good example of a transport provider is the Microsoft Internet transport provider, which connects to remote systems using Windows Sockets and uses SMTP (Simple Mail Transfer Protocol) for outgoing and POP (Post Office Protocol) for incoming messages. Outgoing messages are translated into a readable ASCII form; incoming messages are translated from such form into MAPI message objects.

All providers are represented in the form of DLLs. The set of DLLs that are to be loaded for a MAPI session is determined by MAPI profiles.

MAPI Profiles

The "glue" that holds MAPI components together is the MAPI Spooler. The MAPI Spooler is a separate process that facilitates message receipt and delivery. It is typically the MAPI Spooler that passes submitted messages to transport providers and accepts incoming messages from them. The MAPI Spooler implements a store-and-forward architecture; that is, messages submitted are "spooled" by the spooler to the appropriate transport provider when it becomes available. This capability is vital on systems with large message volumes and many remote connections.

Actually, it is also the MAPI Spooler that is responsible for loading and initializing service providers. But how does the spooler know which service providers to load?

The answer is MAPI profiles. MAPI profiles are registry entries that specify the current MAPI configuration.

These registry entries can be found under the following registry key:

```
HKEY_CURRENT_USER\
    Software\
        Microsoft\
            Windows Messaging Subsystem\
                Profiles
```

Note that the MAPI profile registry entries are generally not readable by human beings and should not be edited manually.

There can be several profiles defined for a user. Each profile describes a series of service providers and their operating parameters. For example, a typical profile may include the Microsoft Personal Information Store (message store provider), the Microsoft Personal Address Book (address book provider), Microsoft Fax (transport provider), and the Microsoft Network Online Service (address book and transport). MAPI profiles can be edited using the Microsoft Exchange client; select the Services command from its Tools menu (Figure 35.2).

FIGURE 35.2.
*Editing a MAPI
profile.*

MAPI APIs

The different APIs serve different types of MAPI applications.

Messaging-aware and messaging-enabled applications can use both Simple MAPI and CMC. The main advantage of using CMC is complete platform independence. It is recommended that newer applications use CMC in place of Simple MAPI.

Messaging-based applications (not to mention service providers) require access to the full MAPI API set and thus should use Extended MAPI.

OLE Messaging is used by Visual Basic and Visual C++ applications. OLE Messaging provides a richer API than CMC or Simple MAPI but falls short of the functionality of the full Extended MAPI set.

Simple MAPI

Simple MAPI provides a series of functions that enable applications to establish a MAPI session, perform messaging functions, and shut down the session.

The simplest way to use Simple MAPI is via the `MAPISendDocuments` function. This function can be used to create a standard MAPI message with one or more file attachments. `MAPISendDocuments` always displays a dialog where the user can specify recipients, sending options, and the message text. This is demonstrated by the program in Listing 35.1. This program sends a message using `MAPISendDocuments` with the file `c:\autoexec.bat` embedded in it. You can compile this program from the command line by typing `cl sendmsg.c user32.lib`.

Listing 35.1. Using `MAPISendDocuments`.

```
#include <windows.h>
#include <mapi.h>
```

```c
LPMAPISENDDOCUMENTS lpfnMAPISendDocuments;

void SendMsg(HWND hwnd)
{
    (*lpfnMAPISendDocuments)((ULONG)hwnd, ";", "C:\\AUTOEXEC.BAT",
                             "AUTOEXEC.BAT", 0);
    MessageBox(hwnd, "Message sent", "", MB_OK);
}

LRESULT CALLBACK WndProc(HWND hwnd, UINT uMsg,
                         WPARAM wParam, LPARAM lParam)
{
    switch(uMsg)
    {
        case WM_LBUTTONDOWN:
            SendMsg(hwnd);
            break;
        case WM_DESTROY:
            PostQuitMessage(0);
            break;
        default:
            return DefWindowProc(hwnd, uMsg, wParam, lParam);
    }
    return 0;
}

int WINAPI WinMain(HINSTANCE hInstance, HINSTANCE hPrevInstance,
                   LPSTR d3, int nCmdShow)
{
    MSG msg;
    HWND hwnd;
    WNDCLASS wndClass;
    HANDLE hMAPILib;

    hMAPILib = LoadLibrary("MAPI32.DLL");
    lpfnMAPISendDocuments = (LPMAPISENDDOCUMENTS)GetProcAddress(
                                hMAPILib, "MAPISendDocuments");
    if (hPrevInstance == NULL)
    {
        memset(&wndClass, 0, sizeof(wndClass));
        wndClass.style = CS_HREDRAW | CS_VREDRAW;
        wndClass.lpfnWndProc = WndProc;
        wndClass.hInstance = hInstance;
        wndClass.hCursor = LoadCursor(NULL, IDC_ARROW);
        wndClass.hbrBackground = (HBRUSH)(COLOR_WINDOW + 1);
        wndClass.lpszClassName = "HELLO";
        if (!RegisterClass(&wndClass)) return FALSE;
    }
    hwnd = CreateWindow("HELLO", "HELLO",
                        WS_OVERLAPPEDWINDOW,
                        CW_USEDEFAULT, 0, CW_USEDEFAULT, 0,
                        NULL, NULL, hInstance, NULL);
    ShowWindow(hwnd, nCmdShow);
    UpdateWindow(hwnd);
    while (GetMessage(&msg, NULL, 0, 0))
        DispatchMessage(&msg);
    FreeLibrary(hMAPILib);
    return msg.wParam;
}
```

A much more flexible way of sending messages is through MAPISendMail. Through a series of structures, you can specify the recipient and contents of the message. MAPISendMail makes it possible to send mail without presenting a user interface whatsoever. Thus, MAPISendMail can also be used, for example, from command-line applications.

MAPISendMail is typically used within a MAPI session that is started by a call to MAPILogon and terminated by calling MAPILogoff. This usage of MAPISendMail is demonstrated by the program in Listing 35.2, which sends a simple text message to president@whitehouse.gov without displaying a user interface. (For the sake of the sanity of Mr. Clinton's staff, do change the mail address before you start experimenting with this program!)

Listing 35.2. Using Simple MAPI in a console application.

```
#include <windows.h>
#include <stdio.h>
#include <mapi.h>

LPMAPILOGON lpfnMAPILogon;
LPMAPISENDMAIL lpfnMAPISendMail;
LPMAPILOGOFF lpfnMAPILogoff;

MapiRecipDesc recipient =
{
    0, MAPI_TO,
    "Bill Clinton", "SMTP:president@whitehouse.gov",
    0, NULL
};

MapiMessage message =
{
    0, "Greetings",
    "Hello, Mr. President!\n",
    NULL, NULL, NULL, 0, NULL, 1, &recipient, 0, NULL
};

void main(void)
{
    LHANDLE lhSession;
    HANDLE hMAPILib;

    hMAPILib = LoadLibrary("MAPI32.DLL");
    lpfnMAPILogon =
        (LPMAPILOGON)GetProcAddress(hMAPILib, "MAPILogon");
    lpfnMAPISendMail =
        (LPMAPISENDMAIL)GetProcAddress(hMAPILib, "MAPISendMail");
    lpfnMAPILogoff =
        (LPMAPILOGOFF)GetProcAddress(hMAPILib, "MAPILogoff");

    (*lpfnMAPILogon)(0, NULL, NULL, MAPI_ALLOW_OTHERS, 0,
                     &lhSession);
    (*lpfnMAPISendMail)(lhSession, 0, &message, 0, 0);
```

```
    (*lpfnMAPILogoff)(lhSession, 0, 0, 0);
    printf("Message to the White House sent.\n");

    FreeLibrary(hMAPILib);
}
```

Simple MAPI can also be used to process incoming messages. Calls like `MAPIFindNext` and `MAPIReadMail` can be used, for example, to examine new messages in the user's Inbox.

Simple MAPI additionally offers a user interface for entering addresses. Instead of using `MAPISendDocuments`, you can utilize the `MAPIAddress` call to enable the user to select and enter addresses.

Common Messaging Calls

Common Messaging Calls is an implementation of the X.400 API Association's Common Messaging Call API. It provides a series of high-level messaging functions that can be used in a fashion similar to Simple MAPI.

Table 35.1 compares CMC functions with Simple MAPI functions.

Table 35.1. CMC and Simple MAPI.

CMC	Simple MAPI	Description
cmc_logon	MAPILogon	Log on to the service
cmc_logoff	MAPILogoff	Log off from the service
cmc_free	MAPIFreeBuffer	Free allocated memory
cmc_send	MAPISendMail	Send a message
cmc_send_documents	MAPISendDocuments	Send files in a message
cmc_list	MAPIFindNext	Find messages
cmc_read	MAPIReadMail	Retrieve messages
cmc_act_on	MAPISaveMail	
	MAPIDeleteMail	Save or delete messages
cmc_look_up	MAPIAddress	
	MAPIDetails	
	MAPIResolveName	Addressing
cmc_query_configuration	N/A	CMC configuration data

The program in Listing 35.3 demonstrates the use of CMC calls from within a console application. You can compile and run this program from the command line. To compile, use `cl cmcmsg.c`.

Listing 35.3. CMC in a console application.

```c
#include <windows.h>
#include <stdio.h>
#include <xcmc.h>

typedef CMC_return_code (FAR PASCAL *LPFNCMCLOGON)(CMC_string,
    CMC_string, CMC_string, CMC_enum, CMC_ui_id, CMC_uint16,
    CMC_flags, CMC_session_id FAR *,CMC_extension FAR *);

typedef CMC_return_code (FAR PASCAL *LPFNCMCSEND)(CMC_session_id,
    CMC_message FAR *, CMC_flags, CMC_ui_id,CMC_extension FAR *);

typedef CMC_return_code (FAR PASCAL *LPFNCMCLOGOFF)(CMC_session_id,
    CMC_ui_id, CMC_flags, CMC_extension FAR *);

LPFNCMCLOGON lpfnCMCLogon;
LPFNCMCSEND lpfnCMCSend;
LPFNCMCLOGOFF lpfnCMCLogoff;

CMC_recipient recipient =
{
    "Bill Clinton", CMC_TYPE_INDIVIDUAL,
    "SMTP:president@whitehouse.gov", CMC_ROLE_TO,
    CMC_RECIP_LAST_ELEMENT, NULL
};

CMC_message message =
{
    NULL, "CMC: IPM", "Greetings", {0, 0, 0, 0, 0, 0, 0, 0, 0, 0},
    "Hello, Mr. President!\n", &recipient, NULL,
    CMC_MSG_LAST_ELEMENT, NULL
};

void main(void)
{
    CMC_session_id session;
    HANDLE hMAPILib;

    hMAPILib = LoadLibrary("MAPI32.DLL");
    lpfnCMCLogon =
        (LPFNCMCLOGON)GetProcAddress(hMAPILib, "cmc_logon");
    lpfnCMCSend =
        (LPFNCMCSEND)GetProcAddress(hMAPILib, "cmc_send");
    lpfnCMCLogoff =
        (LPFNCMCLOGOFF)GetProcAddress(hMAPILib, "cmc_logoff");

    (*lpfnCMCLogon)(NULL, NULL, NULL, (CMC_enum)0, 0, 100,
      CMC_ERROR_UI_ALLOWED | CMC_LOGON_UI_ALLOWED, &session, NULL);
    (*lpfnCMCSend)(session, &message, 0, 0, NULL);
    (*lpfnCMCLogoff)(session, 0,
                CMC_ERROR_UI_ALLOWED | CMC_LOGOFF_UI_ALLOWED, NULL);
```

```
    printf("Message to the White House sent.\n");

    FreeLibrary(hMAPILib);
}
```

Extended MAPI

Extended MAPI is a large, complex object-oriented programming interface to all aspects of MAPI. Its programming model is based on OLE COM, the OLE Component Object Model.

Extended MAPI defines a series of object types, including messages, message stores, folders, attachments, mail users, address books, providers, sessions, and many more supplementary objects. MAPI objects are characterized by a set of properties, themselves implemented as objects. MAPI objects are accessed through interfaces derived from the OLE IUnknown interface. For example, property objects implement the IMAPIProp interface, while message objects implement the IMessage interface.

Extended MAPI programming involves manipulating MAPI objects through their properties and methods and through event notifications. MAPI properties can be manipulated through property objects and the IMAPIProp interface, or through property tables. Methods are the IUnknown-derived interfaces that MAPI objects provide. Event notification is the mechanism of communication between MAPI objects.

Extended MAPI can be used to implement messaging-based applications that require finer control over messaging services than what is available through Simple MAPI or CMC. Extended MAPI can also be used to perform administrative functions, such as selecting and configuring services and creating user profiles.

Another use of Extended MAPI is to program with MAPI forms. MAPI forms represent special types of messages, implemented through a user interface and a form server, which manage the user's interaction with the forms message.

Extended MAPI can also be used to extend the Microsoft Exchange client. Customized versions of the Microsoft Exchange client can provide application-specific views on address books, message stores, and message objects, and can add new searching, addressing, and workgroup features to that application.

Lastly, Extended MAPI also represents the programming interface for creating MAPI service providers. These include address books, message stores, and transports.

OLE Messaging

OLE messaging exposes MAPI objects through the OLE automation interface. As such, it works best with OLE automation clients, such as Visual Basic applications or programs written in Visual Basic for Applications (that is, Microsoft Excel, Access, or Project programs).

Figure 35.3 illustrates the hierarchy of OLE automation objects exposed by OLE messaging.

FIGURE 35.3.

OLE messaging objects.

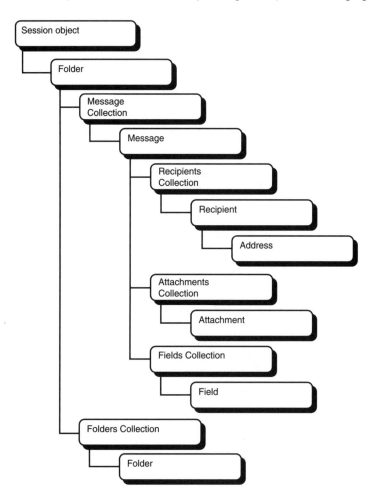

Demonstrating the use of OLE messaging from within Visual C++ is difficult, as it requires constructing an OLE automation client application. In order to demonstrate a simple OLE messaging session, I decided to resort to Visual Basic. The example shown in Listing 35.4 shows how a Visual Basic application can send a simple message without displaying a user interface.

Listing 35.4. OLE messaging example in Visual Basic.

```
Sub Command1_Click ()
    Dim objSession As Object
    Dim objMessage As Object
    Dim objRecip As Object
```

```
    Set objSession = CreateObject("MAPI.Session")
    objSession.Logon "", "", False, False

    Set objMessage = objSession.Outbox.Messages.Add
    objMessage.Subject = "Greetings"
    objMessage.Text = "Hello again, Mr. President!"

    Set objRecip = objMessage.Recipients.Add
    objRecip.Name = "Bill Clinton"
    objRecip.Address = "SMTP:president@whitehouse.gov"
    objRecip.Type = 1
    objRecip.Resolve (False)

    objMessage.Send True, False
    MsgBox "Message to the White House sent"
    objSession.Logoff
    Exit Sub
End Sub
```

To test this simple example, attach this code to a button in a Visual Basic form (you can also use `disptest.exe`, the OLE automation test version of Visual Basic that came as part of your Visual C++ installation), run the program, and click on the button. Oh, and don't forget to change the address before exercising this code!

Note that this test will only work if you have OLE messaging installed on your computer. OLE messaging components are only available at present as part of the MAPI SDK, distributed through the Microsoft Developer Network Level 2 subscription.

MAPI Support in MFC

The Microsoft Foundation Classes Library provides MAPI support through a series of member functions in CDocument. This support, and how this support is incorporated into MFC framework applications, is the subject of the last part of this chapter.

MAPI Support in *CDocument*

The CDocument class supports MAPI through the OnFileSendMail member function.

CDocument::OnFileSendMail serializes the document into a temporary file, and then calls Simple MAPI functions to prepare and send a message with this file as an attachment.

A variant of CDocument::OnFileSendMail is COleDocument::OnFileSendMail; this version handles compound files correctly.

The CDocument::OnUpdateFileSendMail member function determines whether MAPI support is available on the system and updates command items accordingly through a CCmdUI object.

MAPI and AppWizard

The AppWizard can generate skeleton applications with minimal MAPI support. If requested, the AppWizard will add a Send menu item to the new application's File menu. This item will invoke the OnFileSendMail member function of the application's document class. AppWizard will also install a command update handler, referencing the OnUpdateFileSendMail member function.

In other words, if you only wish to make your application messaging-aware, you need not do anything other than enabling MAPI support when creating the application's skeleton with AppWizard. This is all you need to do in order to satisfy the new Windows 95 Logo requirements.

Summary

MAPI, the Messaging Application Programming Interface, represents a comprehensive set of specifications that link messaging applications on the one hand and messaging service providers on the other, forming a messaging architecture.

Messaging applications include messaging-aware, messaging-enabled, and messaging-based programs. Messaging-aware applications such as the Windows 95 WordPad, although they provide some level of MAPI functionality, do not depend on the presence of MAPI for their functionality. Messaging-enabled applications such as Microsoft Schedule+ require the presence of MAPI to perform many of their functions. Messaging-based applications such as the Microsoft Exchange client require MAPI in order to function.

On the service provider side, MAPI recognizes message stores, address books, and transport providers. These providers, acting under the control of the MAPI Spooler, perform the services that together form the messaging system on your computer.

The MAPI configuration is stored in the form of MAPI profiles. MAPI profiles are registry entries that identify active MAPI services and their configuration. A user can have several MAPI profiles, with an active profile selected at the start of the MAPI session.

When developing MAPI applications, one can pick one of several APIs. Simple MAPI provides a set of functions essential for addressing and sending simple messages and retrieving incoming messages. Similar functionality is offered by CMC, the Common Messaging Call API; however, CMC is completely platform-independent. CMC is an implementation of the X.400 API Association's Common Messaging Call API. Visual Basic and Visual C++ applications can also use OLE Messaging for an object-oriented interface to MAPI functions.

The full interface to MAPI, Extended MAPI, is used for developing messaging-based applications, service providers, new message types (MAPI forms), administrative applications, and extensions to the Microsoft Exchange client application.

OLE Control
Development

36

Constructing an OLE custom control used to be a mysterious task best left to gurus who write even their love letters in C++. Version 4 of Visual C++ changes that by adding advanced AppWizard support for OLE control development.

It is now possible to create simple OLE controls with relatively little work. AppWizard provides the OLE custom control framework that consists of control registration and initialization code, and skeleton code for the control's class and property pages.

An OLE control is defined in terms of its appearance, properties, methods, and events. Control properties, methods, and events can be defined through the ClassWizard.

To demonstrate the capabilities of an OLE custom control, I developed a simple control. This control, OCTL, consists of a single button that can have three different shapes (ellipse, rectangle, triangle). When the control is clicked on, it changes its state from deselected to selected or vice versa. When the control is selected, it appears red; otherwise, its color is green. The control generates events whenever its state changes.

Figure 36.1 demonstrates the OCTL custom control in action.

FIGURE 36.1.

The OCTL control in action.

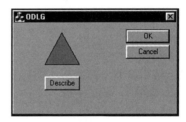

This control, like any other control, can be embedded in dialogs or used otherwise by OLE control container applications. The Developer Studio fully supports the construction of dialogs that contain OLE custom controls and the use of OLE custom controls in applications through wrapper classes.

The steps of creating a custom control are as follows:

1. Create the custom control skeleton through AppWizard.
2. Add the control's properties, methods, and events through ClassWizard.
3. Update the control's representative bitmap using the Developer Studio bitmap editor.
4. Add drawing code to your control.
5. Develop code for methods and events.
6. Create the control's property page.
7. Add code handling to the property page.

In the remainder of this chapter, we review each of these steps in detail. As we proceed, the OCTL control serves as an example of putting the principles into practice.

Creating a Skeleton Control with AppWizard

The first step in constructing an OLE custom control is creating a custom control skeleton through AppWizard—or, to be more precise, through ControlWizard, which is a custom AppWizard developed specifically for the purposes of creating OLE custom controls.

Creating the Skeleton Control

To begin, select New from the Developer Studio File menu, then select Project Workspace in the New dialog. In the New Project Workspace dialog, select OLE ControlWizard as the project type, type in a name for the new project (for example, OCTL), and select a suitable directory (Figure 36.2).

FIGURE 36.2.

Creating the OCTL control.

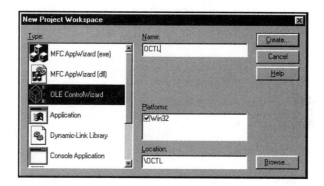

After you click Create, the first page of the two-page OLE ControlWizard appears (Figure 36.3). On this page, you can specify the number of controls in your project (a single OLE control project can contain multiple controls), whether you want licensing support, and whether you want source comments and support for a help file. (Specifying help file support is generally a good idea; it is much easier to throw out code later than trying to add it to your project.)

If you decide to add licensing support, the ControlWizard will create a default LIC file for your control. It will also add functions to your control class that support verification of licensing information. Without a valid license (LIC) file, it will not be possible to use the control in design mode. This is how users of your control should redistribute your control to end users (that is, without the license file); you, on the other hand, provide the control to your users with a valid license file that enables them to do development work with your control.

In the second page of ControlWizard (Figure 36.4), you can review and modify the class names that AppWizard generated for your controls. For every control in your project, AppWizard creates two classes: a control class and a class for the control's property page.

FIGURE 36.3.

*ControlWizard
Page One.*

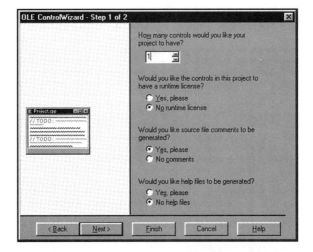

FIGURE 36.4.

*ControlWizard
Page Two.*

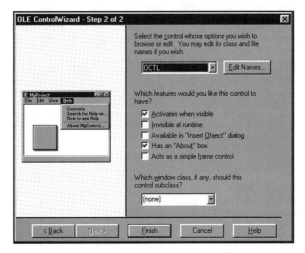

If your control requires more than one property page, don't worry; you will have an opportunity to create additional property pages. Use the ControlWizard to specify the parameters for the first property page.

On this ControlWizard page, several additional properties can also be defined. I would like to bring your attention to two of these. The Invisible at runtime option enables you to create controls (such as the Microsoft Comm control) that do not have a visible interface at runtime. The Available in "Insert Object" dialog option enables you to create a control that can be inserted into OLE container documents. This option should typically remain unchecked; after all, when you create a new button meant to be used in dialogs, you may not want someone to include it in a Word for Windows document!

You can also specify a control class that the new custom control will subclass. For example, you can specify the BUTTON class to create a custom control that inherits some of the behavior of the standard Button control.

The OCTL control was created with all ControlWizard settings left at their default values.

Custom Control Code Overview

Before proceeding, we need to take a look at the code generated by ControlWizard and familiarize ourselves with the new custom control's classes and resources. As always, it is a good idea to develop a basic understanding of these components before proceeding with custom modifications.

If you look at your project in ClassView (Figure 36.5), you can see that the ControlWizard generated three classes for you. One represents the custom control library object; the other two represent the control object and the control's property page. (If you elected to create a project with more than one control, additional pairs of classes were also created by ControlWizard to represent additional control objects and their property pages.)

FIGURE 36.5.

Classes generated by ControlWizard.

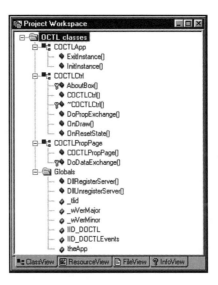

Of the three classes in the OCTL project, the COCTLApp class is perhaps the simplest. Derived from COleControlModule, this class represents the OCX object, that is, the library that contains your OLE custom controls. Only two member functions are declared (Listing 36.1).

Listing 36.1. COCTLApp **class declaration.**

```
class COCTLApp : public COleControlModule
{
public:
    BOOL InitInstance();
    int ExitInstance();
};
```

These functions have a trivial implementation (Listing 36.2). In the same file, OCTL.cpp, there is also a pair of additional functions, DllRegisterServer and DllUnregisterServer. These two functions store and remove OLE registration information for your new controls in the Registry. The redistributable program regsvr32.exe calls these functions to register or unregister OLE custom controls.

Listing 36.2. COCTLApp **class implementation and control registration functions.**

```
/////////////////////////////////////////////////////////////////////
// COCTLApp::InitInstance - DLL initialization

BOOL COCTLApp::InitInstance()
{
    BOOL bInit = COleControlModule::InitInstance();

    if (bInit)
    {
        // TODO: Add your own module initialization code here.
    }

    return bInit;
}


/////////////////////////////////////////////////////////////////////
// COCTLApp::ExitInstance - DLL termination

int COCTLApp::ExitInstance()
{
    // TODO: Add your own module termination code here.

    return COleControlModule::ExitInstance();
}


/////////////////////////////////////////////////////////////////////
// DllRegisterServer - Adds entries to the system registry

STDAPI DllRegisterServer(void)
{
    AFX_MANAGE_STATE(_afxModuleAddrThis);

    if (!AfxOleRegisterTypeLib(AfxGetInstanceHandle(), _tlid))
        return ResultFromScode(SELFREG_E_TYPELIB);
```

```
    if (!COleObjectFactoryEx::UpdateRegistryAll(TRUE))
        return ResultFromScode(SELFREG_E_CLASS);

    return NOERROR;
}


/////////////////////////////////////////////////////////////////////
// DllUnregisterServer - Removes entries from the system registry

STDAPI DllUnregisterServer(void)
{
    AFX_MANAGE_STATE(_afxModuleAddrThis);

    if (!AfxOleUnregisterTypeLib(_tlid))
        return ResultFromScode(SELFREG_E_TYPELIB);

    if (!COleObjectFactoryEx::UpdateRegistryAll(FALSE))
        return ResultFromScode(SELFREG_E_CLASS);

    return NOERROR;
}
```

In terms of simplicity, the COCTRLPropPage class follows. This class implements the property page of the control that design applications (such as the dialog template editor in Developer Studio) can display in a property sheet interface.

The ControlWizard generates a blank property page for you (Figure 36.6). It is up to you to add controls to this property page as they fit the requirements of your control.

FIGURE 36.6.

The default ControlWizard-generated property page.

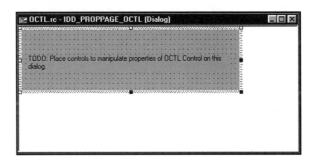

Correspondingly, the default version of the COCTLPropPage is equally simple. The class declaration (Listing 36.3) only contains declarations for a constructor and a DoDataExchange member function. Notice the use of the DECLARE_DYNCREATE and DECLARE_OLECREATE_EX macros; the latter makes the run-time creation of the OLE custom control property page possible.

Listing 36.3. `COCTLPropPage` class declaration.

```
class COCTLPropPage : public COlePropertyPage
{
    DECLARE_DYNCREATE(COCTLPropPage)
    DECLARE_OLECREATE_EX(COCTLPropPage)

// Constructor
public:
    COCTLPropPage();

// Dialog Data
    //{{AFX_DATA(COCTLPropPage)
    enum { IDD = IDD_PROPPAGE_OCTL };
        // NOTE - ClassWizard will add data members here.
 //    DO NOT EDIT what you see in these blocks of generated code !
    //}}AFX_DATA

// Implementation
protected:
    virtual void DoDataExchange(CDataExchange* pDX);

// Message maps
protected:
    //{{AFX_MSG(COCTLPropPage)
        // NOTE - ClassWizard will add and remove member functions
        //   here.  DO NOT EDIT what you see in these blocks of
        //   generated code !
    //}}AFX_MSG
    DECLARE_MESSAGE_MAP()

};
```

Although this class is derived from `COlePropertyPage`, for all practical intents and purposes it works the same way as any `CPropertyPage`-derived class. In particular, you can use the ClassWizard to add member variables that correspond to controls in the property page. However, it is sometimes necessary to use additional data exchange functions and macros (for example, when specifying a persistent custom control property). But more about that later.

The implementation file of `COCTLPropPage` contains, in addition to trivial skeletal definitions of the constructor and the `DoDataExchange` member function, additional OLE-related elements (Listing 36.4). Fortunately, it is rarely necessary to modify these elements manually; where necessary, the ClassWizard will insert items as applicable.

Listing 36.4. `COCTLPropPage` class implementation.

```
IMPLEMENT_DYNCREATE(COCTLPropPage, COlePropertyPage)


/////////////////////////////////////////////////////////////////
// Message map

BEGIN_MESSAGE_MAP(COCTLPropPage, COlePropertyPage)
```

```
    //{{AFX_MSG_MAP(COCTLPropPage)
    // NOTE - ClassWizard will add and remove message map entries
    // DO NOT EDIT what you see in these blocks of generated code !
    //}}AFX_MSG_MAP
END_MESSAGE_MAP()


///////////////////////////////////////////////////////////////////
// Initialize class factory and guid

IMPLEMENT_OLECREATE_EX(COCTLPropPage, "OCTL.OCTLPropPage.1",
                    0xabe328d7, 0xf792, 0x11ce, 0x87, 0xc3, 0,
                    0x40, 0x33, 0x21, 0xbf, 0xac)


///////////////////////////////////////////////////////////////////
// COCTLPropPage::COCTLPropPageFactory::UpdateRegistry -
// Adds or removes system registry entries for COCTLPropPage

BOOL
COCTLPropPage::COCTLPropPageFactory::UpdateRegistry(BOOL bRegister)
{
    if (bRegister)
     return AfxOleRegisterPropertyPageClass(AfxGetInstanceHandle(),
            m_clsid, IDS_OCTL_PPG);
    else
        return AfxOleUnregisterClass(m_clsid, NULL);
}



///////////////////////////////////////////////////////////////////
// COCTLPropPage::COCTLPropPage - Constructor

COCTLPropPage::COCTLPropPage() :
    COlePropertyPage(IDD, IDS_OCTL_PPG_CAPTION)
{
    //{{AFX_DATA_INIT(COCTLPropPage)
    // NOTE: ClassWizard will add member initialization here
    // DO NOT EDIT what you see in these blocks of generated code !
    //}}AFX_DATA_INIT
}



///////////////////////////////////////////////////////////////////
// COCTLPropPage::DoDataExchange -
// Moves data between page and properties

void COCTLPropPage::DoDataExchange(CDataExchange* pDX)
{
    //{{AFX_DATA_MAP(COCTLPropPage)
    // NOTE: ClassWizard will add DDP, DDX, and DDV calls here
    // DO NOT EDIT what you see in these blocks of generated code !
    //}}AFX_DATA_MAP
    DDP_PostProcessing(pDX);
}
```

In fact, under normal circumstances, you will rarely need to edit this code manually at all; code supporting member variables that correspond to controls in the property page will be inserted automatically by ClassWizard. Instances involving the need for manual modification include the case when nonstandard control behavior is desired; but even in those cases, changes are often confined to the DoDataExchange member function.

The last of the three ControlWizard-generated classes for the OCTL control is the class COCTLCtrl. As its name implies, this class encapsulates the overall behavior of the custom control, and as such, can be considered perhaps the central element of the custom control project.

The declaration of the COCTLCtrl class is shown in Listing 36.5. I would like to call your attention to several elements in this declaration.

Listing 36.5. COCTLCtrl class declaration.

```cpp
class COCTLCtrl : public COleControl
{
    DECLARE_DYNCREATE(COCTLCtrl)

// Constructor
public:
    COCTLCtrl();

// Overrides

    // Drawing function
    virtual void OnDraw(
        CDC* pdc, const CRect& rcBounds, const CRect& rcInvalid);

    // Persistence
    virtual void DoPropExchange(CPropExchange* pPX);

    // Reset control state
    virtual void OnResetState();

// Implementation
protected:
    ~COCTLCtrl();

    DECLARE_OLECREATE_EX(COCTLCtrl)      // Class factory and guid
    DECLARE_OLETYPELIB(COCTLCtrl)        // GetTypeInfo
    DECLARE_PROPPAGEIDS(COCTLCtrl)       // Property page IDs
    DECLARE_OLECTLTYPE(COCTLCtrl)        // Type name and misc status

// Message maps
    //{{AFX_MSG(COCTLCtrl)
    // NOTE - ClassWizard will add and remove member functions here.
    //   DO NOT EDIT what you see in these blocks of generated code !
    //}}AFX_MSG
    DECLARE_MESSAGE_MAP()

// Dispatch maps
    //{{AFX_DISPATCH(COCTLCtrl)
    // NOTE - ClassWizard will add and remove member functions here.
```

```
    //  DO NOT EDIT what you see in these blocks of generated code !
    //}}AFX_DISPATCH
    DECLARE_DISPATCH_MAP()

    afx_msg void AboutBox();

// Event maps
    //{{AFX_EVENT(COCTLCtrl)
    // NOTE - ClassWizard will add and remove member functions here.
    //  DO NOT EDIT what you see in these blocks of generated code !
    //}}AFX_EVENT
    DECLARE_EVENT_MAP()

// Dispatch and event IDs
public:
    enum {
    //{{AFX_DISP_ID(COCTLCtrl)
        // NOTE: ClassWizard will add and remove enumeration
        //  elements here.  DO NOT EDIT what you see in these
        //  blocks of generated code !
    //}}AFX_DISP_ID
    };
};
```

The Implementation section of this declaration begins with a series of four macro calls that declare various OLE-related elements. There are corresponding macro calls implementing these elements in the implementation file. Of particular interest is the call to DECLARE_OLECREATE_EX; this macro call is different in the case of an OLE custom control that supports licensing. (It is replaced by a block of function declarations enclosed between a BEGIN_OLEFACTORY and an END_OLEFACTORY macro call.)

In the remainder of the class declaration, the OLE control's message map, dispatch map, event map, and dispatch/event identifiers are declared. These maps are used to route messages and to define the control's OLE interface of properties, methods, and events. The ClassWizard adds items automatically to these sections of code; you rarely need to modify them directly.

The implementation file of class COCTLCtrl (Listing 36.6) contains several elements that you may need to be familiar with.

Listing 36.6. COCTLCtrl class implementation.

```
IMPLEMENT_DYNCREATE(COCTLCtrl, COleControl)


/////////////////////////////////////////////////////////////////////
// Message map

BEGIN_MESSAGE_MAP(COCTLCtrl, COleControl)
    //{{AFX_MSG_MAP(COCTLCtrl)
    // NOTE - ClassWizard will add and remove message map entries
    // DO NOT EDIT what you see in these blocks of generated code !
```

continues

Listing 36.6. continued

```
    //}}AFX_MSG_MAP
    ON_OLEVERB(AFX_IDS_VERB_PROPERTIES, OnProperties)
END_MESSAGE_MAP()


/////////////////////////////////////////////////////////////////////
// Dispatch map

BEGIN_DISPATCH_MAP(COCTLCtrl, COleControl)
    //{{AFX_DISPATCH_MAP(COCTLCtrl)
    // NOTE - ClassWizard will add and remove dispatch map entries
    // DO NOT EDIT what you see in these blocks of generated code !
    //}}AFX_DISPATCH_MAP
    DISP_FUNCTION_ID(COCTLCtrl, "AboutBox", DISPID_ABOUTBOX,
                    AboutBox, VT_EMPTY, VTS_NONE)
END_DISPATCH_MAP()


/////////////////////////////////////////////////////////////////////
// Event map

BEGIN_EVENT_MAP(COCTLCtrl, COleControl)
    //{{AFX_EVENT_MAP(COCTLCtrl)
    // NOTE - ClassWizard will add and remove event map entries
    // DO NOT EDIT what you see in these blocks of generated code !
    //}}AFX_EVENT_MAP
END_EVENT_MAP()


/////////////////////////////////////////////////////////////////////
// Property pages

// TODO: Add more property pages as needed.
//   Remember to increase the count!
BEGIN_PROPPAGEIDS(COCTLCtrl, 1)
    PROPPAGEID(COCTLPropPage::guid)
END_PROPPAGEIDS(COCTLCtrl)


/////////////////////////////////////////////////////////////////////
// Initialize class factory and guid

IMPLEMENT_OLECREATE_EX(COCTLCtrl, "OCTL.OCTLCtrl.1",
                    0x677600e7, 0xf6c5, 0x11ce, 0x87, 0xc3, 0,
                    0x40, 0x33, 0x21, 0xbf, 0xac)


/////////////////////////////////////////////////////////////////////
// Type library ID and version

IMPLEMENT_OLETYPELIB(COCTLCtrl, _tlid, _wVerMajor, _wVerMinor)


/////////////////////////////////////////////////////////////////////
// Interface IDs
```

```
const IID BASED_CODE IID_DOCTL =
                { 0xabe328d5, 0xf792, 0x11ce,
                  { 0x87, 0xc3, 0, 0x40, 0x33, 0x21, 0xbf, 0xac } };
const IID BASED_CODE IID_DOCTLEvents =
                { 0xabe328d6, 0xf792, 0x11ce,
                  { 0x87, 0xc3, 0, 0x40, 0x33, 0x21, 0xbf, 0xac } };


/////////////////////////////////////////////////////////////////
// Control type information

static const DWORD BASED_CODE _dwOCTLOleMisc =
    OLEMISC_ACTIVATEWHENVISIBLE |
    OLEMISC_SETCLIENTSITEFIRST |
    OLEMISC_INSIDEOUT |
    OLEMISC_CANTLINKINSIDE |
    OLEMISC_RECOMPOSEONRESIZE;

IMPLEMENT_OLECTLTYPE(COCTLCtrl, IDS_OCTL, _dwOCTLOleMisc)


/////////////////////////////////////////////////////////////////
// COCTLCtrl::COCTLCtrlFactory::UpdateRegistry -
// Adds or removes system registry entries for COCTLCtrl

BOOL COCTLCtrl::COCTLCtrlFactory::UpdateRegistry(BOOL bRegister)
{
    if (bRegister)
        return AfxOleRegisterControlClass(
            AfxGetInstanceHandle(),
            m_clsid,
            m_lpszProgID,
            IDS_OCTL,
            IDB_OCTL,
            FALSE,                      //  Not insertable
            _dwOCTLOleMisc,
            _tlid,
            _wVerMajor,
            _wVerMinor);
    else
        return AfxOleUnregisterClass(m_clsid, m_lpszProgID);
}


/////////////////////////////////////////////////////////////////
// COCTLCtrl::COCTLCtrl - Constructor

COCTLCtrl::COCTLCtrl()
{
    InitializeIIDs(&IID_DOCTL, &IID_DOCTLEvents);

    // TODO: Initialize your control's instance data here.
}


/////////////////////////////////////////////////////////////////
// COCTLCtrl::~COCTLCtrl - Destructor
```

continues

Listing 36.6. continued

```
COCTLCtrl::~COCTLCtrl()
{
    // TODO: Cleanup your control's instance data here.
}


/////////////////////////////////////////////////////////////////////
// COCTLCtrl::OnDraw - Drawing function

void COCTLCtrl::OnDraw(
          CDC* pdc, const CRect& rcBounds, const CRect& rcInvalid)
{
    // TODO: Replace the following code with your own drawing code.
    pdc->FillRect(rcBounds,
        CBrush::FromHandle((HBRUSH)GetStockObject(WHITE_BRUSH)));
    pdc->Ellipse(rcBounds);
}


/////////////////////////////////////////////////////////////////////
// COCTLCtrl::DoPropExchange - Persistence support

void COCTLCtrl::DoPropExchange(CPropExchange* pPX)
{
    ExchangeVersion(pPX, MAKELONG(_wVerMinor, _wVerMajor));
    COleControl::DoPropExchange(pPX);

    // TODO: Call PX_ functions for each persistent custom property.

}


/////////////////////////////////////////////////////////////////////
// COCTLCtrl::OnResetState - Reset control to default state

void COCTLCtrl::OnResetState()
{
    COleControl::OnResetState();

    // TODO: Reset any other control state here.
}


/////////////////////////////////////////////////////////////////////
// COCTLCtrl::AboutBox - Display an "About" box to the user

void COCTLCtrl::AboutBox()
{
    CDialog dlgAbout(IDD_ABOUTBOX_OCTL);
    dlgAbout.DoModal();
}
```

The Message Map, Dispatch Map, and Event Map sections of this implementation are usually maintained by the ClassWizard. However, should you need to create additional property pages as part of your control's property page interface, you must manually modify the Property Pages section. For example, in a control that has three property pages, this section may contain the following code:

```
BEGIN_PROPPAGEIDS(COCTLCtrl, 3)
    PROPPAGEID(COCTLPropPage1::guid)
    PROPPAGEID(COCTLPropPage2::guid)
    PROPPAGEID(COCTLPropPage3::guid)
END_PROPPAGEIDS(COCTLCtrl)
```

Of the functions defined in this file, three are of importance to the control programmer. The member function OnDraw is used to actually draw the control. The ControlWizard generates this member function with some default drawing instructions in it (either drawing a circle or, in the case of a subclassed control, calling the superclass's drawing function). The member function DoPropExchange implements property persistency; that is, the capability of saving properties at design time and reloading them when the control is displayed at runtime. More about this later. The function OnResetState is used to reset property values to their defaults. Although the call to the base class implementation COleControl::OnResetState resets all persistent properties, it may be necessary to reset other properties manually in OnResetState.

Customizing the Control

Control properties, methods, and events can be added through the ClassWizard.

A property is analogous to a data member of a C++ class, even though control properties are often implemented using get/set methods as opposed to member variables.

A method is analogous to a member function (and is, in fact, implemented as a member function of the control class).

Events are messages that the control can send to its parent window. When you add an event through the ClassWizard, the ClassWizard creates a member function in the control class that fires the event. You can call this member function from your own code as required.

The OCTL control has two properties and one event.

The first of the two properties is the Selected property; this Boolean property reflects the selected/deselected state of the control. Whenever the left mouse button is clicked on the control, the control's state will change from selected to deselected or vice versa. The Selected property will be implemented using get/set methods; this form of implementation enables us to create a read-only control by simply omitting the set method.

The second property, Shape, is an integer property determining the control's shape. Its value can be 0 (elliptical shape), 1 (rectangular shape), or 2 (triangular shape). Although this is a read/write property, we will make it writeable only in design mode. For this reason, this property will also be implemented using get/set methods, with a check for design mode as part of the set method member function.

The single control event, the Select event, indicates to the parent window that the control's state changes. We will fire this event whenever the control receives a left mouse button click. (Needless to say, we must add a handler function for that event first.)

Changing the Control's Bitmap

Before we charge ahead adding code to the control, we must focus on the mundane task of updating the control bitmap. As mundane a task as it is, it should not be neglected; for it is the control bitmap that users of your control will most often see in tool palettes. Figure 36.7 shows the bitmap I drew for the OCTL control. (Okay, okay... I know I am not a graphic artist!)

FIGURE 36.7.

OCTL control bitmap.

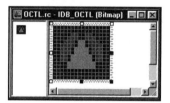

Adding Properties

Now to add the Selected and Shape properties to our control. To do so, invoke the ClassWizard and select the OLE Automation tab. Select the COCTLCtrl class (Figure 36.8).

FIGURE 36.8.

Adding control properties.

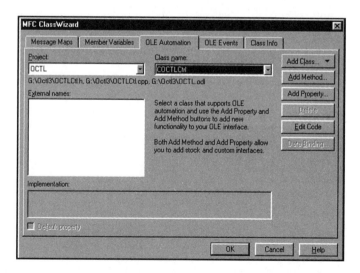

To add the Selected property, click on the Add Property button. In the Add Property dialog, type the name Selected in the External name field; select BOOL as the property type; and select the get/set methods radio button under Implementation. At this point, the dialog automatically generates names for the property's get and set functions. To render this property read-only, simply erase the name of the set function before dismissing the dialog with the OK button (Figure 36.9).

FIGURE 36.9.

Adding the Selected property.

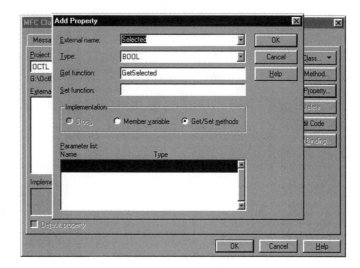

Adding the Shape property is an almost identical process. There are two differences. First, the property's type should be short; second, as this property is a read/write property, you should not erase the name of the set function this time.

At this point, the ClassWizard generates a total of three new member functions in the control class.

To reflect the control's selection state and shape, we must now manually add member variables to the control class declaration. Add the following two declarations to the declaration of the class COCTLCtrl in the header file OCTLctl.h:

```
BOOL m_fSelected;
short m_nShape;
```

It is also necessary to initialize these member variables to reasonable defaults in the constructor of the control class. Add the following lines to COCTLCtrl::COCTLCtrl:

```
m_fSelected = FALSE;
m_nShape = 0;
```

With these member variables at hand, we can proceed with the implementation of the new get/set functions for which ClassWizard created skeletons. The completed functions are shown in Listing 36.7.

Listing 36.7. `COCTLCtrl` **property get/set methods.**

```
short COCTLCtrl::GetShape()
{
    // TODO: Add your property handler here

    return m_nShape;
}

void COCTLCtrl::SetShape(short nNewValue)
{
    // TODO: Add your property handler here
    if (AmbientUserMode())
        ThrowError(CTL_E_SETNOTSUPPORTEDATRUNTIME);
    else if (nNewValue < 0 || nNewValue > 2)
        ThrowError(CTL_E_INVALIDPROPERTYVALUE);
    else
    {
        m_nShape = nNewValue;
        SetModifiedFlag();
        InvalidateControl();
    }
}

BOOL COCTLCtrl::GetSelected()
{
    // TODO: Add your property handler here

    return m_fSelected;
}
```

The functions `GetSelected` and `GetShape` are trivially simple; they just return the value of the `m_fSelected` and `m_nShape` member variables, respectively. The function `SetSelected` is somewhat more complicated; it uses the `AmbientUserMode` function to check whether the control container is in user mode or design mode and disallows changing the control's shape in user mode. Note the use of the `ThrowError` function; this member function of `COleControl` is specifically intended to indicate an error while accessing a property via a get/set method.

The framework provides an implementation for several *stock properties.* Stock properties include, among other things, properties relating to font and color. When adding a stock property, you can elect to use the stock implementation in `COleControl` instead of implementing the property yourself.

Making a Property Persistent

Having added a property is one thing; however, this does not automatically ensure that the property's value is retained when it is set during a design session, for example. To make it happen, we must add a call to a `PX_` function in the `DoPropExchange` member function of the control class.

What does `DoPropExchange` do? Quite simply, this function is used to serialize property values into a *property exchange object.* The property achieves persistence by having its value stored in, and reloaded from, such an object. For example, the Developer Studio dialog editor writes the content of the property exchange object into the application's resource file, from which it is reloaded at runtime.

For every persistent property, a function call of the appropriate `PX_` function must be inserted in `DoPropExchange`. There is a large variety of `PX_` functions corresponding to properties of various types. These are summarized in Table 36.1.

Table 36.1. `PX_` functions.

Function Name	Property Type
PX_Blob	Binary Large Object (BLOB) data
PX_Bool	Boolean value (type BOOL)
PX_Color	Color value (type OLE_COLOR)
PX_Currency	Currency value
PX_Double	Value of type double
PX_Float	Value of type float
PX_Font	A font (pointer to a FONTDESC structure)
PX_IUnknown	An object with an OLE IUnknown-derived interface
PX_Long	Value of type long
PX_Picture	A picture (CPictureHolder reference)
PX_Short	Value of type short
PX_String	A character pointer (type LPCSTR)
PX_ULong	Value of type unsigned long (ULONG)
PX_UShort	Value of type unsigned short
PX_VBXFontConvert	Font-related properties of a VBX control

In the case of OCTL, the one property that we wish to make persistent is the `Shape` property, which is of type `short`. Correspondingly, the following line must be added to the `COCTLCtrl::DoPropExchange` function:

```
PX_Short(pPX, _T("Shape"), m_nShape, 0);
```

Adding Methods

Adding methods to an OLE custom control is similar to adding properties. Methods are also added through the ClassWizard, using the OLE Automation tab.

Although we have not explicitly added any methods to the OCTL control, we have, in fact, added three methods nevertheless; these are the get/set methods that we used for our two properties.

A method can also have a list of parameters. These parameters are also defined through the ClassWizard.

The `COleControl` class supports two stock events: `DoClick` (fires a `Click` event) and `Refresh` (updates the control's appearance).

Adding Events

Events are also added to an OLE custom control through the ClassWizard. To add an event, use the ClassWizard's OLE Events tab (Figure 36.10).

FIGURE 36.10.

Adding OLE events.

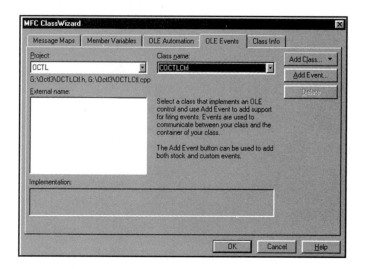

To add the `Select` event, click on the Add Event button. In the Add Event dialog, type `Select` as the event's External name. As you do that, ClassWizard automatically sets the internal name (the name of the function that causes the event to be fired) to `FireSelect`. Make sure to also add the `IsSelected` parameter to this event (this parameter will tell the recipient of the event whether the control has been selected or deselected) and specify this parameter's type as `BOOL` (Figure 36.11).

As I mentioned before, this event will be fired when the control's state changes, that is, when the user clicks on the control with the left mouse button. To implement this behavior, use the ClassWizard to add a handler for the `WM_LBUTTONDOWN` message to the `COCTLCtrl` class. In the handler function, shown in Listing 36.8, we negate the value of the m_fSelected Boolean variable and fire a Select event with this variable's new value. We also ensure that the control is redrawn with the color properly indicating its selection state by calling the InvalidateControl function.

FIGURE 36.11.

Adding the
Select *event.*

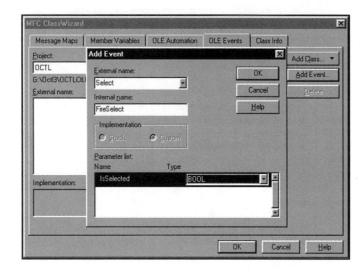

Listing 36.8. Handling a mouse event in OCTL.

```
void COCTLCtrl::OnLButtonDown(UINT nFlags, CPoint point)
{
    // TODO: Add your message handler code here and/or call default

    COleControl::OnLButtonDown(nFlags, point);
    m_fSelected = !m_fSelected;
    InvalidateControl();
    FireSelect(m_fSelected);
}
```

Drawing the Control

There is nothing mysterious about actually drawing a control. When the control class member function OnDraw is called, it receives a pointer to a device context object and a rectangle identifying the control's bounds. With this information at hand, drawing the control is easy.

Naturally, the control's appearance may depend on the values of various member variables representing the control's state. This is certainly the case with the OCTL control, where the m_nShape member variable determines the control's shape, and the m_fSelected member variable determines its color. Listing 36.9 shows my implementation of the OCTL control's drawing function.

Listing 36.9. `COCTLCtrl::OnDraw` **member function.**

```
void COCTLCtrl::OnDraw(
            CDC* pdc, const CRect& rcBounds, const CRect& rcInvalid)
{
    // TODO: Replace the following code with your own drawing code.
//  pdc->FillRect(rcBounds,
//      CBrush::FromHandle((HBRUSH)GetStockObject(WHITE_BRUSH)));
//  pdc->Ellipse(rcBounds);

    CPen pen;
    CBrush foreBrush, backBrush;
    CPoint points[3];
    pdc->SaveDC();
    pen.CreatePen(PS_SOLID, 1, RGB(0, 0, 0));
    backBrush.CreateSolidBrush(TranslateColor(AmbientBackColor()));
    foreBrush.CreateSolidBrush(GetSelected() ? RGB(255, 0, 0) :
                                               RGB(0, 255, 0));
    pdc->FillRect(rcBounds, &backBrush);
    pdc->SelectObject(&pen);
    pdc->SelectObject(&foreBrush);
    switch (m_nShape)
    {
        case 0:
            pdc->Ellipse(rcBounds);
            break;
        case 1:
            pdc->Rectangle(rcBounds);
            break;
        case 2:
            points[0].x = rcBounds.left;
            points[0].y = rcBounds.bottom - 1;
            points[1].x = (rcBounds.left + rcBounds.right - 1) / 2;
            points[1].y = rcBounds.top;
            points[2].x = rcBounds.right - 1;
            points[2].y = rcBounds.bottom - 1;
            pdc->Polygon(points, 3);
            break;
    }
    pdc->RestoreDC(-1);
}
```

Note the use of the function `AmbientBackColor`. This is just one of several functions that can be used to retrieve the control container's *ambient properties*. In this case, we use this function to ensure that the control's background color matches the background color of the control container. Note also that we use the `TranslateColor` function to translate an OLE color into an RGB value. This translation is necessary because the OLE color may occasionally represent a palette index as opposed to an RGB value.

Adding a Property Page Interface

Although implementation of our new control's behavior is complete, our task is not yet done. We must also implement one or more property pages through which our control's property settings can be controlled. These property pages will be used typically by applications in design mode (such as the Developer Studio dialog editor).

The steps are no different from the steps used in implementing an ordinary dialog. We must design the visual appearance of the property page and add the necessary code that connects the controls in the property page to the properties of the control. (As funny as the last sentence sounds, this is indeed the correct terminology. Controls in the property page refer to controls in a dialog; properties of the control refer to properties of the OLE control object. Unfortunately, the terminology of Windows, OLE, C++, and object-oriented programming do conflict at times.)

Editing the Property Page

To change the visual appearance of an OLE custom control's property page, just open the property page's dialog template. Editing it is no different from editing any other dialog resource.

In the case of OCTL's single property page, there are only two controls to be added: a static label and a combo box. The combo box should be of type Drop List, with the identifier IDC_CBSHAPE; the Developer Studio dialog editor can also be used to set its list box values (Figure 36.12). Note that in order to enter multiple values in the area reserved for list box initializers, you must use the Ctrl+Enter key combination to generate a line break, as pressing Enter alone would close the property sheet altogether.

FIGURE 36.12.

Editing the OCTL property page.

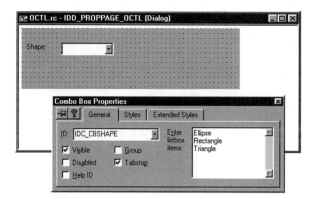

Connecting the Property Page with Control Properties

A member variable for the new property page can be added using regular ClassWizard procedures. What is not regular is how this member variable (that will be a member of the class COCTLPropPage) connects with the appropriate property of the OCTL control. To create this connection, you must also specify the name of the OLE property in ClassWizard's Add Member Variable dialog (Figure 36.13).

FIGURE 36.13.

Connecting a control with an OLE property through ClassWizard.

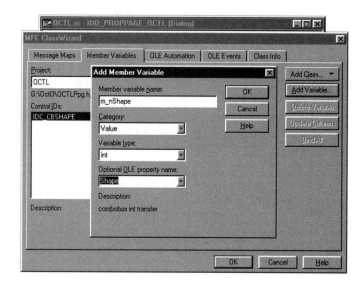

As a result of this, the ClassWizard inserts, in addition to any DDX_ and DDV_ function calls, a set of DDP_ function calls in the DoDataExchange member function of the property page class. This is the line that is inserted for OCTL:

```
DDP_CBIndex(pDX, IDC_CBSHAPE, m_nShape, _T("Shape") );
```

There are several DDP_ functions corresponding to the various control types. These are summarized in Table 36.2.

Table 36.2. DDP_ functions.

Function name	Description
DDP_CBIndex	Combo box int transfer
DDP_CBString	Combo box string transfer
DDP_CBStringExact	Combo box string transfer
DDP_Check	Check box
DDP_LBIndex	List box int transfer
DDP_LBString	List box string transfer
DDP_LBStringExact	List box string transfer
DDP_Radio	Radio button int transfer
DDP_Text	Edit control transfer (string, numeric, and so on)

Additionally, the function `DDP_PostProcessing` should be called after the transfer of control properties through `DDP_` functions has been completed.

Take a look at the result. Figure 36.14 illustrates the OCTL control property page as it appears as part of a property sheet displayed by the Developer Studio dialog editor when an OCTL control is being added to a dialog template.

FIGURE 36.14.

OCTL control property sheet in Developer Studio.

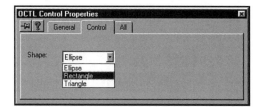

At this point, implementation of the OCTL control is complete. If you have not yet done so, you can recompile the project to create the OCX file. Compiling the project also automatically registers the control.

Additional Property Pages

If your OLE custom control requires additional property pages, those can be created by using the ControlWizard-generated property page as a model. To actually create the class, use the ClassWizard and create a new class derived from `COlePropertyPage`.

In case you are using the stock implementation of the color, font, or picture properties, you can use stock properties pages to provide an interface to them. To use a stock property page, just specify its class identifier when adding property pages in the implementation file of the control class. You do not need to create a class yourself for a stock property page.

Testing, Distributing, and Using a Custom Control

Testing an OLE custom control is an important part of the development process. Not all real-life control projects are as simple as my tiny OCTL control.

As reusable components, OLE custom controls are often created by one programmer but used by others. For this reason, it is important to know how a control can be distributed to its users.

These issues and a brief reminder of how OLE custom controls are used in other applications are described in the remainder of this chapter.

Testing an OLE Custom Control

In order to test an OLE custom control, you do not need to write your own control container application. Instead, you can use the OLE Control Test Container application that is supplied with Visual C++. You can use the Settings command under the Build menu in Developer Studio to specify `tstcon32.exe` as the debug executable; this way, you can exercise your control, set breakpoints, and control its execution through the Visual C++ debugger.

You can also test your OLE custom control by attempting to use it within the Developer Studio dialog editor.

Custom Control Distribution

Distributing a custom control raises two questions. First, which files need to be distributed to control users and, in turn, by control users to end users of their applications? Second, what actions need to be taken during control installation to ensure that the control is correctly registered?

The end user needs only the file with the `.ocx` extension. This file is the actual DLL containing the control's code. Control users (developers), on the other hand, may also need the TLB (type library) file, the EXP file, and the LIB file, all of which are generated when your control project is built.

To register the control, run the server registration program supplied by Microsoft:

```
\msdev\bin\regsvr32.exe /s <controlname>.ocx
```

The `regsvr32.exe` file is freely redistributable. If you are writing a setup program that includes installation of OLE custom controls, you may want to use this file for control installation. However, you could also load the OCX file directly as a DLL, and call its `DllRegisterServer` function.

If you decided to use licensing for your control, remember to include the license (LIC) file with the files supplied to control users. This file should not be redistributed to end users.

Using a Custom Control in Applications

Here is a brief summary of the steps that are required in order to use an OLE custom control in an application:

1. Add OLE control container support by calling `AfxEnableControlContainer` during application initialization.
2. Add the custom control to dialog templates as appropriate.

3. Set the control's initial properties using the control's property page interface.

4. Add member variables to represent the control or its properties as appropriate.

5. Add message handlers to handle messages from the control as appropriate.

Summary

Construction of an OLE custom control has been greatly simplified in Visual C++ 4 thanks to the ControlWizard.

Constructing a custom control involves the following steps:

1. Create the custom control skeleton through ControlWizard.
2. Add the control's properties, methods, and events through ClassWizard.
3. Update the control's bitmap.
4. Add drawing code to your control.
5. Develop code for methods and events.
6. Create the control's property page.
7. Add code handling to the property page.

Custom controls can be tested using the OLE Control Test Container that is supplied with Visual C++.

Distributing a control to end users requires distributing the OCX file. Distributing the control to developers also requires distributing the LIB, TLB, and EXP files. Additionally, if the control is a licensed control, developers also need the license (LIC) file.

Before use, the control must be registered. Registration can be accomplished by using the freely distributable `regsvr32.exe` utility. Alternatively, you can call the control's `DllRegisterServer` function from within your own setup program.

Multimedia Applications

37

It has been several years since Microsoft Windows became a platform of choice for multimedia applications. Since the introduction of multimedia capabilities in Windows 3.1, hardware prices have dropped significantly. Just a few short years ago, multimedia, video, and sound required expensive workstations; now it is available on most home computers. CD-ROM drives, rapidly growing in popularity, provide the means to deliver multimedia presentations to most PCs. In short, multimedia can no longer be ignored by most programmers.

Although multimedia programming under Windows can be quite complex, applications can accomplish many things by a few simple function calls. Nothing demonstrates this better than the MCIWndCreate function, which can be used to replay videos in a single function call. Our review of Windows multimedia programming begins with a closer look at this function; for many simple applications, you may not need anything more sophisticated.

Video Playback with One Function Call

The program shown in Listing 37.1 can perhaps be viewed as the Windows multimedia equivalent of a Hello, World application. This program takes a single command-line parameter, the name of a multimedia file such as an AVI video file, and plays it back in its window. It can also be launched without a parameter; in that case, use the button controls that appear in its window (Figure 37.1) to open a file for playback.

FIGURE 37.1.

AVI playback using
MCIWndCreate.

Listing 37.1. A simple multimedia playback application.

```
#include <windows.h>
#include <vfw.h>

void SetClientRect(HWND hwnd, HWND hwndMCI)
{
    RECT rect;

    GetWindowRect(hwndMCI, &rect);
    AdjustWindowRectEx(&rect, GetWindowLong(hwnd, GWL_STYLE),
                       FALSE, GetWindowLong(hwnd, GWL_EXSTYLE));
    MoveWindow(hwnd, rect.left, rect.top, rect.right - rect.left,
```

```
                      rect.bottom - rect.top, TRUE);
}

LRESULT CALLBACK WndProc(HWND hwnd, UINT uMsg,
                         WPARAM wParam, LPARAM lParam)
{
    switch(uMsg)
    {
        case MCIWNDM_NOTIFYPOS:
        case MCIWNDM_NOTIFYSIZE:
            SetClientRect(hwnd, (HWND)wParam);
            break;
        case WM_DESTROY:
            PostQuitMessage(0);
            break;
        default:
            return DefWindowProc(hwnd, uMsg, wParam, lParam);
    }
    return 0;
}

int WINAPI WinMain(HINSTANCE hInstance, HINSTANCE hPrevInstance,
                   LPSTR lpCmdLine, int nCmdShow)
{
    MSG msg;
    HWND hwnd;
    WNDCLASS wndClass;

    if (hPrevInstance == NULL)
    {
        memset(&wndClass, 0, sizeof(wndClass));
        wndClass.style = CS_HREDRAW | CS_VREDRAW;
        wndClass.lpfnWndProc = WndProc;
        wndClass.hInstance = hInstance;
        wndClass.hCursor = LoadCursor(NULL, IDC_ARROW);
        wndClass.hbrBackground = (HBRUSH)(COLOR_WINDOW + 1);
        wndClass.lpszClassName = "HELLO";
        if (!RegisterClass(&wndClass)) return FALSE;
    }
    hwnd = CreateWindow("HELLO", "HELLO",
                        WS_OVERLAPPED | WS_CAPTION | WS_SYSMENU,
                        CW_USEDEFAULT, 0, CW_USEDEFAULT, 0,
                        NULL, NULL, hInstance, NULL);
    SetClientRect(hwnd, MCIWndCreate(hwnd, hInstance, WS_VISIBLE |
                                     WS_CHILD | MCIWNDF_SHOWALL |
                                     MCIWNDF_NOTIFYSIZE |
                                     MCIWNDF_NOTIFYPOS, lpCmdLine));
    ShowWindow(hwnd, nCmdShow);
    UpdateWindow(hwnd);
    while (GetMessage(&msg, NULL, 0, 0))
        DispatchMessage(&msg);
    return msg.wParam;
}
```

All right, I cheated. In addition to the single function call, we also have a few lines of code handling notification messages. By responding to MCIWNDM_NOTIFYPOS and MCIWNDM_NOTIFYSIZE messages, we can ensure that the application's main window is automatically resized. That way, we end up with a window that is properly sized for video playback. Nevertheless, the application demonstrates the power of MCIWndCreate well; with that one function call, we have been able to create a full-featured video playback application. This simple program can be compiled from the command line by typing cl hello.c user32.lib vfw32.lib.

MCIWndCreate is not the only simple function that can be used for media playback. Another such function is the Playback function; this function can be used to play waveform audio files.

Fundamentals of Multimedia Programming

Multimedia represents the operating system's ability to record and play video and sound. Multimedia programming is accomplished through a series of interfaces, or APIs that applications can utilize for this purpose.

Multimedia Data Formats

Windows recognizes three different multimedia formats: two audio formats and a video format (Figure 37.2).

FIGURE 37.2.

Multimedia in Windows.

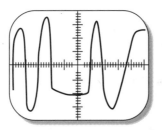

Waveform audio is sampled, digitized audio data. Waveform audio is typically stored in files with the .wav extension. Windows recognizes waveform audio files with mono and stereo data, a variety of sampling rates, and sampling depths. There are also several different compression methods used for the efficient storage of waveform data.

MIDI is the acronym for *Musical Instrument Digital Interface*. This international standard specifies a protocol for interfacing computers and electronic musical instruments. MIDI sequences are data that can be played back on MIDI-compatible instruments. MIDI data is stored under windows in files with the `.mid` extension. MIDI files can be played back on external devices connected to the computer, or on built-in synthesizers that support MIDI capabilities.

AVI is the Audio Video Interleaved file format. AVI files can be used to store a motion video stream and one or more audio channels. Windows recognizes video data at varying resolutions, color depths, and refresh rates. There are also several compression formats that are in wide use.

Although presently Windows does not support recording or playback of MPEG format video files, Microsoft has announced plans to do so in the future.

Windows multimedia functions can also be used for audio-CD playback. Using third-party drivers, recording and playback of other multimedia formats is also possible.

Multimedia Interfaces

Depending on your programming needs, you can choose one of three interface levels to interact with the multimedia subsystem in Windows.

The high-level interface is based on the `MCIWnd` window class. In the example program shown in Listing 37.1, it was an `MCIWnd` function that enabled us to do video playback with only a single function call.

The mid-level interface is the *Media Control Interface*, or MCI. MCI provides a device-independent command-message and command-string interface for the playback and recording of audio and visual data.

At the lowest level, there are several interfaces for waveform audio, AVI video, and MIDI recording and playback. Additional interfaces provide audio mixer capabilities, buffered file I/O, and joystick and timer control.

All these interfaces serve but one purpose: to provide a programming interface between end-user applications on the one hand, and drivers for multimedia hardware on the other. Through these drivers, device-independence in Windows is achieved.

Which interface should you choose for your application? That depends on the needs and requirements of your project.

Applications that require only simple playback capabilities are good candidates for using the `MCIWnd` services. For example, an encyclopedia application that offers video clips accompanying some articles may use an `MCIWnd` window for video playback.

An example for a more demanding multimedia program is an audio recording and playback application. Such a program should probably rely on the services of the Media Control Interface to implement its functionality.

A sophisticated multimedia application, such as a video capture and mixer application, would probably require using low-level video and file services.

Programming with *MCIWnd*

The MCIWnd window class represents the simplest, highest level multimedia programming interface in Windows. Applications that require simple playback capabilities can utilize MCIWnd windows for this purpose; such a window can be created with a single function call, as demonstrated by the program in Listing 37.1.

The *MCIWnd* Window Class

Windows of class MCIWnd provide a user interface that consists of up to four buttons, a trackbar, and an optional playback area (Figure 37.3).

FIGURE 37.3.

MCIWnd Window Controls.

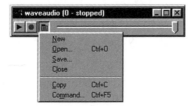

The Play and Stop buttons can be used to start and stop playback. Playback starts at the current position indicated by the trackbar. Special playback effects can be utilized by holding down the Shift or Control keys while clicking on the Play button; holding down the Control key results in full-screen video playback, while holding down the Shift key results in backwards play.

The Menu button can be used to invoke a popup menu. The options in this menu are specific to the type of the media file currently selected. For example, if an AVI file is loaded, the popup menu includes options to set the video playback speed, sound volume, zoom, and video configuration. Other commands enable you to copy the current data to the Windows clipboard and to open another file. Yet another menu option enables you to send an MCI command string directly to the currently active multimedia device.

The Record button can be made available for devices that can record.

The trackbar is used to display the current playback or recording position relative to the size of the file. The trackbar can also be used to move to different locations in the file during playback.

Optimal video playback performance requires that the playback window be aligned on a four-pixel boundary. Normally, Windows aligns the playback window automatically.

MCIWnd Functions

An MCIWnd window is created by a call to MCIWndCreate. A call to this function registers the MCIWnd class and creates an MCIWnd window.

In addition to specifying the handle of the parent window and an instance handle, parameters to this function also specify a set of window styles and an optional filename.

The window style settings control which elements of the MCIWnd window are visible, and how it interacts with the user on the one hand and the application code on the other. For example, by specifying the MCIWNDF_RECORD window style, you can create an MCIWnd window with a visible Record button. Specifying the MCIWNDF_NOTIFYSIZE causes the MCIWnd window to send notification messages to its parent whenever the window's size changes.

MCIWnd windows can be created as child windows or overlapped windows. If created as an overlapped window, an MCIWnd window will have a title bar with contents specified with the appropriate style settings (MCIWNDF_SHOWMODE, MCIWNDF_SHOWNAME, or MCIWNDF_SHOWPOS).

MCIWnd windows can also be created via calls to CreateWindow or CreateWindowEx. Before you can do so, however, you must call MCIWndRegisterClass. This function registers the window class specified by the constant MCIWND_WINDOW_CLASS.

There are two additional functions that use windows of class MCIWnd. The functions GetOpenFileNamePreview and GetSaveFileNamePreview enhance the standard GetOpenFileName and GetSaveFileName functions by adding a multimedia preview window to the standard file open dialog. The preview window that is shown in Figure 37.4 was created using GetOpenFileNamePreview.

FIGURE 37.4.

A file open dialog with a preview window.

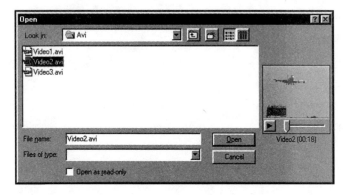

The program in Listing 37.2 demonstrates the use of GetOpenFileNamePreview. To compile this program, type cl ofnp.c vfw32.lib.

Listing 37.2. Using `GetOpenFileNamePreview`.

```
#include <windows.h>
#include <vfw.h>

int WINAPI WinMain(HINSTANCE hInstance, HINSTANCE hPrevInstance,
                                 LPSTR lpCmdLine, int nCmdShow)
{
    OPENFILENAME ofn;
    memset(&ofn, 0, sizeof(ofn));
    ofn.lStructSize = sizeof(ofn);
    GetOpenFileNamePreview(&ofn);
}
```

MCIWnd Macros

Applications can communicate with an MCIWnd window by sending messages to it using the Windows SendMessage function. A large number of helper macros exist that simplify sending most of these messages.

Through these messages, applications can control the appearance and behavior of the MCIWnd window, start and stop playback and recording, close the MCI device or file and open a new file or device for recording or playback, seek specific playback and recording positions, retrieve information on device capabilities and current settings, specify MCI device attributes, and control the MCI device.

Table 37.1 summarizes MCIWnd messages and helper macros.

Table 37.1. MCIWnd messages and macros.

Message	Macro	Description
MCI_CLOSE	MCIWndClose	Close MCI device or file
MCI_OPEN	MCIWndOpenDialog	Open data file
MCI_PAUSE	MCIWndPause	Pause playback or record
MCI_PLAY	MCIWndPlay	Start playback
MCI_RECORD	MCIWndRecord	Start recording
MCI_RESUME	MCIWndResume	Resume playback or record
MCI_SAVE	MCIWndSave	Save content
MCI_SAVE	MCIWndSaveDialog	Save content
MCI_SEEK	MCIWndEnd	Move to end of content
MCI_SEEK	MCIWndHome	Move to start of content
MCI_SEEK	MCIWndSeek	Move to position
MCI_STEP	MCIWndStep	Move position

Message	Macro	Description
MCI_STOP	MCIWndStop	Stop playback or record
MCIWNDM_CAN_CONFIG	MCIWndCanConfig	Can configure device?
MCIWNDM_CAN_EJECT	MCIWndCanEject	Can eject media?
MCIWNDM_CAN_PLAY	MCIWndCanPlay	Can play device?
MCIWNDM_CAN_RECORD	MCIWndCanRecord	Can record on device?
MCIWNDM_CAN_SAVE	MCIWndCanSave	Can save to file?
MCIWNDM_CAN_WINDOW	MCIWndCanWindow	Window commands supported?
MCIWNDM_CHANGESTYLES	MCIWndChangeStyles	Change window style
MCIWNDM_EJECT	MCIWndEject	Eject media
MCIWNDM_GETACTIVETIMER	MCIWndGetActiveTimer	Return update period
MCIWNDM_GETALIAS	MCIWndGetAlias	Return device alias
MCIWNDM_GET_DEST	MCIWndGetDest	Return playback rectangle
MCIWNDM_GETDEVICE	MCIWndGetDevice	Return device name
MCIWNDM_GETDEVICEID	MCIWndGetDeviceID	Return device identifier
MCIWNDM_GETEND	MCIWndGetEnd	Return end location
MCIWNDM_GETERROR	MCIWndGetError	Return last MCI error
MCIWNDM_GETFILENAME	MCIWndGetFileName	Return current filename
MCIWNDM_GETINACTIVETIMER	MCIWndGetInactiveTimer	Return update period
MCIWNDM_GETLENGTH	MCIWndGetLength	Return content length
MCIWNDM_GETMODE	MCIWndGetMode	Return current mode
MCIWNDM_GETPALETTE	MCIWndGetPalette	Return MCI palette handle
MCIWNDM_GETPOSITION	MCIWndGetPosition	Return position
MCIWNDM_GETPOSITION	MCIWndGetPositionString	Return position
MCIWNDM_GETREPEAT	MCIWndGetRepeat	Continuous playback
MCIWNDM_GETSOURCE	MCIWndGetSource	Return cropping rectangle
MCIWNDM_GETSPEED	MCIWndGetSpeed	Return playback speed
MCIWNDM_GETSTART	MCIWndGetStart	Return start location
MCIWNDM_GETSTYLES	MCIWndGetStyles	Return window style
MCIWNDM_GETTIMEFORMAT	MCIWndGetTimeFormat	Return time format
MCIWNDM_GETVOLUME	MCIWndGetVolume	Return volume setting
MCIWNDM_GETZOOM	MCIWndGetZoom	Return zoom setting

continues

Table 37.1. continued

Message	Macro	Description
MCIWNDM_NEW	MCIWndNew	Create new file
MCIWNDM_OPEN	MCIWndOpen	Open MCI device and file
MCIWNDM_OPENINTERFACE	MCIWndOpenInterface	Open IAVI interface
MCIWNDM_PLAYFROM	MCIWndPlayFrom	Playback at position
MCIWNDM_PLAYTO	MCIWndPlayFromTo	Playback range
MCIWNDM_PLAYREVERSE	MCIWndPlayReverse	Playback in reverse
MCIWNDM_PLAYTO	MCIWndPlayTo	Playback to position
MCIWNDM_PUT_DEST	MCIWndPutDest	Change playback rectangle
MCIWNDM_PUT_SOURCE	MCIWndPutSource	Change cropping rectangle
MCIWNDM_REALIZE	MCIWndRealize	Realize MCI palette
MCIWNDM_RETURNSTRING	MCIWndReturnString	Return MCI reply
MCIWNDM_SENDSTRING	MCIWndSendString	Send MCI command
MCIWNDM_SETACTIVETIMER	MCIWndSetActiveTimer	Set update period
MCIWNDM_SETINACTIVETIMER	MCIWndSetInactiveTimer	Set update period
MCIWNDM_SETOWNER	MCIWndSetOwner	Set owner window
MCIWNDM_SETPALETTE	MCIWndSetPalette	Set MCI palette
MCIWNDM_SETREPEAT	MCIWndSetRepeat	Set repeat mode
MCIWNDM_SETSPEED	MCIWndSetSpeed	Set playback speed
MCIWNDM_SETTIMEFORMAT	MCIWndSetTimeFormat	Set time format
MCIWNDM_SETTIMERS	MCIWndSetTimers	Set update period
MCIWNDM_SETVOLUME	MCIWndSetVolume	Set volume
MCIWNDM_SETZOOM	MCIWndSetZoom	Sets video zoom
MCIWNDM_SETTIMEFORMAT	MCIWndUseFrames	Set time format
MCIWNDM_SETTIMEFORMAT	MCIWndUseTime	Set time format
MCIWNDM_VALIDATEMEDIA	MCIWndValidateMedia	Updates positions
WM_CLOSE	MCIWndDestroy	Close MCIWnd window

MCIWnd Notifications

If enabled, MCIWnd windows can send notification messages to their parent windows. Specifically, five types of notification messages can be sent. All five can be enabled by specifying the

MCIWNDF_NOTIFYALL window style when creating the window. Alternatively, notification messages can be enabled individually.

The MCIWNDM_NOTIFYERROR message is sent to the parent window to notify it of MCI errors. This notification can be enabled by specifying the MCIWNDF_NOTIFYERROR window style.

The MCIWNDM_NOTIFYMEDIA message notifies the parent window of any media changes that may have occurred. These messages are enabled by specifying the MCIWNDF_NOTIFYMEDIA window style.

The parent window is notified of changes in the MCIWnd window's position and size through MCIWNDM_NOTIFYPOS and MCIWNDM_NOTIFYSIZE messages. These messages are enabled by the MCIWNDF_NOTIFYPOS and MCIWNDF_NOTIFYSIZE window styles, respectively.

Finally, the parent window is notified of any operating mode changes (for example, changes from play to stop mode) by MCIWNDM_NOTIFYMODE messages. These messages are enabled by the MCIWNDF_NOTIFYMODE window style.

The Media Control Interface

The Media Control Interface (MCI) provides a set of device-independent command messages and command strings for controlling multimedia devices. Command messages and command strings can be used interchangeably. The MCI recognizes a variety of different multimedia devices. These devices are listed in Table 37.2.

Table 37.2. Multimedia devices.

Device name	Description
animation	Animation device
cdaudio	Audio CD player
dat	Digital-audio tape player
digitalvideo	Non GDI-based digital video in a window
other	Undefined device
overlay	Analog video in a window
scanner	Image scanner
sequencer	MIDI sequencer
vcr	Video cassette recorder or player
videodisc	Video disc player
waveaudio	Waveform audio device

Both command messages and command strings can be used to control devices and to retrieve information from devices. Command messages retrieve information in the form of structures, which are easy to interpret in C programs. Command strings retrieve information in the form of strings that must be parsed and interpreted by the application.

All MCI devices support a core set of MCI commands and messages. Many devices support additional, device-specific commands.

Command strings are sent to devices using the mciSendString function. A simple use of this function is demonstrated in Listing 37.3; this application, which takes a single filename as its command-line argument, plays back a multimedia file. For example, if you specify the pathname for an AVI video file, this application will play back the video in full-screen mode. To compile this application, type cl mcistr.c user32.lib winmm.lib.

Listing 37.3. MCI playback using command strings.

```
#include <windows.h>
#include <stdlib.h>

#define CMDSTR "OPEN %s ALIAS MOVIE"

int WINAPI
    WinMain(HINSTANCE d1, HINSTANCE d2, LPSTR lpCmdLine, int d4)
{
    char *pBuf;

    pBuf = malloc(sizeof(CMDSTR) + strlen(lpCmdLine) - 2);
    if (!pBuf) return -1;
    wsprintf(pBuf, CMDSTR, lpCmdLine);
    mciSendString(pBuf, NULL, 0, NULL);
    free(pBuf);
    mciSendString("PLAY MOVIE WAIT", NULL, 0, NULL);
    mciSendString("CLOSE MOVIE", NULL, 0, NULL);
    return 0;
}
```

Command messages are sent to devices using the mciSendCommand function. This function takes several parameters, one of which is a command-specific structure. The structure may either be a general purpose one such as MCI_OPEN_PARMS or a device-specific extension to the general purpose version. Applications fill in this structure as appropriate prior to executing the call to mciSendCommand; commands that return information do so by modifying elements in this structure. The program in Listing 37.4 demonstrates simple playback using the MCI command message interface; this program can be compiled from the command line by typing cl mcimsg.c winmm.lib. Like its command string counterpart, this program also takes the name of a multimedia file on the command line and plays back that file.

Listing 37.4. MCI playback using command messages.

```
#include <windows.h>
#include <stdlib.h>

int WINAPI
    WinMain(HINSTANCE d1, HINSTANCE d2, LPSTR lpCmdLine, int d4)
{
    MCI_OPEN_PARMS mciOpen;
    MCI_PLAY_PARMS mciPlay;
    MCI_GENERIC_PARMS mciClose;

    mciOpen.dwCallback = 0;
    mciOpen.lpstrElementName = lpCmdLine;
    mciOpen.lpstrAlias = "MOVIE";
    mciSendCommand(0, MCI_OPEN, MCI_OPEN_ALIAS ¦ MCI_OPEN_ELEMENT, (DWORD)&mciOp
en);

    mciPlay.dwCallback = 0;
    mciSendCommand(mciOpen.wDeviceID, MCI_PLAY, MCI_WAIT, (DWORD)&mciPlay);

    mciClose.dwCallback = 0;
    mciSendCommand(mciOpen.wDeviceID, MCI_CLOSE, 0, (DWORD)&mciClose);

    return 0;
}
```

MCI Command String Syntax

The generic syntax for MCI command strings is as follows:

command identifier [argument [, argument]]

The *command* portion specifies an MCI command such as PLAY, OPEN, or CLOSE. The *identifier* identifies an MCI device. This may be an MCI device name or an alias name. This identifier represents an instance of the appropriate MCI driver that was created when the device was opened.

Command arguments are used to specify flags and parameters specific to each MCI command.

For example, consider the following MCI command string:

play music from 0 to 100 wait

In this string, play is an MCI command; music is (presumably) an alias that was created when the device was opened; and from 0 to 100 wait is a series of arguments and flags applicable to the play command.

The wait flag in this command specifies that the call to mciSendString should not return before the command is finished. Normally, calls return immediately and the commands are processed in the background.

Another commonly used flag is the notify flag. Specifying this flag causes the MCI to post a multimedia notification (MM_MCINOTIFY) message to the application whenever a command is completed.

Some devices (for example, digital video devices) support the test flag. A command submitted with this flag is not executed; however, the MCI tests whether the command can be executed by the specified device and returns an error if that is not the case.

These flags can also be specified for commands submitted in the form of MCI command messages.

MCI Command Sets

MCI commands fall into different categories. These include system commands, required commands, and optional commands.

The two system commands, break and sysinfo, are recognized and processed by the MCI itself. The break command is used to set a virtual key code that aborts other MCI commands; the sysinfo command returns information on MCI services and devices.

Required commands are those that every MCI device must implement. This set includes the following five commands: capability, close, info, open, and status. The capability, info, and status commands obtain information on the status and capabilities of the device. The open and close commands are used to open or close the device.

Optional commands can be further broken down into two categories; basic commands and extended commands. Basic commands include load and save, play, record, and stop, pause and resume, seek and set, and certain forms of the status command. For most devices, it is reasonable to assume that a subset of these commands applicable to the device is supported. For example, a playback device can reasonably be expected to support at least the play and stop commands; a recording device can be expected to support record and stop.

Extended commands include several additional configuration and editing commands. Your application should not expect that any of these commands are supported; instead, it should use the capability command to find out about the available set of commands.

MCI Functions and Macros

We have already encountered two MCI functions: mciSendCommand is used to send an MCI command message, while mciSendString is used to send an MCI command string.

Another set of three functions can be used to retrieve information about an MCI device. The mciGetCreatorTask function returns the handle of the task that created a specific MCI device. The mciGetDeviceID function returns the MCI device identifier for a named device. The mciGetErrorString returns the error message string corresponding to a specific error code.

Two additional functions, mciGetYieldProc and mciSetYieldProc, can be used to yield proce-dure. The yield procedure is a function that the MCI calls regularly while waiting for the comple-tion of a command that was issued with the wait flag.

The MCI also offers a series of macros that deal with time formats. Various time formats are used in MCI commands to set the recording or playback position, or to read back the current position. Positions can be expressed as time values, track positions, and so on. Time format macros are used to create position values and to retrieve individual elements of a position value. For example, MCI_HMS_HOUR retrieves the hour component of a position expressed in the form of hours, minutes, and seconds (HMS); MCI_MAKE_HMS creates a time value from parameters specifying hours, minutes, and seconds.

MCI Notifications

MCI devices can send two types of messages to the application. The MM_MCINOTIFY message is used to notify the application of the completion of a command. Parameters to this message identify the command and specify whether the command was successfully completed, or whether its execution was interrupted due to an error or some other condition.

The MM_MCISIGNAL message is used specifically in response to the extended MCI command signal. Through this command, applications can request that the MCI send an MM_MCISIGNAL message when a specific spot in the content is reached.

Advanced Interfaces

Windows offers several low-level interfaces for manipulating multimedia.

AVIFile and AVIStream Functions

AVIFile functions and macros offer low-level access to files containing RIFF (Resource Infor-mation File Format) data; examples for such files include digital video and waveform audio files.

AVIFile functions are based on the OLE Component Object Model. AVIFile functions can be used to open and close files, place files to the Windows clipboard, and obtain and manipulate file properties. AVIStream functions can be used to read or write the actual audio or video data.

Custom File and Stream Handlers

For video and audio data sources other than AVI video and waveform audio files, you can write custom file and stream handlers. Custom file and stream handlers are installable drivers that provide access to data in different sources using the OLE Component Object Model.

Custom handlers are dynamic link libraries ("inproc" OLE servers) that implement the `IAVIFile` and `IAVIStream` interfaces. These interfaces are used by the `AVIFile` and `AVIStream` family of functions.

DrawDib Functions

DrawDib functions provide high-performance capabilities for drawing device-independent bitmaps (DIBs) in 8-bit, 16-bit, 24-bit, and 32-bit graphic modes.

DrawDib functions do not rely on the GDI but write directly to video memory. They provide a variety of services ranging from image stretching, dithering, to compression and decompression of many known formats.

The Video Compression Manager

The video compression manager, or VCM, provides access to installable compressors that handle real-time video data.

Applications can use the VCM to compress and decompress video data, and handle the interaction between compressed video data, custom data, and renderers.

Video Capture

Video capture can be accomplished using the `AVICap` window class and a series of related functions and macros.

In the simplest scenario, applications create an `AVICap` window through the `capCreateCaptureWindow` function and send messages to this window to control capturing. A large number of macros exist that simplify the sending of messages to `AVICap` windows and the processing of message results.

Waveform Audio Recording and Playback

Windows offers a series of functions dealing with recording and playback of waveform audio. Simplest among these is the `PlaySound` function that enables you to play audio files that fit into available memory.

Other waveform audio functions can be used to control individual waveform input and output devices.

The Audio Compression Manager

Windows also provides a programming interface to the audio compression manager, or ACM. The ACM provides for the transparent compression and decompression of waveform audio data during recording and playback.

The ACM is installed as a "mapper." This means that the ACM can intercept audio recording and playback requests and decode or encode data as necessary. The ACM can also search for a waveform device or an ACM compressor or decompressor that can handle a specific format.

MIDI Recording and Playback

MIDI file playback is performed by the MCI MIDI sequencer. Low-level MIDI functions enable applications to control MIDI playback and recording, and to process MIDI data.

Audio Mixers

Audio lines can be controlled through mixer devices. Windows offers a series of functions for opening and using mixer devices.

Miscellaneous Multimedia Services

Other multimedia services include a series of functions for low-level buffered file I/O optimized for media recording and playback; file services specific to RIFF (Resource Interchange File Format); functions and notification messages for handling joystick devices; and functions to create and manage high resolution multimedia timers.

Summary

With the rapid deployment of powerful personal computers that are equipped with CD-ROM drives, multimedia has been brought to the masses. The Windows programmer can no longer ignore this area of programming; multimedia, if only in the form of sound effects or tutorial video clips, is quickly becoming a part of most new applications.

Multimedia in windows consists of the capabilities to record and play video and audio files. Windows recognizes one video format (AVI files) and two audio formats (MIDI and waveform audio).

Windows offers multimedia interfaces on three distinct levels. At the highest level is the MCIWnd window class. Through this window class, it is possible to perform video playback with a single function call. The MCIWnd API also offers a large number of macros that utilize the SendMessage function to communicate with an MCIWnd window. These windows can also send notification messages to their parent window.

The mid-level multimedia programming interface is the Media Control Interface, or MCI. MCI offers command strings and command messages for controlling multimedia devices; command strings and command messages can be used interchangeably. All MCI devices recognize a set of core commands; many devices recognize a set of additional, device-specific commands. While using the command string interface is generally simpler, for commands that retrieve information from the device it is often advantageous to use command messages instead. Unlike command strings, which return responses in the form of strings that need to be parsed and interpreted by the application, command messages return information in the form of structures.

Low-level video services include the AVIFile family of functions, interfaces to video compression and video capture, and high performance functions for drawing device-independent bitmaps. For data in nonstandard sources, custom file and stream handler drivers can be developed.

The AVIFile function family as well as custom file and stream handlers are also applicable to waveform audio. Other low-level audio services include functions for recording and playback of waveform audio and MIDI data. Additional interfaces are provided to access the audio compression manager and audio mixer devices.

Other low-level multimedia interfaces include high performance buffered file I/O, joystick control, and multimedia timers.

Implementing Context-Sensitive Help

38

Users of Windows applications expect intuitive user interfaces that enable them to work productively even when they are using an application for the first time. Lengthy learning periods and large, complex user manuals are no longer acceptable features of a new application.

A significant element of a well-thought-out user interface is integrated help. Although many application features are obvious to the experienced user, others are not; furthermore, inexperienced users may not immediately grasp the significance of elements in a menu, window, or dialog.

Windows provides many features that assist the development of professional quality context-sensitive help files. Among these is the WinHelp program, the WinHelp API, and Windows' ability to assign help context identifiers to various user-interface elements.

For MFC applications, AppWizard can be instructed to create a skeleton help file. AppWizard-generated help can also be added to applications that were initially created without context-sensitive help.

Developing help files has never been easier. The Visual C++ development system now includes the Microsoft Help Workshop, an integrated tool that helps you maintain and manage help projects.

In this section, we first examine the features of WinHelp, the Windows help application. Next, we review the rules for constructing help topic files. Lastly, we examine the Help Workshop and touch on the subject of advanced topics.

When authoring a help file, you should always keep in mind your intended audience. Despite a frequently heard myth to the contrary, I do not believe that the contents of help files and printed documentation should be identical. The purpose of these items is fundamentally different; while printed documentation is most often used by users who are new to your application and wish to receive an introduction to its concepts and ideas, help files are more likely to be used by experienced users wishing to obtain specific reference information on a particular topic. The format of the presentation (static, printed text versus online text with hypertext links) also prescribes a different authoring approach.

Help File Development

Help files are hypertext files that are presented by a special Windows application, WinHelp.exe. Constructing a help file is a process of several steps. First, help topic files need to be authored using an editor that is capable of handling rich text format (RTF) files. Next, a help project (HPJ) file must be created; this file identifies the help topic files and other components that comprise a help file project. Next, any additional files (for example, bitmap images) must be created. Finally, the help project file must be compiled using the Microsoft Help Compiler. The final version of the help system may also include dynamic link libraries and a help contents file. Figure 38.1 provides a graphical illustration of this process, identifying the various elements of a help project and the tools used to process them.

FIGURE 38.1.

Help file development.

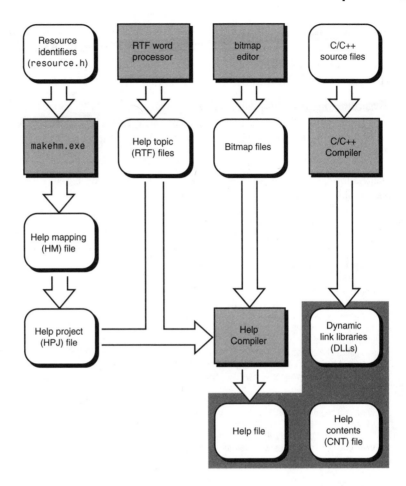

Help files can be invoked from an application in a variety of ways. Applications may invoke help in response to the user's selection of Help menu items, pressing the F1 key, or entering help mode by pressing Shift+F1. In all of these cases, help is actually invoked by a call to the WinHelp function.

Help Topics and the Rich Text Format

I purchased my first Windows SDK back in 1990 or thereabouts. I was a bit disappointed to learn that I needed to make an additional purchase in order to be able to edit rich text format help topic files. Nevertheless, I swallowed the bullet and went out and bought Word for Windows 1.1. What a long way Word has come in five years! Working with Word 1.1 and Windows 3.0 taught me to save my work after every paragraph or so; otherwise, it fell prey to those dreaded Unidentified Application Errors, or UAEs, that crashed Windows every 15 minutes it seemed.

As it turns out, although I never regretted this purchase, there was no need for me to buy Word for Windows to edit help topics. RTF files consist of printable ASCII characters; the file format is not exactly user-friendly, but human-readable. It is possible to edit RTF help topic files using any ASCII text editor.

Regardless of what editor you use, the Windows Help Compiler treats RTF files the same way. It accepts formatted text as its input; however, it interprets certain text attributes in a special way. For example, text that is marked with a double underline is interpreted as text marking a jump to another topic.

Take a look at an example. Listing 38.1 shows a very simple help topic file consisting of only two topics.

Listing 38.1. A simple help topic file.

```
{\rtf1\ansi
{\fonttbl\f0\fswiss MS Sans Serif;}
\deff0\fs20
#{\footnote #H_CONTENTS}
${\footnote $Help Contents}
K{\footnote KContents}
\keepn\brdth\fs28
Help Contents
\par\pard\fs20\sb30
This is the Help Contents page. To see more help, click on
 {\uldb Overview}{\v H_OVERVIEW}.
\par\pard
\page
#{\footnote #H_OVERVIEW}
${\footnote $Help Overview}
K{\footnote KOverview}
!{\footnote !PositionWindow(256,256,512,512,1,"main")}
\keepn\brdrb\fs28
Help Overview
\par\pard\fs20\sb30
This is the Help Overview page. To see more help, click on
 {\uldb Contents}{\v H_CONTENTS}.
\par
To see the a macro at work, click on {\ul About}{\v !About()}.
}
```

At the beginning of this file, `\rtf1\ansi` identifies the RTF version number and the ANSI character set. This part is mandatory for all help topic files.

The next line specifies a font table. The font table of this simple help file consists of only one font. This font is selected as the default font by the `\deff0` statement in line three.

The `\footnote` statements in the next three lines are of crucial importance in help topic files. The help system uses footnotes of different types to index help text and to identify topic-specific information. The type of information specified by the footnote depends on the footnote character. In the present example, the pound sign (#) specifies a context string; the context string is used to refer to the current topic (as in a hypertext link). The 'K' footnote specifies a keyword; the '$' footnote specifies the topic title that will be displayed by the help system as the help window caption.

The topic text that follows is broken by a variety of formatting codes into a scrolling and nonscrolling part. The nonscrolling region appears on top, and can be used, for example, as a topic subtitle (Figure 38.2).

FIGURE 38.2.

Help topic example.

The second part of the topic text contains a hypertext reference to the second topic. The help system recognizes two types of links. Popup links are marked by the `\ul` statement and represent links to topics that appear in a popup window. Links marked with the `\uldb` statement represent links to topics that are displayed in the help system's main window. The link itself is identified by the subsequent `\v` statement.

These codes and most other codes recognized by the help system can easily be generated by an RTF editor. For example, the `\ul` command represents underlined text; `\uldb` represents double underline. For example, the help topics that were presented in Listing 38.1 appear, when edited using Microsoft Word 7.0, as shown in Figure 38.3.

The help system also recognizes commands that are not part of the standard RTF format. These commands are related to bitmaps and DLLs. For example, the `bmc` command can be used to embed a bitmap in text. These help-only commands use a special syntax. The curly braces that normally enclose RTF commands are to be preceded by the backslash character. Furthermore, the backslash character that normally precedes RTF commands should be omitted. For example:

```
\{bmc bitmap.bmp\}
```

This special syntax enables such commands to be included when using an RTF word processor. Simply include the command with the curly braces but *without* the backslashes:

```
{bmc bitmap.bmp}
```

FIGURE 38.3.

Editing a help topic using Word.

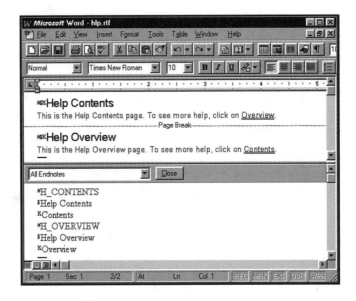

When this text is saved as part of the RTF file, the curly braces are automatically preceded by backslashes to distinguish them from RTF commands.

> **NOTE**
>
> Although the RTF format recognizes embedded pictures through the \pict command, in my experience you are much better off using commands such as bmc to specify bitmaps or metafile pictures in external files. I repeatedly experienced problems with RTF files that grew too large because of the large amounts of picture data embedded within them.

The RTF file shown in Listing 38.1 also contains some macro references. We discuss help macros later in this chapter.

The Help Project File

Every help project must have a help project file. It is this file that is specified when the help compiler is invoked. Help project files usually have the HPJ extension. A typical help project file, the one used to compile the help topics demonstrated earlier, is shown in Listing 38.2.

Listing 38.2. A simple help project file.

```
[OPTIONS]
CONTENTS=H_CONTENTS
```

```
TITLE=Test Help File
COMPRESS=OFF

[WINDOWS]
main=,,,(255,255,192),(192,192,192)

[FILES]
HLP.RTF

[CONFIG]
CreateButton("about", "About", "About()")

[MAP]
H_CONTENTS              10000
H_OVERVIEW              10100
```

Perhaps the most important element in this file is the [FILES] section. It is in this section that the names of the help topic files are specified. Other sections, such as the [OPTIONS] and the [WINDOWS] sections, provide additional parameters specifying the help file's appearance and behavior.

The [WINDOWS] section can also be used to define secondary help windows. Such windows can be referred to in topic files by name, in order to display specific topics in a separate window. A possible use of this capability is to define a window type where sample code can be displayed.

The [CONFIG] section contains macros that are executed when the help file is first opened. More about this later.

The [MAP] section associates context strings with context identifiers. Context identifiers can be passed to WinHelp by the application invoking help. Mappings can be created manually, or, in the case of MFC applications, automatically by using the makehm.exe utility. This utility uses the MFC project's resource.h file to create a mapping for all resource elements in the project.

Help project files can contain #include directives. This is, for example, how AppWizard-generated help project files refer to context mappings that are stored in separate files.

The Help Contents File

The new version of WinHelp, Version 4, can use a separate Table of Contents property page (see Figure 38.4). The table of contents is created from a separate file, one with a name identical to that of the help file but having the CNT extension.

The table of contents file used to generate the table of contents in Figure 38.4 is shown in Listing 38.3.

FIGURE 38.4.

Help table of contents.

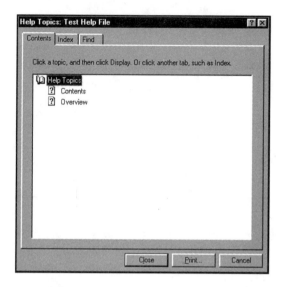

Listing 38.3. A simple help table of contents file.

```
:Base HLP.hlp
1 Help Topics
2 Contents=H_CONTENTS
2 Overview=H_OVERVIEW
```

In addition to specifying the items to appear in the table of contents, this file can contain additional options. For example, it can be used to specify the name of DLLs that specify additional property pages to appear in the Help Topics property sheet next to Contents, Index, and Find.

Compiling Help

In the preceding sections, we have reviewed the elements that comprise a help project. All these elements come together when you invoke the Windows Help Compiler to generate the application's help file.

The name of the new help compiler is `hcrtf.exe`. This program can be invoked by itself, or as part of the Microsoft Help Workshop. To compile a help file from the command line, type a command similar to the following:

```
hcrtf -x hlp.hpj
```

NOTE

Although the `hcrtf` utility can be invoked from the command line (this is how it is invoked from the `makehelp.bat` file generated for MFC application skeletons by AppWizard), it is usually a much better idea to invoke it from within the Microsoft Help Workshop. For one thing, when this utility encounters any errors, it uses a window within the Microsoft Help Workshop to report those.

Macros and DLLs

The Windows help system offers a variety of macros that can be used to enhance the appearance and functionality of a help file. Macros can be utilized in three ways; they can be executed when the help file is first loaded, when a help topic is displayed, or when a hotspot is selected by the user. In addition, some macros (for example, `CreateButton`, `AppendItem`) take macros as arguments; these macros are executed when the item is activated.

To execute a macro at the time the help file is loaded, add the macro to the `[CONFIG]` section of your help project file. For example, the following `[CONFIG]` section in a help project file creates a button that invokes the About dialog:

```
[CONFIG]
CreateButton("about", "About", "About()")
```

To invoke a help macro when a topic is selected, add a footnote to the topic with the exclamation mark (!) as the footnote character. For example, the following footnote, when added to a topic, causes the help window to be centered on the screen every time the topic is invoked:

```
!{\footnote !PositionWindow(256,256,512,512,1,"main")}
```

The third method of invoking a help macro is by adding a macro reference to a hotspot. The following example invokes the Help About dialog when a hotspot is selected by the user:

```
To see the a macro at work, click on {\ul About}{\v !About()}.
```

Wherever you need to specify a macro, you can also specify a macro string. A macro string consists of several macros, separated by semicolons (;).

In addition to macros, help files can also call functions in dynamic link libraries. DLL functions must be registered before use; for registration, use the `RegisterRoutine` macro. Typically, you would invoke this macro from the `[CONFIG]` section of your help project file; this way, the DLL will be registered when the help file is loaded.

For example, if you wish to add a hotspot to your project that plays back a video file, add the following to the help project file:

```
[CONFIG]
RegisterRoutine("MSVFW32.DLL", "MCIWndCreate", "UUUS");
```

Afterwards, you can add a hotspot to a help topic like follows:

```
Click {\ul here}{\v !MCIWndCreate(0,0,0,"myvideo.avi")} for video.
```

Needless to say, you can use functions from system DLLs as well as DLLs that you develop yourself.

DLLs can also be invoked in the context of embedded window references, through the statements ewc, ewl, or ewr that are to be included in your help topic files.

Invoking Help from Applications

Now that we have seen most aspects of help file development, only one question remains: How is help invoked from a C/C++ application?

Regardless of what specific user action causes it, help is always invoked through the WinHelp Windows function. When invoking WinHelp through this function, applications can specify a variety of commands, causing help to appear in a regular or popup window, causing it to display the help contents, a specific topic, and so on.

The simplest way to invoke help is to call WinHelp when the user selects a help command from the application's menu. In this case, simply invoke help by calling WinHelp from the handler of the appropriate WM_COMMAND message.

Handling the F1 key is somewhat more difficult. In order to handle this key regardless of which user-interface element is active, applications used to require a message hook function. In Windows 95, handling F1 is somewhat easier; no hook function is needed because whenever the user presses the F1 key, Windows 95 sends a WM_HELP message to the application.

Windows 95 assists the development of context-sensitive help in other ways. For example, it sends a WM_CONTEXTMENU message whenever the user right-clicks a window. In response to this message, applications can invoke WinHelp with the HELP_CONTEXTMENU command; this causes the popup menu with the "What's This?" menu item to be displayed.

To handle context-help mode, applications must implement a flag indicating that the user has pressed the F1 key or invoked context help through some other means—selecting a toolbar button, for example. When this flag is set, applications must process messages such as command messages differently, invoking WinHelp instead of invoking a command function. If you wish to provide context help on nonclient area components of your application's window, you may also need to intercept the appropriate nonclient area messages as well.

If the application implementing context-help mode is an in-place OLE server or client, care must be taken to ensure that the context-help mode of the server and the client are synchronized. If either the client or the server does not support context-help mode, context-help mode cannot be made available during an in-place session.

For MFC applications, the framework automates invoking the help system with appropriate parameters. Unless you wish to add special effects, you do not need to worry about calling WinHelp yourself.

The Microsoft Help Workshop

The Microsoft Help Workshop is a Windows-based utility for creating and managing help project files and help content files. Using this utility in conjunction with an RTF-capable word processor greatly simplifies help file development.

Editing a Help Project

Figure 38.5 shows the Microsoft Help Workshop with a help project file open. This is the same help project file shown in Listing 38.2. As you can see, the Microsoft Help Workshop adds a series of standard sections and comments to the manually generated file.

FIGURE 38.5.

The Microsoft Help Workshop.

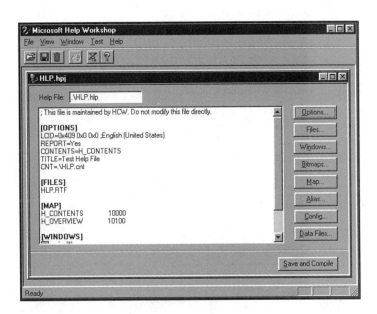

On the right side of the help project window, a series of buttons corresponds to sections of the help project file. Project settings can be modified by either using one of these buttons, or double-clicking on the appropriate item itself. For example, clicking on the Options button or double-clicking on the [OPTIONS] section in the help project file invokes the Options property sheet, shown in Figure 38.6.

FIGURE 38.6.

*Help project
options: the
General page.*

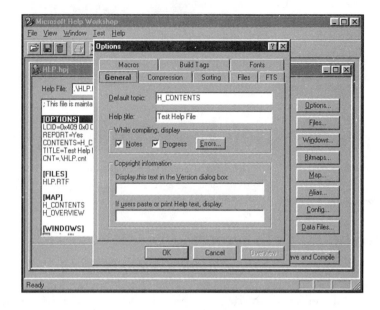

The Files button can be used to identify the help topic (RTF) files that comprise the project (Figure 38.7). You can add or remove files from the file list; you can also specify files that are to be included using the #include directive. A file included here with this directive should contain a list of topic files.

FIGURE 38.7.

*Adding and
removing topic files.*

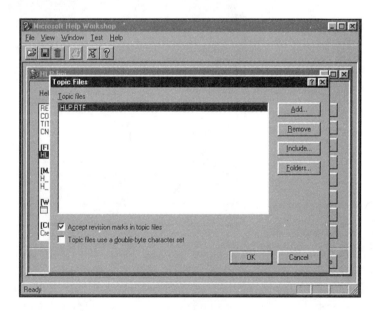

Window options can be set or modified by clicking on the Window button. The property sheet that is displayed (Figure 38.8), can be used to modify window properties such as size, color, caption, standard buttons, and any macros that are to be invoked when the window is displayed. To modify the properties for the main help window, use the window type main; however, you can also define additional window types by using the Add button in the General property page.

FIGURE 38.8.

Help window options: the General page.

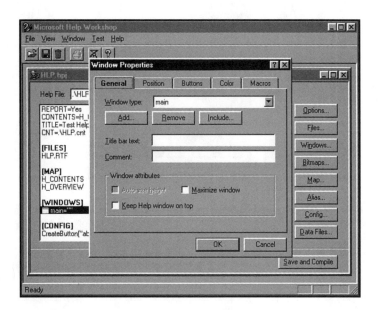

The Bitmaps button can be used to specify the location of bitmap files that are to be included with your help project (Figure 38.9). This option can be used as an alternative to including full pathnames in your help topic files—an approach that would make moving your help project to a different directory difficult.

Help topic mappings (associations of context strings with numeric context identifiers) are added or modified using the Map button (Figure 38.10). A notable feature of this dialog is the Overview button, which invokes the Microsoft Help Workshop help file.

The Alias button can be used to set up topic aliases (Figure 38.11). Topic aliases are particularly useful if you wish to map several user-interface elements to the same topic (for example, a "catchall" topic for error messages).

The Config button can be used to add or modify configuration macros (Figure 38.12). These macros, added to the [CONFIG] section of your help project file, are called when the help file is first loaded.

FIGURE 38.9.

Bitmap directories.

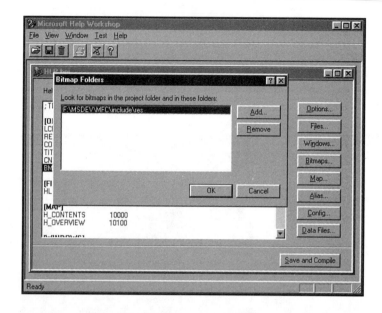

FIGURE 38.10.

Help topic mappings.

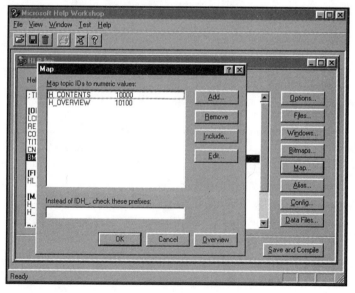

FIGURE 38.11.

*Editing a
topic alias.*

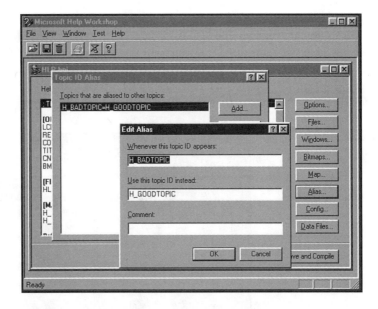

FIGURE 38.12.

*Configuration
Macros dialog.*

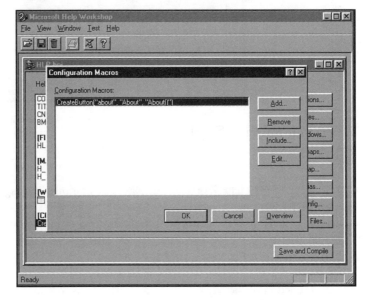

The Data Files button is used to add files to the help project file's [BAGGAGE] section. Files listed in this section are added to the help file's internal file system. WinHelp exposes a set of baggage handling functions that DLLs can use to access these internally stored files. The advantage of using internal files is improved access speed when the help file is loaded from slower media (for example, CD-ROM). A typical use of this capability is to store multimedia files in the help file that are later retrieved and played back by a DLL.

FIGURE 38.13.

Baggage files.

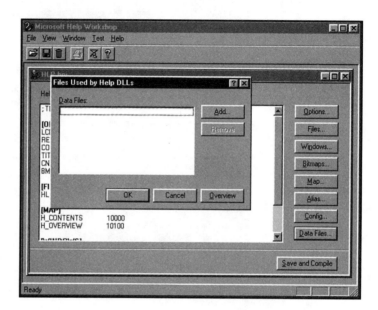

When you wish to recompile a help file, use the Save and Compile button. Clicking on this button causes your modifications to the help project file to be saved and the help compiler, hcrtf.exe, to be started.

Because the Microsoft Help Workshop displays any compiler messages during compilation (Figure 38.14), this is the preferred method for compiling help files. When invoking the help compiler, hcrtf.exe, from the command line, compiler warnings and errors may be lost.

Editing a Help Contents File

The second function of the Microsoft Help Workshop is to maintain help table of contents files (Figure 38.15). These files specify the appearance and contents of the table of contents property page that WinHelp displays when a table of contents file is available and the user selects the Contents button.

FIGURE 38.14.

Help file compilation.

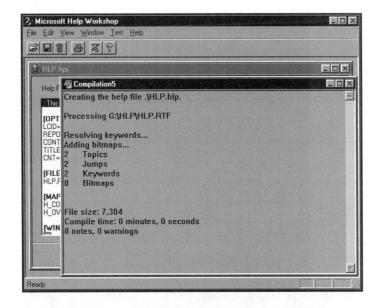

FIGURE 38.15.

Editing a help contents file.

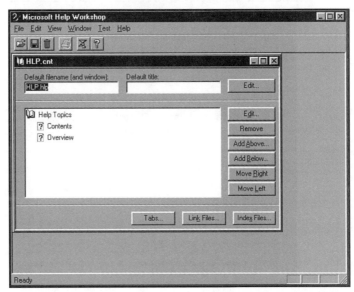

The Edit, Remove, Add Above, Add Below, Move Right, and Move Left buttons can be used to add and remove items as well as to modify the hierarchy of the help table of contents.

The Link Files and the Index Files buttons specify additional help files that are to be included in index searches.

It is possible to add new property pages to the Help Index property sheet by using the Tabs button. A new property page is represented by a DLL that exports the following function:

```
HWND WINAPI OpenTabDialog(HWND, DWORD, DWORD);
```

When called, this function should create a dialog. The first parameter to this function identifies the dialog's parent; the remaining parameters are reserved.

The dialog should be based on a template that is visible, has no borders, and has the WS_CHILD and DS_CONTROL styles set.

You can use the AppWizard to create such a DLL. Create a regular DLL that is statically linked with the MFC library (DLL AppWizard Step 1). Create a new dialog and add a class for the dialog. Next, add an OpenTabDialog function in a separate file (for example, opentab.cpp) that looks similar to the one shown in Listing 38.4.

Listing 38.4. A possible OpenTabDialog implementation file.

```
#include "stdafx.h"
#include "resource.h"
#include "HlpDlg.h"

__declspec(dllexport)
    HWND WINAPI OpenTabDialog(HWND hwnd, DWORD, DWORD)
{
    CHlpDlg *pDlg;
    pDlg = new CHlpDlg;
    pDlg->Create(CHlpDlg::IDD, CWnd::FromHandle(hwnd));
    return pDlg->m_hWnd;
}
```

If your DLL is functioning properly, a new tab is added to the help topics property sheet (Figure 38.16).

You can communicate with WinHelp from your DLL by sending messages to it.

Testing and Running Help

The Microsoft Help Workshop can also be used to test help files. To start WinHelp with a specific help file, use the Run WinHelp command from the File menu. If you select this command, a dialog is displayed (Figure 38.17) where a variety of options can be selected.

The File menu also contains the special Help Author option. When this flag is set, help files are run with debugging enabled. While debugging is enabled, WinHelp displays extra error messages; it also displays the topic identifier in window captions instead of the topic title.

FIGURE 38.16.

Adding a custom tab to the Help Topics property sheet.

FIGURE 38.17.

Starting WinHelp from the Help Workshop.

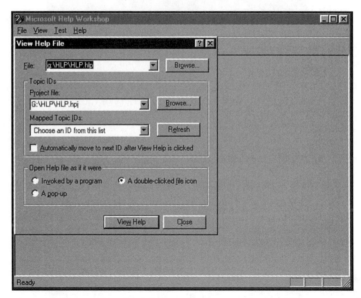

Another useful feature is the WinHelp Messages command in the View menu. This command displays a variety of debugging messages generated by WinHelp while executing a help file.

Finally, several useful test commands are available under the Test menu. The Contents File command tests a help contents file for link integrity. The Close All Help command closes all instances of WinHelp. The Send a macro command executes a macro in the context of the specified help file. Lastly, the WinHelp API command can be used to invoke the WinHelp function with a variety of parameter settings.

AppWizard-Generated Help File Skeletons

For MFC projects that are created with AppWizard with help support requested, the AppWizard can be instructed to create a skeleton set of help files.

The files created include `afxcore.rtf`, `afxprint.rtf`, and a variety of bitmap files. The bitmap files represent toolbar buttons, window portions, and other graphical illustrations used in the help topic files.

Many of the help topics in `afxcore.rtf` and `afxprint.rtf` are complete; others may require modifications. Your application will probably also require a variety of application-specific topics; these you would probably implement in a separate topic file.

In addition to creating the help topic files and bitmaps, the AppWizard also creates a help project file and a help content file for your application. Furthermore, it creates a batch file, `makehelp.bat`, which can be utilized to recompile the help project. This batch file is automatically invoked from your application's make file. However, `makehelp.bat` will not report any errors; if you wish to recompile your help project after extensive changes, I recommend that you use the Microsoft Help Workshop.

Summary

Online context-sensitive help is a mandatory feature for most new Windows applications. Context-sensitive help is developed using a variety of tools and displayed using the `WinHelp.exe` utility.

The files that make up a Windows help project include a help project file, help topic files, and other, optional file components.

Help topic files are in the Microsoft rich-text format. As RTF files consist of printable ASCII characters, they can be edited by most ASCII editors; alternatively, and for convenience, an RTF-compatible word processor, such as Word for Windows, can be used.

The help system interprets specific RTF formatting codes. For example, underlined text represents a hotspot, a hypertext link to another topic in a help topic file. In addition to standard RTF formatting codes, the help system also uses a few help-only codes.

The help project file specifies the files that make up the help project. In addition, this file also specifies a series of settings and attributes for the help file, its windows, and its behavior.

Another help project component is a table of contents file. If such a file exists, the help system uses a special property page for displaying a help file's table of contents.

The help system offers a series of macros. Macros can be nested and chained into macro strings. Macros can be invoked when the help file is first loaded, when a particular help topic is displayed, or when a specific hotspot is selected by the user. In addition to macros, applications can also invoke functions from dynamic-link libraries, assuming that those functions have been previously registered using the `RegisterRoutine` macro.

Applications invoke help using the `WinHelp` Windows function. This function is invoked when the user selects a Help menu command, the F1 key, or when context help mode is selected through the Shift+F1 key. Of these, processing the F1 key requires the use of hook functions, or, alternatively, you can rely on the `WM_HELP` message that is sent to your application under Windows 95.

For MFC applications created with AppWizard, AppWizard automatically adds the functionality to invoke help as appropriate.

A new tool that comes with Visual C++ Version 4 is the Microsoft Help Workshop. This application provides a graphical editing facility for help project and help content files. Use of this application in conjunction with an RTF-capable word processor greatly simplifies the task of help file development.

For MFC application skeletons created with help support, AppWizard creates a series of help-related files. These files contain many complete topics and several other topics that require completion in accordance with the specifics of your application. AppWizard also creates a file, `makehelp.bat`, that is invoked from your application's make file. However, as `makehelp.bat` does not report any errors, it may be useful to compile your help project from within the Microsoft Help Workshop after any significant changes to the help project files.

TCP/IP Programming with WinSock

39

Until the recent information explosion that began a few years ago, not many programmers had heard of TCP/IP, the protocol suite that is used throughout the Internet for internetwork communication (that is, communication between subnetworks).

An obscure protocol a few years back, no new operating system can claim to be complete without it nowadays; Windows is no exception.

The most widely used application programming interface for TCP/IP programming is the Berkeley sockets library. Berkeley sockets have been used throughout the Internet for implementing TCP/IP applications. It was only natural that when the time came, Microsoft picked this API for TCP/IP under Windows.

The use of Berkeley sockets is not limited to TCP/IP programming. Berkeley sockets represent an intertask communication mechanism that may use TCP/IP or other network protocols for the actual transmission of data. However, current WinSock implementations limit the use of the Berkeley socket interface to TCP/IP.

First, here's a review of the fundamentals of TCP/IP networking.

TCP/IP Networks and OSI

I will spare you yet another brief account of the history of TCP/IP. The tale of how it evolved as the protocol suite of ARPANET and later the NSFNET has been told and retold many times.

The Internet Protocol Suite

TCP/IP is somewhat of a misnomer; the internet protocol suite that it usually refers to consists of several components other than TCP and IP. Figure 39.1 provides a brief overview of these in the context of the seven layers of OSI, the Open Systems Interconnect standard.

> **NOTE**
>
> In the phrase "internet protocol," the term internet is used as a generic term and is written in lower case. There can be many internets (for example, the internetwork at a large organization) of which "the" Internet is but one, albeit the biggest by far.

What is behind these strange acronyms?

TCP is the *Transmission Control Protocol*. TCP provides a reliable byte stream between two processes. Reliability in this context means that applications are not required to monitor for lost or corrupted packets. TCP is also a *connection-oriented* protocol. Applications that communicate via TCP establish a logical connection before any exchange of data can take place and terminate the connection when the data exchange has been completed. The term *virtual circuit* is sometimes used for this kind of a logical connection.

FIGURE 39.1.

The internet protocol suite and the OSI layers.

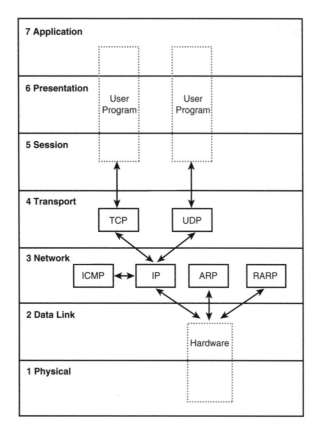

UDP is the *User Datagram Protocol.* UDP is a *connectionless* protocol. Data packets are addressed and delivered individually. UDP is not a reliable protocol; applications must be prepared to handle the loss of packets.

ICMP is the *Internet Control Message Protocol.* This protocol is often used to deliver error and control information on TCP/IP networks. ICMP packets are rarely used by user processes. A notable exception is the ping utility that is used to verify the accessibility of a foreign host by sending an ICMP "echo" packet and monitoring its return.

IP stands for (what else?) *Internet Protocol.* IP provides the packet delivery service on which TCP, UDP, and ICMP rely.

ARP is the *Address Resolution Protocol.* ARP is used to translate a network address to a hardware address.

RARP is the *Reverse Address Resolution Protocol.* RARP is used to translate a hardware address into a network address.

IP Datagrams

At the heart of TCP/IP data transmissions is the *IP datagram*. An IP datagram is a packet that encapsulates source and destination addresses, type of service information, user data, and error correction information.

An IP datagram consists of a header and a block of data. The data can be anything depending on the type of service and the user requirements. The header, on the other hand, contains a set of well-defined fields; this is where we now focus our attention.

IP Headers

The header of an IP datagram, or IP header, usually consists of 20 bytes. Figure 39.2 shows the fields comprising this IP header.

FIGURE 39.2.

The IP Header.

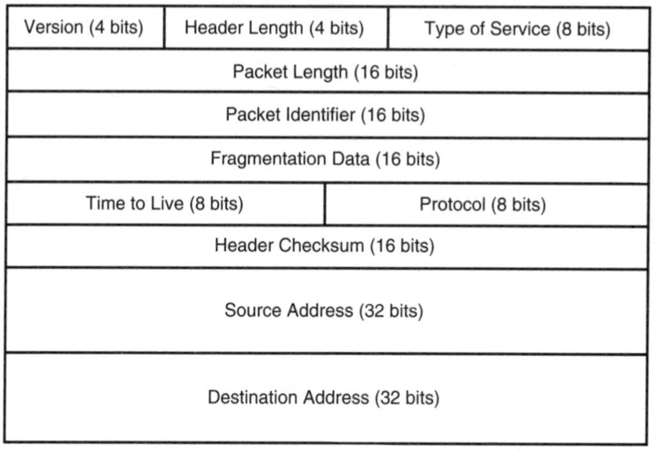

Version (4 bits)	Header Length (4 bits)	Type of Service (8 bits)
Packet Length (16 bits)		
Packet Identifier (16 bits)		
Fragmentation Data (16 bits)		
Time to Live (8 bits)		Protocol (8 bits)
Header Checksum (16 bits)		
Source Address (32 bits)		
Destination Address (32 bits)		

Of the fields shown in Figure 39.2, the ones that are of considerable interest to us include the Protocol, Source Address, and Destination Address fields.

The Protocol field determines how the rest of the IP packet is interpreted. Several dozen values have been defined for this field. For example, a value of 6 implies a TCP packet; a value of 17 implies a UDP packet.

The addresses in a packet represent *host addresses*. Host addresses uniquely identify hosts on an internet.

IP Host Addresses and Routing

An IP host address is a 32-bit number uniquely identifying an internet host. Or, to be more precise, an IP address uniquely identifies a particular interface on an internet host; gateway machines (those which have interfaces on more than one network) routinely have several host addresses.

According to convention, the 4-byte internet host address is usually written down as a set of four decimal numbers: for example, 127.0.0.1.

The internet host address is usually divided into two parts: the *network address* and the actual *host address*. The respective lengths of these two portions of the address vary depending on the most significant byte in the address.

Class A network addresses are those with the most significant byte between 0 and 127. A class A address consists of an 8-bit network address and a 24-bit host address. Because addresses beginning with 0 and 127 are reserved, there can be a maximum of 126 class A subnets on an internet. A class A subnet can contain up to 16,777,214 hosts. (Addresses in the form of nnn.0.0.0 and nnn.255.255.255 are reserved.)

Class B network addresses are those with the most significant byte between 128 and 191. Class B addresses consist of a 16-bit network address and a 16-bit host address. There can be a maximum of 16,383 class B subnets. A class B subnet may contain up to 65,534 hosts. (Again, addresses in the form of nnn.mmm.0.0 and nnn.mmm.255.255 are reserved.)

A class C network address is one with the most significant byte betweeen 192 and 223. This allows a total of 2,097,152 class C subnets. A class C subnet may contain up to 254 hosts. (Addresses in the form of nnn.mmm.kkk.0 and nnn.mmm.kkk.255 are reserved.)

Class D addresses (most significant byte between 224 and 255) are reserved for *IP multicasting*. This limited form of IP broadcasting is of no concern for most WinSock programmers.

Once the destination address of a packet is known, hosts on an internet can *route* the packet as appropriate. For most hosts, routing involves either forwarding a packet to a destination that is known to the host or passing it along a *default route*. For example, if you have a class C subnet that is connected to an Internet service provider via a SLIP or PPP connection, this connection is your default route; any packets that are not addressed to a host on your subnet will be automatically forwarded to your provider.

Larger hosts maintain dynamically updated *routing tables*. Through these tables, the correct route of packets can be identified and in the case of a network error, alternate routes can be found.

Inasmuch as the WinSock programmer is concerned, routing is a transparent activity. You need not be concerned how the Internet accomplishes its magic when delivering a packet to a World Wide Web host in New Zealand or an FTP site in Alaska.

Host Names

It was recognized early during the evolution of the Internet that numeric host addresses may not always be adequate. For one thing, they are difficult to remember; also, if a host's address changes for any reason, the likely result would be endless confusion. Therefore, a naming system was introduced that mapped numeric IP addresses to memorizable host names and vice versa.

In those early days of few hosts on the Internet, every host maintained a file (the hosts file) with a list of all Internet hosts and their addresses. However, as the Internet began its phenomenal growth, this solution quickly proved to be inadequate. First, the naming of Internet hosts had to be standardized; second, a mechanism needed to be found that would eliminate the need to maintain a copy of the hosts file on every Internet-connected computer.

The answer to these problems is the Domain Name System (DNS), development of which began in the early 1980s. DNS is a hierarchical naming system. The format of DNS host names is familiar to everyone who has ever used the Internet: a typical Internet host name is in the form of host.subdomain.domain.

On top of the hierarchy is the *root domain*, denoted by a single period. Next are the *top-level domains*. Top-level domain names have been assigned either by organization (mostly in the United States) or by country name. Organizational top-level domains include the following:

GOV: Government bodies

EDU: Educational institutions

COM: Commercial enterprises

MIL: Military organizations

ORG: Other organizations

Top-level domains by country usually follow the ISO 3166 standard for two-letter country name abbreviations. Examples include US (USA), CA (Canada), DE (Germany).

How is a domain name translated into a numeric IP address and vice versa? DNS defines a distributed name service mechanism whereby hosts can act as *name servers* for various domains. Name servers constantly communicate with each other, supplying each other with information on specific hosts. Without going into too much detail, suffice it to say that when your application requests the IP address for a host name, this request is sent to your default name server, which, in turn, may query other name servers on the Internet to get the requested information. Again, the mechanism is completely transparent to the application programmer.

TCP and UDP Packets, Port Numbers, and Sockets

Clearly, knowing the destination host address of an IP packet is not sufficient for most applications. After all, a host can maintain several open connections, be engaged in several TCP/IP conversations at once. When an IP packet is received, how does the host determine which particular conversation this packet is part of?

In the case of both TCP and UDP packets, in addition to the IP header, the packets also contain additional header information. The first four bytes of both TCP and UDP headers contain a two-byte source and a two-byte destination *port number*.

The port number, together with the IP number, identifies a *socket* that is unique throughout an internet. A pair of sockets uniquely identifies a connection (at least in the case of TCP, a connection-oriented protocol).

> **NOTE**
>
> TCP and UDP ports are not equivalent. For example, TCP port 25 and UDP port 25 refer to two different entities.

Internet Services

There are many types of services on IP networks that are in widespread use. Examples include FTP, telnet, gopher, the WWW, archie, DNS name service, whois, finger, and many others.

The protocols used for these services are defined in the Internet Requests For Comment documents, or RFCs (some of the most relevant RFCs are listed later in this chapter). The services themselves are usually available on *well-known* port numbers. For example, to connect to a telnet server on any host on the Internet, you would make a connection attempt to TCP port 23 on that machine. Well-known ports that a host recognizes are typically identified in the system's services file. This file is used in both UNIX and Windows TCP/IP implementations.

On most systems, TCP and UDP port numbers 0-1023 are reserved for privileged processes.

The WinSock API

The Berkeley sockets interface can be used for communicating using both connection-oriented protocols (TCP) and connectionless protocols (UDP). The programming model is the *client-server* model; servers wait for incoming requests, while clients initiate sessions.

There are some implementation differences between WinSock and the UNIX version of Berkeley sockets. Of these, perhaps the most significant is the fact that socket descriptors and file descriptors cannot be used interchangeably. This has a notable effect when porting applications that make an assumption of this equivalence.

Another difference is that the WinSock library requires initialization. Applications that intend to use WinSock functions must first call the WSAStartup function; when their work with the WinSock library is finished, they should call WSACleanup for proper termination.

The WinSock API also introduces several WinSock-specific functions for performing asynchronous I/O on sockets. This assists in the development of responsive GUI WinSock applications.

WinSock Initialization

The WinSock library is initialized by a call to WSAStartup. The application calling this function provides the address to a WSADATA structure, which will hold initialization information.

During the call to WSAStartup, applications and the WinSock library negotiate a version number. The initialization request fails if there is no overlap between the version number supported by the application and the version number supported by the WinSock library.

If an error occurs, WSAStartup returns a nonzero value. Applications may retrieve extended error information through the function WSAGetLastError.

Creating and Using Sockets

A socket is created by a call to the socket function. Parameters to this function indicate the type of the socket, the type of the network address, and the protocol being used. For example, the call

```
socket(AF_INET, SOCK_STREAM, IPPROTO_TCP)
```

creates a TCP socket.

To associate a socket with an actual host address and port number, applications typically call the bind function. In addition to the socket identifier, or *socket descriptor* (which is returned by the socket call), bind takes a parameter that is a pointer to a structure describing the socket address. This structure is defined as follows:

```
struct sockaddr
{
    u_short sa_family;
    char sa_data[14];
};
```

The sa_family member of this structure specifies the type of the address. For internet addresses, this value is set to AF_INET. The sa_data contains the actual address.

Applications can easily access the various components of the address by referring to it through an sockaddr_in structure (instead of using sockaddr). Here is the definition of this structure:

```
struct sockaddr_in
{
    short sin_family;
    u_short sin_port;
    struct in_addr sin_addr;
    char sin_zero[8];
};
```

Of these members, `sin_port` is the 16-bit port number, while `sin_addr` is the 32-bit host address.

Name Service

In order to assign meaningful values to the host address field in the `sockaddr_in` structure, we must first obtain a 32-bit host address. To obtain an address when the symbolic name of a host is known, use the `gethostbyname` function.

When calling `gethostbyname`, applications pass the symbolic name of the host and receive a pointer to a `hostent` structure in return. The `hostent` structure is defined as follows:

```
struct hostent
{
    char FAR * h_name;
    char FAR * FAR * h_aliases;
    short h_addrtype;
    short h_length;
    char FAR * FAR * h_addr_list;
};
```

This structure is necessary because a host name may be associated with several host addresses (the reverse is also true). In most cases, applications just take the first (often only) address in `h_addr_list`; to make this easier, the symbol `h_addr` is defined as `h_addr_list[0]`.

If an application wishes to use a numeric address instead, it can use the `inet_addr` function to convert a string containing a numeric address into a 32-bit address value. Once that value has been obtained, `gethostbyaddr` can be used to return a `hostent` structure for the specified host.

Byte Ordering

A problem with particular importance when it comes to designing applications that are expected to work on hybrid networks is the issue of *byte ordering*. Some system architectures are *big-endian* (most significant byte comes first); others are *little-endian* (most significant byte comes last). Examples of the latter include the Intel family of processors and DEC CPUs; examples of the former include the Motorola 68000 processor family.

Internet numbers (for example, host addresses) are always big-endian. To ensure correct conversion between machine-independent internet numbers and their machine-dependent representation, you can use the following set of functions: `htonl`, `htons`, `ntohl`, and `ntohs`. These functions connect short or long integers from network to host format or vice versa. Note that these functions may be implemented as macros.

Communication Through Sockets

In the case of the connection-oriented TCP protocol, the server application binds to a specific TCP port and then uses the `listen` function to indicate its willingness to accept incoming connection requests. Immediately after the call to listen, the server calls accept to wait for incoming connections. When accept returns, it provides the address of the peer process.

The client, after creating a socket using the socket call, can immediately initiate a connection using the connect call. It is not necessary to bind the socket to a specific port using bind prior to calling connect.

Once the connection has been successfully initiated, both the client and the server can use the send call to transmit data and the recv call to receive data. The semantics of send and recv are similar to the semantics of the read and write calls for low-level file I/O. Indeed, on UNIX systems it is possible to use the latter pair of functions to perform I/O on sockets. Unfortunately, as I mentioned earlier, this is not possible with WinSock, due to the differences between a file descriptor and a socket descriptor. For the same reason, it is not possible to use the close system call to close a socket; applications must use closesocket when a socket connection is about to be terminated. Either the client or the server can terminate the connection using closesocket.

Figure 39.3 provides an overview of setting up and using a TCP connection.

FIGURE 39.3.

*Socket commun-
ications for
connection-
oriented protocols.*

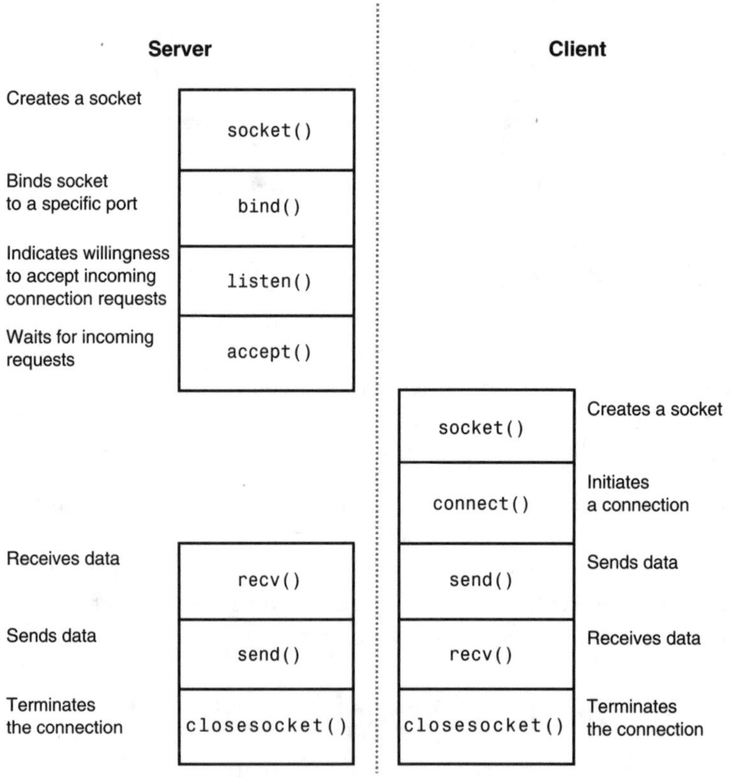

In the case of the connectionless UDP protocol, the sequence of events is somewhat different; the activities of the client and server application are more symmetrical. In this case, both the client and the server create their respective sockets and bind those to specific port numbers. The server then makes a call to the recvfrom function, which waits for any incoming data. The client, in turn, uses the sendto call to send data to a specific address. When this data is received by the server, the recvfrom call returns, and the server also obtains the address from which the data has been received. It can then use this address in a subsequent call to sendto, as it replies to the client. Figure 39.4 presents an overview of this process.

FIGURE 39.4.

Socket communications for connectionless protocols.

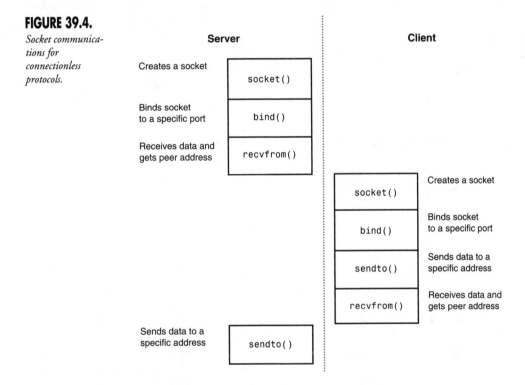

The Blocking Problem and the *select* Call

In the simplistic models shown in Figures 39.3 and 39.4, both the client and the server use *blocking* calls when waiting for data. A blocking call does not return to the calling function until the requested data becomes available. In other words, the application that makes such a call becomes suspended until the call is completed.

While this model will suffice in many simple situations, it is clearly unacceptable for interactive applications. Such an application (for example, a telnet client) cannot simply freeze until data becomes available from the server.

The solution employed by most UNIX TCP/IP applications relies on the select system call. This call makes it possible to wait on multiple (file or socket) descriptors. This way, a UNIX process can easily wait for data on both a socket or the standard input and spring into action whenever data is received on either of them.

Unfortunately, things are not this easy with WinSock. Remember that socket and file descriptors are not interchangeable? Unfortunately, select is no exception; it can only wait on multiple socket descriptors, not on a mix of socket and file descriptors.

While it is possible to monitor a socket while polling, this is not a very efficient solution. Fortunately, Win32's multithreading capability comes to our rescue. A process can easily start additional threads and have a separate thread for each input source. This mechanism works well for both command-line and graphical TCP/IP utilities. Nevertheless, the WinSock library offers yet another family of functions that assist in writing well-behaved TCP/IP applications without having to resort to multithreaded trickery. These asynchronous socket calls can thus also be used in 16-bit programs and programs intended for Win32s.

Asynchronous Socket Calls

Asynchronous socket calls rely on the Windows message passing mechanism to communicate socket events to Windows applications.

At the center of this mechanism is the WSAAsyncSelect function call. Through this function, an application can wait for a combination of socket events. Applications may receive notifications indicating readiness for reading, writing, incoming and completed connections, and socket closure. (This call can also be used for notifications regarding *out of band* data, something that we have not discussed in this section.) The notification takes place in the form of a user-defined message that is posted to a window, also defined in the call to WSAAsyncSelect.

WSAAsyncSelect posts a single message for every event the application expressed an interest in. Once the message has been posted, no further messages will be posted for the same event until the application implicitly resets the event by calling the appropriate socket library function. For example, if a notification for incoming data was posted, no further such notifications will be posted for the given socket until the application retrieves that data with a call to recv or recvfrom.

Other asynchronous socket functions include, for example, asynchronous versions of the standard Berkeley gethostbyname and gethostbyaddr calls: WSAAsyncGetHostByName and WSAAsyncGetHostByAddr. WinSock applications can also influence the blocking mechanism used in the standard Berkeley-style calls by using the WSASetBlockingHook function.

A Simple WinSock Example

It is time to put all this theory into practice. I decided to include a simple WinSock-based command-line utility. This program connects to a well-known service (the *time* service on TCP port 37) on the specified host and retrieves the current time in machine-readable form, which it then formats and displays. With little modification, this application could be used to set the system time from a server that is known to keep reliable time.

The program shown in Listing 39.1 can be compiled from the command line by typing `cl gettime.cpp wsock32.lib`.

Listing 39.1. The gettime command-line utility.

```cpp
#include <iostream.h>
#include <time.h>
#include <winsock.h>

void main(int argc, char *argv[])
{
    time_t t;
    int s;
    struct sockaddr_in a;
    struct hostent *h;
    WSADATA wsaData;

    if (argc != 2)
    {
        cout << "Usage: " << argv[0] << " host\n";
        exit(1);
    }
    if(WSAStartup(0x101, &wsaData))
    {
        cout << "Unable to initialize WinSock library.\n";
        exit(1);
    }
    h = gethostbyname(argv[1]);
    if (h == NULL)
    {
        cout << "Cannot resolve hostname\n";
        WSACleanup();
        exit(1);
    }

    a.sin_family = AF_INET;
    a.sin_port = htons(37);
    memcpy(&(a.sin_addr.s_addr), h->h_addr, sizeof(int));
    s = socket(AF_INET, SOCK_STREAM, IPPROTO_TCP);
    if (s == 0)
    {
        cout << "Cannot establish connection: "
            << WSAGetLastError() << '\n';
        WSACleanup();
        exit(1);
    }
    if (connect(s, (struct sockaddr *)&a, sizeof(a)))
    {
        cout << "Cannot establish connection: "
            << WSAGetLastError() << '\n';
        WSACleanup();
```

continues

Listing 39.1. continued

```
        exit(1);
    }
    if (recv(s, (char *)&t, 4, 0) != 4)
        cout << "Unable to obtain time.\n";
    else
    {
        t = ntohl(t) - 2208988800;
        cout << asctime(localtime(&t));
    }
    closesocket(s);
    WSACleanup();
}
```

The *time service* is described in RFC868. An Internet time server listens to TCP port 37; when it receives a connection request, it sends the current time (GMT) as a 4-byte number representing the number of seconds elapsed since January 1, 1900.

The gettime application in Listing 39.1 requires a single command-line parameter, the name of the host to which it should make a connection attempt. After verifying that this parameter has been supplied, it makes an attempt to initialize the WinSock library.

Next, the host name supplied by the user is converted to a host address. (No attempt is made to resolve numeric addresses that the user might supply.) Next, a socket is created, and a connection attempt is made to the designated host on TCP port 37.

If the connection is successful, the program tries to receive exactly four bytes of data. When the receive operation is complete, the data is converted (ntohl); the time base is corrected (Win32 time functions use January 1, 1970, as the base date for time variables—the number of seconds from January 1, 1900, to January 1, 1970, is 2,208,988,800); and finally, the time is displayed as a human-readable local time on standard output.

Before exiting, the program closes the socket and terminates the session with the WinSock library.

Socket Programming and the Microsoft Foundation Classes

The Microsoft Foundation Classes library encapsulates socket functionality in the CAsyncSocket class. Member functions of CAsyncSocket correspond to many of the standard and asynchronous functions in the WinSock library.

An application wishing to use CAsyncSocket must first initialize the socket library via a call to AfxSocketInit; there is no need to call a corresponding cleanup function.

Typically, applications would derive a class from `CAsyncSocket` and override several callback functions that facilitate asynchronous operations.

CAsyncSocket Example

To see how `CAsyncSocket` works, we can rewrite our gettime application using MFC. This simple program communicates with users using a dialog, shown in Figure 39.5.

FIGURE 39.5.

MFC implementation of the gettime program.

The skeleton for this application can be created through the MFC AppWizard. Create a new project with the name GT. Specify that its user interface be dialog-based. In Step 2, make sure that you check Windows Sockets support. Set the dialog's title to a meaningful text string, such as `"TCP/IP GetTime"`.

After AppWizard has finished creating the skeleton, the first step is to update the application's dialog. Add the fields shown in Figure 39.5. The name of the text field holding the host name should be `IDC_HOST`; the name of the text field holding the time should be `IDC_TIME`. The read-only attribute for `IDC_TIME` should be set. The Connect button's identifier should be `IDC_CONNECT`; the Close button can keep the `IDCANCEL` identifier.

Next, add three member variables using the ClassWizard. Two string variables (`m_sHost` and `m_sTime`) will correspond to the two text fields; the third variable, `m_cConnect`, will be of type `CButton` and correspond to the Connect button.

While using the ClassWizard, add a message handler for the `IDC_CONNECT` button. This handler, `CGTDlg::OnConnect`, should process `BN_CLICKED` messages. It is in this handler function where we add most socket-related code.

To implement our time retrieval functionality, we need to derive a class from `CAsyncSocket` and create an object of this new type when the user clicks on the Connect button. The code that needs to be added to the dialog implementation file `GTDlg.cpp` is shown in Listing 39.2.

Listing 39.2. MFC gettime: the `CGTSocket` class and the `CGTDlg::OnConnect` function.

```
class CGTSocket : public CAsyncSocket
{
public:
    CGTSocket(CGTDlg *pDlg) {m_pDlg = pDlg;};
    virtual void OnReceive(int nErrorCode);
    virtual void OnClose(int nErrorCode);
```

continues

Listing 39.2. continued

```
    CGTDlg *m_pDlg;
    time_t t;
};

void CGTSocket::OnReceive(int nErrorCode)
{
    Receive(&t, 4);
    t = ntohl(t) - 2208988800;
    m_pDlg->m_sTime = asctime(localtime(&t));
    m_pDlg->UpdateData(FALSE);
}

void CGTSocket::OnClose(int nErrorCode)
{
    m_pDlg->m_cConnect.EnableWindow(TRUE);
    delete this;
}

void CGTDlg::OnConnect()
{
    CGTSocket *pSocket;

    pSocket = new CGTSocket(this);
    UpdateData(TRUE);
    m_cConnect.EnableWindow(FALSE);
    pSocket->Create();
    pSocket->AsyncSelect(FD_READ | FD_CLOSE);
    pSocket->Connect(m_sHost, 37);
}
```

In the function CGTDlg::OnConnect, a new object of type CGTSocket is created. This type is derived from CAsyncSocket. The actual socket is created through a call to the Create member function, which is followed by a call to AsyncSelect. This call enables the callback functions OnReceive and OnClose. At this time, the Connect button is also disabled. Finally, the Connect member function is called to initiate a connection to the destination.

When the connection attempt succeeds, the time server immediately sends the time in the form of four data bytes. This triggers execution of the OnReceive function, which reads this data using Receive and uses the result to update the time field in the dialog. After sending the data, the server closes the connection. This results in a call to OnClose, which re-enables the Connect button in the dialog and destroys the CGTSocket object.

Note that in its present form, this program does not perform any error checking and is likely to fail if a network error occurs.

Synchronous Operations and Serialization

The purpose of the CAsyncSocket class is to provide a low-level interface to the WinSock library. In contrast, the CSocket class, which is derived from CAsyncSocket, provides a somewhat higher level of functionality.

Unlike `CAsyncSocket`, `CSocket` provides blocking. Its member functions do not return until a requested operation has been completed.

> **NOTE**
>
> The callback functions `OnConnect` and `OnSend` are never called for `CSocket` objects.

One particular use of `CSocket` objects is in conjunction with `CFileSocket` objects to enable the MFC serialization functions to work on sockets. A `CFileSocket` object can be attached to a `CArchive` and a `CSocket`; afterwards, data can be sent and received by simply using MFC serialization.

Further Information

TCP/IP programming is a very broad subject with a tremendous amount of literature. This chapter is certainly not sufficient to do full justice to this complex topic. Because of this, I decided to include some references that I hope assist you in finding the information you need.

For WinSock, the authoritative reference is Microsoft's WinSock specification, which is published on the Microsoft Developer Network CD-ROM.

There are several good books on the subject. One particularly useful book is Black's *TCP/IP & Related Protocols* (McGraw Hill, 1994). For more information on TCP/IP programming (and, in particular, programming with Berkeley sockets), see *UNIX Network Programming* by W. Richard Stevens (Prentice Hall, 1990). Although the book (as its title implies) is aimed at the UNIX programmer, much of the discussion is not UNIX-specific, simply because the respective APIs are vendor-independent.

The official definitions of most Internet-related standards and protocols are found in the form of RFCs (Requests For Comment). These RFCs are available online. On the World Wide Web, use the following URL: `http://www.cis.ohio-state.edu/htbin/rfc/rfc-index.html`. RFCs can also be requested by Internet e-mail from the InterNIC Directory and Database Services mail server. Send a message to `mailserv@ds.internic.net` with the following command in the message body:

```
document-by-name rfcNNNN
```

To obtain the RFC index, use the command

```
document-by-name rfc-index
```

Several documents can be requested in a single mail if you separate their names with commas or include several `document-by-name` commands in the message body in separate lines.

The RFCs have also been published in CD-ROM format by a number of CD-ROM publishers (the one I use often is the Standards CD-ROM from InfoMagic). If you intend to do serious TCP/IP programming, I strongly recommend that you acquire a low-cost CD-ROM like this one.

Internet RFCs go back a *long* time. The earliest RFC on my CD-ROM, RFC0003, dates back to April 1969! Of course, many of the RFCs have long become obsolete.

RFCs that define the standards most commonly encountered by the WinSock programmer are as follows:

RFC0768, "User Datagram Protocol" (J. Postel, 1980)

RFC0791, "Internet Protocol" (J. Postel, 1981)

RFC0792, "Internet Control Message Protocol" (J. Postel, 1981)

RFC0793, "Transmission Control Protocol" (J. Postel, 1981)

RFC0826, "Ethernet Address Resolution Protocol: Or Converting Network Protocol Addresses to 48.bit Ethernet Address for Transmission on Ethernet Hardware" (D. Plummer, 1982)

RFC0903, "Reverse Address Resolution Protocol" (R. Finlayson, T. Mann, J. Mogul, M. Theimer, 1984)

RFC1034, "Domain names—Concepts and Facilities" (P. Mockapetris, 1987)

RFC1035, "Domain names—Implementation and Specification" (P. Mockapetris, 1987)

Two additional RFCs deserve mentioning. RFC1700 ("Assigned Numbers," J. Reynolds, J. Postel, 1994) contains all "well-known" numbers including protocol identifiers, port numbers, and the like. RFC1800 ("Internet Official Protocol Standards," J. Postel, 1995) is an invaluable reference to all the other RFC standards.

> **NOTE**
>
> A popular misconception is that any material published in the form of an Internet RFC represents a standard. This is not so. In addition to standards, Internet RFCs may contain Informational, Experimental, Standards Track (Proposed Standard, Draft Standard, Internet Standard), or Historic material. The nature of an RFC is usually noted on the front page.

Summary

TCP/IP is the name most often used to refer to the internet protocol suite. This protocol suite, which consists of protocols such as TCP, UDP, ICMP, IP, ARP, and RARP, provides the fundamentals for internetwork communication on the global Internet.

Under Windows, TCP/IP programming is accomplished using the WinSock library. WinSock is an API that closely mimics the Berkeley sockets API used on many UNIX systems. However, there are some differences arising from the fact that Windows and UNIX are very dissimilar architecturally. In particular, the Berkeley sockets library uses socket descriptors that are interchangeable with file descriptors used in low-level I/O operations. For this reason, standard C low-level I/O functions can be used on Berkeley sockets, something that is not true under Windows.

Berkeley sockets can be used to communicate using both connection-oriented protocols, such as TCP, and connectionless protocols, such as TCP/IP. In both cases, fundamental operations include the creation of a socket, binding a socket to a host address and port number, and sending and receiving data.

Host addresses can be obtained using the `gethostbyname` function that resolves symbolic system names into 4-byte TCP/IP addresses. To ensure machine-independent representation of host addresses and other numeric quantities, a set of functions is provided for the translation to and from host byte ordering and internet byte ordering.

Writing responsive applications requires that an application does not remain suspended indefinitely while waiting for socket input. The most generally used Berkeley sockets mechanism, namely the use of the `select` function, has limited utility under Windows as socket and file descriptors are not interchangeable; hence, `select` cannot be used to wait for input on `stdin`, for example. However, Win32 applications can use multiple threads to furnish data exchange on multiple I/O channels simultaneously.

To facilitate the development of responsive applications without relying on the multithreaded capabilities of Windows 95 or Windows NT, applications can use asynchronous socket calls. These calls rely on Windows messaging to deliver information about incoming data or other socket events to the application.

Socket functionality is encapsulated in the `CAsyncSocket` class in the Microsoft Foundation Classes library. With the help of the `CSocket` class, which is derived from `CAsyncSocket` and provides synchronous socket I/O, and the `CSocketFile` class, applications can use MFC serialization functions on a socket interface.

Building Custom AppWizards

40

One of the best features of the Visual C++ development system has always been its capability to build heavily customized skeleton applications. The tool that accomplishes this task is the Visual C++ AppWizard. Through a series of dialogs, AppWizard guides the user through the process of setting up the initial project parameters. It then uses these user-supplied values to customize a set of templates that form the basis of the new project's source.

In Version 4 of Visual C++, application developers are given the power to create customized versions of AppWizard. This customization applies to both the dialogs AppWizard presents to the AppWizard user and the template files from which an application skeleton is created.

If AppWizard is a code generator, then the ability to create custom AppWizards must be called a code generator generator capability, right? To avoid the potential for confusion that is demonstrated by this admittedly uninspired play with words, we should agree on a few terms in advance.

For the purposes of this chapter, the term *developer* means you, the author of a custom AppWizard. The *AppWizard user* is the programmer who uses this custom AppWizard to create a skeleton application. The term *end user* refers to users of the application created by the AppWizard user.

How Does AppWizard Work?

Before we can go about building a custom AppWizard, it is necessary to develop a thorough understanding of the operation of AppWizard.

What exactly happens when you invoke AppWizard? The first thing you see is a series of dialogs that AppWizard presents. Through these dialogs, you can specify many project parameters.

These parameters are stored internally by AppWizard as a series of substitution macros. To this set, another set of internally defined macros is also added.

When AppWizard begins generating a new project, it builds project files from a set of templates. The templates are processed and any macro references in them are expanded with the internally defined or user-supplied values.

Figure 40.1 provides a schematic overview of the AppWizard project creation process.

From here, the method of generalizing AppWizard is obvious. If you could only supply your own wizard dialogs, templates, and macros in place of (or in addition to) those in AppWizard, you could build an application generation customized to your needs. This is exactly how custom AppWizards are constructed.

FIGURE 40.1.
How AppWizard creates a new project.

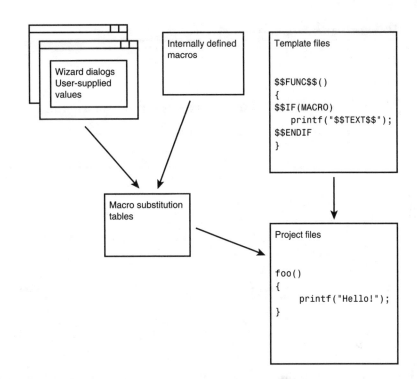

A Working Example: The HelloWizard

I know I am a bore. Could I not find something more entertaining than yet another Hello, World project? Then again, you didn't buy this book for its entertainment value, did you. So perhaps I can be excused for using examples that are admittedly uninspired but help focus on the subject that they are meant to demonstrate. The simpler an example (as long as it is not oversimplified), the better it helps to drive home the point without getting you swamped by unnecessary and irrelevant details.

HelloWizard Overview

On this note, our AppWizard project is a very simple one indeed. Its basis is the program shown in Listing 40.1.

748

Listing 40.1. A simple Hello, World program in Windows.

```
///////////////////////////////////////////////////////////////
// HELLO.CPP

#include <afxwin.h>

int WINAPI WinMain(HINSTANCE d1, HINSTANCE d2, LPSTR d3, int d4)
{
        MessageBox(NULL, "Hello, World!", "HELLO", MB_OK);
        return 0;
}
```

The new AppWizard, HelloWizard, will help the AppWizard user create an application that can display any text, not just this boring "Hello, World!" string. We also would like this revolutionary application to have the proper source comments—that is, we would like to have the name of the actual file appear at the top, which may be different from HELLO.CPP.

Using AppWizard to Create a Custom AppWizard

Custom AppWizard projects are created by, what else? AppWizard, of course. As the first step of creating the new project, select New from the File menu, and specify a new project workspace in the New dialog.

In the New Project dialog, type the name of the new project (for example, HELLO) and select Custom AppWizard as the project type. (Make sure you also specify the correct directory where you want the new project to be located.) Next, click the Create button.

At this time the first of two wizard dialogs (and the only one we use for HelloWizard) appears, shown in Figure 40.2. The first decision you must make is with regard to the starting point from which your new custom AppWizard will be built.

FIGURE 40.2.

*Creating a Custom
AppWizard project
with AppWizard.*

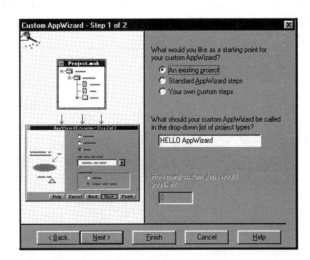

You can base the new custom AppWizard on an existing project. With the help of the new AppWizard, the custom AppWizard user will be able to create projects that are identical copies of the original, except for the project name that will be substituted throughout the project with a name of his choosing.

You can create a custom AppWizard that mimics the standard AppWizard behavior. This is most useful if your goal is to build customized extensions to the standard AppWizard.

Finally, you can create a new custom AppWizard by supplying your own custom steps, bypassing any default AppWizard behavior.

The first two steps are most suitable for applications that are written on the basis of the MFC framework. As our Hello, World program is not such an application, we are restricted to the third choice, the "Your own custom steps" option.

When you click on this option, the editable field towards the lower part of the dialog becomes enabled. In this field, you can specify the number of custom steps (number of wizard dialogs) your custom AppWizard will require. HelloWizard requires only one such step, so you can leave this field at its default setting.

Another change that occurred when you clicked on the "Your own custom steps" option is that the dialog's title changed to "Step 1 of 1" and the Next button became disabled. The second AppWizard step for custom AppWizards is not relevant for custom AppWizards that are based on steps you specify.

Still in this dialog is another field where you can specify the name under which this custom AppWizard will appear. The default is "<projectname> AppWizard" (for example, "HELLO AppWizard"). Change this name to the more elegant HelloWizard. This is purely a cosmetic change; this name is not used for any purpose other than identifying this custom AppWizard when the AppWizard user is about to create a new project workspace.

When you dismiss the wizard dialog by clicking on the Finish button, AppWizard displays a summary of the new custom AppWizard project in the New Project Information dialog. Click on the OK button and the new project is created.

Custom AppWizard Templates

New projects created by a custom AppWizard are defined with the help of templates. When AppWizard created the new custom AppWizard project, it supplied two special template files in the Template subdirectory inside the new custom AppWizard project directory: confirm.inf and newproj.inf. The first of these files, confirm.inf, contains the customizable text that is displayed in the New Project Information dialog when the AppWizard user completes the custom AppWizard steps. Its contents are not used for any other purpose.

In contrast, the other template file, newproj.inf, is perhaps the most important template file in your custom AppWizard project. This is the file that tells AppWizard what other files comprise a skeleton project.

Indeed, what other files are out there? Since we selected a custom AppWizard consisting entirely of steps we build, both `confirm.inf` and `newproj.inf` were created empty. We must supply their content. But before we do that, we turn our attention to our project's single source file, `HELLO.CPP`.

This file, of course, does not exist yet; but you can create it easily by keying in those few lines of code shown in Listing 40.1. But how do you turn this specific program into a generic template that can serve as the starting point for many projects?

The answer is, of course, that you have to use macros at various places throughout this file. We use two such macros, in fact. The first macro is supplied automatically by AppWizard and specifies the name of the application that the AppWizard user is about to create. The second macro is one we create later, and this contains the text that the AppWizard user wishes to include in the new application.

AppWizard macro names are distinguished by prepending and appending two dollar signs to their names. For example, the macro that defines the project name, `ROOT`, should be referred to as `$$ROOT$$` in template files. The same applies to macros we define; in our case, the macro `$$HELLOTEXT$$` that references the value the AppWizard user wishes to output with the new program.

Listing 40.2 shows `HELLO.CPP` in its template version. You can create this file using the integrated editor and save it in the `Template` subdirectory.

Listing 40.2. The Hello, World program as a custom AppWizard template.

```
/////////////////////////////////////////////////////////////////
// $$ROOT$$.CPP

#include <afxwin.h>

int WINAPI WinMain(HINSTANCE d1, HINSTANCE d2, LPSTR d3, int d4)
{
        MessageBox(NULL, "$$HELLOTEXT$$", "$$ROOT$$", MB_OK);
        return 0;
}
```

Notice that the macro substitution takes place regardless where a macro is used (inside a comment, within a pair of quotes).

A custom AppWizard can have *text templates* like our `HELLO.CPP` template, or *binary templates* (for example, a bitmap file). Unlike text templates, binary templates are copied verbatim, with no macro substitution taking place.

As I mentioned, the purpose of the `newproj.inf` template is to list all the templates that a new project consists of. Accordingly, we have to modify the `newproj.inf` template of HelloWizard and include `HELLO.CPP`. This new version of `newproj.inf` is shown in Listing 40.3. To edit `newproj.inf`, open this file through the File Open dialog. It is located in the `Template` subdirectory.

Listing 40.3. The `newproj.inf` template for HelloWizard.

```
$$// newproj.inf = template for list of template files
$$//  format is 'sourceResName' \t 'destFileName'
$$//    The source res name may be preceded by any combination of
$$//    '=', '+', and/or '*'
$$//       '=' => the resource is binary
$$//       '+' => the file should be added to the project
$$//       '*' => bypass custom AppWizard's resources when loading
$$//    if name starts with / => create new subdir


+HELLO.CPP       $$ROOT$$.CPP
```

As the somehow cryptic (AppWizard-generated) header of `newproj.inf` suggests, the name of every file listed in this template may be preceded by a combination of three flags. The flag = indicates a binary resource that is copied verbatim (with no macro processing). The flag specifies that the file should be added to the new project (so for example, you would use this flag with `.CPP` source files, but not with `.H` header files). The meaning of the third flag (*) is somewhat more obscure; it specifies that the custom AppWizard's resources should not be searched for a resource with that name, but instead, the default resource should be used. This is useful if your custom AppWizard contains a template that overrides a default template with the same name, and depending on certain conditions, you may wish to use one or the other.

In our case, we used the + flag because we want the file that is created from the HELLO.CPP template to be automatically added to the AppWizard user's project. The name of the template is followed by a tab character (yes, it must be a single tab character, other whitespace characters are not acceptable), and that is followed by the name this file will have in the AppWizard user's project directory. It goes without saying that macros can be used here as well; we used the $$ROOT$$ macro to specify a filename that is the same as the project name specified by the AppWizard user.

Modification of `confirm.inf` serves purely cosmetic purposes. However, it does give me an opportunity to show some AppWizard template directives (namely the $$IF and $$ENDIF directives) that would not otherwise be required for our simple HelloWizard. Listing 40.4 shows this new version of `confirm.inf`.

Listing 40.4. The `confirm.inf` template for HelloWizard.

```
AppWizard is about to create a new project with the following
settings:

Project name:  $$ROOT$$.MAK
```

continues

Listing 40.4. continued

```
Greeting text: $$HELLOTEXT$$


$$IF(TARGET_INTEL)
The resulting console application can be run inside a DOS box under
both the Windows 95 and the Windows NT operating systems.
$$ENDIF
```

On a minor note, when a macro is referenced in an AppWizard template directive such as $$IF, it is no longer necessary to prepend and append the dollar signs to its name.

Custom AppWizard Resources

We have modified newproj.inf and confirm.inf and we have added a new template, HELLO.CPP. But how do these files find their way into the final custom AppWizard? Indeed, what form does a custom AppWizard take?

The target of the custom AppWizard project is a single file with the .awx extension (in our case, HELLO.awx). Despite the odd extension, this file really is a DLL file that will be called from the Visual C++ Developer Studio when a new project of this type is created. How does the Developer Studio know that this new library is out there? The custom AppWizard, when completed, must be deposited in a special directory location (usually MSDEV\TEMPLATE) where the Developer Studio can locate it.

As I said, the custom AppWizard project is really a DLL project. As such, it also has a resource file. If you open the custom AppWizard project in ResourceView, you will notice a section named "TEMPLATE". In this section, two files that we are already familiar with are specified: confirm.inf, and newproj.inf.

Why did we not simply use ResourceView when editing these files? The problem is, because these files are custom resource files, the Developer Studio makes no assumptions about their content; if you attempt to open them through ResourceView, they will be opened with the binary editor. To open them as text files, you must use the File Open command of the Developer Studio.

The one file that is conspicuously missing from the "TEMPLATE" section is our newly created file, HELLO.CPP. To add this, use the right mouse button over the "TEMPLATE" folder and select the Import command from the popup menu. Select HELLO.CPP in the Template directory and click Import. In the Resource Type dialog that pops up, select "TEMPLATE" as the resource type and click OK.

The Developer Studio opens the file HELLO.CPP for binary editing; you can safely close this window. However, it is necessary to change the identifier of this newly added resource. It was added with the symbolic identifier IDR_TEMPLATE1; we want to change this to the text identifier "HELLO.CPP". For this, simply right-click on the item IDR_TEMPLATE1 in ResourceView, and in the Custom Resource Properties, type "HELLO.CPP" (including the double quotes) over the former ID, IDR_TEMPLATE1.

Doing this should also reveal something about the NEWPROJ.INF file; when we added a reference to HELLO.CPP, what we were referring to was the symbolic name of this resource in our project's resource file, not the actual filename. Of course, it only makes common sense to keep the two identical when possible.

Custom AppWizard Dialogs

Now that we have finished assembling our templates, the nagging question in your mind, no doubt, is just where exactly do user-defined macros acquire their values? It is easy to see how AppWizard, through some internal magic, may set up the values of default macros such as $$ROOT$$ or $$TARGET_INTEL$$; but where does our little macro, $$HELLOTEXT$$, get its value from?

To answer this question, we turn our attention to the dialogs of our custom AppWizard. If you open the Dialog section in ResourceView, you will find exactly one dialog in there: IDD_CUSTOM1. This is because during the initial creation of our custom AppWizard project, we specified that our custom AppWizard should consist of only one step.

Open this dialog by double-clicking. In it, a single static field contains a "TODO" reminder. This must be replaced. HelloWizard requires the user to enter only one text parameter; accordingly, the new version of this dialog should contain a static label and an edit field identified symbolically as IDC_HELLOTEXT. This new, admittedly spartan-looking, dialog is shown in Figure 40.3.

The values from a custom AppWizard's dialog are transferred to member variables through the same dialog data exchange process that is used in other MFC dialogs. To associate a member variable with the new field IDC_HELLOTEXT, invoke the ClassWizard. (This can be done by right-clicking on the edit field and selecting the ClassWizard item in the popup menu.) Select the Member Variables tab, and double-click the IDC_HELLOTEXT item.

The name of the new variable should be m_sHelloText. It is of the Value category and it is of type CString. You do not need to specify a maximum length. Once you have added this variable, you can dismiss the ClassWizard dialog and close all open resources. (It might be a good idea at this time to select the Save All command from the Developer Studio's File menu to ensure that the modified resources are all saved to disk.)

FIGURE 40.3.

HelloWizard's single dialog.

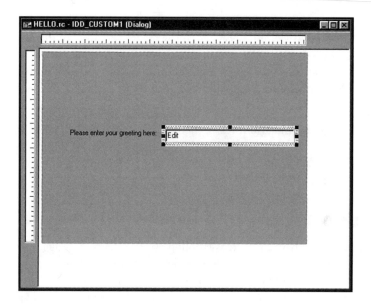

The Macro Dictionary

The new member variable, m_sHelloText, was added to the dialog class corresponding to the dialog IDD_CUSTOM1, the CCustom1Dlg class. It is also through this class that the value assigned to m_sHelloText gets propagated to the custom AppWizard's *macro dictionary*.

Take a look at the class CHELLOAppWiz. This class is derived from the class CCustomAppWiz. CCustomAppWiz has a member variable, m_Dictionary, which is of type CMapStringToString and contains mappings of macro names to macro values. It is this collection of macro name and macro value pairs that we must add our new macro to.

At the end of the file HELLOAw.cpp, a single object of type HELLOAppWiz is declared. It is this global object through which we can access the macro dictionary anywhere in our custom AppWizard.

The place to do it is the OnDismiss member function of the class CCustom1Dlg. This function is called whenever a particular AppWizard dialog is dismissed by the user. We need only add a single line of code that updates the macro dictionary with the new macro value. The modified OnDismiss function is shown in Listing 40.5.

Listing 40.5. Modified version of CCustom1Dlg::OnDismiss.

```
// This is called whenever the user presses Next, Back, or Finish
// with this step present.  Do all validation & data exchange from
// the dialog in this function.
BOOL CCustom1Dlg::OnDismiss()
{
```

```
    if (!UpdateData(TRUE))
        return FALSE;

    // TODO: Set template variables based on the dialog's data.
    HELLOaw.m_Dictionary["HELLOTEXT"] = m_sHelloText;

    return TRUE;
}
```

Believe it or not, this is it. The new HelloWizard is ready for use as soon as it is recompiled and installed in the MSDEV/TEMPLATE directory. You do not have to worry about installing it there yourself; it is done automatically as the last step of building the project.

Testing the New Custom AppWizard

Does our new HelloWizard work as intended? Nothing is simpler than testing this through creating a new project with its help.

To do so, select New from the File menu and specify a new project workspace. Surprise! If you examine the Type drop-down list, you will find HelloWizard as one of the options there. Select it and give the project a name as well (such as GOODBYE). Make sure the project will be created in a directory that is acceptable to you.

As soon as you click OK in the New Project Workspace dialog, the first (and in the case of HelloWizard, only) page of the new AppWizard appears. Enter the text that the new application should display (see Figure 40.4).

FIGURE 40.4.

Creating an application through HelloWizard.

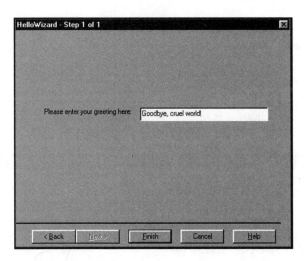

When you dismiss HelloWizard with the Finish button, the New Project Information dialog pops up; in it appears the processed content of confirm.inf (see Figure 40.5). When you click the OK button, the new project is created.

FIGURE 40.5.

*HelloWizard
confirmation
dialog.*

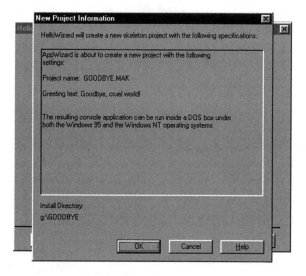

Take a look at the newly created source file, GOODBYE.CPP (shown in Listing 40.6). As you can see, all macro references have been correctly replaced.

Listing 40.6. GOODBYE.CPP, generated by HelloWizard.

```
/////////////////////////////////////////////////////////////////////
// GOODBYE.CPP

#include <afxwin.h>

int WINAPI WinMain(HINSTANCE d1, HINSTANCE d2, LPSTR d3, int d4)
{
    MessageBox(NULL, "Goodbye, cruel world!", "GOODBYE", MB_OK);
    return 0;
}
```

The new application is ready to be compiled.

Other Custom AppWizard Features

Although HelloWizard demonstrates all the major steps of creating a new custom AppWizard, there are a few areas of custom AppWizard development that we have not touched.

AppWizard Classes

Most of the custom AppWizard functionality is implemented through the CCustomAppWiz class. While developing HelloWizard, we have modified the m_Dictionary data member of this class.

In more sophisticated custom AppWizards we can have greater control over how templates are processed by overriding the member functions of this class. For example, by overriding the member function ProcessTemplate, we can modify or completely replace the default AppWizard macro-expansion behavior in a custom AppWizard.

CAppWizStepDlg is a CDialog-derived class that implements the behavior of the AppWizard dialogs. Every AppWizard dialog step has a corresponding CAppWizStepDlg-derived object. Applications usually override the OnDismiss member function of this class (like HelloWizard did) to implement custom behavior, such as updating the contents of the CCustomAppWiz object's dictionary.

When a custom AppWizard project is created, it usually also has another class defined, the CDialogChooser class. This class is not derived from any MFC base class; instead, it serves as a convenient means to access the array of CAppWizStepDlg objects that comprise the custom AppWizard's user interface.

MFCAPWZ.DLL Functions

The AppWizard DLL, MFCAPWZ.DLL, exports a series of functions that custom AppWizards can call. Normally, you do not need to call these functions directly; instead, code that calls them is generated when you first create your custom AppWizard project.

These MFCAPWZ.DLL functions include GetDialog (obtains a pointer to a standard AppWizard step), SetCustomAppWizClass (to provide a pointer to your custom AppWizard class), SetNumberOfSteps, ScanForAvailableLanguages, and SetSupportedLanguages.

Context-Sensitive Help

We neglected to build a help file for HelloWizard despite the fact that our custom AppWizard project already came equipped with a skeleton help file.

The help file must contain a topic for each of the custom AppWizard steps. It must take the form of a WinHelp file; currently, there is no way to integrate a custom AppWizard help file with the Visual C++ help system. The base name of the help file (that is, its filename without the extension) must be identical to the base name of your custom AppWizard (the AWX file). Furthermore, the help file must reside in the same directory as the custom AppWizard (\MSDEV\TEMPLATE).

Debugging a Custom AppWizard

Our HelloWizard was developed in a single edit-compile-run iteration. Not very difficult considering that only a single line of code was added to the AppWizard-generated custom AppWizard project. Unfortunately, real-world projects tend to get complex and messy; otherwise, we wouldn't need symbolic debuggers!

How do you debug a custom AppWizard project when it is a DLL called by the very environment that you would normally use for debugging (that is, the Developer Studio itself)? The answer is obvious: by running a second copy of the Developer Studio. In the Debug tab of the Settings dialog (Build menu), specify the path to the Developer Studio executable (`\MSDEV\BIN\MSDEV.EXE`). Exercise features of your custom AppWizard from this second copy, while using the first copy of Developer Studio as your debugging environment for setting breakpoints, examining the values of variables, or tracing execution.

There is one important difference between the debug version of a custom AppWizard and the debug version of a typical MFC project. As you probably noticed, the custom AppWizard Debug version is labeled Pseudo-Debug. Why this distinction from normal Debug versions?

The reason is that normal Debug targets use a memory allocation that is different from (and incompatible with) the Release target memory allocation mechanism. As you do not have access to the Visual C++ debug binaries, it is necessary to use these Pseudo-Debug targets, which are really Release targets with optimizations disabled and debug information added.

What are the drawbacks of using these types of targets over normal Debug targets? I can think of two such drawbacks. First, not using the Debug memory allocation mechanism makes it less likely that you will catch memory leaks, errors in your custom AppWizard's memory allocation. Second, the ASSERT, VERIFY, and other debugging macros in the release versions of the MFC libraries do nothing; if a condition is encountered that would normally trigger them, you will not see the result. This is not a problem within the custom AppWizard code itself, as the AppWizard-generated custom AppWizard skeleton defines the Pseudo-Debug versions of the appropriate debugging functions.

Of course, if you are really stuck, you can always compile your own version of MFC with similarly defined debugging functions to enable these capabilities in a Pseudo-Debug target.

Custom AppWizard Directives and Macros

There are many custom AppWizard directives and macros that we have not discussed.

In HelloWizard's `confirm.inf` file, we made use of the `$$IF` and `$$ENDIF` directives to add a comment specific to the Intel platform. Other custom AppWizard directives include `$$ELIF`, `$$ELSE`, `$$INCLUDE`, `$$BEGINLOOP`, `$$ENDLOOP`, `$$SET_DEFAULT_LANG`, and `$$//`.

Standard AppWizard macros exist that correspond to each of the standard AppWizard steps. Other standard macros describe the new project, assist in localization (international support), and provide miscellaneous functionality.

Limitations

While the ability to create custom AppWizards is a powerful capability, it is not without some limitations.

The AppWizard technology was initially developed in response to a need to create customized MFC application skeletons. As such, this technology is inherently geared towards constructing MFC applications.

There is no easy way (in other words, I could not find a way that I would not consider a kludge) to directly influence compilation flags in the newly created project file. Thus, whether you like it or not, you are stuck with a project file that assumes your project is an MFC application or DLL. While there is no reason why AppWizard technology could not be used, say, to create console application skeletons, doing so necessitates manual changes to the generated project file after AppWizard has finished its task.

The lack of the capability to directly influence project file settings also imposes other limitations, applicable even for MFC projects. For example, if your project skeleton relies on a nonstandard library, its name must be added to the generated project by the AppWizard user manually; otherwise, compiling the new project will fail.

While these limitations are a matter of fact, they do not diminish the value of custom AppWizards, especially in large organizations. Uses for this capability range from the mundane (such as dropping a company logo on AppWizard-generated dialogs or changing the appearance of the default About dialog) to the sophisticated (such as creating skeletons for components of large, complex projects).

Summary

Custom AppWizards extend the capability of creating project skeletons to skeletons of user-defined project types. The major steps of creating a new custom AppWizard can be summarized as follows:

1. Create a custom AppWizard project using AppWizard. Specify whether you want to base the new AppWizard on standard AppWizard steps, an existing project, or your own custom steps.

2. Modify and add any template files as necessary in your custom AppWizard project's `Template` directory. Add references to any new templates in the `"TEMPLATE"` section of your custom AppWizard's resource file.

3. Create the AppWizard dialogs for your custom AppWizard project. Assign member variables to dialog fields like you would for any dialog based on the `CDialog` class.

4. Modify the `OnDismiss` member function for each of your custom AppWizard dialogs to update the macro dictionary of your custom AppWizard.

5. Add any other code changes as necessary. Recompile your project. The new custom AppWizard will automatically be copied to where it belongs, your `\MSDEV\TEMPLATE` directory, for the Developer Studio to find it there.

6. If necessary, debug your custom AppWizard by launching a second copy of Developer Studio.

7. Write the help file for your custom AppWizard using the help file skeleton that was created for your custom AppWizard project.

The OpenGL Graphics Library

41

OpenGL is a device- and operating system-independent library for three-dimensional graphics and graphics rendering. OpenGL was originally developed by Silicon Graphics, Inc. (SGI) for use on their high-end graphics workstations. Since then, OpenGL has become a widely accepted standard with implementations on many operating system and hardware platforms, including the Windows NT and Windows 95 operating systems.

> **NOTE**
>
> OpenGL support under Windows 95 has just become available recently. The Windows 95 version of the OpenGL development system and redistributable run-time files are available as part of the October 1995 or later release of the Microsoft Developer Library, Level 2. There is no support for OpenGL under Win32s.

In addition to the standard OpenGL Library implementation, Windows also provides a series of functions that integrate OpenGL with the operating system. In particular, functions are provided that associate OpenGL rendering contexts with GDI device contexts. These Windows extensions to the OpenGL Library are identified by names that begin with wgl. In addition to these OpenGL extensions, a series of new Win32 API functions has also been defined to facilitate certain aspects of OpenGL programming.

The OpenGL Library is large and complex. If you wish to have access to a comprehensive set of manuals, you should consider purchasing *The OpenGL Reference Manual* from the OpenGL Architecture Review Board, or *The OpenGL Programming Guide* by Jackie Neider, Tom Davis, and Mason Woo. Both books are published by Addison-Wesley.

In this chapter, in addition to presenting a brief (and far from comprehensive!) overview of the OpenGL Library, I place the focus on using OpenGL from Windows and MFC applications.

OpenGL Overview

The purpose of the OpenGL Library is to render two- and three-dimensional objects into a *frame buffer*, such as the pixel memory of your computer's graphics hardware.

The OpenGL Library is fundamentally procedural. What this means is that in your application, you don't describe what an object looks like; instead, you specify how an object is to be drawn. Complex geometric objects are described in terms of simple elements that your application defines.

The OpenGL Library implementation follows the client-server model. OpenGL clients and servers need not even reside on the same machine.

Basic OpenGL Concepts

At the basic level, the OpenGL Library deals with *vertices*. A vertex is a point, for example the end point of a line, or a corner of a polygon. Vertices can be two- or three-dimensional.

At the next level are *primitives*. Primitives consist of a group of one or more vertices. For example, a rectangle described as a set of four vertices is a primitive.

How vertices are assembled into primitives and how primitives are drawn into a frame buffer are controlled by a variety of settings. For example, applications can specify a three-dimensional transformation matrix that defines how the coordinates of an object are translated into coordinates on the drawing surface.

In addition to its ability to draw points and lines, OpenGL can also draw surfaces, apply lighting specifications, and use texture bitmaps.

Another set of features enables applications to selectively use or discard pixels. For example, drawing a pixel can be made conditional upon properties such as the pixel's depth or its opacity.

A greatly simplified view of how OpenGL works is presented in Figure 41.1.

Initialization

Before the OpenGL Library can be used, a number of initialization steps must be executed.

Every Windows OpenGL application must associate a rendering context with a device context. The device context must be a display device context or a memory device context that is compatible with the display device context. To set up a rendering context, applications must first use the `SetPixelFormat` Win32 function to set up a pixel format for the device; next, they must call `wglCreateContext` with the device context handle as its parameter. If successful, `wglCreateContext` returns a rendering context handle of type `HGLRC`.

> **NOTE**
>
> Windows does not support drawing into a printer device context using the OpenGL Library. If you wish to print an image created with OpenGL, one possible workaround is to draw into a memory device context that is compatible with the display device and then transfer the resulting bitmap to the printer device.

OpenGL under Windows recognizes two types of pixel data modes: RGBA formats and color index-based modes. When the RGBA mode is selected, pixel colors are specified in the form of

RGB color values. When color index mode is selected, pixel colors are selected from the system palette using an index value. These two modes become relevant on palette-based 256-color devices (many VGA-compatible display cards). When your application uses the RGBA mode on such a device, it must manage its own palette and respond to Windows palette notification messages.

FIGURE 41.1.

Simplified overview of OpenGL operations.

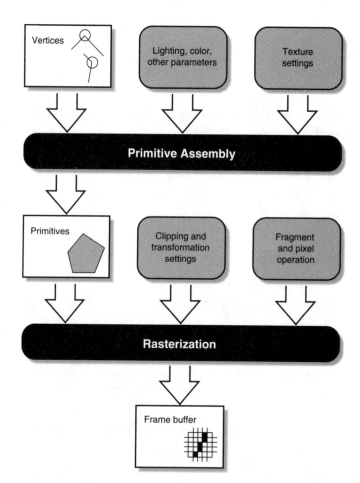

There are specific requirements that must be met by a window that is to be used for OpenGL operations. Specifically, such windows cannot be created using a window class that has the CS_PARENTDC style set. The window itself must have the WS_CLIPCHILDREN and the WS_CLIPSIBLINGS styles in order to be compatible with OpenGL.

Note that to increase your application's performance, you may wish to use a window class that has a null background brush; the window background will be erased through the OpenGL Library anyway.

Before a rendering context can be used, it must be set up as the current context using the wglMakeCurrent function. This function takes two parameters, one of which is a device-context handle. Interestingly, this handle does not need to be identical to the handle used in wglCreateContext—but it must refer to the same device. Thus it is possible, for example, to set up an OpenGL rendering context using a device-context handle returned by GetDC, but use wglMakeCurrent with a device-context handle returned by BeginPaint.

Once a rendering context is ready to accept commands, you may wish to send additional initialization commands; for example, you may wish to erase the frame buffer before drawing, set up coordinate transformations, configure light sources, or enable and disable other options.

One initialization step that cannot be omitted is the call to the glViewport function. Through this function, you can set up or modify the size of the rendering viewport. Typically, you should call this function once when the rendering context is initialized, and subsequently every time your application receives a WM_SIZE message indicating that its window size has changed.

Drawing with OpenGL

Most OpenGL drawing consists of a series of vertex operations enclosed between a pair of glBegin and glEnd calls. The glBegin call identifies the type of primitive that subsequent vertex operations define; glEnd marks the end of constructing the primitive. For example, the following series of calls constructs a pentagon:

```
glBegin(GL_POLYGON);
glVertex2d(0.0, 1.0);
glVertex2d(-0.951057, 0.309017);
glVertex2d(-0.587785, -0.809017);
glVertex2d(0.587785, -0.809017);
glVertex2d(0.951057, 0.309017);
glEnd();
```

The glBegin function can be used to define a variety of primitives. Table 41.1 lists the allowable parameters for this function.

Table 41.1. Primitives constructed through glBegin.

glBegin *Parameter*	*Description*
GL_POINTS	A series of points
GL_LINES	A series of lines
GL_LINE_STRIP	A connected group of line segments
GL_LINE_LOOP	A connected, closed group of line segments
GL_TRIANGLES	A set of triangles
GL_TRIANGLE_STRIP	A set of connected triangles
GL_TRIANGLE_FAN	A set of connected triangles

continues

Table 41.1. continued

`glBegin` *Parameter*	*Description*
`GL_QUADS`	A set of quadrilaterals
`GL_QUAD_STRIP`	A set of connected quadrilaterals
`GL_POLYGON`	A polygon

In the case when `glBegin` defines a set of connected primitives, specific rules govern how vertices of a primitive are reused as vertices of the subsequent primitive. For example, if `GL_LINE_STRIP` is specified, the vertex representing the end point of a line segment also becomes the starting point of the next line segment.

Additional Libraries

In addition to basic OpenGL functions, Microsoft's OpenGL implementation provides two additional OpenGL libraries.

The OpenGL Utility Library (GLU) contains a series of functions that deal with texture support; coordinate transformation; rendering of spheres, disks, and cylinders; B-spline curves and surfaces; and error handling. Additionally, the GLU Library provides *polygon tessellation* functions; these functions can be used to break down complex or concave polygons into simple convex polygons (the only kind that OpenGL can handle).

The OpenGL Programming Guide Auxiliary Library (GLAUX), in addition to providing functions for handling several three-dimensional objects, also provides functions to manage and run an OpenGL application. These functions are most useful for quick porting OpenGL applications from other environments. In particular, these functions provide basic window management, implement a simple message loop, and provide a window procedure for basic message handling. However, these library functions are not intended for use in production applications.

Writing OpenGL Windows Applications in C

Now for a look at a very simple OpenGL application. This application, shown in Listing 41.1, displays a cube. The cube is slightly rotated to show a three-dimensional appearance, and is lit from the side. In its simplicity, this application is the OpenGL version of a Windows Hello, World application.

Listing 41.1. A simple OpenGL application.

```
#include <windows.h>
#include <GL/gl.h>
#include <GL/glu.h>

HGLRC hglrc;

void DrawHello(HWND hwnd)
{
    HDC hDC;
    PAINTSTRUCT paintStruct;
    RECT clientRect;
    GLfloat lightPos[4] = {-1.0F, 2.0F, 0.2F, 0.0F};

    hDC = BeginPaint(hwnd, &paintStruct);
    if (hDC != NULL)
    {
        GetClientRect(hwnd, &clientRect);
        wglMakeCurrent(hDC, hglrc);
        glViewport(0, 0, clientRect.right, clientRect.bottom);
        glLoadIdentity();
        glClear(GL_COLOR_BUFFER_BIT);
        glColor4d(1.0, 1.0, 1.0, 1.0);
        glRotated(30.0, 0.0, 1.0, 0.0);
        glRotated(15.0, 1.0, 0.0, 0.0);
        glEnable(GL_LIGHTING);
        glEnable(GL_LIGHT0);
        glLightfv(GL_LIGHT0, GL_POSITION, lightPos);

        glBegin(GL_QUADS);

        glNormal3d(0.0, -1.0, 0.0);
        glVertex3d(0.5, -0.5, 0.5);
        glVertex3d(-0.5, -0.5, 0.5);
        glVertex3d(-0.5, -0.5, -0.5);
        glVertex3d(0.5, -0.5, -0.5);

        glNormal3d(0.0, 0.0, -1.0);
        glVertex3d(-0.5, -0.5, -0.5);
        glVertex3d(-0.5, 0.5, -0.5);
        glVertex3d(0.5, 0.5, -0.5);
        glVertex3d(0.5, -0.5, -0.5);

        glNormal3d(1.0, 0.0, 0.0);
        glVertex3d(0.5, -0.5, -0.5);
        glVertex3d(0.5, 0.5, -0.5);
        glVertex3d(0.5, 0.5, 0.5);
        glVertex3d(0.5, -0.5, 0.5);

        glNormal3d(0.0, 0.0, 1.0);
        glVertex3d(-0.5, -0.5, 0.5);
        glVertex3d(-0.5, 0.5, 0.5);
        glVertex3d(0.5, 0.5, 0.5);
        glVertex3d(0.5, -0.5, 0.5);
```

continues

Listing 41.1. continued

```
        glNormal3d(-1.0, 0.0, 0.0);
        glVertex3d(-0.5, -0.5, 0.5);
        glVertex3d(-0.5, 0.5, 0.5);
        glVertex3d(-0.5, 0.5, -0.5);
        glVertex3d(-0.5, -0.5, -0.5);

        glNormal3d(0.0, 1.0, 0.0);
        glVertex3d(-0.5, 0.5, 0.5);
        glVertex3d(0.5, 0.5, 0.5);
        glVertex3d(0.5, 0.5, -0.5);
        glVertex3d(-0.5, 0.5, -0.5);

        glEnd();
        glFlush();
        wglMakeCurrent(NULL, NULL);
        EndPaint(hwnd, &paintStruct);
    }
}

LRESULT CALLBACK WndProc(HWND hwnd, UINT uMsg,
                         WPARAM wParam, LPARAM lParam)
{
    switch(uMsg)
    {
        case WM_PAINT:
            DrawHello(hwnd);
            break;
        case WM_DESTROY:
            PostQuitMessage(0);
            break;
        default:
            return DefWindowProc(hwnd, uMsg, wParam, lParam);
    }
    return 0;
}

int WINAPI WinMain(HINSTANCE hInstance, HINSTANCE hPrevInstance,
                   LPSTR d3, int nCmdShow)
{
    MSG msg;
    HWND hwnd;
    WNDCLASS wndClass;
    HDC hDC;
    PIXELFORMATDESCRIPTOR pfd;
    int iPixelFormat;

    if (hPrevInstance == NULL)
    {
        memset(&wndClass, 0, sizeof(wndClass));
        wndClass.style = CS_HREDRAW | CS_VREDRAW;
        wndClass.lpfnWndProc = WndProc;
        wndClass.hInstance = hInstance;
        wndClass.hCursor = LoadCursor(NULL, IDC_ARROW);
        wndClass.lpszClassName = "HELLO";
        if (!RegisterClass(&wndClass)) return FALSE;
```

```
        }
        hwnd = CreateWindow("HELLO", "HELLO",
                WS_OVERLAPPEDWINDOW | WS_CLIPCHILDREN | WS_CLIPSIBLINGS,
                            CW_USEDEFAULT, 0, CW_USEDEFAULT, 0,
                            NULL, NULL, hInstance, NULL);
        hDC = GetDC(hwnd);
        memset(&pfd, 0, sizeof(pfd));
        pfd.nSize = sizeof(pfd);
        pfd.nVersion = 1;
        pfd.dwFlags = PFD_DRAW_TO_WINDOW | PFD_SUPPORT_OPENGL;
        pfd.iPixelType = PFD_TYPE_RGBA;
        pfd.iLayerType = PFD_MAIN_PLANE;
        pfd.cDepthBits = 16;
        iPixelFormat = ChoosePixelFormat(hDC, &pfd);
        SetPixelFormat(hDC, iPixelFormat, &pfd);
        hglrc = wglCreateContext(hDC);
        ReleaseDC(hwnd, hDC);
        ShowWindow(hwnd, nCmdShow);
        UpdateWindow(hwnd);
        while (GetMessage(&msg, NULL, 0, 0))
            DispatchMessage(&msg);
        wglMakeCurrent(NULL, NULL);
        wglDeleteContext(hglrc);
        return msg.wParam;
}
```

The following sections explain this application's method of operation.

Note that for the sake of simplicity, I did not include any palette initialization in this application. For this reason, the application may not behave properly on systems configured for 16 or 256 colors.

OpenGL Initialization

The first series of OpenGL calls in this application begins in WinMain, immediately after the application's window has been created. After obtaining a device-context handle for the client area of this window, the device context's pixel format is set to a pixel format obtained through ChoosePixelFormat. The ChoosePixelFormat function can be used to identify pixel formats for a specific device that best match a set of required characteristics.

Note that although we are using the RGBA data mode, this application does not handle palette notification messages. This is done in order to keep the application as simple as possible; in a production application, you would certainly not want to omit creating and managing a palette that is appropriate for your application.

After the pixel format has been specified, a rendering context is created by a call to wglCreateContext. The rendering context handle is saved in a global variable that will be accessed from within other functions.

When all initializations have been completed, the application enters its message loop. After the message loop terminates, cleanup is performed by calling wglMakeCurrent and wglDeleteContext before the application terminates.

The Window Procedure

The application's simple window procedure processes only two messages: WM_PAINT and WM_DESTROY. When a WM_PAINT message is received, the window procedure calls the DrawHello function; it is in this function where OpenGL drawing operations take place.

The first step in DrawHello is to select the rendering context as the current context and set the viewport size by calling glViewport. The viewport size was obtained by a call to the Win32 GetClientRect function. Next, the frame buffer is erased, and an identity transformation matrix is loaded.

The transformation matrix is changed by two subsequent rotations, specified by calls to glRotated. The first call rotates the view around the vertical axis. The second call tips the view forward by rotating it around the horizontal axis. As a result, we will see the cube from a viewpoint somewhat above and to the left of the cube.

The rotations are followed by calls that enable lighting mode and specify a light source. The code specifies a single light source that illuminates the cube from the left and above.

With all this initialization work complete, actual drawing can begin. A series of six quadrilaterals is drawn, representing the six sides of the cube. For each of the quadrilaterals, the normal vector is defined by a separate call to glNormal3d. When the construction of the six primitives is complete, a call to glFlush is used to ensure that all OpenGL operations are complete, and then the device context is released and the function returns.

Compiling and Running the Application

This application can be compiled simply from the command line. I called the source file cube.c; to compile this file, type the following:

```
cl cube.c user32.lib gdi32.lib opengl32.lib
```

Note that applications that use the GLU Library or the GLAUX Library must also specify glaux.lib or glu32.lib on the command line. And because OpenGL is computation-intensive, it might be a useful idea to compile with the appropriate optimization flags set.

The application should display a window with a three-dimensional image of a cube rendered in it, similar to that shown in Figure 41.2.

FIGURE 41.2.

Running the
cube.exe
Windows
application.

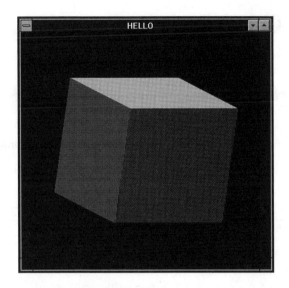

OpenGL in MFC Applications

The OpenGL Library can easily be utilized from MFC applications as well. To enable the OpenGL libraries, add the appropriate library names to your project settings (Figure 41.3).

FIGURE 41.3.

Adding the
OpenGL libraries
to MFC project
settings.

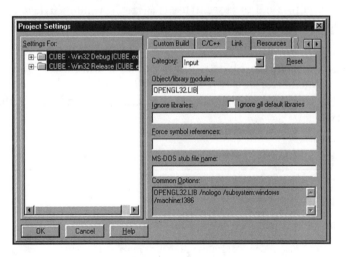

When initializing the OpenGL Library in an MFC application, it is important to remember which window you wish to use for a rendering context. For example, if it is a view window that will serve as the rendering context, it is this window that should be used when the OpenGL rendering context is created.

OpenGL Initialization

The MFC OpenGL application I created is based on an AppWizard-generated single document interface application skeleton.

In this application, we draw a cube identical to the cube drawn in the C application discussed earlier. The cube is drawn into the application's view window. Accordingly, the first task after creating the application's skeleton is to modify the view class's `PreCreateWindow` member function, to ensure that the view window is created with the appropriate flags.

The modified version of this function is shown in Listing 41.2.

Listing 41.2. Modified version of `CCubeView::PreCreateWindow`.

```
BOOL CCUBEView::PreCreateWindow(CREATESTRUCT& cs)
{
    // TODO: Modify the Window class or styles here by modifying
    //   the CREATESTRUCT cs

    cs.style |= WS_CLIPSIBLINGS | WS_CLIPCHILDREN;
    return CView::PreCreateWindow(cs);
}
```

As you can see, the change to this function is simple; it consists only of adding the `WS_CLIPSIBLINGS` and `WS_CLIPCHILDREN` flags to the window style to ensure proper operation of the OpenGL libraries.

Much more extensive initialization work is performed in the view class's `OnCreate` member function. This member function must be added using ClassWizard or the WizardBar, as a handler function for `WM_CREATE` messages. The implementation of this function, shown in Listing 41.3, creates a rendering context after setting a pixel format for the view window's device context.

Listing 41.3. Implementation of `CCubeView::OnCreate`.

```
int CCUBEView::OnCreate(LPCREATESTRUCT lpCreateStruct)
{
    PIXELFORMATDESCRIPTOR pfd;
    int iPixelFormat;
    CDC *pDC;

    if (CView::OnCreate(lpCreateStruct) == -1)
        return -1;

    // TODO: Add your specialized creation code here

    pDC = GetDC();
    memset(&pfd, 0, sizeof(pfd));
    pfd.nSize = sizeof(pfd);
```

```
    pfd.nVersion = 1;
    pfd.dwFlags = PFD_DRAW_TO_WINDOW | PFD_SUPPORT_OPENGL;
    pfd.iPixelType = PFD_TYPE_RGBA;
    pfd.iLayerType = PFD_MAIN_PLANE;
    pfd.cDepthBits = 16;
    iPixelFormat = ChoosePixelFormat(pDC->m_hDC, &pfd);
    SetPixelFormat(pDC->m_hDC, iPixelFormat, &pfd);
    m_hglrc = wglCreateContext(pDC->m_hDC);
    ReleaseDC(pDC);

    return 0;
}
```

The rendering context handle is stored in the member variable m_hglrc. This member variable should be added to the declaration of the view class in the Attributes section, as follows:

```
class CCUBEView : public CView
{
    ...
// Attributes
public:
    CCUBEDoc* GetDocument();
    HGLRC m_hglrc;
    ...
```

Drawing the Cube

The actual drawing of the cube is performed in the OnDraw member function of the view class. This member function, shown in Listing 41.4, is very similar to the DrawHello function of the C application presented earlier in this chapter. After making the rendering context current, the function performs a series of initializations, including setting the size of the viewport, applying coordinate transformations, and setting up lighting. Afterwards, four quadrilaterals that together comprise the cube are drawn.

Listing 41.4. Implementation of CCubeView::OnDraw.

```
void CCUBEView::OnDraw(CDC* pDC)
{
    CRect clientRect;
    GLfloat lightPos[4] = {-1.0F, 2.0F, 0.2F, 0.0F};

    CCUBEDoc* pDoc = GetDocument();
    ASSERT_VALID(pDoc);

    // TODO: add draw code for native data here
    GetClientRect(&clientRect);
    wglMakeCurrent(pDC->m_hDC, m_hglrc);
    glViewport(0, 0, clientRect.right, clientRect.bottom);
    glLoadIdentity();
    glClear(GL_COLOR_BUFFER_BIT);
    glColor4d(1.0, 1.0, 1.0, 1.0);
```

continues

Listing 41.4. continued

```
    glRotated(30.0, 0.0, 1.0, 0.0);
    glRotated(15.0, 1.0, 0.0, 0.0);
    glEnable(GL_LIGHTING);
    glEnable(GL_LIGHT0);
    glLightfv(GL_LIGHT0, GL_POSITION, lightPos);

    glBegin(GL_QUADS);

    glNormal3d(0.0, -1.0, 0.0);
    glVertex3d(0.5, -0.5, 0.5);
    glVertex3d(-0.5, -0.5, 0.5);
    glVertex3d(-0.5, -0.5, -0.5);
    glVertex3d(0.5, -0.5, -0.5);

    glNormal3d(0.0, 0.0, -1.0);
    glVertex3d(-0.5, -0.5, -0.5);
    glVertex3d(-0.5, 0.5, -0.5);
    glVertex3d(0.5, 0.5, -0.5);
    glVertex3d(0.5, -0.5, -0.5);

    glNormal3d(1.0, 0.0, 0.0);
    glVertex3d(0.5, -0.5, -0.5);
    glVertex3d(0.5, 0.5, -0.5);
    glVertex3d(0.5, 0.5, 0.5);
    glVertex3d(0.5, -0.5, 0.5);

    glNormal3d(0.0, 0.0, 1.0);
    glVertex3d(-0.5, -0.5, 0.5);
    glVertex3d(-0.5, 0.5, 0.5);
    glVertex3d(0.5, 0.5, 0.5);
    glVertex3d(0.5, -0.5, 0.5);

    glNormal3d(-1.0, 0.0, 0.0);
    glVertex3d(-0.5, -0.5, 0.5);
    glVertex3d(-0.5, 0.5, 0.5);
    glVertex3d(-0.5, 0.5, -0.5);
    glVertex3d(-0.5, -0.5, -0.5);

    glNormal3d(0.0, 1.0, 0.0);
    glVertex3d(-0.5, 0.5, 0.5);
    glVertex3d(0.5, 0.5, 0.5);
    glVertex3d(0.5, 0.5, -0.5);
    glVertex3d(-0.5, 0.5, -0.5);

    glEnd();
    glFlush();
    wglMakeCurrent(NULL, NULL);
}
```

Note that this implementation does not take into account the fact that the MFC framework also calls the view class's OnDraw function when drawing into a printer-device context. In its present state, attempts to use this application for printing will fail.

Running the Application

To run the application, compile and execute it from the Build menu. The application's window should appear similar to that shown in Figure 41.4.

FIGURE 41.4.

Running the
cube.exe MFC
application.

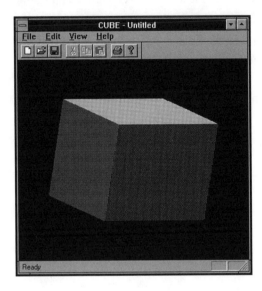

Note that this application, as its non-MFC counterpart, includes no palette initialization and may not work properly on systems configured with 16 or 256 colors.

Summary

OpenGL is a library of high-quality three-dimensional graphics and rendering functions. The library's device- and platform-independence make it a library of choice for developing portable graphical applications.

OpenGL drawings are constructed from primitives; primitives are simple items such as lines or polygons, which in turn are composed of vertices.

The OpenGL Library assembles primitives from vertices while taking into account a variety of settings, such as color, lighting, and texture. Primitives are then processed in accordance with transformations, clipping settings, and other parameters; at the end of the rasterization process is pixel data deposited into a frame buffer.

The Windows implementation of the OpenGL Library consists of the core library, utility functions (GLU), and auxiliary functions (GLAUX). The auxiliary library can be used to easily create simple stand-alone OpenGL applications, as it implements a message loop and a window procedure internally. However, due to the simplicity of implementation, this library should not be used in production applications.

Windows also provides a set of extension functions (WGL) that facilitate the use of OpenGL functions in the context of the Windows GDI. Furthermore, a set of new functions has been added to the Win32 API to support pixel formats and OpenGL double buffering.

The main steps of creating a Windows OpenGL application are as follows:

1. Ensure that your window class is not created with the CS_PARENTDC style. Ensure that your window is created with the styles WM_CLIPCHILDREN and WM_CLIPSIBLINGS set.

2. Create an OpenGL rendering context; a good spot for doing so is in the WM_CREATE handler function for the window that you intend to use with OpenGL.

3. Add appropriate calls in your handler for WM_PAINT messages to draw the OpenGL image.

4. Optionally, add a handler for WM_SIZE messages to reflect changes in the viewport size. Use glViewport to set the viewport size.

5. If you plan to run your application on 256-color devices, add handling for custom palettes.

Telephony Applications with TAPI

42

The Microsoft Telephony API, or TAPI, provides telephony-related services for Win32 applications. TAPI is currently supported on the Windows 3.1 and Windows 95 platforms. In this chapter, we discuss TAPI 1.4, the version that is provided with Windows 95. TAPI is used extensively by those Windows 95 applications that use a modem; for example, the FAX driver and the CompuServe driver in Microsoft Exchange, the Microsoft Network software, or the Windows 95 Phone Dialer and Hyperterminal applications.

TAPI Overview

First, an important note. When most of us hear the term *telephony* in the context of computer communications, we think of data or FAX modems and voice grade telephone lines—and very little else. TAPI goes far beyond these simple concepts and provides a consistent programming interface for a variety of devices operating on voice grade lines, ISDN lines, and private branch exchanges. The devices include modems, FAX modems, voice capable modems, computer-controlled telephone sets, and more.

TAPI provides services for placing outgoing calls, accepting incoming calls, and managing calls and devices. What TAPI does not do is handle the *media stream*; that is, the data that is exchanged during a call. For example, when TAPI is used to place a voice call, it is not TAPI but you, the human operator, who talks; similarly, when TAPI is used to place a data call, it is the communication application that takes over the device and performs I/O operations using standard Win32 file functions.

Assisted TAPI: The Simplest TAPI Application

Before we delve deeper into the TAPI architecture, take a look at the simple program in Listing 42.1. This is about as simple as a TAPI application can get. This program takes a single command-line argument, a telephone number, and dials that number for a voice call.

Listing 42.1. The simplest TAPI application.

```
#include <windows.h>
#include <stdio.h>
#include <tapi.h>

void main(int argc, char *argv[])
{
    if (argc != 2) printf("Usage: %s telephone-number\n", argv[0]);
    else
    {
        printf("Dialing %s...", argv[1]);
        tapiRequestMakeCall(argv[1], NULL, NULL, NULL);
    }
}
```

The actual dialing is performed on behalf of the application by the default *call control application*. An example for a call control application is the Phone Dialer that is provided as part of Windows 95.

The `tapiRequestMakeCall` function that is used in this program is ideally suited for use in scripts. For example, a call to this function can be included as an external DLL call in Visual Basic for Applications.

To compile this application from the command line, type `cl dial.c tapi32.lib`.

The `tapiRequestMakeCall` function is part of TAPI's *Assisted Telephony* features. In the current version of TAPI, there is only one other Assisted Telephony function: the `tapiGetLocationInfo` function can be used to obtain the country code and city code for the user's current location.

TAPI Concepts

TAPI provides a series of *personal telephony* services. Telephony, in this context, refers to technology in general that connects computers with the telephone network.

TAPI services provide for all aspects of usage of the telephone network. This includes connecting to the network, placing and accepting calls, call management features (such as transferring calls, setting up conference calls), use of calling number identification (Caller ID) for identifying incoming calls, and more.

TAPI services are divided into basic, supplementary, and extended services. Basic services are generally supported by all devices; supplementary services may only be available on special devices. Extended services are provider-specific.

For example, TAPI can place a call on all telephone lines; however, call management functions, such as transferring a call, may only be available on devices that specifically support such a feature, and thus is considered a supplementary service.

TAPI is not restricted to what is whimsically referred to by the acronym POTS: Plain Old Telephone Service. POTS is analog service on the *local loop* (the wire connecting the telephone set with the nearest switching office). POTS supports voice calls with a 3.1 kHz bandwidth, or data calls at speeds up to 28.8 kbps using V.34 modems.

In contrast, ISDN (Integrated Services Digital Network) supports up to 128 kbps with its *Basic Rate Interface* (BRI-ISDN); the speed on PRI-ISDN (Primary Rate Interface) is much higher. TAPI supports ISDN as well as other connection types, such as switched 56, or T1/E1. TAPI can also utilize CENTREX features and the features of Private Branch Exchanges (PBXs).

TAPI Devices

TAPI makes a distinction between *line devices* and *phone devices*. A line device is the abstract representation of a physical device that connects your computer to the telephone network. Examples of line devices include modems, FAX modems, or ISDN cards.

A phone device is the abstract representation of a device with the capabilities of a telephone set. A phone device may have a speaker, a microphone, lamps, a display, buttons, and so on. A phone device is not necessarily a physical device; a software emulation that uses the computer's speaker, microphone, sound card hardware, and a voice-capable modem and displays a telephone-like interface on the screen can also act as a phone device.

Figure 42.1 shows a basic configuration consisting of a line device (a data modem) and a phone device (a programmable telephone under TAPI control). Note that the presence of a telephone set does not imply the existence of a TAPI phone device. For example, if you have a plain telephone set that is used in conjunction with a dialer that responds to the Hayes AT command set (or a modem used as a dialer) this configuration is represented by a line device. A phone device is used when TAPI has control over some of the features of the telephone set such as its display, switchhook, ringer, or buttons.

FIGURE 42.1.

TAPI devices.

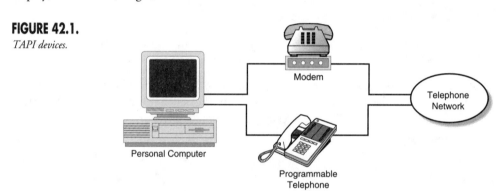

Modem

Telephone Network

Personal Computer

Programmable Telephone

Line devices all provide a basic set of functions (Basic Telephony). In contrast, all phone device functions are part of Supplementary Telephony; this is because there is no minimum set of functions that a phone device is expected to provide.

TAPI Addresses

TAPI distinguishes between the concepts of a line and that of an *address*. The line is the physical entity; the address is, for example, a telephone number assigned to the line.

Although most POTS lines are associated with a single telephone number, this is not always the case. For example, an ordinary telephone line may be configured with more than one telephone number using the telephone company's distinctive ringing service. On digital lines, the use of more than one address on a single line is more common.

A unique feature of telephone numbers is that their actual format is relative to the originating location. Take, for example, a number here in Ottawa, such as 613-555-1234. When I dial this number locally, all I need to dial is the seven digits of the local number, 555-1234. If I call this number from New York City, I need to dial 1-613-555-1234. Calling the same number from Budapest, Hungary, requires dialing 00w1-613-555-1234, where the letter *w* represents waiting for a second dial tone. Calling the same number from a telephone set attached to the PBX of a local company may require dialing the digits 8-555-1234. These differences become especially relevant on portable computers.

TAPI does an excellent job translating telephone numbers. At the heart of its capability is the *canonical address format*. The syntax of a canonical address is as follows:

```
+CountryCode Space [(AreaCode) Space] SubscriberNumber
[¦ SubAddress] [^ Name] CRLF
```

For example, the canonical format of the Ottawa number 555-1234 is as follows:

```
+1 (613) 555-1234
```

The canonical address differs from a *dialable address*. Dialable addresses are those that do not begin with the character +; these numbers are presumed to be dialable on the given line without modification. A canonical address can be translated into a dialable address by the `lineTranslateAddress` TAPI function. The syntax for a dialable number is as follows:

```
DialableNumber [¦ SubAddress] [^ Name] CRLF
```

Dialable addresses can contain, in addition to digits, the DTMF symbols A-D, # (DTMF "gate"), and * (DTMF "star"), and any of a variety of dial modifier characters. Dial modifier characters are based on the Hayes AT command set and include the characters shown in Table 42.1.

Table 42.1. Dial modifier characters used in dialable addresses.

Dial Modifier Character	Description
! (exclamation mark)	flash switchhook
P or p	pulse dial for subsequent digits
T or t	tone dial for subsequent digits
, (comma)	pause
w or W	wait for dial tone
@	wait for quiet answer
$	wait for billing signal
;	indicates incomplete dialable number

TAPI Software Architecture

At the heart of TAPI is the TAPI DLL, the dynamic link library that offers TAPI services to applications. This DLL serves as a layer between telephony applications and TAPI service providers. One such service provider is the UNIMODEM driver; this Universal Modem driver is supplied with Windows 95 and provides TAPI services for modems compatible with the Hayes AT command set.

This basic TAPI architecture is shown in Figure 42.2. In addition to the TAPI DLL and the telephony service providers (drivers), another important, albeit invisible, component of TAPI is the executable program `tapiexe.exe`. This program plays an important role when TAPI sends notifications to the calling application via callback functions.

FIGURE 42.2.

The TAPI software architecture.

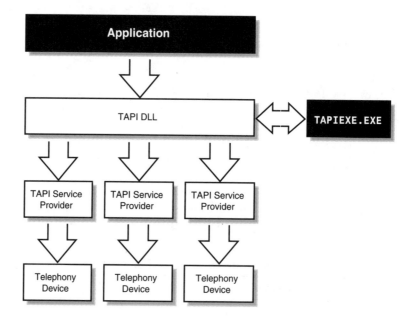

Synchronous and Asynchronous Operations

Many TAPI operations are synchronous; that is, when the TAPI function returns, the operation is either completed or failed, in which case an error code is returned. However, some TAPI operations are asynchronous; the TAPI function returns indicating whether the TAPI operation has been successfully initiated, but the operation is completed in another thread, and the application is notified via a callback function. The callback function is registered with TAPI when the TAPI library is initialized.

The actual callback mechanism deserves a closer examination, especially because it has some consequences as to how TAPI functions operate.

When a service provider wishes to place a notification, it calls the TAPI DLL. In effect, it requests that the DLL notify all concerned applications that a specific event has taken place. This first call to the TAPI DLL takes place in the execution context of the service provider.

The TAPI DLL in turn sends a message to `tapiexe.exe`. This executable program calls the TAPI DLL itself, this time in its own execution context. This call instructs the TAPI DLL to post a Windows message to the applications that need to be modified.

When the application receives and processes the message in its message loop, the message is dispatched to the TAPI DLL again, this time in the application's execution context. The TAPI DLL may in turn call the application's registered TAPI callback function to notify the application of a TAPI event.

The TAPI notification mechanism is shown in Figure 42.3.

FIGURE 42.3.

Processing of TAPI events.

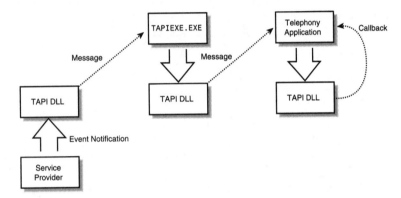

This mechanism has important implications for the architecture of TAPI applications. For one thing, the scenario described here makes it clear that TAPI applications must have a message loop in order to process notifications correctly. Although the use of a callback function may imply that a message loop is unnecessary, this is not the case; the callback function is only called after the application receives a Windows message that the TAPI DLL processes.

Another consequence concerns the use of multiple threads. It is important to realize that in order for TAPI to operate as expected, threads that call asynchronous TAPI functions must have a message loop. The callback function is called in the context of the thread making the asynchronous call; this cannot happen unless the thread processes Windows messages.

While the need for a message loop does not completely rule out the use of TAPI with console applications, it places certain restrictions on them. The console application must have a message loop that processes and dispatches Windows messages. The example presented later in this chapter (Listing 42.2) demonstrates the use of this technique.

Variable-Length Structures

Everywhere throughout TAPI, variable-length structures are frequently used. These structures represent data that is variable in length, such as optional fields or strings.

All TAPI variable-length structures make use of structure members dwTotalSize, dwNeededSize, and dwUsedSize. When a TAPI function is called that is expected to return data in such a structure, your first task is to allocate the structure and fill its dwTotalSize member prior to making the call.

The TAPI documentation refers to structures of this kind as *flattened.* Instead of referred to through pointers, supplementary data fields and variable-length fields are simply appended to the end of the structure. Variable-length fields are referred to in the structure by an offset and a length parameter; the offset specifies the starting position of the field, in bytes, relative to the start of the structure; the length represents the length of the field in bytes.

Suppose a TAPI function called tapiStrangeFunc returns variable-length data in a VARSTRUCT structure. This structure is declared as follows:

```
typedef struct
{
    DWORD dwTotalSize;
    DWORD dwNeededSize;
    DWORD dwUsedSize;
    // other fixed-length elements here
    DWORD dwVarItem1Size;
    DWORD dwVarItem1Offset;
    // more fixed-length elements here
    DWORD dwVarItem2Size;
    DWORD dwVarItem2Offset;
} VARSTRUCT, FAR *LPVARSTRUCT;
```

Before tapiStrangeFunc is called, you must allocate a VARSTRUCT structure. Although you can allocate it as an automatic variable, doing so is not recommended. Instead, use the following mechanism:

```
LPVARSTRUCT pVarStruct;
pVarStruct = (LPVARSTRUCT)malloc(sizeof(pVarStruct));
pVarStruct->dwTotalSize = sizeof(VARSTRUCT);
tapiStrangeFunc(pVarStruct);
```

The description of tapiStrangeFunc may tell you that this function appends an extra DWORD member to this structure. Clearly, this extra member requires additional memory—and so do the two variable-length items identified by the members dwVarItem1Size/dwVarItem1Offset, and dwVarItem2Size/dwVarItem2Offset.

When tapiStrangeFunc returns, this fact is indicated by the value of the dwNeededSize structure member. This member will indicate that additional memory is needed to return all values. A possible response to this would be a reallocation of the structure, and another call to tapiStrangeFunc:

```
pVarStruct = (LPVARSTRUCT)malloc((LPVOID)pVarStruct,
                        pVarStruct->dwNeededSize);
pVarStruct->dwTotalSize = pVarStruct->dwNeededSize;
tapiStrangeFunc(pVarStruct);
```

When this call to tapiStrangeFunc returns, pVarStruct points to a structure in memory as shown in Figure 42.4.

FIGURE 42.4.

An example for a TAPI variable-length structure.

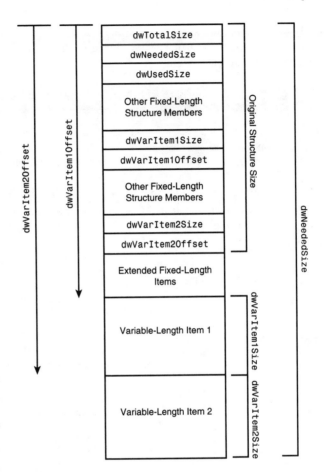

The dwUsedSize field is somewhat of a lesser significance; it comes into play when TAPI could not fill in all the structure members (dwTotalSize was less than dwNeededSize). In this case, rather than truncating a variable-length field, TAPI simply leaves that field empty.

TAPI Services

In addition to the Assisted TAPI services that we have seen already, TAPI provides services that fall into three categories: Basic Telephony, Supplementary Telephony, and Extended Telephony.

Basic Telephony includes all functions that a POTS line can be expected to provide. This minimal set of functions must be supported by all service providers.

Supplementary Telephony includes all standard TAPI services that are not in the Basic Telephony set of functions. These include supplementary services found on most PBXs, such as hold, call transfer, conference calls, and so on. An application can query the set of supplementary services supported by a particular line device or phone device by calling `lineGetDevCaps`, `lineGetAddressCaps`, or `phoneGetDevCaps`.

> **NOTE**
>
> Because there is no minimum set of services that phone devices are expected to support, all phone device services are in the Supplementary Telephony category.

Extended TAPI services are provider-specific. These include all device-specific TAPI extensions. TAPI provides the necessary mechanisms for extending services through variable-length structures, and functions through which service providers can inform applications about the extended services they support.

The TAPI Programming Model

The basic TAPI programming model for line devices is illustrated in Figure 42.5.

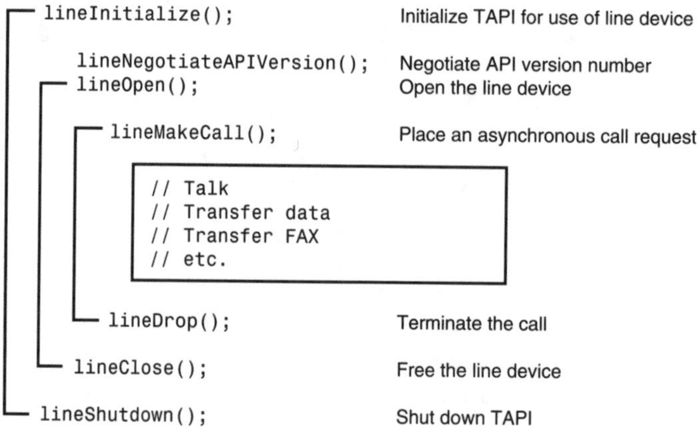

FIGURE 42.5.

The TAPI programming model: calls in a typical TAPI application.

```
  lineInitialize();                          Initialize TAPI for use of line device

      lineNegotiateAPIVersion();             Negotiate API version number
      lineOpen();                            Open the line device

          lineMakeCall();                    Place an asynchronous call request

              // Talk
              // Transfer data
              // Transfer FAX
              // etc.

          lineDrop();                        Terminate the call
      lineClose();                           Free the line device
  lineShutdown();                            Shut down TAPI
```

All TAPI applications that utilize line devices begin by a call to `lineInitialize`. This call initializes TAPI for use with line devices. Note that this call should not be made unless the application actually intends to utilize TAPI services; making this call unnecessarily may use up valuable TAPI resources and cause other applications to fail.

One parameter to `lineInitialize` is the address of a callback function. It is through this function that the application is informed of the completion of asynchronous function requests and other TAPI events.

Before an application can open a specific line device, it must negotiate a TAPI version number by calling `lineNegotiateAPIVersion`. Through this call, the application and the service provider handling the specific device can agree on a version number they can both support. Note that the current TAPI version number is 1.4; only this and an earlier 16-bit version, 1.3, are presently in existence.

The line device is opened by calling `lineOpen`. Afterwards, applications can call a variety of functions that use the open device. One example is the `lineMakeCall` function that is used to place a call on the line device. This function is also an example for an asynchronous function; it returns immediately after the call request has been successfully placed. The application is notified of the completion of the call request through its callback function.

After the call has been placed, an application can do a variety of things with the line depending on its intended function. A number of additional functions can be used to obtain information about the line and the call, configure the line, and manipulate addresses. Supplementary functions can be used to transfer the call, place it on hold, set up conference calls, and so on.

A specific feature offered by TAPI assists data communication applications in particular. Such applications may use the TAPI `lineGetID` function to obtain a handle to the communication device. This handle is opened by TAPI for overlapped I/O and can be used by the application for exchanging data with a remote host.

Using `lineMakeCall` is not the only way to establish a call. Applications may also obtain a call handle by accepting incoming calls. Applications that are set up to accept incoming calls are notified of such calls through their callback function.

When the application wishes to terminate the call, it can use the `lineDrop` function. A call may also be terminated by the remote end; in this case, the application is notified through its callback function.

When the application is finished using the line device, it should call the `lineClose` function to close the device. The `lineShutdown` function can be used to terminate the application's session with TAPI.

The programming model used for phone devices is similar. The key steps of initializing TAPI, negotiating a version number, and opening the device are present. There is no equivalent to placing a call on a phone device; phone device functions exist to manipulate the various components of a telephone, such as its switchhook, display, or buttons.

Applications that wish to use provider-specific Extended Telephony services must call the `lineNegotiateExtVersion` or `phoneNegotiateExtVersion` functions to negotiate the extended version number. Device-specific functions can be executed by calling the escape functions `lineDevSpecific`, `lineDevSpecificFeature` (for switch functions), and `phoneDevSpecific`.

TAPI Media Modes

TAPI provides two concepts that specify the quality of service supported by a line and the type of a call.

The *bearer mode* specifies the quality of service. For example, the voice bearer mode (LINEBEARERMODE_VOICE) indicates a POTS line with a 3.1 kHz analog bandwidth and no provisions for data integrity. Other bearer modes describe ISDN or other data lines.

The *media mode* determines the type of the call. For example, on a voice line it is possible to make voice or data calls; these correspond to the media modes LINEMEDIAMODE_INTERACTIVEVOICE or LINEMEDIAMODE_DATAMODEM.

Multiple Applications

The TAPI architecture enables multiple applications to coexist. This is a very important feature. This makes it possible, for example, for a TAPI FAX application to monitor a line for incoming FAX transmissions while at the same time enabling another TAPI application, such as a data communication application, to use the same line for outgoing calls.

At the heart of this capability is the concept of *call ownership*. Initially, ownership of a call is assigned to one application; it is either the application that originated the call or the application that receives the incoming call. An application can pass ownership of a call to another application through the lineHandoff function. The original application also continues owning the call. It can then choose to remain a co-owner of the call (although doing so is not recommended), deallocate the call handle indicating that it is no longer interested in the call, or use lineSetCallPrivilege to become a *call monitor*. A call monitor is an application cannot control the call's existence, but it can record facts about the call (logging).

> **NOTE**
>
> If a call is co-owned by multiple applications, TAPI offers no mechanism to prevent these applications from interfering with each other.

When handling incoming calls, applications may perform *probing* to determine the nature of the call. Probing can be used, for example, to determine whether an incoming call is a data, FAX, or voice call. Probing is usually done by applications, although some service providers can be configured to auto-answer a call and hand it off to the appropriate application. Note that TAPI does not launch applications to handle specific call types.

Applications can learn about in-progress calls at startup by calling lineGetNewCalls. Through this function, an application can obtain handles with monitoring privilege for all calls that are currently in progress.

Applications can communicate with each other by using the lineSetAppSpecific function. Through this function, they can set the dwAppSpecific field of the LINECALLINFO structure. Other applications that own or monitor the call are informed by receiving a LINE_CALLINFO message.

A Data Communication Example

I decided to put TAPI into practice by modifying a simple console application I wrote earlier. This simple communication application opens a communication port and uses overlapped I/O operations to perform input and output.

In its original version, the application simply opened the port without making any attempt at placing a call. It was up to the user to use the appropriate AT commands to place a call. The communication port was hardcoded in the application.

In the TAPI version presented in Listing 42.2, the call is placed through the TAPI function `lineMakeCall`. Before that happens, the user is given the opportunity to choose a TAPI device.

Listing 42.2. A simple TAPI data communication program.

```
#include <windows.h>
#include <tapi.h>
#include <stdio.h>

volatile BOOL bConnected = FALSE;

VOID FAR PASCAL lineCallback(DWORD hDevice, DWORD dwMsg,
                      DWORD dwCallbackInstance, DWORD dwParam1,
                      DWORD dwParam2, DWORD dwParam3)
{
    if (dwMsg == LINE_CALLSTATE &&
        dwParam1 == LINECALLSTATE_CONNECTED)
            bConnected = TRUE;
}

LINEDEVCAPS *GetDevCaps(HLINEAPP hLineApp, DWORD dwDeviceID,
                      LPDWORD lpdwAPIVersion)
{
    LINEDEVCAPS *pLineDevCaps;
    LINEEXTENSIONID extensionID;

    lineNegotiateAPIVersion(hLineApp, dwDeviceID, 0x10004, 0x10004,
                            lpdwAPIVersion, &extensionID);
    pLineDevCaps = malloc(sizeof(LINEDEVCAPS));
    pLineDevCaps->dwTotalSize = sizeof(LINEDEVCAPS);
    lineGetDevCaps(hLineApp, dwDeviceID, *lpdwAPIVersion, 0,
                    pLineDevCaps);
    if (pLineDevCaps->dwNeededSize > pLineDevCaps->dwTotalSize)
    {
        pLineDevCaps =
            realloc(pLineDevCaps, pLineDevCaps->dwNeededSize);
        pLineDevCaps->dwTotalSize = pLineDevCaps->dwNeededSize;
        lineGetDevCaps(hLineApp, dwDeviceID, *lpdwAPIVersion, 0,
                        pLineDevCaps);
    }
    return pLineDevCaps;
}
```

continues

Listing 42.2. continued

```
HANDLE SelectTAPIDevice(HLINEAPP hLineApp, DWORD dwNumDevs,
                        LPHLINE lphLine, LPHCALL lphCall)
{
    LINEDEVCAPS *pLineDevCaps;
    DWORD dwDeviceID;
    DWORD dwAPIVersion;
    DWORD i;
    LINECALLPARAMS lineCallParams;
    LPVARSTRING lpDeviceID;
    MSG msg;
    char szNumber[81];

    for (i = 0; i < dwNumDevs; i++)
    {
        pLineDevCaps = GetDevCaps(hLineApp, i, &dwAPIVersion);
        if (pLineDevCaps->dwMediaModes & LINEMEDIAMODE_DATAMODEM)
            printf("%d: %s\n", i,
                (char*)pLineDevCaps + pLineDevCaps->dwLineNameOffset);
        free(pLineDevCaps);
    }
    dwDeviceID = 0xFFFFFFFF;
    while (dwDeviceID >= dwNumDevs)
    {
        printf("Select device: ");
        scanf("%d", &dwDeviceID);
        if (dwDeviceID >= dwNumDevs) continue;
        pLineDevCaps =
            GetDevCaps(hLineApp, dwDeviceID, &dwAPIVersion);
        if(!(pLineDevCaps->dwMediaModes & LINEMEDIAMODE_DATAMODEM))
        {
            dwDeviceID = 0xFFFFFFFF;
            free(pLineDevCaps);
        }
    }
    printf("Enter telephone number: ");
    scanf("%s", szNumber);
    printf("Dialing %s on %s...", szNumber,
            (char *)pLineDevCaps + pLineDevCaps->dwLineNameOffset);
    free(pLineDevCaps);
    lineOpen(hLineApp, dwDeviceID, lphLine, dwAPIVersion, 0, 0,
            LINECALLPRIVILEGE_NONE, LINEMEDIAMODE_DATAMODEM, NULL);
    memset(&lineCallParams, 0, sizeof(LINECALLPARAMS));
    lineCallParams.dwTotalSize = sizeof(LINECALLPARAMS);
    lineCallParams.dwMinRate = 2400;
    lineCallParams.dwMaxRate = 57600;
    lineCallParams.dwMediaMode = LINEMEDIAMODE_DATAMODEM;
    lineMakeCall(*lphLine, lphCall, szNumber, 0, &lineCallParams);
    while (!bConnected)
        if (GetMessage(&msg, NULL, 0, 0)) DispatchMessage(&msg);
    putchar('\n');
    lpDeviceID = malloc(sizeof(VARSTRING));
    lpDeviceID->dwTotalSize = sizeof(VARSTRING);
    lineGetID(0, 0, *lphCall, LINECALLSELECT_CALL, lpDeviceID,
            "comm/datamodem");
    if (lpDeviceID->dwNeededSize > lpDeviceID->dwTotalSize)
    {
```

```
            lpDeviceID = realloc(lpDeviceID, lpDeviceID->dwNeededSize);
            lpDeviceID->dwTotalSize = lpDeviceID->dwNeededSize;
            lineGetID(0, 0, *lphCall, LINECALLSELECT_CALL, lpDeviceID,
                        "comm/datamodem");
    }
    return *((LPHANDLE)((char *)lpDeviceID + sizeof(VARSTRING)));
}

void main(void)
{
    HLINEAPP hLineApp;
    HLINE hLine;
    HCALL hCall;
    DWORD dwNumDevs;
    HANDLE hConIn, hConOut, hCommPort;
    HANDLE hEvents[2];
    DWORD dwCount;
    DWORD dwWait;
    COMMTIMEOUTS ctmoCommPort;
    DCB dcbCommPort;
    OVERLAPPED ov;
    INPUT_RECORD irBuffer;
    BOOL fInRead;
    char c;
    int i;

    lineInitialize(&hLineApp, GetModuleHandle(NULL), lineCallback,
                    "Test TAPI Application", &dwNumDevs);
    hCommPort =
        SelectTAPIDevice(hLineApp, dwNumDevs, &hLine, &hCall);
    hConIn = CreateFile("CONIN$", GENERIC_READ | GENERIC_WRITE,
                        FILE_SHARE_READ, NULL, OPEN_EXISTING,
                        FILE_ATTRIBUTE_NORMAL, 0);
    SetConsoleMode(hConIn, 0);
    hConOut = CreateFile("CONOUT$", GENERIC_WRITE,
                        FILE_SHARE_WRITE, NULL, OPEN_EXISTING,
                        FILE_ATTRIBUTE_NORMAL, 0);
    ctmoCommPort.ReadIntervalTimeout = MAXDWORD;
    ctmoCommPort.ReadTotalTimeoutMultiplier = MAXDWORD;
    ctmoCommPort.ReadTotalTimeoutConstant = MAXDWORD;
    ctmoCommPort.WriteTotalTimeoutMultiplier = 0;
    ctmoCommPort.WriteTotalTimeoutConstant = 0;
    SetCommTimeouts(hCommPort, &ctmoCommPort);
    dcbCommPort.DCBlength = sizeof(DCB);
    GetCommState(hCommPort, &dcbCommPort);
    SetCommState(hCommPort, &dcbCommPort);
    SetCommMask(hCommPort, EV_RXCHAR);
    ov.Offset = 0;
    ov.OffsetHigh = 0;
    ov.hEvent = CreateEvent(NULL, TRUE, FALSE, NULL);
    hEvents[0] = ov.hEvent;
    hEvents[1] = hConIn;
    fInRead = FALSE;
    while (1)
    {
        if (!fInRead)
            while (ReadFile(hCommPort, &c, 1, &dwCount, &ov))
                if (dwCount == 1)
```

continues

Listing 42.2. continued

```
                        WriteFile(hConOut, &c, 1, &dwCount, NULL);
            fInRead = TRUE;
            dwWait =
                WaitForMultipleObjects(2, hEvents, FALSE, INFINITE);
            switch (dwWait)
            {
                case WAIT_OBJECT_0:
                    if (GetOverlappedResult(hCommPort, &ov, &dwCount,
                                              FALSE))
                        if (dwCount == 1)
                            WriteFile(hConOut, &c, 1, &dwCount, NULL);
                    fInRead = FALSE;
                    break;
                case WAIT_OBJECT_0 + 1:
                    ReadConsoleInput(hConIn, &irBuffer, 1, &dwCount);
                    if (dwCount == 1 &&
                        irBuffer.EventType == KEY_EVENT &&
                        irBuffer.Event.KeyEvent.bKeyDown)
                      for (i = 0;
                        i < irBuffer.Event.KeyEvent.wRepeatCount; i++)
                    {
                        if (irBuffer.Event.KeyEvent.uChar.AsciiChar)
                        {
                            WriteFile(hCommPort,
                              &irBuffer.Event.KeyEvent.uChar.AsciiChar,
                              1, &dwCount, NULL);
                            if (irBuffer.Event.KeyEvent.uChar.AsciiChar
                                == 24) goto EndLoop;
                        }
                    }
            }
        }
EndLoop:
    CloseHandle(ov.hEvent);
    CloseHandle(hConIn);
    CloseHandle(hConOut);
    CloseHandle(hCommPort);
    lineDrop(hCall, NULL, 0);
    lineClose(hLine);
    lineShutdown(hLineApp);
}
```

The fact that this is a console application represented special challenges. In particular, it was necessary to use a message loop at one point to enable the TAPI callback mechanism to work. Although this approach may be somewhat unorthodox, it demonstrates the TAPI programming model and its traps and pitfalls surprisingly well.

The first call in the applications main function is to the TAPI function lineInitialize. Next, main calls the function SelectTAPIDevice; this high-level function queries the user for a TAPI device and a telephone number, opens the device, places the call, and returns a Win32 handle that the application can use in subsequent I/O calls.

The `SelectTAPIDevice` function first queries all TAPI line devices for the line name. These line names are presented to the user in the form of a numbered list, and the user is requested to choose one of them. When determining the line name, `SelectTAPIDevice` utilizes another function, `GetDevCaps`. Note the duplicate calls to the TAPI function `lineGetDevCaps` in `GetDevCaps`; the first call is used to determine the size of the structure `lineGetDevCaps` would return. The second call is made after a sufficiently large block of memory has been allocated.

After a line device has been selected in `SelectTAPIDevice`, the user is requested to enter a telephone number. This number is then used, after the line has been opened and the appropriate structure initialized, in a call to `lineMakeCall`. Since `lineMakeCall` is an asynchronously executing TAPI function, the return of this function does not indicate completion of the request. In particular, the call handle pointed to by `lphCall` is not yet valid. The application must wait until its callback function is called indicating that the call has been set up; furthermore, it must ensure that the callback mechanism operates as expected by executing a message loop.

The callback function, `lineCallback`, is extremely simplistic; it simply waits for a `LINE_CALLSTATE` message that indicates that the call has been connected. The rest of the application is notified of call completion when the global variable `bConnected` is set to `TRUE` by the callback function. In particular, this change causes the message loop in `SelectTAPIDevice` to terminate.

When `SelectTAPIDevice` is notified of successful call completion through this mechanism, it uses the `lineGetID` function to retrieve a handle to the communication port. Note how `lineGetID` is called twice, first to determine the size of the data structure it is about to return. Note also how an extra structure member of type `HANDLE` is retrieved.

When `SelectTAPIDevice` returns, it passes the communication device handle to `main`. In `main`, this handle is used to configure the communication device and the console for I/O and handle bidirectional data transfer. The application is terminated when the user presses the Ctrl+ X key combination. At this time, the application closes all handles, terminates the TAPI session, and exits.

To compile this application from the command line, type `cl tty.c tapi32.lib user32.lib`. The USER library is required because of the references to the Windows functions `GetMessage` and `DispatchMessage`.

I ran this application on my main desktop computer that has two modems attached to it. An internal FAX modem connects my desktop computer to my data line; an old external pocket modem connects it to my voice line. I mostly use this modem simply as a dialer; however, it comes in handy when I need to test communication applications like this one. Also connected to my data line through its own FAX modem is another computer running Linux (this is my server for Internet mail and TCP/IP connections). This server also accepts incoming data calls, so I can utilize the modem on my voice line to make calls to it.

A sample session using this configuration looked like the following:

```
C:\TTY>tty
0: SupraFAXModem 144i
```

```
1: Practical Peripherals 2400
Select device: 1
Enter telephone number: 555-1234
Dialing 555-1234 on Practical Peripherals 2400...
You have reached a private computer system. Calls to this system
are logged using calling party identification (caller ID).
Unauthorized calls violate my privacy, not to mention the law! If
you have not been specifically authorized by me to access this
system, now would be a great time to terminate your connection.

Viktor

Welcome to Linux 1.1.37.


vtt1!login: vttoth
Password:
Last login: Tue Oct 17 01:57:20 on ttyS0
Linux 1.1.37. (Posix).
vtt1:~$ ^X
C:\TTY>
```

> **NOTE**
>
> This simple application provides absolutely no error handling. In particular, it is
> written with the assumption that the call always succeeds; no provisions are made for
> unsuccessful call attempts, and the application will likely malfunction in such a case.
> Furthermore, the application does not handle the loss of carrier; because it does not
> operate a message loop while it is connected, its TAPI callback function is never
> notified when the call is terminated by the remote end.

Summary

TAPI, the Microsoft Telephony API, provides personal telephony services for Windows applications. TAPI provides abstractions for line devices that connect a computer to a telephone
line, and phone devices, which are telephone sets with a variety of components such as a
switchhook, display, buttons, or ring, that can be manipulated programmatically. (Note that
most commonly used telephone sets cannot be manipulated this way.) A TAPI line device always represents a physical device; in contrast, a phone device can be a software representation
of a telephone that uses the computer's display, keyboard, and sound hardware to provide the
services of a telephone set.

TAPI line devices are not restricted to represent only devices attached to plain old telephone
service (POTS) lines. Line devices can represent hardware connected to ISDN lines, T1/E1
data lines, switched 56 data lines, and other lines.

TAPI provides services to place outgoing calls and accept incoming calls. It is the responsibility of applications to manage the media stream, the actual flow of data during a call. The media stream is a generic term that represents voice, data, FAX images, or other information that flows through a telephone line.

The TAPI DLL represents a layer between applications and device-specific service providers (drivers). Another TAPI component is the `tapiexe.exe` system application that is used in TAPI messaging.

TAPI functions can execute synchronously and asynchronously. Synchronous functions return immediately with a success or failure result. Asynchronous functions, on the other hand, return only to indicate whether a request has been placed successfully; applications are notified of request completion through a callback function. In order for the callback function mechanism to operate, applications must maintain a Windows message loop.

The TAPI interface is broken down into Assisted Telephony, Basic Telephony, Supplementary Telephony, and Extended Telephony.

Assisted Telephony provides a set of simple functions for placing calls. These functions are ideally suited for use in script languages that can call external DLLs.

Basic Telephony consists of those line device functions that all service providers must implement. These include functions to place and accept calls and monitor calls in progress.

Supplementary Telephony consists of functions that require special hardware. For example, special hardware is required for call transfer, conference call, and other call management functions to work. Applications cannot expect that a supplementary function is available; they must query the service provider about the availability of a supplementary function.

Extended Telephony represents device- and provider-specific functionality. Extended functions are accessed through special escape functions that TAPI provides. Before using extended functions, applications must determine their availability by querying the service provider.

Network Programming with Pipes and Remote Procedure Calls

43

Pipes offer an efficient, easy way for two cooperating Windows applications to communicate across a network. Pipes are easy to set up and use; they are one of the favored mechanisms for implementing client-server communications with server software running on Windows NT. Unfortunately, pipe support in Windows 95 is limited to client-side support.

The most often used pipes are *named pipes*. In addition to their other uses, named pipes also represent one of several mechanisms used by *Microsoft Remote Procedure Calls*, or *Microsoft RPC*. RPC is a mechanism that enables applications to call procedures (functions) that are part of another application running (possibly) on a different computer on the network. Apart from some initialization and housekeeping functions, using RPC is almost as simple as calling a local function.

In this chapter, we examine these two communication mechanisms.

Communicating with Pipes

Pipes offer a one- or two-way conduit of communication between cooperating applications. Programming with pipes is based on the client-server model; a typical server application creates a pipe and waits for client applications to request access to the pipe.

Creating Pipes

The Win32 API distinguishes between *named pipes* and *anonymous pipes*. The use of anonymous pipes is somewhat limited. When an application creates an anonymous pipe, it receives two handles; one of these handles must be passed on to another application in order for the two applications to be able to communicate. A possible mechanism for passing a handle is inheritance; therefore, anonymous pipes are often used for communication between a parent and a child process, or between child processes of the same parent process. Because anonymous pipes are identified by handles, they are inherently local (a handle has no validity on another machine on the network). In contrast, named pipes are identified by a UNC name that is valid across the entire network.

Anonymous pipes are created using the CreatePipe function. This function returns two handles: one to the read end of the pipe, and another to its write end.

Named pipes are created by calling the CreateNamedPipe function. Named pipes have names in the following form:

```
\\hostname\\pipe\\pipename
```

Servers cannot create a pipe on another computer. For this reason, the host name component in the pipe name, when the name is used in CreateNamedPipe, must be set to a single period, indicating the local host:

```
\\.\pipe\pipename
```

A named pipe can be one-way or two-way. When the server creates the pipe, it specifies PIPE_ACCESS_DUPLEX, PIPE_ACCESS_INBOUND, or PIPE_ACCESS_OUTBOUND to indicate the directionality of the pipe.

Named pipes support asynchronous (overlapped) I/O operations. However, overlapped I/O is not supported by anonymous pipes.

When a named pipe is created, a server specifies the pipe's type. A pipe can be a byte mode or a message mode pipe. Byte mode pipes treat data as a stream of bytes; message mode pipes treat data as a stream of messages. The pipe's read mode can be byte read mode or message read mode; message mode pipes support both read modes, but byte mode pipes support only the byte read mode.

The pipe's read mode and its wait mode (whether the pipe operates in a blocking or non-blocking mode) can be specified when the pipe is created and later modified using the SetNamedPipeHandleState function. The current state of the pipe can be obtained by calling GetNamedPipeHandleState. Further information about a named pipe can be obtained by calling GetNamedPipeInfo.

Connecting to Named Pipes

When an anonymous pipe is created, the process creating it receives handles for both ends of the pipe. In contrast, when a server creates a named pipe, only one end of the pipe is opened; the server must wait for a client to make an attempt to connect to the pipe before the pipe can be used. An overview of setting up, using, and shutting down named pipes is presented in Figure 43.1.

FIGURE 43.1.

Communicating with named pipes.

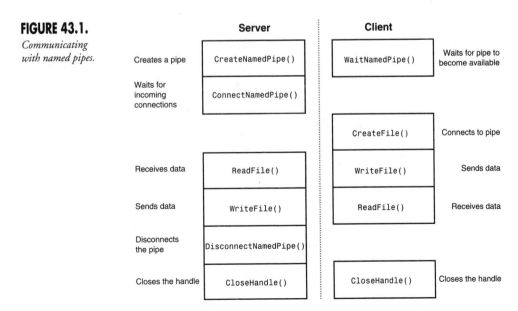

	Server	Client	
Creates a pipe	CreateNamedPipe()	WaitNamedPipe()	Waits for pipe to become available
Waits for incoming connections	ConnectNamedPipe()		
		CreateFile()	Connects to pipe
Receives data	ReadFile()	WriteFile()	Sends data
Sends data	WriteFile()	ReadFile()	Receives data
Disconnects the pipe	DisconnectNamedPipe()		
Closes the handle	CloseHandle()	CloseHandle()	Closes the handle

To wait for a connection, servers issue a call to the ConnectNamedPipe function. This function waits until a client connects to the pipe, identifying the pipe by its name (note that ConnectNamedPipe can also be used asynchronously, in which case the server is free to attend to other tasks while it is waiting for an incoming connection on the pipe).

Clients can determine whether a named pipe is available to be connected to using the WaitNamedPipe function. Once a pipe is available, applications can connect to it using the CreateFile function and giving the name of the pipe as the filename.

An established connection can be broken by the server by calling the DisconnectNamedPipe function. When a server calls this function, the client-side handle of the pipe becomes invalid and all data that was not yet read by the client is discarded. To ensure that the client read all data before DisconnectNamedPipe is called, servers can call the FlushFileBuffers function. After DisconnectNamedPipe returns, servers can either close the pipe handle or reuse it in another call to ConnectNamedPipe.

Clients can break the connection by simply calling CloseHandle on the pipe handle they obtained through calling CreateFile.

Servers can utilize several strategies for handling multiple connections, such as spawning separate threads and using overlapped I/O. A server can create multiple instances of the same pipe by repeatedly calling CreateNamedPipe with the same pipe name.

Transferring Data Through Pipes

Pipes can be written to or read from using WriteFile and ReadFile. Named pipes can also be used for overlapped I/O; in this case, the WriteFileEx and ReadFileEx functions may need to be used.

For message-mode pipes, an alternative mechanism exists for quick and efficient message transfer. Clients can call the TransactNamedPipe function to write a message to and read a message from the specified pipe in a single network operation. The CallNamedPipe function combines into a single operation the calls to WaitNamedPipe, CreateFile, TransactNamedPipe, and CloseHandle. In other words, CallNamedPipe waits for the specified pipe to become available, opens the pipe, exchanges messages, and closes the pipe in a single function call.

A Working Example

This simple example implements a named pipe client and server pair. Listing 43.1 shows the server application.

Listing 43.1. A simple named pipe server.

```
#include <windows.h>
#include <stdio.h>
```

```
void main(void)
{
    HANDLE hPipe;
    DWORD dwRead;
    char c = -1;

    hPipe = CreateNamedPipe("\\\\.\\pipe\\hello",
            PIPE_ACCESS_INBOUND, PIPE_WAIT, PIPE_UNLIMITED_INSTANCES,
            256, 256, 1000, NULL);
    ConnectNamedPipe(hPipe, NULL);
    while (c != '\0')
    {
        ReadFile(hPipe, &c, 1, &dwRead, NULL);
        if (dwRead > 0 && c != 0) putchar(c);
    }
    DisconnectNamedPipe(hPipe);
    CloseHandle(hPipe);
}
```

This application creates the pipe `hello` on the local server. The pipe is created in blocking mode (`PIPE_WAIT`); operations on this pipe will not return until they are completed. Once the pipe has been created, the server calls `ConnectNamedPipe` and waits for incoming client connections.

When a client is connected, the server attempts to read from the pipe. It reads single bytes from the pipe and writes them to standard output until a null character is encountered; at that time, it disconnects the pipe, closes the handle, and terminates.

The client, shown in Listing 43.2, takes two command-line parameters; the first identifies the host that it should connect to, the second represents the string that it sends to the server on that host.

Listing 43.2. A simple named pipe client.

```
#include <windows.h>
#include <string.h>
#include <stdio.h>

void main(int argc, char *argv[])
{
    HANDLE hPipe;
    DWORD dwWritten;
    char *pszPipe;

    if (argc != 3)
    {
        printf("Usage: %s hostname string-to-print\n", argv[0]);
        exit(1);
    }
    pszPipe = malloc(strlen(argv[1]) + 14);
    sprintf(pszPipe, "\\\\%s\\pipe\\hello", argv[1]);
    WaitNamedPipe(pszPipe, NMPWAIT_WAIT_FOREVER);
    hPipe = CreateFile(pszPipe, GENERIC_WRITE, 0, NULL,
```

continues

Listing 43.2. continued

```
                        OPEN_EXISTING, FILE_ATTRIBUTE_NORMAL, NULL);
    free(pszPipe);
    WriteFile(hPipe, argv[2], strlen(argv[2])+1, &dwWritten, NULL);
    CloseHandle(hPipe);
}
```

After processing its command-line parameters, the client begins to wait for the server to become available by calling `WaitNamedPipe`. When `WaitNamedPipe` returns, the client calls `CreateFile` to actually connect to the server; it then uses `WriteFile` to send the string to the server before shutting down the connection by calling `CloseHandle`.

Both the client and the server can easily be compiled from the command line. Type `cl pipes.c` to compile the server and `cl pipec.c` to compile the client.

You can test this application on a single machine running Windows NT (remember that Windows 95 does not support the server end of pipes) or on two machines across a network. If you are using a single machine, start `pipes.exe` in a DOS window and use a separate DOS window for running the client. When using the client, run it with a command line similar to the following:

```
pipec MYHOST "Hello, World!"
```

Microsoft RPC

Microsoft's RPC extends the conceptual elegance and simplicity of a function or subroutine call by providing a similar mechanism for calls across the network. RPC servers can offer a set of functions that can be called by RPC clients.

The RPC mechanism is used widely in Windows. In particular, the RPC mechanism is the basis of Object Linking and Embedding technology.

RPC Fundamentals

Stub functions are key elements in the RPC mechanism. When an RPC client calls an RPC function, it issues a regular function call. However, the function that receives a call is an RPC stub; this stub function converts function arguments for transmission across the network (a procedure referred to as *marshaling*) and transmits the call request and the arguments to the server.

Stub functions on the server side *unmarshal* function arguments and call the server's implementation of the function. When the function returns, its return value is passed back to the client using a reverse mechanism. This entire procedure is illustrated in Figure 43.2.

When developing RPC applications, an element of central importance is the *interface*. Clearly, the stub functions on the client and the server sides must be based on identical function definitions; otherwise, the RPC process will surely fail. The tool that ensures that the stub functions on the two sides are compatible is the Microsoft Interface Development Language (MIDL) compiler.

FIGURE 43.2.

RPC overview.

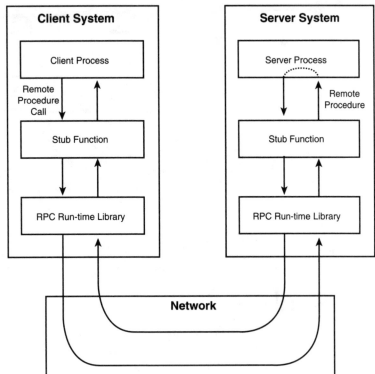

A Simple Example

The next example clarifies the basic concepts of Microsoft RPC. This example, the RPC equivalent of the Hello, World application, implements a simple server function that prints a string received from client applications.

The first step in developing this example is to specify the interface. This is done in the form of two files that represent the input files for the MIDL compiler. The MIDL compiler will produce three files: a header file that must be included in both the client and the server application, and two C source files that implement the client and server stub functions. These files must be linked with our implementation of both the client and the server application to produce the final executables. This process is illustrated in Figure 43.3.

FIGURE 43.3.
RPC development.

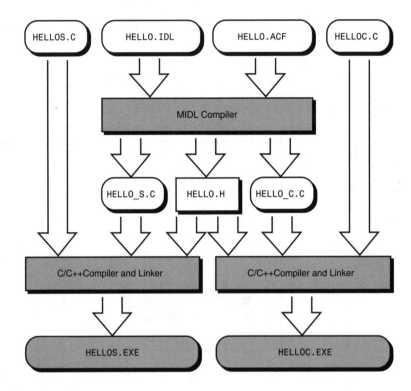

Specifying the Interface

The interface for an RPC implementation is specified in the form of two files: the *Interface Definition Language File* and the *Application Configuration File*. These two files together serve as input for the MIDL compiler.

The Interface Definition Language File for our example application is shown in Listing 43.3.

Listing 43.3. The Interface Definition Language File.

```
[
  uuid (6fdd2ce0-0985-11cf-87c3-00403321bfac),
  version(1.0)
]
interface hello
{
  void HelloProc([in, string] const unsigned char *pszString);
  void Shutdown(void);
}
```

This file consists of two parts: the interface header and the interface body. The interface header has the following syntax:

```
[ interface-attributes ] interface interface-name
```

Perhaps the most important of the interface attributes is the interface's *GUID*, or *globally unique identifier*. The GUID is a 128-bit identifier that is supposed to be world-unique; in other words, no two applications in the world are supposed to have identical identifiers.

The Visual C++ distribution provides a tool, the executable program `guidgen.exe`, that is supposed to create such unique identifiers using, in part, information obtained from your computer's hardware, and in part a randomization algorithm.

The GUID is expressed in the form of a string of 32 hexadecimal digits. The specific form is 8, 4, 4, 4, and 12 digits separated by hyphens. The `guidgen.exe` program generates GUID strings in this form.

In addition to the GUID, another interface attribute specifies the interface's version number. The function of the version number is to identify potentially incompatible versions of the interface.

In the second part of the Interface Definition Language File, function prototypes are defined. The prototype syntax is similar to the syntax of the C language but it also contains extra elements. The `in` keyword indicates to the MIDL compiler that the following parameter is an input-only parameter; that is, it is sent to the server by the client. The `string` keyword indicates that the data sent is a character array.

The Application Configuration File is similar in syntax and appearance to the Interface Definition Language File. However, this file contains information on data and attributes not related to the actual transmission of RPC data.

The Application Configuration File for our project is shown in Listing 43.4.

Listing 43.4. The Application Configuration File.

```
[
    implicit_handle(handle_t hello_IfHandle)
]
interface hello
{
}
```

In this file, we specify a *binding handle* for the interface. This handle is a data object that represents the connection between the client and the server. Because the handle is not transmitted over the network, it is specified in the Application Configuration File.

The use of the keyword `implicit_handle` prescribes a handle that is maintained as a global variable. This handle will be used by the client in calls to RPC run-time functions.

The two files, `hello.idl` and `hello.acf`, can be compiled by the MIDL compiler using a single command:

```
midl hello.idl
```

The result of the compilation is three files produced by the MIDL compiler: `hello_c.c`, `hello_s.c`, and `hello.h`. The files `hello_c.c` and `hello_s.c` provide the client and server-side implementation of stub functions; the `hello.h` header provides necessary declarations.

By looking at these generated files, one can easily see just how much of the network programmer's work is automated by the use of the MIDL compiler. The generated stub functions perform all the required run-time library calls to marshal and unmarshal arguments and to communicate across the network. However, the real beauty and elegant simplicity of the RPC mechanism are yet to become evident when we implement our client and server.

Implementing the Server

The server application's implementation is shown in Listing 43.5.

Listing 43.5. A simple RPC server.

```
#include <stdlib.h>
#include <stdio.h>
#include "hello.h"

void HelloProc(const unsigned char *pszString)
{
    printf("%s\n", pszString);
}

void Shutdown(void)
{
    RpcMgmtStopServerListening(NULL);
    RpcServerUnregisterIf(NULL, NULL, FALSE);
}

void main(int argc, char * argv[])
{
    RpcServerUseProtseqEp("ncacn_ip_tcp", 20, "8000", NULL);
    RpcServerRegisterIf(hello_v1_0_s_ifspec, NULL, NULL);
    RpcServerListen(1, 20, FALSE);
}

void __RPC_FAR * __RPC_USER midl_user_allocate(size_t len)
{
    return(malloc(len));
}

void __RPC_USER midl_user_free(void __RPC_FAR * ptr)
{
    free(ptr);
}
```

The RPC run-time library is initialized and the server is set up to wait for incoming connections through the three RPC run-time library calls in the program's main function. First of these calls is the `RpcServerUseProtseqEp` call; this call defines the network protocol and endpoint that is to be used by the application. In our example, I decided to use the TCP over IP protocol (ncacn_ip_tcp) as a protocol that is supported both under Windows 95 and Windows NT. The RPC mechanism can utilize many other protocols, as shown in Table 43.1.

Table 43.1. RPC protocols.

protocol name	Description
ncacn_ip_tcp	TCP over IP
ncacn_nb_tcp	TCP over NetBIOS
ncacn_nb_ipx	IPX over NetBEUI
ncacn_nb_nb	NetBIOS over NetBEUI
ncacn_np	Named pipes
ncacn_spx	SPX
ncacn_dnet_nsp	DECnet transport
ncadg_ip_udp	UDP over IP
ncadg_ipx	IPX
ncalrpc	local procedure call

Protocols with a name that begins with ncacn are connection-oriented protocols; those with a name that starts with ncadg are datagram (connectionless) protocols.

Because Windows 95 supports named pipes for the client side only, the ncacn_np protocol is only supported for RPC client applications. Windows 95 does not support ncacn_nb_ipx and ncacn_nb_tcp. The ncacn_dnet_nsp protocol is supported only for 16-bit Windows and MS-DOS clients.

The meaning of the endpoint parameter is dependent on the protocol. For example, when the ncacn_ip_tcp protocol is used, the endpoint parameter represents a TPC port number.

Starting up the server consists of two steps. First, the server interface is registered; second, it enters a state where it listens for incoming connections. Registering the server makes it available for incoming client connections.

The actual remote procedure, HelloProc, is implemented the same way as a local function. In fact, it is possible to place the implementation of this function in a separate file; this way, applications that locally call the function could be linked with it, while applications that call this function through RPC link with the client-side stub instead.

Another function, Shutdown, has been provided to facilitate remote shutdown of the server. Server shutdown is accomplished by exiting the listening state and unregistering the server.

In addition to these two functions, the Microsoft RPC specifications require that we implement two additional memory management functions. The `midl_user_allocate` and `midl_user_free` functions are used to allocated a block of memory and to free up allocated memory. In simple cases, these can be mapped to the C run-time functions `malloc` and `free`; however, in large, complex applications these functions enable finer control over memory use. Both of these functions are used when arguments are marshaled or unmarshaled.

To compile the server application, use the following command line:

```
cl hellos.c hello_s.c rpcrt4.lib
```

Implementing the Client

Implementing the RPC client is only slightly more complicated than implementing an application containing a local function call. The client implementation for our example is shown in Listing 43.6.

Listing 43.6. A simple RPC client.

```c
#include <stdlib.h>
#include <stdio.h>
#include <string.h>
#include "hello.h"

void main(int argc, char *argv[])
{
    unsigned char *pszStringBinding;

    if (argc != 3)
    {
        printf("Usage: %s hostname string-to-print\n", argv[0]);
        exit(1);
    }
    RpcStringBindingCompose(NULL, "ncacn_ip_tcp", argv[1], "8000",
    NULL, &pszStringBinding);
    RpcBindingFromStringBinding(pszStringBinding, &hello_IfHandle);
    if (strcmp(argv[2], "SHUTDOWN")) HelloProc(argv[2]);
    else Shutdown();
    RpcStringFree(&pszStringBinding);
    RpcBindingFree(&hello_IfHandle);
    exit(0);
}

void __RPC_FAR * __RPC_USER midl_user_allocate(size_t len)
{
    return(malloc(len));
}

void __RPC_USER midl_user_free(void __RPC_FAR * ptr)
{
    free(ptr);
}
```

This client implementation takes two command-line parameters: the name of the server to connect to and the string to be sent to the server. Because of the protocol being used (TCP over IP), the server name must be the host's internet name or IP address. If you are testing the client and the server on the same host, you can use the default name for the local host, localhost, or its default IP address, 127.0.0.1.

The protocol name, host name, and endpoint are combined into a *string binding* using the RpcStringBindingCompose function. For example, the string binding representing the ncacn_ip_tcp protocol, the local host, and TCP port 8000 would appear as follows:

```
ncacn_ip_tcp:localhost[8000]
```

The RpcStringBindingCompose function is merely a convenience function that frees the programmer from the task of having to assemble the string binding from its components by hand. This string binding is used to obtain the binding handle for the interface in the call to RpcBindingFromStringBinding. The receipt of the binding handle indicates that the connection is ready to be used.

Once the connection is established, using it is simplicity itself. Calling a remote procedure becomes identical to calling a local function. In our client implementation, we call the function HelloProc with the second command-line argument; that is, unless that argument is the string SHUTDOWN, in which case the Shutdown function is called instead to shut down the remote server.

Like the client, the server must also provide its implementations for midl_user_allocate and midl_user_free.

The client application can be compiled using the following command line:

```
cl helloc.c hello_c.c rpcrt4.lib
```

Once you have compiled both the server and the client executables, you can test the two programs from two DOS windows. After you started the server in one of the windows, run the client in the other window as follows:

```
helloc localhost "Hello, World!"
```

To shut down the server from the client side, type:

```
helloc localhost SHUTDOWN
```

RPC Exception Handling

If you attempt to run the client application developed in the previous section alone, without starting up a server, a serious deficiency of our implementation becomes evident. Neither the client nor the server in this example performs any error handling; in particular, this means that the client does not respond well to situations when no server is available.

Unlike other errors, the unavailability of a server should be considered a likely occurrence that must be handled. (Not that I am suggesting that handling of other errors can or should be neglected in production applications!) The Microsoft RPC implementation provides a special mechanism for this purpose that is very similar in its appearance to Win32 structured exceptions or C++ exception handling.

By protecting the remote procedure calls using the RPC exception handling macros, one can ensure graceful handling of network error conditions by a client application. For example, in our Hello, World application, the calls to HelloProc and Shutdown on the client side could be protected as follows:

```
RpcTryExcept {
    if (strcmp(argv[2], "SHUTDOWN")) HelloProc(argv[2]);
    else Shutdown();
}
RpcExcept(1) {
    printf("RPC run-time exception %08.8X\n", RpcExceptionCode());
}
RpcEndExcept
```

If you recompile the client application with this change, it will no longer crash when the server is not available; it will gracefully terminate, printing the exception number.

Advanced RPC Features

Although this example application demonstrates the simplicity of using Microsoft RPC adequately, it only hints at the power and rich features of the RPC mechanism. This section mentions a few of the most notable features of Microsoft RPC.

The MIDL compiler can be used for specifying remote procedures that accept all kinds of arguments. This includes pointers and arrays; however, pointers and arrays require special consideration. Because the RPC stub functions must not only marshal the pointer arguments themselves but also the data they point to, it is necessary to define the size of the memory block a pointer points to in the interface specification. A series of attributes is available for specifying an array's size. For example, consider a remote procedure that takes the size of an array and a pointer to it as its parameters:

```
void myproc(short s, double *d);
```

You can identify the interface for such a procedure in your IDL file as follows:

```
void myproc([in] short s, [in, out, size_is(d)] double d[]);
```

This informs the MIDL to generate stub code that marshals s number of array elements.

The size_is attribute is not the only attribute that assists in specifying array arguments. Others include length_is, first_is, last_is, and max_is.

The RPC mechanism can utilize the Microsoft RPC Name Service Provider on Windows NT.

Through this mechanism, it is possible for clients to locate an RPC server by name. In particular, the use of RPC Name Service enables you to develop clients that do not use an explicit binding handle (like our Hello,World example did). Such clients would contain no RPC run-time library calls whatsoever and, apart from being linked with the client-side stub, they look no different from programs that use local functions.

The MIDL syntax enables you to define interfaces that are derived from other interfaces. The syntax is similar to that used for deriving classes in C++:

```
[attributes] interface interface-name : base-interface
```

The derived interface inherits member functions, status codes, and interface attributes from the base interface.

Summary

Pipes represent a simple, efficient interapplication communication mechanism supported by Windows 95 (client side only) and Windows NT.

Pipes can be named and unnamed. Anonymous pipes are typically used between a parent and a child process or two sibling processes. The use of anonymous pipes requires communicating a pipe handle from one process to another (for example, by inheriting the handle). Because anonymous pipes are identified by handle alone, they cannot be used for communication across a network.

Unlike anonymous pipes, named pipes support overlapped I/O operations. A server can use a combination of techniques including overlapped I/O and using separate threads to serve several clients simultaneously.

Both servers and clients communicate on a named pipe using the pipe's handle and standard Win32 input and output functions.

Microsoft RPC is a mechanism for applications to call functions remotely. It provides a transparent interface where client applications can call remote functions in a fashion that is very similar to the calling of local functions.

The key to Microsoft RPC, in addition to the RPC run-time library, is the Microsoft Interface Definition Language (MIDL) compiler. The interface between a client and a server can be specified using a simple C-like syntax, from which the MIDL compiler generates server and client-side stub functions, freeing the programmer from the burden of complex network programming tasks and from having to maintain compatible versions of these functions on the server and client sides.

The actual implementation is through these stub functions. When a client calls a remote procedure, the call is handled by the corresponding client-side stub function. The stub function, in turn, calls the RPC run-time library that uses the underlying network transport to invoke stub functions on the server side. The client-side stub function also marshals function arguments for transmission over the network. The server-side stub function unmarshals these arguments and calls the actual function implementation. When the function returns, this process is played out in reverse, as return values are transported back to the client application.

Advanced RPC features include RPC Name Service, pointer and array function arguments, derived interfaces, and much more.

High-Performance Graphics and Sound: The Game SDK

44

Early in my career I had the opportunity to spend almost a year as a member of a programmer team working on games for the Commodore 64 home computer. Although we barely earned enough to eat, I have the fondest memories of this period. I don't think I ever had as much fun with computers as I did then, designing green dragons, writing a real-time executive, coding Bartok's Allegro Barbaro on the C64's primitive sound synthesizer, and learning about high-performance drawing algorithms. Game programming is probably the most technically challenging form of programming for desktop systems, and the joy of seeing your creation come to life is a reward by itself.

Games under Windows are as old as Windows itself; I vaguely remember playing Reversi with a machine that had Windows 1.0 installed. However, creating true arcade-style games with real-time animation and sound under Windows proved to be an elusive target until now—despite the fact that the benefits of using the Windows platform for game development are enormous. Under Windows, you no longer need to contend with the multitude of graphics accelerators, sound cards, TSR drivers, and the rest of the paraphernalia that make developing even the simplest graphic application under MS-DOS a nightmare. Windows' device-independence takes care of it all.

One reason game development under Windows has lagged so far behind the DOS platform is speed. The GDI, although great on device-independence, is not very efficient; updating a window of a relatively large surface area takes a considerable amount of time.

In the past, Microsoft has attempted to provide high-efficiency graphics libraries and other tools for game developers. However, nothing compares to their latest product, the Windows 95 Game SDK. At the heart of this product is the family of DirectX libraries for graphics, sound, joystick control, and communications (for multiple-player games). These libraries are based on Microsoft's Common Object Model, the foundation of Microsoft's OLE technology.

The Game SDK is not part of Visual C++; it is available separately, as part of the Microsoft Developer Network Level 2 subscription.

The DirectX APIs

The Windows 95 Game SDK consists of a series of APIs. The names of these APIs begin with the word Direct, and thus they are collectively referred to as the *DirectX APIs*.

The first of these APIs, *DirectDraw*, provides a low-level, high-speed interface to your computer's graphics hardware. Through DirectDraw, it is possible to write games that use real-time animation in a window; the API also provides the capability to write full-screen graphical applications.

The *DirectSound* API provides low-level access to your computer's sound hardware. The most important capabilities of this API include the ability to play sounds continuously in a loop and the ability to mix sounds.

The *DirectPlay* API provides a game-oriented communication interface to facilitate multiplayer gaming across a modem, network connection, or through an online service.

The *DirectInput* API provides improved, more reliable access to joystick services.

Lastly, the *DirectSetup* API provides a single-function setup capability for DirectX run-time components.

DirectX and the Common Object Model

The DirectDraw, DirectSound, and DirectPlay APIs provide services using the Common Object Model (COM). A COM object is exposed to the outside world through one or more interfaces; each interface is essentially a table of function pointers representing the object's *methods*. Thus, the interface resembles the implementation of a pure virtual class in C++; the actual implementations of these functions are provided by the object itself.

The similarity to C++ classes ends, however, when it comes to inheritance. Although it is possible to create a new interface using an old interface, the new interface will not inherit the implementation of the old interface's methods. For example, although all COM interfaces are derived from the basic interface, IUnknown, they must individually implement mandatory IUnknown methods.

COM interfaces are compatible with the implementation of C++ classes. The table of methods in a COM interface easily translates into virtual member functions of the C++ class representing the interface. When applications use COM interfaces from the C language, they must refer to the interface's virtual function table (vtable) explicitly. The DirectX API header files provide convenience macros for all DirectX methods.

As I mentioned, all COM interfaces are derived from IUnknown. The IUnknown interface has three methods. The first of these methods, QueryInterface, can be used to determine if a particular interface is present. AddRef and Release implement reference counting for objects as they are created, referred to from other objects, or released. These methods must be implemented by all IUnknown-derived COM interfaces.

By convention, the names of COM interfaces begin with the uppercase letter I. Also by convention, interface methods are referenced using a C++ syntax even though they can also be accessed from C using an explicit vtable reference.

DirectDraw

DirectDraw is a client to the services provided by the DirectDraw HAL (Hardware Abstraction Layer) and HEL (Hardware Emulation Layer). DirectDraw is implemented in the dynamic link library ddraw.dll. The DirectDraw HAL implements device-dependent functions; it only implements functions that are supported by the device. For unsupported functions, the HAL simply reports that they are unavailable. The HAL performs no parameter validation; all parameter validation is performed by DirectDraw.

The DirectDraw HEL appears to DirectDraw just like the DirectDraw HAL and provides software emulation for capabilities not implemented in hardware. The DirectDraw HAL and DirectDraw HEL are implemented in the form of driver libraries like `ati.vxd` and `atim32.drv`.

The DirectDraw API provides access to low-level graphics services through a series of COM interfaces. These interfaces and their relationships are schematically depicted in Figure 44.1.

FIGURE 44.1.

DirectDraw COM interfaces.

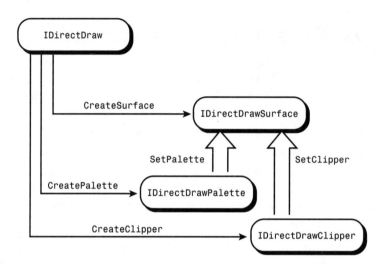

The first of these interfaces, `IDirectDraw`, represents the graphics hardware (accelerator card) in your computer. Applications that use DirectDraw services begin their operation by creating a DirectDraw object using the `DirectDrawCreate` function. `DirectDrawCreate` returns a pointer to an `IDirectDraw` interface. Before doing any other work, applications must also call `IDirectDraw::SetCooperativeLevel`. Applications that request exclusive access to the computer's graphics hardware through `IDirectDraw::SetCooperativeLevel` can change the video mode and implement full-screen graphics and animation; other applications are restricted to the current video mode and should confine their graphic activity to windows they own.

The `IDirectDraw::CreateSurface` method creates a DirectDrawSurface object and returns a pointer to an `IDirectDrawSurface` interface. DirectDrawSurface objects represent rectangular areas in memory (typically, video memory) where applications can draw. The primary drawing surface is the visible display surface; secondary drawing surfaces may exist in video memory or the computer's main memory and are used for off-screen drawing.

Drawing onto a surface is possible through any of a variety of bit blit methods provided by the `IDirectDrawSurface` interface or by using ordinary GDI functions. The `IDirectDrawSurface::GetDC` method can be used to obtain a device-context handle to the surface. GDI will treat this handle as a handle to a memory-device context—even when the surface is the primary drawing surface.

`IDirectDrawSurface` supports smooth animation with back-buffer surfaces. The `IDirectDrawSurface::Flip` method can be used to switch the contents of the primary surface and the back-buffer surface. Applications can use the back-buffer surface to perform off-screen drawing, flip the two surfaces when drawing is finished, and start drawing the next frame in the back buffer. Of course, this is only one of several techniques that can be used to achieve smooth animation. If only small portions of the display surface are updated at any given time, another technique (such as the technique using multiple buffers implemented by the example shown later in this chapter) may be more beneficial.

Another interface, `IDirectDrawPalette`, provides access to palette services. This interface represents the hardware palette and bypasses Windows palettes. Because of this, use of `IDirectDrawPalette` requires exclusive access to the video hardware. `IDirectDrawPalette` can be used for many effects, including palette animation. Note that this interface may not be available on systems that do not support a hardware palette.

An `IDirectDrawPalette` interface is created by a call to `IDirectDraw::CreatePalette`. The palette must be attached to a display surface through `IDirectDrawSurface::SetPalette`.

The `IDirectDrawClipper` interface represents clip lists. A clip list can be attached to a DirectDrawSurface object and used during bit blit operations. A window handle can also be attached to a clip list, in which case the clip list represents the clipping rectangles of the window.

An `IDirectDrawClipper` interface is created by calling `IDirectDraw::CreateClipper` and attached to a drawing surface by calling `IDirectDrawSurface::SetClipper`.

The DirectDraw API can be used to represent not only the primary video hardware in your computer but also secondary display devices that are not normally recognized by Windows. For example, consider a development system that has a secondary display card and monitor for testing purposes. An `IDirectDraw` interface representing this secondary device can be created by a call to `DirectDrawCreate`. The first parameter of this function represents the GUID (globally unique identifier) of a display driver; when it is set to NULL, `DirectDrawCreate` creates an interface representing the active display driver. However, you can also specify an explicit GUID representing any secondary device that may be installed on your system.

DirectSound

The DirectSound API provides access to your computer's waveform sound hardware. The sound device is represented by the `IDirectSound` interface; individual buffers are represented by `IDirectSoundBuffer`.

NOTE

DirectSound does not provide MIDI functionality. To utilize your sound hardware's MIDI capability, use the standard Win32 multimedia APIs for MIDI.

The most important DirectSound capability is wave mixing. It is accomplished by using a series of primary and secondary sound buffers.

A primary buffer represents the hardware buffer of the sound device; that is, the buffer that is currently playing. Secondary buffers may represent different audio streams that are mixed together into the primary buffer for playback. This mechanism is depicted schematically in Figure 44.2.

FIGURE 44.2.

DirectSound wave mixing.

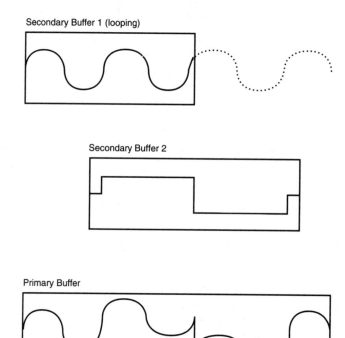

An IDirectSound interface is created by calling DirectSoundCreate. Before the interface can be used, you must also call DirectSoundCreate::SetCooperativeLevel to specify the level of access you require to the sound card. For most applications, this should be DSSCL_NORMAL. This level of access ensures smooth cooperation between applications that compete for the same hardware resources.

A sound buffer is allocated by calling IDirectSound::CreateSoundBuffer. An interface to the sound buffer is returned in the form of an IDirectSoundBuffer pointer. Applications do not normally need to allocate a primary sound buffer; this buffer is allocated implicitly when the contents of secondary buffers are played back.

When a secondary buffer is allocated, you must specify the size of the buffer. Afterwards, you can use `IDirectSoundBuffer::Lock` to obtain a pointer to this buffer. You can then use standard C library functions to copy waveform information into this buffer.

The content of a buffer is played back using the `IDirectSoundBuffer::Play` method. Calling this function while a buffer is playing will update playback flags but will not affect playback otherwise (for example, it will not cause playback to restart at the beginning of the buffer). To change the playback position, use `IDirectSoundBuffer::SetCurrentPosition`.

`IDirectSoundBuffer::Play` can also be used for continuous (looping) playback. This capability is ideal to provide background sounds, such as the engine sounds in an aircraft simulation game.

DirectPlay

Game-oriented communication services are provided through the DirectPlay API.

The DirectPlay API consists of two components: the `IDirectPlay` interface and the DirectPlay server. Microsoft provides DirectPlay servers for modem and network connections; other servers (for example, servers for online services) are provided by third party developers. To find out what DirectPlay servers are installed on a computer, use the `DirectPlayEnumerate` function.

A DirectPlay object is created by the `DirectPlayCreate` function. You must pass the GUID of the selected DirectPlay server to this function. In turn, `DirectPlayCreate` returns a pointer to an `IDirectPlay` interface.

You can enumerate existing DirectPlay sessions by calling `IDirectPlay::EnumSessions`. This method must be called after the DirectPlay object has been created.

You can create a DirectPlay session or connect to an existing session using the `IDirectPlay::Open` method. This method actually establishes the communication link. DirectPlay invokes the necessary user interface for configuring the communication protocol; for example, if a modem connection is requested, DirectPlay will invoke a dialog requesting the telephone number and other dialing information.

Games using DirectPlay must be identified by a globally unique identifier, a GUID. You can generate a GUID using the `guidgen.exe` utility that is part of Visual C++.

After you have connected to a session, you must create players. A player is created through `IDirectPlay::CreatePlayer`. You can obtain the list of players in the session by calling `IDirectPlay::EnumPlayers`.

To actually exchange messages between players, you can use `IDirectPlay::Send` and `IDirectPlay::Receive`.

Other methods exist for managing sessions, players, groups of players, and messages. Players are destroyed using `IDirectPlay::DestroyPlayer`; a session is terminated by calling `IDirectPlay::Close`.

DirectInput

The DirectInput API consists of joystick-related Win32 services. These include the `joyGetPosEx` function that can return position and button state information for joysticks with six degrees of freedom (axes) and 32 buttons. They also include functions for querying device capabilities: `joyGetDevCaps`, `joyGetNumDevs`, and `joyConfigChanged`.

DirectSetup

The DirectSetup API provides a single-function setup capability for DirectX redistributable components.

When distributing applications that use the DirectX APIs, you must distribute with them the contents of the `redist` subdirectory that is part of your Windows 95 Game SDK distribution. The contents of the `redist` directory must be redistributed in unaltered form, in accordance with the license Windows 95 Game SDK license agreement. Included in this subdirectory are the DirectSetup DLLs that implement the `DirectXSetup` function.

`DirectXSetup` is called with parameters that specify the installation root path and flags that specify which DirectX components to install. Although it is possible to install only selected components, Microsoft recommends that you do not do so; disk space savings would be minimal due to interdependencies among the DirectX components.

The existence of `DirectXSetup` is more than a convenience. Because of the complexities of DirectX installation, developers should not attempt to perform a manual installation.

A Simple Example

The application shown in Listing 44.1 uses DirectDraw and DirectSound services to implement a noisy bouncing ball.

Listing 44.1. Simple DirectX application.

```
#include <windows.h>
#include <ddraw.h>
#include <dsound.h>

IDirectDraw *dd;
IDirectDrawSurface *dds0, *dds1, *dds2, *dds3;
IDirectDrawClipper *ddc;

IDirectSound *ds;
IDirectSoundBuffer *dsb1, *dsb2;
```

```
int x = 20, y = 20;
int vx = 5, vy = 3;

void MoveBall(HWND hwnd, BOOL bMove)
{
    BOOL bBounce = FALSE;
    RECT rectSrc, rectDest;
    int ox, oy, nx, ny;

    GetClientRect(hwnd, &rectDest);
    ClientToScreen(hwnd, (POINT *)&rectDest.left);
    ClientToScreen(hwnd, (POINT *)&rectDest.right);
    if (bMove)
    {
        ox = rectDest.left +
            MulDiv(rectDest.right - rectDest.left - 32, x, 500);
        oy = rectDest.top +
            MulDiv(rectDest.bottom - rectDest.top - 32, y, 500);
        x += vx;
        y += vy;
        if (x < 0) { x = 0; vx = -vx; bBounce = TRUE; }
        if (x >= 500) { x = 1000 - x; vx = -vx; bBounce = TRUE; }
        if (y < 0) { y = -y; vy = -vy; bBounce = TRUE; }
        if (y >= 500) { y = 1000 - y; vy = -vy; bBounce = TRUE; }
        if (bBounce)
        {
            dsb1->SetCurrentPosition(0);
            dsb1->Play(0, 0, 0);
        }
    }
    nx = rectDest.left +
        MulDiv(rectDest.right - rectDest.left - 32, x, 500);
    ny = rectDest.top +
        MulDiv(rectDest.bottom - rectDest.top - 32, y, 500);

    rectSrc.left = rectSrc.top = 0;
    rectSrc.right = rectSrc.bottom = 32;

    if (bMove)
    {
        rectDest.left = rectDest.top = 0;
        rectDest.right = rectDest.bottom = 32;
        dds2->Blt(&rectDest, dds3, &rectSrc, DDBLT_WAIT, NULL);

        if (abs(nx - ox) < 32 && abs(ny - oy) < 32)
        {
            if (nx < ox)
            {
                rectSrc.left = ox - nx;
                rectSrc.right = 32;
                rectDest.left = 0;
                rectDest.right = 32 - rectSrc.left;
            }
            else
            {
                rectDest.left = nx - ox;
                rectDest.right = 32;
```

continues

Listing 44.1. continued

```
                rectSrc.left = 0;
                rectSrc.right = 32 - rectDest.left;
            }
            if (ny < oy)
            {
                rectSrc.top = oy - ny;
                rectSrc.bottom = 32;
                rectDest.top = 0;
                rectDest.bottom = 32 - rectSrc.top;
            }
            else
            {
                rectDest.top = ny - oy;
                rectDest.bottom = 32;
                rectSrc.top = 0;
                rectSrc.bottom = 32 - rectDest.top;
            }
            dds2->Blt(&rectDest, dds1, &rectSrc, DDBLT_WAIT, NULL);
        }

        rectSrc.left = rectSrc.top = 0;
        rectSrc.right = rectSrc.bottom = 32;
        rectDest.left = ox;
        rectDest.top = oy;
        rectDest.right = rectDest.left + 32;
        rectDest.bottom = rectDest.top + 32;
        dds0->Blt(&rectDest, dds2, &rectSrc, DDBLT_WAIT, NULL);
    }

    rectDest.left = nx;
    rectDest.top = ny;
    rectDest.right = rectDest.left + 32;
    rectDest.bottom = rectDest.top + 32;
    dds0->Blt(&rectDest, dds1, &rectSrc, DDBLT_WAIT, NULL);
}

LRESULT CALLBACK WndProc(HWND hwnd, UINT uMsg,
                         WPARAM wParam, LPARAM lParam)
{
    HDC hDC;
    PAINTSTRUCT paintStruct;

    switch(uMsg)
    {
        case WM_PAINT:
            hDC = BeginPaint(hwnd, &paintStruct);
            if (hDC != NULL)
            {
                MoveBall(hwnd, FALSE);
                EndPaint(hwnd, &paintStruct);
            }
            break;
        case WM_TIMER:
            MoveBall(hwnd, TRUE);
            break;
        case WM_KEYDOWN:
```

```
            switch (wParam)
            {
                case VK_LEFT: vx--; break;
                case VK_UP: vy--; break;
                case VK_RIGHT: vx++; break;
                case VK_DOWN: vy++; break;
                case VK_ESCAPE: PostMessage(hwnd, WM_CLOSE, 0, 0);
            }
            break;
        case WM_DESTROY:
            PostQuitMessage(0);
            break;
        default:
            return DefWindowProc(hwnd, uMsg, wParam, lParam);
    }
    return 0;
}

int WINAPI WinMain(HINSTANCE hInstance, HINSTANCE hPrevInstance,
                                  LPSTR d3, int nCmdShow)
{
    MSG msg;
    HWND hwnd;
    WNDCLASS wndClass;
    DDSURFACEDESC ddsd;
    DSBUFFERDESC dsbd;
    HDC hddDC;
    RECT rect;
    HRSRC hrsrc;
    HGLOBAL hRData;
    DWORD *pRData;
    LPBYTE pMem1, pMem2;
    DWORD dwSize1, dwSize2;

    if (hPrevInstance == NULL)
    {
        memset(&wndClass, 0, sizeof(wndClass));
        wndClass.style = CS_HREDRAW | CS_VREDRAW;
        wndClass.lpfnWndProc = WndProc;
        wndClass.hInstance = hInstance;
        wndClass.hCursor = LoadCursor(NULL, IDC_ARROW);
        wndClass.hbrBackground = (HBRUSH)(COLOR_WINDOW + 1);
        wndClass.lpszClassName = "BOUNCE";
        if (!RegisterClass(&wndClass)) return FALSE;
    }
    hwnd = CreateWindow("BOUNCE", "BOUNCE",
                        WS_OVERLAPPEDWINDOW,
                        CW_USEDEFAULT, 0, CW_USEDEFAULT, 0,
                        NULL, NULL, hInstance, NULL);

    DirectDrawCreate(NULL, &dd, NULL);
    dd->SetCooperativeLevel(hwnd,
                        DDSCL_NORMAL | DDSCL_NOWINDOWCHANGES);
    memset(&ddsd, 0, sizeof(DDSURFACEDESC));
    ddsd.dwSize = sizeof(DDSURFACEDESC);
    ddsd.ddsCaps.dwCaps = DDSCAPS_PRIMARYSURFACE;
    ddsd.dwFlags = DDSD_CAPS;
    dd->CreateSurface(&ddsd, &dds0, NULL);
```

continues

Listing 44.1. continued

```
dd->CreateClipper(0, &ddc, NULL);
dds0->SetClipper(ddc);
ddc->SetHWnd(0, hwnd);

ddsd.ddsCaps.dwCaps = DDSCAPS_OFFSCREENPLAIN;
ddsd.dwHeight = 32;
ddsd.dwWidth = 32;
ddsd.dwFlags = DDSD_CAPS ¦ DDSD_HEIGHT ¦ DDSD_WIDTH;
dd->CreateSurface(&ddsd, &dds1, NULL);
dd->CreateSurface(&ddsd, &dds2, NULL);
dd->CreateSurface(&ddsd, &dds3, NULL);

dds1->GetDC(&hddDC);
SaveDC(hddDC);
rect.left = rect.top = 0;
rect.right = rect.bottom = 32;
FillRect(hddDC, &rect, (HBRUSH)(COLOR_WINDOW + 1));
SelectObject(hddDC, GetStockObject(BLACK_BRUSH));
SelectObject(hddDC, GetStockObject(BLACK_PEN));
Ellipse(hddDC, 0, 0, 32, 32);
RestoreDC(hddDC, -1);
dds1->ReleaseDC(hddDC);

dds3->GetDC(&hddDC);
FillRect(hddDC, &rect, (HBRUSH)(COLOR_WINDOW + 1));
dds3->ReleaseDC(hddDC);

DirectSoundCreate(NULL, &ds, NULL);
ds->SetCooperativeLevel(hwnd, DSSCL_NORMAL);

memset(&dsbd, 0, sizeof(DSBUFFERDESC));
dsbd.dwSize = sizeof(DSBUFFERDESC);
dsbd.dwFlags = DSBCAPS_STATIC ¦ DSBCAPS_CTRLDEFAULT;

hrsrc = FindResource(hInstance, "BOUNCE.WAV", "WAVE");
hRData = LoadResource(hInstance, hrsrc);
pRData = (DWORD *)LockResource(hRData);
dsbd.dwBufferBytes = *(pRData + 10);
dsbd.lpwfxFormat = (LPWAVEFORMATEX)(pRData + 5);

ds->CreateSoundBuffer(&dsbd, &dsb1, NULL);

dsb1->Lock(0, dsbd.dwBufferBytes, &pMem1, &dwSize1,
                                  &pMem2, &dwSize2, 0);
memcpy(pMem1, (LPBYTE)(pRData + 11), dwSize1);
if (dwSize2 != 0)
    memcpy(pMem2, (LPBYTE)(pRData + 11) + dwSize1, dwSize2);
dsb1->Unlock(pMem1, dwSize1, pMem2, dwSize2);

hrsrc = FindResource(hInstance, "HUM.WAV", "WAVE");
hRData = LoadResource(hInstance, hrsrc);
pRData = (DWORD *)LockResource(hRData);
dsbd.dwBufferBytes = *(pRData + 10);
dsbd.lpwfxFormat = (LPWAVEFORMATEX)(pRData + 5);
```

```
    ds->CreateSoundBuffer(&dsbd, &dsb2, NULL);

    dsb2->Lock(0, dsbd.dwBufferBytes, &pMem1, &dwSize1,
                                      &pMem2, &dwSize2, 0);
    memcpy(pMem1, (LPBYTE)(pRData + 11), dwSize1);
    if (dwSize2 != 0)
        memcpy(pMem2, (LPBYTE)(pRData + 11) + dwSize1, dwSize2);
    dsb2->Unlock(pMem1, dwSize1, pMem2, dwSize2);

    dsb2->Play(0, 0, DSBPLAY_LOOPING);

    ShowWindow(hwnd, nCmdShow);
    UpdateWindow(hwnd);

    SetTimer(hwnd, 1, 100, NULL);
    while (GetMessage(&msg, NULL, 0, 0))
        DispatchMessage(&msg);
    KillTimer(hwnd, 1);
    return msg.wParam;
}
```

This application uses both DirectDraw and DirectSound services. Its execution begins in WinMain, where first a perfectly ordinary window class is registered and the application's window is created.

Next, DirectDrawCreate is called to create an IDirectDraw interface to the display hardware. This interface is used to create a primary display surface. Then a clip list is created using IDirectDraw::CreateClipper and attached to this primary surface. The window handle of the application's window is attached to this clip list, ensuring that subsequent bit blit operations into the primary surface will operate correctly when the window is partially covered.

Next, a series of secondary display surfaces is created. These secondary surfaces are used in a special algorithm that ensures smooth repainting of the bouncing ball. Two of these surfaces are initialized, one with the image of the ball (created through the GDI Ellipse function), the other with the background color.

When initialization of the drawing surfaces is complete, an interface to the computer's sound hardware is created using DirectSoundCreate. Two secondary sound buffers are then created using IDirectSound::CreateBuffer. One is used to store the audio stream for the background hum, the other stores the stream for the bouncing noise. Continuous playing of the background sound is started by calling IDirectSoundBuffer::Play with the DSBPLAY_LOOPING parameter.

Before we enter the application's main message loop, a call is made to SetTimer to set up a 100-millisecond timer. This timer is used to periodically update the bouncing ball's position and redraw the display.

When a WM_TIMER event is received, the application's window procedure calls the MoveBall function. This function calculates the ball's new position based on the global velocity values vx and vy. The ball's position is expressed in the form of integers running between 0 and 500; these are then translated into screen coordinates using the MulDiv function.

Redrawing the ball is a complex process involving three secondary buffers. Why is this complexity necessary?

Obviously, if we are to update the ball's position on the screen, we have to do two things: erase the ball at its old position and draw it at its new position. However, unless the ball moves very fast, chances are that its old and new positions overlap. Simply erasing the ball at its old position would cause unwanted flicker, as those screen pixels that are covered by the ball at both its old and its new position also turn briefly white.

To avoid this, instead of simply erasing the ball at its old position, we create a secondary buffer that represents the ball's old position. Into this buffer we draw portions of the ball that will be visible after the ball is at its new position. We copy this buffer at the ball's old position; we also copy the entire ball at its new position. Figure 44.3 shows a schematic representation of this multistep process. When your application updates only small areas of its window, this procedure may yield better performance than updating a back-buffer and using the `IDirectDrawBuffer::Flip` function.

FIGURE 44.3.

Smooth screen update using multiple buffers.

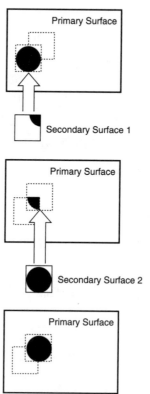

The application also responds to keyboard events. The arrow keys can be used to accelerate or decelerate the ball in the horizontal or vertical direction. Hitting the Escape key causes the application to terminate.

The two sounds that the application uses are in the waveform files hum.wav and bounce.wav. These files are referenced in the application's tiny resource file, shown in Listing 44.2.

Listing 44.2. Simple DirectX application resource file.

BOUNCE.WAV	WAVE	DISCARDABLE	"bounce.wav"
HUM.WAV	WAVE	DISCARDABLE	"hum.wav"

Note that in order to keep the application simple, some explicit assumptions were made as to the contents and structure of these waveform files. If you wish to utilize another file, you may be well advised to look at some of the Game SDK samples for ideas as to how to provide a generic parsing capability. The application can be compiled from the command line using the C/C++ compiler of Visual C++:

```
rc bounce.rc
cl bounce.cpp bounce.res user32.lib gdi32.lib ddraw.lib dsound.lib
```

Note that in order for the compilation to succeed, you must have the Windows 95 Game SDK already installed on your system.

The completed application looks similar to Figure 44.4. To run the application, you must have the DirectX run-time libraries installed.

FIGURE 44.4.

The bouncing ball application.

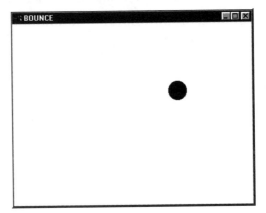

Summary

Recognizing the need for a high-performance interface for real-time Windows game applications, Microsoft developed the Windows 95 Game SDK. The Game SDK provides a family of APIs, collectively referred to as the DirectX APIs, for access to the computer's video, sound, communication, and joystick hardware.

The basis for many elements in the DirectX APIs is Microsoft's Component Object Model. Several of the interfaces in the DirectX APIs are derived from the COM `IUnknown` interface.

Video hardware is represented by DirectDraw objects, accessed through the `IDirectDraw` interface. Through a DirectDraw object, applications can create drawing surfaces, palettes, and clip lists. The interface to drawing surfaces, `IDirectDrawSurface`, provides high-performance bit blit capabilities. The `IDirectDraw` interface can be used to manipulate the display hardware in a variety of ways; this includes exclusive access to the display hardware for games that provide full-screen graphics and animation. A special use of `IDirectDraw` is to provide access to secondary video hardware not normally recognized by Windows itself.

Access to sound hardware is provided through the `IDirectSound` interface. Applications typically use the sound hardware by creating a series of secondary sound buffers; the contents of these buffers are mixed into the primary buffer and played back by DirectSound. This wave mixing capability as well as the capability to play back in looping mode are the key game-related capabilities of DirectSound.

DirectPlay provides communication services for multiplayer applications. Such applications can communicate through networks, modems, or online services. DirectPlay provides a simple send-receive functionality for game programs that participate in game sessions.

The DirectInput API consists of Win32 joystick services such as `joyGetPosEx` that can return position and other information for multibutton, multiaxis control devices.

Setting up the DirectX API is a complex task. A single-function interface that performs DirectX setup from the standard redistributable directories is provided in the form of the `DirectXSetup` function.

Bibliography

Black, Uyless. *TCP/IP & Related Protocols*, Second Edition, McGraw-Hill, New York, New York, 1994.

Bronstein, I.N., and K.A.Semendayev. *Spravotchnik po Matematike*. Gostechizdat, Moscow, 1954; Hungarian translation, *Matematikai Zsebkönyv*, Műszaki Könyvkiadó, Budapest, 1963.

Date, C.J. *A Guide to the SQL Standard*, Second Edition, Addison-Wesley Publishing Company, Reading, MA, 1989.

Ellis, Margaret A. and Bjarne Stroustrup. *The Annotated C++ Reference Manual*, Addison-Wesley Publishing Company, Reading, MA, 1991.

Kernighan, Brian W., and Dennis M. Ritchie. *The C Programming Language*, Second Edition, Prentice Hall, Englewood Cliffs, NJ, 1988.

Microsoft Corporation. *Microsoft Developer Network Developer Library*, July, 1995.

Microsoft Corporation. *Windows 95 Game SDK*, 1995.

Press, William H., Saul A. Teukolsky, William T. Vettering, and Brian P. Flannery. *Numerical Recipes in C*, Second Edition, Cambridge University Press, 1992.

SAMS Publishing, multiple authors. *Programming Windows 95 Unleashed*, Sams Publishing, Indianapolis, IN., 1995.

Shirley, John and Ward Rosenberry. *Microsoft RPC Programming Guide*, O'Reilly & Associates, Sebastopol, CA, 1995.

Stevens, W. Richard. *UNIX Network Programming*, Prentice Hall, Inc., Englewood Cliffs, NJ, 1990.

Stroustrup, Bjarne. *The C++ Programming Language*, Second Edition, Addison-Wesley Publishing Company, Reading, MA, 1991.

INDEX

Add to Your Sams Library Today with the Best Books for Programming, Operating Systems, and New Technologies

The easiest way to order is to pick up the phone and call

1-800-428-5331

between 9:00 a.m. and 5:00 p.m. EST.
For faster service please have your credit card available.

ISBN	Quantity	Description of Item	Unit Cost	Total Cost
0-672-30602-6		Programming Windows 95 Unleashed (book/CD)	$49.99	
0-672-30474-0		Windows 95 Unleashed (book/CD)	$39.99	
0-672-30611-5		Your Windows 95 Consultant, Pre-Release Edition	$19.99	
0-672-30685-9		Windows NT 3.5 Unleashed, Second Edition	$39.99	
0-672-30462-7		Teach Yourself MFC in 21 Days	$29.99	
0-672-30568-2		Teach Yourself OLE Programming in 21 Days (book/CD)	$39.99	
0-672-30594-1		Programming WinSock (book/disk)	$35.00	
0-672-30655-7		Developing Your Own 32-Bit Operating System (book/CD)	$49.99	
0-672-30593-3		Develop a Professional Visual C++ Application in 21 Days (book/CD)	$35.00	
0-672-30737-5		World Wide Web Unleashed, Second Edition	$39.99	
0-672-30765-0		Navigating the Internet with Windows 95	$25.00	
		Shipping and Handling: See information below.		
		TOTAL		

❏ 3 ½" Disk

❏ 5 ¼" Disk

Shipping and Handling: $4.00 for the first book, and $1.75 for each additional book. Floppy disk: add $1.75 for shipping and handling. If you need to have it NOW, we can ship product to you in 24 hours for an additional charge of approximately $18.00, and you will receive your item overnight or in two days. Overseas shipping and handling adds $2.00 per book and $8.00 for up to three disks. Prices subject to change. Call for availability and pricing information on latest editions.

201 W. 103rd Street, Indianapolis, Indiana 46290

1-800-428-5331 — Orders   1-800-835-3202 — FAX   1-800-858-7674 — Customer Service

Book ISBN 0-672-30874-6

Introducing *EditPro* 4.1

The Power Programmers Editor

Upgrade Now for Only $89.00 - that's a $180.00 Savings

When it comes to Speed, Power, and Flexibility EditPro tops the list. New for this release, along with its award-winning Windows 3.x product, EditPro comes bundled with Windows 95 and Windows NT versions all for the same affordable price.

Take a Test Drive on Us...

We're so convinced you'll flip for EditPro that we've included our full EditPro Version 3.5 **FREE** on the enclosed CD. Try it out, then let us know what you think. Remember, we offer a full 30-day money back guarantee if you're not completely satisfied.

Feature List

- Bundle supports Windows, Windows 95, Windows NT
- Syntax Color Coding for over 20 Languages and Data Files
- Open, Create, Add, and Extract Industry Standard PKZIP files
- Project Management for C and C++ with Project Browser and HyperLink Jumps
- Complete Image Processing Package supports 40 File Formats and Pixel Editing
- File Differencing
- Edit Binary files with Search, Replace, Insert, and Overstrike
- GREP file Search
- C-style Macro Language
- BRIEF and CUA Keystrokes

"EditPro has an incredible color-coding scheme which knows about Classes, Types, and Constants to aid in writing code and finding errors before you compile. EditPro also includes one of the most comprehensive and easy-to-use GREP functions that you'll ever see."
     Scott Gellerman, Xerox Corporation

"I've used several editors and seen a lot of Windows products but EditPro is the best in its class, ..., I use EditPro for all my Windows NT development."
     Jeffrey Gross, Microsoft Corporation

EditPro Corporation

9974 Scripps Ranch Blvd., Suite 307
San Diego, CA 92131
Phone: 619/549-8081 FAX: 619/549-2082 Internet: sales@editpro.com

EditPro is a Registered Trademark of EditPro Corporation.

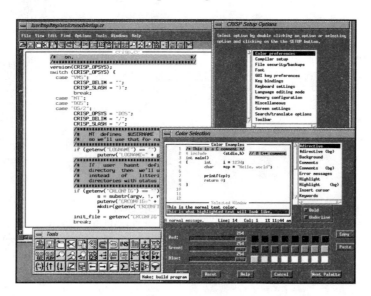

What's on the CD-ROM

The companion CD-ROM contains software developed by the author, plus an assortment of third-party tools and product demos. The disc is designed to be explored using a browser program. Using the browser, you can view information concerning products and companies, and you can install programs with a single click of the mouse. To install the browser, read the instructions on the following page.

> **NOTE**
>
> The browser program requires at least 256 colors. For best results, set your monitor to display between 256 and 64,000 colors. A screen resolution of 640×480 pixels is also recommended. If necessary, adjust your monitor settings before using the CD-ROM.

Windows 3.1 Installation Instructions:

1. Insert the CD-ROM disc into your CD-ROM drive.

2. From File Manager or Program Manager, choose Run from the File menu.

3. Type <drive>\setup and press Enter, where <drive> corresponds to the drive letter of your CD-ROM. For example, if your CD-ROM is drive D:, type D:\SETUP and Press enter.

4. Installation creates a program manager group named "Visual C++ 4 Unleashed." To browse the CD-ROM, double click on the "Guide to the CD-ROM" icon inside this program manager group.

Windows 95 Installation Instructions:

1. Insert the CD-ROM disc into your CD-ROM drive.

2. If the Autorun feature is disabled, from the Windows 95 desktop, double-click on the "My Computer" icon.

3. Double-click on the icon representing your CD-ROM drive.

4. Double-click on the icon titled "Setup.exe" to run the installation program.

5. Installation creates a program group named "Visual C++ 4 Unleashed." To browse the CD-ROM, press the Start Button and select Programs. Then choose "Visual C++ Unleashed," followed by "Guide to the CD-ROM" to run the browser program.

Windows NT Installation Instructions:

1. Insert the CD-ROM disc into your CD-ROM drive.

2. From File Manager or Program Manager, choose Run from the File menu.

3. Type <drive>\setup and press Enter, where <drive> corresponds to the drive letter of your CD-ROM drive. For example, if your CD-ROM is drive D:, type D:\setup and press Enter.

   The installation creates a Program Manager group named "Visual C++ 4 Unleashed." To browse the CD-ROM, double-click the "Guide to the CD-ROM" icon inside this program manager group.

   NOTE: The browser program requires at least 256 colors. For best results, set your monitor to display between 256 and 64,000 colors. A screen resolution of 640 by 480 pixels is also recommended. If necessary, adjust your monitor settings before using the CD-ROM.